Microcomputer Operation, Troubleshooting, and Repair

Microcomputer Operation, Troubleshooting, and Repair

ROBERT T. PAYNTER

Senior CET
Electronics Technicians Association

Senior Electronics Instructor
ITT

PRENTICE-HALL, Englewood Cliffs, New Jersey 07632

Library of Congress Cataloging-in-Publication Data

PAYNTER, ROBERT T. (date)
  Microcomputer operation, troubleshooting, and repair.

  Bibliography: p. 408
  Includes index.
  1. Microcomputers—Maintenance and repair.
I. Title.
TK7887.P39 1986   621.391 ′6   85-28254
ISBN 0-13-580341-1

Editorial/production supervision
and interior design: *Theresa A. Soler*
Cover design: *Diane Saxe*
Manufacturing buyer: *Gordon Osbourne*

Printed in the United States of America

10 9 8 7 6 5 4 3

0-13-580341-1 025

PRENTICE-HALL INTERNATIONAL (UK) LIMITED, *London*
PRENTICE-HALL OF AUSTRALIA PTY. LIMITED, *Sydney*
PRENTICE-HALL CANADA INC., *Toronto*
PRENTICE-HALL HISPANOAMERICANA, S.A., *Mexico*
PRENTICE-HALL OF INDIA PRIVATE LIMITED, *New Delhi*
PRENTICE-HALL OF JAPAN, INC., *Tokyo*
PRENTICE-HALL OF SOUTHEAST ASIA PTE. LTD., *Singapore*
EDITORA PRENTICE-HALL DO BRASIL, LTDA., *Rio de Janeiro*
WHITEHALL BOOKS LIMITED, *WELLINGTON, New Zealand*

This work is dedicated
to my grandparents,

Frank and Clare Bick

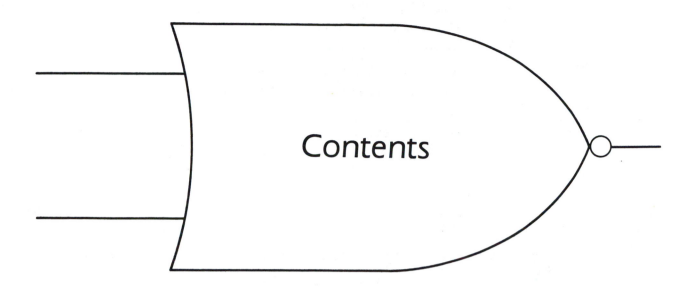

Contents

PREFACE   **xiii**

PART I   DIGITAL FUNDAMENTALS   1

1 **INTRODUCTION TO DIGITAL COMPUTERS**   1

1.1   What Is a Computer?   1
1.2   Basic Digital Computer Operation and Architecture   2
1.3   Representing Information in Digital Systems   5
1.4   Two-State Output Circuits   5
       Summary   9
       Questions   9

2 **DIGITAL NUMBER SYSTEMS**   11

2.1   Introduction to Number Systems   11
2.2   The Decimal Number System   11
2.3   The Binary Number System   13
2.4   Basic Binary Arithmetic   16
2.5   Binary-Based Codes   20
2.6   The Octal Number System   24
2.7   The Hexadecimal Number System   25
       Questions   26
       Problems   27

3 **BASIC LOGIC CIRCUITS**   **30**

3.1   Basic Logic Operations and Gates   30

3.2   Combining the Basic Logic Gates   37

3.3   The XOR and XNOR Gates   39

3.4   Alternate Logic Gate Symbols   41

3.5   Active versus Inactive Output States   41

3.6   Common Faults in Basic Logic Gates   45

Summary   47

Questions   47

Problems   48

PART II   ELECTRONIC FUNDAMENTALS   50

4 **REVIEW OF BASIC ELECTRONIC CIRCUITS**   **50**

4.1   Resistive–Capacitive Circuits   50

4.2   Digital Applications of *RC* Circuits   57

4.3   Transistor Operation   59

4.4   Common Transistor Applications in Digital Systems   63

Summary   66

Questions   67

5 **INTEGRATED CIRCUITS**   **68**

5.1   Basic Concepts   68

5.2   Dependency Logic Notation   70

5.3   Transistor-Transistor Logic   76

5.4   TTL Subfamilies   84

5.5   Three-State Logic   87

5.6   Open-Collector Logic   89

5.7   MOS Logic   90

5.8   CMOS Logic   93

5.9   Emitter-Coupled Logic and Integrated Injection Logic   96

Summary   98

Questions   98

6 **TEST EQUIPMENT**   **100**

6.1   Digital Testing with an Oscilloscope   100

6.2   Logic Probes   109

6.3   Logic Analyzers   110

PART III   COMMON DIGITAL CIRCUITS   111

7 SIGNAL SOURCES AND FLIP-FLOPS   111

7.1   What Is a Clock?   111

7.2   The 555 Timer   112

7.3   Crystal-Controlled Oscillators   116

7.4   Monostable Multivibrators (One-Shots)   118

7.5   One-Shot Applications   121

7.6   Bistable Multivibrators (Flip-Flops)   123

7.7   Flip-Flop Applications   129

Summary   133

Questions   133

8 COUNTERS AND REGISTERS   135

8.1   Counters   135

8.2   Down Counters and Up/Down Counters   139

8.3   IC Counters   142

8.4   Analyzing and Troubleshooting Counters   149

8.5   Registers   151

8.6   Troubleshooting Shift Register Circuits   157

Summary   159

Questions   159

9 COMMON MSI LOGIC CIRCUITS   161

9.1   Multiplexers   161

9.2   Demultiplexers   167

9.3   Encoders   173

Summary   176

Questions   177

PART IV   MICROCOMPUTERS   178

10 MEMORY CIRCUITS   178

10.1   Introduction to Memory and Memory Terminology   178

10.2   General Memory Organization   180

10.3   Read-Only Memory   182

10.4   ROM Applications   187

10.5   Static RAM   188

10.6   Dynamic RAM   192

10.7   Memory Addressing Techniques   193

10.8   Memory Maps   204

10.9   Testing and Troubleshooting the Entire Memory Unit   204

Summary   207

Questions   208

11 MICROCOMPUTERS AND MICROPROCESSORS   209

11.1   The Complete Microcomputer   209

11.2   The Microprocessor as the Control Unit: The MC6800   212

11.3   A Working Microcomputer System: The ET–3400 Trainer   217

11.4   When the CPU Malfunctions   230

Summary   231

Questions   231

12 MICROPROCESSOR ARCHITECTURE   232

12.1   The Internal Registers   233

12.2   The ALU   238

12.3   The Instruction Cycle   238

12.4   Data Transfer Operations   239

12.5   A Word about the CPU Internal Control Circuitry   241

Summary   242

Questions   242

13 MACHINE-LEVEL PROGRAMMING   244

13.1   Introduction to Machine-Level Programming   244

13.2   The MC6800 Instruction Set   248

13.3   Program Examples   258

13.4   Subroutines   265

13.5   Higher-Level Languages   268

Summary   269

Questions   270

Problems   270

14 I/O DEVICES   273

14.1   Introduction to Input/Output Interfacing   274

14.2   Keyboards and Keyboard Encoding   278

14.3   CRT Operation, Control, and Troubleshooting   289

14.4   Serial I/O for Printers and Modems   304

Questions   312

15   **PRINTERS AND DISK DRIVES**   **313**

15.1   Introduction to Line Printers   313

15.2   Microcomputer/Printer Interfacing   316

15.3   The Heath WH14 Printer   321

15.4   Printer Troubleshooting   336

15.5   Introduction to Floppy Disks   339

15.6   Disk Drive Units and Disk Drive Interfacing   343

A Final Word   345

Questions   346

16   **ANALYZING AND TROUBLESHOOTING THE SYSTEM**   **347**

16.1   The Step-by-Step Procedure   347

16.2   Breaking Down the Logic Diagram   351

16.3   Initial Checkout Procedures   352

16.4   Isolating the Problem to a Section   356

16.5   Isolating the Problem to a Component   361

16.6   When All Else Fails   365

16.7   Removing and Replacing the Faulty IC   366

Summary   369

A Final Note   371

Questions   371

17   **INTRODUCTION TO 16-BIT MICROPROCESSORS:
THE MC68000**   **372**

17.1   Introductory Concepts   372

17.2   Internal Construction and Data Storage   378

17.3   Common CPU Operations   382

Summary   385

References   385

APPENDIX   DEPENDENCY LOGIC NOTATION   **386**

BIBLIOGRAPHY   **408**

INDEX   **409**

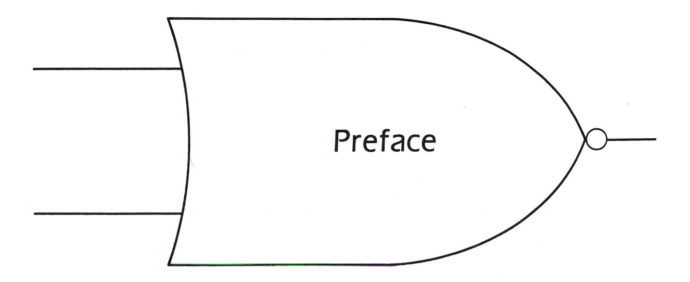

Preface

The objective of this work is simple: To take the reader from the introductory concepts of microcomputer operation to analyzing complete microcomputer systems. The emphasis is always placed on practical applications, fault symptoms, and fault analysis. Conventional design techniques, such as Boolean algebra and Karnaugh maps, have been eliminated from the discussion on basic logic gates, counters, and registers. Instead, the basic digital circuits discussed have been approached from the standpoint of the *purposes* they serve in digital systems.

A knowledge of basic electronics, with some background in solid-state electronics, is assumed in this text. The reader needs no previous exposure to digital electronics to understand the concepts covered.

Chapter 1 serves to remove some of the "mystique" that surrounds computer operation. The microcomputer is introduced as a basic machine that processes specific types of information. The foundation is established for the second chapter, so that the reader knows *why* the study of number systems and binary codes is important.

Chapter 3 covers basic logic gates. The emphasis is placed on why a given gate would be used in a microcomputer. Working examples of basic circuits and circuit combinations are used throughout the chapter. The reader is also introduced to the ways in which faulty logic circuits are isolated by waveform analysis.

Chapter 4 reviews some of the fundamental concepts of practical electronics: specifically, *RC* circuits and transistor operation. In both cases, the reader is introduced to the ways in which the circuits discussed are used in practical microcomputer systems. The discussion on *RC* circuits and transistor operation also helps lay the foundation for Chapter 5.

Chapter 5 covers logic families and their operation parameters. The emphasis is placed on TTL, since this logic family is still the predominant logic family in microcomputers.

The main topic of discussion in Chapter 6 is troubleshooting with an oscilloscope. Although there is a brief mention of logic probes and logic analyzers, the oscilloscope is emphasized. Learning to troubleshoot microcomputers effectively with an oscilloscope allows the reader to be able to practice the techniques taught with a minimum investment in troubleshooting equipment.

Chapters 7, 8, and 9 introduce the reader to the circuits that make up a majority of microcomputer components. Monostable and bistable multivibrators, counters, registers, multiplexers, demultiplexers, and encoders are all covered from the same practical viewpoint as the earlier logic gates. Again, the emphasis is placed on applications, fault indications, and troubleshooting procedures.

Chapter 10 introduces memory circuits, memory addressing techniques, internal and external memory decoding, memory maps, and memory troubleshooting. At this point, the reader is first exposed to a working microcomputer memory system in order to demonstrate the principles covered. Just enough information is given on the control unit at this point to allow the reader to see how it controls the operation of the memory unit.

Chapter 11 introduces the microprocessor as a ''black box'' source of control signals. The microprocessor is viewed as a device that constantly performs read/write operations and responds to interrupt inputs. There is little discussion at this point of the internal operations of the microprocessor. The reader is also introduced for the first time to a complete microcomputer system. This system, the Heath ET–3400 microcomputer trainer, is simple enough for the reader to use as a starting point for microcomputer system analysis, and at the same time, complete enough to be used to demonstrate all of the principles of microcomputer operation covered up to this point. The microprocessor discussed is the MC6800, an 8-bit microprocessor that works well for introducing the reader to the basic principles of microprocessor operation.

Chapters 12 and 13 are used to provide a more in-depth analysis of microprocessor operation. These two chapters deal with the internal operation of the CPU and with machine-level programming. Since a knowledge of machine-level programming is not absolutely necessary for microcomputer troubleshooting, Chapter 13 may be skipped by the reader without loss of continuity. Chapter 13 is provided for those readers who wish to gain more insight as to the types of operations that a microcomputer performs on data and how these operations are combined to perform a useful function.

Chapter 14 introduces the reader to the most common input output (I/O) devices: the keyboard, CRT, and serial I/O interfaces. The circuits analyzed are those contained in the Heath H-89A, since these circuits are simple enough to be used to demonstrate the principles of operation covered, and complex enough to begin to challenge the reader. Again, the emphasis is placed on component-level troubleshooting.

Chapter 15 introduces the reader to the basic operation principles of printers and disk drives. The emphasis is placed on electronic operation and troubleshooting rather than on the mechanical makeup of these two devices. The section on disk drives introduces the reader to the principles of operation of floppy disks, discussing the microcomputer/disk drive interface while treating the disk drive unit as a device that should be removed and replaced (when faulty), rather than as a device to be repaired on sight.

Chapter 16 introduces some techniques that the reader can use to effectively troubleshoot any microcomputer system. The emphasis in this chapter is placed on analyzing and troubleshooting systems with which the reader is unfamiliar. The analysis goes from gaining information from the user, to replacing the faulty component. These techniques, once mastered, all allow the reader to effectively analyze and troubleshoot any microcomputer system, regardless of any previous experience with that system.

The final chapter introduces the reader to 16-bit microprocessors. Although it is acknowledged that these devices are steadily making their way into more and more microcomputer systems, the discussion on them is delayed until this point for two reasons. First, it is easier for the reader to understand the concepts of 16-bit operation *after* thoroughly covering the techniques used in 8-bit systems. Also, while 16-bit CPUs are becoming more and more common, a majority of the home microcomputer systems being used are still 8-bit systems.

The appendix is included to provide the reader with a method of analyzing the dependency logic notation symbols that may be encountered in more and more everyday applications.

One final note: It is understood that the tendency in the industry today is to use software diagnostics for field service work on microcomputer systems. Many people believe that learning to troubleshoot a microcomputer to the component level is unnecessary and not cost-effective. It is my belief, however, that it is better to have knowledge of a subject and not always need it than to need the knowledge and not have it. Although software diagnostics can isolate a majority of problems, there are always those problems which the software diagnostic program will not be able to find. When this occurs, the technician who is able to troubleshoot to the component level will become as valuable as any technician could possibly be.

ACKNOWLEDGMENTS

I would like to gratefully acknowledge the following people who, at some point or another, have contributed to the completion of this book: Jerome S. Padak, Alan Dixon, Dan Merkel, William R. Miller, Johnny M. Clark, Michael Kelly, and Steve Forbes.

I would also like to acknowledge the members of the electronics staff of ITT Bailey Technical School, the finest group of electronics professionals that I have ever had the pleasure of being associated with: Ed Moore, Guy Turner, Bob Fleischmann, Richard Parrett, Dwight Holtman, Terry Stivers, Larry Johnson, George Johnson, Ted Widel, and Cliff Clark. Without their constant help and encouragement, this book would have never been completed.

Finally, a special thanks goes out to Wilson Miller for the photography, and to Ron Engeling for the barroom crash course on determination.

Robert T. Paynter

PART I
DIGITAL FUNDAMENTALS

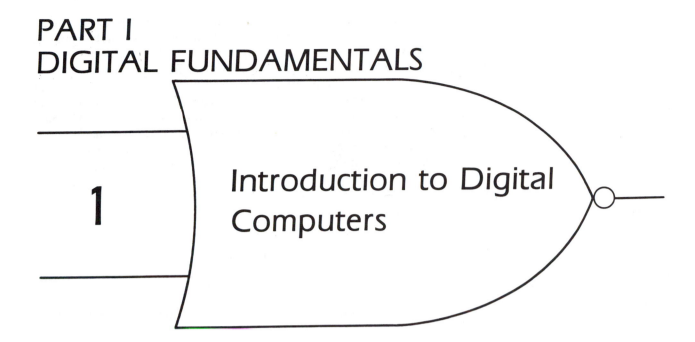

1 Introduction to Digital Computers

1.1 WHAT IS A COMPUTER?

A computer is *an electronic device that accepts information, processes that information, and produces a desired output.* The concept of a machine built to process information is not as strange as it may seem at first. A radio, for example, accepts a transmitted signal (information), converts the signal to a series of audio tones, and produces music (the desired output). It would follow, then, that computers serve the same overall purpose as any other type of electronic device. They do, however, differ from more conventional electronic systems in two respects:

1. They use specific voltage sequences rather than modulated signals to represent information.
2. They use circuits that act as switches to process that information.

A study of computers focuses on the ways in which information is represented and the circuits used to process that information. Once you understand both of these topics, you have the foundation necessary to troubleshoot and repair almost any computer malfunction.

Electronic computers fall into one of two categories, *analog* or *digital*. Analog computers deal with continuously changing quantities that vary within a set range. The main building block of the analog computer is the operational amplifier. Analog computers are not covered in this book, since microcomputers are not analog devices. Digital computers differ from analog systems in that they deal with quantities that must assume one of two possible values. These two-level, or *binary*, quantities are represented by voltage levels within the computer. Groups of these binary quantities are used to represent information. These signals may appear in sequence on one given wire, or they may appear simultaneously on a group of parallel wires.

The two voltage levels that are used to represent information in a digital computer are referred to as *logic levels*. The typical digital circuit will be constantly switching back and forth between these two levels and is referred to as a *logic circuit.* Logic circuits are composed mainly of transistors that are being switched rapidly from one output state to another, usually between saturation and cutoff. The idea of a transistor being used as a switch is covered in detail in Chapter 4.

The difference between digital computer signals and other types of signals can be seen in Figure 1.1. The analog signal shown is changing at a continuous rate, while the digital signal is remaining at one dc level for a period of time, then switching almost instantly to another dc level. *These dc levels usually correspond closely to the V_{cc} and ground levels for the system.* The waveform itself is called a *pulse waveform,* and is the basis for all digital computer operation. With all of this in mind, we can redefine the digital computer as *an information-processing device that is composed mainly of high-speed electronically controlled switches that respond to pulse waveforms.*

Analog   Digital   **Figure 1.1**   Basic signals.

1.2 BASIC DIGITAL COMPUTER OPERATION AND ARCHITECTURE

Information, as it applies to digital computer, is classified as one of two types. *Data* is all the information, numeric or otherwise, that can be processed by the computer. *Instructions* are the codes that tell the computer exactly what is to be done to the data. Suppose that a computer is given the task of adding the number 2 to the number 4. The numbers (2 and 4) are the data and *add* is the instruction. The actual sequence of instructions needed to add these two numbers might look something more like this:

```
LOAD (2)
LOAD (4)
ADD
OUTPUT (sum)
```

The first line contains the instruction LOAD, which tells the computer to get the first data value (2). The second line also contains the LOAD instruction, which causes the computer to get the second value (4). The third line contains only the ADD instruction, which causes the computer to add the two numbers that were loaded. The fourth line tells the computer to provide the user with the sum of the numbers.

A sequence of instructions like the one just discussed is called a *program* and causes the computer to perform a specific task. Programs range in length from a few instructions to thousands of instructions, depending on the difficulty of the task to be performed. Programs may be stored in the computer until needed by the user, or they may be stored on some type of magnetic recording medium, such as a cassette tape or a magnetic disk.

Hardware versus Software

Software is a term that is used to refer to the programs that are run by the computer. When you buy software from a retailer, you are simply buying prewritten programs. The instructions that make up these programs are recorded on tapes or disks in much the same way that music is. *Hardware,* on the other hand, refers to the actual electronic circuitry and mechanical parts that make up the computer. The hardware is designed to perform many general-purpose functions. It is the software that causes these functions to be performed in such an order as to accomplish a specific purpose. A computer without software is about as useful as software without a computer.

Complete courses are written that deal exclusively with computer software. In fact, you do not need a background in electronics at all to be a computer programmer or to understand how a program accomplishes its purpose. Most people involved in computer operation have very little, if any, understanding of how a computer processes the instructions and data electronically. Fortunately for the electronics technician, you actually need to know very little of how the software works to determine the source of a computer malfunction. All you need is a solid understanding of how the logic circuits work, what they tend to do when they do not work, and how they are wired together to form a complete system.

Basic Computer Architecture

Digital computers come in a variety of shapes and sizes, from pocket calculators to giant mainframe systems. Their applications are as varied as our imaginations will allow them to be. But no matter what their size or function, they all stem from the same basic block diagram. This basic block diagram is shown in Figure 1.2. Each block in this diagram represents a group of logic circuits that are dedicated to performing a specific function in the overall operation of the system.

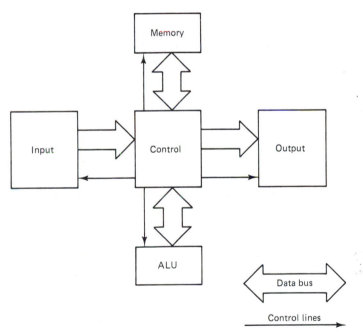

Figure 1.2 Basic computer.

The *input* unit is that part of the system that accepts information. It may consist of a joystick, a keyboard, or any number of other devices designed to allow the user to enter programs and data into the system. This unit also contains the circuitry that is used to initially process the information that is being entered into the system.

The *output* unit is that part of the system which provides the user with the results of a given operation. These results may be anything from information displayed on a cathode-ray tube (CRT) to a series of motor control signals. The input and output units of a computer contain almost all of the mechanical parts of the system. Since mechanical parts are almost always slower than electronic circuits, these two units are the slowest parts of the computer system. In fact, the overall speed of a given digital computer is determined primarily by the speed of its input and output units.

The *memory* unit is used to store instructions and data until they are needed by the system. There are two basic types of memory: memory that loses the information it is storing when power is removed, and memory that retains information whether or not power is applied. For example, information that is stored on a cassette tape is not lost when the tape is removed from the system. At the same time, most internal computer memory is automatically "erased" when the system is turned off. The various types of memory are covered in detail in Chapter 10. It should be noted that the input and output units each contain a relatively small amount of memory that is used mainly to store data temporarily as it is being dealt with by these units. This memory circuitry is usually not considered to be a part of the memory unit.

The *control* unit is the part of the system that directs and synchronizes the activities of the other system units. It gets the program instructions from memory, interprets those instructions, and causes the other units of the computer to carry them out. It also provides the basic timing signals for the other sections of the computer. This section is considered by many computer professionals to be the "brains" of the computer. However, without the memory unit, this "brain" would be useless.

The *arithmetic/logic unit* (ALU) performs all the mathematical operations called for by the program. It also performs another group of operations, called *logic operations*. These operations are covered in detail in Chapter 13. Just like all the other units, the ALU is directed by the control unit. When a program calls for an arithmetic or logic operation, the control unit sends the appropriate control signals and data to the ALU. The ALU then performs the operation called for and sends the results back to the control unit, or to either the memory or output units. The destination for the result data is also determined by the control unit.

The final part of Figure 1.2 is the *data bus*. A *bus* is a group of wires that carry signals which are related to each other by function. The data bus is used to allow data to be transferred from one unit of the computer to another. For example, the control unit could not get instructions from memory if there were not a path for those signals. Also, the input unit could not be used to load data and instructions in memory if there were not a physical connection between those two units. The data bus, together with several other types of microcomputer buses, are covered in Chapter 11.

One of the biggest problems with troubleshooting any microcomputer system stems from the way in which the units of the system are wired together. In the typical computer system, a failure in one section of the system will cause all the other sections of the computer to act as if they are also malfunctioning. For example, a given program is entered into a computer and the computer does not provide the user with the results. This could be caused by any of the following circumstances:

1. The input unit is down (malfunctioning), so the computer never received the instructions in the first place.
2. The memory unit is down, so the data and instructions that were entered into the computer were never stored and thus could not be processed.
3. The control unit is down, so there is no way for the computer to run the program.
4. The output unit is down. In this case, the computer has actually run the program but has no way of providing the user with the results.

As you can see, troubleshooting a down computer would seem to be a formidable task. However, in this book you will be taught some very reliable methods of isolating a fault to one unit of the system. Once this is done, some very basic steps will lead you to the component responsible for the trouble.

1.3 REPRESENTING INFORMATION IN DIGITAL SYSTEMS

All languages use specific symbols to represent information. In English, we use various combinations of the letters A through Z to represent spoken words. In contrast, the ancient Egyptians used drawings to represent spoken words. These two methods of representing information, however different, share one very important characteristic: *The symbols used to represent information have meaning only because there is general agreement on that meaning.* For example, we could use the letter combination ''xlpqrz'' to mean ''hello,'' provided that everyone agreed on that meaning. The point here is that any type of symbols can be used to represent information, provided that the symbols and their various combinations are agreed upon by those that use them. To bring this idea a little closer to home, consider the resistor color code. The standard resistor color code can be used by any technician, simply because there is agreement on the value of the colors and the significance of the color band positions.

Digital computers use only the symbols ''1'' and ''0'' to represent information. However, various combinations of ones and zeros have meaning because those who design and operate computers agree on their meaning. For example, the American Standard Code for Information Interchange (ASCII code) is a universally recognized code that is used to represent letters, numbers, and other information in digital computers. In this code, the combination of 1000001 is used to represent the letter A. When you enter the letter A into a digital computer, the input circuitry converts the letter into the combination 1000001, which the computer has been designed to recognize and treat as the letter A. Each character that can be entered into the computer has a different *binary digit, or bit,* combination. Using all of these bits to represent a single character may not seem to be too efficient at first, but you must remember one very important point: *A digital computer can only deal with ones and zeros and the signals used to represent them.* We must therefore use various combinations of these two values to represent all information. This requirement does not really pose a problem, since there is agreement on the meanings of the various bit combinations used.

It may interest you to know that computers cannot recognize English. Nor do they understand what the various commands used by the operator mean. They are simply designed and programmed to respond to specific sequences of bit combinations in a very predictable way. For example, a given computer has been programmed to respond to the command ''PRINT'' by sending data to a printer. When the operator enters the word PRINT, the input unit translates the word into a series of ASCII codes. The exact sequence of bit combinations would be

$$1010000\text{-}1010010\text{-}1001001\text{-}1001110\text{-}1010100$$
$$\text{P} \qquad \text{R} \qquad \text{I} \qquad \text{N} \qquad \text{T}$$

Although the word PRINT has no meaning to the computer, the sequence of bit combinations shown causes the computer to send data to its printer. The computer has not done anything that requires intelligence; it simply responded to the bit combinations in the way that it was designed to respond. By the same token, other sequences of bits would cause the computer to perform other functions, simply because it was designed to respond to them in certain ways.

1.4 TWO-STATE OUTPUT CIRCUITS

As we stated earlier, logic circuits deal with signals that must have one of two possible values. Although we use the terms *logic 1* and *logic 0* to discuss the inputs and outputs of digital circuits, we are actually dealing with voltage levels. In terms of circuit operation, *logic 1* is used to refer to one specific voltage range, and *logic 0* is used to refer to another. For example, one type of logic circuit that has been very common for several years uses the following voltage ranges to represent logic states:

1. *Logic 1:* +2 to +5 V dc
2. *Logic 0:* 0 to +0.8 V dc

The voltage arrangement can be seen in Figure 1.3. Assuming that the circuit is operating properly, the output will always be in one of these two voltage ranges. For this type of circuit, it does not matter if the output from a given circuit is +2 V dc, +3.889 V dc, or +5 V dc. All are defined as a logic 1 output. By the same token, any output between 0 and +0.8 V dc is defined as a logic 0. Under normal operating conditions, the output voltage would always be in one of these two ranges, or making a rapid transition between the two. The output range +0.8 to +2 V dc would never be used to represent information in this system.

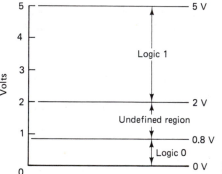

Figure 1.3 Logic levels.

There is a special output condition for the circuit just discussed, called the *high-impedance*, or *three-state*, condition. This condition, which is neither a logic 1 nor a logic 0, is discussed in detail in Chapter 5. For now, it is important that you understand that there are only two output states that are used to represent information, and that these states correspond to distinct voltage ranges.

It was stated ealier that digital computers deal with pulse waveforms. A *pulse* is *a waveform that consists of rapid transitions between two or more dc voltage levels.* Since digital computers deal with pulses, it is important that you have a solid understanding of the characteristics of these waveforms.

Pulse Waveform Characteristics

The pulse shown in Figure 1.4 is an *ideal* pulse. In an ideal pulse, the transition from one dc level to the other is assumed to happen instantaneously. The *pulse amplitude* is simply the difference between the two dc levels. The transition *away* from the reference voltage is the *leading edge*. If the waveform normally sits at 0 V dc, the

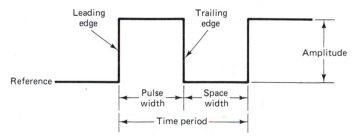

Figure 1.4 Ideal pulse.

transition to $+5$ V dc would be the leading edge. If the waveform normally sits at $+5$ V dc, the transition to 0 V dc would be the leading edge. In both cases, the leading edge is the transition away from the normal state of the signal. It should be noted that many technicians refer to the transition away from ground as the leading edge, regardless of the normal state of the signal.

The transition that is made when returning *to* the reference voltage is called the *trailing edge*. The time between the leading and trailing edges is called the *pulse width* of the waveform. The time between the trailing edge and the next leading edge is called the *space width*. Both of these characteristics are measured in units of time. The sum of these times is the *time period* of the pulse. Time period is to a pulse what cycle time is to a sine wave. Therefore, the reciprocal ($1/x$) of the time period is the frequency, or *pulse-repetition rate* (PRR), of the pulse.

EXAMPLE 1.1.

The pulse waveform shown in Figure 1.5 normally sits at 0 V dc. Calculate the pulse amplitude, pulse width, space width, time period, and pulse-repetition rate for the waveform.

Solution: Since the normal state for the waveform is 0 V dc, transition a is the leading edge and transition b is the trailing edge. Transition c would be the leading edge of the next pulse.

pulse amplitude $= +10$ V dc $-$ OV dc $= +10$ V dc
pulse width $=$ time from a to b $= 20$ (μs)
space width $=$ time from b to c $= 30$ μs
time period $=$ pulse width $+$ space width $= 50$ μs

$$\text{PRR} = \frac{1}{\text{time period}} = \frac{1}{50 \ \mu s} = 20 \text{ kHz}$$

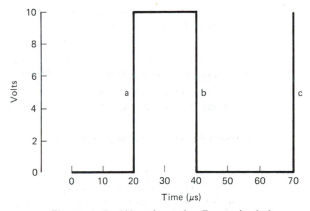

Figure 1.5 Waveform for Example 1.1.

There are two basic types of pulses, *positive going* and *negative going*. Both of these types of pulses, together with their appropriate labels, are shown in Figure 1.6. Note that in both cases the transitions are labeled with respect to the normal state of the waveform. As you can see, pulse width is simply the time spent away from the reference voltage, and space width is the time spent at the reference voltage. The purpose of making the distinction between these two types of pulses has to do with the fact that some digital circuits normally have a *low* (ground) output, and some digital circuits normally have a *high* (V_{cc}) output. In both cases, the transition away from the normal output state is called the leading edge of the output waveform.

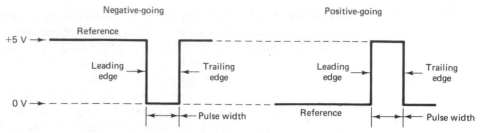

Figure 1.6 Positive-going versus negative-going pulses.

Another important characteristic of a pulse is its *duty cycle*. The duty cycle of a pulse is the percentage of the total time period that is taken by the pulse width. By formula,

$$\text{duty cycle} = \frac{\text{pulse width}}{\text{time period}} \times 100\%$$

Many digital circuits have a maximum duty-cycle rating, so you should know what the duty cycle of a waveform is. However, if you are not planning to work with prototype circuits (i.e., circuits that are in the first stages of development), you will rarely find system malfunctions that are caused by exceeding the duty cycle of a given circuit. These problems are worked out long before a computer system ever goes to market.

EXAMPLE 1.2

Find the duty cycle of the waveform analyzed in Example 1.1.

Solution:

$$\text{Duty cycle} = \frac{\text{pulse width}}{\text{time period}} \times 100\% = \frac{20 \ \mu s}{50 \ \mu s} \times 100\%$$
$$= 0.4 \times 100\%$$
$$= 40\%$$

This means that the pulse width took 40% of the total time period of the pulse. Therefore, any circuit that used this pulse would have to have a maximum duty-cycle rating of 40% or greater. If this condition was not met, the result would be a severely distorted output from the circuit.

Up until now, our discussion has been limited to an ideal pulse. Although the ideal pulse would have an instantaneous transition from one level to the other, the actual transitions do take some time to occur. These transitions are shown in Figure 1.7. *Delay time* is the time required for the pulse to go from 0% to 10% of its transition. *Rise time* is the time it takes the waveform to go from 10% to 90% of its transition. *Storage time* is the time required for the waveform to go from 100% to 90% on the trailing edge. *Fall time* is the time required for the waveform to go from 90% to 10% on the trailing edge. All of these times are caused by the switching characteristics of transistors and are discussed in detail in Chapter 4. For now, it is important that you understand that pulse waveforms are not perfect. It does take some time for the transitions to occur.

So, where do you measure pulse width and space width? This was no problem with the ideal pulse. However, as you can see, if you measured pulse width at the bottom of the pulse, you would obtain a different value than you would if you measured it at the top of the pulse. As a standard, pulse width and space width are both measured at the 50% point on the transition. In this way, any technician measuring these two times should obtain the same value.

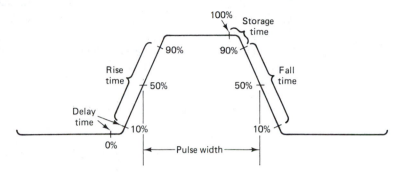

Figure 1.7 Pulse characteristics.

SUMMARY

Digital computers are information-processing devices that are based on pulse waveforms and their effect on transistor switching circuits. Information is represented by groups of bits in the system, with each bit having only one of two possible values. The meaning of these bit groups is determined by agreement on those meanings by the people who design and use the systems.

Bits are processed electronically by logic circuits. Those circuits are designed to handle input signals that have only two possible values. At any given time, the output of these circuits should be at one logic level or the other, or making a rapid transition between the two.

Information falls into one of the two categories. *Data* is the information to be processed, and *instructions* tell the computer what to do with the data. Instructions are grouped together in a *program* that causes the computer to perform a useful function. The programs written for a given computer are referred to as its *software*. The electronic and mechanical parts that make up the system are referred to as its *hardware*.

The hardware of a given digital computer is broken down into five functional units. The input and output units are used to transfer information from user to computer and computer to user. These two units are the slowest parts of the computer. The memory stores information and the control unit directs and synchronizes the other parts of the system. The ALU performs all the mathematical and logic operations called for in the program. The computer buses are used to provide paths for information transfers within the computer. The wiring of these buses and functional units causes a malfunction in one section of the system to display itself in such a way as to lead the unexperienced technician to believe that all units are down.

QUESTIONS

1. What is a computer?
2. How do computers differ from other types of electronic devices?
3. What is the difference between analog and digital computers?
4. What are logic levels? What are logic circuits?
5. What are pulse waveforms?

6. What are the two types of information found in digital computers? Define each.

7. What is a program? What is software?

8. What is hardware?

9. List the five functional units of a computer and state the function of each.

10. A computer operator enters a command into the computer. How does the computer interpret this command?

11. Refer to Figure 1.3. For each voltage level listed below, state whether the voltage is a logic 1, a logic 0, or neither.
    (a) +2.7 V dc
    (b) +1.5 V dc
    (c) +0.667 V dc
    (d) +0.9 V dc
    (e) +4.5 V dc

12. Draw a positive-going pulse and a negative-going pulse. On each waveform, label the leading edge, the trailing edge, the pulse width, and the space width.

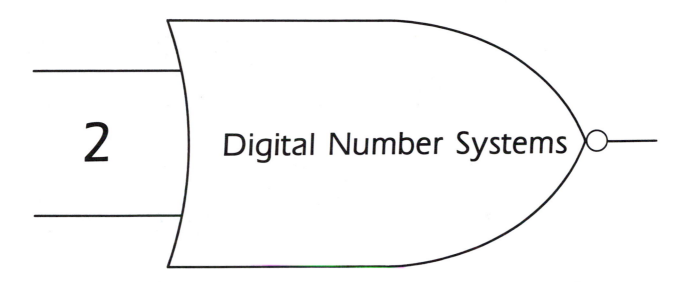

2 Digital Number Systems

2.1 INTRODUCTION TO NUMBER SYSTEMS

We all grew up using the decimal number system. We have always understood that you count by ones up to 10, then by tens up to 100, then by hundreds up to 1000, and so on. And nobody would argue the fact that we use 10 symbols (0 through 9) to represent quantity. There are, however, number systems that do not use the same symbols or counting progression that are used in the decimal number system. There are three of these number systems with which any digital technician must be familiar. One of these is the *binary* number system. This number system uses only two symbols, 0 and 1. All internal computer operations are based on the binary number system. The other two number systems that are used in digital applications are the *octal* number system and the *hexadecimal* number system. These number systems use 8 and 16 symbols, respectively, and are used almost exclusively for computer input/output (I/O) operations.

This chapter covers the four number systems just mentioned and the methods used to convert a number in one system to its equivalent value in another. We also discuss the basic principles of binary arithmetic and some of the more common binary codes.

2.2 THE DECIMAL NUMBER SYSTEM

The *base* of a number system is the number of symbols used in that system. In the decimal number system, 10 symbols are used: 0, 1, 2, 3, 4, 5, 6, 7, 8, and 9. It is therefore referred to as the "base 10" number system. All quantities in the base 10 number system are represented using some combination of these 10 symbols. However, the symbols alone do not determine the value of a given number. The position that a symbol holds in the overall number is also important. For example, look at the number 7 in each of the following numbers:

$$7492$$

$$3766$$

$$6453.7$$

In each number, the 7 has a different actual value due to its position in the overall number. The other digits also have implied values due to their relative positions. If we were to take the number 7492 and break it down by position, we would have

$$(7 \times 1000) + (4 \times 100) + (9 \times 10) + (2 \times 1)$$

which equals

$$(7 \times 10^3) + (4 \times 10^2) + (9 \times 10^1) + (2 \times 10^0)$$

Note that as you go left from the least significant digit, each place represents an increasing power of 10. If you go to the right from any digit position, you decrease the power of 10 from each digit to the next. This can be seen in the following power structure:

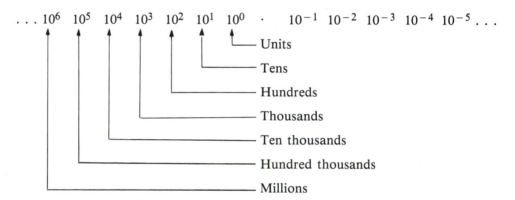

As you can see, the base 10 number system uses progressing powers of 10 for the position weights. *A digit in any position is multiplied by the weight of that position to obtain the actual value of the number.* This setup is the same for any number system. In the binary (base 2) number system, you have progressing powers of 2, and in the octal (base 8) number system, you have progressing powers of 8, and so on.

Counting

Although everyone can count, there are a few points about what happens as you count up that need to be discussed because they will help in understanding the count sequence in binary, octal, and hexadecimal. Consider the count progression for the units position in decimal. When you count up to nine, nothing that is noteworthy happens. However, after nine is reached, the count to 10 shows one important characteristic of count sequences:

$$9$$

$$10$$

Note that the units position *resets* (returns to zero), and the next column, the tens position, advances by one. As you continue counting up, the same thing will eventually happen. After the count of 19, the units position resets, and the tens position counts up by one to obtain the number 20. This pattern will reoccur every time any digit position reaches its maximum value. Any time that the maximum count is reached for one position, the number resets and the next column advances by one.

Another point to be made is that *a position will not be advanced until all previous positions have reached their maximum count.* This can be seen in the following number pairs:

99	999	9999	99999	999999
100	1000	10000	100000	1000000

Note that just before the most significant position to a 1, all previous position contained their maximum value, 9. This situation holds true for all number systems. In summary:

1. When you add one to the highest value for a given position, that position resets, and the next position counts up by one.
2. A position will not advance by one until all previous positions have reached their maximum count.

Although the points that have been made regarding the decimal number system may seem to be a matter of common sense, you must remember that they apply to all number systems and are better understood if first discussed in terms of the decimal number system.

2.3 THE BINARY NUMBER SYSTEM

The binary, or base 2, number system uses only two symbols to represent quantity. Sound familiar? The fact that both digital computers and the binary number system use two-value quantities makes them suited perfectly for each other.

Binary numbers can be pretty frightening at first because of their strange appearance, but they are really not that difficult to deal with. You can determine the value of any binary number in exactly the same way that you determine the value of a given decimal number. Simply take each bit in the number and multiply it by the weight for that position. Remember that, in this case, we are dealing with powers of 2 instead of powers of 10. For example,

$$1101_2 = (1 \times 2^3) + (1 \times 2^2) + (0 \times 2^1) + (1 \times 2^0)$$
$$= (1 \times 8) + (1 \times 4) + (0 \times 2) + (1 \times 1)$$
$$= 8 + 4 + 0 + 1$$
$$= 13_{10}$$

Thus 1101 in binary equals 13 in decimal. The power structure for the binary number system is essentially the same as that for the decimal number system, except that each position represents a power of 2. Because of this, each position carries a different weight than in the decimal number system. This can be seen in Table 2.1. Note that the 2^n column doubles in value from each line to the next. If the sequence is continued, the increasing powers of 2 are determined as $2^6 = 64$, $2^7 = 128$, and so on.

TABLE 2.1

n	10^n	2^n
0	1	1
1	10	2
2	100	4
3	1,000	8
4	10,000	16
5	100,000	32

A faster method of converting binary numbers to decimal numbers is to simply ignore the bit positions that contain a zero and perform the multiplication only on the positions that contain a 1.

EXAMPLE 2.1

Convert the binary number 11010110 to decimal.

Solution:

$$11010110 = (1 \times 2^7) + (1 \times 2^6) + (1 \times 2^4) + (1 \times 2^2) + (1 \times 2^1)$$

$$= 128 + 64 + 16 + 4 + 2$$

$$= 214_{10}$$

With a bit of practice, you should have no trouble in converting any binary number to its decimal equivalent. Be sure to work the problems on conversion of binary numbers to decimal at the end of the chapter.

Binary Counting

Although the count sequence for binary numbers may seem strange at first, an examination of the count sequence will show that it works exactly the same way that a decimal count sequence works. Consider the count sequence for a 4-bit binary value:

Decimal	Binary	Decimal	Binary
0	0000	8	1000
1	0001	9	1001
2	0010	10	1010
3	0011	11	1011
4	0100	12	1100
5	0101	13	1101
6	0110	14	1110
7	0111	15	1111

Each bit position is counted up to its maximum value (1), and is then reset to zero at a later count. At that time, the next bit position is incremented (counted up) by one. Also note that each bit position is incremented only after all previous bits equal a 1. For example, look at the change that occurs between the numbers 7 and 8. In line 7, the three least significant bits all equal one. On the next count, they all reset, and the most significant bit increments by one.

Another point can be made at this time. Note that there are 16 possible combinations of 4 bits (including the combination of 0000). *If you raise 2 to the power equal to the number of bits in the value, you will get the number of possible combinations for that number of bits.* For example, $2^4 = 16$, the number of combinations in the table. This works for any number of bits. Thus with 8 bits you have $2^8 = 256$ combinations, with 16 bits you have $2^{16} = 65,536$ combinations, and so on. This means that a 16-bit binary number has 65,536 different bit combinations, ranging from

$$0000000000000000 \quad \text{to} \quad 1111111111111111$$

If you want to determine the number of bits required to represent a given number of combinations, simply use the following formula:

$$n = \frac{\log X}{\log 2}$$

where

$$n = \text{ number of bits that are required}$$

$$X = \text{ number of desired combinations}$$

EXAMPLE 2.2

Determine the number of bits required to provide 16,384 combinations.

Solution:

$$n = \frac{\log 16,384}{\log 2} = \frac{4.2144199}{0.30103} = 14$$

Thus 14 bits are required to provide 16,384 possible bit combinations. Note that if the problem works out with any fractional value, you must round the number up. Therefore, if the formula yielded an answer of 4.0874627, you would need 5 bits.

Decimal-to-Binary Conversion

The process of converting a decimal number to binary is relatively simple, using a *divide-remainder* method. Divide the decimal number by 2 and note whether or not there is a remainder. If there is, write a 1. If not, write a 0. Then repeat this process on the quotient, and continue until the quotient equals zero. For example, if we wanted to convert the decimal number 23 to binary, the sequence of divisions would look like this:

$$\frac{23}{2} = 11 \qquad \text{remainder} = 1$$

$$\frac{11}{2} = 5 \qquad \text{remainder} = 1$$

$$\frac{5}{2} = 2 \qquad \text{remainder} = 1$$

$$\frac{2}{2} = 1 \qquad \text{remainder} = 0$$

$$\frac{1}{2} = 0 \qquad \text{remainder} = 1$$

Now read the remainders *from bottom to top,* in this case 10111. This is the binary equivalent of the decimal number 23. It should be noted that in the division process we are concerned only with *whole-number quotients.* Any fractional component in the quotient is dropped and a remainder is assumed to exist. The process is repeated in the following example.

EXAMPLE 2.3

Convert the decimal number 76 to binary.

Solution:

$$\frac{76}{2} = 38 \qquad \text{remainder} = 0$$

$$\frac{38}{2} = 19 \qquad \text{remainder} = 0$$

$$\frac{19}{2} = 9 \qquad \text{remainder} = 1$$

$$\frac{9}{2} = 4 \qquad \text{remainder} = 1$$

$$\frac{4}{2} = 2 \qquad \text{remainder} = 0$$

$$\frac{2}{2} = 1 \qquad \text{remainder} = 0$$

$$\frac{1}{2} = 0 \qquad \text{remainder} = 1$$

Reading the remainders from bottom to top gives the number 1001100. This is the binary equivalent of the decimal number 76.

The processes of number system conversion that have been covered are best learned through practice. By working the problems at the end of the chapter, you will gain a better understanding of how these processes work.

2.4 BASIC BINARY ARITHMETIC

An understanding of binary arithmetic is not required for you to be able to effectively troubleshoot and repair a microcomputer, but it will help you if you plan to continue your studies beyond the scope of this book. For those who do not wish to cover basic binary arithmetic, this section may be skipped without losing continuity.

Binary Addition

There are four rules for binary addition which cover all the possibilities that arise when adding two binary numbers of any length. These rules are as follows:

$$0 + 0 = 0$$
$$0 + 1 = 1$$
$$1 + 1 = 10$$
$$1 + 1 + 1 = 11$$

All of these rules apply in the following addition problem:

$$
\begin{array}{rl}
111 \quad 1 & \text{carry bits} \\
10110011 & \text{augend} \\
+ \ \underline{11110010} & \text{addend} \\
110100101 & \text{sum} \\
B_7 \qquad B_0 & \text{bit positions}
\end{array}
$$

In the B_1 position, the addition of two 1's results in a sum of 0, with a carry bit being generated. This is just like adding 1 to 9; you end up with a sum of 0 and a carry is generated into the next position. In the B_4 position, the addition of three 1's results in a sum of 1 and a carry is generated. When adding two binary numbers, you will never encounter a situation that takes you beyond the addition of three 1's.

So, what happens if you are adding more than two binary numbers? Add them the way that microcomputers do. Add two of the numbers, then add the third number to the result of the first addition, and so on. This will greatly simplify the whole situation.

Binary Subtraction

The rules for binary subtraction are a bit more difficult than those for addition, but if you relate them to the rules for decimal subtraction, they are not that difficult to understand. The rules for binary subtraction are as follows:

$$
\begin{array}{l}
0 - 0 = 0 \\
1 - 0 = 1 \\
1 - 1 = 0 \\
0 - 1 = 1 \quad \text{(with a borrow)}
\end{array}
$$

When a borrow is generated, it is carried to the next line, just as in decimal subtraction. The following problem demonstrates all the rules of binary subtraction:

$$
\begin{array}{rl}
1 \quad 1 & \text{borrow bits} \\
10110110 & \text{minuend} \\
- \ \underline{01101100} & \text{subtrahend} \\
01001010 & \text{difference}
\end{array}
$$

With borrows being propagated throughout the problem, your standard binary subtraction problem can become a true nightmare. Fortunately, there is a relatively painless method of subtracting one binary number from another, called the *two's-complement* method of subtraction.

Two's-Complement Arithmetic

Two's-complement arithmetic was developed out of a need to be able to express negative numbers in digital computers. The first method used to express negative numbers was called *sign-magnitude* notation. In this system, the most significant bit (MSB) is used to represent the sign of the number (positive versus negative), and the rest of the number represents the magnitude of the number. If the MSB = 0, the number is positive. If the MSB = 1, the number is negative. For example, in a system that uses 8-bit numbers, the two representations for the number 4 would be

$$00000100 = +4$$
$$10000100 = -4$$

While this system seems simple enough, it is not without its problems. The two main problems are:

1. When adding a positive number to a negative number, you get the wrong answer.
2. The system allows for both a positive zero and a negative zero.

The first point can be seen by simply adding the two numbers listed above. As any third-grade math teacher would tell you, the sum of +4 and −4 is zero. However, if you add the two signed-magnitude numbers, you get

$$00000100 + 10000100 = 10001000 = -8$$

Although there is circuitry that will detect and correct this problem, it is really more trouble than it is worth for microcomputers.

The second problem can be seen by looking at the following 8-bit numbers, which both equal zero:

$$00000000 \quad \text{and} \quad 10000000$$

Having two versions of zero is absurd, to say the least. The two's-complement system of arithmetic, however, solves both of these problems.

The two's-complement (negative) value of a binary number is found using the following process:

1. Complement the number. This means to simply change all the ones to zeros and all the zeros to ones.
2. Add one to the complemented number.

The number obtained is the negative value of the original number.

EXAMPLE 2.4

Find the 8-bit value for −4.

Solution: Complementing the number 00000100 gives you 11111011. Adding one to this number gives you 11111100. This is the two's-complement value for −4.

The process for subtracting with two's-complement numbers is a lot simpler than standard binary subtraction:

1. Find the two's complement of the subtrahend.
2. Add the complemented subtrahend to the minuend. Drop any carry out of the MSB position.

Let's try adding +4 to −4 using two's-complement arithmetic and see if we get the right answer. The value of −4 was already determined to be 11111100. Adding this to 00000100 gives

$$
\begin{array}{ll}
 00000100 & \text{minuend} \\
+\ \underline{11111100} & \text{subtrahend} \\
100000000 & \text{sum}
\end{array}
$$

If the carry-out is ignored, you have 00000000, which equals zero, of course. Here is the problem that was used to demonstrate the rules of binary subtraction, but this time it is being solved using two's-complement arithmetic. First the two's-complement of the subtrahend is found, then it is added to the minuend to solve the problem. Remember that the carry-out is ignored:

$$
\begin{array}{ll}
 01101100 & \text{subtrahend} \\
 10010100 & \text{complemented subtrahend} \\
+\ \underline{10110110} & \text{minuend} \\
 01001010 & \text{difference}
\end{array}
$$

As you can see, the same answer was obtained using both methods of subtraction. When using two's-complement arithmetic, however, you must take one precaution. *If the subtrahend has fewer bits than the minuend, you must add zeros to the most significant positions of the subtrahend so that the two numbers have the same number of bits.* This must be done *before* complementing the subtrahend.

EXAMPLE 2.5

Solve the problem shown using two's-complement arithmetic.

$$
\begin{array}{r}
01111010 \\
-\ \underline{10111} \\
\end{array}
$$

Solution: The subtrahend is rewritten as 00010111 so that it has the same number of bits as the minuend. Now the two's complement of the number is found: 11101001. This is added to the minuend, as follows:

$$
\begin{array}{ll}
 01111010 & \text{minuend} \\
+\ \underline{11101001} & \text{complemented minuend} \\
 01100011 & \text{difference}
\end{array}
$$

Remember the zero problem with signed-magnitude notation? If the number 00000000 is two's-complemented, the result is 00000000. Try it.

A few more points need to be made about two's-complement arithmetic. If the result of a subtraction problem is negative, the MSB will equal a 1. To get the actual magnitude of the number, simply two's-complement the result. Also, all positive numbers must have a zero in the MSB position. For example, if you want to use 8 bits to represent positive numbers, the highest value you can have is 01111111, which equals 127. You must reserve the MSB for a 0.

Binary Multiplication and Division

Binary multiplication and division are usually performed using *algorithms* in microcomputers. An algorithm is a logical program that simulates a mathematical process. Algorithms are used because most computers are not capable of multiplying or dividing. Binary multiplication and division are tedious processes that are really not worth the trouble, especially when you consider that the algorithms are actually easier to perform. The algorithms for binary multiplication are covered in Chapter 13.

2.5 BINARY-BASED CODES

There are probably enough binary-based codes to fill an entire book. It seems that for every application, there is a special binary code that someone, somewhere, is using. These binary codes were all created so that there would be a way to represent certain types of information using binary numbers. For example, the ASCII code was created to provide a standard code for alphanumeric characters. Although it is not possible to cover every binary code that is in use in this section, we will touch on some of the more commonly used codes, together with their applications and limitations.

Binary-Coded Decimal

Binary-coded decimal (BCD) is a code that was developed to allow decimal numbers to be entered directly into a computer with a keyboard. In BCD, each decimal digit is translated into a 4-bit value called a *decade*. The most common BCD code is the 8421 code. In this code, each decimal digit is translated directly into the standard 4-bit value for that digit. For example, the number 749 would be translated as follows:

$$7 \qquad 4 \qquad 9$$

$$0111 \quad 0100 \quad 1001$$

So the number 749 would be entered into the computer as 011101001001. If you were to take that number and determine its value treating it as a true binary number, you would see that 011101001001 = 1865. As you can see, BCD numbers cannot be treated as standard binary numbers. In fact, the main disadvantage of BCD is that BCD numbers must be converted to standard binary within the system. So why use BCD? Simply because it allows a keyboard to be wired so that the same code is generated no matter when the key is pressed. Consider the situation where you want to enter two different decimal values into a computer: 12 and 18. If you wanted the keyboard to provide standard binary numbers, it would have to provide the following numbers:

$$12 = 01100$$

$$18 = 10010$$

In this case, the "1" key would have to be translated differently for the two numbers. Computers just are not capable of doing this without having to go to an extreme amount of trouble. If the two numbers above had been entered using the 8421 BCD code, the results would have been

$$12 = 00010010$$

$$18 = 00011000$$

Note that in both cases, the "1" key was translated directly as 0001. This greatly simplifies the keyboard circuitry.

As we stated earlier, the 8421 code is the most common BCD code. In fact, when most people refer to "BCD," you can be fairly certain that they are referring to the 8421 code. There are, however, other BCD codes, as can be seen in Table 2.2. The 2421 code and the 5421 code translate each decimal digit in the same manner as does the 8421 code. The excess-3 code has values that are determined by taking the 8421 value for a given decimal digit and adding 3 to that value. Thus the decimal number 436 would be coded as follows:

4	3	6	decimal digits
0011	0011	0011	8421 value
+ 0011	+ 0011	+ 0011	offset value
0111	0110	1001	excess-3 code

Each of the BCD codes shown in Table 2.2 has its own applications. Most microcomputers, however, no longer use BCD. Most keyboards are now being encoded in ASCII, due to the availability of circuits that generate ASCII codes.

TABLE 2.2
Binary-Coded-Decimal Values

Decimal	8421	2421	XS-3	Bi-quinary
0	0000	0000	0011	01–00001
1	0001	0001	0100	01–00010
2	0010	0010	0101	01–00100
3	0011	0011	0110	01–01000
4	0100	0100	0111	01–10000
5	0101	1011	1000	10–00001
6	0110	1100	1001	10–00010
7	0111	1101	1010	10–00100
8	1000	1110	1011	10–01000
9	1001	1111	1100	10–10000

Alphanumeric Codes

An alphanumeric code is one in which letters and punctuation marks, as well as numbers, are represented. This allows any type of information to be stored, processed, and transmitted by digital computers.

By far the most common alphanumeric code for microcomputer applications is the ASCII code. This code uses 7-bit values to represent all types of characters. The ASCII code is shown in Table 2.3. The code for each character can be found by putting together the row and column values for that character. For example, the letter A has row values of 100 and column values of 0001. Putting these values together forms the value 1000001, which is the ASCII code for the letter A.

The ASCII code is so common that it would be difficult to find a microcomputer on the market that does not use it. We will work with the ASCII code some more later in our discussion of keyboard circuitry.

Another common alphanumeric code is the Hollerith code, which has its principal applications in larger computer systems. Those holes that you find in U.S. government checks are used to encode data in Hollerith. A punched card is shown in Figure 2.1.

The punched card is set up in a 12-row by 80-column format. Each character fills one column position, so up to 80 characters can be encoded on a single card. A given character is represented by one or more holes punched in the row positions. The 10 basic row positions are numbered 0 through 9. There are also two unnumbered

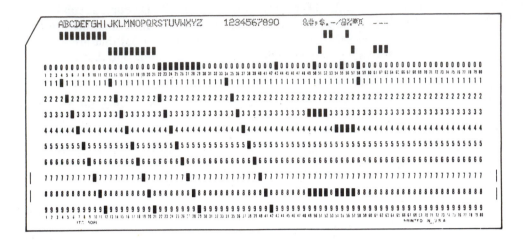

Figure 2.1 The Hollerith code.

rows at the top, called *zones*. Combinations of row and zone punches represent the various alphanumeric characters. For example, the letters A through I are represented by a hole in zone 1, and a progression of holes punched in rows 0 through 9. The row progression is repeated for the letters J through R, but the second zone is now punched, and so on.

As we stated earlier, this code does not really have much to do with microcomputers. However, it is a code with which you should be familiar if you plan to go to work in the computer repair field.

The Gray Code

The Gray code is a binary code that was created for use in analog-to-digital and digital-to-analog conversion. In this code, only one bit changes from each decimal value to the next. This can be seen in Table 2.4. The Gray code is an *unweighted* code. This means that there are no set weights for the column positions. This means that Gray code values must be converted into standard weighted values within the computer system.

TABLE 2.4

Gray Code Listing

Decimal	Binary	Gray
0	0000	0000
1	0001	0001
2	0010	0011
3	0011	0010
4	0100	0110
5	0101	0111
6	0110	0101
7	0111	0100
8	1000	1100
9	1001	1101
10	1010	1111
11	1011	1110
12	1100	1010
13	1101	1011
14	1110	1001
15	1111	1000

TABLE 2.3

The ASCII Code[a]

	0000	0001	0010	0011	0100	0101	0110	0111	1000	1001	1010	1011	1100	1101	1110	1111
000	Null	SOM	EOA	EOM	EOT	WRU	RU	Bell	FE	HT	LF	VT	Form	CR	SO	SI
001	DC0	DC1	DC2	DC3	DC4	Err	Sync	LEM	S0	S1	S2	S3	S4	S5	S6	S7
010	Sp	!	"	#	$	%	&	′	(	)	*	+	,	–	.	/
011	0	1	2	3	4	5	6	7	8	9	:	;	<	=	>	?
100	@	A	B	C	D	E	F	G	H	I	J	K	L	M	N	O
101	P	Q	R	S	T	U	V	W	X	Y	Z	[	\	]	↑	←
110																
111														Ack		Esc

[a]SOM, start of message; EOA, end of address; EOM, end of message; EOT, end of transmission; WRU, who are you?; RU, are you . . . ?; Bell, bell; FE, format effector; HT, horizontal tabulation; LF, line feed; VT, vertical tabulation; Form, form feed; CR, carriage return; SO, shift out; SI, shift in; DC0–DC4, device control; Err, error; Sync, synchronize idle; LEM, logical end of media; SO–S7, separator; Sp, space; Ack, acknowledge; Esc, escape

Parity

Parity is a method by which a computer can ensure the integrity of the data that it is transmitting or receiving. It involves the addition of a single bit to each data word so that all data words have either an even or odd number of ones. For example, the following 7-bit values have each had a bit added to the MSB position to provide an even number of ones in that word.

Parity bit	Word
1	0110100
0	1101001
1	1000000
0	0000000

Notice how each word that had an odd number of ones had a one added to make the number of ones even, and the numbers with an even number of ones had a zero added to keep it that way. If odd parity had been used, the bits added would have been the opposite of those shown.

Most microcomputer systems allow you to pick which type of parity you wish to use, or you may choose to use none at all. This choice is usually made by setting an internal switch, or set of switches. This sets up the system to add an even- or odd-parity bit to data that it is transmitting, and check for the same type of parity in the data that it is receiving. If an error is detected, the computer will signal the user that a data error has occurred. An error is detected if a system using even parity gets a data word with an odd number of ones, or vice versa. You must therefore be sure that when communications are set up between two computers, both of them are set up for the same type of parity.

2.6 THE OCTAL NUMBER SYSTEM

Imagine that you are trying to check the binary codes that are in a group of memory locations. You enter a special command into the computer, and the computer responds by putting about 200 8-bit binary numbers on the CRT. Now, you try to compare these binary numbers to a list of about 200 binary numbers that you have sitting on the table. After about 15 numbers, your eyes start to blur and you get a headache. After about 100 numbers, you seriously contemplate suicide. Sound far fetched? Try reading that many binary numbers some time.

Luckily enough, this situation is rarely encountered. This is due to the fact that there is a number system that relates so closely to the binary number system that the computer has virtually no problem in converting from one number system to the other. This number system is the base 8, or *octal* number system.

The octal number system uses eight symbols to represent quantity. These eight symbols are 0, 1, 2, 3, 4, 5, 6, and 7. The great value of the octal number system lies in the fact that each octal digit translates directly into a 3-bit binary value, as follows:

Octal digit	Binary equivalent
0	000
1	001
2	010
3	011
4	100
5	101
6	110
7	111

If you want to translate an octal number into binary, you simply write the 3-bit code for each octal digit. For example, $176_8 = 001\ 111\ 110$. The process for converting binary to octal is not all that different. Divide the binary number into groups of 3 bits, *starting at the binary point*. Then convert each group to its octal equivalent.

EXAMPLE 2.6

Convert the binary number 110101101011 to octal.

Solution: The binary number is divided into groups as shown:

$$110\ 101\ 101\ 011$$

Each group is now rewritten as its octal equivalent to obtain the number 6553_8

Octal numbers can be converted to decimal in the same way that binary numbers are converted to decimal. Simply take each octal digit and multiply it by the weight of its position, then add the results together. You must remember, however, that just as the base 2 system uses powers of 2, and the decimal system uses powers of 10, the octal system uses progressive powers of 8. Therefore, the octal number 377 would be converted to decimal as follows:

$$
\begin{aligned}
377_8 &= (3 \times 8^2) + (7 \times 8^1) + (7 \times 8^0) \\
&= 192 + 56 + 7 \\
&= 255
\end{aligned}
$$

Incidentally, both of the numbers above are equal to the binary number 11111111. This shows that values can be written in any one of the three number systems.

Many microcomputers have octal keyboards to enable the programmer to enter binary values directly into the computer. In an 8-bit microcomputer, each 8-bit word is entered using three octal digits. This greatly simplifies the whole programming process.

2.7 THE HEXADECIMAL NUMBER SYSTEM

Another number system that converts directly to and from binary is the hexadecimal, or base 16, number system. This number system uses 16 symbols to represent quantity: 0, 1, 2, 3, 4, 5, 6, 7, 8, 9, A, B, C, D, E, and F. The main difference between hexadecimal and octal is that hex digits translate into 4-bit binary values. A list of the 16 hex symbols, together with their equivalent decimal, octal, and binary values, is presented in Table 2.5. Hex digits would be translated into binary in the same manner as octal digits are, except that each hex digit is converted to a 4-bit binary value. Thus the hex number 7F would equal the binary number 01111111. Binary numbers are converted to hexadecimal by breaking the binary number into groups of 4 bits and rewriting each group as its hex equivalent.

EXAMPLE 2.7

Convert the binary number 110101101011 into hexadecimal.

Solution: The binary number is divided into groups as shown:

$$1101 \quad 0110 \quad 1011$$

Each group is now rewritten as its hexadecimal equivalent to obtain the number $D6B_{16}$.

The advantage of using hexadecimal over octal to represent binary numbers lies in the fact that a given binary number will convert to fewer hex digits than octal digits. For example, an 8-bit binary value converts to a three-digit octal value or a two-digit hex value. This advantage grows as binary numbers increase in length.

It should be noted that neither the octal number system nor the hexadecimal system would be of any value at all if it were not for the fact that they provide a greatly simplified means of recording and reading binary data values. As we progress in our discussion of digital systems, we will begin to refer more and more to binary values in terms of their hexadecimal equivalents.

TABLE 2.5
Number System Equivalents

Decimal	Octal	Hexidecimal	Binary
0	00	0	0000
1	01	1	0001
2	02	2	0001
3	03	3	0011
4	04	4	0100
5	05	5	0101
6	06	6	0110
7	07	7	0111
8	10	8	1000
9	11	9	1001
10	12	A	1010
11	13	B	1011
12	14	C	1100
13	15	D	1101
14	16	E	1110
15	17	F	1111

QUESTIONS

1. What is the base of a number system?
2. What two factors determine the actual value of a digit in a given number?
3. What is meant by the term *reset*?

4. How do you find the number of possible combinations for a given number of binary bits?

5. How do you determine the number of bits required to represent a given number of combinations?

6. How are numbers represented in signed-magnitude notation?

7. What are the disadvantages of using signed-magnitude notation?

8. What is the main disadvantage of using BCD?

9. What is an alphanumeric code?

10. What is the most common alphanumeric code in microcomputer applications?

11. What is the Hollerith code? What is it used for?

12. What is parity?

PROBLEMS

1. Write each of the decimal numbers listed as a sum of its powers.
   (a) 653
   (b) 17834
   (c) 3542
   (d) 534.32

2. Write each of the binary numbers below as a sum of its powers.
   (a) 1101011
   (b) 100100110
   (c) 11110001
   (d) 10100101001

3. Convert the following binary numbers to decimal.
   (a) 101101
   (b) 111000
   (c) 11010110
   (d) 10101100

4. Determine the number of possible combinations in binary numbers having
   (a) 12 bits
   (b) 7 bits
   (c) 8 bits
   (d) 32 bits

5. Determine the number of bits required to provide
   (a) 736 combinations
   (b) 450 combinations
   (c) 1036 combinations
   (d) 126 combinations

6. Convert the following decimal numbers to binary.
   (a) 236
   (b) 54
   (c) 747
   (d) 254

7. Add the following sets of binary numbers.

   (a)   101101110
      + 11101100

   (b)   11101001
      + 11000111

   (c)   11010101
      + 11111011

   (d)   11111111
      + 11110111

8. Find the two's-complement negative value for each of the numbers listed.
   (a) 01101001
   (b) 01110111
   (c) 00000100
   (d) 01010101

9. Solve each of the following subtraction problems using two's complement arithmetic.

   (a)   01101101   **(b)**   00110011
            − 01011010   −   11001

   (c)   01101111   **(d)**   01111111
            − 110000   − 01010011

10. Write each of the following decimal numbers as an 8421 BCD value.
    (a) 5683
    (b) 1024
    (c) 79,466
    (d) 1963

11. Determine the ASCII code for each of the characters listed using Table 2.3.
    (a) D
    (b) 6
    (c) &
    (d) R

12. Determine the message encoded on the punched card shown in Figure 2.2.

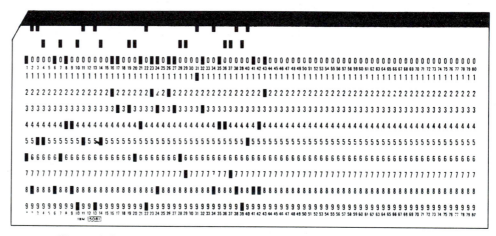

Figure 2.2 Punched card for problem 12.

13. Add a bit in the MSB position to each of the binary words listed to provide even parity; to provide odd parity.
    (a) 0111010
    (b) 0001110
    (c) 0101010
    (d) 1111111

14. Convert the following binary numbers to octal.
    (a) 110101101011
    (b) 101110010100
    (c) 000111010110
    (d) 010100011110

15. Convert the following octal numbers to binary.
    (a) 7462
    (b) 2315
    (c) 1074
    (d) 4351

16. Convert the following binary numbers to hexadecimal.
    (a) 1101011011111100
    (b) 0100001100001101
    (c) 011010101101110
    (d) 001010010101011

17. Convert the following hexadecimal numbers to binary.
    (a) 746F
    (b) B9A3
    (c) 1COE
    (d) 2F48

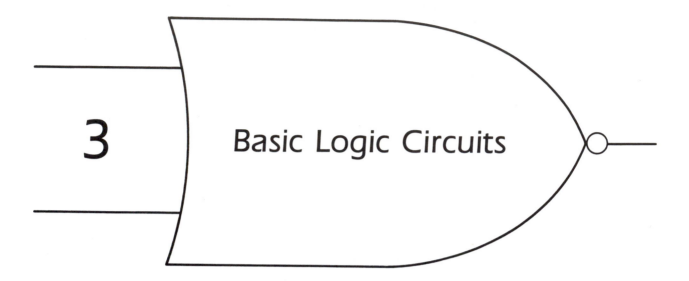

3 Basic Logic Circuits

All digital circuits, no matter how complex, have evolved from three basic operations. These operations are the AND, OR, and COMPLEMENT operations. Combinations of these operations allow the digital computer to solve arithmetic problems, process data, and make logical decisions. Yet these operations are so simple that anyone is capable of understanding them and how they work. This chapter deals with these operations, as well as with the circuits that perform them. These circuits are called *logic gates*. Each of the basic logic gates either performs one of these logic operations, or a combination of several logic operations.

Up until now, we have referred to the two logic levels in a digital computer as logic 1 and logic 0. It has also been understood that these two levels corresponded closely to V_{cc} and ground. Although these two points still hold true, we will now be using some new terms to describe these levels. A *high* input or output is one that is in the logic 1 state. A *low* input or output is one that is in the logic 0 state. These states are still assumed to correspond to V_{cc} and ground, respectively.

3.1 BASIC LOGIC OPERATIONS AND GATES

At this point, logic gates will be represented only by their "block diagram" symbols. These symbols, which show only inputs and outputs, are called *logic symbols*. Each type of logic gate can be identified by its logic symbol. In computer schematics, or *logic diagrams*, the basic logic gates are always represented using these symbols. Recognition of these logic symbols is therefore a definite requirement for reading logic diagrams.

The Inverter

The inverter is a logic gate that is used to change a signal from one logic level to the other. *A high input to an inverter will always provide a low output, and a low input will always provide a high output*. This changing of logic levels from input to output is called the *complement* operation. The output is therefore called the complement of the input.

The logic symbol for the inverter, together with its truth table, can be seen in Figure 3.1. A *truth table* is a table that shows the input/output relationship for a given logic circuit. As the truth table for the inverter indicates, the output for this gate should never equal its input.

The input to the inverter in Figure 3.1 is labeled "A." The A is used to represent the signal at that point. Since this signal may be high at one time, and low at another, it is easier to simply represent it as a variable, A. This allows us to discuss the signal without assigning a specific logic level to it. As you can see, the output from the inverter is labeled $\overline{A}$. This represents the complemented input, and is called "not A." This means that this output will not equal A. This relationship is always used to describe the operation of the inverter. If a given inverter had an input signal labeled D7, the output would be labeled $\overline{D7}$ to indicate that the output would not equal the input, D7.

A	$\overline{A}$
0	1
1	0

Figure 3.1 Inverter.

Inverters are used at times for a reason other than complementing a signal. When two inverters are wired in series, as shown in Figure 3.2, they are being used to amplify the current level of a signal. In this case, the output current can be as high as 10 times the amount of current that was provided at the input. The reason for using two inverters is to put the final output signal in the same phase as the original input signal. This is done because the inverters were being used strictly to amplify the current levels of A, not to complement the signal. As the truth table in Figure 3.2 indicates, the final output signal equals the original input signal. Only the current level of this signal was changed.

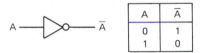

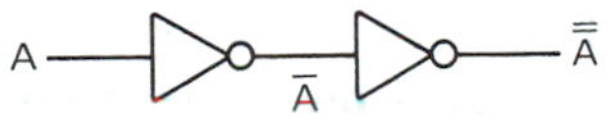

A	$\overline{A}$	$\overline{\overline{A}}$
0	1	0
1	0	1

Figure 3.2 Series inverters.

The Buffer

Another logic gate that can be used to amplify current is the *buffer*. This gate performs no logic function as such. It simply increases the current level of a given signal. The logic symbol and truth table for a buffer can be seen in Figure 3.3.

At this point, you may be wondering why anyone would use two inverters to amplify current if one buffer will do the job. The answer is actually pretty simple. If you have ever looked at a computer printed-circuit board, you have seen that most of the circuitry is made up of small black boxes with seven or more leads coming out of them. These boxes, or *chips*, contain the logic gates. Assume that a design engineer needs to amplify the current level of a given signal. The engineer sees that a chip containing six inverters is in the circuit, and that only three of the six inverters

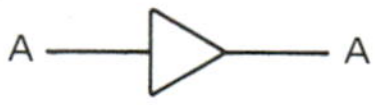

A	A
0	0
1	1

Figure 3.3 Buffer.

are being used. Rather than put a buffer chip in the circuit to amplify the signal, the engineer uses two of the available inverters. This saves time and lowers production costs for the system, because the engineer has used a chip that was already in the circuit rather than adding another.

The AND Gate

The AND gate is a circuit that provides a high output only when *all* of its inputs are high. If any input into an AND gate is low, the output will be low. The logic symbol and the truth table for the AND gate can be seen in Figure 3.4. With inputs labeled A and B, the output is labeled AB. When two variables are written in this manner, it means that they were joined together by the AND function. This again allows us to describe the function of the gate in terms of its inputs without having to assign specific values to those inputs. As the truth table indicates, the output is high only when both inputs are high. This holds true for AND gates with any number of inputs. An eight-input AND gate would have a high output only if all eight inputs were high. As soon as any input went low, the output would also go low.

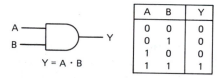

A	B	Y
0	0	0
0	1	0
1	0	0
1	1	1

$Y = A \cdot B$

Figure 3.4 AND gate.

The AND gate has many practical applications in digital systems. The first one we will discuss is the AND gate being used to pass or block another signal. This application can be seen in Figure 3.5. In Figure 3.5a, the control signal, B, is being held at a constant zero. Because of this, the output of the AND gate is also being held at a constant low. In this case, signal A is not being allowed to pass through the gate. In Figure 3.5b, the high input to the gate is allowing signal A to pass through the gate. The reason that signal A is making it to the output can be better understood by referring back to the truth table. Look at the cases where the B input was high. In both of these cases, the output from the gate equals the A input. This is precisely what is happening in Figure 3.5b.

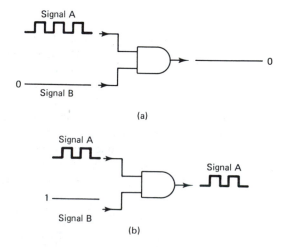

Figure 3.5 AND-gate applications.

The purpose for this type of setup would be to allow one circuit to determine whether or not another circuit was to receive signal A. This allows one circuit to enable or disable the operation of another circuit.

Another common use of the AND gate can be seen in Figure 3.6. In this circuit, the AND gate is being used to enable circuit C when the output from circuit A is low, or the output from circuit B is low. In either case, a low input to the AND gate causes a low output. This low is needed to enable the operation of circuit C. The $\overline{E}$ input on circuit C is the "enable" input. The bar over the letter means, in this case, that a low signal is required for the circuit to operate.

The AND gate has other applications that will be introduced as required throughout this book. The two cases just discussed are two of the more common AND-gate applications in microcomputers.

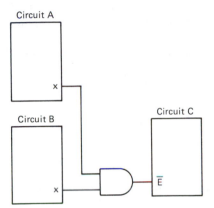

Figure 3.6 Another AND-gate application.

The OR Gate

The OR gate is a circuit that will provide a high output if *any* of its inputs are at a high level. The only time that the output of an OR gate will be low is when *all* of its inputs are low. The logic symbol and truth table for the OR gate are shown in Figure 3.7. The output from the OR gate is labeled A + B, with the "+" sign indicating the OR operation. This should always be read as "A or B" to prevent it from being mistaken as addition. While the first three lines of the OR-gate truth table do follow the rules of binary addition from input to output, the final line of the truth table does not. For this reason, you should be sure to distinguish the OR operation from addition.

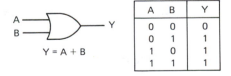

A	B	Y
0	0	0
0	1	1
1	0	1
1	1	1

$Y = A + B$

Figure 3.7 OR gate.

Recall the circuit in Figure 3.5a. When signal B was low, the output was also low. But what if you needed for the output signal, Y, to be high when signal A was being blocked. This could be done by using an OR gate instead of the AND gate. This circuit is shown in Figure 3.8. In Figure 3.8a, signal B is high, which blocks signal A and provides the required high output. When signal B goes low, signal A passes through the gate. Note from the OR-gate truth table that the output of the gate will equal A whenever B is low. For this reason, signal A is passed through the OR gate with no change in logic levels.

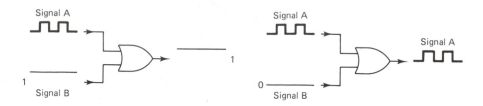

Figure 3.8 OR-gate applications.

Figure 3.6 showed the AND gate being used to provide a low enable signal whenever the output from one of two control circuits was low. If circuit C was to be enabled only when *both* control outputs were low, an OR gate could be used instead of an AND gate. The redrawn circuit is shown in Figure 3.9. Since the OR gate will provide a low output only when all of its inputs are low, circuits A and B must *both* provide a low output to enable circuit C.

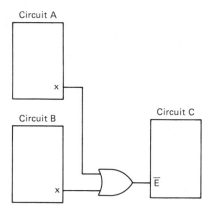

Figure 3.9 Another OR-gate application.

We have now covered the three basic logic operations. All other logic operations are built from various combinations of these three operations. These operations are summarized as follows:

1. The *complement* operation changes either logic level to the other.
2. The AND operation provides a high output only when *all* inputs are high. If any input goes low, the output will also go low.
3. The OR operation will provide a high output if any input is high. It will provide a low output only if all the inputs are low.

We will now start to combine these operations in various ways to produce other logic gates.

The NAND Gate

Figure 3.10a shows the result of taking an AND gate and following it with an inverter. The output from the inverter will be low only when *all* of the AND gate inputs are high. If you combined these two gates into one circuit, you would have the Not-AND, or NAND gate. The logic symbol and truth table for the NAND gate are shown in Figure 3.10b. As the truth table shows, the output from the NAND gate will be high if any of the inputs are low.

The NAND gate is probably the most often used of the basic logic gates. This is due to the fact that you can use NAND gates to implement any of the basic logic

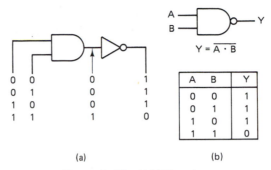

$$Y = \overline{A \cdot B}$$

A	B	Y
0	0	1
0	1	1
1	0	1
1	1	0

(a)   (b)

Figure 3.10 NAND gate.

operations simply by wiring them together in various ways. The NAND-gate circuits that will perform the complement, AND, and OR operations are shown in Figure 3.11. Figure 3.11a shows the NAND gate wired as an inverter. If signal A is high, then both NAND-gate inputs are high, and the resulting output is low. If signal A is low, then both inputs are low, and the resulting output is high. The end result is that the signal has been inverted. The same operation will be accomplished using the circuit shown in Figure 3.11b. In this case, the second NAND-gate input is tied to V_{cc} via a *pull-up resistor*. This puts a permanent high at that input. Now, look at the NAND gate truth table in Figure 3.10b. According to the truth table, the output will not equal A when B = 1. Therefore, if B is tied high, the output will be the complement of signal A. Again, we have an inverter.

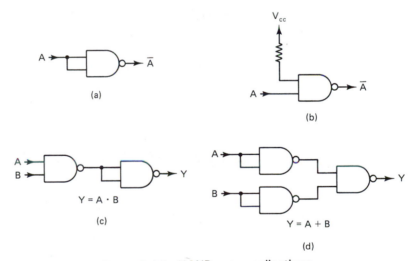

Figure 3.11 NAND-gate applications.

Figure 3.11c shows two NAND gates connected to act as an AND gate. This circuit will act according to the following truth table:

A	B	X	Y
0	0	1	0
0	1	1	0
1	0	1	0
1	1	0	1

Note the relationship between the final output, Y, and the inputs, A and B. This follows the truth table for the AND gate that was shown in Figure 3.4.

The circuit in Figure 3.11d will function as an OR gate. If either signal A or signal B is high, the output from the corresponding NAND gate will be low. This low will go to the output gate, causing the final output to be high. If both input signals are low, the inputs to the final gate will both be high. This will cause the final output to be low. By truth table:

A	B	C	D	E
0	0	1	1	0
0	1	1	0	1
1	0	0	1	1
1	1	0	0	1

The final output in this case is exactly the same as the output column for the OR-gate truth table in Figure 3.7.

The NAND gate can be used in so many applications that it is referred to as the *universal gate*. You will see NAND gates performing all sorts of duties in any given microcomputer. The importance of NAND gates will become more and more evident as your study of microcomputer systems continues.

The NOR Gate

If you follow an OR gate with an inverter, you will be building a circuit that provides a high output only when *all* inputs are low. This is the same function that is performed by the Not-OR, or NOR, gate. The logic symbol and truth table for the NOR gate are shown in Figure 3.12. As is shown by the truth table, the NOR gate will have a low output if any of its inputs are high. This is just the opposite of the OR gate.

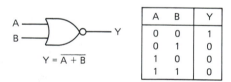

$$Y = \overline{A + B}$$

A	B	Y
0	0	1
0	1	0
1	0	0
1	1	0

Figure 3.12 NOR gate.

Keeping the logic operations for all of these circuits straight may seem at first to be a difficult task. However, there is a relatively simple way to remember them all. Each logic gate has a unique output condition. There is one input combination that will cause a different output than the other three input conditions. To help you see this, the truth table below has been constructed to show how each of the logic gates will react to two signals, A and B.

A	B	AND	OR	NAND	NOR
0	0	0	0	1	1
0	1	0	1	1	0
1	0	0	1	1	0
1	1	1	1	0	0

The statements listed below are the keys to remembering how each gate works. After reading each statement, look at the output column for that gate to help visualize what is being said.

1. The AND gate will have a high output only when *all* inputs are high.
2. The OR gate will have a low output only when *all* inputs are low.
3. The NAND gate will have a low output only when *all* inputs are high.
4. The NOR gate will have a high output only when *all* inputs are low.
5. The buffer has an output that equals its input.
6. The inverter has an output that does not equal its input.

Added exposure to these basic gates will make it much easier for you to remember which gate does what operation. For now, committing the points listed above to memory is your best bet.

3.2 COMBINING THE BASIC LOGIC GATES

The next step is to learn how to determine the output from a circuit that is composed of several of the basic logic gates. To determine the output from such a circuit, simply determine the output for each gate, in order, until the final output is reached. The following series of examples will demonstrate just how this is done.

EXAMPLE 3.1

Determine the output of the gating circuit shown in Figure 3.13.

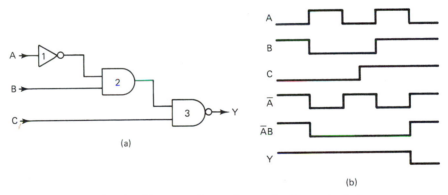

Figure 3.13   Circuit and waveforms for Example 3.1.

Solution: Signal A is first inverted by gate 1. This results in the waveform shown in Figure 3.13b, line 4. This waveform ($\overline{A}$) is applied to the AND gate with signal B. The resulting waveform ($\overline{A}B$) is shown in line 5. Note that this output is high only when both $\overline{A}$ and B are high. This waveform is now combined with single C at the NAND gate. Note that the output from the NAND gate is low only when both inputs are high.

EXAMPLE 3.2

Determine the final output from the gating circuit shown in Figure 3.14.

Solution: The NOR gate is wired to act as an inverter. As the truth table for the NOR gate shows (Figure 3.12), the output from the NOR gate equals $\overline{A}$ when signal B is low. In this case, the output from the NOR gate equals $\overline{A1}$. This signal is now applied to the OR gate with signal A2. The output from the OR gate will be high whenever either of the inputs signals are high. The resulting waveform is labeled "X." This waveform is then inverted by gate 3, resulting in the $\overline{X}$

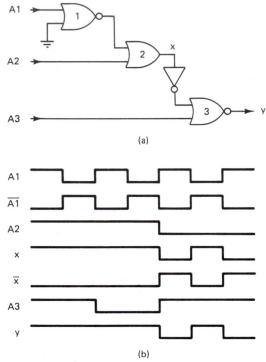

(a)

(b)

Figure 3.14 Circuit and waveforms for Example 3.2.

waveform. This signal is now combined with signal A3 by the NAND gate. The final output is shown as waveform Y.

EXAMPLE 3.3

Prove by waveform analysis that the two circuits shown in Figure 3.15 perform the same function.

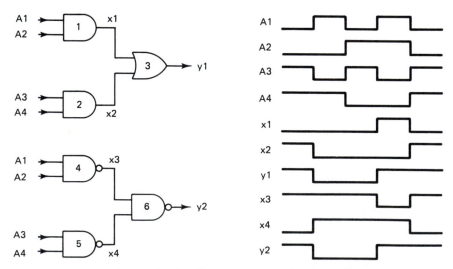

Figure 3.15 Circuit and waveforms for Example 3.3.

Solution: Signals A1 and A2 are combined by gate 1 to produce waveform X1. In the same manner, signals A3 and A4 are combined by gate 2 to produce waveform X2. These two signals (X1 and X2) are now combined by the OR gate to produce waveform Y1. As you can see, each of these gates has acted exactly as stated in their respective truth tables. Now A1 and A2 are applied to gate 4. The resulting waveform is labeled X3. Note that this output goes low only when both inputs are high. Signals A3 and A4 are combined in the same manner by gate 5. The resulting waveform is labeled X4. These two waveforms (X3 and X4) are now combined using gate 6 to produce waveform Y2.

Now compare waveforms Y1 and Y2. As you can see, these two waveforms are exactly the same for the same input signals. When two different gating circuits produce the same output waveform, as these two circuits have, the circuits are proven to be equivalent circuits. Again, it has been shown that NAND gates can be used to perform the same functions as the other basic logic gates.

With practice, it should be easy for you to predict the output from any combination of basic logic gates. Working the problems in waveform analysis at the end of this chapter should help strengthen your understanding of how logic gates combine signals. You should be sure to work these problems, since you must be able to determine what should be coming out of a logic gating circuit before you can determine when the circuit is inoperative. If you cannot determine what should be at a given point, you cannot determine what should not be there either.

3.3 THE XOR AND XNOR GATES

There are two more basic logic gates. These are the *exclusive-OR* (XOR) and the *exclusive-NOR* (XNOR) gates. These gates differ from the other basic logic gates in that there is not a single input condition that will result in an output that is unique for that condition.

The XOR Gate

The XOR gate is a logic circuit that will have a high output only when its inputs are unequal. In other words, one of the two inputs must be a one and the other must be a zero for the gate to have a high output. The logic symbol and truth table for the XOR gate can be seen in Figure 3.16. As the truth table shows, the output will

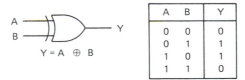

$$Y = A \oplus B$$

A	B	Y
0	0	0
0	1	1
1	0	1
1	1	0

Figure 3.16   XOR gate.

be low whenever signal A equals signal B. Because of this input/output relationship, the XOR gate can be used for some applications that would take several of the other basic logic gates. Several of these XOR circuits are shown in Figure 3.17.

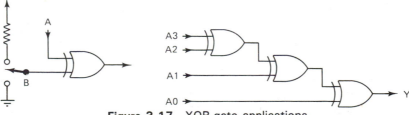

Figure 3.17   XOR-gate applications.

The XOR gate can be used as a "programmable inverter" when wired as the circuit in Figure 3.17a. To understand how this circuit operates, refer to the XOR truth table in Figure 3.16. According to the truth table, the output of the XOR gate will equal signal A when signal B is low. When signal B is high, the output of the gate will equal $\overline{A}$. By connecting the switch in Figure 3.17a to the ground position, the output will equal signal A, and by connecting it to the pull-up resistor, the output signal will equal $\overline{A}$. This allows us to use the XOR gate as an inverter at one point in time and as a buffer at another.

The circuit shown in Figure 3.17b can be used to determine whether the number of ones in the input word is even or odd. If the number of ones in the input word is odd, the circuit will have a high output. If the number of ones in the input word is even, the output from the circuit will be low. You can cascade any number of XOR gates and the results will be the same. This makes the XOR gate very useful in circuits that are used to check and generate parity bits.

The circuit shown in Figure 3.18 would be used to generate even or odd parity, depending on the position of the parity switch. See if you can figure out how this circuit would be used to check a data word and generate the desired parity bit.

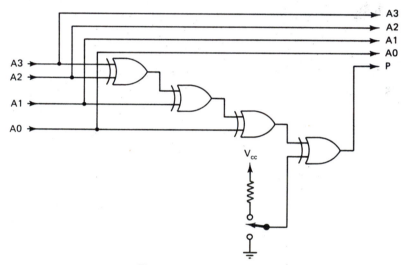

Figure 3.18   Even/odd parity generator.

The XNOR Gate

The XNOR gate is the opposite of the XOR gate in that it will have a high output only when the inputs are equal. For this reason, the XNOR gate is often referred to as the *equality gate*. The logic symbol and truth table for the XNOR gate are shown in Figure 3.19. As the truth table indicates, the output of the XNOR gate will be low whenever the inputs are unequal. This is just the opposite of the XOR gate.

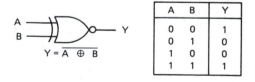

A	B	Y
0	0	1
0	1	0
1	0	0
1	1	1

$Y = \overline{A \oplus B}$

Figure 3.19   XNOR gate.

3.4 ALTERNATE LOGIC GATE SYMBOLS

Each of the basic logic gates (with the exception of the XOR and XNOR gates) has an alternate logic symbol. These logic symbols are meant to be used to tell the technician the purpose that a given logic gate serves in a system. This point is discussed further in Section 3.5.

The method used to find the alternate symbol for any logic gate is simple. First, you change the basic function shape of the gate. This means that the AND shape is changed to the OR shape, and vice versa. Next, you reverse all "bubble" positions. This means to put bubbles where there were none and to remove any bubbles that were in the original symbol. For example, the two logic symbols for the NAND gate are shown in Figure 3.20. To obtain the alternate symbol for the NAND gate, the AND symbol was changed to an OR symbol and the bubble positions were reversed. Just as the NAND symbol in Figure 3.20a was composed of an AND gate followed by an inverter, the NAND symbol in Figure 3.20 could be considered to be an OR gate with inverters on the inputs. The following truth table shows the equivalence of these two circuits.

| | (a) | | | (b) | | **Figure 3.20** NAND-gate symbols. |

A	B	$\overline{AB}$	$\overline{A}$	$\overline{B}$	$\overline{A} + \overline{B}$
0	0	1	1	1	1
0	1	1	1	0	1
1	0	1	0	1	1
1	1	0	0	0	0

As the truth table indicates, the two circuits shown in Figure 3.20 are equal. This allows us to use the alternate logic symbol shown to represent the NAND gate. The alternate logic symbols for the NOR, OR, and AND gates are shown in Figure 3.21. See if you can follow the process that was used to derive each of these symbols.

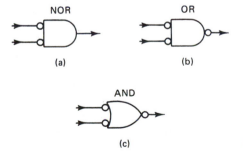

(c)   **Figure 3.21** Other alternate symbols.

3.5 ACTIVE VERSUS INACTIVE OUTPUT STATES

Every logic gate serves a specific purpose in the overall microcomputer system. Each gate is there to provide a specific signal at a specific time, under a specific set of circumstances. Some circuits are there to provide a low signal at one ɪoint in time, and simply sit at a high potential the rest of the time. Some circuits work just the opposite way. They supply a high signal at one specific point in time, and simply sit at a low potential the rest of the time. When a signal is providing the signal that it was put there to supply, it is said to be in its *active* output state. The rest of the time, it is in its *inactive* output state. The point of active versus inactive output states is important, so we will discuss each of the basic logic gates in this light.

The AND gate is designed to have a high output when all inputs are high, and a low output otherwise. The AND gate would therefore serve one of two purposes:

1. To provide a high output if all of its inputs go high
2. To provide a low output if any of its inputs go low

In the first condition, the high output is the active output and the low output is the inactive output. In the second condition, the low output is the active output and the high output is the inactive output. Both of these conditions describe the AND function, but they do so in terms of the specific purpose that a given gate serves.

This point can be better understood by looking at the circuits shown in Figure 3.22. These two circuits are used to light a red LED when certain conditions exist. The circuit in Figure 3.22a is being used to light the LED if any of its three inputs go *low*. A low input to this gate will cause its output to go low. This will supply the LED with the ground path that it needs to light. In this case, the output from the AND gate is said to be *active-low*, since this is what is needed to light the LED. Since a low input causes this low-output state, the inputs are also said to be active-low. The circuit in Figure 3.22b is being used to light the LED only when all three AND-gate inputs are high. Thus the output is said to be *active-high*. The active input levels would also be high, since they must all be high for the output to go to its active-high state.

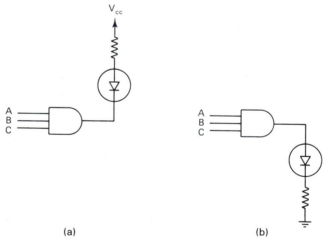

Figure 3.22   AND-gate LED driver.

The OR gate can be used to provide an active-low output when *all* of its inputs are low, or to provide an active-high output when any of its inputs are high. These two circuits can be seen in Figure 3.23.

Before reading on, see if you can determine which purpose is served by each of the circuits shown. Since the LED in Figure 3.23a needs a high voltage level to light, the OR gate must be providing an active-high output. Since it needs a high input to have a high output, its inputs must also be active-high. The LED in Figure 3.23b needs a low voltage to light, so the OR gate must have an active-low output. This means that the inputs must also be active-low.

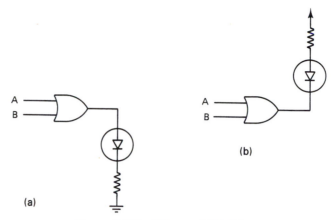

Figure 3.23 OR-gate LED driver.

The NAND gate can be used for one of the following two purposes:

1. To provide a high output when any of its inputs are low
2. To provide a low output when all of its inputs are high

In the same manner, the NOR gate can be used for one of the following purposes:

1. To provide a high output when *all* of its inputs are low
2. To provide a low output if any of its inputs are high

The Use of Alternate Logic Symbols

The advantage of using alternate logic symbols is that the purpose for a given gate can be determined by looking at the schematic if these symbols are used. To see how this works, refer back to Figure 3.20, which shows the two symbols that are used to represent the NAND gate. Assume that the presence of a bubble indicates a low-active state and the lack of a bubble indicates a high-active state. If both of these symbols are used, the symbol in Figure 3.20a would indicate that the circuit was being used to provide a low output when input signal A *AND* input signal B are high. The circuit in Figure 3.20b would be used to indicate that the circuit was used to provide a high output if signal A *OR* signal B was low. In this manner, circuit analysis could be done simply looking at the logic symbols. Unfortunately, most logic diagrams do not incorporate alternate logic symbols. This means that other methods must be used to determine the purpose that is served by a given logic gate.

Figure 3.24 shows how each of the other logic symbols could be used to indicate the purpose that is served by that gate. In each case, try to match the bubble positions and functional shape of the gate to its purpose.

Even when alternate logic symbols are not used, it is still possible to determine the purpose that is served by a given logic gate. A look at Figure 3.25 will help you see how this is done. A few points must be made regarding U1 in Figure 3.25. This rectangle is being used to represent a logic circuit that is far more sophisticated than the basic logic gates. This method of representing such a circuit is standard in logic diagrams. In later chapters we discuss these types of logic circuits and how to deal with them. For now, you will need to know that the inputs and outputs for such a circuit can be identified as being active-high or active-low in one of two ways:

1. An input or output is active-low if a bubble is present.
2. An input or output is active-low if there is a bar over the identifying label for that line. For example, $\overline{X1}$ would be assumed to be active-low.

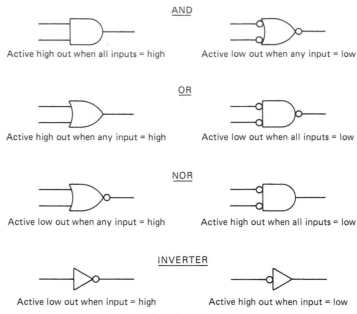

Figure 3.24   Alternate symbols.

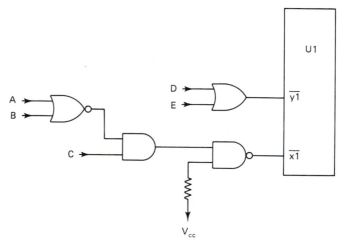

Figure 3.25

Also, you can usually determine whether a given line is an input or an output by seeing what is connected to the other end of the wire. If the line is an input, the wire that is drawn will certainly lead to the output of another circuit. If it is an output, it will lead to the input of another circuit.

Tracing the wire from $\overline{X1}$ leads to the output of the NAND gate, so $\overline{X1}$ must be an input. Since it is active-low, the output from the NAND gate must also be active-low. Two high inputs are required by the NAND gate to have a low output, so the inputs to this gate must be active-high. Input A is being provided by an AND gate, so the AND gate must have an active-high output. Two high inputs are required to provide the high output, so both inputs must also be active-high. This leads to the NOR gate, which must have a high output to provide the active level required by the AND gate. Since two low inputs are required by the NOR gate to have an active-high output, signal A and signal B must be active-low. Based on this reasoning, $\overline{X1}$ will receive its active input (low) only when signal A and signal B are low and signal C is high. If any of these signals malfunctioned, $\overline{X1}$ could not receive its active input signal. This would prevent U1 from working. U1 could also be prevented from working by a bad signal at its $\overline{Y1}$ input. Since this input is active low, the output from the OR gate is also active-low. Two low inputs are required to get a low output from an OR gate, so signals D and E are also active low. If any of the five input signals go bad, or one of the logic gates goes bad, U1 will not work.

By using the same signal tracing method just used, you can determine the purpose served by almost any logic gate. You may have to follow a line of inputs and outputs for a longer string of circuits, but with a little patience it can be done.

If you were troubleshooting a circuit such as the one just discussed, you would first need to determine which input to U1 was not going to its active level. You would then trace the signal back until you found the point at which the input/output relationship was bad. The odds would be good that the chip with the bad input/output relationship was the source of the problem.

3.6 COMMON FAULTS IN BASIC LOGIC GATES

As we stated earlier, the output from a digital circuit should be high, low, or making a rapid transition between the two. These transitions may, in practice, occur at a megahertz rate. A digital input or output will rarely stay at one logic level or the other for any length of time. Some inputs are wired directly to V_{cc} or ground, and thus will stay at one logic level permanently. Most of them, however, will be constantly changing. For these inputs and outputs, high or low levels that last for more than a few seconds usually indicate that there is a problem. A problem may also be indicated when an input or output is at a constant voltage that is between the high and low levels for the system. Each of these fault-indicating voltages, together with the possible causes for each, is covered in this section. In each case, we will discuss outputs only, since fault levels that appear at inputs are usually caused by a previous output. In those cases where the inputs themselves are bad, a few simple tests will verify that the problem is indeed the input.

Held-Low Outputs

An output from a basic logic gate may be held at a constant low by one of several conditions:

1. All digital logic chips have internal connections to ground. An output may be shorted to ground by the internal wiring of the chip. In this case, removal and replacement of the chip will eliminate the problem.

2. Solder bridges on printed-circuit boards can cause an output to be held at a constant low level. In this case, the problem is not actually being caused by the chip, so replacement of the chip will *not* solve the problem. You can verify that a solder bridge to a ground run on the circuit board exists by removing the chip from its socket and checking for continuity from the socket to ground using an ohmmeter. If the ohmmeter indicates that the resistance from the socket to ground is low, then you have a solder bridge, or some other shorting connection. In either case, the cause of the short must be located and removed. In most cases, the chip will also have to be removed and replaced, since a short to ground from an output usually destroys the chip.

3. All chips have one pin that is connected to ground and one pin that is connected to V_{cc}. These pins are used to supply the power connections that are required for the circuitry inside the chip to work. If there is a break

in the V_{cc} connection to the chip, all outputs from the chip will constantly be held low. Checking the voltage at the V_{cc} pin will quickly verify whether or not this is the problem. In this case, the chip is not the cause of the problem, and again, replacing the chip will not solve the problem.

4. The chip may not be receiving the signals that it is supposed to receive. In this case, further signal tracing is required, since you have not yet arrived at the source of the problem.

5. On rare occasions, an output from a given chip can be held low by the input pin to which it is connected. For example, refer back to Figure 3.25. If the input pin $\overline{Y1}$ was internally shorted to ground, it would appear as if the output from the OR gate was faulty. There are two ways that you could verify whether this condition exists. One of these methods is to use a device called a *current tracer*. Another method would involve removing the chip with the questionable input, bending the suspect pin up and outward from the chip, and putting it back in the circuit. If the output from the basic gate started working, the input is at fault. If not, the input is not at fault.

As you can see, a constantly low output can be caused by one of several conditions. If you cannot determine which condition is causing the problem, try to determine which ones are not. Using a process of elimination is as valid a technique for troubleshooting as any.

Held-High Outputs

There are several conditions that will cause the output from a given logic gate to be held constantly at a high level. These conditions are as follows:

1. An output pin may be internally shorted to V_{cc}. In this case, remove and replace the chip.

2. A solder bridge from the output run on the printed circuit board to a V_{cc} run could cause the output to be held high constantly. This condition will usually cause the chip to be destroyed the first time that the output tries to go low. You can again verify the bridge using an ohmmeter, but this time, the continuity check should be made to the V_{cc} connection to the board.

3. A break in the chip connection to ground may result in the output being held at a constant high level. When this condition exists, an oscilloscope will show the output to be trying to change logic levels, but not making it. For example, the output may be showing transitions, but these transitions would only be a few millivolts. Also, a continuity check from the ground pin to the ground connection to the board can be performed to verify whether or not there is any connection. There is still a third way to check this problem. Connect a properly grounded oscilloscope probe to the ground pin. If the pin is properly connected to ground, the trace on the oscilloscope will not move. If the trace jumps, there is a strong possibility that the pin is open. It should be noted that this test will work only if the oscilloscope is set up for dc operation.

4. A constantly high output may be caused by improper inputs to the chip. Again, further signal tracing is required at this point.

The output from a given logic gate will *not* be held high by a problem with the input that it is feeding. This simplifies the troubleshooting procedure for this type of problem. Again, when you cannot find the condition that is causing the problem, figure out which ones are not. It should be noted that the problem of an output being constantly held high does not happen as often as the problem of an output being constantly held low.

Constant Outputs That Are Neither High nor Low

Sometimes, the output from a given logic circuit will be held at a constant voltage that is neither high nor low, but rather, lies somewhere between the two. This problem also has several possible causes, as follows:

1. Either a bad V_{cc} connection or a bad ground connection, or both, can cause this problem. In this case, the output is being held in this voltage region, called the *prohibited region*, by components that are external to the logic gates themselves (i.e., resistors, capacitors, etc.). Again, a quick check of the V_{cc} and ground pin voltages will verify whether or not this is the problem.

2. Inputs that are in the prohibited region will cause the output of a gate to go into the prohibited region under some circumstances. For example, if a two-input NAND gate gets one high input and one input that is in the prohibited region, the output will go into the prohibited region. Exactly when an input can cause the output of a basic gate to go into the prohibited region is extremely unpredictable. As a rule of thumb, if the inputs to such a gate look the least bit strange, further signal tracing is probably required.

SUMMARY

As you can see, there are quite a few things that can go wrong when dealing with basic logic gates. All of these problems, however, can be found using an oscilloscope and an ohmmeter. While the various pieces of test equipment that are on the market do help considerably in determining the cause of a system malfunction, a bit of thought and good testing techniques will enable you to troubleshoot basic logic systems with standard test equipment.

QUESTIONS

1. When is the output from an AND gate high?
2. When is the output from an OR gate high?
3. When is the output from a NOR gate low?
4. When is the output for a NAND gate low?
5. When is the output from an XOR gate high?
6. When is the output from an XNOR gate high?
7. What is a truth table?
8. What is a logic symbol? What is a logic diagram?
9. What are the three basic logic operations?
10. Which logic gate is known as the universal gate? What does this name mean?
11. Which operation does the (+) sign represent?
12. Which operation would the expression (AB) imply?
13. Which logic gate can be used as a programmable inverter?
14. In each output column in the truth table, determine which logic operation is being represented.

Input		Output			
A	B	AB	A + B	$\overline{AB}$	$\overline{A + B}$
O	O	O	O	1	1
O	1	O	1	1	O
1	O	O	1	1	O
1	1	1	1	O	O

15. What task would be made easier by using alternate logic symbols?

16. What is the process for determining the alternate logic symbol for a given logic gate?

17. What are the most common causes for held-low outputs?

18. What are the most common causes for held-high outputs?

PROBLEMS

1. In Figure 3.26, determine the active input and output levels for all of the basic logic gates.

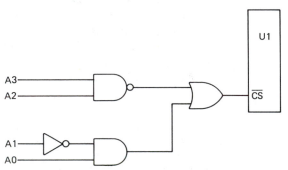

Figure 3.26 Circuit for problem 1.

2. For each of the circuits shown in Figure 3.27, determine which logic gate(s) have faulty input/output relationships.

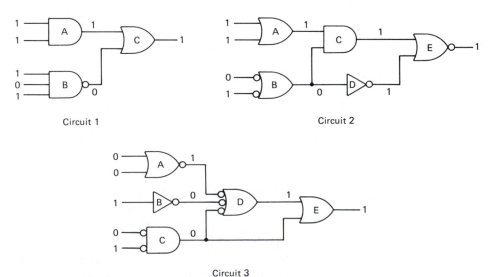

Circuit 1   Circuit 2

Circuit 3

Figure 3.27 Circuit for problem 2.

3. With the input waveforms shown in Figure 3.28, determine the waveforms that should appear at each of the test points indicated.

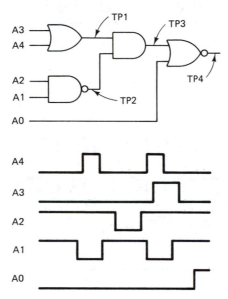

Figure 3.28 Circuit for problem 3.

PART II
ELECTRONIC FUNDAMENTALS

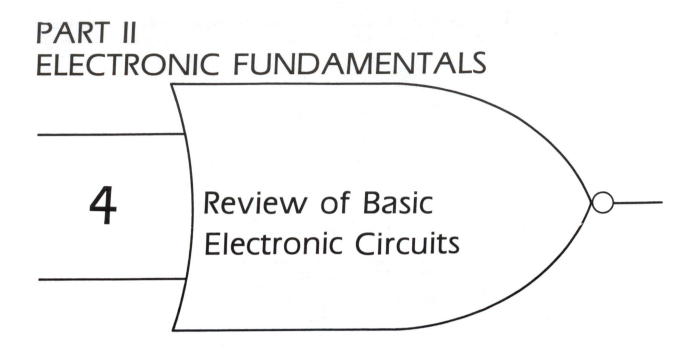

4

Review of Basic Electronic Circuits

Microcomputer systems are made up of a wide variety of electronic components, just like any other type of electronic system. The components that are encountered most often in microcomputer systems are diodes, transistors, and *RC* (resistive–capacitive) circuits. Inductive circuits are rarely encountered in digital circuits, but the subject of inductance becomes important when dealing with speakers and mechanical relays that are being driven by digital circuits. In this chapter we focus on these components and circuits, their applications in microcomputer systems, and the testing procedures for each.

4.1 RESISTIVE-CAPACITIVE CIRCUITS

In most analog devices, such as radios and televisions, *RC* circuits are used in high-pass or low-pass filters. These circuits pass certain frequencies while rejecting others. In digital applications, however, they are usually used for one of two purposes:

1. They are used for *pulse shaping*.
2. They are used to provide a time delay.

Both of these applications are made possible by the way in which *RC* circuits react to pulse waveform inputs. In order to understand the way in which *RC* circuits respond to pulses, we must first review the basic operation of a capacitor.

The fundamental rule of capacitor operation is that *a capacitor cannot change its plate-to-plate charge instantaneously*. If a given capacitor has a plate-to-plate charge of zero, and a voltage is applied to it, the plate-to-plate charge will change after a given period of time. In the circuit shown in Figure 4.1, a dc voltage is being applied to a circuit that consists of a capacitor and a resistor and a switch. Assume that the switch is initially open and that the capacitor has a plate-to-plate charge (voltage) of zero. When SW1 is closed, C_1 will start to accept a charge. It is important to remember that this charge has a polarity that *opposes* the charging voltage. Therefore, the circuit current at any given point in time can be calculated using the formula

$$i_c = \frac{E - E_c}{R}$$

where, i_c = circuit current, and thus the capacitor current

E = applied voltage

E_c = opposing charge on the capacitor

R = circuit resistance

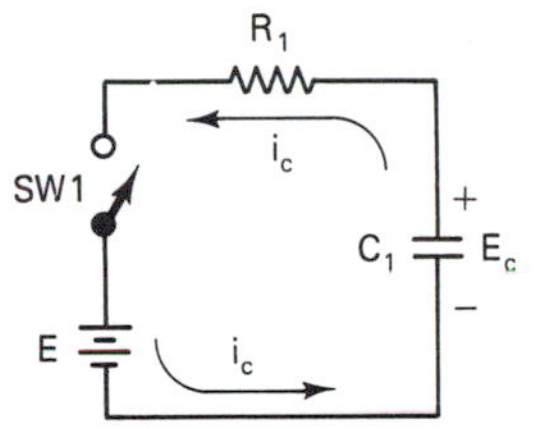

By substituting increasing values for E_c into the formula, you can see that i_c decreases. For example, using the values shown in Figure 4.1, and using the values of 1, 2, 3, 4, and 5 V for E_c you get the following corresponding values of i_c:

Figure 4.1 A simple RC circuit.

E_c(V)	$E - E_c$(V)	i_c(mA)
0	5	5
1	4	4
2	3	3
3	2	2
4	1	1
5	0	0

At the point at which E_c equals the applied voltage, circuit current stops flowing. This would make perfect sense, since there would no longer be a difference of potential across the resistor. With a full charge across the capacitor, you have two equal and opposing voltage sources, so the net voltage across the resistor is zero and no current can flow through it. This stops the charging current to the capacitor.

The catch to this circuit lies in the fact that the capacitor does not accept a charge at a linear rate. *The rate at which the charge on a capacitor increases is related directly to the amount of charging current.* As the circuit current decreases, the change in capacitor charge also decreases. For example, assume that C_1 in Figure 4.1 accepts a full charge (+ 5 V) in five equal time periods. Assume also that during each time period, the capacitor is charged by an amount equal to 63% of the voltage across the resistor. A graph of capacitor charge versus the five time periods would then look like the graph shown in Figure 4.2. An analysis of this graph would proceed as follows:

T_0-T_1:

$$V_R = E - E_c = +5 \text{ V} - 0 \text{ V} = +5 \text{ V}$$
$$\Delta E_c = V_R \times 63\% = 3.15 \text{ V}$$
$$E_c = E_c + \Delta E_c = 0 \text{ V} + 3.15 \text{ V} = 3.15 \text{ V}$$

T_1–T_2:

$$V_R = E - E_c = +5 \text{ V} - 3.15 \text{ V} = 1.85 \text{ V}$$
$$\Delta E_c = V_R \times 63\% = 1.17 \text{ V}$$
$$E_c = E_c + \Delta E_c = 3.15 \text{ V} + 1.17 \text{ V} = 4.32 \text{ V}$$

T_2–T_3:

$$V_R = E - E_c = +5 \text{ V} - 4.32 \text{ V} = 0.68 \text{ V}$$
$$\Delta E_c = 0.68 \text{ V} \times 63\% = 0.43 \text{ V}$$
$$E_c = E_c + \Delta E_c = 4.32 \text{ V} + 0.43 \text{ V} = 4.75 \text{ V}$$

T_3–T_4:

$$V_R = E - E_c = +5 \text{ V} - 4.75 \text{ V} = 0.25 \text{ V}$$
$$\Delta E_c = V_R \times 63\% = 0.16 \text{ V}$$
$$E_c = E_c + \Delta E_c = 4.75 \text{ V} + 0.16 \text{ V} = 4.91 \text{ V}$$

T_4–T_5:

$$V_R = E - E_c = +5 \text{ V} - 4.91 \text{ V} = 0.09 \text{ V}$$
$$\Delta E_c = V_R \times 63\% = 0.06 \text{ V}$$
$$E_c = E_c + \Delta E_c = 4.91 \text{ V} + 0.06 \text{ V} = 4.97 \text{ V}$$

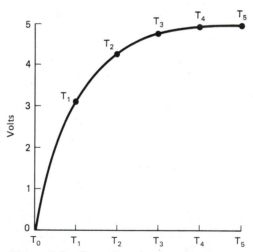

Figure 4.2 Capacitor dc charge curve.

As the graph and analysis both show, the amount by which the capacitor charges is not linear. The rate of change in E_c is constant, but since the available charging voltage decreases, the amount by which E_c changes also decreases. In fact, the capacitor in Figure 4.1 theoretically would never charge to the total value of the applied voltage. For all practical purposes, however, the capacitor could be considered to be fully charged after five time periods, like those used in the example that was just discussed.

Time Constants

The value of 63% used to determine the graph in Figure 4.2 was not chosen by chance. The time it takes for a capacitor to charge to approximately 63% of the resistor voltage in an *RC* circuit is referred to as the *time constant* for that circuit. In a given *RC* circuit, the capacitor will reach approximately 99% of its total potential charge in five time constants. A capacitor will also discharge at the same rate. In a given *RC* circuit, the capacitor will charge or discharge its total potential voltage by the following percentages:

Time constant	Percent of charge
1	63.2
2	86.5
3	95.03
4	98.17
5	99.33

The chart shows the amount by which the capacitor will have charged or discharged at the end of the given time constants. Thus an *RC* circuit with an applied voltage of 10 V will charge to 95.03% of the total potential (10 V) at the end of three time constants, for a total charge of approximately 9.5 V. The chart is based on the physical properties of the capacitor and thus is accurate for any *RC* network and for any applied dc voltage. The one thing that is not constant is the amount of time that we call a time constant. This real period of time varies from one *RC* circuit to the next. The method for determining the time constant for a given *RC* circuit is to multiply the value of its resistance by the value of its capacitance. By formula,

$$T = R \times C$$

where, T = time constant for the circuit

R = resistance of the circuit, in ohms (Ω)

C = capacitance of the circuit, in farads (F)

In a circuit having values of $R = 1\ k\Omega$ and $C = 0.01\ \mu F$, the time constant for the circuit would be found as

$$
\begin{aligned}
T &= R \times C \\
&= (1 \times 10^3) \times (0.01 \times 10^{-6}) \\
&= 10\ \mu s
\end{aligned}
$$

The capacitor in this circuit would therefore charge to approximately the applied voltage in 50 μs, the time required for five time constants. For any *RC* circuit, you can determine the time for the capacitor to charge or discharge by determining its time constant ($R \times C$), then multiplying that time by 5. In this period of time, the capacitor will charge to the value of the applied voltage, or discharge its total plate-to-plate charge.

EXAMPLE 4.1

For the circuit shown in Figure 4.3, determine the amount of time required for the capacitor to charge to the total applied voltage when the switch is closed.

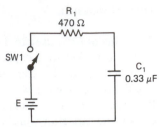

Figure 4.3 Circuit for Example 4.1.

Assume that the initial charge on the capacitor is 0 V.

Solution: The time constant for the circuit is found as follows:

$$T = R \times C$$
$$= (470) \times (0.33 \times 10^{-6})$$
$$= 155.1 \ \mu s$$

The time required for the capacitor to fully charge is equal to five time constants, so it will take 775.5 μs for the capacitor to fully charge.

EXAMPLE 4.2

If the applied voltage in Figure 4.3 is +5 V, approximately how long will it take for the capacitor voltage to reach 4.5 V?

Solution: 4.5 V is approximately 90% of the applied voltage. Since the capacitor will charge to approximately 90% of the applied voltage in about 2.5 time constants, the time required for C_1 to reach 4.5 V will be about 387 μs. This time would be valid only for purposes of approximation, since the change of 90% would not occur at exactly 2.5 time constants.

Pulse Inputs

There is a very important relationship between the pulse width of a given waveform and the time constant of the *RC* circuit to which it is being applied. Consider the waveform and *RC* circuit shown in Figure 4.4. For the circuit shown in Figure 4.4b, the *RC* time constant is equal to 220 μs. This means that the capacitor will reach its full charge in 1.1 ms. The pulse width for the input waveform shown in Figure 4.4a is 1.5 ms. This means that the capacitor will barely have enough time to charge before the pulse input is gone. The result is the badly distorted waveform shown in

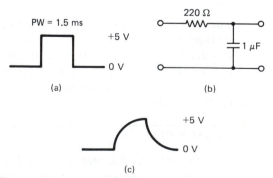

Figure 4.4 *RC* circuit response to pulse inputs.

Figure 4.4c. The rounding off of the leading edge is due to the charge time required by the capacitor in this circuit. The slope on the trailing edge of the output waveform is due to the discharge time required. The input waveform shown in Figure 4.4a would have been coupled with little or no distortion by the circuit shown in Figure 4.5. The time constant for the circuit in Figure 4.5a is equal to 1 μs, so the capacitor will reach full charge in approximately 5 μs. This is a much faster charge time than the circuit in Figure 4.4b. In fact, the capacitor in Figure 4.5a would reach full charge before 0.45% of the pulse width for the input waveform had expired. The output waveform would therefore look like the waveform in Figure 4.5b. When viewing both waveforms in the same time frame, there will appear to be very little, if any, distortion created by the *RC* circuit.

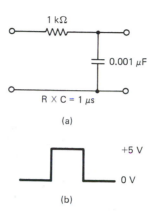

Figure 4.5 Pulse coupling by a short time constant *RC* circuit.

In contrast to the circuit just discussed, consider an *RC* circuit with a time constant that is approximately 10 times the pulse width of the input. In such a circuit, the capacitor would have virtually no time to charge, and the output would be almost a flat line. The circuit would therefore all but eliminate the input waveform.

The three circuits discussed have shown that there definitely is an important relationship between the time constant of an *RC* circuit and the pulse width (PW) of its input waveform. To describe these relationships, we refer to time constants as being *long, medium,* or *short* time constants. Each type of time constant is defined in terms of the pulse input, as follows:

1. If $R \times C \leqslant 0.1 \times \text{PW}$, the time constant is said to be a *short time constant.*
2. If $R \times C \geqslant 10 \times \text{PW}$, the time constant is said to be a *long time constant.*
3. Anything between these two is generally referred to as a *medium time constant.*

The circuit in Figure 4.4b had a medium time constant, which caused an undesirable, but usually acceptable, amount of distortion. The ideal time constant was found in Figure 4.5a. This was a short time constant and caused no distortion to the input waveform. The circuit that virtually eliminates the input waveform would be a long time constant. For an *RC* circuit with the output being taken across the capacitor, this type of time constant is totally unacceptable if the input is a pulse waveform.

The circuit configuration we have been discussing has had the output taken across the capacitor. This configuration is called an *integrator.* Another configuration would be to have the input applied to the capacitor and the output taken across the resistor. This type of circuit is called a *differentiator.* The basic configuration for the differentiator can be seen in Figure 4.6.

Up until now, we have ignored the waveform that appears across the resistor in an *RC* circuit. However, since this waveform is the output waveform for the differentiator, we must now determine what it looks like. The resistor waveform can be derived by taking the basic capacitor waveform and subtracting its instantaneous values from the applied dc input. Doing this with the waveform shown in Figure 4.6b would result in the waveform shown in Figure 4.6c. As you can see, the resistor waveform looks exactly like the discharge waveform for the capacitors in the previous examples.

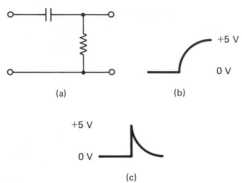

Figure 4.6 (a) Differentiator; (b) capacitor waveform; (c) resistor waveform.

A differentiator with a short time constant produces a waveform that requires a bit of explaining. The input and output waveforms for a differentiator with a short time constant can be seen in Figure 4.7. At the end of the fifth time constant, the capacitor has accepted a full charge and therefore has a plate-to-plate charge of 5 V. This means that the right plate is sitting at a potential that is 5 V more *negative* than the left plate. Now, recall that this plate-to-plate voltage relationship cannot be changed instantly. Thus, when the left plate is suddenly driven to 0 V, the right plate must go to − 5 V to maintain the plate-to-plate charge. The capacitor then discharges to ground through the resistor, causing the resistor voltage to return to zero. In a digital system having circuit limits of 0 and + 5 V, this negative spike could destroy the chips connected to this circuit. Because of this, a differentiator with a short time constant usually requires some type of additional circuitry to protect the logic gates from this spike. This circuitry will be covered at a later point.

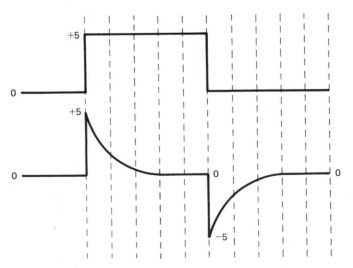

Figure 4.7 Circuit response of a short time constant differentiator.

The differentiator with a long time constant couples a signal as well as an integrator with a short time constant. The reason for this is relatively simple. With a long time constant, the capacitor in the circuit will maintain its plate-to-plate charge of zero, since it has no time to charge. This means that the output plate of the capacitor will follow the input plate during its voltage transitions. If the input plate goes to + 5 V, the output plate will do the same to maintain the plate-to-plate voltage relationship. This voltage on the output plate is felt across the resistor, so it also has a waveform that exactly follows the input waveform.

A summary of the input/output relationships for integrators and differentiators with long, medium, and short time constants is presented in Figure 4.8.

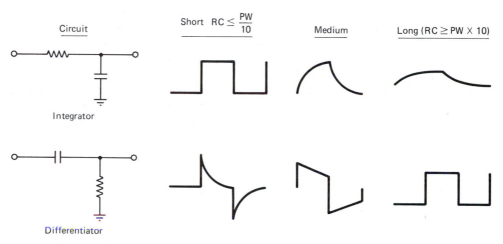

Figure 4.8   Summary of input/output relationships of *RC* circuits.

4.2 DIGITAL APPLICATIONS OF RC CIRCUITS

As we stated earlier, *RC* circuits are used primarily as time-delay circuits and pulse shapers in digital applications. The first application that we will look at is the integrator as a delay circuit. The circuit shown in Figure 4.9 uses an integrator with a medium time constant with an AND gate to delay the leading edge of a given pulse. The waveforms for the circuit in Figure 4.9a are shown in Figure 4.9b. When the output from gate 1 goes high, input A of gate 2 instantly goes high. As you can see,

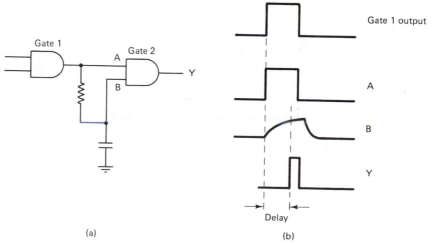

Figure 4.9   *RC* delay circuit and waveforms.

input B of gate 2 is connected to the output of gate 1 by way of an *RC* integrator. The input voltage at input B is equal to the voltage across the capacitor when measured with respect to ground. This capacitor will take some time to charge, and thus the initial input to gate 2 at input B is low. When the capacitor finally charges to the high input potential, gate 2 will have two high inputs. At that time, the output will go high. The *RC* circuit therefore caused a delay equal to the time required for the capacitor to charge to the logic 1 voltage level.

Another *RC* time-delay circuit can be seen in Figure 4.10. This circuit is used to supply a $\overline{\text{RESET}}$ signal when power is first applied to the system. A $\overline{\text{RESET}}$ is an active-low signal that causes a given circuit to go to a "starting point" in its operation. The exact purpose that is served by a $\overline{\text{RESET}}$ signal will be covered in a later chapter. What you need to know now is that this signal is needed by some digital circuits when power is first applied in a system. The circuit used to supply this signal is shown in Figure 4.10. When V_{cc} is first applied, circuit X receives the +5 V it needs to operate. At the same time, it needs the $\overline{\text{RESET}}$ signal to initialize its operation. The RC circuit at its $\overline{\text{RESET}}$ input will provide this signal for the time required for the capacitor to charge to the logic 1 voltage level. At that time, the $\overline{\text{RESET}}$ input will go to its inactive level. This type of circuit is called a *power-up reset circuit* and is very common in digital systems.

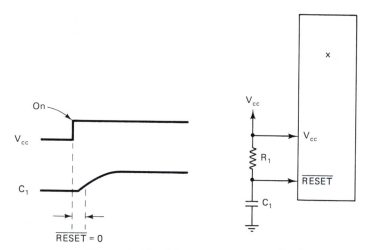

Figure 4.10 *RC* power-up reset circuit.

Pulse Shapers

A differentiator can be used to change a square wave into a series of rapid pulses that have a very short duration. A differentiator used for this purpose is shown in Figure 4.11. The differentiator shown in Figure 4.11 has a short time constant and thus has the spiked output that is shown. The purpose of D_1 is to short the negative spikes normally produced by a differentiator to ground. This protects the inputs to the circuit that the differentiator is feeding.

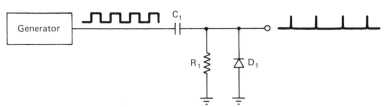

Figure 4.11 *RC* pulse shaping circuit.

There is another application for an *RC* circuit that does not really fall into either the time-delay application category or the pulse-shaper category, but rather, is sort of a combination of the two. This circuit, shown in Figure 4.12, is a *pulse generator*. With only a dc input, this circuit will supply a pulse waveform output. To understand how this circuit works, we will assume that the initial input to the first inverter is zero, due to there being no charge on C_1. This low inverted three times, so the output from the third gate is high. This high is applied to the *RC* circuit and causes C_1 to start to charge. When the charge on C_1 reaches the logic 1 level, the output from the first inverter goes low, which eventually causes the output from the third gate to also go low. This removes the charging voltage from the *RC* circuit, and the capacitor starts to discharge. When the charge on the C_1 reaches zero, the output of the final inverter goes high again, and the cycle repeats itself. The output frequency from the circuit will depend on the time constant of the *RC* circuit. Generally, the time constant must be long for the output waveform to have sharp leading and trailing edges. Three inverters are used in the circuit to provide enough of a delay from the input of the first gate to the output of the last to allow the circuit to work.

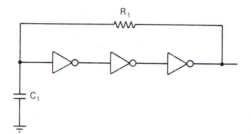

Figure 4.12 A simple square wave generator.

There are several types of signal sources in digital systems and most of them use *RC* networks to determine their output frequency. These circuits are described in Chapter 7.

4.3 TRANSISTOR OPERATION

In communications electronics, transistors are operated in their active region to provide linear amplification of sinusoidal waveforms. In these applications, transistors are not permitted to enter saturation or cutoff, since these two regions of operation are disastrous for class A amplifiers. In digital applications, however, transistors are operated almost exclusively in saturation and cutoff. In fact, the less time that a transistor spends in the active region, the better the overall operation of the digital circuit that contains the transistor.

To better understand the role that is played by the transistor in digital switching circuits, it is necessary to review the characteristics of a transistor that is in saturation or cutoff.

Saturation versus Cutoff

One of the simplest ways to view a transistor is to consider it to be an electronically variable resistor. The emitter-to-collector resistance can be varied from approximately zero ohms to what is, for all practical purposes, infinite ohms. This resistance is controlled by the base current, I_b. Figure 4.13a shows a basic common-emitter amplifier. When I_b increases, the resistance from emitter to collector decreases. When I_b decreases, the emitter-to-collector resistance increases.

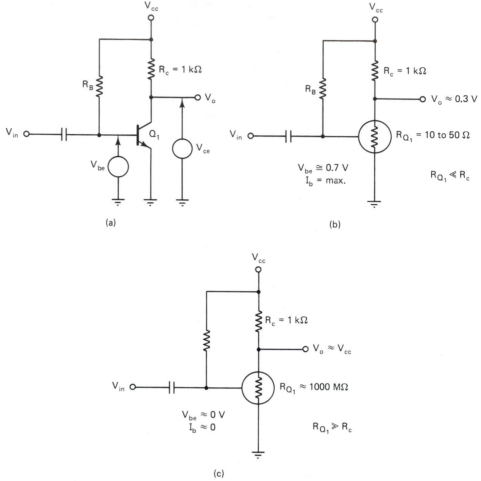

Figure 4.13 (a) Common-emitter amplifier; (b) saturation: transistor as a low resistance value; (c) cutoff: transistor as a high resistance value.

Saturation is the condition where, for all practical purposes, the emitter-to-collector resistance of the device equals zero ohms. This condition, caused by a high value of I_b, is represented in Figure 4.13b. When a transistor is in saturation, maximum electron flow from emitter to collector occurs, since the resistance between the two terminals is so low. A saturated transistor will have an emitter-to-base voltage (V_{be}) of approximately 0.6 to 0.7 V. With the low emitter-to-collector resistance, very little voltage will be developed across the emitter and collector terminals. This voltage, V_{ce}, will be approximately 0.3 V, assuming that the transistor is silicon.* For all practical purposes, the collector voltage of the saturated transistor shown in Figure 4.13b is zero volts.

Cutoff is the condition where the emitter-to-collector resistance of the device equals infinite ohms, for all practical purposes. This condition is caused by having an I_b of nearly zero and is represented in Figure 4.13c. In this condition, virtually no electron flow occurs in the emitter-to-collector circuit. You can, in this case, consider the device to be an open circuit. This means that virtually all of V_{cc} will be dropped across the transistor, so the output voltage will be approximately equal to V_{cc}. The collector current will be very near zero in this case.

---

*For our discussion we will assume that the transistors are silicon NPN transistors, since these are the ones that are most commonly used in digital circuits.

The characteristics for saturation and cutoff are summarized below. Be sure to commit these characteristics to memory, as they are extremely critical if a solid understanding of the operation of digital circuits is to be gained.

State	V_{be}	V_{ce}	I_c	Voltage provided to next stage
Saturation	High	Low	High	Low
Cutoff	Low	High	Low	High

Transistor Switching

In digital applications, transistors are used as high-speed electronically controlled switches that are being switched rapidly between saturation and cutoff. For this application, the time that is spent in the active region (the region of operation between saturation and cutoff) is held to an absolute minimum.

The circuit in Figure 4.13a can be used as a switch by applying a pulse to the base of the transistor. The pulse that would be applied in this case would vary between V_{cc} and ground. When the input to the transistor is equal to V_{cc}, the transistor will saturate, since V_{be} will be greater than 0.7 V. This will cause the output voltage of the transistor to be low. When the input voltage goes low, the transistor will go into cutoff. This will cause the output voltage of the transistor to be high. The time spent in the active region is determined by the rise and fall times of the input signal. The faster the rise and fall times of the input, the less time the transistor will spend in its active region.

As you may have guessed by now, a single common-emitter amplifier that is being used as a switch acts like an inverter. While inverters that are used are actually more sophisticated internally than a single transistor, the transistor gives a good indication of how inverters work. Now, take a look at a series of switching transistors, as can be seen in Figure 4.14. This circuit contains three transistors that are being used as switches. The input to Q_1 is high, causing that transistor to saturate. Since it is saturated, its collector voltage is approximately 0.3 V. This voltage is being applied to the base of Q_2. With 0.3 V on the base of Q_2, it is in cutoff. This means that its collector voltage is very high. This high collector voltage is applied to the base of Q_3, which saturates. The output voltage from Q_3 is therefore very low.

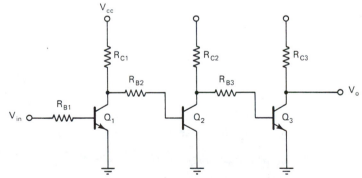

Figure 4.14   Transistor switches.

There is a quick rule of thumb for switching transistors. When they are wired together like those seen in Figure 4.14, a saturated transistor is always followed by a cutoff transistor, and vice versa. Knowing this eliminates some analysis time for this type of circuit. Using this rule, it is easy to see that a low input to Q_1 would put it in cutoff, causing Q_2 to saturate, causing Q_3 to be in cutoff. The final output voltage would therefore be high.

Another point to be made about switching transistors is that their power dissipation is relatively low. In fact, the ideal switching transistor will dissipate no power at all. According to the formula

$$P_d = I_c \times V_{ce}$$

you need some measurable value of I_c and V_{ce} in order to dissipate any power in a transistor. When a transistor is in cutoff, I_c is approximately zero, so P_d is approximately zero. When a transistor is saturated, V_{ce} is approximately zero, so again, P_d is approximately zero. The only time that a switching transistor dissipates any measurable amount of power is when it is switching between the cutoff and saturation states. During this time, both I_c and V_{ce} are measurable quantities, and as a result, P_d is also a measurable quantity. This presents another good reason for assuring that switching time is held to a minimum. The less time that is spent switching from one state to the other, the less power will be dissipated by the circuits.

The Effects of Switching Transistors on Pulse Waveforms

In Chapter 1, rise time, fall time, delay time, and storage time were all attributed to the physical characteristics of switching transistors. It is time to look at these pulse characteristics and their causes. To start, we will look at what is actually happening in a switching transistor. Figure 4.15 shows the physical transistor in its various states of operation.

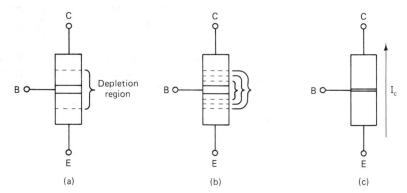

Figure 4.15   (a) Cutoff; (b) changing region size as V_{BE} increases; (c) saturation.

As you may recall from your basic courses in solid-state theory, the transistor is made up of two PN junctions that are biased either on or off. When a transistor is in cutoff, both junctions are off, and an insulating area, called the *depletion region*, is at its maximum physical size. This region surrounds the base and causes the resistance of the device to be at maximum from any one terminal to any other. This condition is shown in Figure 4.15a. Note that the depletion region is blocking the path of current flow through the device. When the input starts to go positive, the depletion region starts to shrink. When it gets small enough, current can flow through it. As it continues to get smaller, the current through it continues to increase. This changing is represented in Figure 4.15b. Eventually, the depletion region becomes so small that it virtually does not exist. At this point, there is no opposition to current flow through the transistor, and the transistor saturates. When the transistor is saturated, the base region is flooded with electrons, as can be seen in Figure 4.15c.

With these points in mind, we can now discuss the various time delays that a pulse waveform has.

Delay time is caused when the transistor is first being turned on from the cutoff region of operation. When the input signal to a cutoff transistor goes positive, it takes a period of time for the depletion region to dissolve to the point that it will let current flow through the device. How long this process takes depends on two things:

1. How much current is being supplied by the input signal
2. How large the depletion region was to begin with

Transistors are *current-controlled* devices. It is current, not voltage, that causes the depletion region to dissolve. The more current that is available at the input, the faster the depletion region will dissolve. The size of the depletion region at the start is also important. The larger it is, the longer it will take to make it small enough to allow current to pass through. The size of the depletion region depends on the initial amount of reverse bias on the device. When the input of the transistor makes its transition, the depletion region will shrink, thus letting current flow. This causes the output of the transistor to also start to make a transition. Delay time is the time required for 10% of this output transition to occur, starting at the point when the input made its transition. Therefore, delay time can be said to be the time required for the depletion region of a transistor to dissolve to the point that it will allow current to flow. It is measured at the 10% point of the transition merely as a matter of agreement as to where it should be measured.

Rise time and *fall time* are the times required for the transistor to complete the transition from one state to the other. These are controlled by the physical characteristics of the transistor and the rise and fall times of the input signal to the transistor. The only thing that can really be done to improve the rise and fall times of the transistor is to improve the rise and fall times of the input signal.

Storage time is the time required for the electrons to be removed from the base region when a saturated transistor is turned off. When the input signal to a saturated transistor goes low, it takes a period of time for all the electrons in the base region to be removed. These electrons must flow out of the base region before a depletion region can start to develop. Of all the time delays, this one is the worst. The only way to reduce or eliminate storage time is to ensure that the transistor never really saturates. Some logic circuits do this to eliminate storage time. These circuits are discussed in detail in Chapter 5.

4.4 COMMON TRANSISTOR APPLICATIONS IN DIGITAL SYSTEMS

Without a doubt, the most common application for discrete transistors in digital systems is when transistors are being used as a substitute for inverters. This application can be seen in Figure 4.16. In this circuit, circuit X has active high outputs. However, active-low signals are required to drive the indicator LEDs. Rather than use several inverter chips to change the active-highs to active-lows, discrete transistors are used. In about nine out of ten cases, the transistor is being used for this purpose if it is in the common-emitter configuration.

Sometimes, transistors are used as *current amplifiers* in digital systems. When a discrete transistor is being used as a current amplifier, it is usually wired in the emitter-follower configuration. In this configuration, the input is on the transistor base and the output is taken from the emitter. This eliminates the inverting process, since there is no phase shift from base to emitter in a transistor. The voltage gain for this circuit is approximately unity (1), and the current level of the input signal is increased significantly. In this case, the transistor is being used in place of a buffer.

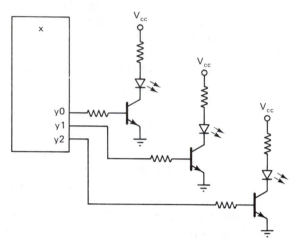

Figure 4.16   Transistor inverters.

High-Current Outputs

In many cases, digital circuits are used to drive circuits with high current requirements, such as mechanical relays. When the device that is being driven requires more current than the digital circuit is capable of producing, high power transistors or Darlington pairs are used. You may recall that a Darlington pair is a device that is used because of its high-current-amplification characteristics. A Darlington pair, which is shown in Figure 4.17, has a current gain equal to the product of the individual beta ratings for the transistors. Figure 4.17 shows a Darlington pair being used to

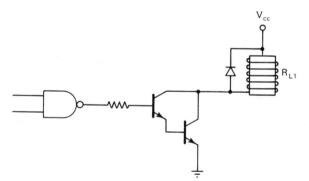

Figure 4.17   Darlington pair driver.

drive a mechanical relay. When the output from the NAND gate is high, the Darlington pair saturates. This provides the ground path necessary to activate the relay. Note that the relay has a diode in parallel with the relay coil. This is used to protect the Darlington pair from the "back *EMF*" produced when the relay turns off. Without this diode, this reverse voltage would destroy the Darlington pair. Any time that a digital circuit is driving a coil of any type, whether in a relay or a speaker, the coil will have a diode in parallel with it to protect the digital output driver.

In-Circuit Transistor Testing

Most transistors in digital circuits can be checked in-circuit using an oscilloscope, an ohmmeter, or both. When you suspect that a given transistor is not functioning, you should first check it while the circuit is on. Using a dual-trace oscilloscope, you can check to see if the output of a common-emitter transistor is the complement of its input. For example, consider the circuit shown in Figure 4.18. In this circuit, the transistor is being used to invert the output from the AND gate to provide an active-low input to the NOR gate. If the transistor is operating properly, the input to the NOR gate should always be the opposite of the AND-gate output. This could be checked using a dual-trace oscilloscope. You would not want to check at the leads of the transistor itself, since the base voltage on the transistor will be very close to the collector voltage when the device is saturated. If the AND-gate output and the NOR-gate input are not always opposites, there is sufficient reason to check the transistor further.

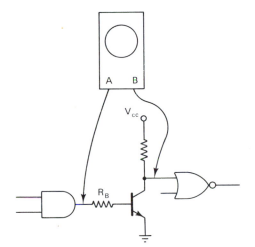

Figure 4.18 In-circuit transistor check.

You can further check a transistor in-circuit using an ohmmeter. However, there is one major precaution. *When using an ohmmeter to test a transistor in-circuit, you must be sure that the system is turned off and you must remove all chips that are connected to the transistor prior to performing the check!* The reason for turning off the system is simple. If the system is on, you will probably destroy the meter, since this is a resistance check you will be performing. The reason for removing all the chips connected to the transistor has to do with protecting those chips. Almost all chips have transistors or diodes at their inputs. These transistors and diodes are much more sensitive than your everyday discrete transistor. In fact, forward biasing these transistors and diodes without having V_{cc} and ground applied to the system can destroy them. Since the ohmmeter is a current supply, it may forward bias the inputs to the chips, causing the chips to be ruined.

Once the power is off and the chips have been removed, you may check the transistor in the method shown in Figure 4.19. When using the ohmmeter to check transistors, you should be sure to remember that the red lead on the meter is positive and the black lead is common (negative). Figure 4.19a shows the ohmmeter being used to check the emitter–base junction. In this case, the junction will be forward biased by the meter and the meter should read a *low* resistance. This resistance will typically be less than 1000 Ω. Now, reverse the leads, as shown in Figure 4.19b, to measure the reverse resistance of the emitter–base junction. In this test, you should read a very *high* resistance on the meter, typically greater than 100 kΩ. If both of these tests indicate that the transistor is okay, you check the collector–base junction in the same manner. Figure 4.19c shows the collector–base junction being checked in the forward-bias condition, which should read less than 1000 Ω, and Figure 4.19d shows the collector–base junction being checked in the reverse-bias condition, with a good reading being over 100 kΩ. If all of these tests show the transistor to be good, you have two more checks to make. Connect the meter leads to the emitter and collector. You should read a very high resistance in both directions. If all of these tests show the transistor to be good, your problem most likely lies elsewhere. If the transistor fails any of these tests, it is bad and must be replaced.

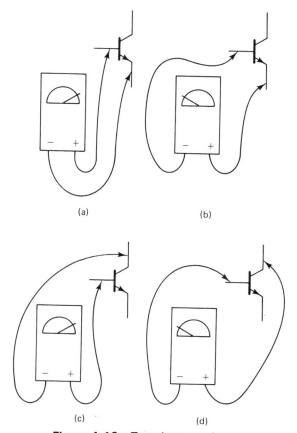

(a)   (b)

(c)   (d)

Figure 4.19 Transistor testing.

SUMMARY

The components and circuits discussed in this chapter are as critical to the operation of a computer as are the chips themselves. And, as often as not, it will be the discrete components that go bad rather than the chips. If you feel that you need more exposure to these concepts than has been presented here, you should check your references on basic and solid-state electronics. You may even consider a refresher course on these topics if you have been out of school for a while.

When looking at a logic diagram for the first time, remember the common applications that have been discussed in this chapter. They may help you to quickly determine the purpose that these circuits are serving. Above all, try the transistor checking methods discussed in this chapter. You will find that they work just as well for analog devices as they do for digital circuits.

QUESTIONS

1. What are the most common applications for *RC* circuits?
2. What is the fundamental rule for capacitor action?
3. Why doesn't the charge on a capacitor in an *RC* circuit change at a linear rate?
4. What happens to circuit current when a capacitor reaches full charge in a dc circuit?
5. Refer to Figure 4.2. What will be the charge on the capacitor at the end of each time interval if the applied voltage is 15 V?
6. What is a time constant? How many time constants does it take for a capacitor to reach maximum charge?
7. What is the percent of charge on a capacitor after each of the five time constants?
8. Which edge of a pulse will be distorted by a medium time constant?
9. What is a short time constant?
10. What is a long time constant?
11. What is an integrator? What are the most common applications for integrators?
12. What is a differentiator? What are the most common differentiator applications?
13. What must be done to protect digital circuits from the negative spikes that are produced by differentiators?
14. Which type of time constant is needed to make a coupler out of an integrator? A differentiator?
15. What is a $\overline{\text{RESET}}$ signal? What is a power-up reset signal?
16. Which two transistor operating regions are used most often in digital electronics? Why are these two regions used?
17. What are the operating characteristics of a saturated transistor?
18. What are the operating characteristics of a cutoff transistor?
19. What controls the emitter-to-collector resistance of a transistor?
20. Why doesn't a transistor that is operating in saturation and cutoff dissipate much power?
21. When does a switching transistor dissipate the most power?
22. What causes delay time? What can be done to reduce it?
23. What causes rise and fall times? What can be done to reduce these delays?
24. What causes storage time? What can be done to reduce it?
25. What is the most common application for common-emitter transistors in digital systems?
26. Why are emitter followers used in digital circuits?
27. When are Darlington pairs used in digital systems?
28. Why are diodes placed in parallel with relay coils and speakers when they are being driven by digital circuits?
29. What is the process for checking a transistor in-circuit with an oscilloscope?
30. What precautions must be taken before checking an in-circuit transistor with an ohmmeter?
31. What measurements are taken when checking a transistor with an ohmmeter? What should you read for each of these measurements?

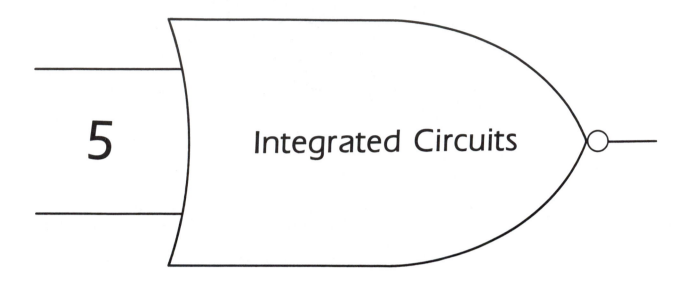

5 Integrated Circuits

An *integrated circuit* (IC) is an electronic device which contains up to thousands of solid-state components that have been constructed on a single chip of semiconductor material. Anyone who has worked on any type of electronic device during the past 10 years has come into contact with ICs at one time or another. The 741 operational amplifier, for example, is an integrated circuit that contains a number of transistors, resistors, diodes, and capacitors. All of these components have been constructed on a single chip of semiconductor material.

ICs are always easy to recognize. They are those "black boxes" that you see with all the pins on the sides. If you have ever looked at the circuitry of a microcomputer, you have seen that these components come in a variety of sizes, with the typical IC having anywhere from 8 pins up to 40 pins and more. Just as their size varies, so does the complexity of the functions that they perform. The simplest ICs contain nothing but solid-state resistors. The most complex IC, the *microprocessor*, contains the entire ALU and control units of a computer and is the basis of the microcomputer.

This chapter deals with integrated circuits and their electronic characteristics. We also show you how to determine what a given IC is, how to determine its operating characteristics, and how to read IC specification sheets.

5.1 BASIC CONCEPTS

As we stated earlier, integrated circuits are constructed on a single piece of semiconductor material. In most cases, this material is silicon. Silicon is preferred over germanium for IC construction because it is much more tolerant of heat.

The process by which ICs are produced is long and complex and thus will not be covered in great detail. The basic principle, however, is that components are "burned" into chips of semiconductor material that are typically less than 1/1000 of an inch thick. Transistors, diodes, resistors, and capacitors can all be manufactured on these chips, allowing virtually any type of electronic function to be performed by them.

Levels of Integration

There are four levels of circuit integration. Each level is identified by the number of basic gates that are made on a single chip. As the level of integration increases, the complexity of the circuit function also increases. The four levels of integration are as follows:

1. *Small-scale integration (SSI)*: These chips typically contain up to 10 gates per chip. All of the basic logic gates are made using SSI, which is the simplest type of IC to manufacture.
2. *Medium-scale integration (MSI)*: These chips contain from 10 to 100 gates per chip.
3. *Large-scale integration (LSI)*: These chips contain from 100 to 1000 gates per chip. They are mostly composed of metal-oxide semiconductor (MOS) devices, since MOS transistors take less physical space than bipolar transistors.
4. *Very-large-scale integration (VLSI)*: These chips contain over 1000 gates per chip and are by far the most complex and difficult to produce. VLSI technology has made it possible to produce single memory chips that can store over 256,000 bits of information.

Classifying the levels of integration by the number of gates that each contains can be somewhat misleading. A single gate can contain from four to six transistors, a variety of resistors and diodes, and some capacitors. If you consider a basic gate to contain an average of 10 components, VLSI chips can be classified as containing over 10,000 components on a single chip. That is pretty remarkable when you consider the fact that most of these chips are not much more than 1 cm in diameter.

Integrated circuits are a dream come true for the electronics technician who is faced with fixing a down computer. Imagine what it would be like to have to troubleshoot a microcomputer that had no integrated circuits. Instead of having to determine which of about 100 chips was not working, you would have to determine which of about 500,000 or more discrete components was causing the problem! Luckily enough, you only need to worry about whether the ICs are working in terms of their input/output functions. You do not need to worry about which component inside the chip is bad. You simply need to determine which chip is bad, then replace the whole chip.

Logic Families

A group of ICs that are all composed of circuits that share similar structure and operating characteristics is referred to as a *logic family*. All of the circuits in a given logic family will be compatible in supply voltage requirements, current requirements, and other circuit requirements.

Some logic families are electronically compatible with other logic families, and some are not. When two logic families are compatible, they can easily be wired together, or *interfaced*. When two logic families are not compatible, special circuitry is required to allow them to be interfaced. This chapter will identify those logic families that are compatible and cover the circuitry required to interface those that are not.

Some of the more popular logic families today are *transistor-transistor logic* (TTL), *complementary MOSFET logic* (CMOS), *emitter-coupled logic* (ECL), and *integrated injection logic* (I^2L). Each of these is covered in detail in this chapter, starting with the most common of the logic families, TTL.

IC Packaging

As we stated earlier, the semiconductor chips that contain the integrated circuits are packaged in various types of cases. The most popular type of IC casing is the dual-in-line package (DIP). This type of case is made of nonconducting plastic, with the size of the package being much larger than that of the chip it contains. The relative size of the package is determined by the number of pins required to connect the silicon

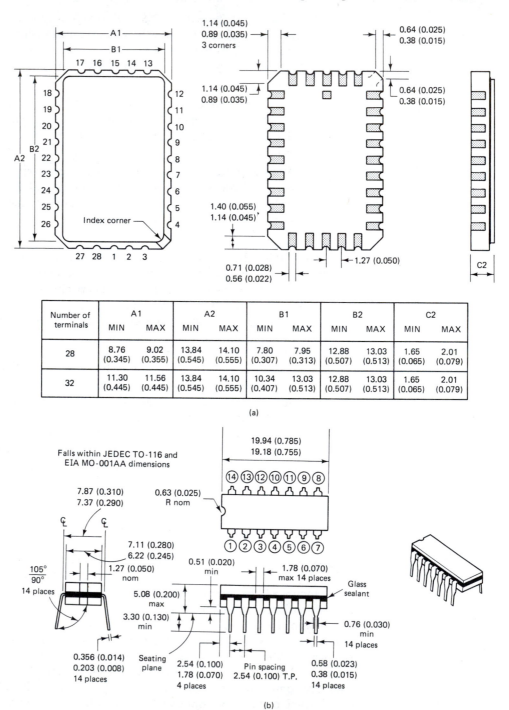

Number of terminals	A1		A2		B1		B2		C2	
	MIN	MAX	MIN	MAX	MIN	MAX	MIN	MAX	MIN	MAX
28	8.76 (0.345)	9.02 (0.355)	13.84 (0.545)	14.10 (0.555)	7.80 (0.307)	7.95 (0.313)	12.88 (0.507)	13.03 (0.513)	1.65 (0.065)	2.01 (0.079)
32	11.30 (0.445)	11.56 (0.445)	13.84 (0.545)	14.10 (0.555)	10.34 (0.407)	13.03 (0.513)	12.88 (0.507)	13.03 (0.513)	1.65 (0.065)	2.01 (0.079)

(a)

(b)

Figure 5.1 IC packages: (a) Rectangular FE ceramic chip carrier package (28-terminal package); (b) 14-pin J ceramic. (All dimensions are in millimeters and paranthetically in inches.) *(Courtesy of Texas Instruments, Inc.)*

chip inside to all the external circuitry. The size of the package also provides a source of heat dissipation, since the heat produced by the integrated circuit is spread out over the physical case in which it is housed.

Another type of IC package is the *carrier package*. This type of IC package is designed so that the chip is mounted on the surface of the printed circuit board, with the top of the IC being much closer to the actual surface of the board. Since these chips lay much closer to the surface of the board, less space is required between the various boards that are contained in the microcomputer.

Most carrier cases have no leads (pins on the IC). Instead, they have small metal contacts on the sides and bottom of the case that are connected to solder lands on the printed circuit board. Both of these types of packages, the DIP and the carrier case, can be seen in Figure 5.1.

The most common IC packages have 8, 14, 16, 20, 24, or 40 pins. Almost all of the basic logic gates are housed in 14-pin packages. Generally, the more pins or contacts an IC has, the more complex its function. This will become more evident as your study of digital electronics continues.

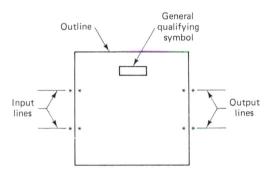

*Possible positions for qualifying symbols relating to inputs and outputs

Figure 5.2   Basic DLN symbol configuration.

5.2   DEPENDENCY LOGIC NOTATION

There is a type of logic symbology that is used for the purpose of improving the readability of logic diagrams. This symbology, called *dependency logic notation*, allows the technician or engineer to determine the function of a given circuit, generally without having to refer to some source of IC documentation to determine what type of IC is being dealt with.

With dependency logic notation (DLN), every IC is represented by a block that contains specific information as to the function performed by each input, the active input and output levels, and the relationship between the inputs and outputs. The basic format for DLN is shown in Figure 5.2. The outer block represents the circuit itself. At the top of the block will be a symbol, called a *general qualifying symbol*, that is used to indicate the type of circuit that is contained in the IC. Inputs are always on the left and outputs are always on the right, unless arrows are placed on the lines indicating a right-to-left direction of signal flow.

To give you an idea of how DLN works, consider the two circuits that are shown in Figure 5.3. Both of these diagrams are used to represent the 7400 TTL NAND IC. Figure 5.3a shows the conventional representation of the NAND gate. As you can see, the first gate has two inputs (pins 1 and 2), and the output is on pin 3. The NAND function is easily identified by the NAND symbols in the block. The DLN diagram for the same chip is shown in Figure 5.3b. Each block within the symbol represents one of the NAND gates within the IC. Identification of this chip as being a NAND gate is done in the same basic way as you identify the conventional NAND

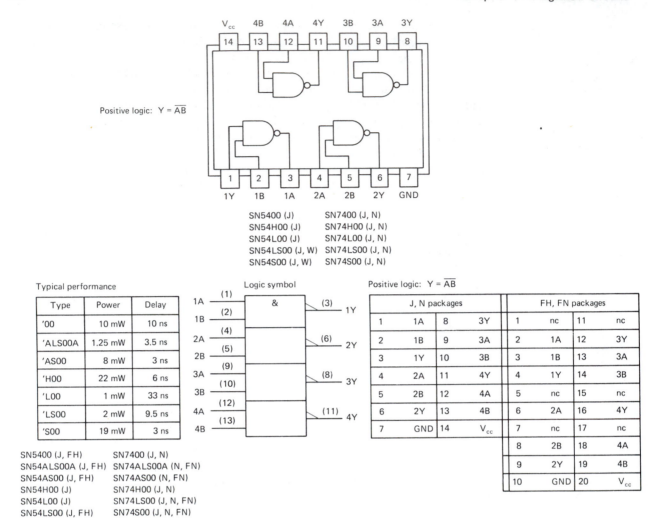

Positive logic: $Y = \overline{AB}$

SN5400 (J)   SN7400 (J, N)
SN54H00 (J)   SN74H00 (J, N)
SN54L00 (J)   SN74L00 (J, N)
SN54LS00 (J, W)   SN74LS00 (J, N)
SN54S00 (J, W)   SN74S00 (J, N)

Typical performance

Type	Power	Delay
'00	10 mW	10 ns
'ALS00A	1.25 mW	3.5 ns
'AS00	8 mW	3 ns
'H00	22 mW	6 ns
'L00	1 mW	33 ns
'LS00	2 mW	9.5 ns
'S00	19 mW	3 ns

SN5400 (J, FH)   SN7400 (J, N)
SN54ALS00A (J, FH)   SN74ALS00A (N, FN)
SN54AS00 (J, FH)   SN74AS00 (N, FN)
SN54H00 (J)   SN74H00 (J, N)
SN54L00 (J)   SN74LS00 (J, N, FN)
SN54LS00 (J, FH)   SN74S00 (J, N, FN)
SN54S00 (J, FH)

Logic symbol

Positive logic: $Y = \overline{AB}$

J, N packages				FH, FN packages			
1	1A	8	3Y	1	nc	11	nc
2	1B	9	3A	2	1A	12	3Y
3	1Y	10	3B	3	1B	13	3A
4	2A	11	4Y	4	1Y	14	3B
5	2B	12	4A	5	nc	15	nc
6	2Y	13	4B	6	2A	16	4Y
7	GND	14	V_{cc}	7	nc	17	nc
				8	2B	18	4A
				9	2Y	19	4B
				10	GND	20	V_{cc}

Figure 5.3 Conventional and DLN symbols for the SN7400.
(Courtesy of Texas Instruments, Inc.)

gate. The "&" qualifying symbol indicates an AND function, as does the shape of the symbol in Figure 5.3a. The "◁" sign on the output represents an inversion, as does the bubble on the conventional logic symbol. When the "◁" sign is present, an active-low is indicated. An active-high is indicated when the symbol is missing. Thus for the NAND gate in Figure 5.3b, an active-low output is achieved when inputs 1 & (AND) 2 are active-high. This relationship describes the NAND gate, which will have a low output only when all inputs are high. Under any other set of input conditions, the output will be high.

The qualifying symbols for the three basic logic functions (AND, OR, INVERT) are as follows:

Symbol	Function
&	AND
≥1	OR
1	INVERT[a]

[a]When an active-low " " symbol is shown on the output.

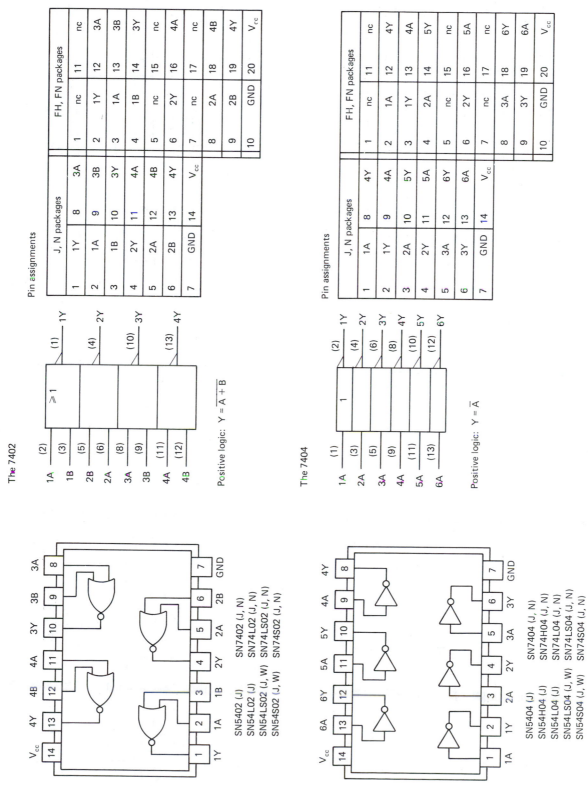

Figure 5.4 Basic logic gate pin and DLN diagrams. *(Courtesy of Texas Instruments, Inc.)*

73

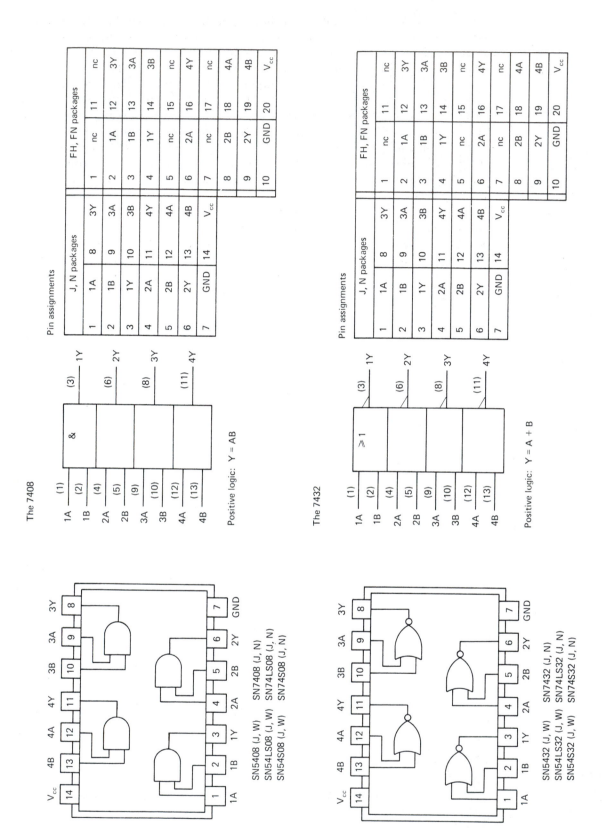

Figure 5.4 (Continued)

The OR symbol indicates that the output of the gate will be active when the *sum* of the inputs is greater than or equal to 1. This will occur if one or more inputs are at a logic 1 state. The "greater than or equal to" sign distinguishes the OR function from the XOR function, whose qualifying symbol is " = 1." The " = 1" symbol for the XOR gate indicates that the output will be active only when the sum of the inputs equals 1, meaning that only one of the inputs can be at the logic 1 state to produce a high output. Any other inputs must be low. The DLN symbols of the other basic logic gates are shown in Figure 5.4 on pages 73 and 74, together with the conventional diagrams for the same ICs. In the case of the 7408 AND gate, the "&" qualifying symbol is used. This, together with the lack of the "   " symbol on the output, indicates that each gate will have an active-high output only when all the inputs are high. Each of the gate symbols can be analyzed in the same basic fashion.

Figures 5.5 through 5.7 show all the symbols that are used in DLN. These symbols will each be explained as needed throughout the course of this text. Whenever possible, a given logic symbol will be accompanied by the DLN symbol for the IC, with an explanation of the DLN symbol used. A complete reproduction of the Texas Instruments publication on DLN appears in Appendix A. Refer to this appendix whenever you are not sure how to interpret a given DLN symbol.

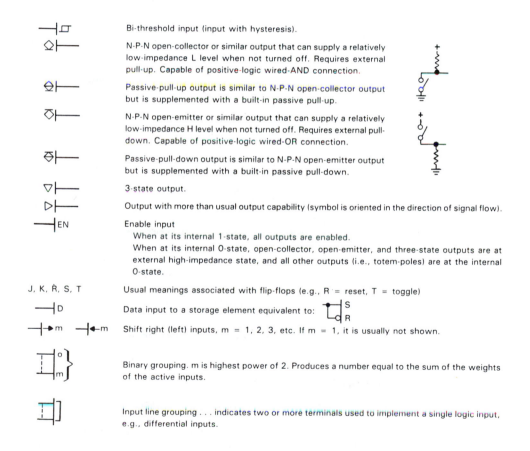

Bi-threshold input (input with hysteresis).

N-P-N open-collector or similar output that can supply a relatively low-impedance L level when not turned off. Requires external pull-up. Capable of positive-logic wired-AND connection.

Passive-pull-up output is similar to N-P-N open-collector output but is supplemented with a built-in passive pull-up.

N-P-N open-emitter or similar output that can supply a relatively low-impedance H level when not turned off. Requires external pull-down. Capable of positive-logic wired-OR connection.

Passive-pull-down output is similar to N-P-N open-emitter output but is supplemented with a built-in passive pull-down.

3-state output.

Output with more than usual output capability (symbol is oriented in the direction of signal flow).

Enable input
   When at its internal 1-state, all outputs are enabled.
   When at its internal 0-state, open-collector, open-emitter, and three-state outputs are at external high-impedance state, and all other outputs (i.e., totem-poles) are at the internal 0-state.

J, K, R̄, S, T   Usual meanings associated with flip-flops (e.g., R = reset, T = toggle)

Data input to a storage element equivalent to:

Shift right (left) inputs, m = 1, 2, 3, etc. If m = 1, it is usually not shown.

Binary grouping. m is highest power of 2. Produces a number equal to the sum of the weights of the active inputs.

Input line grouping . . . indicates two or more terminals used to implement a single logic input, e.g., differential inputs.

Figure 5.5 Symbols inside the outline. *(Courtesy of Texas Instruments, Inc.)*

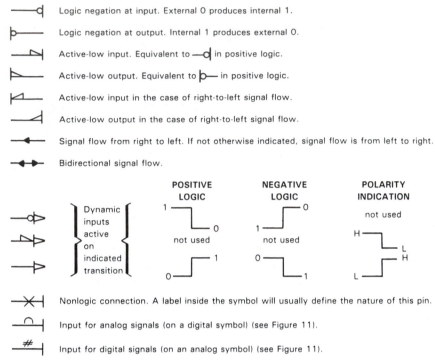

Logic negation at input. External 0 produces internal 1.

Logic negation at output. Internal 1 produces external 0.

Active-low input. Equivalent to ─o in positive logic.

Active-low output. Equivalent to o─ in positive logic.

Active-low input in the case of right-to-left signal flow.

Active-low output in the case of right-to-left signal flow.

Signal flow from right to left. If not otherwise indicated, signal flow is from left to right.

Bidirectional signal flow.

	POSITIVE LOGIC	NEGATIVE LOGIC	POLARITY INDICATION

Dynamic inputs active on indicated transition

Nonlogic connection. A label inside the symbol will usually define the nature of this pin.

Input for analog signals (on a digital symbol) (see Figure 11).

Input for digital signals (on an analog symbol) (see Figure 11).

Figure 5.6 Qualifying symbols for inputs and outputs. *(Courtesy of Texas Instruments, Inc.)*

SYMBOL	DESCRIPTION
&	AND gate or function.
≥ 1	OR gate or function. The symbol was chosen to indicate that at least one active input is needed to activate the output.
= 1	Exclusive OR. One and only one input must be active to activate the output.
1	The one input must be active.
▷ or ◁	A buffer or element with more than usual output capability (symbol is oriented in the direction of signal flow).
⎍	Schmitt trigger; element with hysteresis.
X/Y	Coder, code converter, level converter.
	The following are examples of subsets of this general class of qualifying symbol used in this book:
	BCD/7-SEG — BCD to 7-segment display driver.
	TTL/MOS — TTL to MOS level converter.
	CMOS/PLASMA DISP — Plasma-display driver with CMOS-compatible inputs.
	MOS/LED — Light-emitting-diode driver with MOS-compatible inputs.
	CMOS/VAC FLUOR DISP — Vacuum-fluorescent display driver with CMOS-compatible inputs.
	CMOS/EL DISP — Electroluminescent display driver with CMOS-compatible inputs.
	TTL/GAS DISCH DISPLAY — Gas-discharge display driver with TTL-compatible inputs.
SRGm	Shift register. m is the number of bits.

Figure 5.7 General qualifying symbols. *(Courtesy of Texas Instruments, Inc.)*

5.3 TRANSISTOR-TRANSISTOR LOGIC

TTL is by far the most common logic family in use today. This logic family was developed in the early 1970s and has become the standard for most SSI and MSI circuits. The name TTL signifies that the input and output components are transistors. These transistors are NPN bipolar transistors, as can be seen in Figure 5.8. The circuit shown here is the TTL two-input NAND gate. As you can see, the input signals (A and B) are applied to a transistor, and the output (Y) is taken from the collector of a transistor: thus the name "transistor-transistor logic." All TTL circuits have this type of input/output setup. The standard supply voltage (V_{cc}) for TTL circuitry is + 5 V, which is the V_{cc} value that we have been using for all of our discussions up to this point.

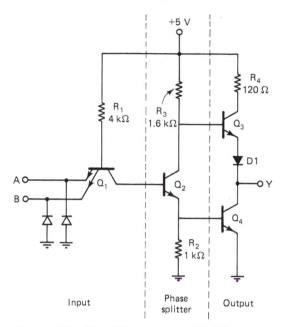

Figure 5.8 The TTL two-input NAND gate.

To help you understand how TTL circuits work, we will discuss the operation of this NAND gate in depth. This discussion should also remove some of the mystery surrounding the operation of basic logic gates. While the schematics for the other basic gates are somewhat different than the NAND gate schematic, they work in the same basic manner.

TTL Circuit Analysis

The circuit shown in Figure 5.8 can be broken down into three sections. Q_1 is a *multi-emitter transistor* that is used as the input to the circuit. The combination of Q_3 and Q_4 forms what is called the *totem-pole pair*, which is used to provide the final output from the gate. Q_2 is called the *phasesplitter*, which is used to determine which transistor in the totem-pole pair will be on at any given point in time.

As a start, we look at the totem-pole pair. These transistors (Q_3 and Q_4) are wired so that only one of the two transistors can be saturated. If Q_3 is on, Q_4 will be off, and vice versa. If Q_3 is on and Q_4 is off, the output is effectively connected to V_{cc} through D_1, Q_3, and R_4. In this case, the output will typically be between 3.0 and 4.5 V, which is considered to be a logic 1. If Q_4 is on and Q_3 is off, the output is effectively connected to ground. In this case, the output will typically be between 0.4 and 0.8 V. *If the circuit is operating properly, these two transistors will never both be saturated or cut off.* Which transistor is on will be determined by the phasesplitter, Q_2. If Q_2 is in saturation, Q_4 will be on and Q_3 will be off. If Q_2 is in cutoff, Q_3 will be on and Q_4 will be off. Each of these Q_2 operating states and their results will now be looked at in greater detail.

Q_2 saturated. When Q_2 is in saturation, current flows from its emitter to its collector. This current causes approximately 1 V to be developed across R_2. This voltage causes Q_4's emitter–base junction to be forward biased, which turns Q_4 on. At this time, the emitter of Q_2 is clamped to approximately 0.7 V by the base of

Q_4. Since Q_2 is saturated, its collector will be approximately 0.3 V more positive than its emitter. The collector of Q_2 will therefore be at around 1 V, since its emitter is at approximately 0.7V. This would be enough voltage to turn on Q_3 if it were not for the Q_3 emitter circuit. The emitter circuit for Q_3 contains D_1 and Q_4. To turn Q_3 on, the potential applied to its base would have to equal the sum of the V_{ce} of Q_4, the forward voltage drop of D_1, and the 0.7 V (V_{be}) needed to turn on Q_3. This means that with Q_4 on, it would take 1.7 V to turn on Q_3. Since there is only 1 V on the base of Q_3, it is biased off. Thus, with Q_2 on, Q_4 is on and Q_3 is off.

Q_2 *cutoff.* When Q_2 is off, there is no current flowing in its emitter circuit, since an off transistor acts like an open switch. With no current in the emitter circuit of Q_2, there is no voltage developed across R_2, and Q_4 will be off. Since there is no current flow in the collector circuit of Q_2, the full value of V_{cc} (+ 5 V) is felt at the base of Q_3. This turns both Q_3 and D_1 on, connecting the output to V_{cc}. The relative states of Q_2, Q_3, and Q_4 can now be summarized as follows:

Q_2	Q_3	Q_4
On	Off	On
Off	On	Off

Just remember that the operating states of Q_2 and Q_4 are always the same, and Q_3 is always in the opposite state. All we need to cover now is the way in which Q_2 is turned on and off.

As was stated earlier, Q_1 is a multi-emitter transistor that is used as the input to the logic circuit. As you can see in Figure 5.8, the inputs are applied to the emitters of Q_1. If any emitter to Q_1 is grounded, the transistor will saturate, since its base is connected to V_{cc} through R_1. If *all* of the Q_1 emitters are at + 5 V, V_{be} of Q_1 will equal 0 volts and Q_1 will be off. *The key to turning Q_1 on is to supply any one of its emitters with a ground path.* If either emitter is at ground, Q_1 will saturate. This will drop its collector to approximately 0.3 V. With 0.3 V being applied to the base of Q_2, Q_2 will be off. If *all* of the emitters of Q_1 are at + 5 V, Q_1 will be off and its collector will rise toward + 5 V. This voltage will be applied to the base of Q_2, turning it on. A summary of all the transistor operating states is as follows:

Q_1	Q_2	Q_3	Q_4
On	Off	On	Off
Off	On	Off	On

As you can see, the operating states for Q_1 and Q_3 are always the same. The operating states for Q_2 and Q_4 are equal to each other and opposite to the operating states for the other two transistors. The operation of this circuit will follow the NAND-gate truth table. If any input is low (at ground), Q_1 will be on, which leads to Q_3 being on. This provides a high output. The only time that Q_4 is on, providing a low output, is when all of the Q_1 inputs are high.

It may interest you to know that the TTL inverter differs from the NAND gate just discussed in only one aspect. The TTL inverter has only one input to Q_1. Except for that, the circuit is exactly the same. By the same token, the three-input NAND gate has three emitters on Q_1, the four-input NAND gate has four emitters on Q_1, and the eight-input NAND gate has eight emitters on Q_1. Except for that, these circuits are all exactly the same internally.

A Few Important Points Concerning TTL

Now that we have discussed the basic operation of a TTL gate, there are a few points that should be made regarding the operation of TTL circuits in general:

1. *All TTL circuits respond to ground paths at their inputs.* The key to the operation of the circuit in Figure 5.8 was to provide a ground path to Q_1 so that it will saturate. This will cause the output to go high. If Q_1 is not allowed to saturate, the output will be low. In other words, anything that prevents Q_1 from saturating will cause the output to be low. *Leaving the inputs open will prevent Q_1 from saturating just as putting them at $+5$ V will prevent it from saturating.* In both cases, the result is the same. The bottom line is that *open TTL inputs almost always act as a logic 1.* You must therefore be careful when leaving TTL inputs open. If, for example, you leave an input to an OR gate open, the output from that gate will never go low, since a high input (or open input) will cause the output from the OR gate to be high.

2. At this point, we need to redefine the terms *logic 1* and *logic 0.* Recall that the circuit in Figure 5.8 had a logic 1 output when Q_3 was on. At that time, the output was connected to V_{cc} through a circuit that had a relatively small amount of impedance. When the output was at a logic 0 ($Q_4 =$ on), the output was connected to ground through Q_4, which has very little impedance when saturated. With these points in mind, we will now redefine logic 1 and logic 0 as follows:

    logic 1: a low impedance path to V_{cc}

    logic 0: a low impedance path to ground

    The reason for using these definitions of logic 1 and logic 0 will become evident in our discussion of three-state logic later in this chapter.

TTL IC Numbering

Standard TTL logic circuits are numbered in one of two formats. They are either 7400 series ICs or 5400 series ICs. The 74 and 54 indicate that the chip is TTL, and the last two (and sometimes three) numbers indicate which TTL chip it is. The 74 series chips are the standard commercial TTL chips, and the 54 series chips are military-application chips. The 54 series ICs have a tolerance for a wider range of operating temperatures. This point will be discussed further in the next section. One important point, however, is that for each of the 74 series chips, there is an exact 54 series equivalent. For example, the military hex inverter is numbered 5404 instead of 7404. Other than the chip number (54 versus 74) and the operating characteristic differences, these two chips are exactly the same. Their pin configurations are also the same, so in most cases, one can be substituted for the other.

There are quite a few manufacturers of standard TTL ICs. All of these manufacturers, however, use the same basic numbering system. So if you have a 7432 that needs to be replaced, you can replace it with a 7432 from any of the manufacturers of standard TTL chips. They all have the same pin configurations and numbering systems.

Data books are available for the TTL logic family. These data books show the pin configurations for all the TTL chips and provide the spec sheets for each chip. Any digital technician must have one of these data books, as they are an indispensable tool for working with digital systems. There are also data books available for the other logic families.

We will now discuss the parameters that are listed on typical TTL spec sheets. These parameters apply not only to TTL, but to all the logic families. The numerical values for the parameters may change from one logic family to another, but the parameters themselves will not. Therefore, if you can read the spec sheet for one logic family, you can read the spec sheet for any other.

TTL Parameters

A parameter is simply a limit. All logic circuits have certain operating limits. The parameters for a given circuit are all listed on its spec sheet. The typical TTL spec sheet can be seen in Figure 5.9. This is the spec sheet for the NAND gates and the inverter. Since the basic circuit construction for all of these gates is the same, the electrical characteristics will not change from one gate to another. For our discus-

Recommended operating conditions

Parameter	54 FAMILY / 74 FAMILY	SERIES 54 / SERIES 74 ('00, '04, '10, '20, '30)			SERIES 54H / SERIES 74H ('H00, 'H04, 'H10, 'H20, 'H30)			SERIES 54L / SERIES 74L ('L00, 'L04, 'L10, 'L20, 'L30)			SERIES 54LS / SERIES 74LS ('LS00, 'LS04, 'LS10, 'LS20, 'LS30)			SERIES 54S / SERIES 74S ('S00, 'S04, 'S10, 'S20, 'S30, 'S133)			UNIT
		MIN.	NOM.	MAX.	MIN.	NOM.	MAX.	MIN.	NOM	MAX.	MIN.	NOM.	MAX.	MIN.	NOM.	MAX.	
Supply voltage, V_{cc}	54 Family	4.5	5	5.5	4.5	5	5.5	4.5	5	5.5	4.5	5	5.5	4.5	5	5.5	V
	74 Family	4.75	5	5.25	4.75	5	5.25	4.75	5	5.25	4.75	5	5.25	4.75	5	5.25	
High-level output current, I_{OH}	54 Family			−400			−500			−100			−400			−1000	µA
	74 Family			−400			−500			−200			−400			−1000	
Low-level output current, I_{OL}	54 Family			16			20			2			4			20	mA
	74 Family			16			20			3.6			8			20	
Operating free-air temperature, T_A	54 Family	−55		125	−55		125	−55		125	−55		125	−55		125	°C
	74 Family	0		70	0		70	0		70	0		70	0		70	

Electrical characteristics over recommended operating free-air temperature range (unless otherwise noted)

Parameter	Test figure	Test conditions[†]		SERIES 54 / SERIES 74 ('00, '04, '10, '20, '30)			SERIES 54H / SERIES 74H ('H00, 'H04, 'H10, 'H20, 'H30)			SERIES 54L / SERIES 74L ('L00, 'L04, 'L10, 'L20, 'L30)			SERIES 54LS / SERIES 74LS ('LS00, 'LS04, 'LS10, 'LS20, 'LS30)			SERIES 54S / SERIES 74S ('S00, 'S04, 'S10, 'S20, 'S30, 'S133)			UNIT
				MIN.	TYP[‡]	MAX.	MIN.	TYP[‡]	MAX.	MIN.	TYP[‡]	MAX.	MIN.	TYP[‡]	MAX.	MIN.	TYP[‡]	MAX.	
High-level input voltage, V_{IH}	1, 2			2			2			2			2			2			V
Low-level input voltage, V_{IL}	1, 2		54 Family			0.8			0.8			0.7			0.7			0.8	V
			74 Family			0.8			0.8			0.7			0.8			0.8	
Input clamp voltage, V_{IK}	3	V_{cc} = MIN., I_I = [§]				−1.5			−1.5						−1.5			−1.2	V
High-level output voltage, V_{OH}	1	V_{cc} = MIN., V_{IL} = V_{IL} max, I_{OH} = MAX.	54 Family	2.4	3.4		2.4	3.5		2.4	3.3		2.5	3.4		2.5	3.4		V
			74 Family	2.4	3.4		2.4	3.5		2.4	3.2		2.7	3.4		2.7	3.4		
Low-level output voltage, V_{OL}	2	V_{cc} = MIN., V_{IH} = 2 V, I_{OL} = MAX.	54 Family		0.2	0.4		0.2	0.4		0.15	0.3		0.25	0.4			0.5	V
			74 Family		0.2	0.4		0.2	0.4		0.2	0.4		0.25	0.5			0.5	
		I_{OL} = 4 mA	Series 74LS												0.4				
Input current at maximum input voltage, I_I	4	V_{cc} = MAX.	V_I = 5.5 V			1			1			0.1						1	mA
			V_I = 7 V												0.1				
High-level input current, I_{IH}	4	V_{cc} = MAX.	V_{IH} = 2.4 V			40			50			10							µA
			V_{IH} = 2.7 V												20			50	
Low-level input current, I_{IL}	5	V_{cc} = MAX.	V_{IL} = 0.3 V									−0.18							mA
			V_{IL} = 0.4 V						−1.6			−2			−0.4				
			V_{IL} = 0.5 V															−2	
Short circuit output current*, I_{OS}	6	V_{cc} = MAX.	54 Family	−20		−55	−40		−100	−3		−15	−20		−100	−40		−100	mA
			74 Family	−18		−55	−40		−100	−3		−15	−20		−100	−40		−100	
Supply current, I_{CC}	7	V_{cc} = MAX.																	mA

[†] For conditions shown as MIN. or MAX., use the appropriate value specified under recommended operating conditions.
[‡] All typical values are at V_{cc} = 5 V, T_A = 25°C.
[§] I_I = −12 mA for SN54'/SN74', −8 mA for SN54H'/SN74H', and −18 mA for SN54LS'/SN74LS' and SN54S'/SN74S'.
*Not more than one output should be shorted at a time, and for SN54H'/SN74H', SN54LS'/SN74LS', and SN54S'/SN74S', duration of short-circuit should not exceed 1 second.

Figure 5.9   The TI 7400 NAND gate specification sheet. *(Courtesy of Texas Instruments, Inc.)*

sion, we will be concerned only with the "series 54/series 74" column in the chart shown. The other columns deal with TTL subfamilies and are covered in the next section.

It was stated earlier that the 54 series TTL chips have a wider range of acceptable supply voltages and operating temperatures than do the 74 series chips. This can be seen in the ratings listed in Figure 5.9. Note that the 54 series has a V_{cc} range of 4.5 to 5.5 V, while the range for the 74 series is 4.75 to 5.25 V. Also, the 54 series has an ambient temperature range of -55 to 125 °C, while the 74 series has a range of 0 to 70 °C. Other than for these two ratings, there is little, if any, difference between the series.

The *high-level input voltage* (V_{IH}) is the minimum input voltage guaranteed to be recognized as a logic 1 by the gate. Any voltage higher than this will be recognized as a logic 1 by the inputs. The *high-level output voltage* (V_{OH}) is the lowest output voltage that will be produced when the output is high. For the 7400, these two values are as follows:

$$V_{OH} = +2.4 \text{ V}$$

$$V_{IH} = +2.0 \text{ V}$$

Notice that there is a 400-mV difference between the lowest logic 1 output and the lowest recognizable logic 1 input. This difference is referred to as the *high-level noise margin* for the circuit. A 400-mV noise margin means that up to 400 mV of the output of one gate could be attenuated and still be recognized as a logic 1 at the input of the next gate. This noise margin (400 mV) is the worst-case value for these gates.

The *low-level output voltage* (V_{OL}) is the maximum output voltage that the gate will produce when in the low-output condition. The *low-level input voltage* (V_{IL}) is the highest voltage that will be recognized to be low by an input. As Figure 5.9 indicates, these values are as follows:

$$V_{OL} = +0.4 \text{ V}$$

$$V_{IL} = +0.8 \text{ V}$$

Again, you have a 400 mV difference between the input and output levels. This noise margin is referred to as the *low-level noise margin*. For the 7400, up to 400 mV of noise can be generated in a line between two gates without affecting a low signal level.

The *input clamp voltage* (V_{IK}) is the maximum negative voltage that can be clamped to ground through the protective diodes at the gate's inputs. If any signal is received that is more negative than this value, the gate will probably be destroyed.

Fanout

As the table in Figure 5.9 indicates, the *high-level input current* (I_{IH}) is equal to 40 µA for the 7400. At the same time, the *high-level output current* (I_{OH}) for the 7400 is 400 µA. This would indicate that the output of one 7400 is capable of supplying the current required by 10 inputs. The number of inputs that can be driven by a single output is referred to as the *fanout* for the gate. While the fanout gives the driving capability of a gate under worst-case conditions, it should never be exceeded, as the circuit operation could become erratic. For example, assume that the 7400, which has a fanout of 10, was being used to drive 12 other 7400s as shown in Figure 5.10. If the inputs each require a 40-µA current flow, the output from the driving gate will not be able to provide a path for this current. This would cause the noise margins to decrease and the propagation delay to increase for the gates that are being driven. To determine the fanout for a given logic family, simply divide the output current

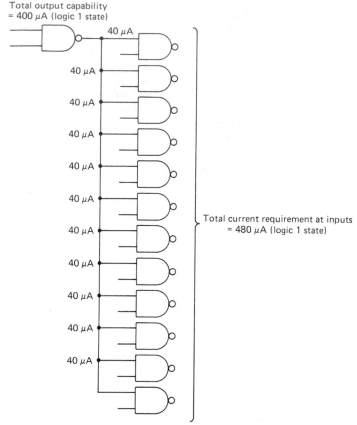

Figure 5.10   Fanout illustration.

by the input current of the inverter for that logic family. This will give you a typical fanout value for that logic family. *Note that the fanout for the gate must be determined for both the high output current values and the low output current values.* If the results are not equal, you must take the lower of the two numbers. For example, look at the input and output current levels for the 74S series chips in Figure 5.9. The current levels for the 74S series are as follows:

$$\text{high-level output current } (I_{OH}) \quad = \quad 1000 \ \mu A$$

$$\text{high-level input current } (I_{IH}) \quad = \quad 50 \ \mu A$$

$$\text{low-level output current } (I_{OH}) \quad = \quad 20 \ mA$$

$$\text{low-level input current } (I_{IL}) \quad = \quad 2 \ mA$$

Dividing the current levels shown yields the following two results:

$$\text{fanout for high output} \quad = \quad \frac{I_{OH}}{I_{IH}} \ = \ 20$$

$$\text{fanout for low output} \quad = \quad \frac{I_{OL}}{I_{IL}} \ = \ 10$$

Since the fanout for the low-output state is the lower of the two numbers, you would have to assume that the maximum fanout for the 74S series is 10. This is due to the fact that the output from one of these gates must under all circumstances be able to drive all inputs to which it is connected.

Propagation Delay

Propagation delay is the time from when the input of a gate makes 50% of its transition until the output of the gate makes 50% of its transition. The propagation delay of the 7404 inverter can be seen in Figure 5.11. For the 7404, the propagation delay from a low to a high output, t_{PLH}, is typically 12 ns. This means that approximately 12 ns after the input to the 7404 reaches the 50% point in its transition from high to low, the output will have made 50% of its transition from low to high. The propagation delay from a high to a low output, t_{PHL}, is typically 8 ns for this gate. Again, the delay is measured at the 50% point on the transitions.

As you can see, the two propagation delays in Figure 5.11 are not equal. The reason for this is actually very simple. During the propagation delay from low to high, t_{PLH}, transistor Q_4 in the totem-pole pair is turning off. This transistor usually has up to 16 mA of current flowing through it, so its storage time is relatively long. During the propagation delay time from high to low, t_{PHL}, transistor Q_3 is turning off. Since this transistor normally has up to 400 μA of current flowing through it, its storage time is relatively short. Recall that storage time is the time it takes to clear all the free electrons out of the base region of a saturated transistor so that a depletion region can start to form. This was discussed in Chapter 1.

When the propagation delay times are not equal, you take the average of the two to determine the average propagation delay. When troubleshooting a given digital system, you will not usually encounter any problems with propagation delay, since delay-time problems are worked out long before a system goes to market.

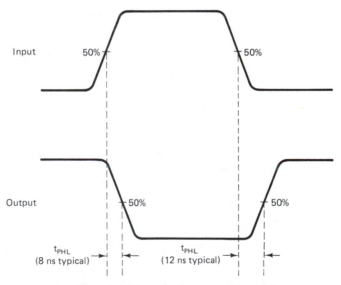

Figure 5.11   7404 propagation delay.

Power Dissipation

Another parameter for logic circuits is power dissipation. This rating, usually in mW per gate, is proportional to the current that is used by the logic gate. This leads to an interesting problem.

A transistor is turned on by current. The more current you supply to the transistor input, the faster it will turn on. This means that the logic circuits that use higher current levels are faster than those with low current levels. However, the higher current levels also mean that the logic gate will dissipate more power. Higher power dissipation can cause problems in systems where the ICs must be mounted very close together. The bottom line is that you have a trade-off between power dissipation and speed. If you want high speed, you are stuck with relatively high power dissipation. If you want low power dissipation, you are stuck with relatively low speed.

A figure of merit for ICs that is based on this trade-off is the *speed–power product*. The speed–power product for a given gate is found by multiplying the average propagation delay for the gate (in ns) by the power dissipation for a single gate (in mW). The lower the speed–power product for a given logic circuit, the better. We will encounter the speed–power product figure of merit again in our discussion of TTL subfamilies.

5.4   TTL SUBFAMILIES

Take a look at the column headings in Figure 5.9. As you can see, the column headings are similar except for the letter or letters that follow the 74 or 54. These letters are used to indicate to which of the TTL subfamilies the chip belongs. A *subfamily* is a group of chips that, while belonging to the same logic family as other chips, shares unique speed and/or power characteristics. The members of a given subfamily may be faster or dissipate less power, for example, than other chips in the same basic logic family. These variations in speed and power ratings are brought about by changing the component values, or in some cases, the component types. At the same time, the overall circuit makeup of the subfamily is the same as the other chips in the logic family, so the subfamilies are all compatible in terms of supply voltages.

The first TTL subfamily we discuss is *high-speed* TTL, the 74H series. The schematic for the 74H00 can be seen in Figure 5.12a. Note that the resistor values have all been decreased. Because of this, the circuit currents are higher than the currents in standard TTL circuits. Increased current levels cause the transistors to switch on faster, thus increasing the overall speed of the circuit. The one drawback with this subfamily is the fact that increased current levels also means increased power dissipation. These chips tend to run hotter than standard TTL chips and thus tend to have a shorter life.

Another TTL subfamily is the *low-power* TTL, or 74L series. The schematic for the 74L00 NAND gate is shown in Figure 5.12b. As you can see, the resistor values have all been drastically increased for this chip. Because of this, the current levels for the chip are lower, and thus less power is dissipated. Unfortunately, this lower current also means that the circuit is slower, since the transistors take longer to switch states. These chips are useful where power dissipation is a more important consideration than speed.

The 74S series, or *Schottky* TTL, uses Schottky clamped transistors to increase the speed of the logic circuits. The 74S00, shown in Figure 5.12c, needs a bit of explaining. First of all, the transistor symbols shown represent transistors that have a Schottky barrier diode connected from the base to the emitter, as shown in Figure 5.12d. This diode turns on when the potential is approximately 0.3 V. This prevents the collector of the transistor from ever being more than 0.3 V more negative than the base.

Recall that the collector of a saturated transistor is usually 0.4 V more negative than the base. With the Schottky barrier diode, the collector of this transistor will pull down the base potential of the transistor as the device approaches saturation. This decreases the base current and prevents the transistor from saturating. The first key to the operation of this circuit is the fact that the transistors never saturate. Now, recall that the biggest contributor to propagation delay is storage time, which is caused by the transistor saturating. If you keep the transistor from actually entering saturation, you eliminate storage time, which decreases the propagation delay of the circuit. This is precisely how Schottky TTL works. The Schottky barrier diode prevents

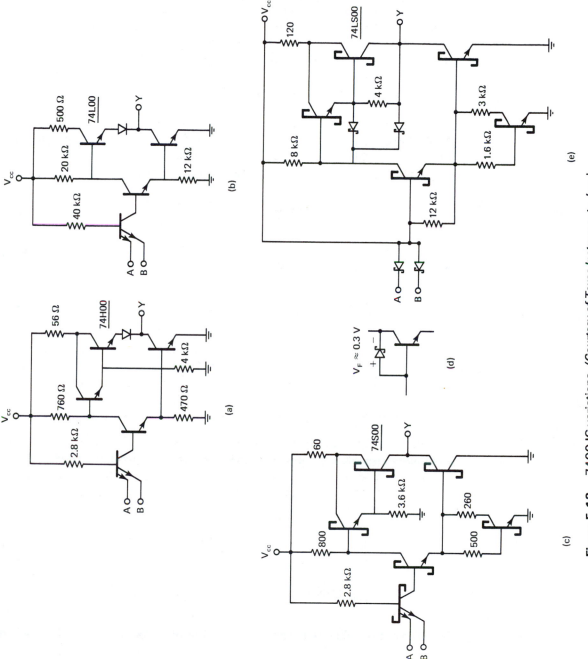

Figure 5.12. 7400 IC variations. *(Courtesy of Texas Instruments, Inc.)*

the transistors from actually entering saturation, which eliminates storage time, thus decreasing the propagation delay of the circuit. t_{PLH} and t_{PHL} for the 74S series chip are nearly identical. This is due to the fact that storage time has been eliminated for all practical purposes.

Another TTL subfamily is the *low-power Schottky* TTL, or 74LS series. This subfamily uses higher resistor values and Schottky clamped transistors to produce circuits that are fast, yet have a relatively low power dissipation rating. The basic LS series NAND gate can be seen in Figure 5.12e. The LS series has the best speed–power product of any of the TTL families. For this reason, it is in the process of replacing most of the other TTL subfamilies.

Interfacing TTL Subfamilies

As we stated earlier, all of the TTL subfamilies are compatible in terms of supply voltages and logic levels. The problem in interfacing the various subfamilies lies in their fanout capabilities. Recall that fanout is a rating of the current driving capability of a given logic family and is found using the formula

$$fanout = \frac{output\ current}{input\ current}$$

As can be seen in the table shown in Figure 5.9, the various TTL subfamilies have different input and output current ratings. These variations in current levels can cause problems when replacing one TTL chip with another that is not from the same subfamily. For example, look at the following current ratings for the H series and the L series:

Subfamily	I_{OL} (mA)	I_{IL} (mA)	I_{OH} (μA)	I_{IH} (μA)
H series	20	2	500	50
L series	3.6	0.18	200	10

Using the values listed, it can be determined that one H series chip can drive 10 other H series chips, and one L series chip can drive 20 other L series chips. When interfacing these two TTL subfamilies, we have to consider the fanout from one sub-family to the other. When driving L series chips with H series chips, the fanout is determined as follows:

$$fanout\ (high) = \frac{I_{OH}\ (H\ series)}{I_{IH}\ (L\ series)} = \frac{500\ \mu A}{10\ \mu A} = 50$$

$$fanout\ (low) = \frac{I_{OL}\ (H\ series)}{I_{IL}\ (L\ series)} = \frac{20\ mA}{0.18\ mA} = 111$$

Since you must take the lower number of the two, the H series-to-L series fanout rating would be 50. This means that one H series chip can reliably drive 50 L series chips. The same formulas would be used to determine the L series-to-H series fanout, except that the L series output currents would be divided by the H series input currents. Performing these divisions yields the following results:

$$fanout\ (high) = 4$$

$$fanout\ (low) = 1$$

Note that the low fanout rating (1) is the result of rounding the actual result (1.8) *down*. You must always round the result of a division down to the nearest whole number, as stated earlier. The fanout from L series to H series is only 1. This could lead to problems when attempting to replace an H series chip with an L series chip. For example, refer to the circuit shown in Figure 5.13. This simple circuit contains three H series chips. Assume that IC1 has burned out and needs to be replaced. If you replace it with an L series chip, the current capabilities of the chip will not be sufficient to drive IC2 and IC3. This would cause the circuit to continue to malfunction, which may lead you to believe that another chip was actually the cause of the problem. Well, you had the right problem, just the wrong replacement. Believe it or not, this happens more often than anyone would care to admit. The bottom line is that you must be very careful when mixing TTL subfamilies, as the current differences between the subfamilies may cause problems.

You may want to consider constructing a fanout chart that shows the fanout from each of the TTL subfamilies to each of the others. This chart may save you a great deal of time and trouble when actually determining suitable chip replacements.

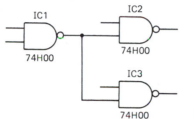

Figure 5.13

5.5 THREE-STATE LOGIC

Earlier in this chapter, logic 0 was redefined as being a low-impedance path to ground, and logic 1 was redefined as being a low-impedance path to the supply. There is a third output state, called the *disabled state*. When a logic circuit is in the disabled state, its output acts as an open circuit, which forms *a high-impedance path to both ground and the supply*. A logic circuit that is capable of being disabled is called a *three-state gate*. When a three-state gate is disabled, its output is said to be *floating*. The logic symbol and schematic for a three-state inverter are shown in Figure 5.14. As you can see, the three-state inverter has an "enable" input. This input must be low for the circuit to operate as a normal inverter. When the enable input is high, the output from the inverter will be floating, or disabled. To help you see this, refer to the circuit shown in Figure 5.14. When the enable input is low, the output from the inverter (U1) is high. This will reverse bias both of the diodes that are connected to the U1 output, and they will not affect circuit action. When the enable input goes high, the output of U1 goes low. This low causes two things to happen:

1. Q_1 is turned on by the low applied to its emitter through D_2. Turning on Q_1 causes Q_2 and Q_4 to both turn off, as stated in Section 5.2. With Q_4 off, there is a high-impedance path between the output and ground.

2. With Q_2 off, Q_3 would normally turn on, since the voltage on its base would be high. However, D_3 has a low on its cathode and thus will start to conduct. When D_3 conducts, it drops the base voltage of Q_3, which prevents Q_3 from turning on. With Q_3 being off, there is a high-impedance path between the output and the supply.

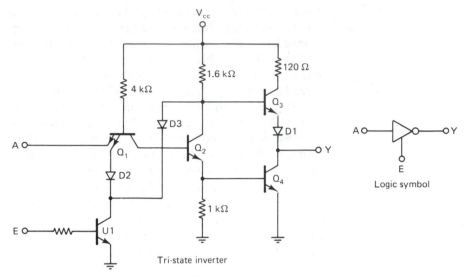

Figure 5.14

With both Q_4 and Q_3 off, the output of the circuit is essentially an open circuit, since there is no path for any current to flow. In effect, the circuit is electrically isolated from the line to which it is connected. *An output that is in the disabled state will normally read between 0.8 and 1.8 V when measured with an oscilloscope.*

Three-state logic is very useful, especially in a circuit like the one shown in Figure 5.15. This circuit is using three-state buffers to protect the outputs of circuits A, B, and C. The overall purpose of the circuit shown is unimportant at this point; however,

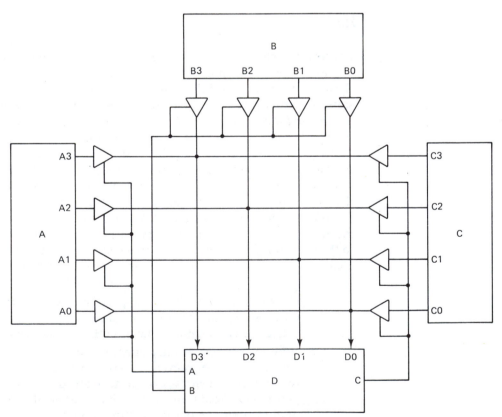

Figure 5.15 A simple circuit incorporating three-state logic.

for the sake of discussion, we will state that the purpose of circuit D is to get information from one of the other three circuits. In other words, at one point circuit D may be getting data from circuit A, from circuit B at another time, and so on.

The problem with this configuration lies in the fact that the outputs from circuits A, B, and C share the same lines to circuit D. If circuit A had all *low* outputs, and circuit B had all *high* outputs, the power supply would essentially be shorted to ground through the circuit outputs. This would cause either circuit A or circuit B (or both) to be destroyed. However, by using three-state buffers, circuit D can enable only the output from which it needs data, while disabling the other two. This would be done using the A, B, and C outputs from circuit D. For example, if circuit D needs to get data from circuit A, it would drive line A low while leaving lines B and C high. This would enable the outputs from circuit A while isolating circuits B and C from the bus. If the data were to be gotten from circuit B, circuit D would drive output B low while keeping the other lines high. In any case, the buffers with the low enable inputs will work as normal buffers, while the buffers with high enable inputs will have their outputs floated. This effectively isolates them from the bus wires.

Three-state circuits are extremely useful because they allow many circuits to be connected to common wires, or buses, as was just shown. This greatly reduces the number of wires that must be used in a given digital system.

Most LSI and VLSI chips have three-state inputs and outputs. When a given LSI or VLSI chip has three-state inputs and outputs, the lines will be controlled by one or more inputs. The inputs will be labeled either $\overline{E}$ (enable) or $\overline{CE}$ (chip enable) or $\overline{CS}$ (chip select). When low, these inputs allow the chip to work as usual, and when high, they cause the three-state lines to be floated. This will be seen more and more as we start to cover the more sophisticated digital circuits.

Troubleshooting Three-State Gates

When a three-state gate is enabled, it works just like any other logic circuit and thus would require the same troubleshooting techniques as any other basic gate. When you have a three-state gate whose output is constantly floating, check to see what the enable input is doing. If it is constantly high, you need to check the source of the enable signal. If it is constantly low, or changing at different intervals, and the output from the three-state gate does not change, you should replace the three-state gate. Remember that a floating output will read between 0.8 and 1.8 V when measured with an oscilloscope. Any other readings would not indicate that the outputs are floating under most circumstances.

5.6 OPEN-COLLECTOR LOGIC

Open-collector logic has been replaced for the most part by three-state gates. However, there are still systems that use open-collector circuits, so they do need to be discussed. Open-collector circuits were designed so that you could wire the outputs of several gates together, something that you cannot do with standard TTL gates. The schematic for the open-collector inverter can be seen in Figure 5.16a. Note that this gate is exactly like the standard TTL inverter, except that the Q_3 circuitry is missing. With the Q_3 circuitry missing, this gate has either a low output or no output at all. Because it cannot have a high output, the output pin must be connected to V_{cc} via a pull-up resistor, as shown in Figure 5.16b. This resistor ensures that the output pin is high when Q_4 is not turned on.

You can connect more than one open-collector gate to one line, as shown in Figure 5.16c. If all the outputs are high, Y will be high. If any of the open-collector gates has a low output, point Y will also be low. This circuit configuration is referred to as a *wire-AND*, since all the open-collector gates must have a high output in order for point Y to be high. Wire-ANDing is acceptable with open-collector and three-state gates, but not with standard TTL chips.

Open-collector chips have fallen by the wayside for several reasons. One is that they are much slower than standard TTL. They are also more susceptible to noise. The biggest problem, however, is that a circuit that is based on open-collector chips is extremely difficult to troubleshoot. For example, assume that the circuit shown in Figure 5.16c has an output (Y) that is held constantly low. With all of the gate outputs being tied to point Y, it is extremely difficult to determine which gate is causing this point to be held low. To determine which gate is faulty, you would have to disconnect the gates from point Y, one at a time, until point Y went high again. The last gate that was disconnected before point Y went high was the faulty gate.

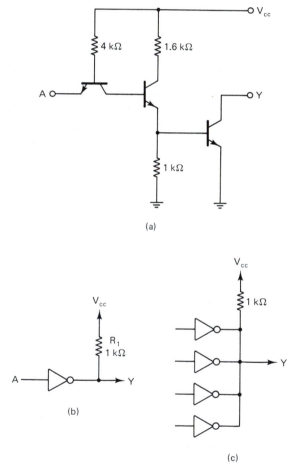

Figure 5.16   Open collector logic.

5.7   MOS LOGIC

There is a group of logic circuits that are constructed with MOSFETs. These logic families have some distinct advantages over TTL circuits:

1. They take up less physical space to build, so more of these gates can be constructed on a single chip. For this reason, they are very useful in VLSI applications.

2. They have very low input current levels, so their fanout ratings are very high, typically 400 and up.

3. They dissipate very little power.

While MOS circuits do have these advantages over TTL circuits, they also have several disadvantages. These disadvantages are discussed later in this section.

Review of MOS Transistors

We'll start our discussion of MOS logic circuits by reviewing the basic operating characteristics of MOSFETs. The structure of the most common types of MOSFET can be seen in Figure 5.17. Figure 5.17a shows the *enhancement-mode* MOSFET, which is the most commonly used in digital applications. This device has a gate which is electrically isolated from the rest of the device by a small oxide coating between the aluminum and the P-type material. Current flow through the device is normally from source to drain. However, as the device is drawn in Figure 5.17a, no current can flow between these two terminals, since the two N-type terminals form back-to-back diodes with the P-type material between them. The only way to get current flow from source to drain would be to somehow cause an N-type channel to form between the two terminals. Current could then flow into the source, through the induced N-type channel, and out the drain. The gate is used to cause such a channel to form. If the gate is made positive, the electrons in the P-type material will start to be pulled toward the gate and the holes will start to be repelled from the gate. When enough electrons are pulled toward the gate, they will form an N-type channel that will bridge the gap between the source and drain terminals. This channel will allow current to flow from source to drain. The voltage that causes the channel to form is called the *threshold voltage*, or $V_{GS(TH)}$. The typical value for the threshold voltage is about 2.5 V. After this voltage is reached, any further increases in gate voltage cause a rapid increase in drain current until saturation is reached. If the gate voltage goes below the threshold voltage, drain current is reduced to near zero.

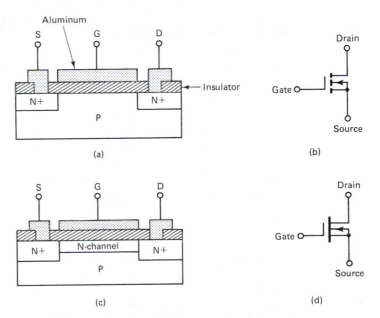

Figure 5.17 (a) N-type enhancement-mode MOSFET; (b) schematic symbol; (c) N-type depletion-mode MOSFET; (d) schematic symbol.

Because of the insulating layer (oxide) between the gate and the substrate, no current enters the device through the gate. This means that the gate has almost no current draw on the output that is driving the MOSFET. This is the reason MOS circuits have such a high fanout rating. With no current being drawn by the input, you can connect a virtually unlimited number of these gates to a single output.

Basically, you can look at the enhancement-mode MOSFET in much the same way as an NPN transistor when dealing with digital circuits. If the enhancement-mode MOSFET gets a high-enough positive voltage at the gate, it will saturate just like an NPN transistor with a high input voltage. The main difference between the two is the fact that the MOSFET will have little or no input current.

The *depletion-mode* MOSFET, shown in Figure 5.17c, has a physically constructed channel between the source and drain. When the gate voltage is zero or something more positive, current will flow from source to drain. When the gate goes negative with respect to the source, the channel will begin to narrow. This will reduce the source-to-drain current. When a negative gate voltage, called $V_{GS,\text{off}}$ is reached, current will no longer flow through the device. The off voltage is a physical characteristic of the device. The key to the operation of this device is that current will flow from the source to the drain as long as V_{GS} is more positive than $V_{GS,\text{off}}$.

Both of these devices have little or no input current, and both are relatively easy to construct in IC form. However, both of them have one very major drawback. *The insulating layer in the gate is extremely sensitive to static charges*. In fact, the static electricity from your hand can destroy a MOS circuit. Because of this, you have to be very careful how you handle a MOS circuit. You should never touch the pins on a MOS IC. If necessary, pick the IC up with a needlenose pliers and place it in the IC socket before touching it. You must also be careful never to store a MOS IC in styrofoam; they must be stored in conductive foam or static-resistant plastic. One more precaution—which should be followed no matter which logic family you are dealing with—is never to remove ICs from their sockets while the power is applied. This will surely destroy a MOS IC.

MOS Logic Families

MOS logic circuits have a much greater *packing density* than that of TTL chips. This means that many more MOS gates than TTL gates can be constructed in a given amount of space. One of the reasons for this is that MOS circuits contain no resistors. Resistors are not needed in MOS logic circuits because MOSFETs can be used as resistors. The source-to-drain resistance of a MOSFET can be varied from approximately 1000 Ω to hundreds of megohms simply by setting the gate potential. A saturated MOSFET will have approximately 1000 Ω of resistance from source to drain and therefore makes a convenient current-limiting resistor.

In bipolar logic circuits, the biggest "space user" is the resistor. It takes more physical space on an IC to construct a resistor than any other component. Since MOS logic families do not need resistors, more gates can be constructed in a given amount of space. As you will see later in this section, none of the MOS logic circuits contain resistors.

NMOS Logic

This logic group uses N-channel MOSFETs. NMOS is currently used in most MOS memory circuits and in many microprocessors. The basic NMOS inverter can be seen in Figure 5.18a. In this circuit, Q_1 is being used as the drain resistor. Since its gate is connected to V_{dd}, it is biased to saturation and has a source-to-drain resistance of approximately 1000 Ω. Q_2 is the input device. It is turned on when the input goes high, and turned off when the input goes low. When Q_2 is on, the output is essentially pulled down to ground. When it is off, the output is pulled up to V_{dd}. Since NMOS can use the same supply voltage as TTL, it is often used in LSI and VLSI circuits that must be interfaced with TTL. These LSI and VLSI circuits usually have internal TTL buffers on their output pins to ensure that the output current is sufficient to drive a TTL gate. This point is discussed further in Chapter 12.

PMOS Logic

PMOS logic circuits use P-channel MOSFETs. The supply voltages for PMOS are usually negative, which does not make PMOS a logic family that is easily interfaced with TTL. A variation on standard PMOS, called *low-threshold PMOS*, can be used in systems with TTL supply voltages. The basic PMOS NOR gate is shown in Figure 5.18b.

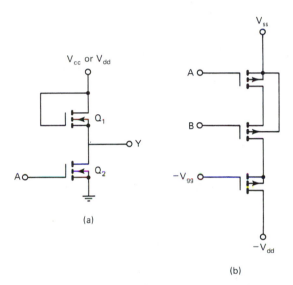

Figure 5.18 (a) N-MOS inverter; (b) P-MOS NOR gate.

5.8 CMOS LOGIC

By far the most common MOS logic family is *complementary MOS* (CMOS) logic. CMOS uses a combination of NMOS and PMOS devices to produce logic gates. The basic CMOS inverter can be seen in Figure 5.19a. This inverter is constructed with one PMOS device (Q_1) and one NMOS device (Q_2). Assuming that the input will be either $+5$ V or ground, one of the devices will be turned off by the input while the other is turned on. For example, if the input is at ground, Q_1 will be turned on (since its gate is negative) and Q_2 will be off. This means that there will be about 1000 Ω between the output and the supply, and virtually infinite ohms between the output and ground. If the input goes high, Q_2 will be turned on and Q_1 will be turned off. This reverses the impedance relationship just stated, and the output will be low. One of the advantages of this circuit lies in the fact that virtually all of the supply voltage is dropped across the off transistor. This means that the output will be almost exactly V_{dd} or almost exactly at ground.

The CMOS NAND gate can be seen in Figure 5.19b. Note that Q_1 and Q_2 are PMOS transistors and Q_3 and Q_4 are NMOS transistors. If input A goes low, Q_1 will be turned on and Q_4 will be turned off. This puts the off transistor between the output and ground, and the on transistor between the output and V_{dd}. The output is therefore approximately equal to V_{dd}. If input B is low, Q_2 is turned on and Q_3

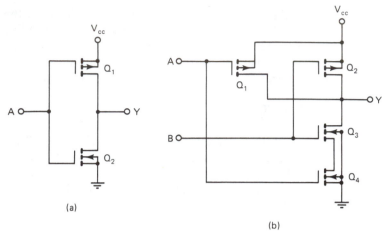

Figure 5.19 Basic CMOS circuits. (a) Inverter; (b) NAND gate

is turned off. This has the same overall effect as having the A input low. If both inputs go high, Q_1 and Q_2 will be off and Q_3 and Q_4 will be on. This ties the input to ground through Q_3 and Q_4. At the same time, almost all of V_{dd} will be dropped across Q_1 and Q_2.

The NAND gate has the same voltage-output characteristics as the inverter. Due to the extremely high impedance in series with a relatively low impedance, the output will be within a few tenths of a volt of V_{dd} or ground. As you will see in the discussion on CMOS characteristics, this output voltage characteristic gives CMOS an excellent noise margin.

CMOS Characteristics

To give you an idea of the operating characteristics of CMOS circuits in general, we will take a look at the specifications for the CD4001, which is a quad two-input NOR gate chip. The specifications for this chip are shown in Figure 5.20. Note that the operating V_{dd} range for this chip is stated to be "V_{ss} + 3.0 V to V_{ss} + 15 V." This means that V_{dd} can be anywhere between + 3 and + 15 volts when V_{ss} is equal to ground. We will look at the characteristics listed for $V_{dd} = 5$ V, since this supply voltage is TTL compatible.

The first two characteristics listed are the quiescent device current and quiescent device dissipation per package. These two characteristics are both measured with the inputs being low. The values listed with a + 5-V power supply are 0.5 μA for current and 2.5 μW for power. Both of these ratings are considerably lower than their TTL counterparts. Remember that CMOS devices use less current because of their impedance, and thus dissipate less power than TTL.

The next two characteristics listed are the high and low output voltages. Note that the maximum low output voltage is 0.01 V and the minimum high output voltage is 4.99 V. This goes along with what was said earlier about the outputs being very nearly V_{dd} or ground.

The noise immunity of the gate is rated at being at least 1.5 V. This would appear at first to be a much better noise margin than TTL. However, you must remember that CMOS circuits are very susceptible to noise in their lines, so this wider noise margin is needed. In general, the typical noise margin is approximately equal to one-third of V_{dd} (minimum) for CMOS circuits.

The output and input current ratings show why CMOS circuitry has such a high fanout rating. The minimum output current, regardless of which state the output is in, is 300 μA. The typical input current is approximately 10 pA. This means that

Absolute maximum ratings

Voltage at any pin*	$V_{ss} - 0.3$ V to $V_{dd} + 0.3$ V
Operating temperature range	
CD4001M	-55 to $+125°C$
CD4001C	-40 to $+85°C$
Storage temperature range	-65 to $+150°C$
Package dissipation	500 mW
Operating V_{dd} range	$V_{ss} + 3.0$ V to $V_{ss} + 15$ V
Lead temperature (soldering, 10 seconds)	$300°C$

DC electrical characteristics CD4001C

Parameter	Conditions	Limits −40°C Min.	−40°C Typ.	−40°C Max.	25°C Min.	25°C Typ.	25°C Max.	85°C Min.	85°C Typ.	85°C Max.	Units
Quiescent device current, I_L	$V_{dd} = 5$ V			0.5		0.005	0.5			15	µA
	$V_{dd} = 10$ V			5		0.005	5			30	µA
Quiescent device dissipation/package, P_D	$V_{dd} = 5$ V			2.5		0.025	2.5			75	µW
	$V_{dd} = 10$ V			50		0.05	50			300	µW
Output voltage low level, V_{OL}	$V_{dd} = 5$ V, $V_I = V_{dd}$, $I_O = 0$ A			0.01		0	0.01			0.05	V
	$V_{dd} = 10$ V, $V_I = V_{dd}$, $I_O = 0$ A			0.01		0	0.01			0.05	V
Output voltage high level, V_{OH}	$V_{dd} = 5$ V, $V_I = V_{ss}$, $I_O = 0$ A	4.99			4.99	5		4.95			V
	$V_{dd} = 10$ V, $V_I = V_{ss}$, $I_O = 0$ A	9.99			9.99	10		9.95			V
Noise immunity, V_{NL} (all inputs)	$V_{dd} = 5$ V, $V_O = 3.6$ V, $I_O = 0$ A	1.5			1.5	2.25		1.4			V
	$V_{dd} = 10$ V, $V_O = 7.2$ V, $I_O = 0$ A	3			3	4.5		2.9			V
Noise immunity, V_{NH} (all inputs)	$V_{dd} = 5$ V, $V_O = 0.95$ V, $I_O = 0$ A	1.4			1.5	2.25		1.5			V
	$V_{dd} = 10$ V, $V_O = 2.9$ V, $I_O = 0$ A	2.9			3	4.5		3			V
Output drive current, N-channel, I_D N	$V_{dd} = 5$ V, $V_O = 0.4$ V, $V_I = V_{dd}$	0.35			0.3	1		0.24			mA
	$V_{dd} = 10$ V, $V_O = 0.5$ V, $V_I = V_{dd}$	0.72			0.6	2.5		0.48			mA
Output drive current, P-channel, I_D P	$V_{dd} = 5$ V, $V_O = 2.5$ V, $V_I = V_{ss}$	−0.35			−0.3	−2		−0.24			mA
	$V_{dd} = 10$ V, $V_O = 9.5$ V, $V_I = V_{ss}$	−0.3			−0.25	−1		−0.2			mA
Input current, I_I						10					pA

Figure 5.20 TI CMOS specification sheet. *(Courtesy of Texas Instruments, Inc.)*

*This device should not be connected to circuits with the power on because high transient voltages may cause permanent damage.

for this chip, the minimum fanout is far greater than any reasonable circuit would ever require.

As the specifications have shown, CMOS definitely works better than TTL in terms of fanout, current requirements, and power dissipation. However, you still have the IC handling problems. You can expect to accidentally destroy at least one CMOS IC in your career, but with time and practice at handling these ICs, you will come to have relatively little trouble with them.

5.9 EMITTER-COUPLED LOGIC AND INTEGRATED INJECTION LOGIC

There are two more logic families that should be mentioned, ECL and I^{4}L. Neither of these two logic families is used very extensively in microcomputers, so we will not go through an in-depth circuit analysis of their basic circuits. Rather, we will discuss some of their input and output characteristics, together with their advantages and limitations.

Emitter-Coupled Logic

ECL is by far the fastest commercially available logic family today. The typical rise time for ECL circuits is approximately 1 ns compared with 3 to 30 ns for TTL and 20 to 175 ns for CMOS. The relatively high speed of ECL can be attributed to three factors:

1. ECL has a very small logic swing. There is less than 1-V difference between logic 1 and logic 0. Typically, a logic 0 is anything between -1.85 and -1.63 V, and a logic 1 is anything between -0.81 and -0.98 V.

2. ECL logic gates have a very low output impedance. Because of this, circuit stray capacitances are charged and discharged very rapidly. This greatly reduces propagation delay.

3. ECL is a *nonsaturated* logic family. Since its transistors are never allowed to saturate, storage time is eliminated, which increases the internal speed of the device.

The first point above shows one of the major limitations of ECL. *The logic levels for ECL are not TTL compatible.* In fact, levels translators are required in any system that utilizes both ECL and TTL. The fact that ECL is not compatible with TTL circuits has been a major factor in ECL's failure to catch on as a feasible microcomputer logic family.

The other problem with ECL is a bit more difficult to understand. Because of the high speed of ECL circuits, copper runs or wires that are more than a few inches long must be treated as transmission lines. The explanation for this is lengthy and probably not worth the trouble, but the bottom line is that any connections between ECL circuits longer than a few inches in length must be terminated with a resistor to ground, as shown in Figure 5.21. If lines are not terminated with a shunt resistor like the one shown in Figure 5.21, the lines will have standing waves, just like a mismatched transmission line. Implementing these terminating resistors is expensive and time consuming. This increases the cost of ECL systems.

Although ECL is an extremely fast logic family, the problems associated with its logic levels and transmission-line characteristics cannot be ignored. In all probability, ECL will never catch on as a feasible microcomputer logic family.

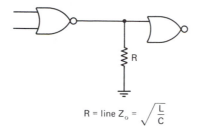

$$R = \text{line } Z_o = \sqrt{\frac{L}{C}}$$

Figure 5.21 ECL gates with terminating resistor.

Integrated Injection Logic

I^2L is a bipolar logic family that is used exclusively in LSI and VLSI applications. At this time, SSI gates are not commercially available in I^2L circuitry. I^2L has the following advantages:

1. Current levels are constant, which eliminates switching transients.
2. Current levels can be set using an external current-limiting resistor. This allows you to set up I^2L circuits for a predetermined speed and/or power dissipation rating.

To understand the first advantage of I^2L circuits better, refer back to the schematic of the TTL NAND gate shown in Figure 5.8. Recall that the totem-pole pair, Q_3 and Q_4, are always at opposite states. One will be on and the other will be off. However, there is a small period of time, when the output is switching states, that both Q_3 and Q_4 are on. During the time that they are both on, there is a relatively low impedance path from V_{cc} to ground through the two transistors. At that time, a current transient is produced on the V_{cc} line. In other words, the current in the V_{cc} line surges for an instant because it is effectively being shorted to ground. This transient can cause some problems if not corrected.

The switching transient is not an exclusive problem for TTL. The same thing happens with both CMOS and ECL. To correct the problem, all ICs from these logic families must have a capacitor connected between the V_{cc} and the ground pin to "short-out" the current transient. This bypass capacitor should have a value of between 0.1 and 0.01 μF.

Since I^2L does not have these switching transients, it does not need any capacitive bypass circuitry. This cuts down the overall number of components required in a system.

The fact that you can program the internal current levels of I^2L circuits is another advantage. If you need high speed, a low-value external resistor will provide the current required to bring up the speed of the device. Remember that increased currents increase the speed of a logic circuit. If you need low power dissipation, a high-value external resistor will decrease current levels and thus reduce power consumption. As always, speed and power dissipation are a trade-off.

One additional advantage of I^2L circuits is the fact that this logic family is TTL compatible. It is also compatible with CMOS circuitry.

The one problem with I^2L circuitry is that it is more difficult than MOS circuitry to manufacture. MOS circuitry is the main competitor of I^2L. Since MOS circuits are easier to produce, they are usually preferred over I^2L circuits.

SUMMARY

Most logic circuits are now manufactured in integrated-circuit form. An integrated circuit is a device, usually made of silicon, that contains anywhere from several to thousands of logic circuits. Integrated circuits are separated into groups called *logic families*. The members of a given logic family share similar construction and operating characteristics. The most popular logic family is the TTL group. Another popular logic family is CMOS. Although these two logic families have many distinct characteristics, it is not uncommon to find them both in the same microcomputer.

ICs are also grouped by the number of gates they contain and the type of package used. SSI chips contain up to 10 gates, MSI chips contain from 10 to 100 chips, LSI chips contain from 100 to 1000 gates, and VLSI chips contain over 1000 gates. LSI and VLSI chips are usually made of MOS and I^2L circuits, since these logic families utilize smaller circuits that dissipate less power. The two most common types of IC package are the *dual-in-line package* (DIP), and the *flatpack*.

The TTL logic family is subdivided into groups called *subfamilies*. While all of the TTL subfamilies are compatible in terms of supply voltages and logic levels, they have different current, power, and speed characteristics. The figure of merit for the subfamilies is the *speed–power product*.

There are five TTL subfamilies: standard TTL, the L series, and H series, the S series, and the LS series. Of the five, the LS series has the best speed–power product. When mixing TTL subfamilies, you must be careful not to exceed the fanout rating of the chips. *Fanout* is the number of loads that can be driven by a single source and is found by dividing the output current of the driving chip by the total current required by the load chips. If the fanout for a given chip is exceeded, the noise margins will be reduced, propagation delay will increase, and the chips may have intermittent problems.

A type of logic circuit that allows several logic gates to be tied to a common input and/or output line is called *three-state logic*. A three-state gate has a high-impedance output state that effectively removes the gate from the circuit. When a given input or output is in this high-impedance state, it is said to be *floating* and will typically measure between 0.8 and 1.8 V when checked with an oscilloscope. Open-collector chips were used to perform this function, but they have been replaced for the most part by three-state gates, because open-collector gates are slow, noisy, and very difficult to troubleshoot.

MOS circuits have lower power dissipation ratings and better packing density than TTL and are thus better suited for LSI and VLSI applications. The major drawback to MOS circuits is that they are very static sensitive. You must be very careful to avoid touching the pins of a MOS chip when handling them, because under certain circumstances, the static from your hand can destroy them. Also, they should be stored in static-resistant plastic or conductive foam.

QUESTIONS

1. What is an integrated circuit?
2. Why is silicon usually preferred to germanium for IC construction?
3. What are the four levels of integration? How many gates are typically contained in each?
4. What is a logic family? What are the most common logic families?
5. What is interfacing?
6. What are the two types of IC packaging?
7. What are the standard TTL supply and logic voltage ratings?

8. Refer to Figure 5.3. Explain how this circuit works.

9. Why do open TTL inputs almost always act as a logic 1?

10. How are logic 0 and logic 1 defined in term of impedance paths?

11. What are the differences between the 54 series and 74 series TTL chips?

12. What is a parameter? Where are parameters found?

13. What is fanout? How do you determine the fanout rating for a given logic circuit?

14. What is affected by exceeding the fanout rating for a given logic circuit?

15. Why is the propagation delay shorter for a nonsaturated logic circuit than it is for a saturated logic circuit?

16. What is the speed–power product? How is the speed–power product found for a given logic family?

17. List the TTL subfamilies and the characteristics of each.

18. What must you be careful of when interfacing TTL subfamilies? Why?

19. What purpose is served by three-state logic?

20. What is meant by the term *floating*? What does a floating line measure in terms of voltage?

21. How do you troubleshoot three-state gates?

22. What is open-collector logic? What connection must be made when using open-collector gates?

23. Why are three-state gates preferred over open-collector gates?

24. Why do MOS circuits have a higher packing density than TTL circuits?

25. Why do MOS circuits have such high fanout ratings?

26. Why are MOS circuits so static sensitive?

27. Which MOS logic family is the most popular?

28. Why haven't ECL circuits gained the popularity of TTL and CMOS in microcomputer applications?

29. What advantage does ECL have over TTL and CMOS circuits?

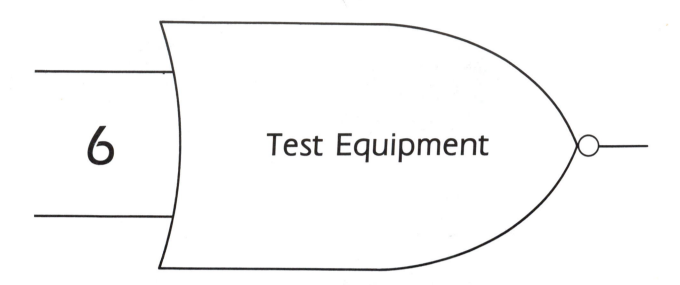

6 Test Equipment

As every experienced technician knows, there is a specialized piece of test equipment for almost every application you could think of. It is also possible to buy test equipment that is so sophisticated it will almost do all of your troubleshooting for you. However, most technicians either prefer not to use such test equipment or simply cannot afford it. This chapter is written for those technicians.

6.1 DIGITAL TESTING WITH AN OSCILLOSCOPE

The oscilloscope is without a doubt one of the most versatile pieces of test equipment made. You can make over 90% of the tests that you will ever need to make using an oscilloscope. Although research and development applications require more sophisticated test procedures and equipment, the field technician should be able to find almost every microcomputer problem using an oscilloscope and a multimeter if the proper procedures are used.

Microcomputer troubleshooting requires different oscilloscope setup and analysis techniques than those that are used when troubleshooting analog systems. For this reason, we will review the oscilloscope controls and their functions as they relate to digital troubleshooting.

Review of Oscilloscope Controls and Operation

In our review of the oscilloscope controls and operation, we will focus on the Tektronix model T922 oscilloscope. Although we are using a particular oscilloscope model, it should be remembered that the controls discussed are standard controls, so this discussion will help you regardless of which model you actually use.

The control panel and CRT of the T922 are shown in Figure 6.1. The oscilloscope

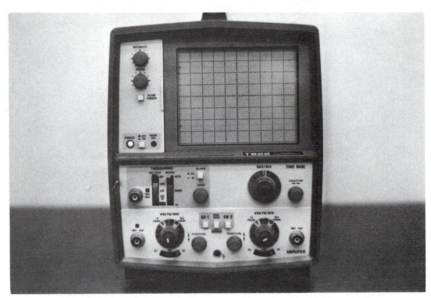

Figure 6.1   Tektronix T922 oscilloscope *(Courtesy of Tektronix, Inc.)*

controls can be classified as one of two types: *horizontal* or *vertical*. The horizontal controls affect the "length" of the waveform, and the vertical controls affect the "height" of the waveform. The basic horizontal controls are as follows:

TRIGGERING SOURCE: This switch determines the source of the signal on which the oscilloscope will trigger. When in the INT (internal) position, the oscilloscope will trigger on the waveform that is being displayed. When in the LINE position, the oscilloscope will trigger on the 60-Hz line input. When in the EXT (external) position, the oscilloscope will trigger on a signal provided at the X input. The EXT/10 position works the same as the EXT position, except that it divides the input amplitude by 10. This allows you to trigger the oscilloscope on a signal that has too high an amplitude to normally be applied to the X input. The X-Y position puts the oscilloscope in a graphical mode. This trigger source has no common application in digital troubleshooting. In most microcomputer troubleshooting applications, it is best to set the triggering source switch in the EXT position. This will allow you to trigger the oscilloscope on a signal from inside the microcomputer. The signal you want to use for triggering the oscilloscope must have a relatively high frequency and be a *stable* signal. A stable signal is one that repeats at a constant rate. One such signal in a microcomputer is the signal that is applied to the clock input of the microprocessor. Assuming that this signal is not malfunctioning, it will provide a good time base from which to view all the system signals. If it is malfunctioning, put the triggering source switch in the INT position. This will cause the oscilloscope to trigger on whatever signal you are viewing at the time. Note that you should disconnect the X input when using the oscilloscope in the INT triggering source condition.

TRIGGERING MODE: This switch is usually in either the AUTO or NORM position for digital troubleshooting. There really is not much of a difference between the two, except that the NORM position will cause the oscilloscope to blank the CRT if the signal is not suitable for triggering or if the LEVEL control is out of adjustment. If either of these conditions exist and the oscilloscope is in the AUTO mode, the display will not be blanked and you will see a signal that is not triggered.

SLOPE: This switch determines whether the oscilloscope triggers on the rising or falling edge of the input signal.

LEVEL: This control "fine tunes" the triggering section of the oscilloscope. If you have a display that the oscilloscope is having trouble keeping stable, adjust the level control.

SEC/DIV.: This switch determines the horizontal sweep frequency of the oscilloscope. When the sweep frequency increases, the time represented by one division on the CRT decreases, and vice versa. Decreasing the time per division will increase the "length" of the displayed waveform. Note that this control has a calibration control in its center. This control should be rotated fully counterclockwise for the T922. It may be clockwise for your oscilloscope, but either way, you must be sure to check its position. If the calibration control is not in the right position, your time measurements will all be wrong.

Remember that the horizontal controls just covered affect the "length" of the signal and have nothing to do with its amplitude. There is another point that should be made at this time in regard to digital troubleshooting. In our discussions of digital waveforms, digital waveforms are represented as nice clear waveforms. In actual practice, however, these waveforms are not usually so neat in appearance. Two actual digital waveforms can be seen in Figure 6.2. The waveform in Figure 6.2a is a clock signal. As you can see, it is a stable waveform. The signal in Figure 6.2b was taken from an output pin of a microprocessor. Note that the oscilloscope cannot lock in on this signal. This is because the signal changes at a varying rate. This is the way this signal should look, and does not indicate a problem. When you see a signal like this, do not assume that there is something wrong with the oscilloscope.

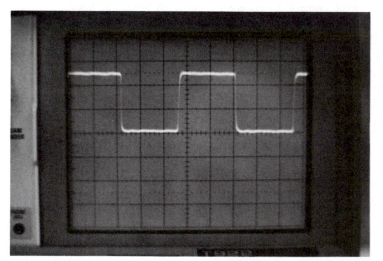 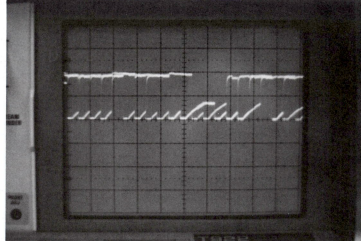

Figure 6.2 Digital waveforms: (a) repetitive; (b) nonrepetitive.

As we stated earlier, the vertical controls affect the apparent amplitude of the waveform. In a dual-trace oscilloscope, there are two separate vertical inputs to the oscilloscope, each with its own set of vertical controls. These controls are as follows:

VOLTS/DIV.: The "volts per division" control determines how many volts are represented by each vertical division on the CRT. When first checking an unknown signal, this control should always be set at its highest setting. Even when you feel that you know what the voltage is at a certain point, you should still set this control at its highest setting, since a power supply problem can increase the voltage at that point. After you have determined that the signal is not at a higher-than-usual value, you can turn this control down to obtain a better waveform. This switch is also calibrated by an additional calibration control. Be sure to calibrate it before making any measurements. Many a technician has sworn that a power supply was dead, only to find out later that the VOLTS/DIV control was not calibrated. Talk about feeling stupid!

AC/GND/DC.: This switch determines the type of input coupling to the oscilloscope that is being used. When in the AC position, the probe is put in series with a dc blocking capacitor inside the oscilloscope. This blocks the dc value of the input waveform, which results in the waveform being centered around zero volts. When in the GND position, the oscilloscope will display a flat line at the ground position on the CRT. When in the DC position, the probe is coupled directly to the internal vertical circuitry of the oscilloscope. This results in the dc component of the waveform being displayed. This can be seen better by looking at the displays in Figure 6.3. The input signal to the oscilloscope is the same signal that was used in Figure 6.2a. The only difference is the setting of the AC/GND/DC switch. In Figure 6.3a, the switch is in the GND (ground) position. This establishes the center line as the ground position on the

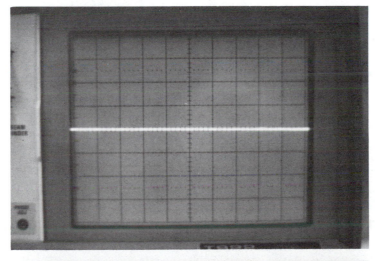

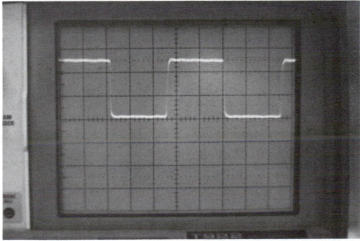

Figure 6.3 (a) AC/GND/DC = GND; (b) AC/GND/DC = DC; (c) AC/GND/DC = AC.

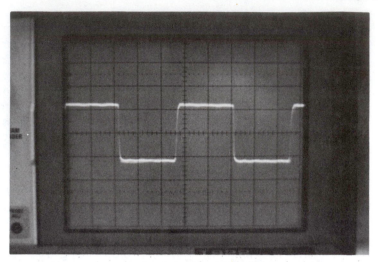

Figure 6.3   (Continued)

CRT. Figure 6.3b shows the signal when the switch is in the DC position. Note that the waveform varies from ground to +5 V (the oscilloscope is set at 2 volts per division). In Figure 6.3c, the switch is in the AC position. In this position, the dc component of the waveform has been removed and the waveform has been centered around zero. Since dc levels are often critical in the proper operation of digital circuits, you should always have this switch in the DC position. That way, you can tell whether or not a given signal is reaching its correct logic levels.

Digital Testing

When properly set up and used, the oscilloscope can locate almost every problem that will ever arise in a microcomputer. The recommended procedure for setting up the oscilloscope for digital troubleshooting is as follows:

1. *Before turning the oscilloscope on,* turn the intensity control fully counterclockwise and set the VOLTS/DIV switch at its maximum value. Now, turn on the oscilloscope and allow it approximately 5 minutes to warm up. After that time, turn the intensity up so that the trace is visible but not very bright. Having the intensity way up shortens the life of the CRT, so you should keep the intensity setting as low as is practical.

2. Check to make sure that all calibration controls are in the calibrated position. If there is a procedure given for calibrating your oscilloscope, follow it at this time.

3. Establish the ground position for your trace. This is done by putting the AC/GND/DC switch in the GND position, then using the vertical adjustment control to set the trace at the desired position. After setting the desired ground position, set the AC/GND/DC switch in the DC position. Leave the switch in this position for all measurements. If you are using a single-trace oscilloscope, it is recommended that you use the center line on the CRT for a ground position. If you are using a dual-trace oscilloscope, try using the center line as the ground position for one trace, and the second line from the bottom for the second trace. This will allow enough space between the traces for your measurements.

4. Set the TRIGGER SOURCE in the EXT (external) position and connect

a probe from the clock source to the X input. If a clock source is not available, use internal triggering. Also, set the TRIGGER MODE switch to the AUTO position.

Once the oscilloscope is set up properly, it is recommended that you immediately check all supply voltages in the system. By doing this, you are ensuring that you do not run into any surprises while troubleshooting. Besides, you might get lucky and find the problem right off the bat. Remember, *keep the VOLTS/DIV control at its maximum setting while checking supply voltages.* This will prevent you from damaging the oscilloscope from checking voltages that are too high. If you need to check a voltage that is higher than the oscilloscope is designed to handle, use a X10 probe. This will attenuate the input signal by 90%, so that only 10% of the signal amplitude will be displayed. Remember, however, that when using a X10 probe, you must multiply all voltage readings by 10 to get the actual voltage.

When checking dc power supplies, the trace will stay level, but will move a given distance from the ground reference, as shown in Figure 6.4. In both of these measurements, the center of the graticule was established as the ground point. In Figure 6.4a, the VOLTS/DIV control is set for 5 volts per division. As you can see, the trace has moved 2.5 divisions from the ground point (center). The voltage measured is therefore found to be

$$2.5 \text{ divisions} \times 5 \text{ V/div} = 12.5 \text{ V}$$

The voltage is known to be positive, because the trace moved in the positive direction from the center line. In Figure 6.4b, the VOLTS/DIV is set for 2 V/div. The trace has moved 1 division in the negative direction, so the voltage is found to be

$$1 \text{ division} \times 2 \text{ V/div} = -2 \text{ V}$$

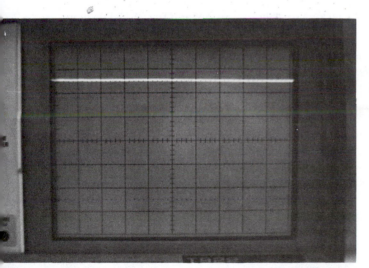 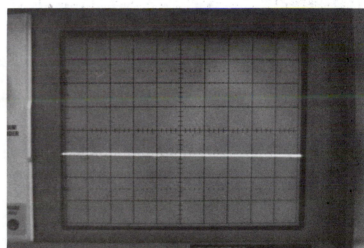

Figure 6.4 Stable dc voltage displays

Note that both of these measurements were taken *after* measuring the supply voltages with the VOLTS/DIV switch set to 20 V/div. After the supply voltages were seen to be low, the VOLTS/DIV setting was decreased to give a more accurate reading. *Note that whenever you change the VOLTS/DIV setting, you must recheck the ground position to be sure that it has not shifted.*

After checking the supply voltages, you will be ready to check the signals in the microcomputer. There are a few things to remember before you start to check these signals:

1. Digital signals are rarely stable waveforms. This was shown in Figure 6.2. More often than not, a "junk signal" like the one shown is an indication that the circuit is working perfectly.
2. Digital inputs and outputs rarely stay at either ground or V_{cc}. If an input or output is staying at one logic level or another, it usually indicates that something is wrong. The exception to this is an input that is tied to either ground or V_{cc}.
3. Malfunctions in commercial microcomputers are rarely caused by timing problems. These problems are worked out by research and development teams long before the microcomputer goes to market. Because of this, the SEC/DIV setting of an oscilloscope is not that critical, as long as you can see the entire waveform.

What follows here is a series of case histories that are being used to show you some of the problems encountered when troubleshooting digital circuits with an oscilloscope, together with their solutions:

CASE 1

A technician was troubleshooting a digital system with a single-trace oscilloscope. When checking out the input and output waveforms from an inverter, the technician saw the waveforms shown in Figure 6.5a and b, respectively. The technician came to the conclusion that the inverter was not inverting, and thus was a bad circuit. This conclusion was reached because both waveforms showed a rising edge at the center of the graticule, so the technician assumed that the two signals were in phase. The oscilloscope was set for internal triggering in the auto mode. The VOLTS/DIV control was set to 2 V and the SEC/DIV control was set to 10 μs.

Observation: There was nothing wrong with the inverter. The problem was the way in which the oscilloscope was set up. With the oscilloscope being set for internal triggering, it triggered on the rising edge of both waveforms. The result is that the output waveform was shifted so that the rising edge would occur at the left of the CRT, just as the input waveform was shifted.

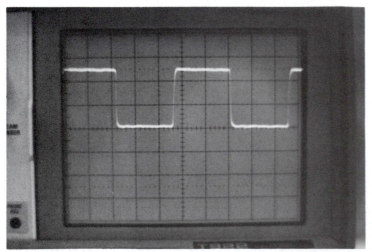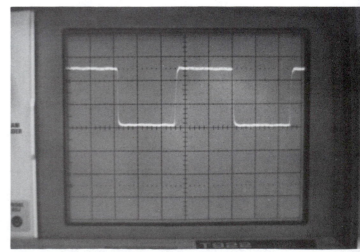

Figure 6.5 Waveforms for troubleshooting Case 1.

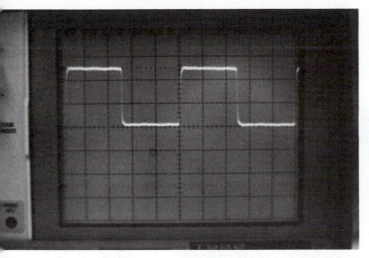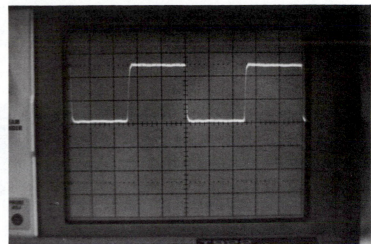

Figure 6.5 (Continued)

Solution: Use the external triggering mode, to trigger the oscilloscope on the inverter input. Now, recheck the input and output waveforms. The results can be seen in Figure 6.5c and d. Note how the output waveform (Figure 6.5d) now can be seen to be 180° out of phase with the input by comparing the two signals at the center of the graticule. All is well, and the inverter is doing its job. By the way, this problem would not occur with a dual-trace oscilloscope. In the dual-trace mode, the oscilloscope would show the two signals in their proper phase relationship.

CASE 2

A circuit is being held in the disabled state, and a check of the $\overline{CS}$ input results in the signal level shown in Figure 6.6a. Since the signal is at 0.6 V (1 V/div), which is less than the 0.8 V maximum for a logic 0, the technician concludes that the chip must be bad because it is not responding to the active low at the $\overline{CS}$ input. Replacing the chip does not resolve the problem. The new chip acts just like the old one.

Observation: There was nothing wrong with the chip. The problem was that the $\overline{CS}$ input was open. When an input is open, it usually reflects a voltage that was inside the chip. As a result, the oscilloscope trace jumped when this input was checked. While an open input will read some voltage when checked with an oscilloscope, don't be fooled. TTL circuits respond to ground paths, and an open input is certainly no ground path. So, while the pin may appear to be at a logic 0, the circuit did not respond because there was no ground path.

Solution: So, how can you tell an open input from a legitimate logic 0? The key is to observe the trace *as you first connect the probe to the input*. An open input will cause the trace to make a definite jump. This jump rarely occurs when the input is a legitimate logic 0. If the trace makes this jump, you can conclude, with a high degree of accuracy, that the input is open. Another indication would be if the input read between 0.8 and 1.8 V while the output that feeds the input was at a logic 1 or logic 0.

CASE 3

A 10-MHz oscilloscope is being used to check a signal that goes low every 10 µs for a duration of 500 ns. When checking the signal with an oscilloscope, the technician sees the waveform shown in Figure 6.6b. The conclusion reached

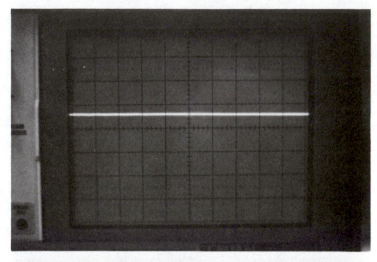

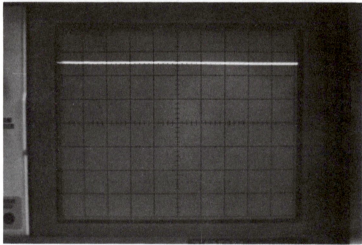

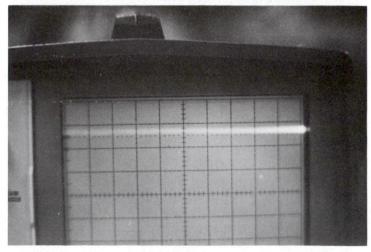

Figure 6.6 Displays for troubleshooting Cases 2 & 3.

is that the low pulse is not occurring.

Observation: The low pulse is occurring, it just isn't showing up on the oscilloscope.

Solution: Set the SEC/DIV control on the oscilloscope to its lowest setting and turn the beam intensity way up. Although this is not the recommended intensity setting, it is only temporary and will not damage the oscilloscope. The resulting trace can be seen in Figure 6.6c. Note the small ''pips'' that are occurring. This is what the technician was looking for.

The cases just discussed here do not cover the variety of situations that you may encounter when troubleshooting with an oscilloscope, but they do cover some of the more common ones. As with any troubleshooting technique, only time and experience will give you the insight needed to determine when you have a legitimate logic malfunction or just an oscilloscope problem.

As your study of troubleshooting microcomputers advance, you will be shown other tests and waveforms that will increase your understanding of digital troubleshooting with an oscilloscope. For now, it is important that you understand how to set up the oscilloscope, how to check signals, and how to avoid some of the common problems that inexperienced digital technicians run into.

6.2 LOGIC PROBES

A logic probe is a device that allows you to check the logic levels at a given point without an oscilloscope. A logic probe contains LED indicators that will verify whether a given point is at logic 0, logic 1, or pulsing. They will also indicate an open pin. The B & K Model DT-51 logic probe is shown in Figure 6.7. Note that the probe has three LEDs, indicating whether a tested point is high, low, or pulsing. An open pin will be indicated by a dimly lit LED.

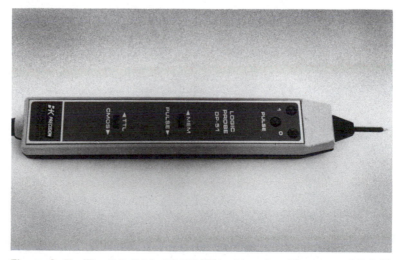

Figure 6–7   The B & K Model DT-57 logic probe. (*Courtesy of B & K*)

The Model DT-51 has another useful feature. As shown in Figure 6.7, the probe has a switch labeled MEM/PULSE. For normal operation, this switch is in the PULSE position. When switched to the MEM position, the probe will register any transient pulses that occur on a given line. For example, one problem that is extremely difficult to diagnose is a ''glitch'' that occurs on a V_{cc} line. A glitch is a rapid change of state that occurs at irregular intervals and thus is extremely difficult to catch on an oscilloscope. The probe, when in the MEM mode of operation, will light the pulse LED when a glitch occurs. You would now know that you were troubleshooting a transient problem on the power lines and could adjust your test procedures accordingly.

Every digital technician should have a logic probe. Although their prices and capabilities vary, a basic probe, such as the one just discussed, should be sufficient. The operation and connection procedures vary from probe to probe, so be sure to carefully read the instructions that come with the probe that you decide to use.

6.3 LOGIC ANALYZERS

A logic analyzer is an expensive but very useful piece of test equipment. The simplest way to describe a logic analyzer is to call it an "oscilloscope with memory." With a logic analyzer, you can view up to 32 waveforms simultaneously, even after those waveforms have stopped. This allows you to analyze the operation of an entire group of circuits with only one test.

Most logic analyzers have a variety of display formats. You can view the actual waveforms themselves, or you can have the circuit operation displayed in binary, hexadecimal, or octal numbers.

The cost of a logic analyzer puts them out of reach of most technicians. Although they can perform some very sophisticated tests, they simply are not worth the cost for most bench technicians. Their primary application is in research and development departments because of their usefulness in detecting timing problems. However, as was stated earlier, these problems are usually worked out long before a given microcomputer reaches the market. For the bench technician, this eliminates the major advantage of owning a logic analyzer.

PART III
COMMON DIGITAL CIRCUITS

7   Signal Sources and Flip-Flops

A majority of microcomputer operations involve clock sources and bistable multivibrators, or flip-flops. Clock sources are used to synchronize the operations of the microcomputer components and units. Flip-flops have a variety of applications, the two most common being *data storage* and *frequency division*.

Most of the circuits discussed in this chapter belong to a general class of transistor circuit called the *multivibrator*. A multivibrator is a dual-transistor oscillator that produces pulse waveform outputs. A multivibrator will produce two output waveforms that are always 180° out of phase.

The *free-running*, or *astable multivibrator* will have two outputs that are constantly changing states. This type of circuit is useful as a square-wave generator. The *monostable multivibrator*, or *one-shot*, has one stable output state. When given a "trigger" signal, the output will change from one logic level to another for a brief period of time, then will automatically revert back to the original output logic level. The *bistable multivibrator*, or *flip-flop*, has two stable output states. When given a trigger signal, the output will go from one logic level to the other, and will stay there until another trigger signal causes it to revert back to its original state. Each of these three types of circuits is covered in detail in this chapter.

7.1 WHAT IS A CLOCK?

A *clock* is *a signal that repeats itself at a constant rate, which is used to synchronize the operation of two or more circuits in a digital system*. A clock signal can come from one of several types of sources, but it must meet some general requirements:

1. A clock signal must repeat at set intervals. This means that the clock source must have a very stable output frequency.
2. It must have a fanout that is high enough to drive all the circuits to which it is connected. If the fanout of the clock source is not high enough, the output logic levels may fall out of the acceptable ranges.

111

3. The clock frequency must be higher than the minimum allowable clock frequency for any circuit it is driving. Some digital circuits have a minimum clock frequency rating. Operating below this rating can cause the chip to malfunction.

There are several types of clock sources. The most common microcomputer clock source is the *crystal-controlled oscillator*. Crystals have very stable output frequencies and thus are perfectly suited for clock applications. Crystal-controlled oscillators are described in Section 7.4.

Clock circuits are not very difficult to understand, but their operation is critical in microcomputer systems. If the clock source malfunctions in a given microcomputer, the entire system will malfunction. For example, refer back to Figure 1.2 in Chapter 1. This figure shows the functional units of the microcomputer. All of these units must be synchronized to operate as a system. The control unit must synchronize the input and memory units so that when data is entered into the system the memory will accept the data. This means that the control unit must have the memory ready to accept data at the same time that it has the input unit putting the data on the data bus. If the memory unit was not synchronized correctly, it may try to accept data before it was available. This would cause the overall system to malfunction.

As you have probably guessed by now, the clock is considered to be a part of the control unit of the microcomputer. The control unit takes the main clock frequency and applies it to the other parts of the system at the proper times. In most cases, the signals that are applied to the other sections of the micrcomputer are at a lower frequency than the main clock frequency. For example, the control unit may take a clock signal of 10 MHz and divide it into lower frequencies of 5, 2.5, and 1.25 MHz. These signals would then be applied to the circuits that required them. Although the three frequencies are not the same, they are synchronized to each other because they were all derived from the same original 10-MHz signal. The methods by which this is accomplished are covered later in this chapter and in Chapter 8. For now, it is important that you understand that all microcomputer timing comes from an original clock source, and that if that clock source goes bad, the entire microcomputer system will be inoperational.

7.2 THE 555 TIMER

The 555 timer is an eight-pin IC that can be used as either an astable multivibrator or a monostable multivibrator, depending on the external circuitry to which it is connected. The block diagram of the 555 internal circuitry is shown in Figure. 7.1 The main operating components of the 555 timer are the two input comparators and the S-R flip-flop. The operation of both of these circuits is really very simple. The comparators have two inputs, a " + " input and a " − " input. When the polarities of these two inputs are correct in relationship to each other, the output from the comparator will be high. When they are reversed, the output will be low. For example, note that comparator 1 has its " − " input connected to a voltage divider. Assuming that $V_{cc} = + 5$ V, the voltage at this input will equal approximately + 3.34 V. If the " + " input of the comparator is more positive than + 3.34 V, the output from the comparator will be high. If the " + " input is less than + 3.34 V, the output from the comparator will be low. Comparator 2 works in the same basic fashion. Its " + " input is connected to the voltage divider and has a set potential of + 1.67 V. If the " − " input to comparator 2 is less than + 1.67 V, the output from the comparator will be high. If not, the output from the comparator will be low.

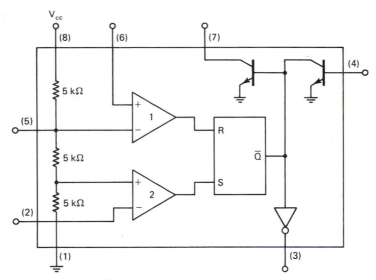

Figure 7.1   The 555 timer internal structure.

The other component of importance is the S-R flip-flop. While flip-flops are covered in detail later in this chapter, the operation of this circuit is summarized as follows to help you understand the 555 timer:

1. If the S input goes *high*, the output ($\overline{Q}$) will go *low*.
2. If the R input goes *high*, the output will go *high*.
3. If the output is low, it will stay low until the R input goes high, regardless of what happens at the S input.
4. If the output is high, it will stay high until the S input goes high, regardless of what happens at the R input.

As we discuss the overall operation of the 555 timer, keep referring back to the discussion of the comparators and the S-R flip-flop to help you follow the theory of operation.

Assume that the output from the S-R flip-flop is initially high. This high is inverted, and appears as a low at the output of the timer (pin 3). The high output from the flip-flop also biases Q_1 on, since it is an NPN transistor. If pin 2 goes low, comparator 2 will have a high output. This puts a high to the S input of the flip-flop, causing its output to go low. This low is inverted and appears as a high at the timer output (pin 3). It also biases Q_1 off. If pin 6 now goes higher than +3.34 V, the output from comparator 1 will also go high. This will put a high at the R input of the flip-flop, causing its output to go high again. All the other levels discussed will now return to their original levels. In summary, if pin 2 goes low, the output from the timer will go high. It will stay that way until pin 6 goes high. At that point, the output will go low again. Now, we need to consider the external circuitry that is used to control the 555 timer.

Figure 7.2 shows the 555 timer wired to act as a monostable multivibrator, or one-shot. Recall that the output from a one-shot will be at one logic level until a trigger signal is received. At that time, the output will change states for a predetermined period of time, then revert automatically to the original output state. In the case of the 555 timer one-shot shown, the output will be low when the one-shot is in its resting state. When a trigger signal is received, the output will go high for a specified period of time, then will automatically go low again. It will then remain low until another trigger signal is received. The initial conditions for the circuit in Figure 7.2 are as follows:

1. The trigger input (pin 2) is high, so the output from comparator 2 is low.
2. The output from the flip-flop is high, so the timer output (pin 3) is low and Q_1 is biased on. This shorts the upper plate of C_1 to ground.
3. With pin 6 being low, comparator 1 has a low output, which is applied to the R input of the flip-flop.

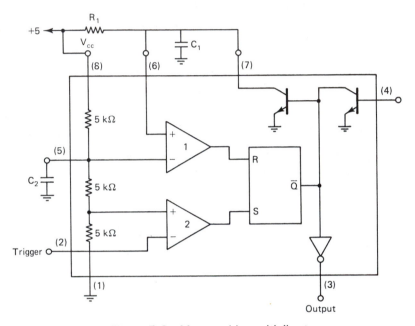

Figure 7.2 Monostable multivibrator.

When a negative-going trigger signal is applied to pin 2, the following occurs:

1. The low input to pin 2 causes the output from comparator 2 to go high.
2. The high input to the S input of the flip-flop causes the output of the flip-flop to go low. This low is inverted and causes the output of the timer (pin 3) to go high. At the same time, the low out of the flip-flop turns Q_1 off.
3. C_1 will now start to charge, since it is connected to V_{cc} via R_1. When the capacitor charge reaches approximately $+3.34$ V, this voltage will cause comparator 1 to produce a high output.
4. The high output from comparator 1 is applied to the R input of the flip-flop. This will cause the output of the flip-flop to go high, returning the circuit to its original resting state. The circuit will now stay in this resting state until another trigger signal is applied to pin 2.

So, how long does the output stay high? The duration of the output pulse is determined by the *RC* network connected to the timer and can be found using the formula

$$T = 1.1 \times R_1 \times C_1$$

The method by which this formula is derived is unimportant at this point. A note of caution: Capacitors can vary in actual value by as much as 20% below to 100%

above their rated value. For this reason, the calculated pulse width from a one-shot may be way off the actual pulse width. Before replacing a bad capacitor in a one-shot circuit, be sure that the replacement capacitor will provide the required pulse width from the circuit.

The applications for one-shots are covered in Section 7.7. The 555 timer is only one of many one-shot circuits, and these other circuits will also be discussed in detail. The other application that a 555 timer is commonly used for is a free-running, or astable multivibrator. This application will be covered next.

The 555 Timer as a Clock Source

As we stated earlier, a free-running, or astable multivibrator is a circuit that produces a pulse waveform output with only a dc input. With the proper external circuitry, the 555 timer can be made to operate as an astable multivibrator. This astable circuit can be seen in Figure 7.3. The main difference between this circuit and the 555 one-shot is the connection between pins 2 and 6. Another resistor has been added, and pin 7 has been connected between the two resistors.

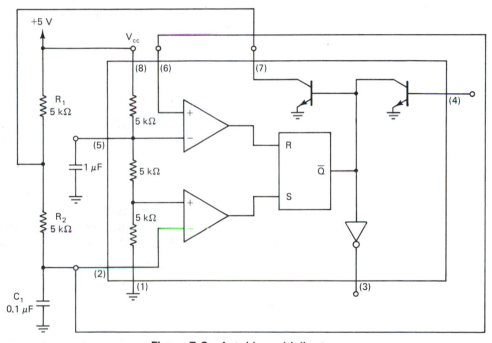

Figure 7.3 Astable multivibrator.

We are going to make some assumptions to start our discussion of the operation of this circuit. Assume that C_1 had charged to a potential equal to V_{cc} and is now in the process of discharging. The circuit operation at this point is as follows:

1. When the potential on C_1 goes below approximately $+1.67$ V, pin 2 will cause comparator 2 to have a high output. This high is applied to the S input of the flip-flop, causing its output to go low.
2. The low output from the flip-flop is inverted and applied to the output of the timer (pin 3). It also causes Q_1 to turn off.
3. With Q_1 off, C_1 starts to charge toward V_{cc} through R_1 and R_2. When the potential across C_1 reaches approximately $+3.34$ V, comparator 1 is activated by the potential at pin 6 of the timer.

4. When the output from comparator 1 goes high, this high is applied to the R input of the flip-flop, causing the output of the flip-flop to go high.

5. The high output from the flip-flop is inverted, and produces a low at the timer output. It also causes Q_1 to turn on. This provides a discharge path for C_1, and C_1 starts to discharge.

6. This brings us back to the starting point in the circuit operation.

With both pin 2 and pin 6 being connected to the C_1 circuit, C_1 will provide both of the triggering signals needed by the 555 timer. The output frequency for the circuit can be found using the formula

$$f = \frac{1.44}{[R_1 + (2 \times R_2)] \, C_1}$$

Again, the method by which the formula was derived is not important for our purposes, and again, the actual value of C_1 will have a great effect on the accuracy of the formula.

The 555 timer astable circuit is fine to use as a clock source for some digital circuits, but most microcomputers will not use this circuit. There are several reasons for this:

1. The maximum output frequency for this circuit is not high enough for most microcomputer applications. While the circuit can produce frequencies in the hundreds of kHz, most microcomputers require frequencies in the MHz region.

2. As the circuit heats up, its output frequency tends to change. This is unacceptable, since microcomputers depend on stable clock frequencies to operate correctly.

The main application for free-running 555 timer circuits can be found in small, dedicated digital circuits. A dedicated circuit is one that performs one specific function only. An example may be a digital alarm circuit. Such a circuit may well use a free-running 555 timer circuit for a clock source, since timing in such a circuit is not as critical as timing in a microcomputer.

7.3 CRYSTAL-CONTROLLED OSCILLATORS

One of the most common types of microcomputer clock sources is the crystal-controlled oscillator (CCO). CCOs are used for several reasons. First, they have extremely stable output frequencies and are available in a wide variety of frequency ratings. Second, crystals have a relatively long life, which makes CCOs a highly reliable timing source. A practical CCO can be seen in Figure 7.4. This is the clock circuit from the Heath H-89A. The timing basis for the circuit is Y501, the 12.288-MHz crystal. The *RC* network is used to provide filtering of low-frequency harmonics and to make sure that the clock signal changes states at a linear rate. U501A provides an output that is within acceptable TTL voltage limits. U501B is used to improve the current levels of the clock signal while improving the rise and fall times of the signal. The output waveform from U501B can be seen in Figure 7.5. This waveform was measured with the oscilloscope being set to 1 V/div. The oscilloscope ground was set at the bottom of the graticule. As you can see, the clock signal is hardly a square wave. Instead, it resembles a triangular waveform. This wave shape is acceptable because of its high frequency. At much lower frequencies, a signal like this could cause the

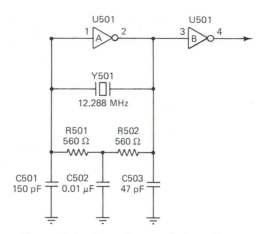

Figure 7.4 Crystal-controlled oscillator.

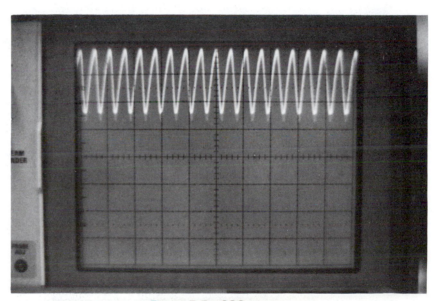

Figure 7.5 CCO output.

ICs to overheat. Also note that the signal barely passes the minimum acceptable logic 1 and the maximum acceptable logic 0 voltage levels. This is also acceptable, since the circuits that are connected to the output of U501B are able to respond to the signal. The small voltage transition out of U501B is due to the operating frequency of the crystal.

Troubleshooting a CCO is not difficult at all. If the final output from the circuit shown in Figure 7.4 is dead, odds are that the TTL circuits that are being driven by the crystal are defective. Since these gates operate mainly in the voltage region between logic 0 and logic 1, they produce a relatively high amount of heat. This tends to shorten the life of the gate. If the logic gates are not the cause of the problem, check the crystal. For the circuit shown in Figure 7.4, this can be done by checking the input to U501A. If the input is not changing states, the crystal is probably defective and should be replaced. If the circuit has an output, but the signal has dropped considerably in frequency, check C502. This capacitor is responsible for filtering out the lower harmonics produced in the circuit. If the clock is putting out a signal, but that signal is not within acceptable TTL voltage levels, check R501 and R502.

Of all the problems that could arise in this and other CCOs, the most common problem is the clock signal going completely dead. This is good news for the technician, since this problem is the easiest one to detect and correct.

7.4 MONOSTABLE MULTIVIBRATORS (ONE-SHOTS)

As was stated earlier, a one-shot is a circuit that has one stable (resting) output state. When it receives a trigger signal, it switches to the other output state for a predetermined period of time, then automatically reverts back to the stable output state. Although we have already covered the 555 timer as a one-shot, we will now cover some of the other common TTL one-shots. This will include a discussion of their circuit action, parameters, and circuit requirements.

The 74121

The 74121 is a one-shot that has "Schmitt-trigger" inputs. A Schmitt-trigger input is one that is transition sensitive rather than level sensitive. This means that the transition past a certain threshold voltage will trigger the device. The pin diagram and truth table for the 74121 can be seen in Figure 7.6. The operation of the circuit can best be understood by taking a look at the truth table. The device has two outputs, labeled Q and $\overline{Q}$. These two outputs are always in the opposite states, as can be seen in the output columns of the truth table.

The key to triggering the 74121 is to cause a transition at the output of the internal AND gate. This AND gate is a Schmitt-trigger gate, as is denoted by the hysteresis symbol in the logic symbol. Any time that you see this symbol, you are dealing with a Schmitt-trigger circuit, which responds to transitions rather than the logic levels themselves. To help you understand this better, compare the first four lines of the truth table to the last five lines. In the first four lines of the table, there are no ($\uparrow$,$\downarrow$) symbols in the input columns. This symbol represents a transition. Note that with no transition, the output from the 74121 is always Q = 0 and $\overline{Q}$ = 1, regardless of the actual input logic levels. In the last five lines of the table, the inputs all show a transition at one point or another. In each case, the output is shown to change from one state to the other, then back again.

Let's take a look at how the trigger inputs (A1, A2, and B) affect the circuit. First, take a look at the B input. This input is tied directly to the internal AND gate. If this input is held low, there is no way that the one-shot can be triggered. This is because it takes a positive-going transition out of the AND gate to trigger the circuit. If one of the inputs is held low, there is no way that this positive-going transition can occur. Thus, with the B input tied low, the circuit is inhibited, regardless of what happens at the A1 and A2 inputs. This can be seen in the third line of the truth table. The "×" in this line means that the input has no effect on the overall circuit action. The circuit can also be inhibited by keeping A1 and A2 at a high level. Note that these two inputs are applied to a NAND gate. With both NAND gate inputs high, its output is low. This puts a low into the AND gate, which again will keep its output low. As the fourth line of the truth table indicates, the B input is ineffective when A1 = 1 and A2 = 1.

As the first two lines of the truth table indicate, there is another way of inhibiting the circuit. This involves tying the B input high and either one of the A inputs low. If either A input is low, the output from the NAND gate is at a constant high. This constant high, together with the constant high from the B input, causes the output of the AND gate at a constant high. Now, remember that this circuit responds to positive-going *transitions,* not the actual high level itself. If the output from the AND gate is at a constant high, the one-shot itself cannot get the transition that it needs to trigger. It is therefore effectively inhibited.

Function table

Inputs			Outputs	
A1	A2	B	Q	$\overline{Q}$
L	X	H	L	H
X	L	H	L*	H*
X	X	L	L*	H*
H	H	X	L*	H*
H	↓	H	⊓	⊔
↓	H	H	⊓	⊔
↓	↓	H	⊓	⊔
L	X	↑	⊓	⊔
X	L	↑	⊓	⊔

Notes: 1. An external capacitor may be connected between C_{ext} (positive) and R_{ext}/C_{ext}.

2. To use the internal timing resistor, connect R_{int} to V_{cc}. For improved pulse width accuracy and repeatability, connect an external resistor between R_{ext}/C_{ext} and V_{cc} with R_{int} open-circuited.

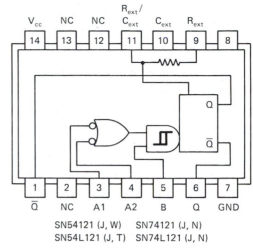

SN54121 (J, W)   SN74121 (J, N)
SN54L121 (J, T)   SN74L121 (J, N)

'121 . . . R_{int} = 2 kΩ NOM.
'L121 . . . R_{int} = 4 kΩ NOM.

NC — No internal connection.

*These lines of the function table assume that the indicated steady-state conditions at the A and B inputs have been set up long enough to complete any pulse started before the setup.

(a)

Typical performance

Type	No. of inputs		Output pulse range	Total power
	HI	LO		
'121	1	2	40 ns–28 s	90 mW
'L121	1	2	40 ns–28 s	40 mW

SN54121 (J)   SN74121 (J, N)
SN54L121 (J)

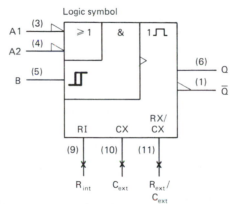

Logic symbol

Pin assignments

J, N packages			
1	$\overline{Q}$	8	nc
2	nc	9	R_{int}
3	A1	10	C_{ext}
4	A2	11	R_{ext}/C_{ext}
5	B	12	nc
6	Q	13	nc
7	GND	14	V_{cc}

'121 . . . R_{int} = 2 kΩ nominal
'L121 . . . R_{int} = 4 kΩ nominal

(b)

Figure 7.6 74121: (a) conventional symbol; (b) DLM symbol. *(Courtesy of Texas Instruments, Inc.)*

Now, we will take a look at the active triggering conditions. These are represented in the last five lines of the truth table and will be covered individually.

Line 5: With the B input tied high, the key to getting the positive-going transition at the one-shot is to cause the output from the NAND gate to go high. Line 5 indicates that this can be done by tying the A1 input high, then causing a negative-going transition at the A2 input. When A2 goes low, the output from the NAND gate will make a positive-going transition. This transition is applied to the upper input and the AND gate, causing its output to also make a positive-going transition. This will trigger the one-shot.

Line 6: This line of the truth table is identical in operation to line 5, except that the negative-going transition is being applied to the A1 input while the A2 input is being tied high. As far as the rest of the circuit action goes, this has the same effect as line 5 of the table.

Line 7: This line shows a negative-going transition being applied to both of the A inputs simultaneously, with the B input being held high. When the A inputs both make the negative-going transition, the output from the NAND gate will make a positive going transition. The output from the AND gate will therefore make the same transition, triggering the one-shot.

Line 8: This line shows the transition being applied to the B input while the A1 input is tied low. With A1 being held low, the output from the NAND gate is constantly high. When the positive-going transition occurs at the B input, the AND gate output will make its transition, and the one-shot will be triggered.

Line 9: This is exactly the same as line 8, except that the A2 input is the NAND input that is held low. Otherwise, nothing has changed.

As you can see, there must be a transition at either one of the A inputs, or at the B input, for the one-shot to be triggered. Having the circuit constructed as it is gives the system designer a choice. Notice how the transitions on the A inputs were all negative-going while the transitions on the B input were all positive-going. This gives the system designer a choice of which type of signal to use as a trigger. Figure 7.7 shows the 74121 wired for a positive-going trigger and for a negative-going trigger. Try to relate these two circuits to the truth table to see which truth table lines apply to the operation of the circuits.

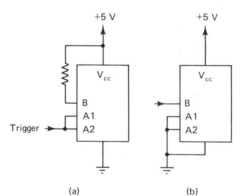

Figure 7.7 (a) Negative-edge trigger; (b) Positive-edge trigger.

Now that we have determined the methods by which the 74121 can be triggered, let's take a look at how the pulse width of the output is determined. As with all one shots, the pulse width of the output is determined by the external wiring of the circuit. The 74121 has a pulse-width range of approximately 35 ns to 28 s, depending on how the device is wired.

There are three inputs to the device which are used in setting the device timing. These inputs are R_{ext}/C_{ext} (pin 11), C_{ext} (pin10), and R_{int} (pin 9). Two methods of wiring these inputs are shown in Figure 7.8. In Figure 7.8a, the internal resistor of the 74121 is being used to set the circuit timing. When wired this way, the pulse width of the output will be typically 35 to 40 ns. The pulse width can be varied over a much wider range by wiring the 74121 as shown in Figure 7.8b. The external *RC* circuit will now determine the pulse width of the output. When wired this way, the pulse width of the output can be determined using the formula

$$t_{W(out)} = 0.7C_{ext}R_T$$

There are limits to the values that may be used for the external timing components. The range of values for the capacitor are 0 to 1000 μF, and the limits for the resistor are from 1.4 to 40 kΩ. Using the maximum allowable values for both *R* and *C,* the pulse width obtained will be approximately 28 s.

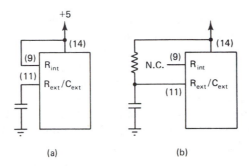

(a) (b) **Figure 7.8** *RC* connections.

One of the major limitations of the 74121 is the fact that it is not a *retriggerable* one-shot. This means that the circuit cannot receive another trigger while it is in its output pulse condition. If the output is in its active state, and another trigger is applied to the circuit, the output may become very unstable. This could cause any circuits that are being driven by this gate to malfunction. There are retriggerable one-shots. The 74122 is a retriggerable one-shot. By applying a series of trigger pulses to its inputs, the 74122 can be used to produce extremely long output pulses.

There are many commercially available one-shots in almost every logic family. Although we could not possibly hope to cover them all here, the 74121 is one of the more common ones and should give you a good idea how they all work. We will now discuss some of the more common applications for one-shots.

7.5 ONE-SHOT APPLICATIONS

One of the more common applications for a one-shot is as a signal controller. In this application, the one-shot is being used to allow a clock signal to be applied to a circuit for a specified period of time. For example, look at the circuit shown in Figure 7.9. In the circuit shown, the one-shot is used to allow the 1-kHz signal to

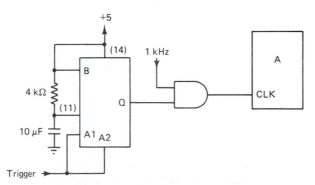

Figure 7.9 Clock-enabling circuit.

be applied to circuit A for approximately 28 ms. When circuit B drives its B1 output low, the 74121 is triggered. At that time, the Q output from the 74121 goes high, with this high being applied to one of the AND gate inputs. With the 1-kHz signal being applied to the other AND gate input, the output from the AND gate will now also be a 1-kHz signal. After approximately 28 ms, the Q output of the 74121 will go low again. This will disable the AND gate, preventing the 1-kHz signal from being applied to circuit A. The waveforms for the circuit are shown in Figure 7.9b.

Another application for the one-shot is as a "pulse-narrowing" circuit. This circuit would be used to take a relatively long input pulse and convert it to a pulse with a much smaller pulse width. Such a circuit is shown in Figure 7.10a. As the waveforms in Figure 7.10b indicate, the input signal to the 74121 has a pulse width of 20 ms. The 74121, which triggers on the positive-going transition of the input, has an output pulse width of approximately 154 μs. When the input signal first goes high, the one-shot triggers and produces a 154-μs pulse that is in phase with the input signal. Since the one-shot is positive-edge triggered (i.e., requires a positive-going signal to trigger), it will not trigger again until the input signal has gone and makes another positive-going transition. The end result is that circuit A will receive a 154-μs pulse instead of the original 20-ms pulse that was being used. This type of circuit is useful, because there are digital circuits that have maximum input pulse duration ratings. When a given circuit has such a rating, and its input signal exceeds that rating, a circuit like the one shown in Figure 7.10 can be used to solve the problem.

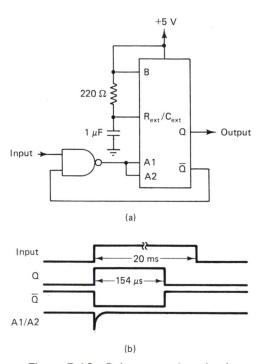

Figure 7.10   Pulse-narrowing circuit.

One-Shot Troubleshooting

One-shot circuits can be somewhat tricky when it comes to troubleshooting. The problem lies in the fact that most one-shots are not used at regular intervals. When a given one-shot is used at regular intervals, you simply connect an oscilloscope to its output to see if the output is changing states whenever the device is triggered. If it is not changing states, the one-shot is probably defective and should be replaced. If this does not solve the problem, change the *RC* network that is connected to the circuit.

When a one-shot is not used at regular intervals, a bit of additional work may be required to determine if the device is working or not. Refer back to the circuit in Figure 7.9. Assume that this circuit was used only at given times while the microcomputer was operating. If you could not get the computer to produce the conditions under which the one-shot is used, you could use the following series of tests to determine whether or not the device is working:

1. Disconnect the trigger input . This could be done by removing circuit B from its socket and bending the pin out, then replacing the IC into its socket.

2. Disconnect the output from the one-shot so that no other circuits will be affected by the test. This can be done in the same way that B1 was disconnected.

3. Attach a pulse generator to the trigger input of the one-shot and observe the output of the device with an oscilloscope. If all of the input requirements for the one-shot have been met, and the device still does not trigger, it is defective, and should be replaced.

> **CAUTION:** Make sure that you never inject a signal into a circuit before removing all ICs that are not being tested and might be affected by the testing procedure!

All you need is to destroy a dozen chips while testing one. If a given circuit is not being tested, remove it. This may take a few extra minutes of your time, but the possible results of not removing the chips could cost you a few extra hours of repair time.

7.6 BISTABLE MULTIVIBRATORS (FLIP-FLOPS)

A flip-flop is a circuit that has two stable states. These states are referred to as SET ($Q = 1$) and RESET ($Q = 0$). Each flip-flop has two outputs, Q and $\overline{Q}$, just like the 74121. When an input signal causes a flip-flop to SET, it will remain in the SET condition until caused to return to the RESET condition. Similarly, if an input signal causes a flip-flop to RESET, it will stay in the RESET condition until caused to return to the SET condition. In either case, the state of the flip-flop is indicated at the Q output. The $\overline{Q}$ is simply a complemented output.

There are several types of flip-flops. While they all have the same output characteristics (SET versus RESET), their input characteristics are different. In other words, the various types of flip-flops will change states under varying conditions. In this section we discuss the various types of flip-flops and the triggering requirements for each.

NOR-Gate and NAND-Gate S-R Flip-Flops

The simplest flip-flops are the NOR- and NAND-gate S-R (SET-RESET) flip-flops. The NOR-gate S-R flip-flop can be seen, together with its truth table, in Figure 7.11.

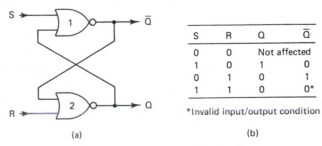

S	R	Q	$\overline{Q}$
0	0	Not affected	
1	0	1	0
0	1	0	1
1	1	0	0*

*Invalid input/output condition

(a)   (b)

Figure 7.11 NOR-gate SR flip-flop.

As you can see, the flip-flop consists of nothing but cross-coupled NOR gates. The output of each gate is internally wired to the input of the other. The external inputs to the NOR gates are used to change the state of the device. To see how this works, we will start by assuming that the flip-flop is in the RESET ($Q = 0$, $\overline{Q} = 1$) condition. Also assume that the external inputs are at their inactive (0) level. With the output of gate 2 being connected to gate 1, gate 1 will have two zeros being applied to its inputs. Its output is therefore a logic 1. This one is tied to the input of gate 2, holding its output at zero. As long as no signal is applied to the external inputs, the flip-flop will stay in this condition. This is indicated by the first line of the truth table, which states that, with two zeros in, the Q and $\overline{Q}$ outputs will equal whatever value they were at previously.

Line 1 of the truth table shows the input levels that are referred to as the SET input. This means that if S = 1, and R = 0, the flip-flop will SET. If the S input goes to a 1, the output from gate 1 will now go low. With two zeros into gate 2, the output from gate 2 will now go high. This high, coupled back to the input of gate 1, will cause the output of gate 1 to be low, even after the S input returns to zero. The result of this SET input is that the Q output has gone to a 1, which is the SET output condition for the circuit.

An interesting point can now be made. With the flip-flop now in the SET condition, note what would happen if we applied another SET input to the circuit. When the S input goes high, there is no effect on the circuit, since the internal connection to gate 1 is already holding the output of gate 1 low. This leads to a general statement about the operation of all flip-flops. *A previously SET flip-flop will not respond to a SET input. Similarly, a previously RESET flip-flop will not respond to a RESET input.*

Now, let's consider what happens when a SET flip-flop receives a RESET input. The RESET input condition is covered in line 3 of the truth table. When the R input goes high, the output from gate 2 goes low. This low is coupled back to the internal input of gate 1. With two lows into gate 1, its output goes high. This high is coupled internally back to the input of gate 2, so the output of gate 2 is held low, even after the high input at R is removed. The flip-flop has now returned to the RESET (Q = 0) condition.

The last line of the truth table indicates an *invalid* input condition. If both inputs were to go high, both outputs would go low. This is an invalid output condition and must not be allowed to occur. Under normal circumstances, this input condition would never be allowed to occur. If it does occur, it is due to a problem with the circuit that is providing the inputs to the flip-flop.

The NAND-gate S-R flip-flop works in the same basic fashion as the NOR gate circuit, except that the active input level is low instead of high. The NAND-gate S-R flip-flop and its truth table can be seen in Figure 7.12. Again, we will start our circuit analysis with the assumption that the flip-flop is in the RESET condition. The external inputs are in their inactive state, which, in this case, is high. With the output of gate 1 being high, gate 2 has two high inputs. The output from gate 2 is therefore low. This low is coupled internally back to the input of gate 1, holding its output high. The flip-flop will stay in this state until a SET input is received.

The active SET input for the circuit is shown in line 2 of the truth table. If the S input to the circuit goes low, the output from gate 2 will go high. This high

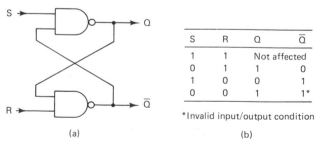

S	R	Q	$\overline{Q}$
1	1	Not affected	
0	1	1	0
1	0	0	1
0	0	1	1*

*Invalid input/output condition

(a)   (b)

Figure 7.12 NAND-gate S-R flip-flop.

is coupled back to the input of gate 1, so gate 1 will now have two high inputs. With two high inputs, the output from gate 1 will now go low. This low is coupled back to gate 2, so its output will stay high, even after the SET signal is removed from the input. Again, applying another SET input at this point will have no effect on the circuit.

If a RESET signal is applied to the circuit, as shown in line 3 of the truth table, the low into gate 1 will cause its output to go high. This high will be fed back to the input of gate 2, causing the output of gate 2 to go low. The low out of gate 2 will be fed back to the internal input to gate 1, ensuring that its output stays high, even after the RESET input is removed.

Line 4 of the truth table again indicates an invalid input condition. Under normal circumstances, the inputs to the NAND S-R flip-flop will never both go low, as this will cause an invalid output state ($Q = \overline{Q} = 1$).

The NAND- and NOR-gate S-R flip-flops are usually represented by the logic diagrams shown in Figure 7.13. Note that the NAND S-R flip-flop has inputs that are labeled $\overline{S}$ and $\overline{R}$. This indicates the active-low inputs that are required to cause the circuit to change states.

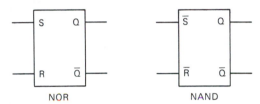

Figure 7.13 S-R flip-flop logic symbols.

We will cover some of the applications for NAND and NOR S-R flip-flops in Section 7.7. Incidentally, the basic flip-flops just discussed are often referred to as *latches*. Whenver you hear someone discussing NAND latches or NOR latches, they are talking about the NAND and NOR S-R flip-flops.

D-Type Flip-Flops

The most commonly used flip-flop is the D-type flip-flop, or D-latch. The logic symbol and truth table for the D-latch are shown in Figure 7.14. The basic operation for this circuit is very simple. When a clock signal is received by the latch, whatever value is at the D input will be sent to the Q output and held there until another clock signal is received. Again, a complemented ($\overline{Q}$) output is provided.

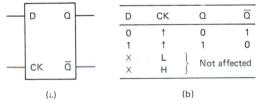

Figure 7.14 D-type flip-flop: (a) logic symbol; (b) truth table.

If a D-latch is RESET, and a low is clocked in, the device will remain RESET. If a high is clocked into a RESET D-latch, the circuit will switch to the SET condition. If a high is clocked into a SET D-latch, the device will remain SET. However, if a low is clocked into a SET D-latch, the device will RESET. Just remember, if

D is low when a clock is applied, Q will be low. If D is high when a clock is applied, Q will be high. Simple enough?

The most commonly used TTL D-type flip-flop is the 7474. This is a *positive-edge-triggered* flip-flop. This means that the level at the D input is transferred to the Q output on the positive-going transition of the clock signal. This can be seen by looking at the waveforms shown in Figure 7.15. As you can see, the positive-going transitions of the clock are labeled T_0 through T_3. At each one of these transitions, the Q output changes to the logic level that is present at the D input. Note that there is no change in the output state of the circuit at time T_2. This is due to the fact that a low is being applied to the D input when the Q output is already low.

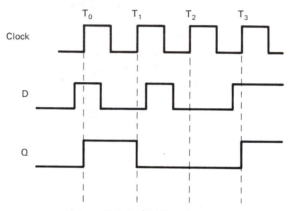

Figure 7.15 7474 timing.

D-type latches have another type of input, called an *asynchronous* input. An asynchronous input works independently of the clock, as opposed to a synchronous input, which depends on a clock signal to work. The D input would be a synchronous input, since it has no effect on the circuit until the clock signal is received.

The asynchronous inputs to the D-type flip-flop are called the *preset* and *clear* inputs. The preset input will cause the flip-flop to SET, regardless of what is happening to the D input. The clear input will cause the flip-flop to RESET, regardless of what is happening at the D input. *Both of these asynchronous inputs are active-low inputs and both will override the clock input.* The revised logic diagram and truth table for the D-type flip-flop are shown in Figure 7.16. Note that, according to the truth table, the preset and clear inputs to the circuit override the D and clock inputs. As long as the asynchronous inputs are being used, the D and clock inputs are ineffective.

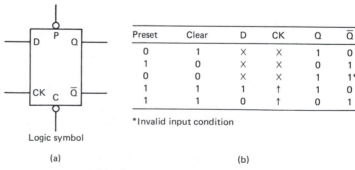

Preset	Clear	D	CK	Q	$\overline{Q}$
0	1	X	X	1	0
1	0	X	X	0	1
0	0	X	X	1	1*
1	1	1	↑	1	0
1	1	0	↑	0	1

*Invalid input condition

Logic symbol

(a)   (b)

Figure 7.16 D-type flip-flop.

One important point: *The preset and clear inputs to the flip-flop must never both be activated at the same time.* This would cause an invalid output state. Again, if the circuitry that is driving the flip-flop is working correctly, these two inputs will never be activated at the same time. Also note that when these asynchronous inputs are not being used in a given circuit, they are usually tied high to prevent accidental SET or RESET operations.

J-K Flip-Flops

Another type of flip-flop is the J-K flip-flop. The truth table and logic symbol for the J-K are shown in Figure 7.17. The J-K has two data inputs rather than the single D input that the D-type has. Both of these inputs must be at specified levels to cause the device to change states. When both inputs are at their correct logic levels and the device receives a clock signal, the output will go to the appropriate logic state.

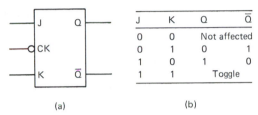

J	K	Q	$\overline{Q}$
0	0	Not affected	
0	1	0	1
1	0	1	0
1	1	Toggle	

(a)   (b)

Figure 7.17   J-K flip-flop.

The first line of the truth table shows the inactive input condition. If $J = 0$ and $K = 0$, the device will not change states when the clock signal occurs. If the device is SET, it will remain SET. If the device is RESET, it will remain RESET.

The second line of the truth table shows the RESET input condition. If $J = 0$ and $K = 1$, the device will be in the RESET condition after the clock signal occurs, regardless of the previous state of the device.

The third line of the table indicates the SET input condition. If $J = 1$ and $K = 0$, the device will SET when the clock signal occurs, regardless of the previous state of the device.

The final line indicates an input condition that is unique for the J-K flip-flop. This is called the *toggle* input. When $J = 1$ and $K = 1$, the next clock signal will cause the flip-flop to switch from its current output state to the other. If the device is SET, it will RESET. If the device is RESET, it will SET. This has some interesting applications, as will be seen in Section 7.7 and in Chapter 8.

J-K flip-flops are available with preset and clear inputs, just like the D-type latch. These asynchronous inputs are active low and will override the clocked inputs.

There is a special type of J-K flip-flop, called a *master-slave* J-K flip-flop. This device works just like the J-K just discussed, with one exception. This exception can be seen by looking at the timing diagrams in Figure 7.18. The timing waveforms shown in Figure 7.18a are those for a conventional J-K, while the waveforms in Figure 7.18b are those for a master-slave flip-flop. Note that the output from the conventional J-K changes on the negative-going transition of the clock, while the output from the M-S flip-flop changes on the positive-going transition. Although both devices are triggered on the negative-going transition, the M-S flip-flop will not change its output until the next positive-going transition. This can be seen better by looking at the waveforms shown in Figure 7.19a. At time T_0, the data that is at the J and K inputs is entered into the flip-flop. As the waveform shows, this SET input has not been reflected at the output of the device. At the next positive-going transition (T_1), the

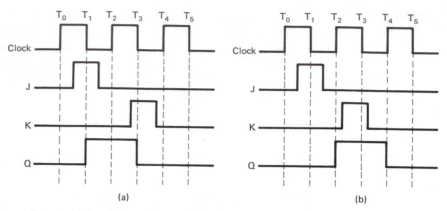

Figure 7.18 J-K flip-flop waveforms: (a) conventional; (b) master-slave.

data that appeared at the J and K inputs is clocked to the output. Since the device had received a SET input at the negative-going transition, the output goes to the SET condition on the next positive-going transition. So, while the conventional J-K flip-flop immediately changes its output state when it receives a clock signal, the M-S flip-flop waits until the next positive-going transition of the clock to change its output.

Figure 7.19b shows an addition to the basic logic symbol for the J-K flip-flop. Note that the clock input has a bubble and a small triangle inside the block. The bubble indicates that the input is active low, while the triangle indicates that the device is edge-triggered. The combination of the two indicates that the device triggers on the negative-going edge of the clock signal.

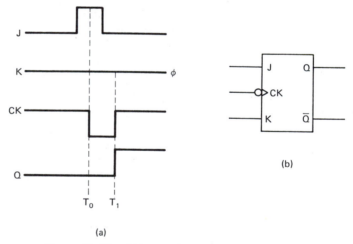

Figure 7.19 J-K waveforms and logic symbol.

J-K flip-flops are not used as frequently as D-type flip-flops because they require two input signals (J and K) rather than one (D). However, you will still run into many systems that use mainly J-K flip-flops or a combination of J-K flip-flops and D-type flip-flops. In the next section we will discuss some of the applications of these devices. For each application that can be performed by either type of flip-flop, a diagram is provided showing both types of flip-flop wired to perform the application. You should try to remember these wiring diagrams, since the wiring of a flip-flop is often your best indicator of the function that the device is being used to perform.

7.7 FLIP-FLOP APPLICATIONS

The applications for flip-flops in microcomputers are almost endless. There is not a single area in the microcomputer where you will not find at least one flip-flop being used. However, all flip-flop applications fall into one of three categories. Regardless of the area where you find a flip-flop, it is being used as a *one-bit memory,* a *frequency divider,* or an *operation sequencer.* These three general categories of flip-flop applications are covered in this section.

One-Bit Memory

A flip-flop can be seen to be a one-bit memory circuit if you look at the relationship between the Q output and the last input received by the device. For example, recall that when the D-type latch receives a 1 at the D input, the Q output goes to a 1. It was shown that the Q output stayed at a 1, even after the 1 at the D input was gone. In essence, the flip-flop "remembered" the last value clocked into the D input. Based on this operating principle, the following statements about flip-flops in general are made:

> A flip-flop that is in the SET condition is said to be storing a logic 1.
>
> A flip-flop that is in the RESET condition is said to be storing a logic 0.

It is easy to wire the D-type as a one-bit memory. Simply apply the data you want stored to the D input of the device. But what if you want to store a single data bit into a J-K flip-flop? You can control the J-K flip-flop with a single input data bit by wiring the device as shown in Figure 7.20a. If a 1 is applied to the J input of the circuit shown, it will be inverted and applied to the K input of the device. This gives you the input condition of J = 1 and K = 0. With this input condition, the device will SET on the next transition of the clock, and will be storing a logic 1. If a 0 is

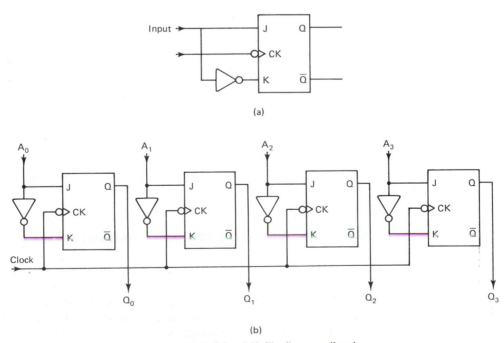

(a)

(b)

Figure 7.20 J-K flip-flop applications.

applied to the J input, it will be inverted and applied to the K input. This gives you the input condition of J = 0 and K = 1. On the next clock transition, the device will RESET and will be storing a logic 0. Note that in both conditions, the Q output will equal the value at the J input after the clock signal occurs. This essentially is the same circuit operation as the D-type flip-flop.

Figure 7.20b shows four J-K flip-flops wired to store a 4-bit word. The four data inputs (A_0 through A_3) are applied to the J inputs. When a given value appears at these inputs and a clock signal occurs, the data word will be stored in the circuit. Driving the clear input low would cause the flip-flops to RESET, eliminating the word that is being stored. Groups of these circuits could be used to store several 4-bit words. When several flip-flops are wired in parallel like this, the circuit is referred to as a *shift register*. Shift registers will be covered in detail in Chapter 8.

Frequency Divider

Flip-flops are often used to divide a clock frequency by some power of 2, to produce a lower frequency signal. A single J-K flip-flop, wired to act as a "divide-by-2" circuit, is shown in Figure 7.21a. This circuit will produce a square-wave output that is equal to one-half of the clock frequency. Note that the circuit in Figure 7.21a is

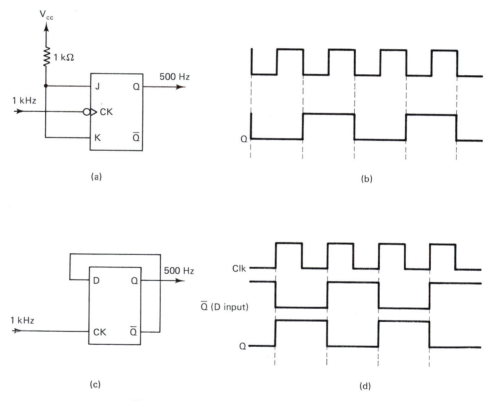

Figure 7.21 Flip-flop frequency dividers.

wired for the toggle input condition. This means that the circuit will change output states on every negative-going transition of the clock. Assuming that the circuit is initially RESET, the first transition of the clock causes the flip-flop to toggle to the SET condition and the Q output goes high. On the next transition of the input clock, the flip-flop toggles again, this time going to the RESET condition. The Q output now goes low, and so on. The clock and Q waveforms for this circuit can be seen in Figure 7.21b. Note that the waveform at the Q output goes through one complete cycle for every two clock cycles. This waveform is therefore equal to one-half of the clock frequency. If the input frequency is 1 kHz, the frequency at the Q output is equal to 500 Hz. The same function is performed by the D-type flip-flop shown in Figure 7.21c.

Assume that the D latch shown is initially in the RESET condition. This means that Q = 0 and $\overline{Q}$ = 1. On the positive transition of the clock, the 1 at the D input of the device will be clocked in. At this time, the Q output is high and the $\overline{Q}$ output is low. This low is tied back to the D input and is clocked into the flip-flop on the next clock transition. The flip-flop is now RESET and the cycle repeats itself. The key to the operation of this circuit is the fact that the D input is being driven by the $\overline{Q}$ output of the flip-flop. After each transition, the D input automatically goes to the opposite state of the one that was just entered. So the output of this circuit changes once for each input clock cycle. The waveforms for the circuit are shown in Figure 7.21d.

What if you needed a frequency that was equal to one-fourth of the input clock frequency? You could wire two flip-flops together, as shown in Figure 7.22. In the circuit shown in Figure 7.22a, the Q output from the first flip-flop is driving the clock input of the second. Both flip-flops are wired for the toggle input condition, so both

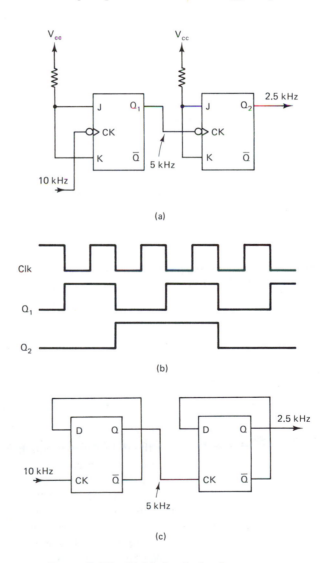

Figure 7.22 Divide-by-4 circuits.

will divide their input frequency by 2. The output frequency from the first flip-flop will be equal to 5 kHz (10 kHz/2 = 5 kHz). This 5-kHz signal is the clock for the second flip-flop. Since this second flip-flop divides its clock frequency by 2, it will have an output frequency of 2.5 kHz. This is equal to one-fourth of the original clock frequency. The waveforms for the circuit are shown in Figure 7.22b.

The same divide-by-4 action can be performed by wiring two D-type flip-flops together, as shown in Figure 7.22c. Again, the first flip-flop is dividing the original clock frequency by 2, and this new frequency is being used to clock the second divide-by-2 circuit. With 10 kHz in, this circuit will also have a 2.5-kHz output.

When flip-flops are wired together for frequency division, such as these two circuits here, the total circuit is referred to as a *counter*. Counters use series-wired rather than parallel-wired flip-flops. Counters are also covered in detail in Chapter 8.

Operation Sequencer

A flip-flop can be used to ensure that one operation occurs after another. For example, consider the circuit shown in Figure 7.23. In this system, circuit C is to accept

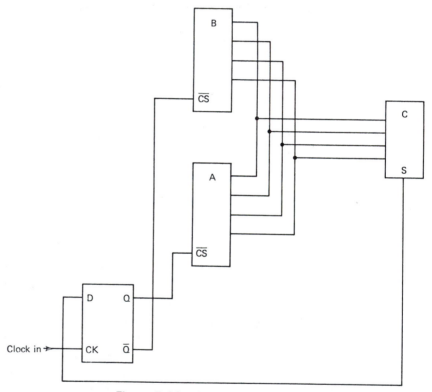

Figure 7.23 Operation sequencer.

data from circuits A and B. However, the data from circuit A must be applied to circuit C before the data from circuit B is. The D-type flip-flop is used to ensure that this sequence of data transfers occurs. Note that the Q output from the flip-flop is connected to the $\overline{CS}$ input of circuit A, while the $\overline{Q}$ output from the flip-flop is connected to the $\overline{CS}$ input of circuit B. As has been stated, the $\overline{CS}$ (chip select) input is an input that three-state circuits use to enable their outputs. When this input is low, the output is enabled and will work like any other circuit. When disabled, the outputs from the three-state gate will act as open circuits.

In the circuit shown, circuit A is enabled and circuit B is disabled when the flip-flop is RESET. The opposite condition exists when the flip-flop is SET. When circuit C requires data from circuit A, it drives its S output low. This causes the flip-flop to RESET on the next clock pulse. Circuit A is now enabled, so its data appear on the D inputs of circuit C. After circuit C gets the available data, it drives its S output high. This causes the flip-flop to set on the next clock pulse. The low out of the $\overline{Q}$ output now enables circuit B, so its data appears on the D inputs to circuit C.

The D-type flip-flop has been used to ensure that the correct data arrive at the right place at the right time. This is a very common application for flip-flops, as you will see when we start discussing entire microcomputer systems.

SUMMARY

Two of the most important components in a given microcomputer are the clock source and flip-flops. The most commonly used clock source is the crystal-controlled oscillator, although some circuits use an astable multivibrator instead. An astable multivibrator is a circuit that produces a pulse waveform output with only a dc input, and the most commonly used a stable source is the 555 timer.

The 555 timer can be used as either an astable or monostable multivibrator, depending on how it is wired in the circuit. A monostable multivibrator is a circuit that has one stable output state. When it receives a trigger, it switches to the other output state for a previously determined period of time, then automatically reverts back to the original output state. Another name for the monostable multivibrator is the one-shot.

A bistable multivibrator, or flip-flop, is a circuit that has two stable output states. It will stay in the SET (1) state or the RESET (0) state until a signal causes it to change states. The most commonly used flip-flops are the D-type flip-flop, or D latch, and the J-K flip-flop. Both of these circuits are commonly used as one-bit memories, frequency dividers, or operation sequencers.

QUESTIONS

1. What is a multivibrator?
2. What are the three types of multivibrators? What are the output characteristics of each?
3. What is the other name for a monostable multivibrator? For a bistable multivibrator?
4. What is a clock signal?
5. What is a clock signal used for?
6. What are the three requirements for a clock source?
7. What is the most commonly used clock source? Why?
8. Which microcomputer unit contains the system clock?
9. Describe the internal operation of the 555 timer.
10. Refer to Figure 7.2. If $C = 0.01 \mu F$ and $R = 10 k\Omega$, what is the pulse width out of the circuit?
11. Refer to Figure 7.3. With the circuit values shown, what is the output frequency of the circuit?
12. Why isn't the 555 timer astable circuit used for most microcomputer timing applications?
13. Why are crystal-controlled oscillators the most commonly used microcomputer timing source?
14. How does a Schmitt-trigger input differ from a conventional input?
15. What is a *retriggerable* one-shot?
16. Why can troubleshooting one-shots be a difficult task? How is the problem corrected?
17. When a given flip-flop is SET, what does its Q output equal? When it's RESET?

18. What is the difference between the NOR- and NAND-gate S-R flip-flops, in terms of inputs?

19. Discuss the D-type flip-flop truth table shown in Figure 7.14.

20. What is an asynchronous input? What is the relationship between these inputs and clocked inputs?

21. Discuss the truth table for the J-K flip-flop shown in Figure 7.17.

22. What is the difference between the standard J-K flip-flop and a master-slave flip-flop?

23. Explain how the circuit shown in Figure 7.21c would be used as a frequency divider.

24. Draw three J-K flip-flops wired in series, as the two are in Figure 7.22, and explain how the three would combine to form a divide-by-8 circuit.

8 | Counters and Registers

Counters and registers are two of the most commonly used circuit configurations in microcomputers. Counters are used primarily for frequency division and operation sequencing. Registers are used to temporarily store binary information and to perform a type of logic operation, called a *shift operation*.

Both counters and registers are made up of flip-flops. Counters are made by wiring flip-flops in series, while registers are made by wiring flip-flops in parallel. Both types of circuits are available in MSI form (i.e., there are many single-chip counters and registers). Some of the more common single-chip counters and registers will be covered in this chapter.

8.1 COUNTERS

Before discussing the circuit operation of counters, let's take a look at typical counter output. The count sequence and waveforms shown in Figure 8.1 are those produced by a 4-bit binary counter. In Figure 8.1a, the standard 4-bit binary count sequence is shown. Note that the LSB, A, changes from each bit to the next. The value of B changes at intervals of two, while the values of C and D change at intervals of four and eight, respectively. If you read the numbers from top to bottom, you will see that the numbers progress from 0000 to 1111 as they advance across the page. This is a standard count progression for 4 binary bits.

The same count progression appears in Figure 8.1b, but waveforms for each of the bits (A, B, C, and D) have been added. These waveforms have been labeled Q_A through Q_D since they are actually the outputs from flip-flops. Note that Q_A changes with each count, while Q_B, Q_C, and Q_D change at rates of two counts, four counts, and eight counts, respectively. The waveforms can therefore be seen to represent the count sequence shown in Figure 8.1a. This is the manner in which a counter counts. It produces an output waveform that is representative of a specific binary count sequence. It may count from 0000 to 1111, as in the count sequence just shown, or it may count from zero to just about any number you could think of. The count progression from a given counter depends on its construction, as will be seen throughout this section.

So, what do counters count? They count cycles of the input clock. For each complete cycle of the input clock, a counter will advance its output count by one. When the counter reaches its maximum count, the next clock cycle will cause the counter to return to an output count of zero. For example, the count sequence shown in Figure 8.1 counted up to 1111. If the counter that produced this count were to receive another clock cycle, its output would return to 0000.

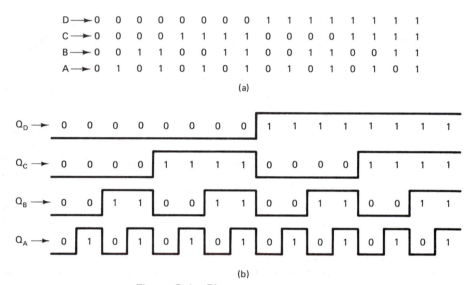

(a)

(b)

Figure 8.1 Binary count sequences.

Counters are usually referred to as *divide-by-N* circuits, where N is the number of clock cycles required to cause the counter to return to the zero state. In the count sequence just discussed, the counter would be referred to as a divide-by-16 counter, since it took 16 clock cycles to cause the counter to count from 0000 to 1111 and then return to 0000. For any given counter, the highest output count will be $N - 1$, as it was in the count sequence in Figure 8.1. So, if you had a divide-by-10 counter, the highest output count from the circuit would be 10-1, or 1001 (9). This holds true for all counters, as will be seen throughout our discussion of counters.

A Simple Four-Bit Counter

We will now take a look at the counter that produced the waveforms shown in Figure 8.1. This counter, which consists of four J-K flip-flops, is shown in Figure 8.2. Note that each flip-flop is wired so that the inputs are always J = 1 and K = 1. This is the toggle input for the J-K, which causes the flip-flop to change output state each time that a clock signal is received. This mode of operation for the J-K was covered in Chapter 7. Also note that the Q output from each flip-flop is being used to clock the next flip-flop.

Let's take a look at the way in which flip-flop A produces the Q_A waveform shown in Figure 8.1b. Assuming that the flip-flop is initially RESET (Q = 0), the first negative-going transition of the input clock will cause the flip-flop to SET (Q = 1). The next negative-going transition of the input clock will cause the flip-flop to RESET again. This back-and-forth action will continue as long as there is an input clock being received.

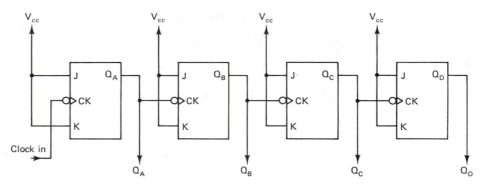

Figure 8.2 Four-bit ripple counter.

Flip-flop B works in exactly the same fashion, except that it is being clocked by the Q_A output. It will therefore change its output state each time that Q_A makes a negative-going transition. As you can see in Figure 8.1b, Q_B changes each time that Q_A goes to the zero state, a negative-going transition. By the same operating principle, the negative-going transition of Q_B causes Q_C to change states, and the negative-going transition of Q_C causes Q_D to change states. On the sixteenth cycle of the input clock, each of the flip-flops RESETs, causing the next flip-flop to also RESET. The end result is that the counter has returned to a count of 0000. This completes the waveforms shown in Figure 8.1b.

Take a look at the waveforms in Figure 8.1b again. As the waveforms indicate, each flip-flop has an output frequency that is one-half of its input frequency. For example, Q_B goes through one complete cycle for every two complete cycles of Q_A. The same relationship exists for the other waveforms. Assuming that the original clock frequency for this counter is 16 kHz, the following frequency relationships would exist:

$$\text{clock} = 16 \text{ kHz}$$

$$Q_A = \frac{16 \text{ kHz}}{2} = 8 \text{ kHz}$$

$$Q_B = \frac{8 \text{ kHz}}{2} = 4 \text{ kHz}$$

$$Q_C = \frac{4 \text{ kHz}}{2} = 2 \text{ kHz}$$

$$Q_D = \frac{2 \text{ kHz}}{2} = 1 \text{ kHz}$$

We could therefore use this counter to produce these frequencies, giving us several clock frequencies from a single original clock source. This is one of the most common applications for counters in microcomputers. It should be noted that not all counter outputs must be used when a given counter is being used as a frequency divider. For example, suppose that the counter in Figure 8.2 is being used to provide a 32-kHz signal and an 8-kHz signal from an original clock frequency of 64 kHz. The original clock would be fed to the clock input of the counter, and the Q_A and Q_C outputs would be used to provide the required output frequencies. Since these outputs are the only ones needed to fulfill the frequency-division requirements, they are the only ones used. The Q_B and Q_D outputs would not be used.

Ripple versus Synchronous Counters

The counter just discussed is called a *ripple counter*, since the original clock signal "rippled" through the counter. Another type of counter is the *synchronous* counter. In this type of counter, the original clock signal is applied to all the flip-flops in the counter. A synchronous 4-bit binary counter is shown in Figure 8.3. The counter

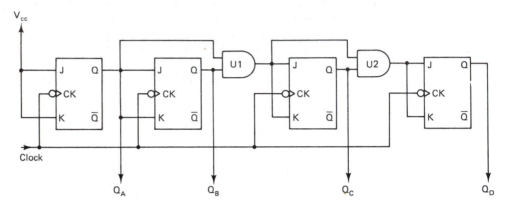

Figure 8.3 Synchronous 4-bit counter.

shown will produce the same output waveforms as those shown in Figure 8.1b. To understand this counter, we must take a look at the waveforms again. Note that the Q_B waveform changes at the end of each SET output of Q_A. Q_C changes after Q_A *and* Q_B are SET. Q_D changes after *all* previous Q outputs are SET. It can be stated, then, that a given flip-flop in the counter will change states only after *all* previous flip-flops have SET.

Now, look at the counter in Figure 8.3. First, it can be determined to be a synchronous counter, because the original input clock is applied to *all* of the flip-flops. Flip-flop A is connected to flip-flop B in such a way as to cause flip-flop B to change states on the clock signal after A is SET. When A is SET, two 1's are applied to flip-flop B, and on the next clock signal, flip-flop B toggles. When both flip-flop A and flip-flop B are SET, the output from U1 is high, applying a toggle input to flip-flop C. On the next clock transition, flip-flop C will SET. When all three flip-flops are SET (A, B, and C), the output from U2 will be high, causing flip-flop D to toggle on the next clock signal. The result is that each flip-flop will change states on the clock transition after *all* previous flip-flops have SET. This produces the waveforms shown in Figure 8.1b.

It probably seems that this circuit would be more trouble than it is worth. After all, it produces the same output waveforms as the less complicated ripple counter shown in Figure 8.2. However, this circuit does have its advantages. Assume that the propagation delay of a single J-K flip-flop is 25 ns. The ripple counter would have a total propagation delay of 100 ns, since the signals would have to work their way through all of the flip-flops. For example, on the transition from 1111 to 0000, each flip-flop would have to RESET before the next one did, so it would take 100 ns for the entire circuit to RESET. With the synchronous counter, all of the flip-flops would RESET simultaneously, so the entire propagation delay for the circuit would be equal to the delay for one flip-flop, 25 ns. This means that the synchronous counter can operate at much higher frequencies than its ripple counterpart.

Most standard IC counters are ripple counters, since their maximum operating frequency is high enough for most applications. However, when building a counter from individual flip-flops, it is advantagous to build a synchronous counter if the circuit is to operate at high frequencies.

Decade Counters

Not all counters are made to count by even powers of 2. One common counter that does not count by even powers of 2 is the *divide-by-10*, or *decade counter*. This counter, shown in Figure 8.4a, counts from 0000 to 1001 and then resets to 0000. Assume that this counter has counted up to 1001 in the normal fashion. On the next clock input, the counter will go to 1010. At that time, the output from U1 will go *low*, clearing all the flip-flops. The count will now be 0000. While the flip-flop did go to 1010, this output condition would last just long enough for U1 to produce a low output. This typically takes about 5 ns, so the 1010 count does not occur for all practical purposes.

The decade counter has many applications, the most common of which is in a real-time digital clock. This application is discussed later in the section on counter applications.

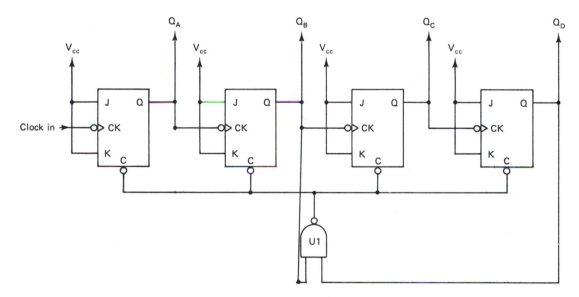

Figure 8.4   Decade counter.

8.2 DOWN COUNTERS AND UP/DOWN COUNTERS

There are circuits which require a counter that counts down or that can count both up and down. A down counter is one that counts from its maximum count down to zero, and an up/down counter is one that is capable of counting in either direction.

A 4-bit down counter is shown in Figure 8.5. This counter will count from 1111 down to 0000. Then, on the next cycle of the input clock, it will go back to 1111 and start the down count again. The main difference between this down counter and a 4-bit up counter is the fact that each flip-flop is being driven by the $\overline{Q}$ output of the previous flip-flop instead of the Q output. The resulting waveforms are shown in Figure 8.5b. The key to understanding these waveforms lies in the fact that the flip-flops will now trigger on the positive-going edge of the Q output, since the $\overline{Q}$ makes a negative-going transition at that time. As you can see, the count sequence is shown to be starting at 0000. At T_O, flip-flop A SETs. This causes its $\overline{Q}$ output to make a negative-going transition, causing flip-flop B to SET, and so on. The end result is that all flip-flops SET, so the output count is now at 1111. The count now progresses, with each flip-flop changing states when the Q output of the previous flip-flop makes a positive-going transition. The result is the down-count waveforms shown in Figure 8.5b.

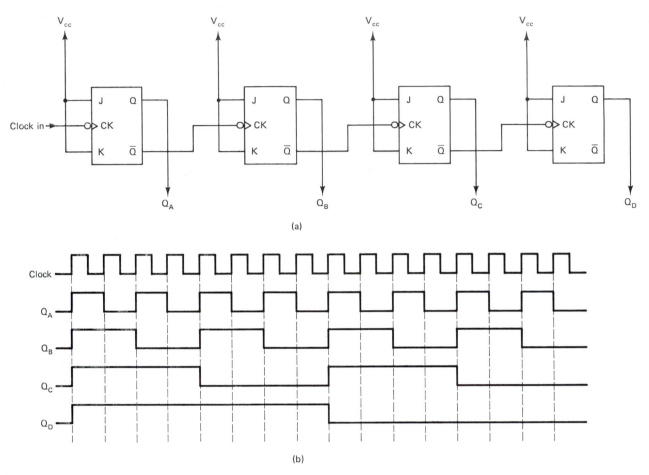

(a)

(b)

Figure 8.5 Down counter.

A synchronous down counter is produced by using the $\overline{Q}$ outputs instead of the Q outputs, as shown in Figure 8.6. This counter works on the principle that all

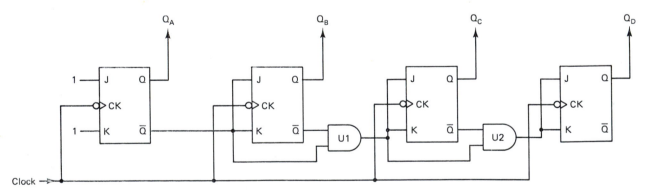

Figure 8.6 Synchronous down-counter.

previous Q outputs must be *low* to cause a flip-flop to toggle. For example, when flip-flops A, B, and C are RESET (Q = 0), their $\overline{Q}$ outputs are high. This causes the output from U2 to be high, which will cause flip-flop D to toggle on the next

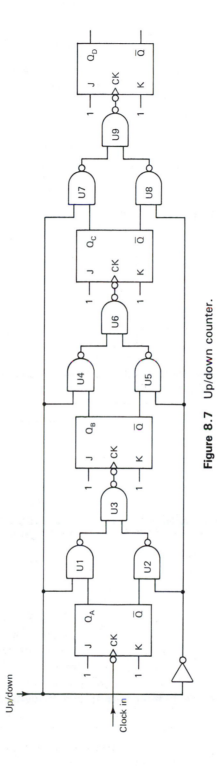

Figure 8.7 Up/down counter.

clock cycle. Each of the flip-flops works in this manner. The resulting waveform is the same as that in Figure 8.5b.

An up/down counter is one that is capable of counting either up or down, depending on a single control input. An up/down counter is shown in Figure 8.7. Note that an up/down control has been added to the basic counter, together with a more sophisticated connection between flip-flops. You may recall from previous discussions that the NAND gate configurations shown act as AND gates followed by OR gates. This was shown in Example 3.3. Whenever all of the inputs to U1 are high, for example, its output will be low. This will cause the output from U3 to be high, which provides the B flip-flop with a toggle input.

The up/down control will provide a 1 to U1, U4, and U7 when the input to the control line is high. At the same time, this high is inverted and applied to U2, U5, and U8. With a low input, the outputs from U2, U5, and U8 will always be high and thus will not affect the NAND gates they feed. However, U1, U4, and U7 will be enabled, so that when their other inputs are high, their outputs will be low. This will cause a toggle input to be applied to the next flip-flop. For example, assume that the control input is high and that $Q_A = Q_B = Q_C = 1$. With these conditions, all the inputs to U7 are high, so its output will be low. This low causes the output from U9 to be high, which provides a toggle input to flip-flop D. Flip-flop D will therefore toggle on the next clock input.

The key here is that the counter will act as an up counter when U1, U4, and U7 are enabled and will act as a down counter when U2, U5, and U8 are enabled. In either case, the inputs to the controlling NAND gates must all be high in order to have a low output. When the output from the controlling gate goes low, the next flip-flop will receive a toggle input.

Down counters and up/down counters are not used in many microcomputers, except for some of the counters in the control circuitry. However, these counters are usually contained inside the microprocessor circuitry, so you will rarely run into a down counter or up/down counter troubleshooting problem.

8.3 IC COUNTERS

There are many available counters that are contained in a single IC. These counters vary in count sequence and in their preset and clear capabilities. In this section we discuss some of the more common TTL counters in terms of their construction, operation, and applications.

The 7490 Decade Counter

The 7490 is a decade counter that actually consists of a single divide-by-2 counter and a single divide-by-5 counter that must be connected externally in order to obtain a divide-by-10 count sequence. The pin configuration, logic diagram, and truth table for the 7490 are shown in Figure 8.8.

Take a look at the logic diagram for the 7490. The B, C, and D flip-flops are wired together internally to form a divide-by-5 counter. If you were to apply a clock signal to the B input (pin 1), the Q_B, Q_C, and Q_D outputs would continually count from 000 to 100 and RESET to 000. Q_A forms a separate divide-by-2 circuit. To get the counter to act as a decade counter, you must connect the Q_A output (pin 12) to the B input and apply the clock signal to the A input (pin 14). This wiring method can be seen in Figure 8.9a. Note that the RO(1) and RO(2) inputs are wired to ground. These inputs will cause the counter to RESET if they both go high, so one or the other of them must be wired to ground if you want the counter to work. Wiring them both to ground is also acceptable. By the same token, either R9(1) or R9(2) must

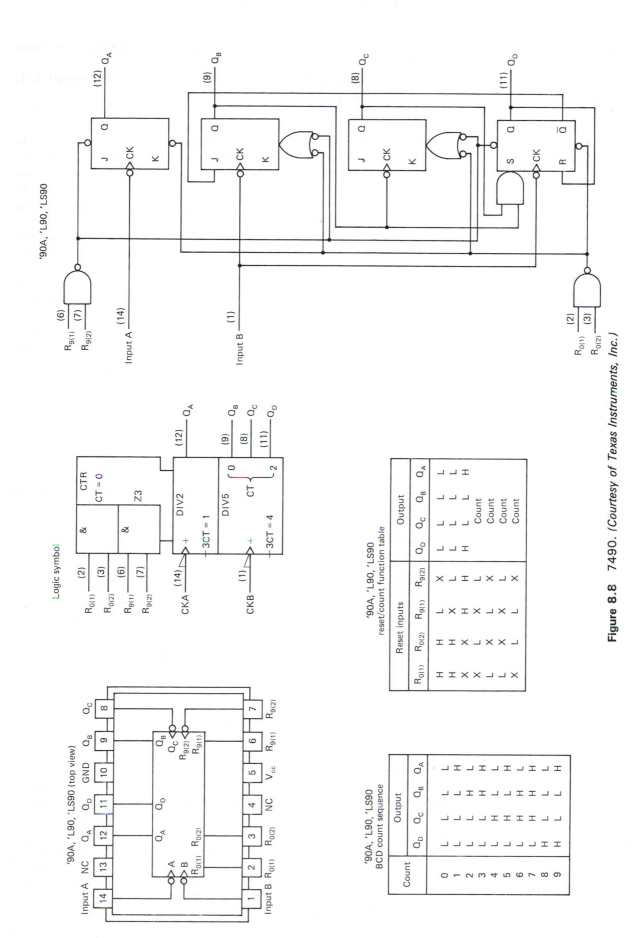

Figure 8.8 7490. *(Courtesy of Texas Instruments, Inc.)*

'90A, 'L90, 'LS90
reset/count function table

Reset inputs				Output			
$R_{0(1)}$	$R_{0(2)}$	$R_{9(1)}$	$R_{9(2)}$	Q_D	Q_C	Q_B	Q_A
H	H	L	X	L	L	L	L
H	H	X	L	L	L	L	L
X	X	H	H	H	L	L	H
X	L	X	L	Count			
L	X	L	X	Count			
X	L	L	X	Count			
L	X	X	L	Count			

'90A, 'L90, 'LS90
BCD count sequence

Count	Output			
	Q_D	Q_C	Q_B	Q_A
0	L	L	L	L
1	L	L	L	H
2	L	L	H	L
3	L	L	H	H
4	L	H	L	L
5	L	H	L	H
6	L	H	H	L
7	L	H	H	H
8	H	L	L	L
9	H	L	L	H

be wired to ground. If they both go high, the counter will be forced into the 1001 output condition. With the 7490 wired exactly as shown, the counter will provide the desired divide-by-10 output count.

Another way of wiring the 7490 can be seen in Figure 8.9b. In this circuit, the clock signal is applied to the B input, and the Q_D output is wired to the A input. Although this method of wiring will not provide a correct count sequence of 0000 through 1001, it does have its application, as will be seen in the following example.

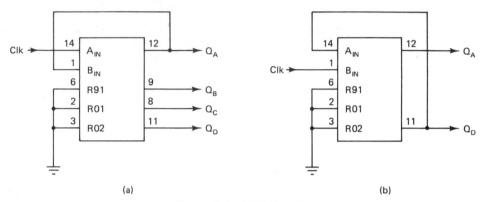

(a)   (b)

Figure 8.9   7490 wiring.

EXAMPLE 8.1

A given circuit has a clock frequency of 100 kHz. From this frequency, two signals must be generated. The frequencies needed are 20 kHz and 10 kHz. The circuit shown in Figure 8.9b can be used to provide the necessary signals. With 100 kHz being applied to the B input, the frequency at pin 11 (Q_D) will be 20 kHz, since this part of the chip forms a divide-by-5 counter. This 20 kHz is then fed back to the A input. Since flip-flop A forms a divide-by-2 circuit, Q_A will have a frequency of 10 kHz. If the circuit had been wired as shown in Figure 8.9a, there would have been no way to produce the 20-kHz signal.

The 7492 Divide-by-12 Counter

The 7492 forms a divide-by-12 counter by using a divide-by-2 circuit and a divide-by-6 circuit. The pin configuration, logic diagram, and truth table for the 7492 can be seen in Figure 8.10. This counter works in the same manner as the 7490, except for the fact that flip-flops B, C, and D form a divide-by-6 circuit rather than a divide-by-5 circuit. Again, you must wire either the RO(1) or RO(2) input to ground in order for the counter to work. Also, you must connect the divide-by-2 circuit to the rest of the circuit in order to obtain a divide-by-12 count. This counter is used mainly as a frequency divider, as will be seen in later examples.

Presettable Counters

Some counters are *presettable*, which means that they can be set to a specific count sequence. One example of this type of circuit is the 74176 presettable decade counter. The pin configuration for the 74176 is shown in Figure 8.11. This counter consists of independent divide-by-2 and divide-by-5 circuits, just like the 7490. For a standard divide-by-10 count, the clock signal should be applied to clock 1 (pin 8), and the Q_A output should be connected to the clock 2 input (pin 6).

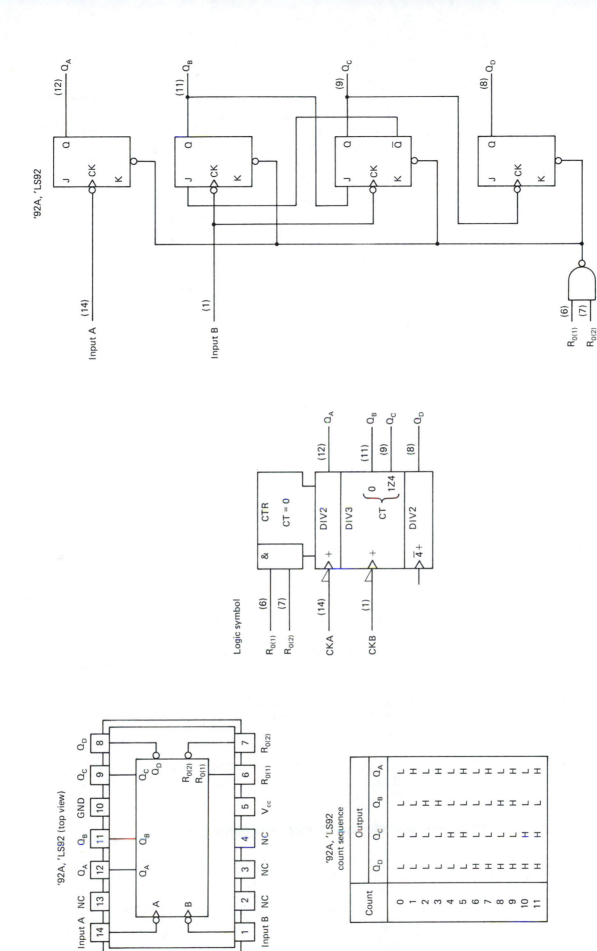

Figure 8.10 7492. *(Courtesy of Texas Instruments, Inc.)*

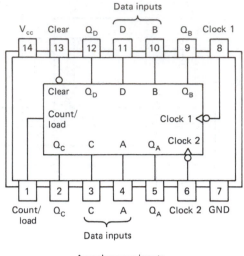

Asynchronous input:
Low input to clear sets
Q_A, Q_B, Q_C, and Q_D low.

Logic symbol, '176

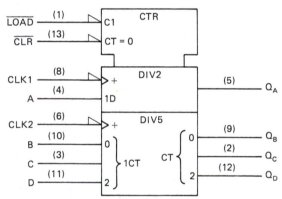

Figure 8.11 74176. *(Courtesy of Texas Instruments, Inc.)*

The *count/load* input affects the circuit as follows:

1. When this input is *high*, the counter will count as any decade counter.
2. When this input is *low*, the flip-flops will be set to the number that appears at the A, B, C, and D inputs. The counter will stay at this value until the count/load input goes high again.

This type of counter allows you to start the count sequence at any given value. We will see a typical application for presettable counters when we start discussing entire microcomputer systems.

IC Counter Applications: A Real-Time Clock

Figure 8.12 shows a real-time clock that is divided into three sections: seconds, minutes, and hours. The clock is made up almost entirely of 7490s and 7492s. The 7490s are being used as divide-by-10 counters, and the 7492s are being used as divide-by-6 counters in the seconds and minutes sections, while the 7492 in the hours section is being used as a divide-by-12 counter. Note that the original clock signal for the circuit is a 1-Hz square wave.

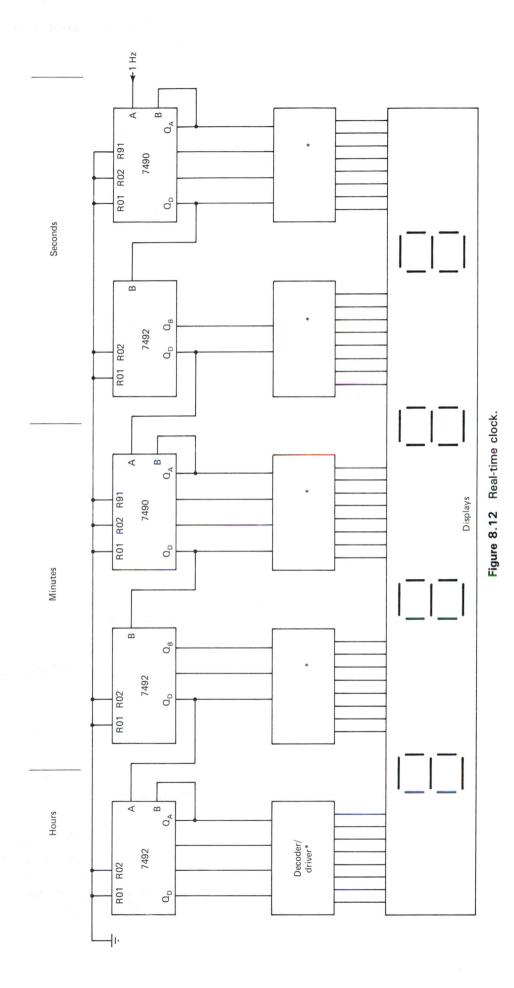

Figure 8.12 Real-time clock.

The displays are driven by a series of chips labeled "decoder/driver." Since we have not discussed this type of chip yet, we will simply assume that they cause the binary outputs from the counters to be displayed as decimal numbers. Decoder/drivers are discussed in Chapter 9.

Now, let's take a look at the "seconds" section. This section consists of a 7490 that is wired as a decade counter and a 7492 that is wired as a divide-by-6 counter. As you can see, the Q_D output of the 7490 is driving the clock input of the 7492. Since the 7492 is negative-edge triggered, it will advance its count by one each time that the Q_D output of the 7490 makes a transition from one to zero. The only time that this happens is when the 7490 counts from 1001 to 0000. So the 7492 will advance by one when the 7490 RESETs to zero. The combination of the decade counter followed by a divide-by-6 counter forms a divide-by-60 counter that will count from zero to 59, then RESET to zero again, just like the seconds hand on a clock.

Each time that the 7492 in the seconds section counts from 101 to 000, a negative-going clock signal is supplied to the 7490 in the "minutes" section. This means that the minutes will count up one for each complete cycle of the seconds section. The minutes section is identical to the seconds section, so it works in the exact same manner. The only difference is that the minutes section is clocked at a rate of one pulse per minute, rather than one pulse per second. After the minutes section has counted to 59, it will RESET to zero, providing a clock signal to the "hours" section. The hours section consists of a single 7492, wired to act as a divide-by-12 counter. The output of this counter is decoded by some special circuitry to display the numbers 1 through 12 as the counter is advanced.

There are many applications for counters other than the ones which have been discussed so far. However, determining the purpose served by a given counter is not as difficult as it may seem at first.

Determining the Purpose Served by a Given Counter

You will see a wide variety of counters in a given microcomputer, and each of these counters will be serving a specific purpose in the overall operation of the system. However, the purpose served by all the counters will fall into one of two general categories:

1. Frequency dividers
2. Binary count generators

The first category includes those counters which are being used to generate a needed frequency from a higher-order frequency. Such a counter was discussed in Example 8.1. The second category includes those counters that are being used to provide sequences of binary numbers, such as the counters in the real-time clock that was discussed. (*Note:* You may have noticed that the counters in the real-time clock were also providing frequency division from one counter to the next; however, their main purpose was to provide a time display of advancing numbers.)

It is relatively easy to determine which of the two categories a given counter falls into without having to do a lot of research. Simply use the following guidelines when looking at the schematic:

1. If a given counter is wired so that only some of its outputs are being used, or is wired so that its outputs go to different sections of the computer, it is being used as a frequency divider.
2. If all the outputs of a given counter go to a group of common inputs on one or more other ICs, the counter is being used to provide a binary count sequence.

These two points may be better understood by looking at the two counter circuits shown in Figure 8.13. The counter shown in Figure 8.13a is being used as a

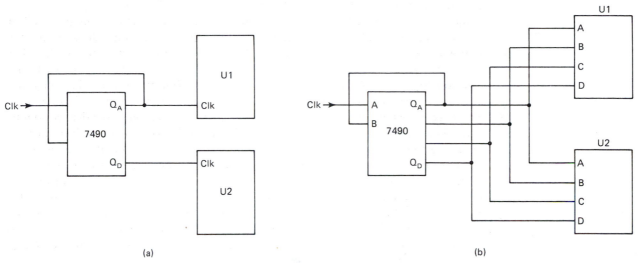

Figure 8.13 Counter versus frequency-divider wiring.

frequency divider. This is determined by the fact that only two of the counter outputs are being used, and those two outputs are going to different circuits. In this case, the counter is obviously not providing another circuit with a binary count sequence. In the circuit shown in Figure 8.13b, the counter outputs are all going to inputs on the other two chips that share similar input labels. In this case, the counter is being used to provide a count sequence to the other chips, in much the same way as they provided a count sequence to the decoder/drivers in the real-time clock.

A few points should be made at this time. First, a counter may be being used to provide a count sequence, without all of its outputs being used. For example, the 7492s that were being used in the seconds and minutes sections of the real-time clock used only the Q_B, Q_C, and Q_D outputs. However, since the circuits were being used as divide-by-6 counters, the Q_A outputs were not needed. You could therefore determine that the counters were being used to provide a count sequence because all of the outputs from the divide-by-6 section were being used, and because these outputs went to similar inputs on the decoder/drivers.

Another point is that there is a dead giveaway to some counters that are being used as frequency dividers. If the two internal counters are being used as separate circuits, the counter is definitely a frequency divider. For example, if a 7490 has its divide-by-2 counter being used by one group of circuits, and its divide-by-5 counter being used by another, it is definitely a frequency divider. This mode of operation is entirely possible, since these two internal counters work independently of each other unless connected externally.

With a little practice, you will be able to determine which category a given counter falls into just by looking at the system schematic. A few basic steps will then enable you to analyze and troubleshoot the circuit.

8.4 ANALYZING AND TROUBLESHOOTING COUNTERS

In most cases, troubleshooting a counter circuit is a very simple process. What makes them relatively simple to troubleshoot is the fact that *counters do not change count sequences*. A divide-by-12 counter would never start putting out a divide-by-10 sequence because of a circuit malfunction. When counters go bad, one or more of the counter outputs will go out completely. This means that the bad output will be either high or low or somewhere between the two. When this happens, you check all of the clock and control inputs, and the V_{cc} and ground connections to the chip. If all of these inputs are good and the counter output is bad, replace it. Although this may seem simple enough (and usually it is), there are some points that must be covered to prepare you for practical counter analysis and troubleshooting.

Counter Input and Output Labels

You may be able to save some research time when troubleshooting counter circuits if you have a well-labeled schematic. Although not all counters are labeled using the exact same labels, they do follow a somewhat standard form. The following chart shows some of the more common labels for counter inputs and outputs.

Input/output	Common labels
Clock[a]	Clk, Ck
Reset[b]	C_1, RO(1), (2), RESET
Load (presettable)[b]	LD
Data inputs	A, B, C, D, etc.
Counter outputs	$Q_A, Q_B, \ldots$ or $Q_1, Q_2, \ldots$

[a]Usually negative-edge triggered.
[b]Usually active-low.

Having the counter outputs labeled in the $(Q_1, Q_2, \ldots)$ manner can definitely save you some time, because these output labels indicate the power of 2 by which the clock is being divided. For example, if you have a counter that has a clock frequency of 128 kHz and you are checking the Q_8 output, you should see a signal that is equal to $128 \text{ kHz}/2^8$, or 500 Hz.

If you see labels that you recognize on a counter in a given schematic, use those labels when troubleshooting. If not, you have to go to the documentation.

Presettable Counters

You can run into a bit of difficulty when troubleshooting presettable counters. The main problem is that they are seldom used to provide their entire count sequence. For example, look at the circuit shown in Figure 8.14. The counter shown is a preset-

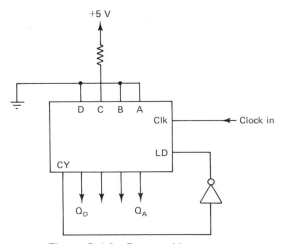

Figure 8.14 Presettable counter.

table 4-bit binary counter. It also has a "carry" output which goes high when the counter RESETs from 1111 to 0000. In this diagram, the carry output is being inverted and applied to the load input of the counter. The value at the load inputs is 0100, as can be determined by reading the inputs in alphabetical order.

Whenever the carry output of the counter goes high, the load input is activated. This causes the counter to load the value 0100 and proceed to count from there. In effect, this causes the counter to act as a divide-by-12 counter, since it counts from 0100 to 1111, then goes back to 0100 when the counter RESETs.

To determine what a presettable counter is supposed to be doing, first figure out what value is supposed to be loaded into the counter. Then determine what the highest count for the device will be. Next, subtract the loaded value from the highest count and then add one to your answer. This will give you the divide-by-N value for the counter. (*Note:* The reason that the one is added is to account for the turnover to zero.)

EXAMPLE 8.2

The counter shown in Figure 8.14 is changed so that the value being loaded into the counter is 0111. What would the divide-by-N value for the counter be?

Solution: The highest count for the counter is 1111, so the divide-by-N value of the counter would be found as

$$1111 - 0111 + 0001 = 1001$$

So, the counter would be acting as a divide-by-9 counter. The Q_D frequency would be equal to one-ninth of the clock frequency. Note that while the device is being used as a divide-by-9 counter, it would *not* count from 0000 to 1000, then RESET. Rather, it would count from 1000 to 1111 and then return to 1000.

In most cases, you will probably have to go to a logic data book to get some needed information on a counter that you are troubleshooting. However, in those cases where the system schematic is properly labeled, you may be able to save yourself some time by using the information and analysis techniques that have been covered in this section.

8.5 REGISTERS

A register is a circuit that is used to temporarily store data. These circuits, composed of flip-flops wired in parallel, are often used to perform a special type of logic operation, called a *shift* operation. For this reason, they are usually referred to as *shift registers*. In a shift operation, all of the bits in the data are shifted either one place to the left or one place to the right. The shift operation is covered in our discussion of the basic shift register shown in Figure 8.15.

The register shown consists of eight D-type flip-flops wired so that the Q output of each flip-flop is connected to the D input of the next. With this configuration, each clock pulse will cause the data bit being stored in any flip-flop to be loaded into the flip-flop on its immediate right. For example, if the data word stored in the register is 10010010 and the bit being applied to D1 is a 1, the clock will cause each bit to be loaded in the flip-flop immediately to its right, resulting in the data value in the register being 11001001. The zero that was stored in FF8 before the shift has been replaced with the 1 from FF7. The 1 from FF7 has been replaced with the zero from FF6, and so on. A look at the waveforms in Figure 8.16 will help make the operation of the register a little clearer. At T_O, the Q outputs of the register are show-

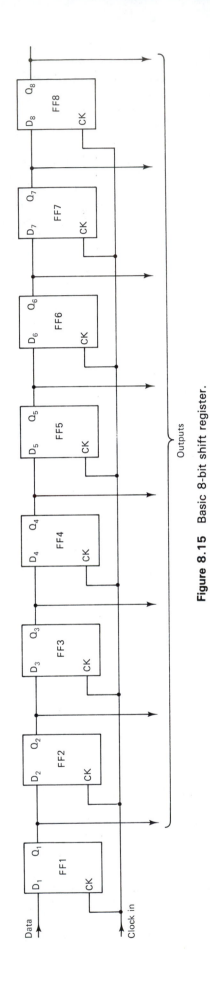

Figure 8.15 Basic 8-bit shift register.

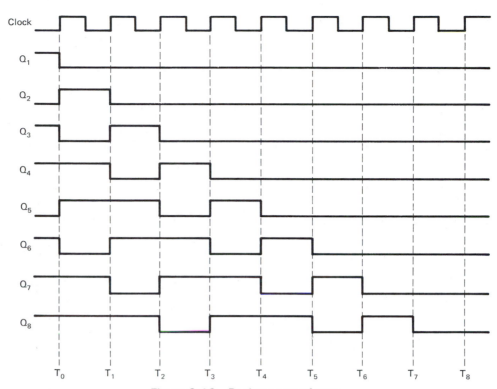

Figure 8.16 Register waveforms.

ing the register to be storing the binary value 10110111. For the waveforms shown, we are assuming that the input to D_1 is constantly at a logic zero. At T_1, the data bits are all shifted one place to the right and a zero is entered into FF1. At T_2, the bits have all been shifted one place to the right again. Following the waveforms through T_8 shows the same process to be occurring at each clock input to the register.

A *shift-left* register would work in the same manner, except that each bit would be shifted one place to the left for each cycle of the clock, rather than being shifted right. A *shift-left/right* register has the capability of shifting in either direction. The direction of the shift is determined by an input bit to the register. Neither of these registers will be discussed as circuits composed of flip-flops and basic gates, since most of them are produced in MSI form. You will very rarely run into a register that is made up of SSI logic circuits because MSI registers are available in every configuration and are much easier to deal with. We cover these MSI register types next.

MSI Shift Registers

MSI shift registers are register circuits that are contained in a single chip. These registers come in one of four basic types:

> parallel in/parallel out
> parallel in/serial out
> serial in/parallel out
> serial in/serial out

These types describe the type of inputs and outputs that the register has. Note that all MSI registers have one of these input/output relationships, or a combination of two or more, as will be seen in the following discussions.

The 7495 is a TTL *parallel in/parallel out* shift register. This means that all flip-flop data bits are loaded in simultaneously and read out simultaneously. The block diagram and truth table for the 7495 are shown in Figure 8.17. The four in-

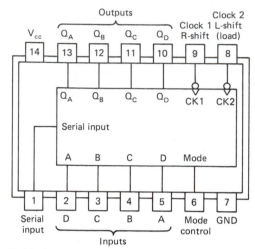

Positive logic: see function table

Function table

Mode control	Clocks		Serial	Parallel				Outputs			
	2(L)	1(R)		A	B	C	D	Q_A	Q_B	Q_C	Q_D
H	H	X	X	X	X	X	X	Q_{A0}	Q_{B0}	Q_{C0}	Q_{D0}
H	↓	X	X	a	b	c	d	a	b	c	d
H	↓	X	X	$Q_B{}^\dagger$	$Q_C{}^\dagger$	$Q_D{}^\dagger$	d	Q_{Bn}	Q_{Cn}	Q_{Dn}	d
L	L	H	X	X	X	X	X	Q_{A0}	Q_{B0}	Q_{C0}	Q_{D0}
L	X	↓	H	X	X	X	X	H	Q_{An}	Q_{Bn}	Q_{Cn}
L	X	↓	L	X	X	X	X	L	Q_{An}	Q_{Bn}	Q_{Cn}
↑	L	L	X	X	X	X	X	Q_{A0}	Q_{B0}	Q_{C0}	Q_{D0}
↓	L	L	X	X	X	X	X	Q_{A0}	Q_{B0}	Q_{C0}	Q_{D0}
↓	L	H	X	X	X	X	X	Q_{A0}	Q_{B0}	Q_{C0}	Q_{D0}
↑	H	L	X	X	X	X	X	Q_{A0}	Q_{B0}	Q_{C0}	Q_{D0}
↑	H	H	X	X	X	X	X	Q_{A0}	Q_{B0}	Q_{C0}	Q_{D0}

Figure 8.17   7495. *(Courtesy of Texas Instruments, Inc.)*

puts, A, B, C, and D, are connected to the inputs of the flip-flops that have outputs labeled Q_A, Q_B, Q_C, and Q_D, respectively. The bits in the register are shifted to the right (from Q_A toward Q_D) or shifted left, depending on which clock input is used. If the circuit is wired so that the clock is being applied to pin 9, it is being used as a shift-right register. If the clock is being applied to pin 8, it is being used as a shift-left register. Note that the *mode control* (pin 6) must be low for shift-right operation and high for shift-left operation. The operation of these three inputs is summarized as follows:

1. If the mode control is low, the register will shift right on the negative-going transition of the clock signal at pin 9.
2. If the mode control is low, the values at A, B, C, and D will be loaded into the register by a negative-going transition at pin 8.
3. If the mode control is high, the register will shift left on the negative-going transition of the clock signal at pin 8.

In any of the cases above, the register outputs will immediately reflect the results of the operation. For example, if the mode control is low and the input at pin 8 goes low, the values at A, B, C, and D will immediately be loaded into the register and will be seen at the outputs. In other words, Q_A will equal A, Q_B will equal B, and so on.

The 7495 also has a serial input that allows it to be used as a *serial in/parallel out* shift register. In this mode of operation, any data values that are to be entered into the register are done so one bit at a time, starting with the MSB of the data word being entered into the A flip-flop. To use the register as a serial in/parallel out shift register, the mode of operation for shift-right operation must be followed, and the bits to be entered must be applied, in order, at pin 1. For example, look at the circuit and waveforms shown in Figure 8.18. The 7495 shown is wired to operate

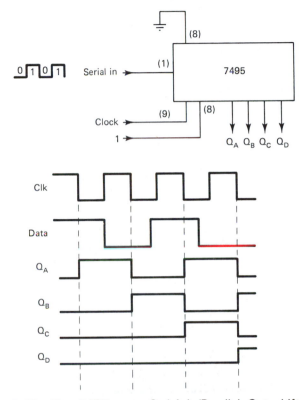

Figure 8.18   The 7495 as a Serial In/Parallel Out shift register.

as a serial in/parallel out shift register. The value 1010 is being applied to pin 1, the mode control is low, and the clock is being applied to pin 9. The latter two conditions are the operating requirements for a shift-right register.

On the first negative-going transition at pin 9, the first data bit (1) is entered into the register. This results in a register output of 0001, reading Q_D as the MSB. On the second transition of the clock, the Q_A value is shifted one place to the right, and the second data value (0) is entered. The output is now 0010. On the third transition, the two data bits that are already in the register are shifted to the right again, and the third data value (1) is entered, resulting in an output of 0101. On the fourth transition, the register data is shifted to the right again, and the last data value (0) is entered into the register. The final output is 1010, the original value that was to be entered. This may seem like a lot of trouble to go through to enter a data word into a register, but it does have one very important application. A register in this configuration can be used to convert serial data into parallel. Serial-to-parallel data conversion is needed when a computer needs to get information from any device that transmits data bit by bit. When a given device transmits data one bit at a time and the computer gets that information, it usually uses a serial in/parallel out register to convert the data into parallel form, which is the method in which data is handled within the computer.

The parallel in/parallel out mode of operation is used when a register is being used as a temporary storage location for a given data word. For example, if a given microcomputer needs to store a value that is used in several mathematical operations, it may store the word in a parallel in/parallel out shift register for as long as it is needed. When the word is no longer needed, it can be replaced by another by simply loading the new data word into the register. Both of the applications just discussed will be seen when we start covering microcomputer units. In the meantime, it is sufficient that you understand the difference between these two modes of entering data into a register.

The 7495 could also be used as a *parallel in/serial out* shift register by wiring it as shown in Figure 8.19a. With this wiring configuration, only the Q_D output is connected to the external circuitry. The other Q outputs are simply left open. The

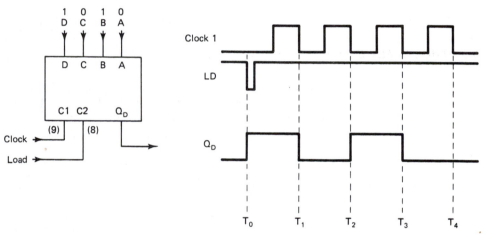

Figure 8.19   The 7495 as a Parallel In/Serial Out shift register.

operation of this circuit configuration involves using both the load and shift-right modes. The waveforms shown in Figure 8.19b show the process in converting the value 1010 into serial data using the 7495. At T_O, pin 1 is low and pin 8 makes a negative-going transition, resulting in the value 1010 being loaded into the register. Note that the D input is immediately sent to the Q_D output. At T_1, pin 9 makes a transition, resulting in the internal data word being shifted to the right (toward Q_D). The output bit is now 0, the second bit from the original data value. On the next transition at pin 9, the internal data word is shifted right again and the Q_D output will equal 1, the third data bit of the original value. On the fourth transition at pin 9, the final data bit goes to the Q_D output. The result of the entire operation is that the original data value (1010) has been sent one bit at a time, in order, to the external circuitry. This data conversion is also used for microcomputer input and output operations.

The final mode of operation for a shift register is the *serial in/ serial* out mode. The 7495 can also be wired for this mode . To operate as a serial in/serial out register, all data is entered into the register through pin 1 and read out only at the Q_D output. The device is operated as a shift-right register only. As each negative-going clock transition occurs, the value at pin 1 is entered into the register and another internal bit is shifted to the Q_D output. Thus the data bits that are entered into the chip eventually appear, in order, at the Q_D output.

There are many MSI registers available in the TTL series. The most commonly used are 8-bit shift registers. These registers work in the same basic manner as the

7495. Although their control signal labels may vary, they perform the same basic functions, as will be seen in later discussions of microcomputer units.

Most shift registers have CLEAR inputs that RESET all flip-flops in the register when activated. These inputs are almost always active-low and are used for one of two purposes:

1. A register may be cleared to eliminate a data value when it is no longer needed by the system.
2. A register may be cleared *before* a data word is entered to ensure that the register will not give a false output.

The second case above normally applies to a register that is being used to convert serial data to parallel data. When a register is being used for this purpose, it is necessary to ensure that the first bit that comes from the register is the first bit of the data word. Clearing the register before the data word is entered ensures that this requirement is met.

8.6 TROUBLESHOOTING SHIFT REGISTER CIRCUITS

Shift registers can be really tricky circuits to troubleshoot. Their outputs are not as predictable as counters or basic logic gates, since registers may be shifting at one time and loading the next. There are some points, however, that may make troubleshooting shift registers a bit easier:

1. *Most shift registers are used for temporary data storage and are therefore operated in the parallel in/parallel out mode.* This helps, because this mode of operation is the easiest to verify. Check the load input. If this input is happening at regular intervals, connect the external trigger of the oscilloscope to this input. Then, with your oscilloscope in dual-trace operation, check each of the input/output pairs in turn (i.e., check input A and Q_A, input B and Q_B, and so on). These pairs should be identical at each negative-going transition of the load signal. If they are not, the chip is faulty and must be replaced.

2. *Serial in/parallel out shift registers tend to malfunction in one of two ways.* Either the serial value will not be loaded at all, or a single Q output will not reflect the entered data value. In the first case, all of the Q outputs will stay at stable output levels. If this occurs, check the clock input to the register and all control inputs. If they are correct, be sure that the serial input has data being applied to it. In almost every case, data at the serial input are verified as good if you see a digital waveform at this input that the oscilloscope is having trouble locking in on. This is due to the uneven rate at which the serial data change states. Once the serial input is verified as being there, check all the outputs. If they are all changing at uneven rates, the chip is good (assuming that the output levels are correct). If any output pin is staying at a stable logic level, the chip is probably bad and should be replaced. If replacing the chip does not correct the problem, make sure that another circuit is not holding that output at the bad logic level.

3. *Serial in/serial out shift registers can be the most difficult to troubleshoot.* Fortunately, they are hardly, if ever, used. The only way to check a serial in/serial out shift register is to verify that any data value entered appears at the output N cycles later, where N is equal to the number of flip-flops in the register. For example, with the 7495 register (4-bit), any data bit

entered at the serial input should appear at the serial output after four transitions of the clock. This is due to the fact that the bit has to go through four flip-flops to get to the output.

4. *Parallel in/serial out shift registers must be checked one bit at a time.* Assuming that all control, clock, and power connections to a parallel in/serial out shift register are good, the output must be compared to the inputs one at a time. This is a bit more involved than it may seem at first. To effectively compare the signals, follow the procedure outlined here:

   a. Trigger the oscilloscope on the LOAD input.
   b. While observing the clock input, adjust the TIME/DIV calibrator so that one complete cycle of the input clock takes one division to occur.
   c. Set the HORIZONTAL POSITION so that the negative-going transition of the clock marks the beginning of each time division.
   d. Now compare the inputs, one at a time, to the output. The number of divisions it will take for a given input bit to appear at the output is N, where N is the number of flip-flops between the input and the output. For example, if the 7495 is being used as a parallel in/serial out register and you are checking the B input, the value at B will appear at the Q_D output after two clock cycles. Therefore, the B input should always be at the same level as the Q_D output is two time divisions later. This relationship can be better understood by looking at Figure 8.20. The clock signal is included to show what the trace should look like after setting the clock as described in steps (b) and (c). Position X indicates the relative location of a given input bit (A through D). The divisions labeled A through D are the points to observe and compare to X. For example, when checking input B, position B should always be the same as that input. When input B changes, position B should change to the same value.

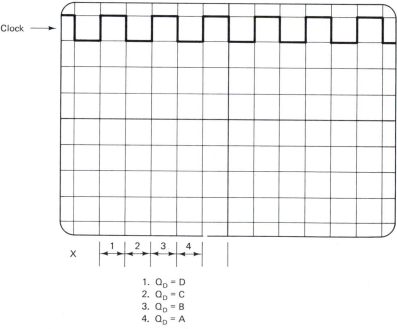

1. $Q_D = D$
2. $Q_D = C$
3. $Q_D = B$
4. $Q_D = A$

Figure 8.20 Oscilloscope display positions for checking register outputs.

As you can see, you have your work cut out for you when troubleshooting registers. However, with practice, you will be able to find a very high percentage of the register malfunctions. *One note:* If you test a given register, and still have a gut-level feeling that it is not working despite test results that say otherwise, go ahead and replace it. Sometimes "chip swapping" is the best tool you have.

SUMMARY

Counters and registers are involved in over 90% of the operations performed in microcomputers. Although they are not extremely difficult to understand, they can be some of the most difficult circuits to troubleshoot. Counters can be difficult to troubleshoot because of the many configurations in which they can be used. Registers can be difficult to troubleshoot because of the fact that they may be shifting at one time and loading at another.

Most technicians will be able to effectively troubleshoot counters and registers only after tripping over themselves for a period of time. However, being able to deal effectively with these circuits is worth the trouble, since they are used so extensively.

QUESTIONS

1. How are flip-flops wired to produce a counter? How are they wired to produce a shift register?
2. How are count progressions represented by counters?
3. Describe the outputs of a divide-by-13 counter. What would be the highest count the counter would reach?
4. A 6-bit binary counter has an input frequency of 256 kHz. What would the six output frequencies equal?
5. Refer to Figure 8.21. What would the output frequency of the counter equal?

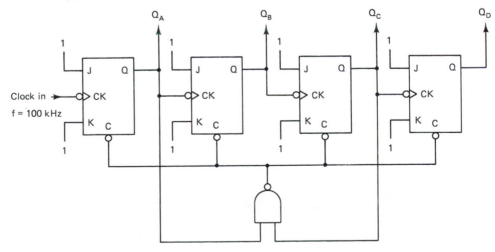

Figure 8.21   Circuit for question 5.

6. What is the difference between a ripple counter and a synchronous counter? What are the advantages and disadvantages of each?

7. Refer to the counter shown in Figure 8.22. What is its divide-by-N value?

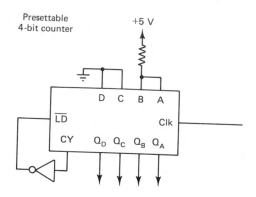

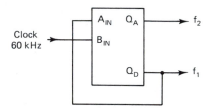

Figure 8.22 Circuit for question 7.

8. Refer to the 7492 shown in Figure 8.23. What are the two output frequencies?

Figure 8.23 Circuit for question 8.

9. What are the four types of shift registers?

10. Draw and describe the 7495 wired to act as each of the four types of shift register. Can you come up with a quick way to determine what mode of operation a given register is using just by looking at the circuit diagram?

11. What useful function is performed by parallel in/serial out registers? By serial in/parallel out registers?

12. Describe the techniques used to troubleshoot registers. What is the major difficulty encountered with troubleshooting each of the register operation modes?

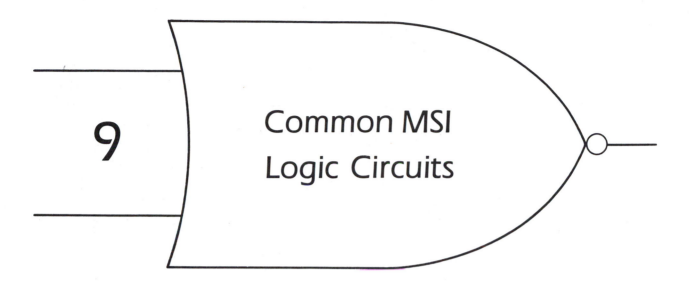

9 Common MSI Logic Circuits

There are several types of common MSI logic circuits other than counters and registers. These medium-scale integrated circuits are used in a variety of systems, and perform a variety of useful functions. The three basic types of circuits we will discuss are *multiplexers, demultiplexers (decoders),* and encoders. Although these circuits do not really fall into any of the circuit categories we have covered thus far, such as counters and registers, no microcomputer would work without them.

9.1 MULTIPLEXERS

A multiplexer is *a circuit that accepts data from one of several inputs and sends that data to a single output.* The logic symbol and truth table for the 74151 8-line-to-1-line multiplexer is shown in Figure 9.1. The 74151 is used to select data from one of eight input lines and send that data to the Y output (pin 5). The input is determined by the select inputs to the chip. These inputs are driven by the circuit that is controlling the chip.

The operation of this multiplexer is typical of all multiplexers and is actually very simple. A binary code is applied to the select inputs. The input that corresponds to the value of the binary select code will be connected to the output. For example, if the select code equals 000, input DO will be connected to the output. If the select code equals 101 (5), input D5 will be connected to the output, and so on. When a given input is connected to the output, whatever waveform appears on that input will appear at the output.

The 74151 has a W output that equals $\overline{Y}$. This allows the user to choose between inverted and noninverted data. The chip also has a STROBE input that must be low in order for the chip to work. This input is nothing more than an enable input. In most applications, the strobe input to the 74151 will be tied low.

Another multiplexer that is commonly used is the 74153 dual 4-line-to-1-line multiplexer. The logic symbol and truth table for this circuit are shown in Figure

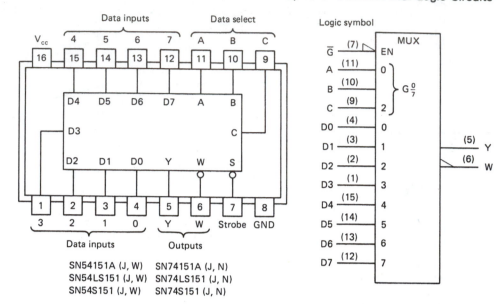

Figure 9.1   74151. *(Courtesy of Texas Instruments, Inc.)*

9.2. Note that the inputs and output associated with the first multiplexer are labeled with 1's and those associated with the second multiplexer are labeled with 2's. Each circuit has its own strobe input and data output. Since each of the internal multiplexers has only four inputs, only two select lines are needed. While the select lines are common to both multiplexers, the strobe inputs will determine which internal multiplexer responds to the select codes. For example, if the select code equals 10 (2), and strobe $\overline{G1}$ is low, output Y1 (pin 7) will provide the data that appear at input 1C2 (pin 4).

In many applications, both of the multiplexers in the 74153 will be used. When both are used, the strobe inputs are tied to ground. The data from each of the multiplexers appear at their respective outputs. An application for the 74153 can be seen in Figure 9.3. This circuit is used to provide circuit X with one of four 4-bit words. The 4-bit words are provided by circuits A through D. The select inputs are being driven by circuit X. This allows circuit X to determine which 4-bit word it is to receive. When the select output of circuit X equals 00, the C0 inputs of all the 74153 multiplexers are connected to the outputs. This results in word zero (W00 through W03) being sent to circuit X. The select code 01 causes word 1 (W10 through W13) to be sent to circuit X, and so on.

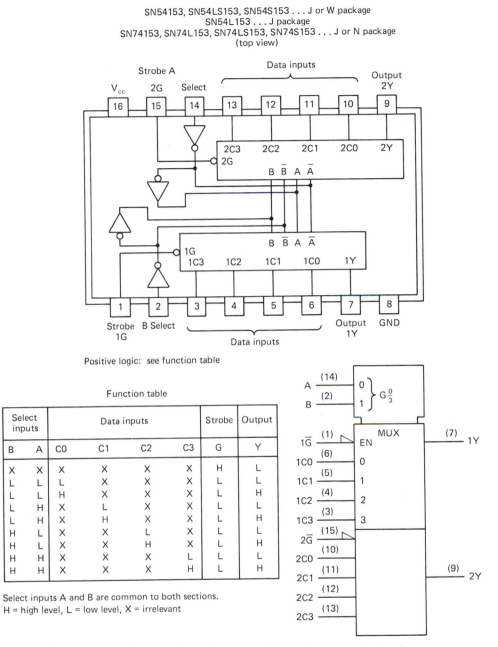

SN54153, SN54LS153, SN54S153 . . . J or W package
SN54L153 . . . J package
SN74153, SN74L153, SN74LS153, SN74S153 . . . J or N package
(top view)

Positive logic: see function table

Function table

Select inputs		Data inputs				Strobe	Output
B	A	C0	C1	C2	C3	G	Y
X	X	X	X	X	X	H	L
L	L	L	X	X	X	L	L
L	L	H	X	X	X	L	H
L	H	X	L	X	X	L	L
L	H	X	H	X	X	L	H
H	L	X	X	L	X	L	L
H	L	X	X	H	X	L	H
H	H	X	X	X	L	L	L
H	H	X	X	X	H	L	H

Select inputs A and B are common to both sections.
H = high level, L = low level, X = irrelevant

Figure 9.2 74153. *(Courtesy of Texas Instruments, Inc.)*

The most common application for multiplexers is to select one of several words, as was done in the circuit just discussed. Another application would be to use the multiplexer to check several individual lines. For example, a given system might require that the control unit ''scan'' several lines to determine if any of those lines had gone low. A multiplexer could be used to perform this function. The lines to be scanned would be connected to the inputs of the multiplexer, and the select lines of the multiplexer would be driven by the control unit. When the control unit detected

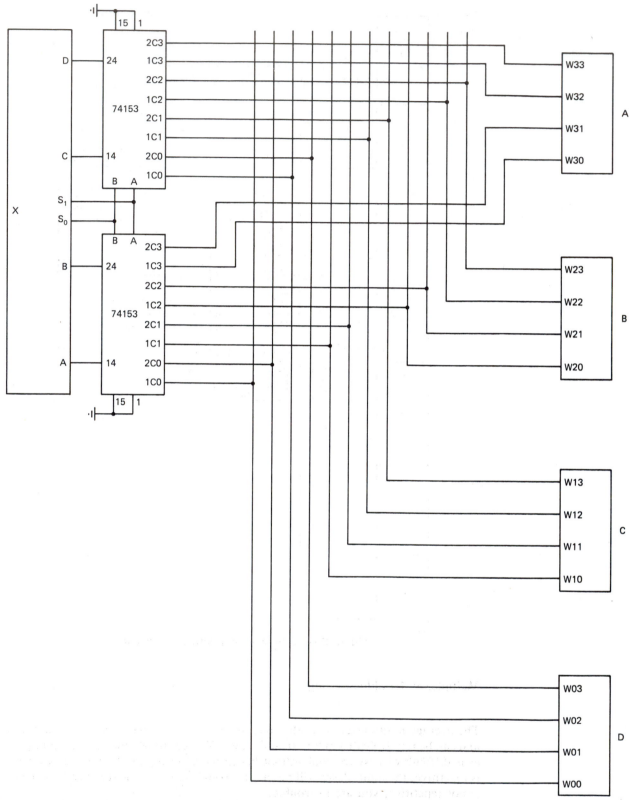

Figure 9.3 Typical multiplexer application.

that an input to the multiplexer was low, it would check its own select code to determine which input line to the multiplexer had the low on it. Such a circuit is shown in Figure 9.4.

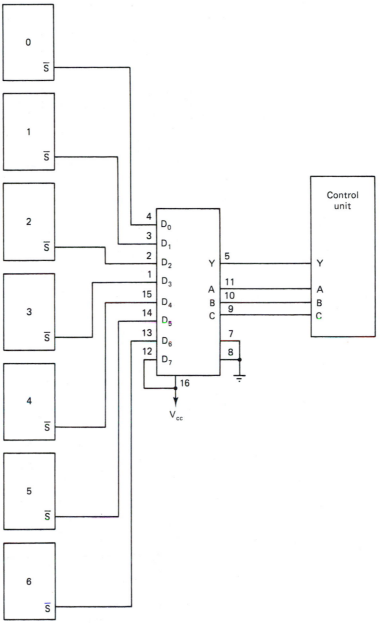

Figure 9.4 Line scanning with a multiplexer.

Multiplexer Troubleshooting

The average multiplexer is another one of those circuits that is easy to understand and can be relatively difficult to troubleshoot. The key to whether a given multiplexer is difficult or easy to troubleshoot lies in its select inputs. If the code sequence is repetitive, the multiplexer will be easy to troubleshoot. If the select code sequence is not repetitive, you are in trouble.

A repetitive code sequence is one that repeats itself in even cycles. The input codes may not be in numeric order, but as long as they repeat in the exact same series of codes, they are repetitive and you are in luck. When you determine that the codes are repetitive, use your oscilloscope to determine the exact sequence of numbers. This is done using the following procedure:

1. Trigger the oscilloscope on the MSB of the select code using the external trigger. This input is usually the lowest and most stable frequency and thus is the easiest for the oscilloscope to trigger on. After triggering on this input, view the signal on one trace of the scope. If you get a stable trace, you can use this input for a trigger. If not, you must use another select input for the scope trigger.

2. After establishing a trigger base for the scope, view all of the select inputs, in order, from the MSB to the LSB. As you view each waveform, sketch the waveform on a piece of paper in its proper time frame. This can be done by comparing the transitions of the signals to relative positions on the oscilloscope graticule. If you draw a sketch of the graticule on your paper, then show the transitions as they appear on the actual oscilloscope graticule, they will be drawn in the proper relationship to each other. Graph paper might not be a bad idea in this case.

3. Determine the binary code being generated across the waveforms at each change of the input code. This will give you the number sequence at the select inputs of the multiplexer.

EXAMPLE 9.1

A 74151 is showing signs of being defective, so the technician decides to take a closer look. Quick observation of the select inputs to the chip indicate that the code sequence is repetitive, since all waveforms can be locked into the oscilloscope. The technician triggered the oscilloscope on the MSB of the select inputs, then viewed and sketched the waveforms shown in Figure 9.5. Analyz-

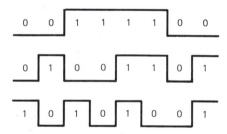

Figure 9.5 Select input waveforms for Example 9.1.

ing the three inputs for each time period shown resulted in the three bit codes written below each time period. The sequence of codes was therefore 1, 2, 5, 4, 7, 6, 0, 3.

Knowing the select code sequence is half the battle in troubleshooting the multiplexer. Provided that all input signals check out to be working properly, the final check is to determine if the output bits are correct for the input lines. This can be done using the following procedure:

1. *Do not change the external trigger!* Since this was used to determine the order in which the input lines were selected, you need to use this reference.

2. At each time division on the oscilloscope, compare the output to the input line that corresponds to that time division. For example, in Example 9.1, the fifth time division had the select code for input D7. While viewing the output on one trace, check input D7 on the other trace. At time division five, these two signals should be the same.

3. Repeat the procedure above for all of the inputs. If any of the input/output relationships do not match, the multiplexer is defective and should be replaced.

So much for the easy stuff. What if the multiplexer select codes are not repetitive? First, check all of the control inputs and make sure that they are working. If they are, you are better off simply replacing the chip. There is not really any way to be 100% sure if the multiplexer is doing its job when the select codes are not repetitive. You could test the circuit by removing it from the system and checking it out using other signal sources, but that would take a lot longer than simply replacing the chip and thus is not cost-effective.

9.2 DEMULTIPLEXERS

A demultiplexer is *a circuit that will take the data from a single input and send it to one of several output lines*. This is exactly the opposite function of that of the multiplexer. The logic symbol and truth table for the 74138 demultiplexer is shown in Figure 9.6. The demultiplexer (decoder) shown will drive one of eight output lines low, with the low output being determined by the select code. All of the lines that are not selected will automatically be high. For example, if the input code is 100 (4), output line Y4 (pin 11) will be low, and all of the other output lines will be high. If the output select code is 111 (7), output line Y7 (pin 7) will be low and all of the others will be high, and so on.

The 74138 has three enable inputs which must *all* be at their active level for the chip to work. This means that pins 4 and 5 must be low and pin 6 must be high. If any enable input is not at its active level, the outputs from the 74138 will all be high.

A very common application for decoders can be seen in Figure 9.7. In this circuit, the control unit is using the decoder to enable one of eight circuits. In this configuration, the control unit is to work with only one of the circuits shown at any given time. When the control unit wants to work with a given circuit, it sends the proper select code to the decoder, which then sends an active-low enable signal to that circuit. The circuit is then able to communicate with the control unit.

An interesting combination of multiplexers and decoders can be seen in the circuit in Figure 9.8. This circuit is actually a combination of the circuits shown in Figures 9.4 and 9.7. In this configuration, the control unit uses the multiplexer to scan the Y outputs of the circuits. If one of the circuits needs to communicate with the control unit, it drives its Y output low. If, as the scanning is performed, the control unit detects a low output from any circuit, it sends the appropriate select code to the decoder. The decoder then sends an active-low enable signal to the proper circuit. For example, the control unit, when sending out the code 010 (2), receives a low input. In response to this input, the control unit places the same select code on its A3, A4, and A5 outputs. This code causes the decoder to drive its output line 2 low while keeping the others high. This results in the signaling circuit being enabled, and communications between the two units have been established.

There are several types of decoders. Some have active-low outputs, like the 74138, and some have active-high outputs. Almost all decoders have enable inputs, and all work along the same lines as the 74138.

Decoder Troubleshooting

Decoders are made relatively simple to troubleshoot by the way in which they are constructed and used. A decoder may be used to enable only a few circuits, and thus may have only a small percentage of its outputs being used. When this is the case,

'LS138, 'S138
function table

| Inputs | | | | | Outputs | | | | | | | |
| Enable | | Select | | | | | | | | | | |
G1	G2*	C	B	A	Y0	Y1	Y2	Y3	Y4	Y5	Y6	Y7
X	H	X	X	X	H	H	H	H	H	H	H	H
L	X	X	X	X	H	H	H	H	H	H	H	H
H	L	L	L	L	L	H	H	H	H	H	H	H
H	L	L	L	H	H	L	H	H	H	H	H	H
H	L	L	H	L	H	H	L	H	H	H	H	H
H	L	L	H	H	H	H	H	L	H	H	H	H
H	L	H	L	L	H	H	H	H	L	H	H	H
H	L	H	L	H	H	H	H	H	H	L	H	H
H	L	H	H	L	H	H	H	H	H	H	L	H
H	L	H	H	H	H	H	H	H	H	H	H	L

*G2 = G2A + G2B
H = high level, L = low level, X = irrelevant

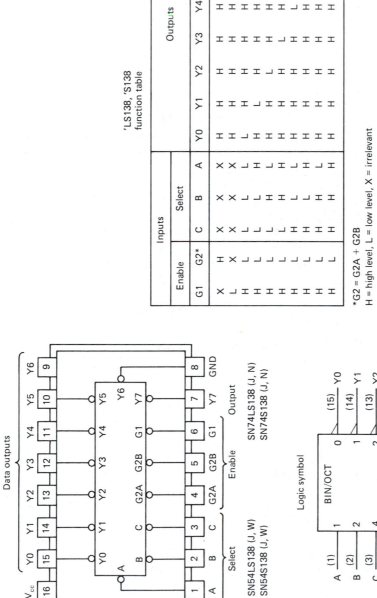

Figure 9.6 74138. *(Courtesy of Texas Instruments, Inc.)*

168

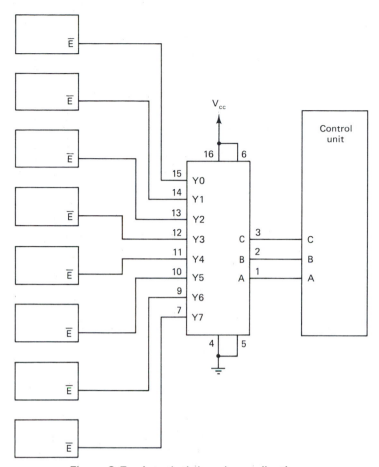

Figure 9.7 A typical decoder application.

problems could develop in the unused outputs and not affect the overall performance of the device. In contrast, a counter must have all of its internal components working in order to work as a unit. When only part of a circuit is being used, there is less that can go wrong and less circuitry to analyze.

If you suspect that a given decoder may be causing trouble, check all of the outputs that are being used. In most cases, the outputs of a given decoder will be pulsing low (or high if the device has active-high outputs) at odd intervals. Decoders rarely have repetitive outputs. If all of the usable outputs are pulsing, odds are that the device is working as it should.

A little common sense will also help. For example, look at the block diagram in Figure 9.9. In the diagram, the control unit is using a decoder to enable the different input/output sections. When the control unit needs to send information to the CRT circuitry, it sends a code to the decoder that is intended to select, or *address*, the CRT. The decoder, if it is operating properly, then sends out an active-low enable to the CRT circuitry.

Now, say that trouble has developed in the CRT circuitry. Preliminary tests indicate that the keyboard, disk drive, and printer are all working and that the problem is related directly to the CRT circuitry. There is no need to go haywire troubleshooting the entire decoder, since the other input/output devices are all receiving the enable signals they need to work. Only the CRT circuitry is not working, so only the decoder output that goes to the CRT circuitry needs to be checked. If that output is pulsing, the decoder is not the cause of the problem.

An important point has been made here with regard to troubleshooting in general. *Check only those signals and circuits that are relevant to the symptoms and*

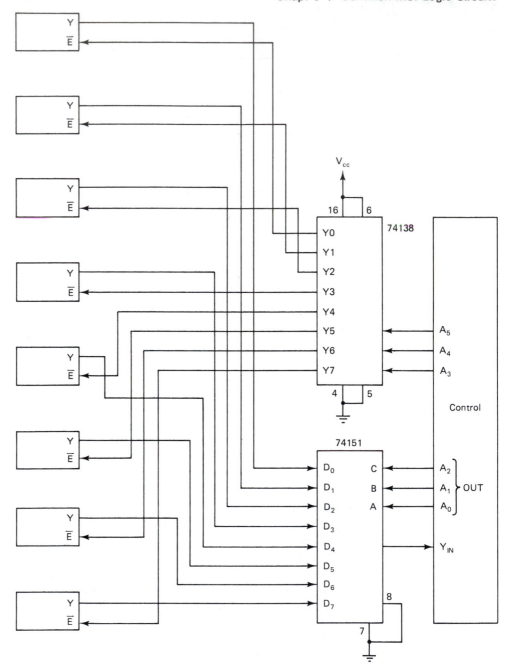

Figure 9.8 Combining scan and enabling circuits.

the trouble area. In the circuit in Figure 9.9, it would have been necessary to check the entire decoder only if *all* of the input/output devices had failed. If this had been the case, the decoder would have been suspect, because it is the point at which all the failed devices are tied together.

Decoder/Drivers

A decoder/driver is a decoder that is used to drive a seven-segment display. These decoders differ from standard decoders in that they will drive several outputs low (or high) for a given input code, rather than driving only one output to its active level. The 7447 decoder/driver is shown connected to a seven-segment display in Figure 9.10. The truth table for the 7447 is also shown.

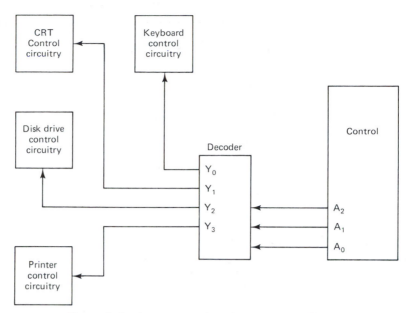

Figure 9.9 A common decoder wiring configuration.

First, a word about seven-segment displays. A seven-segment display consists of seven LEDs that are all tied to a common ground or common supply connection. When the LEDs are connected to a common supply point, the display is called *common anode*. When the LEDs are connected to a common ground point, the display is called *common cathode*. In a common-anode display, each of the LEDs must be supplied with individual ground connections in order to light. Conversely, common-cathode displays require individual V_{cc} connections to light the displays. In both cases, current-limiting resistors must be connected between the individual inputs and their voltage sources to prevent the LEDs from overheating.

In the circuit shown in Figure 9.10, the display is a common-anode display, which means that each LED must be supplied with a ground path from the decoder/driver in order to light. The inputs to the display are labeled (a) through (g) to show which segment in the display is driven by each input. For example, when input line (g) goes low, segment (g) will light. By driving combinations of segment input lines low, numbers appear on the displays. The combination of (a), (b), and (c) going low would cause the corresponding segments to light, and the number 7 would appear on the display. Any combination of segments can be lighted by supplying the correct combination of low signals to the display. This is where the decoder/driver comes in.

The 7447 is a BCD decoder/driver with active-low outputs. As the truth table indicates, various BCD inputs cause specific output lines to go low. For example, when the 7447 gets an input code of 0000, the first line of the truth table indicates that a low will be supplied to all but the (g) displays. This causes the number 0 to appear on the display. If you go through the truth table line by line, you will see that the input combinations of 0000 through 1001 cause the numbers 0 through 9 to light on the display.

The input combinations 1010 through 1110 cause some rather strange combinations of segments to light, while the input 1111 causes the display to go completely blank. Under normal operating circumstances, these code combinations will not be fed to the decoder/driver. If any of these patterns appear on the displays (with the exception of the display being blank), there is a faulty input being fed to the decoder/driver.

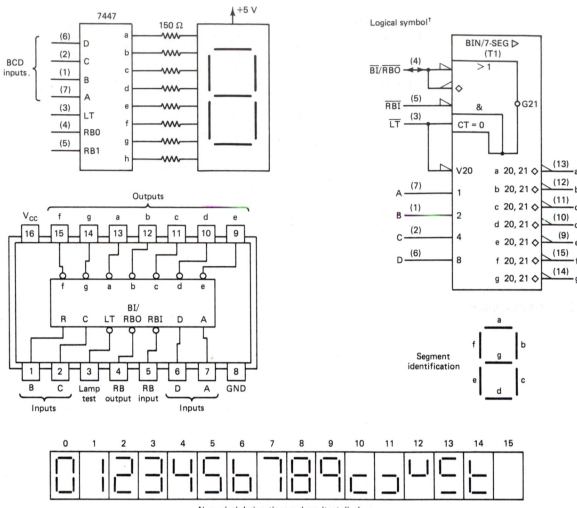

Numerical designations and resultant displays

'46A, '47A, 'L46, 'L47, 'LS47 function table

Decimal or function	Inputs						BI/RBO†	Outputs							Note
	LT	RBI	D	C	B	A		a	b	c	d	e	f	g	
0	H	H	L	L	L	L	H	ON	ON	ON	ON	ON	ON	OFF	
1	H	X	L	L	L	H	H	OFF	ON	ON	OFF	OFF	OFF	OFF	
2	H	X	L	L	H	L	H	ON	ON	OFF	ON	ON	OFF	ON	
3	H	X	L	L	H	H	H	ON	ON	ON	ON	OFF	OFF	ON	
4	H	X	L	H	L	L	H	OFF	ON	ON	OFF	OFF	ON	ON	
5	H	X	L	H	L	H	H	ON	OFF	ON	ON	OFF	ON	ON	
6	H	X	L	H	H	L	H	OFF	OFF	ON	ON	ON	ON	ON	
7	H	X	L	H	H	H	H	ON	ON	ON	OFF	OFF	OFF	OFF	
8	H	X	H	L	L	L	H	ON	ON	ON	ON	ON	ON	ON	1
9	H	X	H	L	L	H	H	ON	ON	ON	OFF	OFF	ON	ON	
10	H	X	H	L	H	L	H	OFF	OFF	OFF	ON	ON	OFF	ON	
11	H	X	H	L	H	H	H	OFF	OFF	ON	ON	OFF	OFF	ON	
12	H	X	H	H	L	L	H	OFF	ON	OFF	OFF	OFF	ON	ON	
13	H	X	H	H	L	H	H	ON	OFF	OFF	ON	OFF	ON	ON	
14	H	X	H	H	H	L	H	OFF	OFF	OFF	ON	ON	ON	ON	
15	H	X	H	H	H	H	H	OFF	OFF	OFF	OFF	OFF	OFF	OFF	
BI	X	X	X	X	X	X	L	OFF	OFF	OFF	OFF	OFF	OFF	OFF	2
RBI	H	L	L	L	L	L	L	OFF	OFF	OFF	OFF	OFF	OFF	OFF	3
LT	L	X	X	X	X	X	H	ON	ON	ON	ON	ON	ON	ON	4

Figure 9.10 The 7447 Decoder/driver and 7-segment display. *(Courtesy of Texas Instruments, Inc.)*

The RBI input to the display will cause the display to be blank when it is low. This is used to blank displays that are not being used for a given number display. For example, if you have six displays and are lighting the number 1479, you want the two most significant displays to be blank, since they are not used in the number. The RBI input for a given display is usually connected to the RBO output of the previous display.

The LT (lamp test) input to the display will cause all the displays to light when it is low. This provides a quick method of checking the display segments to make sure that they are all good.

Decoder/drivers are very common circuits. The 7448 is the companion chip to the 7447 and has active-high outputs that are used to drive common-cathode displays.

There is no problem at all in troubleshooting decoder/drivers. If a given display is lit in a strange pattern, check the inputs to the decoder/driver. If they are good, replace the decoder/driver. If a single LED fails to light, activate the LT input to the decoder/driver. If the LED still does not light, replace the display. If it does, replace the decoder/driver.

9.3 ENCODERS

An encoder is *a circuit that detects when any of its input lines goes low and provides an output code indicating which input line has gone low.* The logic symbol and truth table for the 74148 priority encoder are shown in Figure 9.11. A *priority encoder* is an encoder that assigns priority to its inputs. In most cases, the higher-numbered input has the priority. For example, if input 7 and input 5 to the 74148 were to go low at the same time, the chip would respond to input 7, since it is the higher-numbered input.

The inputs to the 74148 are numbered 0 through 7 and the outputs are labeled A0, A1, and A2. These outputs are referred to as *address* outputs, because they produce a unique binary code that is used to identify a specific input, much in the same way that your address is used to identify your house. The term *address* is one that you will come to be very familiar with as your study of digital electronics continues.

It would seem that the address supplied by the outputs of the 74148 would correspond directly to the number of the input. However, as the truth table indicates, the address codes for the inputs do not numerically equal the number of the input. For example, if input 7 goes low, the output address from the chip is 000. This binary number obviously does not equal 7. However, if you were to invert the address bits, the address codes would equal the input numbers. Most encoders work this way, and it is not uncommon to see their address outputs followed by inverters that change the output codes into exact binary equivalents of the input numbers.

The 74148 also has an input/output pair labeled EI and EO. These inputs are used to allow you to cascade several encoders. If you needed a priority encoder for 16 lines, you could connect two 74148s together to form a 16-line priority encoder. To understand how this works, look at the first line of the truth table. This line indicates that when EI (enable input) is high, the outputs from the chip are all high, regardless of what is going on at the inputs. The chip is therefore effectively disabled. This allows you to cascade 74148s, as shown in Figure 9.12. The key to the operation of the 16-line priority encoder shown in Figure 9.12 is the connection of EO (enable output) from chip A being connected to EI of chip B. The EO output will go high whenever any input to the encoder is activated. This will disable chip B. For example, if input 6 of chip A goes low, the chip will respond by putting the address code for input 6 on the address outputs and driving EO high. This high output on EO immediately disables chip B. All lower-priority inputs are now disabled. If there is

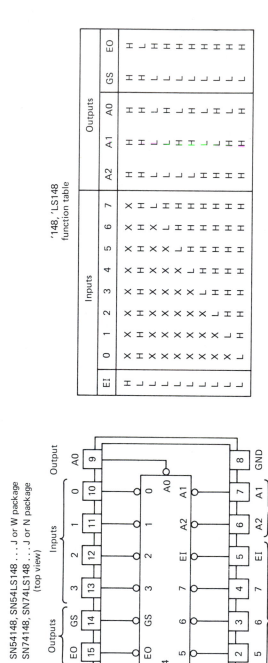

Figure 9.11 74148. *(Courtesy of Texas Instruments, Inc.)*

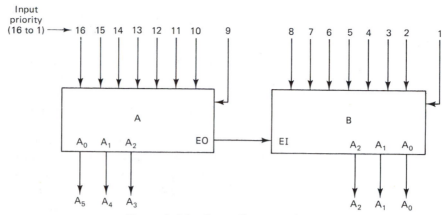

Figure 9.12 Cascading encoders.

no input to chip A, its EO output is low and chip B can function. The end result is that you have a 16-line priority encoder where an input will affect the circuit only if all higher-priority inputs are inactive.

A practical application for a priority encoder can be seen in Figure 9.13. In this circuit, the encoder is being used to inform the control unit when an input device needs to communicate with it, and which input device it is. The inputs to the 74148 are connected to the various input devices. These input devices are assigned priority by the designing engineers. The basis for the priority assignment is unimportant at this point and will be covered in later chapters on complete microcomputer systems. For now, it is important to understand that the higher-priority input devices have been connected to the higher-priority inputs of the 74148. In this case, the EI pin of the 74148 has been tied to ground to permanently enable the chip.

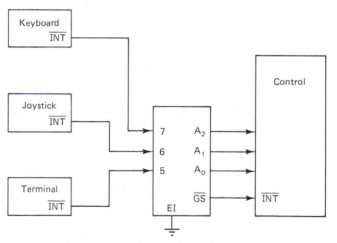

Figure 9.13 Input identification circuit.

Another output pin on the 74148 is the GS output. This output goes low when any input occurs and has been connected to the control unit. This gives the control unit a method of knowing when a given input device is attempting to establish communications. For example, if the keyboard needs to communicate with the control unit, it will drive its INT output low. The 74148 responds by driving its GS output low and putting the address code for the keyboard input on its address outputs. When the control unit detects the low at its INT input, it checks the address outputs of the 74148 to determine which device is requesting communications. The control unit would then respond by sending the proper code to the decoder to enable the keyboard.

This circuit serves the same overall purpose as the circuit shown in Figure 9.8. There is, however, one very important difference. In the circuit shown in Figure 9.8, the control unit constantly scanned the circuits to see if any of them needed to establish communications. That scanning process would tie up the control unit for a considerable period of time. In the circuit shown in Figure 9.13, the control unit does not need to scan the input devices. It can go about its business until the $\overline{INT}$ input is driven low. Then it responds to the input device that caused the signal. A signal of this nature is called an *interrupt*. When the control unit detects that an *interrupt* signal has occurred, it stops whatever it is doing and responds to the interrupting device. Interrupt signals are covered in great detail in Chapters 11 and 12.

Incidentally, if a lower-priority input device in Figure 9.13 needed to communicate with the control unit while the keyboard was sending a higher-priority signal out, the lower-priority device would simply keep its $\overline{INT}$ output low. Then, as soon as the low input to the 74148 from the keyboard disappeared, the 74148 would respond to the lower-priority input and repeat the interrupt to the control unit.

Troubleshooting Encoders

Most encoders work in the same manner as the 74148. Some have output address codes that correspond directly to the input number, but overall, their operating principles are the same.

The easiest way to troubleshoot an encoder is outlined in the following procedure:

1. Verify that all control inputs to the encoder are at their proper levels.
2. Verify that the data inputs to the encoder are being driven low.
3. Locate the output address pins and be ready to check them quickly with your oscilloscope.
4. Ground the highest-priority input and rapidly check the address outputs to see if they go to the correct levels for that input.
5. Remove the ground *immediately* after verifying the value on the address outputs.

Some digital technicians would roll over in their graves over the suggestion that you ground a chip input that is still in the system, because in doing so, you are also tying the output that normally drives that input to ground. This could burn up the output if the ground connection was left for any length of time. However, if you check the address outputs *quickly* after making the ground connection, you will not do any damage to any other chip.

If the chip responds to the test by putting out the correct address code, repeat the process for each of the inputs, going from the highest-priority inputs down to the lowest. In most cases, you can determine whether or not the chip is functioning correctly by using this test procedure. Again, if you get through the test and all other evidence still points to the encoder as being the source of the trouble, go ahead and replace it. There may be a current-level problem that your testing did not show.

SUMMARY

Multiplexers, decoders, and encoders are three very common circuits that are used to allow the control unit to distinguish the origin or destination of various signals. These circuits are used primarily in processing enable or interrupt signals.

You will see decoders and encoders in almost every microcomputer unit. Multiplexers tend to be used more in the input and output units than any others. Decoders are used by the control unit to provide enable signals for various circuits, and encoders are used to inform the control unit that communications are being requested by one device or another.

As you get used to working with the circuits discussed in this section, it will become obvious to you that although some aspects change from decoder to decoder, encoder to encoder, and multiplexer to multiplexer, the operation of a given type of circuit does not vary considerably from one chip to another. After a while, they will become as easy for you to deal with as any other digital circuit.

QUESTIONS

1. What is a multiplexer?
2. What determines which multiplexer input is connected to the output?
3. What is the procedure for troubleshooting a multiplexer with repetitive select input codes?
4. The waveforms shown in Figure 9.14 were obtained from the select lines of a multiplexer. What is the select code sequence if the top waveform is from the MSB of the select input?

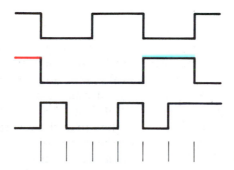
Figure 9.14 Waveforms for question 4.

5. What is a demultiplexer? What is another name for the demultiplexer?
6. Refer to Figure 9.9. If the keyboard is not working, which decoder output(s) should be checked? Why?
7. What is a decoder/driver? How does a decoder/driver differ from a conventional decoder?
8. What is the procedure for troubleshooting a decoder/driver?
9. What are the two types of seven-segment displays? How do they differ in their construction and input signal requirements?
10. What is an encoder? What is a priority encoder?
11. Referring to Figure 9.12, draw a 24-line priority encoder made of 74148s, and describe how it works.
12. What is an interrupt? Why are interrupts used?

PART IV
MICROCOMPUTERS

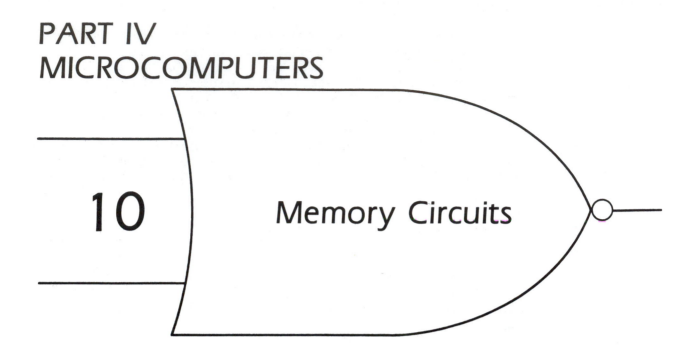

10   Memory Circuits

Microcomputers must be able to store digital information if they are to perform any useful function at all. The storage of digital information in its binary form is accomplished by the memory unit. Basically, a memory circuit is a circuit that can "remember" the last input it received. A good example of a memory circuit is a flip-flop, which can "remember" if it was last SET or RESET. In fact, a *memory cell*, the most basic memory unit, is nothing more than the electronic equivalent of a flip-flop. A memory cell is a memory unit that is capable of storing one bit. Like a flip-flop, it is either SET or RESET. The actual circuitry of a memory cell, however, is simpler than that of a flip-flop.

Although memory plays an extremely important function in the overall operation of a microcomputer, it seems to be one of the least understood of the computer units, and is by far the most difficult to troubleshoot. In fact, the greatest indication that a computer's memory has malfunctioned can be summed up as follows: *When everything works, but nothing works, the problem is memory.* For example, assume that you have been troubleshooting a down microcomputer system. Tests have indicated that all the units of the computer are working, but the overall system still does not work as it should. Since the circuits all work, but the overall system does not, the problem is in memory. This problem may either be due to faulty circuitry or faulty programming. Some testing will tell you which problem it is.

Although memory can be a very frustrating section of the microcomputer to deal with, you will see that like the other circuits covered so far, some common sense analysis and solid test procedures will render any problem solvable.

10.1   INTRODUCTION TO MEMORY AND MEMORY TERMINOLOGY

A typical memory unit consists of up to hundreds of thousands of locations that are used to store binary data. Each location works in much the same way as a register.

For this group of data storage locations to be of any use, the microcomputer must provide several things:

1. A method by which the control unit can select one of the many locations
2. A method by which the control unit can enter data into each location
3. A method by which the control unit can retrieve data from each location

The control unit of a microcomputer selects the individual memory locations using a binary code called an *address*. Each memory location has a unique address. Address codes are applied to the memory unit by means of a group of wires called the *address bus*. The address bus is connected to every memory circuit in the system and is never used for anything other than providing a path for these binary address codes.

Data is transferred to and from the memory unit by way of the *data bus*. This group of wires is connected to the control unit and the individual memory circuits in the same fashion as the address bus. The data bus is capable of carrying data in two directions (from memory to control and from control to memory), and is thus referred to as *bidirectional*. Although data cannot be transferred in both directions at the same time, the direction can be changed as required by the control unit. How the direction of data flow is determined is discussed in Section 10.2.

There are only two operations that the control unit performs that involve memory. These two operations are referred to as the *read* and *write* operations. A read operation is the process by which the control unit obtains data from memory. The steps involved in performing a read operation are summarized as follows:

1. The control unit sends out the address of the memory register that contains the required data.
2. The memory unit connects the output lines of the addressed register to the data bus.
3. The control unit gets the data from the data bus.

The process is actually a bit more involved than this, but as a basis, the process described will be sufficient for now.

The time it takes for the first two steps listed above to be completed is called *access time*. Access time starts when the control unit first places the address on the address bus, and ends when the data become available to the control unit. Access time is usually rated in nanoseconds and is a critical factor in the overall rating of a given memory type. The lower the access time, the better the memory type. Note that access time deals only with read operations.

The steps involved in performing a write operation are summarized as follows:

1. The control unit sends out the address of the memory register in which the data is to be stored.
2. The memory unit connects the input lines of the addressed register to the data bus.
3. The control unit enters the data into the register by way of the data bus.

Note the similarity between the read and write operations. *In both cases, the operation starts with the control unit addressing the memory register that will be involved in the operation.* The rest of the operation then involves a data transfer either to or from the memory.

It should be mentioned that our discussions on memory in this chapter deal with those memory circuits that are an internal part of the microcomputer system. There are external data storage devices, such as cassette tapes and magnetic disks, but these are not discussed in this chapter.

Memory Terminology

There are several terms that are used in discussions on memory. These terms are defined here:

Memory word: the group of bits that are stored in a single memory location. The number of bits in a memory word is equal to the number of memory cells in each given location. For example, in a memory system having eight bit registers, the system would be said to be storing 8-bit words. A word is treated as a single unit within the system, not as individual bits.

Random access memory: a memory unit in which the access time for all memory locations is the same. In other words, it takes the same amount of time to retrieve data, regardless of where that data is stored in the memory. This type of memory is referred to as RAM.

Sequential access memory: a memory unit in which the access time varies from location to location: for example, a cassette tape. If data needs to be read from the last location on the tape, the control unit must go through all other locations to get to the last one. This would take considerably longer than reading data from the first location on the tape.

Volatile memory: a memory type that loses the data it is storing when power is removed. This type of memory must be reprogrammed when the microcomputer is turned on. Any data that is in the memory when the power is turned off is lost, so any critical data must be stored elsewhere before turning off the computer.

Nonvolatile memory: a memory type that retains its data when power is removed. This type of memory is usually used for long-term storage of data.

Read/write memory: a type of memory that can be written into and read from during the normal course of a program run. This type of memory is usually used to store data and instructions that are being used in a specific program. This enables the system to reprogram the locations after they have been used for their purpose.

Read-only memory: a memory type that cannot be written into by the control unit. This type of memory is preprogrammed before it is placed into a microcomputer, and stores data that is crucial for the proper operation of the system.

10.2 GENERAL MEMORY ORGANIZATION

The basic organization for a typical microcomputer memory can be seen in Figure 10.1. This memory is shown to be composed of ROM and read/write (R/$\overline{\text{W}}$) memory.

In Figure 10.1, the address bus and the data bus are connected to the outer block of the memory, indicating that they are connected to every memory location, regardless of whether that location is a R/$\overline{\text{W}}$ or a ROM location. The data bus is shown to be an 8-bit bus. This indicates two things:

1. There are eight separate lines in the data bus. This allows 8 bits to be simultaneously transferred between control and memory.
2. Each memory location holds an 8-bit word. Since memory words are treated as a group and the data bus has eight lines, you can assume that the system has 8-bit words.

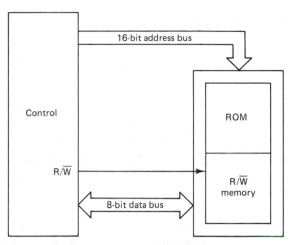

Figure 10.1 General memory organization.

You can always tell the size of the memory words by the number of lines in the data bus. By the same token, the number of lines in the address bus will tell you the maximum number of memory locations possible for the system.

In the first chapter it was stated that the number of possible combinations of n number of bits was equal to 2^n. Thus, with 10 bits, for example, the number of possible bit combinations equals $2^{10} = 1024$. In a microcomputer with n address lines, you can find the maximum number of address-bit combinations using the same 2^n method. In the system shown, there are 16 address lines, which means that the system uses 16-bit address codes. With 16 bits, the maximum number of address codes is found to be $2^{16} = 65,536$. Since each memory location must have its own unique address, the maximum number of memory locations for this system is 65,536. Note that this value is the *maximum* number of memory locations. The system may actually use less than that.

There is an important point that should be made here. You have probably noticed at one time or another that computer memory is referred to in terms of k. One computer is said to have a 64k memory, another has a 256k memory, and so on. While "k" is used in standard electronics to mean 1000, it takes on a different meaning when being used to discuss computer memory. In this context, k = 2^{10}, or 1024. A 64k memory would actually have 64 $\times$ 2^{10} = 65,536 locations. The actual size of any memory listed in k values is found in the same way.

The memory shown in Figure 10.1 would be referred to as a 64k $\times$ 8 memory, where 64k is the number of memory locations and 8 is the number of bits stored in each location. In many technical manuals, memory units are described in this fashion. The first number always indicates the number of locations, and the second number always indicates the number of bits per location.

The R/$\overline{\text{W}}$ line is a control line that the control unit uses to determine the direction of data flow during a read or write operation. When the control unit is performing a read operation, the R/$\overline{\text{W}}$ line is driven high. This puts the addressed location in the output mode. While performing a write operation, the control unit drives the R/$\overline{\text{W}}$ line low, which puts the addressed location in the input mode.

Note that the R/$\overline{\text{W}}$ line is not connected to the ROM. This is due to the fact that the control unit cannot enter data into the ROM. There is therefore no reason to have the R/$\overline{\text{W}}$ line go to this section. ROM is always in the output mode, as will be shown in the next section.

The memory organization discussed here is simplified, but accurate. We cover the finer details of memory organization in a later section, after covering the types of internal memory and the circuits that make them up.

10.3 READ-ONLY MEMORY

Read-only memory is a vital part of every computer made. This type of memory stores information that is used in almost every computer operation. ROM is nonvolatile, and thus it lends itself to storing data that must be used by the control unit every time that the computer is used. For example, a given microcomputer may be set up so that "hello" is printed on the CRT every time that the computer is turned on. To be able to do this, the control unit needs two things; it must have the program to tell it to send the characters to the CRT, and it must have the correct sequence of ASCII characters. Both the program and the ASCII characters would be stored in ROM so that the required data would be available when the computer was first turned on.

A ROM chip is programmed before it is put into the microcomputer that will use it, using one of several methods of programming. These methods of programming are associated with physical characteristics of the ROM chip and are discussed later in this section. *It should be noted, however, that the programs and data that are stored in a given ROM chip are never changed while the chip is in the microcomputer that is using it.* The principle is almost the same as cassette tape with the recoding tab removed. A cassette player can get music from the tape, but cannot record any new music onto it. While the construction of the ROM and cassette tape are radically different, their operating principles are basically the same. The data recorded in a ROM cannot be changed by the microcomputer using it any more than the music on the cassette can be changed by the recorder playing it.

Basic ROM Construction

All ROMs are constructed so that a given input address will cause a specific data word to appear at the data outputs. Although not all ROMs are constructed in the same way as the one shown in Figure 10.2, the one shown will give you a good idea of how ROMs work in general.

As you can see, the ROM shown is constructed of diodes, resistors, and a decoder. The output lines, D0 through D3, are connected to V_{cc} via the 1-kΩ resistors and connected to the decoder via the diodes. When a given decoder output line is low, that low is applied to the output lines that are connected to the decoder output and not the others. The decoder is driven by the address inputs A0 through A3.

Let's take a look at what happens when the address inputs to the ROM equal 0101. With an address input of 0101, output line 5 of the decoder goes low. This line is tied to line D3 through the diode. With line 5 low, the diode is forward biased, causing line D3 to go low. None of the other D lines are connected to line 5, so they all remain high. The result is that the ROM has an output of 0111 at D3 through D0. The output code for each decoder line is labeled by that line. See if you can determine how each address input causes the appropriate output data word to be developed.

The ROM chip shown in Figure 10.2 can be given three state outputs by adding three-state buffers to the data lines. The new circuit is shown in Figure 10.3. The three-state buffers are being controlled by the $\overline{CS}$ (chip select) line. When this line is low, the three-state buffers are enabled and the D outputs are connected to the diode matrix. When $\overline{CS} = 1$, the buffers are disabled and the ROM will have no output. All the D lines will be floating at around 1 to 1.8 V.

Now consider the ROM chip just covered and its relationship to the operating principles of ROM in general. The circuit shown in Figure 10.2 has its data permanently determined by the diode matrix construction. Once the diodes have been constructed in the matrix, the outputs will not change for a given address. If this chip were to be placed into a microcomputer, the control unit would be able to address the chip

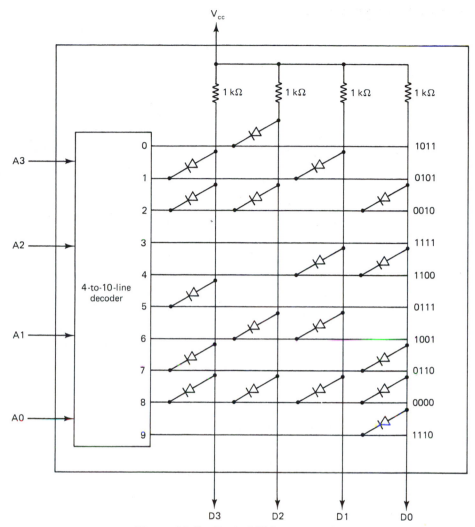

Figure 10.2 Basic ROM construction.

and get data from it, but it would not be able to change the data that is in the chip. This is the basis of ROM.

Two of the chips shown in Figure 10.2 could be wired in parallel to provide output words that were 8 bits long. This circuit configuration is shown in Figure 10.4. The ROM chips have been drawn as blocks, but the operating principles are the same.

Note that the $\overline{CS}$ pins for the two chips have been tied together, as well as the address lines. This ensures that both chips will receive the same address and $\overline{CS}$ signal at any given point in time. Now take a look at the wiring of the data outputs of the two chips. The data lines from U1 have been wired to the D7 through D4 input lines to control, while the data lines from U2 have been wired to the D3 through D0 lines. This means that the control unit is getting half of its data word from U1 and the other half from U2. For example, assume that the data word at address 0000 is 1011 in U1 and 0100 in U2. The control unit, when it addresses location 0000, would drive the $\overline{CS}$ inputs of U1 and U2 low. At that time, the output from U1 would be 1011 and the output from U2 would be 0100. These values would appear simultaneously on inputs D7 through D0 of the control unit. The data received by the control unit would be 10110100. This data value would be treated as a single word by the control unit. What the control unit would do with that word is a topic that is left for later

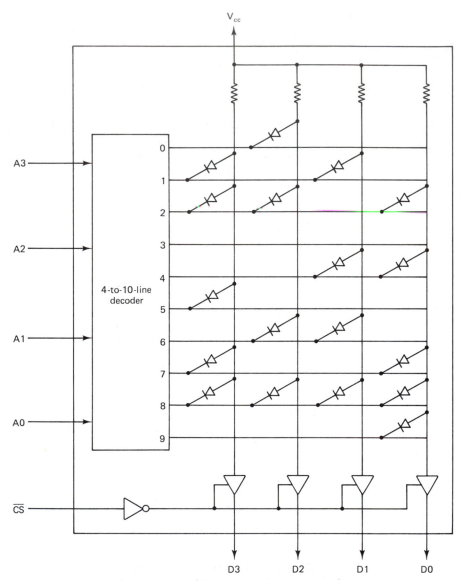

Figure 10.3 ROM with three-state outputs.

discussions. However, for now, realize that these data values have some importance to the control circuitry, and that they can be obtained from, but not written into, ROM.

Mask-Programmed ROM

As we stated earlier, there are several methods by which ROM is constructed and programmed. One of these ROM types is the *mask-programmed ROM*. The mask-programmed ROM has its data permanently burned into its physical construction when the chip is first produced. Although the process may seem strange, it is relatively simple as IC manufacturing techniques go.

Recall that circuits are "burned" into semiconductor materials when ICs are manufactured. The easiest of the circuits to produce is the diode. Now, picture the circuit shown in Figure 10.2 being produced in IC form. The diode matrix could be formed by burning diodes in certain positions and not in others. This is how a mask-programmed ROM is made. A "mask" is used to prevent the laser that is used to

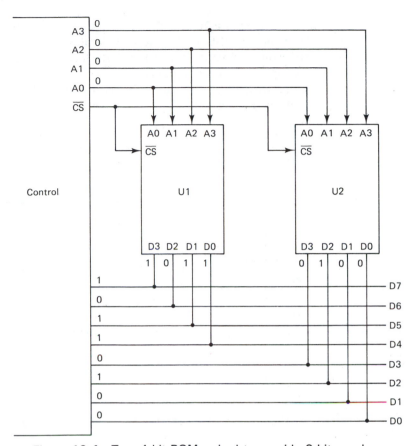

Figure 10.4 Two 4-bit ROMs wired to provide 8-bit words.

burn the circuits from burning diodes in certain positions. Any position not blocked by the mask will have a diode burned in. After the matrix is formed, the rest of the circuitry is burned in and the chip is complete. Although this is an extremely simplified explanation of the actual production process used for mask programmed ROMs, it is sufficient for understanding some of the more important points regarding mask programmed ROMs.

First, the data contained in a mask-programmed ROM is permanent. Once the chip is produced, there is nothing that can be done to change the data. Second, mask programmed ROMs must be programmed by the manufacturer. This means that an individual mask must be made for a given ROM chip, since not all ROMs contain the same information. These masks are extremely expensive, so the only way to make a mask-programmed ROM cost-effective is to produce a great number of them. That way, the cost of the mask is spread out over the cost of all the chips. In fact, if a sufficient number of chips are produced, the mask-programmed ROM will be the least expensive type of ROM to use. For example, if a given microcomputer manufacturer expects to sell 50,000 systems, that manufacturer would use mask-programmed ROMs, since, at that number of chips, they would be the least expensive to use.

Programmable ROM (PROM)

A PROM is a permanent ROM that is programmed by the system manufacturer rather than by the IC manufacturer. These ROM chips are cheaper to use when relatively few chips containing a given data set are needed.

When a PROM is first made, all memory cells are in the logic 0 state. This is because the cells are basically made up of semiconductor fuses that are connected to ground. To program a PROM, the location is addressed, and a large current pulse is applied to the output pins where you want a logic 1 to appear. This blows the semiconductor fuse, eliminating the ground path. The circuit shown in Figure 10.5 will help you understand the process better.

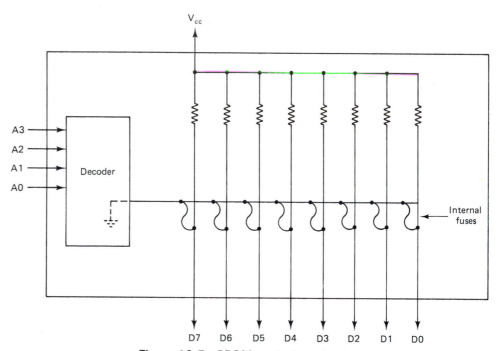

Figure 10.5 PROM equivalent circuit.

The circuit shown represents a single 8-bit memory location. As you can see, the D lines are all connected to ground through their respective fuses. If you wanted to program the value 11010011 into this particular location, you would first apply the correct address to the address pins on the chip. You would then apply a large current pulse to lines D7, D6, D4, D1, and D0. This would eliminate the fuses on the appropriate lines, and they would then be held at a logic 1. From that point on, whenever that particular location was addressed, the output would be 11010011.

Without the need of a program mask, PROMs are cheaper in small quantities than are mask-programmed ROMs and with the use of PROM programmers, they can be produced at a relatively rapid rate. A PROM programmer is a machine that addresses and programs each location automatically. When the PROM programmer has been supplied with the needed address/data information, a PROM is inserted and the PROM is automatically programmed.

On the average, PROMs are used more often than mask-programmed ROMs, since their initial outlay is lower. Also, if a microcomputer manufacturer decides to modify the contents of a given system's ROM, a new mask is not needed. The manufacturer simply changes the contents of the next series of chips produced.

There are some disadvantages to using PROMs. First, if a mistake is made while programming a PROM, the chip is ruined. There is no way to amend a given data set once it is programmed into the PROM. Another problem lies in the fact that the semiconductor fuses can redevelop over a long period of time. This causes the PROM to give out faulty data and will cause the system to malfunction.

Erasable PROM (EPROM)

The second type of PROM is the EPROM. The EPROM stores data as pockets of charge that can be erased with a high-intensity ultraviolet light. The method by which an EPROM stores a charge is rather involved, but an adequate explanation is that a charge is trapped between two insulators. The presence of a charge represents a logic 1, and the absence of a charge represents a logic 0.

An EPROM can always be identified by the presence of a small quartz window on the top of the chip. It is through this window that the EPROM is erased. When a high-intensity ultraviolet light is passed through the window, the pockets of charge are removed, which clears the memory chip. *Note that the entire chip is erased by the light when it is applied; it is not possible to erase a single location in the chip.*

Because the chip can be erased through the quartz window, it is usually covered with opaque tape when the chip is programmed. This prevents the chip from slowly being erased by ordinary light, which has some ultraviolet light in it.

EPROMs are used mainly in prototype situations. When a given ROM data set has not been proven to work, it is best to use an EPROM to test it. That way, if the programs and data contained in the chip are faulty, the manufacturer can simply erase the chip and start again.

All three types of ROM come in various sizes, and all three can be found in the average microcomputer. As will be shown in the next section, ROMs have a wide variety of applications. All of these applications are based on one important point—the fact that ROMs retain their data when power is removed.

10.4 ROM APPLICATIONS

ROM is used in almost every aspect of microcomputer operation. The applications of ROM are so widespread that ROM can be found in almost every functional unit of the computer. This section will touch on most of those applications.

Computer Memory

The most common application for ROM is the storing of binary program instructions and data. One of the most common examples of this is the storing of a given microcomputer's *bootstrap* program. A bootstrap program is a list of binary instructions that the computer runs when it is first turned on. You see, a computer is incapable of doing anything that is not spelled out clearly in one program or another. This includes such things as getting data from a keyboard, sending information to the CRT, accepting data from a disk drive, and so on. This means that some sort of program must be run when the computer is first turned on. Otherwise, the system would be incapable of accepting any instructions or data from the user. This would render the system useless.

Code Converter

ROM is also used in code-conversion applications. For example, a 4-bit ROM can be used as a binary-to-Gray code converter by using a given binary value as the address, and storing the Gray code equivalent of the address in the selected location. ROM can also be used to convert binary to ASCII (and vice versa), and so on.

Character Generator

If you have ever looked closely at a microcomputer CRT, you may have noticed that the letters are made up of very small dots. It takes a series of these "dot patterns" (binary codes that light or do not light dots) to form a single letter. This process is covered in detail in a later chapter. However, for now, it will suffice to say that up to thirteen 8-bit words are required to display a single letter on the CRT. These dot patterns are fixed, meaning that the same series of dot patterns is required every time a given letter is to be displayed on the CRT. The patterns also vary from character to character.

Dot patterns are stored in a special ROM, called a *character generator*. When the character generator receives the ASCII code for a given character, it uses the code, together with other codes, to provide the required dot pattern. The ASCII character is used as the address and the data out of the ROM is the appropriate dot pattern. This is discussed in more detail in Chapter 14.

The three applications discussed here form the bulk of ROM applications. Most other applications fall into one of these three categories, as will be seen when we start discussing entire microcomputer systems.

10.5   STATIC RAM

As we stated earlier, RAM is *random access memory*. This means that the access time for all memory locations is the same. Although this definition also holds true for ROM (ROM access times tend to be equal), RAM is a term that is usually used to refer to random access *read/write memory*. Whenever a technical publication refers to RAM, it is actually referring to the read/write memory that the system contains. Read/write memory is memory that the control unit can both retrieve data from (read) and enter data into (write). Since a majority of computer operations involve instructions and data that are required on a temporary basis, RAM makes up a vast majority of microcomputer memory.

Static RAM is *read/write memory that will preserve its data as long as power is applied*. In contrast, *dynamic RAM* (which will be covered in the next section) must have its data rewritten into memory periodically, or the data will be lost. As long as the control unit does nothing to change a given data word in static RAM, that word will be in its given memory location for as long as power is applied to the system.

Most static RAM is volatile; that is its data is lost when power is turned off. For this reason, RAM must be programmed every time the microcomputer is turned on. Any critical information stored in RAM is usually stored on a magnetic disk or cassette tape before the system is turned off so that the information will be saved for later use.

RAM chips come in a wide variety of sizes, from 256 × 4 bits to 256k × 1 bit. The way by which these chips are wired into the circuit depends on the configuration of the chips themselves. An example of a RAM memory configuration can be seen in Figure 10.6. This is a 16k × 8 bit memory, consisting of eight 16k × 1 RAM chips.

The address bus coming from the control unit has 14 address lines. This enables the control unit to address $2^{14} = 16,384$ (16k) locations. The address lines are connected to all of the RAM chips so that they are always addressed as a group. The control unit data bus is wired so that each 16k × 1 chip is connected to a single data line. The $\overline{CS}$ pins of the chips are all connected to a single control input, as are the $R/\overline{W}$ pins. This allows the control unit to enable/disable the entire RAM unit, as well as determine the direction of data flow.

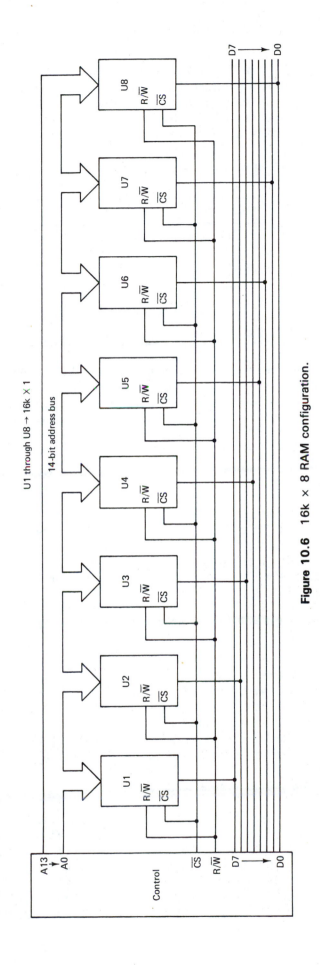

Figure 10.6 16k × 8 RAM configuration.

With the D (data) input/output pins wired as they are, a given 8-bit word is stored across the eight chips. For example, assume that the control unit is storing the value 10110110 in address 11100010011100 (389C-hexadecimal). The address value 389C is put out on the address bus. Both the $\overline{CS}$ and R/$\overline{W}$ lines are then driven low. This enables the chips and puts them in the input (write) mode. Now, the control unit places the value to be stored, 10110110, on the data bus. Each bit of the word to be stored goes to one of the memory chips, according to the following list:

Data value	Goes to:	By way of line:
1	U1	D7
0	U2	D6
1	U3	D5
1	U4	D4
0	U5	D3
1	U6	D2
1	U7	D1
0	U8	D0

After the write operation is complete, the entire 8-bit word has been stored, with one bit being held in each of the memory chips.

In the memory configuration shown, the most significant bit (MSB) of every word would be stored in U1. The second bit of every word would be stored in U2, and so on. This means that if a given chip in the unit goes bad, every data word will be affected. This is discussed in greater detail in Section 10.9.

TTL RAM

TTL circuitry is used mainly for smaller RAM systems, due to the relatively large size of the basic TTL RAM cell. Although a TTL RAM cell is actually smaller than a standard flip-flop, it is still rather large by comparison to other logic family RAM cells. The larger size of the circuit means that less cells can be placed on a single chip. This makes TTL impractical for large memory units, since it would take entirely too many IC chips.

MOS RAM

For the most part, microcomputers use MOS RAM chips. Because the average MOS circuit takes less space to build and consumes much less power than TTL, MOS RAM is by far a more practical logic circuit to use. MOS RAM chips are capable of storing quite a few bits of information in a single chip. In fact, the 16k × 1 chips used in Figure 10.6 would probably have been MOS chips, since TTL chips of that size are not produced. The power dissipated by a MOS RAM is typically less than one-half of that dissipated by an equivalent TTL RAM.

Memory Chip Internal Address Decoding

Most memory chips in use in microcomputers these days contain thousands of 1-bit locations. Some of the more common sizes are 16k × 1 and 64k × 1; and 256k × 1 chips are being developed. Each of these chips requires internal address decoding circuitry to select one memory location out of the thousands that they contain. A typical decoding circuitry setup can be seen in Figure 10.7. Although this is only a 16-bit configuration, the principle is the same for much larger chips. Each square in the figure represents a single memory cell. For simplification, the data input and

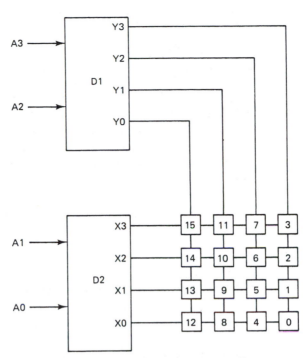

Figure 10.7 Internal RAM cell decoding.

output lines have been eliminated. The cells themselves have been arranged in an X-Y matrix, with each cell being connected to one X line and one Y line. In order for a given cell to be enabled, both its X select line and its Y select line must be low. If they are not both low, the cell cannot be read from or written into.

The decoders are used to drive one of their respective output lines low while keeping all the others high. Both decoders work according to the following truth table:

Input code		Low output line
A1	A0	
0	0	0
0	1	1
1	0	2
1	1	3

To see how the overall decoding operation works, assume that the input address to the chip is A3 = 1, A2 = 1, A1 = 0, A0 = 0 (1100). Decoder D1 has an input code of 11, so output line 3 is low. Decoder D2 has an input code of 00, so output line 0 is low. These two lines intersect at memory cell 10. This memory cell, and no other, would be enabled. Any read or write operation involving this chip would involve only this memory cell.

In the same manner, every memory cell can be addressed and selected. By increasing the number of X-Y lines and intersections, the total number of cells in the chip can be increased. The 16k × 1 chips in Figure 10.6, for example, would contain two 7-to-128 line decoders. This would provide 128 X select lines and 128 Y select lines. The total number of intersections would equal 128 × 128 = 16,384. This corresponds to the number of memory cells in the chips.

With memory chips having such high storage capacities, additional external addressing techniques are required. These are discussed in Section 10.7.

10.6 DYNAMIC RAM

Dynamic RAM differs from static RAM in that it stores data as pockets of charge. These pockets of charge must be amplified, or *refreshed* periodically, or the data that is contained in the memory chip is lost. Although the need to refresh a dynamic memory is indeed a disadvantage, dynamic memory does have its advantage. Dynamic RAM cells are the smallest and simplest to produce, so many more cells can be manufactured on a single chip. This results in a great saving in manufacturing costs to the manufacturer. Assume that a 64k memory can be constructed using half as many dynamic RAM chips as it would take using static RAM chips. Now add the difference over, say, 25,000 systems. As you can see, the savings would be considerable if dynamic RAM were used.

Another point must be taken into consideration. The refresh process is not something that happens by itself. It takes, in some cases, special circuitry, and that circuitry costs money to produce. However, in large memory systems (those over 4k), dynamic RAM still has the cost advantage over static RAM. In systems that contain less than 4k of memory, the cost of the refresh circuitry prevents dynamic RAM from being cost-effective. So, in smaller systems, you will rarely encounter dynamic RAM.

Outside of the need for a refresh cycle, dynamic RAM works in the same manner as static RAM. It is addressed in the same way, controlled in the same way, and so on. For most dynamic RAM chips, the refresh circuitry is internal. This means that the system need only supply certain control signals at given time intervals to accomplish the data refresh. We will now discuss some of the refresh methods currently used.

$\overline{\text{RAS}}$-Only Refresh

There are two inputs that can be found on many RAM chips, called *row-address strobe* ($\overline{\text{RAS}}$) and *column-address strobe* ($\overline{\text{CAS}}$). These two inputs are used mainly in address multiplexing operations, which are covered in Section 10.7. For now, simply remember that $\overline{\text{RAS}}$ would act as an enable for the X select lines, and $\overline{\text{CAS}}$ would act as an enable for the Y select lines. Recall that these select lines were shown in Figure 10.7.

In $\overline{\text{RAS}}$-only refresh, the following sequence of events must occur to refresh the memory chip:

1. $\overline{\text{RAS}}$ goes low, while $\overline{\text{CAS}}$ and $\overline{\text{RFSH}}$ (the refresh input) are held high.
2. The addressed X select line is activated, and the refresh pulse is internally generated.
3. $\overline{\text{RAS}}$ goes high, the address is advanced, and the cycle is repeated.

This process applies a current pulse to all memory cells on a given X select line. That pulse refreshes the data in all memory cells on that line. The advantage of using this technique is that the entire refresh cycle for the chip can be accomplished in a relatively short period of time. For example, it was stated earlier that a 16k $\times$ 1 chip would be arranged as a 128 $\times$ 128 select line matrix. Using $\overline{\text{RAS}}$-only refresh, it would take 128 cycles to refresh the entire chip since there are 128 rows of memory cells in the chip. Each chip must be refreshed at least once every 2 ms. With 128 rows being refreshed every 2 ms, a relatively small period of time is actually involved in refresh operations.

Automatic Refresh

An automatic refresh is similar to the $\overline{\text{RAS}}$-only refresh. However, in this case, $\overline{\text{RAS}}$ is held high, and $\overline{\text{RFSH}}$ is driven low by the control unit to refresh the device. An internal counter is used to advance between rows, so the control unit is freed from this task. This type of refresh is also referred to as *hidden refresh*, since no elaborate external addressing circuitry is required.

Summary of Dynamic RAM

The refresh process of dynamic RAM is probably one of the least understood of the memory functions. However, here is a summary of what you need to know to be able to deal effectively with dynamic RAM:

1. Dynamic RAM must be refreshed (rewritten) at least once every 2 ms, or its internal data will be lost.
2. The amount of time required to perform one refresh cycle varies with the size of the chip and the technique being used, usually up to 300 ns.
3. The control unit must provide the $\overline{\text{RAS}}$ and $\overline{\text{RFSH}}$ at the proper time and in the proper sequence.

10.7 MEMORY ADDRESSING TECHNIQUES

Up until now, we have confined our discussions to a relatively small (16k) memory. The average microcomputer has a 16-bit address bus and thus can address 64k of memory. This 64k includes both RAM and ROM. We will now take a look at a typical 64k memory configuration. The memory unit shown in Figure 10.8 is made up of memory groups, called *banks*. Each memory bank is made up of 16k of memory, with the four banks totaling 64k. Bank 0 contains RAM and ROM and is discussed later in this section.

Memory banks 1, 2, and 3 are made up exclusively of read/write random access memory. Each of these banks is wired in the same fashion as the 16k unit shown in Figure 10.6 and works according to the same principles. A common R/$\overline{\text{W}}$ control line determines the data flow direction for all RAM chips. The $\overline{\text{CS}}$ lines are used to select one of the four memory banks. The reason for needing to select only one of the four banks lies in the way in which the banks are wired to the data bus. You may recall from the discussion on the basic 16k RAM that the eight 16k × 1 chips are wired so that each chip stores one bit of a given 8-bit word. With this wiring configuration, it is necessary to enable all of the chips in a given bank at the same time, in order to write in the entire word. However, *no more than one bank can be enabled at any given time*. Consider what would happen if banks 2 and 3 were enabled at the same time. With both banks enabled, there would be two enabled chip outputs connected to each wire on the data bus. This could cause one or more of the RAM chips in each of the banks to be destroyed, since a wire-AND situation would exist.

The addressing system is actually relatively simple. The first 14 address bits are connected to the address inputs of all of the 16k × 1 RAM chips. The two most significant address bits (A14 and A15) are used to drive a 2- to 4-line decoder. As with all of the decoders we have discussed thus far, one output line of the decoder will be low and the others will remain high. The low output is determined by the inputs to the decoder.

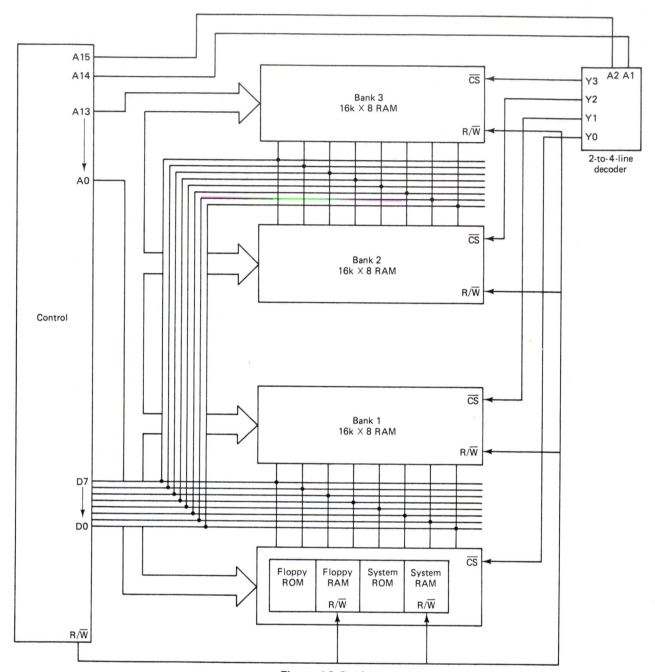

Figure 10.8 64k memory configuration.

Each decoder output is connected to all of the $\overline{\text{CS}}$ inputs of all the chips within a given bank. For example, if output line Y1 is low, all the RAM chips in bank one are enabled. The rest of the chips within the memory unit are disabled and will not respond to any other control or address signals.

Addressing a Specific Memory Location

The 16 address bits are used to select one out of the 65,536 memory locations. To show how this is done, consider the case in which the control unit is addressing location C479-H. The binary outputs from the control unit would be as follows:

A15	A14	A13	A12	A11	A10	A9	A8	A7	A6	A5	A4	A3	A2	A1	A0
1	1	0	0	0	1	0	0	0	1	1	1	1	0	0	1

Address bits A15 and A14 cause the input code to the decoder to equal 3, so output line 3 of the decoder will be low, enabling all the chips in bank 3. The rest of the address bits would then address location 10001111001 (479-H) in that bank. In this same manner, the control unit can address every location between 0000000000000000 (0000-H) and 1111111111111111 (FFFF-H). This covers the entire 64k range of memory.

Bank 0 operates a little differently than the rest of the banks and thus requires some special decoding circuitry. Within bank 0, there are several memory chips that are serving some dedicated purpose. These chips, with their respective functions, are listed below:

Floppy ROM: contains all programs and instructions associated with the operation of the floppy disk drive.

Floppy RAM: used to temporarily store the data and instructions that are transferred to or from the disk drive unit.

System ROM: contains the instructions and data that the control unit requires in order to perform its functions.

System RAM: used as a temporary storage location for the control unit. In it, the control unit stores only that data that is used when running the programs in the system ROM. It can be looked upon as a piece of scratch paper that the control unit has for its own use.

Data would not be placed in the system RAM or floppy RAM by the programmer. These chips are for the exclusive use of the control unit. It is common for a system to have memory that is used exclusively by the control unit, as will be seen in chapters 11 and 12. For now, there are several points that must be made:

1. The chips in this section of memory are not bound together as the chips in the other banks are. Each is a separate memory entity, capable of storing 8-bit words.
2. Because the chips have independent functions, they are enabled at different times. This means that bank 0 requires its own memory decoding circuitry.

Figure 10.9 shows the wiring of bank 0. As you can see, its wiring is significantly different from that of the rest of the memory unit. Each of the chips in bank 0 is constructed in a 4k × 8 configuration. This configuration requires 12 address bits to select a single location within a given chip. The address bits from the control unit are broken down as follows:

A15 and A14: used to decode the bank

A13 and A12: used to decode the chip within bank 0

A11 through A0: used to select the location within the selected chip

The output line from the main memory decoder is used to enable the bank 0 decoder, D2. When the $\overline{CS}$ input to D2 is low, one output from the chip will go low, depending on the values at A13 and A12. The low out of the decoder will enable one of the chips within bank 0 and disable the rest. The rest of the address bits will then select a single location within the selected chip. For example, consider the decoding of the address 0A44-H. The address bits applied to the memory would be as follows:

A15	*A14*	*A13*	*A12*	*A11*	*A10*	*A9*	*A8*	*A7*	*A6*	*A5*	*A4*	*A3*	*A2*	*A1*	*A0*
0	0	0	0	1	0	1	0	0	1	0	0	0	1	0	0

Bits A15 and A14 are at 00, so decoder D1 enables decoder D2. A13 and A12 are also at 00, so line 0 from decoder D2 is low, enabling system ROM. The rest of the address bits would then decode location 101001000100 (A44-H) within the system ROM chip.

When and why the control unit would decode a specific memory location is a subject that is discussed in Chapter 13. For now, it is important that you under-

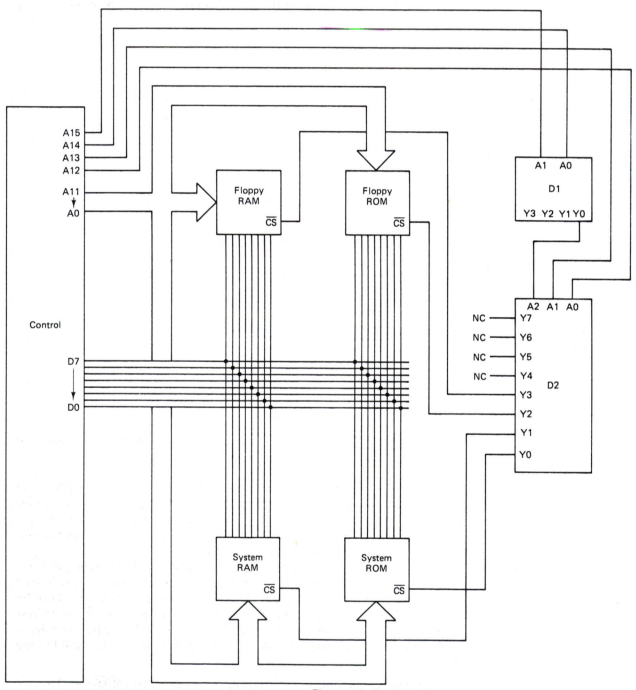

Figure 10.9 Bank 0 wiring.

stand how the address bits are used to decode a specific memory location. Once a location is selected, the control unit will either enter information into that location or get information from it, depending on the operation being performed and the type of chip that has been addressed. Before going beyond this point, make sure that you understand the circuits shown in Figures 10.8 and 10.9.

Address Multiplexing

With many memory chips, the number of address input pins are limited by the size of the chip. For example, the MCM6664 is a 64k × 1 RAM chip that is contained in a 16-pin DIP. The pin diagram of the chip is shown in Figure 10.10. As you can

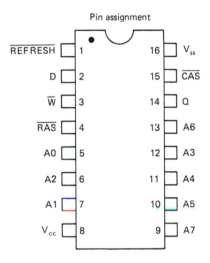

Pin assignment

$\overline{\text{REFRESH}}$	1	16	V_{ss}
D	2	15	$\overline{\text{CAS}}$
$\overline{W}$	3	14	Q
$\overline{\text{RAS}}$	4	13	A6
A0	5	12	A3
A2	6	11	A4
A1	7	10	A5
V_{cc}	8	9	A7

Pin names	
REFRESH	Refresh
A0–A7	Address input
D	Data in
Q	Data out
$\overline{W}$	Read-write input
$\overline{\text{RAS}}$	Row address strobe
$\overline{\text{CAS}}$	Column address strobe
V_{cc}	Power (+5 V)
V_{ss}	Ground

Figure 10.10 MCM6664. *(Courtesy of Motorola, Inc.)*

see, there are only eight address pins on the chip. Since 16 address bits are required to address 64k locations, the address bits must be applied to the chip in two groups of 8 bits. This is accomplished using *address multiplexing*. With address multiplexing, the 16 address bits are applied as two 8-bit words, while the $\overline{\text{RAS}}$ and $\overline{\text{CAS}}$ inputs are used to control the addressing operation.

The 64k locations are constructed in a matrix fashion within the chip, in much the same way as the circuit shown in Figure 10.7. This matrix, however, is formed as a 256 × 256 line matrix to give the required 65,536 (64k) intersections. In order to drive one of 256 lines low, you need 8 address bits. Thus 8 bits of the address are used to control the row address lines, and 8 bits are used to drive the column address lines. When the control unit addresses the chip, it does so in the following sequence:

1. The control unit puts out the 16 address bits and drives $\overline{\text{RAS}}$ low. The row address bits are now entered into the chip.

2. After a specified period of time (in nanoseconds), the $\overline{\text{RAS}}$ is returned to its inactive high level and $\overline{\text{CAS}}$ is driven low. The remaining 8 address bits are now entered into the chip.

The data bit stored in the addressed location will now appear at the output if the operation being performed is a read operation. If it is a write operation, the addressed location will now be in the input mode. As usual, this is controlled by the R/$\overline{\text{W}}$ line. The chip can be determined to be a dynamic RAM chip by the $\overline{\text{REFRESH}}$ input.

Using address multiplexing requires extra memory decoding circuitry, but it is worth it. Consider the case of a system based on 64k × 1 chips, each using address multiplexing. To provide 64k 8-bit RAM locations, eight such chips would be needed. A given amount of room on a circuit board would be required for the eight 16-pin chips. Now consider the space requirements of the same type of memory setup, without address multiplexing. The chips needed would now have to be 24-pin chips. The extra chips would be needed to accommodate the extra address bits. This group of chips would require a much larger amount of space on the circuit board. Space conservation is important, especially when you consider the fact that the average microcomputer can contain up to hundreds of ICs. The bottom line is that conserving physical space on printed-circuit boards is a goal in system design, and address multiplexing helps meet that goal, since physically smaller chips can be used with address multiplexing. A multiplexed memory system can be seen in the discussion on a real memory unit.

A Working Memory System

We are going to take a fairly major leap now and discuss a working memory system. This memory system, shown in Figure 10.11, is the memory unit of the Heath H-89A microcomputer. We will be going into a certain amount of depth in our discussion, so be sure that you follow the schematic closely. This will help you follow the operation of the unit as a whole.

The CPU (central processing unit), U504, makes up over 90% of the control circuitry. It is a *microprocessor*, a device that runs the programs stored in memory. Microprocessors are the subject of another chapter. For now, we will summarize the major points of the operation of this CPU as they relate to the operation of the memory circuitry:

1. The CPU supplies the address codes at its A0 through A15 outputs.
2. The $\overline{\text{MREQ}}$ output of the CPU goes low every time that it addresses memory.
3. The CPU has separate $\overline{\text{RD}}$ (read) and $\overline{\text{WR}}$ (write) outputs. One of these two outputs will be low, indicating a read or write operation. *They are never both low at the same time.*
4. The $\overline{\text{RFSH}}$ (refresh) output of the CPU is used to refresh the dynamic RAM.
5. The data pins on the CPU are bidirectional (i.e., they act as both inputs to and outputs from the CPU).

These are the only CPU outputs with which we will concern ourselves at this time. As the summary indicates, they act just as the control outputs that we have covered in previous discussions. Again, do not worry about when and why the CPU performs a given read or write operation. These points are covered in Chapter 14. For now, we are concerned only with the operation of the control, data, and address lines listed above and their relationship to the memory unit.

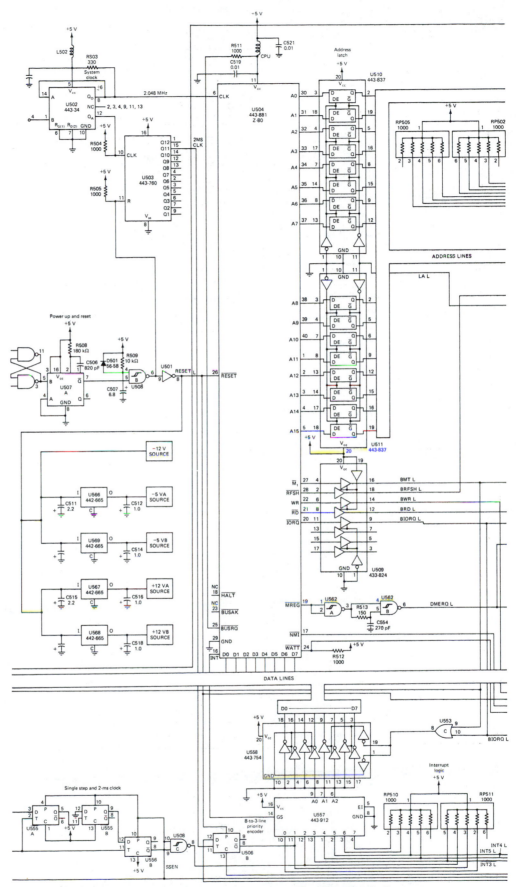

Figure 10.11 A complete memory unit. (© *1981 Heath Company.*
Reprinted by permission of Heath Company.)

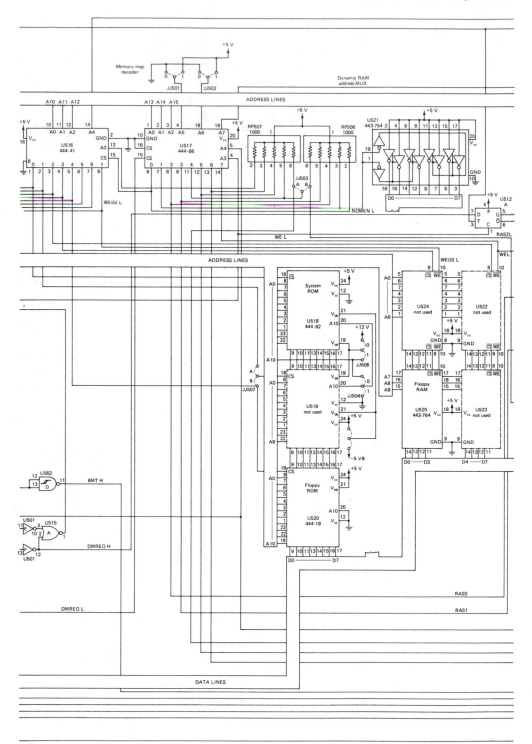

Figure 10.11   (Continued)

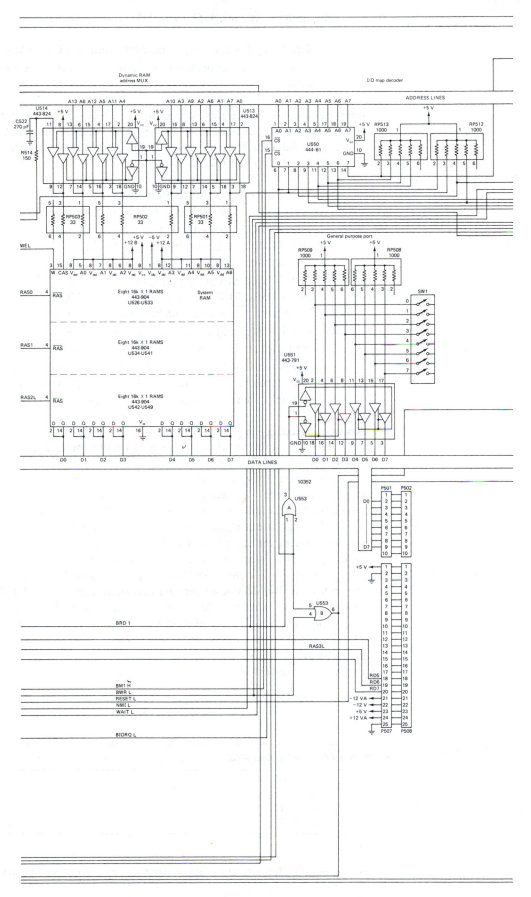

Figure 10.11 (Continued)

The *address latches*, U510 and U511, serve two purposes:

1. They amplify the output current from the CPU address outputs.
2. They hold the address values long enough for the memory to respond to them.

Since the address output pins have a fanout of 1 (a standard CPU address line fanout value) and the latches have a fanout of 10, current amplification is a natural result of using the latches. The way in which the latches hold an address is covered in the following operation summary:

1. When the CPU needs to address memory, it simultaneously places the address code on the address bus and drives $\overline{MREQ}$ low.
2. The $\overline{MREQ}$ is applied to a delay circuit, composed of U562A, U562B, R513, and C554. This circuit works just like the circuit discussed on page 57. The only difference is that the active output level is low.
3. The delayed $\overline{MREQ}$ signal (DMREQ L)[*] is applied to the address latches by way of U501F (Inverter) and U515A (NOR gate). The output from the NOR gate is the *latch address* (LA L) signal.
4. The LA L signal causes the address latches to accept the address bits at their inputs. The outputs of the address latches do not change at this time.
5. $\overline{MREQ}$ returns to the logic 1 state. This causes LA L to go high again. When LA L goes high, the address latch outputs change to the values that were entered. These values will stay until the foregoing process is repeated.

The delay used in the DMREQ L circuitry is there to provide time for the address bits to become stable on the address pins before the latches attempt to latch them. This entire process occurs every time that the CPU addresses memory.

The DMREQ is used for another purpose. If you trace the line past the U501 tie-off, you will see that this same signal is applied to U517. U517 is one of the memory decoders. This decoder is used to select the memory banks and needs a low input at pin 15 to operate. Immediately to the left of U517 is U516, another decoder that is used to select certain chips in bank zero. Both of the decoders are PROMs that are programmed to act as decoders. PROMs were used in place of decoders in this system to allow their input/output relationships to be changed if the system were ever modified. But do not let the fact that these chips are PROMs scare you. In this system, they act exactly as decoders. Based on the logic states of the A15 and A14 inputs (pins 4 and 3), U517 will enable either bank 1, bank 2, bank 3, or U516. When U516 is enabled by the zero output of U517 (pin 6), it decodes address bits A12, A11, and A10 to select a specific chip within bank zero. The input/output relationships of the two decoders are as follows:

For the U517:

Inputs (A15, A14, and A13)	Active output	Enabled memory
0 0 0	0	Bank 0 (U516)
0 1 0	2	Bank 1
0 1 1	3	Bank 2
1 0 0	4	Bank 3

[*]In this schematic, L is used to indicate an active-low line and H is used to indicate an active-high line.

For the U516:

Inputs (A12, A11, and A10)	Active output	Enabled memory
0 0 0	0	System ROM (U518)
0 0 1	1	U519 (not used)[a]
0 1 0	2	U522 (not used)
0 1 1	3	Floppy RAM (U525)[b]
1 0 0	4	Floppy ROM (U520)

[a]These sockets are provided for future additions to the machine.
[b]U525 receives its signal via the empty U524 socket, as shown on the bottom of the U524 socket in the diagram.

The rest of the outputs from the two chips are not used for the system configuration as it is. At this time, trace the outputs from the decoder PROMs to their destinations, and relate the wiring to the charts above.

Bank zero is shown as a group of separate chips in the schematic, while banks 1, 2, and 3 are shown in eight 16k × 1 blocks. Each block is essentially wired as the 16k × 8 blocks previously discussed. This system, however, uses address multiplexing to address RAM. As the schematic indicates, the RAM chips themselves have only seven address inputs. The 14 address bits needed to select one of the 16k locations in a given bank are multiplexed to the seven address pins via U513 and U514. These two chips are controlled by U512A.

As the schematic shows, the enable inputs (pins 1 and 19) are all wired together and controlled by the Q output of U512A. When U512A-5 (U512A, pin 5) is high, the buffers connected to A13, A12, A11, A10, A9, A8, and A7 are enabled by pin 19 on the buffer chips. The buffers connected to A6, A5, A4, A3, A2, A1, and A0 are disabled by pin 1. This is due to the fact that pin 19 is an active-high enable and pin 1 is an active-low enable. When the Q output (U512A-5) goes low, the situation is reversed. This means that when U512A is high, address bits A13 through A7 are applied to the RAM chips, and when U512A-5 is low, address bits A6 through A0 are applied to the RAM chips. U512A, then, determines when the groups of address bits are applied to RAM. At the same time, U512A performs another important operation: It provides the $\overline{CAS}$ signals for the RAM chips. When the Q output of U512A is high, the $\overline{Q}$ output of U512A (U512A-6) is low. This low is applied to the input to the leftmost buffer in U514. Since this buffer is enabled (by the high input at U514-19), the low is applied to the $\overline{CAS}$ input of the RAM chips. This signal, together with the other U513 and U514 outputs, provides the column addresses needed by the RAM chips. Note that when U512A-6 is high and U514-1 is low, an inactive-high level is applied to the $\overline{CAS}$ input of the RAM chips. This occurs while the row address is being applied to the chips.

Let's look now at how all of these circuits work in conjunction to select a given address:

1. The CPU provides the address select code and drives its $\overline{MREQ}$ output low. The low $\overline{MREQ}$ signal causes several things to happen:
   a. LA L is provided (via U501F and U515A) to the address latches (U510 and U511), causing the address bits to be entered into the latches.
   b. The DMREQ L signal enables U517.
   c. DMREQ H (the output of U501F) causes U512A to set. The flip-flop will actually change to the set condition after the next trigger input is provided by the system clock at the T input (U512A-3).
2. $\overline{MREQ}$ goes high again, causing the output of the address latches to change. At the same time, the decoders apply the $\overline{RAS}$ signal to the RAM, and the D input of U512A (U512A-2) goes low.

3. While the D input to U512A is low, the output of the chip is still Q = 1, since the next transition of the clock will be needed to RESET the flip-flop. With U512A-5 being high, the column address bits are entered into the RAM chips, as discussed previously.

4. When the next transition of the system clock causes U512A to RESET, the Q output goes low and the row address bits are passed through U513 and U514.

Once the desired location has been addressed, the read or write signal must be applied to the chips. Both of these signals are provided by U517. As the schematic shows, the $\overline{RD}$ and $\overline{RFSH}$ outputs from the CPU are applied to the A4 and A3 inputs of U517, respectively. If the $\overline{RD}$ output is low, U517-5 is low, and U517 responds by driving output line 7 (U517-14) high. This disables the $\overline{W}$ (write) input on the RAM chips. If the $\overline{RFSH}$ line goes low, the same results occur. If neither CPU line is low when memory is addressed, U517-14 goes low to write enable RAM. The logic behind this operation is actually relatively simple. The CPU addresses memory for one of three reasons: to get information from it (read), to refresh it, or to write information into it. If memory is being addressed and neither a read nor a refresh operation is being performed, it must be a write operation. The only other time that this line will be disabled (high), is when bank 0 is being addressed. If bank 0 is being addressed, there is no reason to write enable the other memory banks, so U517-14 will be high when bank 0 is addressed.

The system we have been discussing is far more complex than anything covered thus far. For this reason, you should go through this section several times over to be sure that you can follow the operation of the memory unit.

10.8   MEMORY MAPS

A memory map is a chart that is included in the documentation of a given computer, indicating which memory addresses are used for the given types of memory. Figure 10.12 shows the memory map for the H-89A. As the memory map indicates, the lowest 8K of memory is reserved for system memory (i.e., system RAM and ROM, and floppy RAM and ROM). The next 48k of memory is divided into three groups of 16k memory (banks 1, 2, and 3). The top 8k of memory is reserved for input/output device addresses and special programs. A breakdown of this section is shown as the I/O port map. We will not go into these addresses in depth at this point. We will only say that they are used to address input and output devices and to store the basic operating program for the entire system.

As the memory map indicates, no 64k system truly has 65,536 memory locations. Part of the address range must be used to address input and output locations. However, the number of addresses taken up for these devices is relatively small in most systems.

10.9   TESTING AND TROUBLESHOOTING THE ENTIRE UNIT

Let's face it. Troubleshooting a memory unit can lead to nervous disorders. The most difficult problems to find in a microcomputer all seem to enjoy hanging around in memory. But while prayer has often been suggested as the first step in troubleshooting memory, you will find that following a proven procedure will almost always do the trick.

Troubleshooting memory usually boils down to finding out not what the problem is, but what it isn't. If you can eliminate 90% of the logic circuits as the cause

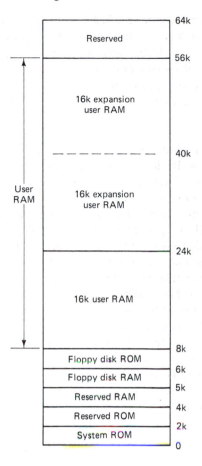

Figure 10.12 Heath H-89A memory map, illustrating the use of the specified memory locations. (© *1981 Heath Company. Reprinted by permission of Heath Company.)*

of the problem, you can play "chip swapping" with the rest in a relatively short period of time. Although chip swapping is considered to be the easy way out in troubleshooting in general, you will find that there is almost no way to get around it when troubleshooting memory. About the only way to get around it is to invest in a logic analyzer or a new computer, and neither of those options is nearly cost-effective enough.

The basic procedure for troubleshooting memory involves several steps that are designed to eliminate the major groups of possible problems in a systematic order. The series of checks that should be made are listed here in the order in which they should be performed:

1. Perform a sensory check of the entire memory unit.
2. Check the V_{cc} and ground connections within the unit.
3. Check all control lines in the unit.
4. Check all address lines.
5. Check all data lines.

The first three checks are not only the easiest to perform, but they eliminate the majority of possible problems. Whatever you do, never skip any of these checks, as you may increase your work load considerably as a result. We will now cover each type of check, how it is performed, and what to look for.

Sensory Checks

A great deal of time and trouble can be saved by using the two natural troubleshooting tools that every technician has: your sense of sight and your sense of touch.

A visual check of the following should be a standard check, regardless of which unit of the microcomputer is being tested. Look for:

Burned or split copper runs on the printed-circuit board
Burned resistors and capacitors
Burned IC chips
Touching components
Loose connectors
Wires loose in their sockets

Burned copper runs and components will be easily visible. When a burned copper run is seen, be sure to replace all chips that are connected to that run if no bad chip can be seen. This must be done to ensure that the component which caused the copper run to burn is removed and replaced. A burned copper run is easily repaired by bridging the burned point with 22- or 24-gage wire. Be sure to remove the copper that has lifted from the board before bridging the gap.

A group of circuits can be made to malfunction by two or more components touching each other. Check to be sure that no components are shorting out.

Touching the ICs in the circuit can tell you if any of them are drawing excessive current. *Be careful to touch the ICs quickly and lightly, as prolonged contact with hot ICs can cause severe burns!* If you feel an extremely hot IC, replace it. Realize that most ICs get fairly hot in the course of normal operation. The clue to a given IC drawing excessive current is that the IC will be much hotter than any other IC in the area. If none of these checks produces any tangible results, you must continue with the procedure given for troubleshooting the unit.

Checking the Control Lines

After checking the V_{cc} and ground connections in the memory unit, you should check the control lines. As with all signal checks, V_{cc}, ground, and the control line signals should be checked using an oscilloscope, as outlined in Chapter 6. Also, remember that *all electronic signals should be checked directly on the IC chip pins whenever possible.* Just because a signal is getting to a socket does not necessarily mean that it is getting to the IC. IC sockets and pins can oxidize over a period of time, having the same effect as an open circuit. When this happens, try using contact cleaner on the socket and the IC pins. If that does not work, both the IC and the socket may have to be replaced.

The first step in checking the control signals is to identify *every* one of them. Missing a single control signal can cause you to miss the fault completely. For example, refer back to the circuit in Figure 10.11. In this circuit, the following points should be checked:

U510-11	U511-11	U517-15	U517-4	U517-5	U516-15
U514-19	U514-1	U513-19	U513-1		

For the circuit shown, these are the main control lines and would have the largest overall effect on the memory unit. After these are checked, you would check the $\overline{CS}$ and R/$\overline{W}$ signal on all the chips, together with the $\overline{CAS}$ and $\overline{RAS}$ signals. If at any point, you detect a bad signal, trace the bad signal back to its origin, using the techniques discussed in Chapter 3.

In any system, the main control lines are those which enable buffers, latches, and decoders. These are the types of control lines that were listed above. Once the main control lines are eliminated, check the individual chip control lines. If all the control lines in the memory unit prove themselves to be good, you must go on to the next step in the overall procedure.

Checking the Address Lines

The address lines must be checked at every IC to which they are connected. Under normal circumstances, these lines will display signals that resemble the "garbage" signals discussed in Chapter 6. There are, however, some differences. First, the address signals decrease in frequency as the number of the address line increases. For example, A15 would have a much lower frequency than Al. Therefore, you must constantly change the TIME/DIV setting on your oscilloscope as you go higher on the bus. Otherwise, you may think that an address line is stuck at a given level when it is not. Also, the address bus of a given microcomputer will be made up of three-state lines. If one address pin on a memory chip seems to be floating, there is probably a problem at the chip. If all address bus lines are floating, the control unit is the source of the trouble, not the memory unit.

Checking the Data Lines

If you have gotten to this point in the troubleshooting procedure and still have not found the problem, you are in deep trouble. The main difficulty in troubleshooting data lines is the fact that there a bad signal on any line could be coming from either the control unit or any one of the other circuits that are connected to it. As a result, it is difficult and time consuming to determine the source of a fault on a given data line.

Data lines are the same as the others. Their signals will appear as strange or stranger than any of the control or address lines. If a data line is bad, it will be stuck at one level or another. When you detect a bad data line, take a known good RAM chip and use it to replace the other chips. Each time you put the chip in, try to run the computer. If it does not run, you have replaced a good chip and must replace the next. This process should continue until every RAM chip has been removed and replaced by a good chip once, or until the problem corrects itself. If the problem corrects itself, you have located the bad chip. If all chips have been systematically replaced and the memory still does not work, the ROM chips must be replaced.

SUMMARY

Troubleshooting memory is one of the hardest procedures to master, due to the fact that a majority of the lines in memory are common to all of the memory chips. Luckily, most microcomputer malfunctions are located in the other units of the system. Memory chips in general draw little current, and thus tend to last a long time. However, when memory chips do go bad, a long and tiring troubleshooting procedure is usually required.

There are some microcomputer symptoms that tend to be caused by memory malfunctions. Although they are not always caused by memory, they are in a majority of cases. The first symptom is the random printing of characters on the CRT. These will be all types of characters, with no rhyme or reason as to where they appear. This problem is usually caused by RAM malfunctions. Another symptom is random audio tones. Almost every microcomputer has an audio tone that is sounded whenever a key is pressed. If this tone occurs at random intervals without any keys being pressed, the problem is *probably* memory. A third symptom is output devices turning on and off. For example, the disk drive or printer may turn on and off for no apparent reason.

The biggest key to troubleshooting memory is to be patient. If you get frustrated, you will stop thinking. If while troubleshooting any system or circuit, you feel yourself getting frustrated, leave the problem for awhile. You may find that the problem will be much easier to find after you return.

QUESTIONS

1. What is a memory cell?
2. What indicates a memory problem?
3. What is an address?
4. What is a bidirectional bus?
5. What two microcomputer operations are performed on memory?
6. What are the steps involved in a read operation? A write operation?
7. What is a memory word?
8. What is random access memory? What is it usually called?
9. What is meant by the term *volatile*? *Nonvolatile*?
10. What type of internal memory is volatile? Which is nonvolatile?
11. What type of control signal is not sent to ROM?
12. In terms of memory, what does "k" stand for?
13. How many bits would be stored in a 64k $\times$ 8 memory? What does "64k $\times$ 8" mean?
14. Discuss the ROM applications.
15. What are the three types of ROM? When is each used?
16. How can you identify an EPROM?
17. How are each of the ROM types programmed?
18. What is a bootstrap program?
19. What is static RAM?
20. What is dynamic RAM? When is dynamic RAM used?
21. What is the advantage of using dynamic RAM? The disadvantage?
22. What is a refresh cycle?
23. Discuss the address decoding in the circuit shown in Figure 10.8.
24. Explain why only one bank in Figure 10.8 can be enabled at any given point in time.
25. In the circuit in Figure 10.8, why is special decoding needed for bank 0?
26. What is *address multiplexing*? Why is it used?
27. Refer to Figure 10.11. Trace back to its origin the signal at each of the circuit points listed below.

U512A-2	U526-4	U510-11	U534-4
U526-6	U523-10	U527-15	U513-19

28. What is a memory map? What is it used for?
29. List and discuss each of the steps involved in troubleshooting a memory unit.

11

Microcomputers and Microprocessors

A microcomputer is a complete data processing machine that is housed in a relatively small physical casing. This machine contains all five of the functional units of a computer: the control unit, the ALU, the input unit, the output unit, and memory. Advances in integrated circuit technology have made the microcomputer possible by drastically increasing the number of circuits that can be constructed in a single chip. But of all the advances, none have matched the advent of the *microprocessor*. The microprocessor, or *central processing unit* (CPU), is a single chip that contains both the control unit and the ALU of the computer. Two units of the computer that once made up a large bulk of the system are now housed within a single chip.

This chapter deals with the microprocessor and how it controls the various units of the microcomputer. Although emphasis is placed on a specific microprocessor, the Motorola MC6800, the principles covered relate in one way or another to the vast majority of the general-purpose CPUs on the market today.

11.1 THE COMPLETE MICROCOMPUTER

Before discussing the microprocessor as a control unit, we must first take a look at how each of the functional units of the microcomputer relates to the control unit. Since each of the units has its own specific purpose and operating characteristics, each requires a special type of signal relationship with the CPU. In this section we discuss these signal requirements and the way in which the CPU deals with them.

The Memory Unit

Chapter 10 introduced you to the signals that the CPU supplies to memory and the types of operations that the CPU performs on memory. As a summary, the CPU must be able to:

1. Address memory locations.
2. Read data from and write data into memory.
3. Determine the direction of data flow.
4. Enable the chips as required to perform a given operation.
5. Interpret the information read from memory to determine whether it is data or an instruction to be performed.
6. When retrieving an instruction from memory, the CPU must be able to perform the operation called for.

Most of the requirements listed above can be met by the address bus, the R/$\overline{\text{W}}$ line, and the enable signals provided by the CPU. The data bus is used to transfer information to and from the memory unit as well as the input/output (I/O) devices. As the last two requirements would indicate, the CPU must be able to do more than provide control and addressing signals. It must also be able to *fetch* (read) and *execute* (perform) instructions. How the CPU responds to the various instructions that are stored in memory is the subject of Chapter 13. This topic can be very interesting, and has been the subject of entire books. However you do not really need to know how or why the CPU responds to a given instruction to be able to fix a down system. Although a knowledge of the internal workings of the CPU is a valuable asset, the microcomputer can still be dealt with effectively by the technician who has only a "black box" understanding of the microprocessor. Treating the microprocessor as a black box means that it is treated strictly as a source of signals that the rest of the system needs. At this level of analysis, the only information required by the technician can be summed up as follows:

1. What are the control signals, and what do they do?
2. How are these control signals wired into the system?
3. When the control signals are at their active levels, are the circuits to which they are connected responding as they should?

Having the answers to these questions will allow the technician to troubleshoot the system effectively.

We are going to start our analysis of microprocessors on the basis of this black box approach. In following chapters we take a more in-depth approach. In terms of memory, a black box approach views the CPU as a source of the signals required to fulfill the first four items listed at the start of this section. These requirements can be met using the address bus, the data bus, the R/$\overline{\text{W}}$ line, and a $\overline{\text{CS}}$ line. As long as the CPU is providing the needed signals on these lines, it is fulfilling its signal requirements for memory.

The Input Unit

The input unit of the microcomputer must be able to enter information into the system when the user is ready to do so. This means that the input devices must not only be able to transfer information to the CPU or memory, but must also be able to let the CPU know that there is information to be entered into the system. The input unit does this using a signal called an *interrupt*. An interrupt signal is simply a logic level that is placed on a specific control input to the CPU. When the CPU receives an interrupt signal, it responds by sending back a signal called an *interrupt acknowledge*. In many cases, the interrupt acknowledge is nothing more than a $\overline{\text{CS}}$ signal that is sent to the input unit. When this acknowledge signal is received by the input unit, it transfers the information that the user entered to the CPU. For example, assume that you are starting to enter information into a microcomputer using the system's keyboard. The general sequence of events within the system would be as follows:

1. The input circuitry detects that a key has been pressed.
2. The input circuitry simultaneously accepts the keyboard input, decodes it, and sends an interrupt signal to the CPU, indicating that information is available.
3. The CPU stops its present activities and sends an interrupt acknowledge signal back to the input unit, indicating that it is ready to accept the information.
4. The input device transfers the information to the CPU, then goes back to the keyboard to get the next value. If there is another one, the process above is repeated.

Outside of the interrupt sequence, the process above is basically a read operation. For all practical purposes, the CPU is providing a $\overline{CS}$ signal to a memory location (in this case, the input unit) and reading the information that is available from that location. When a given system treats the input and output locations like a memory location, the setup is called *memory-mapped I/O*. In memory-mapped I/O, the CPU does nothing to distinguish an input or output device from any memory location. The CPU would always read an input device by selecting it, sending it the equivalent of a read signal, and then taking in the data that the device puts on the data bus.

The situation is somewhat complicated by the fact that there is usually more than one input device on a given microcomputer. This means that the CPU must be able to distinguish which device is interrupting it and to deal with that device in its own special way. A disk drive, for example, would have to be treated differently than a keyboard, since the disk drive has a totally different data transfer method.

The bottom line is that the CPU must be able to do several things in order to deal effectively with the various input devices that the system may have. The CPU must be able to:

1. Accept interrupt signals
2. Determine the source of the interrupt
3. Acknowledge the interrupt signal
4. Read the input device as it would a memory location

In terms of physical connections, the CPU must therefore use the address bus, the data bus, and have an interrupt input and an interrupt acknowledge output.

The Output Unit

Just as a given system usually has more than one input device, it usually has more than one output device. Again, an addressing and data transfer capability is required. However, the output devices are handled in a manner opposite to that of the input devices. Rather than reading data from an output device, the CPU only writes data into it.

There is no need to have an interrupt input from an output device, but the CPU must be capable of enabling the device. This is usually done with a $\overline{CS}$ signal.

The control unit needs no special wiring to the ALU (arithmetic/logic unit) in a microcomputer, since both are housed in the microprocessor. However, the list of what the microprocessor must be able to do with the external microcomputer units is extensive enough. A summary of CPU functions is as follows:

1. The CPU must be able to address *all* memory, input, and output locations.
2. The CPU must be able to perform data transfers between itself and all external computer units.
3. The CPU must be able to respond to interrupt inputs.
4. The CPU must be able to enable any chips necessary to complete a given operation.
5. The CPU must be able to interpret instructions and carry them out.

Exactly when the CPU does each and every one of the foregoing operations is determined by the programming of the system. Microcomputer programming is covered in a later chapter. For now, we will look only at those signals and signal paths that are provided by the CPU.

11.2 THE MICROPROCESSOR AS THE CONTROL UNIT: THE MC6800

The Motorola MC6800 is an 8-bit microprocessor with 64k addressing capability. An 8-bit CPU is one that handles 8-bit data words and instructions. The Intel 8080, the Zilog Z80, and the MC6800 are three of the most popular 8-bit CPUs on the market. Although they do not all operate in the same fashion, you will see that they are very similar—so similar, in fact, that the average technician, after learning the operation of one, can work effectively on any system containing any of the three.

The MC6800 pin configuration is shown in Figure 11.1. The arrow directions indicate whether a given line is an input or an output. No arrow indicates that the pin is either a supply pin or is not used.

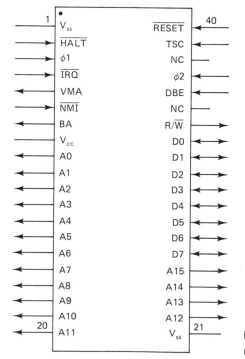

Figure 11.1 MC6800 microprocessor. *(Courtesy of Motorola, Inc.)*

As you can see, the MC6800 has 40 pins. Of these, 16 are address pins, 8 are bidirectional data pins, 8 are control inputs, 3 are control outputs, and 3 are voltage supply pins. Two pins on the chip (pins 35 and 38) are not internally connected and are left as open pins in the circuit. In discussing the MC6800, we will break the pins down into several groups and deal with these groups on an individual basis. The pin groups are:

Voltage supply pins
Clock pins
Control inputs
Control outputs
Address and data buses

Voltage Supply Pins

The MC6800 is a TTL-compatible CPU, and thus uses TTL-level supply voltages. Pin 8 is the V_{cc} connection and is wired to the system's $+5$-V supply. There are two ground (V_{ss}) pins, pins 1 and 21. These two pins must *both* be wired to ground in order for the device to work. This is due to the internal construction of the chip. Pin 1 supplies a ground path to one half of the chip, and pin 21 provides the ground path for the rest. If either of these pins are open, the device will malfunction.

Clock Pins

The MC6800 has two clock inputs, labeled $\phi1$ (pin 3) and $\phi2$ (pin 37). The clock signals fed to these two inputs must be 180° out of phase and must be *nonoverlapping*. This means that they cannot *both* be at a logic 1 level at any point in time. Two nonoverlapping clock signals can be seen in Figure 11.2. Note that although they can be changing states at the same time, they are always at opposite logic levels. The two-phase clock signal used by the MC6800 is usually generated by some type of external clock generating circuit. One such circuit, the MC6875, is covered later. For now, the important point is the fact that the CPU requires two clock signals that are 180° out of phase.

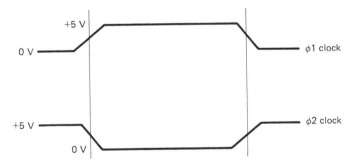

Figure 11.2 Two-phase nonoverlapping clock.

Control Inputs

At this point, we will not go into an extensive discussion of the uses for each of the control inputs. Specific applications are discussed later in the chapter. For now, we will only identify each of the lines.

$\overline{RESET}$ *(pin 40):* Causes the CPU to restart its operation when low. The CPU responds to this input by going indirectly to a specified program and running that program. This input is usually activated when the system is first turned on.

$\overline{HALT}$ (pin 2):	Causes the CPU to go into an "idle" state. When this input goes low, the CPU will finish its current operation and will then float its address pins, data pins, and R/$\overline{W}$ line, all of which are three-state pins. The chip will stay in this idle state until the low at pin 2 is removed.
DBE (pin 36):	*Data bus enable.* This input, which is normally tied high, causes the CPU to float its data bus and R/$\overline{W}$ line when low.
TSC (pin 39):	*Three-state control.* This input, when high, causes the CPU to float the address bus and the R/$\overline{W}$ line.
$\overline{IRQ}$ (pin 4):	*Interrupt request.* This interrupt causes the CPU to go indirectly to a specified memory address and start running the program that starts at that address.
$\overline{NMI}$ (pin 6):	*Nonmaskable interrupt.* Another interrupt input that does basically the same thing as $\overline{IRQ}$. This input, however, has priority over the other interrupt and goes to a different address to gets its instructions.

The interrupt inputs are discussed in detail in a later section, as will applications of the other control inputs.

The Control Outputs

The control outputs are pins that carry signals which are used to direct the activities of the external circuits. As you will see, there are not a great number of them. However, they combine to perform all the external signaling capability that the chip needs.

BA (pin 7):	*Bus available.* This signal is used to indicate to the external devices that the CPU has floated its buses and R/$\overline{W}$ line.
VMA (pin 5):	*Valid memory address.* This signal indicates that the CPU has a valid address on its address bus. It is an active-high output.
$\overline{READ/WRITE}$ (pin 34):	Directs the direction of data flow within the computer. Goes high during a read operation and low during a write operation. This is a three-state line.

The Address Bus and Data Bus

The address and data bus pins are all three-state in nature and will be floated under the circumstances discussed previously. The address bus is unidirectional (i.e., the signal flow is always out of the chip). The data bus is bidirectional and the R/$\overline{W}$ line always indicates which state the bus is in. If R/$\overline{W}$ = 1, the CPU is performing a read operation and the data bus is in the input mode, as seen from the CPU. If R/$\overline{W}$ = 0, the CPU is in the write mode and the data pins are acting as CPU outputs.

The address and data pins all have a TTL fanout of 1. This means that one of these pins can drive only one TTL input. For this reason the address bus is usually buffered, increasing the fanout to 10. The data bus does not need to be buffered, since only one circuit will be connected to it at any given point in time. For example, refer to Figure 11.3. This shows the basic address and data bus connections in a block form. It has been stated before that the control unit (in this case, the CPU) will enable only one of the circuits connected to its data bus at a time. Because only one circuit

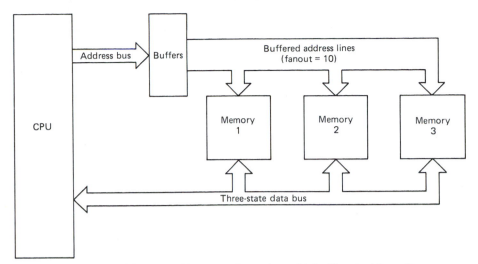

Figure 11.3   Memory address configuration with buffered address lines.

will be enabled and the rest will be in the three-state condition, the fanout of the data bus does not need to be any greater than 1. The address bus, on the other hand, must supply addresses to all the circuits at the same time. In the case of the circuit shown, the required fanout from the address pins on the CPU would be 3. To supply this needed driving current, buffers would have to be placed on the address bus. Otherwise, the CPU would not be able to drive the address inputs of the various circuits to which it is connected.

Again, we will not concern ourselves at this point with how the CPU knows when to perform certain operations. We will deal only with how the various lines can be used to control the other units of the computer. These control-line applications will be discussed next. Although they do not cover every possible application for every control line, they will help you better understand how they are used in a typical system.

Control Line Applications

Figure 11.4 shows the MC6800 being used as the control unit of a simple microcomputer system. For ease of discussion, all of the other microcomputer units have been represented in block form, and only those lines necessary to complete the control requirements discussed previously have been included.

The memory unit is connected, as usual, to the address and data buses. Also, the $R/\overline{W}$ output (pin 34) has been connected to all RAM locations. The decoder, D1, is being used to enable one of the four memory banks. The decoder itself is three-state in nature and is enabled by the VMA output (pin 5) of the CPU. Recall that this output goes high whenever there is a valid address on the address bus. This high is inverted and connected to the enable input of the memory decoder. This will prevent the decoder from having an output when there is no valid address on the address bus. These connections take care of the signals required by the memory unit.

The input unit needs a method by which it can interrupt the CPU, as was stated earlier. This requirement has been met by the $\overline{IRQ}$ and $\overline{NMI}$ inputs to the CPU, pins 4 and 6, respectively. The disk drive has been connected to the $\overline{IRQ}$ input, and the keyboard has been connected to the $\overline{NMI}$ input. Since the $\overline{NMI}$ input is the higher-priority input, the keyboard has the higher priority. Priority of the input devices is a condition that is determined by the system designer (i.e., the input devices that are connected to the priority interrupts are determined by the system designer). The priority of the inputs themselves is a function of the internal wiring of the MC6800.

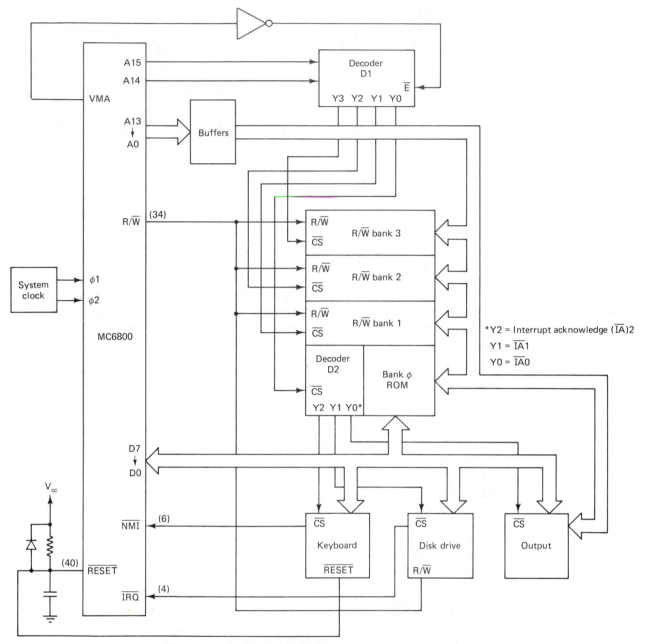

Figure 11.4 Basic MC6800 microcomputer system.

When an interrupt is received by the CPU, it sets an internal flip-flop, called a *flag*. When the interrupt flag is SET, the interrupt input ($\overline{\text{IRQ}}$) is disabled, or *masked*. The $\overline{\text{NMI}}$ input cannot be blocked by this mask—thus the name "nonmaskable interrupt." While an input at the $\overline{\text{NMI}}$ input will SET the interrupt flag, the input itself will not be blocked by it. Only the $\overline{\text{IRQ}}$ pin will be affected. In summary:

1. The $\overline{\text{NMI}}$ input will set the interrupt flag, which will prevent any input at the $\overline{\text{IRQ}}$ input from being accepted.

2. An input at the $\overline{\text{IRQ}}$ input will set the interrupt flag, which will prevent another $\overline{\text{IRQ}}$ input from being accepted but will not stop a $\overline{\text{NMI}}$ input.

When the CPU has run the program to "service" the interrupting device, it RESETs the interrupt flag automatically, enabling another $\overline{\text{IRQ}}$ input to be accepted.

The interrupt acknowledge is nothing more than a $\overline{CS}$ signal. The input circuitry will not be able to transfer information to the CPU until this signal is received. The address and data buses are connected to the input devices just as they are to the other units.

The output unit is connected just like a memory location, except that it needs no R/$\overline{W}$ connection. This is because the output unit only accepts information from the CPU. It never transfers data *to* the CPU. There are other connections that would be used in a more sophisticated system, but for now, the system just discussed will make the necessary points.

The clock inputs are shown to be driven by the system clock. Although the system clock may also be connected to the other microcomputer units, it is not shown in this configuration. The clock circuit shown would generate the needed two-phase clock system, thus supplying both the $\phi1$ and the $\phi2$ clock signals.

The $\overline{RESET}$ input to the CPU is connected to both the keyboard and a power-up circuit. This circuit, which was discussed in Chapter 4, is used to RESET the CPU at power-up. This would cause the system to run its bootstrap program. Recall that the bootstrap program is the initial program required by the computer in order to operate correctly when power is first applied.

In the circuit in Figure 11.4, the DBE, BA, and TSC inputs to the CPU are not connected to anything. These inputs would only be used in a computer system that contained other circuits that needed to take control of the address and data buses. Such a system is discussed in a later chapter.

The MC6800 has been shown to be capable of supplying the basic control signals needed by a simple microcomputer system. As we progress in our discussion of microprocessors and microcomputers, increasingly sophisticated connections between the CPU and the rest of the system units will be shown and discussed.

11.3 A WORKING MICROCOMPUTER SYSTEM: THE ET-3400 TRAINER

The ET-3400 is an educational microcomputer designed and manufactured by Heath Company. The system is designed to be simple, yet contain all of the basic working elements of a complete microcomputer system. The schematic diagram of the ET-3400 is shown in Figure 11.5. For our discussion, we will break the ET-3400 down into five groups of circuits:

The control unit (IC11, IC19, IC4, IC5, IC7, IC8, and IC6)

The memory unit (IC12, IC14, and IC15)

The input unit (IC13 and the keyboard)

The output unit (IC23 through IC28, and the seven-segment displays)

The memory decoding circuitry (IC2, IC3, IC20, IC21, and IC22)

As you can see, there are many more chips and circuits on the schematic than are listed above. These circuits, although part of the system, are not a part of the units that we are attempting to analyze. For this reason, their functions are mentioned briefly at the end of this section. At this point, we will discuss the units listed above.

The Memory Unit

Memory for this system is comprised of ROM (IC12) and RAM (IC14 and IC15). The ROM is a 1024 × 8-bit ROM. This can be determined by the fact that it has 10 address inputs (A0 through A9)* and eight data inputs (D0 through D7). With

---

*The rest of the address connections to the ROM are CS inputs and are not used to address internal locations.

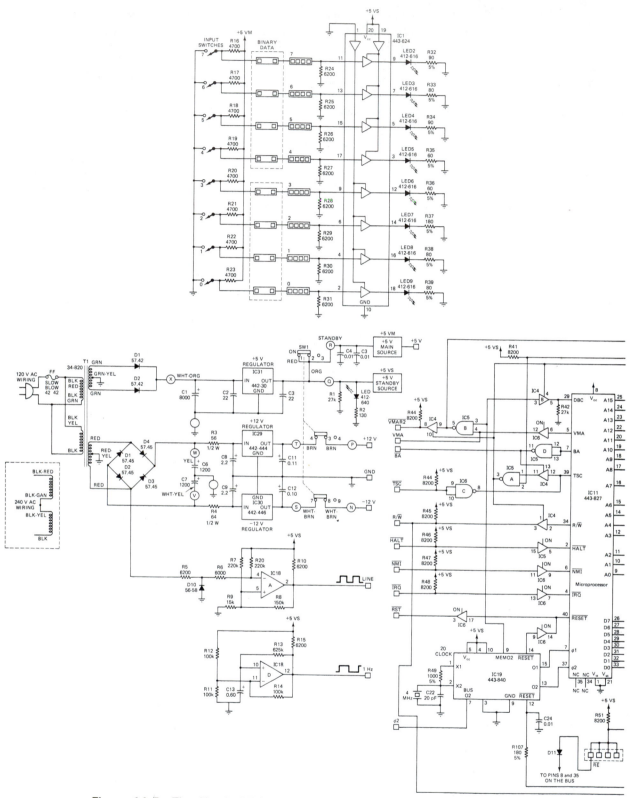

Figure 11.5 The Heath ET-3400 microcomputer. (© 1981 Heath Company. Reprinted by permission of Heath Company.)

10 address inputs, you have $2^{10} = 1024$ locations; and the eight data pins indicate that each word is 8 bits.

The RAM can be analyzed in the same basic fashion. With eight address inputs, there must be $2^8 = 256$ locations. It would appear at first that the system is using 4-bit words (judging by the number of data pins on the RAM chips), but the system is using 8-bit words. If you look closely, you will see that data bits D0 through D3 are being stored in IC15, and data bits D4 through D7 are being stored in IC14. The system therefore has a 256×8 RAM setup.

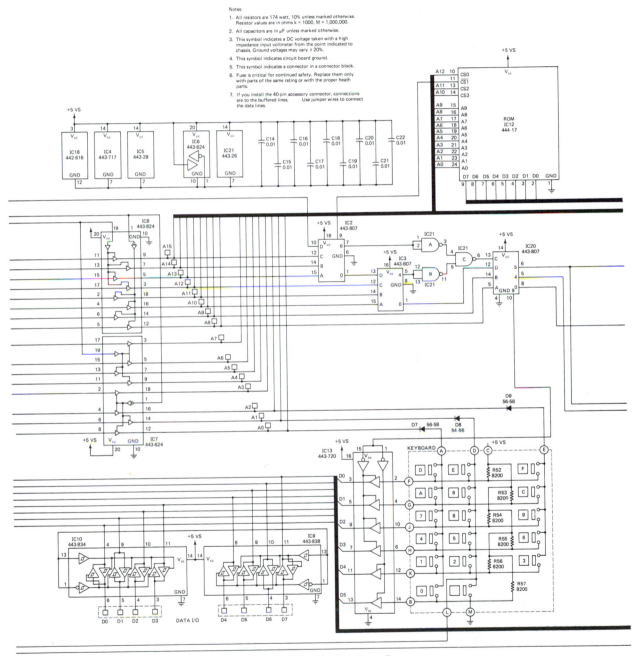

Figure 11.5 (Continued)

The enable lines for the two memory groups come from the memory decoding circuitry. First, take a look at the ROM, IC12. This chip has four CS inputs, labeled CS0 through CS3. Of the four, three are active-high inputs and one is an active-low input ($\overline{CS1}$). Note how the active-high CS inputs are all tied to their active level, while

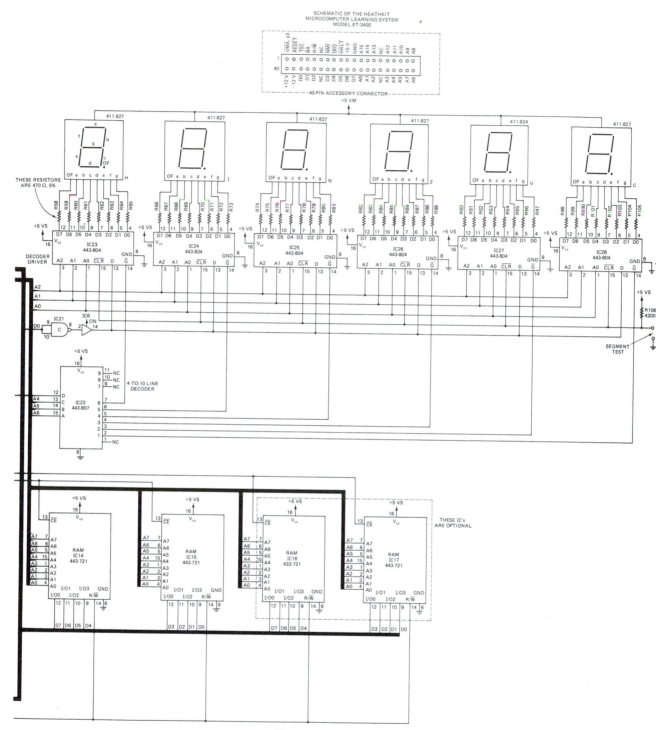

Figure 11.5 (Continued)

the active-low CS input is the one tied to the memory decoding circuitry. This configuration is not at all uncommon. Many ROM chips have several CS inputs, some of which are active-high and some of which are low. *When more than one CS input is present, the active-low input is always the one that is driven by the memory decoding circuitry.* This prevents the chip from ever being enabled by an open wire, which will act as a logic 1 in a TTL system. In this system, the active-low $\overline{CS1}$ input to ROM is driven by IC2-9. Even though the $\overline{CS1}$ input looks like it is connected to the address bus, it actually continues on the other side of it.

The $\overline{\text{CE}}$ (chip enable) inputs to the RAM chips are driven by IC20-5. Note that the $\overline{\text{CE}}$ inputs to the two chips are tied together, so they will always be in the same operating state (i.e., they will both be either enabled or disabled). The R/$\overline{\text{W}}$ inputs to RAM (pin 14) are connected to IC11 (the CPU) via IC4A. The output from pin 34 of the CPU is buffered by IC4A to increase its fanout before being applied to the RAM chips.

The Input Unit

The input unit consists solely of the keyboard and IC13. Although this is a relatively small amount of circuitry to have to deal with, the operation of the unit takes a bit of explaining.

First, take a look at the keyboard. The keyboard is set up in a column-by-row matrix, consisting of three columns and six rows. At the intersection of each row and column, there is a key that will connect the two wires when pressed. For example, if the "8" key is pressed, the "D" column wire will be connected to the "J" row wire. The "0" key will cause a connection between the "C" column wire and the "B" row wire when pressed. (Note that the "0" key is the only key connected to the "B" wire. The RESET key bypasses the wire, as will be discussed.)

When the CPU is checking the keyboard for an input, it does so by "scanning" the columns. This is done by putting the following sequence of addresses on the A2, A1, and A0 lines:

A2	A1	A0
0	1	1
1	1	0
1	0	1

In this address code sequence, only one of the three columns will have a low on it at any given time. When you press a given key, the low will go through that key to one of the row wires. With IC13 being enabled, that low will be applied to one of the data inputs of the CPU, indicating that a key has been pressed. The CPU then uses the address value and the data value to determine which key has been pressed. For example, the sequence of events that would occur when the "C" key is pressed would be as follows:

1. The key is pressed, connecting the "E" column wire to the "G" row wire.
2. The CPU enables IC13 (using the memory decoding circuitry) and puts its data pins into the input mode.
3. The first address code (011) is placed on the three least significant bits of the address bus. Since the 0 is not applied to the column containing the pressed key, it cannot get to IC13. This is due to the fact that the zero must get to one of the row wires to be applied to IC13, and the zero can get to the row wires only if a key is pressed in that column. As a result, the output from IC13 is 111111, which the CPU will ignore.
4. The next code is applied to the address bus. The 110 combination of bits puts a zero on the "E" column. This low goes through the "C" key to the "G" row wire, and on to the IC13-4 (D1) input. The output code from the buffer is then 111101.
5. The CPU detects the 0 on the data bus and determines that a key has been pressed. It then uses the address code and the data value to determine which key has been pressed.

IC13 is a three-state buffer that is enabled by IC20-10. When this line is low, IC13 is enabled and the CPU will scan the keyboard for an input. When it does not need to scan the keyboard, the CPU will disable IC13 through the memory decoding circuitry. Since IC13 is connected only to the keyboard, it should be obvious that it is used only when the keyboard is being scanned by the CPU.

The keyboard itself is a hexadecimal keyboard that is decoded by the CPU into 4 bit values. The C key, for example, would be decoded by the CPU as 1100. . ., the binary equivalent of the hexadecimal value C. All of the other keys would be decoded the same way, so two keys must be pressed to enter an 8-bit value into the microcomputer. For example, assume that you wanted to enter the value 10110010 into the system. This would be entered by pressing B2 on the keyboard. The CPU would decode the two keys into their individual 4-bit values, then combine the two to form an 8-bit word. This, again, is a function of the system programming.

The Output Unit

The output unit consists of six seven-segment displays, six decoder/drivers, and IC22, an enable decoder. IC22 is a 4-to-10-line decoder which will drive one of its output lines low, depending on the binary input at A through D. For example, if the input code is 0110, output line 6 (pin 7) will be low and the rest of the output lines will be high. The output lines from the decoder go to the enable ($\overline{G}$) inputs of the decoder/drivers. They are used in this case to enable the decoder/driver inputs, not the outputs.

The decoder/drivers are actually octal D-type flip-flops, meaning that each chip consists of eight D-type flip-flops. Data bits are stored in the flip-flops to either turn on or turn off a given display segment. For example, refer to the blown up IC23 and display configuration shown in Figure 11.6. Each Q output from IC23 is used to drive a specific segment in the display. At each Q output, a low causes the appropriate segment to light, and a high causes the segment to be off. Tracing the wires out of IC23 to the display inputs will show you which Q output drives a specific segment. For example, the Q_7 output is connected to the DP (decimal point) input of the display. If Q_7 is low, the DP LED will light. If Q_7 is high, the DP LED will be off. An entire value is displayed by having the proper LEDs in a given segment lit. For example, to display the number "2" on the display, the following conditions must exist:

$$DP = Q_7 = \text{off} \quad (1)$$
$$A = Q_6 = \text{on} \quad (0)$$
$$B = Q_5 = \text{on} \quad (0)$$
$$C = Q_4 = \text{off} \quad (1)$$
$$D = Q_3 = \text{on} \quad (0)$$
$$E = Q_2 = \text{on} \quad (0)$$
$$F = Q_1 = \text{off} \quad (1)$$
$$G = Q_0 = \text{on} \quad (0)$$

Note that the low outputs correspond to the segments that would have to be lit for the display to show the number 2. This means that the values 10010010 would have to be stored in IC23 in order to display the desired value. These bits are stored in the decoder/drivers by the CPU performing the following sequence of operations:

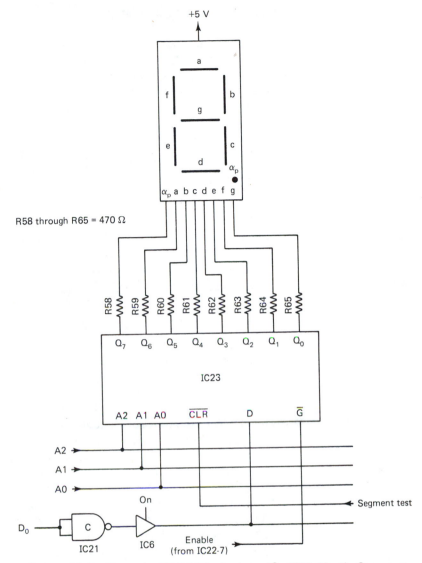

Figure 11.6 Example ET-3400 display. (© *1981 Heath Company. Reprinted by permission of Heath Company.*)

1. The CPU would enable the inputs to the decoder by driving U22-7 low. This is done through the memory decoding circuitry.

2. With IC23 enabled, the CPU addresses each flip-flop in the chip using the A2, A1, and A0 connections to the chip. With three address bits connected to IC23, the CPU can address $2^3 = 8$ locations—the number of flip-flops within the chip. As each location is addressed, the CPU enters the needed value into the decoder/driver.

3. After all bits have been written into the decoder/driver, the CPU enables the next decoder/driver, and repeats the process using the needed values for the display.

4. After all displays have been lit using the needed values, the CPU disables IC22. This decoder will remain disabled until the CPU needs to enter new values in the display decoder/drivers.

The foregoing process is a function of another program in the system. This program is run only when the CPU needs to enter data into the displays.

The Memory Decoding Circuitry

The memory decoding circuitry is made up of three 4-to-10-line decoders (IC2, IC3, and IC20), and the NAND gates (IC21). The memory decoding circuitry is used to supply a $\overline{CS}$ signal to the proper parts of the system when needed. To help in our discussion of this circuitry, refer to the address chart shown in Figure 11.7. This is the address breakdown for the ET-3400. The memory chart shows the values required

		A_{15}	A_{14}	A_{13}	A_{12}	A_{11}	A_{10}	A_9	A_8	A_7	A_6	A_5	A_4	A_3	A_2	A_1	A_0
ROM IC12	FFXX FCxx	1	1	1	1	1	1	X	X	X	X	X	X	X	X	X	X
RAM (optional) IC16, IC17	01XX	0	0	0	0	0	0	0	1	X	X	X	X	X	X	X	X
RAM IC14, IC15	00XX	0	0	0	0	0	0	0	0	X	X	X	X	X	X	X	X
Keyboard	C0-X	1	1	0	0	0	0	0	0	–	–	–	–	–	X	X	X
Displays	C1XX	1	1	0	0	0	0	0	1	–	X	X	X	–	X	X	X

1, logic 1; 0, logic 0; –, does not care; X, functioning address

Figure 11.7 ET3400 memory decoding. (© 1981 Heath Company. Reprinted by permission of Heath Company.)

on the given address lines to decode a specific device. A 1 or a 0 in a specific position indicates the logic level required on that address line. An "×" indicates that the address bit is part of the functioning address, meaning that the bit is not being used by the decoding circuitry. A line in a given position indicates that the value on that address line is not being used for either address decoding or as part of a functioning address. For that reason, the system "does not care" what value is on that line.

The chart shows the address ranges for ROM, RAM, the keyboard, and the displays. In each case, there are specific bits that are required to decode the desired area, and several bits that are used to address specific locations within the selected area. The hexadecimal values for the given address ranges are listed in the first column, together with the name of the area. These hexadecimal values are found by determining the total range of the binary values listed. For example, ROM is shown to have the following address range:

$$1\ 1\ 1\ 1\ 1\ 1\ \times\ \times\ \times\ \times\ \times\ \times\ \times\ \times\ \times\ \times$$

Since the × values can range from all 0's up to all 1's, the total range of addresses in ROM is

$$1111110000000000 \quad\quad \text{to} \quad\quad 1111111111111111$$

or

$$\text{FC00} \quad\quad \text{to} \quad\quad \text{FFFF}$$

The address range is determined in the same way for each section.

Let's take a look at how the address bits are used to decode ROM. Remember that when ROM is selected, it must get a low $\overline{CS}$ signal, and the remainder of the microcomputer units must have an inactive-high $\overline{CS}$ input. Trace the bits through the circuit shown in Figure 11.8. This figure is a condensed schematic of the ET-3400 decoding circuitry. IC2-12, the D input, is the pin that will enable or disable the en-

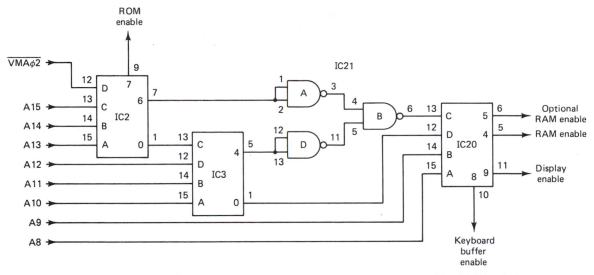

Figure 11.8 ET-3400 memory decoding circuitry. (© *1981 Heath Company. Reprinted by permission of Heath Company.)*

tire memory decoding circuitry. The reason for this will be shown later in this section. For now, just remember that *the D input to IC2 must be low for the memory decoding circuitry to work.* Assuming that this input is low and that the CPU is putting the proper values (111111) on A15 through A10, the inputs to IC2 will be

$$D = 0 \quad C = 1 \quad B = 1 \quad A = 1$$

With the binary value 7 being applied to IC2, a 4-to-10-line decoder, output 7 (pin 9) from the decoder will be low. This low is applied to the ROM chip, together with bits A12, A11, and A10, which all equal 1. The ROM now has all of its CS inputs, so it is enabled. Now, the rest of the decoding circuitry must make sure that the rest of the system is disabled. Let's take a look at how this is accomplished.

Since pin 9 of IC2 is low, the rest of the outputs must be high. With IC2-1 being high, the inputs to IC3 are

$$D = 1 \quad C = 1 \quad B = 1 \quad A = 1$$

With this input, all outputs from IC3 will be high, since the input code must equal 1001 or less for the decoder to have any output low. Now take a look at the IC21 configuration. These three NAND gates are wired so that a high into either IC21A or IC21D will cause the output of IC21B to be high. The three gates work as an OR gate, for all practical purposes. With this configuration, the high output at IC3-5 causes the output at IC21B to be high. The input code to IC20 is therefore

$$D = 1 \quad C = 1 \quad B = 1 \quad A = 1$$

With this input code, all the IC20 outputs will be high. The high output from IC20-10 will disable IC13 in the keyboard circuitry, so the input to the system is disabled. Output IC20-5 will disable both of the RAM chips, and IC20-11 will apply a high input to the D input of IC22. Since all of the output lines from this decoder that are used need the condition of D = 0 to be low, the display inputs are disabled.

Table 11.1 shows the binary inputs and outputs for the memory decoding circuitry with each of the microcomputer sections being decoded. Go through this chart and trace each of the bit combinations through the circuit shown in Figure 11.8. The asterisk (*) in each row shows the output that actually enables the desired unit of the system. The last line in the table shows what happens if IC2-12 is high. Note how every section of the microcomputer is disabled with this input condition. The low required at this input is supplied by the control unit when it is addressing any unit in the system. How this signal is provided is discussed in the next section.

The Control Unit

The control circuitry for the ET-3400 is simpler than the control circuitry in many other systems, simply because the interrupt inputs are not utilized. The $\overline{\text{IRQ}}$, $\overline{\text{NMI}}$, TSC, and HALT inputs to the CPU are all held at their inactive levels. $\overline{\text{IRQ}}$, $\overline{\text{NMI}}$, and $\overline{\text{HALT}}$ are all connected to pull-up resistors at the left side of the schematic. The blocks shown are inputs to the system that can be wired to different circuits for experiment purposes. The pulled-high lines all go to buffers (IC6) that are wired to be enabled. The outputs from these buffers are high, tying the $\overline{\text{IRQ}}$, $\overline{\text{NMI}}$, and $\overline{\text{HALT}}$ inputs to the CPU to their inactive-high level. The TSC input to the CPU is controlled by a circuit that is a bit different than the other control input circuits. The TSC input at the left side of the schematic is tied high, causing the output from IC6C to be low. This is the inactive level for the TSC input to the CPU.

The clock signals for the CPU are provided by IC19. Note how the ϕ1 and ϕ2 outputs from IC19 are connected to the ϕ1 and ϕ2 inputs to the CPU. The frequency at these two pins equals 500 kHz. IC19 also controls the $\overline{\text{RESET}}$ input to the CPU. As you can see, there are two lines labeled $\overline{\text{RESET}}$ on IC19. IC19-12 is its $\overline{\text{RESET}}$ input, and IC19-14 is its $\overline{\text{RESET}}$ output. Follow the input pin back to the RESET key on the keyboard. This key connects the line to ground when pressed. Assuming that the key has been pressed, the low input at IC19-12 causes the output IC19-14 to go low. This low is applied to the $\overline{\text{RESET}}$ input to the CPU. When the CPU gets this low input, it runs a special program designed to prepare the system for a user input. There are two results that are visible to the technician of this program running:

1. The displays will say "CPU UP," meaning that the CPU is working.
2. The CPU will scan the keyboard. This scanning will continue until there is an input.

Both of these actions are a result of the $\overline{\text{RESET}}$ program being run. If there is a system malfunction that prevents the program from running, the actions listed above will not occur.

The resistor (R107) and capacitor (C24) in the RESET input line to IC19 are there to improve the response time of the input. The MEMϕ2 output from IC19 is a clock output that is in phase with the ϕ2 output. It has a higher current level than the ϕ2 output, but beyond that there is little difference between the two. This output is applied to several circuits. It goes to:

1. The DBE input to the CPU, via IC4B
2. IC5B-5

The reason that it goes to the DBE input of the CPU has to do with the internal workings of the MC6800. The MC6800 addresses memory and transfers data during the high cycle of the ϕ2 clock. Whenever the ϕ2 clock is high, the CPU will use the data bus, if needed, but will not use the data bus when the ϕ2 clock is low. The DBE input disables the data bus and the R/$\overline{\text{W}}$ line when the ϕ2 clock is low. Since the CPU will not use it during this time, IC19 disables the data bus.

When the ϕ2 clock is high, the CPU not only performs any data transfer operations, it also does the following:

TABLE 11.1

ET-3400 Address Decoding

Address (HEX)	IC: 2							3						21					20							
Pin:	12	13	14	15	9	7	1	13	12	14	15	5	1	1,2	12,13	3	11	6	13	12	14	15	6	4	11	10
FCxx (ROM)	0	0	1	1	0	0	1	1	1	1	1	1	1	1	1	0	0	1	1	1	1	1	1	1	1	1
01xx (RAM)	0	0	0	0	1	1	0	0	0	0	0	1	0	1	1	0	0	1	1	1	0	0	0*	1	1	1
00xx (RAM)	0	0	0	0	1	1	0	0	0	0	0	1	0	0	0	0	0	1	0	0	0	0	1	0*	1	1
C0-x (keyboard)	0	1	1	0	1	0	1	1	0	0	0	0	1	0	0	1	1	0	0	0	0	0	1	1	1	0*
C1xx (displays)	0	1	1	0	1	0	1	1	0	0	0	0	1	0	0	1	1	0	1	1	1	1	1	1	0*	1
FCxx (ROM)	1	1	1	1	1	1	1	1	1	1	1	1	1	1	1	0	0	1	1	1	1	1	1	1	1	1

Note: The last line denotes the effect of IC2-12 being high during an address decoding operation. Asterisks denote the enabling output from the address decoding circuitry.

1. It addresses memory of an input/output device.
2. It drives its VMA output high if it is addressing any location.

Now assume that the CPU is addressing a memory location. On the positive half cycle of the $\phi2$ clock, it puts an address on the address bus and drives VMA high. This high is applied to IC5B together with the high MEM$\phi2$ signal. With two high inputs, the output from IC5B will be low. This low goes to IC2-12, enabling the memory decoding circuitry. This ensures that the memory decoding circuitry is enabled only during that time when the CPU is addressing some location within the system. During the $\phi1 = 1$ cycle, and when the CPU is not addressing any location, the output from IC5B will be high, disabling the memory decoding circuitry.

IC5A is used to disable the buffers on the R/$\overline{W}$ line (IC4A) and on the address bus (IC7 and IC8) when the TSC input to the CPU is high. The reason for this is to protect the buffers themselves. Earlier, it was said that the address bus and R/$\overline{W}$ lines required buffers because they had a fanout of 1. With buffers on the line, the fanouts were increased to 10. Now, consider what would happen if these buffers were not three-state buffers and the TSC input to the CPU went high. The address bus and R/$\overline{W}$ outputs from the CPU would be floated because of the TSC = 1 input. These floating outputs would act as open inputs to the buffers on the lines. Since TTL circuits treat open inputs like a logic 1, the buffers would put a logic 1 on the address bus lines and on the R/$\overline{W}$ line. This could cause trouble if some other device tried to drive these lines low. To prevent this type of situation from occurring, the TSC input is also used to disable the buffers on the lines. That way, they are protected when their inputs are open.

Without having an ET-3400 trainer to check the signals discussed in this section, it is naturally difficult to understand how all of these signals tie together to perform some useful function. The objective at this point, however, should be to follow through the discussion to see how the control unit can address any section with which it needs to communicate, and perform the required function. For example, if you want to determine what happens during a read operation from RAM, go through Table 11.1 to see how the address bits decode RAM, and trace the R/$\overline{W}$ signal to the proper chips.

Troubleshooting the System

Before we discuss the methods by which you would find a fault in a microcomputer, let's take a look at the bottom line of what will be going on in this system when it is working. When this or any other microcomputer system is working properly, the control unit is going to be continually doing three things:

1. Addressing memory locations, inputs, or outputs
2. Transferring data
3. Supplying the control signals required to transfer data

In terms of signals, if you look around in the ET-3400 with an oscilloscope, you should see several things, assuming that the system is working:

1. The address lines should be changing at various intervals.
2. The data bus should be showing almost continual changes in logic states.
3. VMA, R/$\overline{W}$ and DBE should be continually changing.
4. $\overline{\text{RESET}}$ should be at a high level at the CPU unless the RESET key is pressed.
5. TSC should be low at the CPU.

6. $\overline{IRQ}$, $\overline{NMI}$, and $\overline{HALT}$ should all be high at the CPU.
7. The various units of the system should be getting $\overline{CS}$ signals at odd intervals.

When the system is not functioning normally, one or more of the foregoing signal conditions will not be present. The key to finding the trouble is to find the signal that is not as it should be. For example, if you were to troubleshoot a down system, you may find that the keyboard buffers (IC13) are not getting the low pulses required to be enabled. This would indicate that there is a problem either in control or the memory decoding circuitry. If all of the inputs to the memory decoding circuitry are as they should be, the problem is in the memory decoding circuitry. You would then have to troubleshoot this part of the system.

The basic procedure for troubleshooting this system is the same as it is for any electronic device. First, isolate the problem down to a section. Then isolate the problem down to the component. In this system, isolating the section can be done with some simple checks and using a little common sense, as can be seen in the following example.

EXAMPLE 11.1

A down ET-3400 shows the following symptoms:

> Garbage on the displays (bad characters)
> Pressing the RESET key does not change the display

So, where do you start?

Solution: The best place to begin would be at IC13-1 and IC13-15. The reason for this is that the system should be doing *two* things after running the RESET program: changing the displays and scanning the keyboard. If the CPU is scanning the keyboard, you have already isolated the problem down to the output circuitry. Why? Because the control unit and memory decoding circuitry must be working for the CPU to be scanning the keyboard. ROM must also be good, because it is a program in ROM that causes the CPU to scan the keyboard. Since RAM is used by the CPU when running the ROM programs, RAM must also be good. The problem would therefore have to be in the output section.

Now, the section was isolated by taking one measurement and taking a moment to think about what that signal meant. If the enable signal had not been present at IC13, you could safely assume that there was nothing wrong with the output circuitry. Why? Because a problem in the output circuitry would not prevent the keyboard from being scanned, but a problem in one of the other units would cause *both* of the sections to not work. Since the keyboard is not being scanned *and* the displays are not working, the problem must be in an area that could affect both. The next step would be to see if the memory decoding circuitry is enabling anything at all. If it was enabling only ROM, the odds are that the problem is in the later part of the decoding circuitry. If it was not enabling anything, odds are that the problem is somewhere in control, since control determines what the memory decoding circuitry does. Determining whether the problem was in the decoding circuitry or in the control circuitry would be done by checking the inputs to the decoding circuitry. If they are all good, the problem is in the decoding circuitry itself. If not, there is a problem in control.

There is a point which should be made at this point in time regarding microcomputer troubleshooting in general. When troubleshooting a down system, it helps a great deal if you have some knowledge of how the good signals should look. That way, you have something with which to compare the signals you are getting. A good practice is to learn the signals that are present in a working system *after the RESET has been performed*. The reason for this is simple. Almost every microcomputer contains a circuit that causes the system to reset at power up. If you know what the system signals should look like after the system RESET occurs, you can start checking out the system immediately after turning it on. You do not need to perform any special procedures before troubleshooting. Besides, the system may be in such a condition as to make any operation other than a RESET impossible. In this case, if you need signals other than those which appear after a RESET, you may be in big trouble.

11.4 WHEN THE CPU MALFUNCTIONS

In most cases, when a major CPU malfunction occurs, nothing will work. The address bus will have no signals, or the control lines will go out, and so on. But how do you diagnose a CPU problem that is not quite so obvious?

There are several telltale signs that there is a CPU problem. First, give the CPU itself a visual and touch check. A CPU with an internal problem will usually get extremely hot. While CPUs tend to run hotter than other ICs to begin with, they should not be so hot that you cannot stand to touch them. If a CPU feels this hot to you and you have reason to believe that it is not working correctly, go ahead and change it.

Another sign is a color change in one or more of the leads coming from the CPU. If any of these runs appear to be turning brown, there is a good chance that the CPU is drawing or supplying too much current. If this is the case on one line, the high current draw may not be high enough to cause the entire chip to overheat, but the problem is there regardless. This is why you need to check the lines even though the CPU does not seem to be too hot.

A bad interrupt input can usually be diagnosed by simple observation of the system as a whole. If none of the input devices connected to a given interrupt input seem to be working, the interrupt input is probably the cause of the problem. For example, assume that a given system will not accept information from its keyboard. If the keyboard keeps putting out its interrupt signal but the CPU does not respond, check the interrupt circuitry. If no problem is found there, the CPU should be replaced, as its interrupt input is probably bad.

Before replacing the CPU in any system, you should perform a few checks to be sure that the reason the CPU is malfunctioning is the CPU itself. You should always check the following before replacing the CPU:

1. The V_{cc} and ground connections to the CPU
2. The $\overline{\text{RESET}}$ input
3. The system clock
4. Any WAIT or HOLD input, any interrupt inputs, and any enable inputs

The control inputs listed above will prevent the CPU from working if they are stuck at their active levels. The system clock will stop the entire system if it fails, and no chip can work without the proper V_{cc} and ground connections. The bottom line is that the CPU should be replaced only under two conditions:

1. There seems to be a mass failure of the CPU, as evidenced by the address bus going dead, or overheating, and so on.
2. All tests indicate that the inputs to the CPU are good, and a failure such as one of those listed above is present.

SUMMARY

The microcomputer has been made possible by the advent of the microprocessor, a single chip that contains both the control circuitry and the ALU. This single chip performs many complicated internal operations, such as interpreting and executing instructions that it reads from memory. Although these functions should be understood by the technician to gain an insight into the operation of the system, the microcomputer can still be dealt with effectively by treating the CPU as a black box source of signals. Some of the most common signals are the $R/\overline{W}$, the $\overline{CS}$, and the address and data signals. Another important signal to understand is the interrupt signal. This signal is generated by input devices when they need to communicate with the CPU.

In most cases, the signals listed above tend to change at uneven intervals, meaning that they appear to be garbage signals that the oscilloscope cannot lock in on. When the signals coming from the CPU seem to be inoperative, the power and control inputs to the CPU should be checked. If they are all there and the CPU still seems to be inoperative, the CPU should be replaced. Another indication of a CPU failure is the overheating of the CPU or burning of copper runs around the device.

The keys to effective troubleshooting of any microcomputer system are familiarity with the system and a systematic approach. When attempting to familiarize yourself with a system, you should observe the system operation that occurs immediately after a RESET operation occurs. This allows you to troubleshoot the system when it responds to nothing but the power-up RESET. When using a systematic approach, the following steps should be used:

1. Isolate the problem to a section of the system by checking the signals that interconnect the sections and by observing the obvious problem indicators, such as a failure in the keyboard circuitry.
2. Check the control lines within a section to determine if any control signal is missing.
3. Check the V_{cc} and ground connections to any chip that is suspect.
4. Check the address and/or data inputs to any chip that is suspect.
5. If all inputs to a given chip are present and the chip still does not have an output, replace the chip.

QUESTIONS

1. What is contained in the CPU?
2. What operations must be performed by the CPU when dealing with memory? Which CPU outputs would be involved with these operations?
3. What do the terms *fetch* and *execute* mean?
4. If you are treating the CPU as a "black box," what are you doing?
5. What is an interrupt? Which unit generates interrupt signals?
6. What does the CPU do when it receives an interrupt?
7. What is memory-mapped I/O?
8. What operations must the CPU be capable of performing to deal effectively with the input unit?
9. List and describe each of the pin functions of the MC6800.
10. What is the relationship between the $\overline{IRQ}$ and $\overline{NMI}$ inputs to the MC6800?
11. What is an interrupt flag?
12. What is the systematic approach to troubleshooting a microcomputer?
13. What are the indicators that a given CPU has failed? When should the CPU be replaced?

12

Microprocessor

Architecture

In Chapter 11 the CPU was introduced as nothing more than a source of microcomputer control signals. But how does the CPU know to which device to send a particular signal? How does it know when to do so? Obviously, the CPU must be an extremely sophisticated device, capable of interpreting and following the instructions contained in its program. In this chapter we focus on the internal makeup of the CPU, with the emphasis being, again, on the MC6800.

The CPU must be able to perform a variety of functions internally in order to accomplish the goals of the program. For example, consider the steps that are involved in the CPU fetching an instruction from memory. First, the CPU must know where in memory to go to get the instruction. After determining the instruction location, the address and the proper control signals must be provided to the memory unit. Then the CPU must put its data pins into the input mode and latch the data when it becomes available.

What the CPU is capable of doing depends on its internal physical construction. The construction of the CPU determines the type of instructions to which it is capable of responding. The point of all this is simple: *The CPU is not an intelligent being. It simply responds to certain signal combinations in the way that it was designed to do,* much as a radio responds to transmitted signals. In the case of the CPU, the signals that it responds to are the instructions contained in the program, and the circuitry used to do so is made up of a complex control network and a series of registers. These registers are each associated with a particular CPU function, and almost all of them are used in each CPU operation. It's almost like an automobile engine. The engine is made up of hundreds of parts that each perform a unique function. Yet all of these parts are involved in every revolution that the engine makes.

In this chapter we look at this internal CPU construction. We focus on the way in which the internal parts of the CPU work together to perform a given CPU operation.

12.1 THE INTERNAL REGISTERS

Figure 12.1 shows the internal makeup of the MC6800. With the exception of the *instruction decode and control* circuits and the *ALU,* the entire block diagram is made up of registers. Registers, you may recall, are temporary storage locations for data. In the case of the CPU, the term *register* also includes counters. Since the counters contained in the CPU can be preset to certain values, they are considered to be registers. In this section we take a look at the registers that are contained in the MC6800 and discuss the functions performed by each.

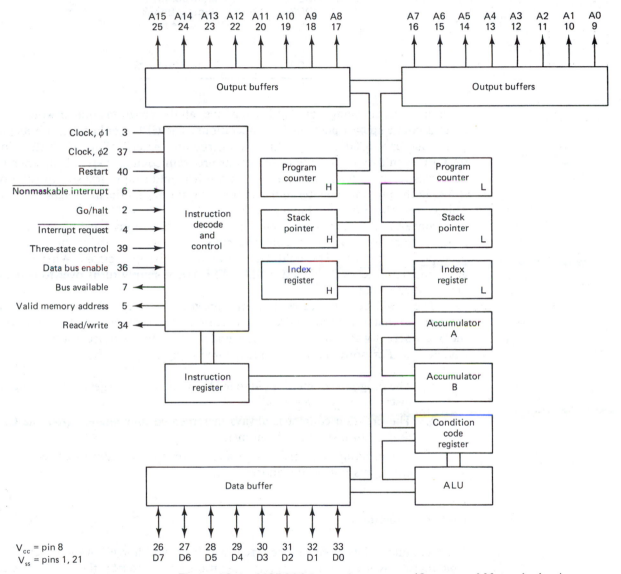

Figure 12.1 MC6800 internal structure. *(Courtesy of Motorola, Inc.)*

The Program Counter

The program counter is a 16-bit counter that is responsible for providing the addresses required to fetch instructions from memory. Although this may seem like an enormous task at first, it is made simpler by one fact: *Program instructions are stored in successive locations in memory.* When a given program is stored in memory, each instruction is stored in the next higher memory location than the previous one. For example, assume that a program made up of 10 instructions was to be stored in memory. The program would probably be stored in the following manner:

Address	Contents
0000	Instruction 1
0001	Instruction 2
0002	Instruction 3
•	•
•	•
•	•
0009	Instruction 10

With the program being stored as listed above, all the program counter would have to do is count up by 1 between fetch operations. The CPU would start with its program counter at 0000, and fetch the first instruction. After fetching the instruction, the CPU would automatically increment its program counter 0001. Then, when the CPU was ready to fetch the next instruction, it would simply transfer the number stored in the program counter to the address bus and repeat the increment function. This is how the program counter works.

Since the program counter must be able to address any location in memory, it stands to reason that it must contain a number of bits equal to the number of address pins on the CPU. This holds true for all 8-bit microprocessors. When the program counter reaches its highest count (FFFF-H), it simply turns over to 0000, as any counter would.

There will be some cases when the program counter will have its contents changed, so that it will start addressing an entirely different section of memory than the one where it was. The circumstances under which this will occur are covered in Chapter 13. For now, simply remember three things:

1. The program counter is used to tell the CPU where to get the next program instruction from memory.
2. The program counter is always incremented immediately *after* the CPU fetches an instruction from memory.
3. The program counter is the primary source of the address codes that the CPU puts out on the address bus.

The Accumulator

The accumulator has often been referred to as the "workhorse" of the system. This 8-bit register is used in almost every operation performed by the CPU. The accumulator is a "scratch-pad" register, which means that it is used by the CPU in much the same way as you would use scratch paper. When the CPU needs to transfer information from one memory location to another, it gets the value from the first location and stores it in the accumulator until the second location has been addressed and is ready to accept the data.

The MC6800 has two accumulators, *accumulator A* and *accumulator B*. The CPU will use either one of the accumulators, or both, depending on the instruction it is performing. Every instruction that involves accumulator A has an equivalent instruction that involves accumulator B. So the choice of which accumulator is used by the CPU is actually up to the programmer, since the programmer decides which instructions are contained in the program.

Some of the operations that can be performed involving the accumulators are as follows:

Transferring data from accumulator A to accumulator B

Transferring data from accumulator B to accumulator A

Adding the values in the two accumulators

Adding an outside value to the value contained in either accumulator

The Condition Code Register

In Chapter 11, reference was made to the interrupt flag: a flip-flop that contained a single bit, used to indicate that an interrupt had occurred. The CPU has a number of flags, each of which indicate that a given condition exists. These flags are grouped together to form the condition code register.

While the flags that make up the CCR are physically in the same location, they are influenced by different factors and operate independently of each other. The flags in the MC6800 condition code register are as follows:

Bit position:	5	4	3	2	1	0
	H	I	N	Z	V	C

Half-carry flag. (H): This bit is used to indicate whether or not there was a carry out of the bit 3 position of the accumulator. It is used only when the CPU is performing BCD arithmetic.

Interrupt flag. (I): This bit is set when an interrupt is received by the CPU and is cleared after the CPU is finished servicing the interrupting device. It will prevent the $\overline{IRQ}$ input from working when it is set.

Negative flag. (N): This flag will set when the result of a given operation causes the MSB of the accumulator to set. In two's-complement arithmetic, the condition of MSB = 1 indicates a negative result.

Zero flag. (Z): This flag will set when the contents of the accumulator equals zero, and reset otherwise.

Overflow flag. (V): This flag will set if the result of a two's-complement operation causes the accumulator to go over the maximum legal value of ± 127.

Carry flag. (C): This flag will set when there is a carry out of the MSB position of the accumulator. It is cleared otherwise.

The *half-carry* flag is used only in BCD arithmetic because 4-bit values are used in this number system. Recall that in BCD, decimal digits are represented by 4-bit values. When these values are stored in the accumulator, an 8-bit register, two decimal values are stored at a time. For example, consider the following two numbers being stored in the two accumulators:

accumulator A = 78 = 0111   1000

accumulator B = 28 = 0010   1000

If the two values listed were to be added together, the system would need to know if there was a carry from the bit 3 to the bit 4 position in the accumulators, since this would indicate a carry from the decimal units to the decimal tens position. The half-carry flag fulfills this need. In most other CPU functions, this flag is not used.

The *negative* flag is used in two's-complement arithmetic. Recall that in two's-complement arithmetic, negative numbers are indicated by a 1 in the MSB position of the value. When the CPU is performing two's-complement arithmetic, the N flag is used to indicate that the value stored in the accumulator is negative.

The *overflow* flag is another flag that is used in two's-complement arithmetic. To understand the significance of this flag, refer back to Section 2.4, the discussion on two's-complement arithmetic. It was stated in that section that the maximum positive number that can be represented by 8 bits is 01111111, or 127. By the same token, the maximum negative number that can be represented by 8 bits is 10000001, or −127. Both of these limits are determined by the fact that the MSB of the number is used only to show the sign of the number. This setup leads to an interesting problem. Consider the addition of the following two positive two's-complement numbers:

$$
\begin{array}{r}
01111000 \\
+\ 01000111 \\
\hline
10111111 \quad \text{sum}
\end{array}
$$

The MSB of the sum would indicate that the number is negative, which we know not to be the case. What has occurred is a situation called an *overflow;* that is, the sum is too large to be represented in two's-complement form. In the MC6800, the overflow flag would set if this situation occurred, and the CPU would then treat the number as its actual binary value, not as a two's-complement number.

The *interrupt, carry,* and *zero* flags would each set under the conditions stated. They would be reset otherwise. All of the flags will be discussed in Chapter 13 more in terms of their applications. As will be shown, they are used in the decision-making processes of the CPU.

The Instruction Register

The instruction register is used to store the instructions that the CPU fetches from memory. As shown in Figure 12.1, the instruction register is connected to the *instruction decode and control* circuitry of the CPU. When a given instruction is fetched from memory, it is stored in the instruction register, where the decoding circuitry then begins to respond to it. This register is an 8-bit register, which corresponds to the length, in bits, of any given MC6800 instruction.

The Index Register

The index register could, for all practical purposes, be considered a 16-bit accumulator. This register is used for a wide variety of functions, including adding, temporary storage of information, counting, and a special form of memory addressing. This memory addressing technique, called *index addressing,* is covered in detail in Chapter 13.

The Stack Pointer

Picture the CPU running a program and having critical data associated with that program in all its internal registers. Now, an interrupt is received. After the CPU finishes the instruction it is currently executing, it must stop, acknowledge the interrupt, and run another program that was written to service the interrupting device. But what happens to the data that the CPU had in its registers from the program on which it was originally working? In order for the CPU to be able to return to its original program after the interrupt routine is complete, it must be able to retrieve all the data that it had in its registers when the program was interrupted.

When the CPU receives an interrupt and completes its current instruction, it stores all its internal register data in a special area of memory called the *stack*. Then, after the interrupt service routine has been run, the CPU returns to the stack, transfers the information stored back to its internal registers, and continues with the original program at the point where it left off. The *stack pointer* (SP), a 16-bit register, tells the CPU where the stack is located and is used to address the locations that are there. To help you understand how this is done, we will go through the process step by step. Assume that the CPU is running a program and an interrupt is received. For the sake of discussion, we will assume that the original value in the stack pointer is the hexadecimal value A04C. Now, here is what happens when the interrupt is received.

1. The stack pointer value (A04C) is placed on the address bus. The CPU then stores (writes) the 8-bit value contained in the low byte* of the program counter at this location. The stack pointer is now decremented bv one to A04B.

2. The SP (stack pointer) value A04B is placed on the address bus and the high byte* of the program counter is stored at this location. The SP is again decremented to A04A.

3. The SP value A04A is placed on the address bus and the low byte of the index register is stored. The SP is now decremented to A049.

4. The SP value A049 is placed on the address bus and the high byte of the index register is stored. The SP is now decremented to A048.

5. The SP value A048 is placed on the address bus and the contents of accumulator A are stored. The SP is now decremented to A047.

6. The SP value A047 is placed on the address bus and the contents of accumulator B are stored. The SP is now decremented to A046.

7. The SP value A046 is placed on the address bus and the contents of the CCR (condition code register) are stored. The SP is *not* decremented.

The data from each of the internal registers has now been stored in memory. The locations used and their contents are shown in Figure 12.2. You may have noticed that the value contained in the stack pointer was not stored in memory. This is because the CPU will use the value as soon as the interrupt has been serviced.

After the CPU runs the program associated with the interrupt it received, the data in its registers is no longer useful, so it does not need to be stored. The CPU will, at this point, reverse the process just covered. It will start at the lowest SP address value (A046) and load (read) the information in that location into the CCR. It will then *increment* the SP to A047 and place that value on the address bus. The contents from that location will be loaded into accumulator B. The process is repeated until the SP is at its orignal value (A04B) and all data has been returned to its original CPU register. Now the CPU continues with its original program at the exact point where it left off.

The location of the stack in memory is up to the system designer. During the power-up (bootstrap) program, the starting address of the stack is loaded into the SP. The fact that this value is determined by the person who wrote the program allows a great deal of freedom as to where the stack will be located.

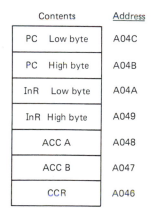

Contents	Address
PC Low byte	A04C
PC High byte	A04B
InR Low byte	A04A
InR High byte	A049
ACC A	A048
ACC B	A047
CCR	A046

Figure 12.2   Stack organization.

*Whenever the contents of a 16-bit register are discussed, the least significant 8 bits are referred to as the *low byte,* and the most significant 8 bits are referred to as the *high byte.*

12.2 THE ALU

The ALU is that part of the CPU which performs all arithmetic and logic operations. This part of the CPU circuitry interacts primarily with the accumulators and thus performs most of its functions on the data contained in either or both of these registers.

In terms of arithmetic operations, the ALU is capable of performing only two operations: addition and subtraction. All mathematical operations performed by the computer must be made up of these two operations and one or more logic operations.

The basic logic operations performed by the ALU are the AND, OR, and COMPLEMENT operations. These three logic operations are combined to perform more complex operations when required by a given program.

With the ALU being limited to these five basic operations, it should not be surprising to discover that the microcomputer must usually perform hundreds of steps to accomplish anything useful. How these steps are combined to accomplish a given task is the subject of Chapter 13.

12.3 THE INSTRUCTION CYCLE

An *instruction cycle* is the time required for the CPU to fetch one instruction from memory and perform the task that the instruction calls for. As we stated earlier, the process of reading the instruction from memory is called a *fetch,* and the process of performing the operation called for in the instruction is called the *execution*. The instruction cycle is therefore broken down into two cycles: the *fetch cycle* and the *execution cycle*. During the fetch cycle, the CPU reads the instruction from memory and places it in the instruction register. During the execution cycle, the CPU performs the operation called for in the instruction. The breakdown is shown in Figure 12.3. Some critical points in the instruction cycle are numbered. Each of these times corresponds to the point at which an internal CPU operation always occurs, regardless of the instruction. These operations are as follows:

1. At T1, the value in the program counter, index register, or stack pointer is placed on the address bus. The source of the address code depends on the circumstances involved; but regardless of where the address comes from, it is sent to the address bus at this time.

2. At T2, the source of the address is incremented. When the program counter is the source of the address (which is usually the case), it is incremented at the end of the fetch cycle.

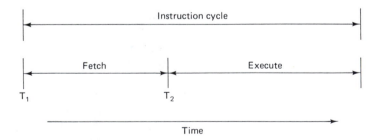

Figure 12.3 Instruction cycle.

The fetch and execution cycles are broken down further into *machine cycles*. The machine cycle is the time required for the CPU to perform one basic operation.

For example, the instruction ADD, which causes the CPU to add a value stored in memory to the value in the accumulator, takes three machine cycles to perform:

Machine cycle 1: The instruction is fetched from memory.
Machine cycle 2: The data value to be added is read from memory.
Machine cycle 3: The two values are added.

As you can see, only one operation was performed during each machine cycle. The example above also demonstrates two important points about machine cycles in general:

1. *The instruction is always fetched during the first machine cycle of every instruction cycle.*
2. *There are usually more machine cycles involved in executing an instruction than in fetching it.*

Fetching an instruction always requires a single machine cycle, but executing an instruction can require up to nine machine cycles, depending on the complexity of the instruction.

The machine cycle is broken down into clock cycles. For the MC6800 it takes one complete cycle of the $\phi1$ and $\phi2$ clocks to complete a machine cycle. The total breakdown of the instruction cycle can be seen in Figure 12.4. Knowing the number of machine cycles involved in running a given program and the length of time required for a machine cycle allows you to determine the time required for the program to run. For example, if a program took 940 machine cycles to run and a clock

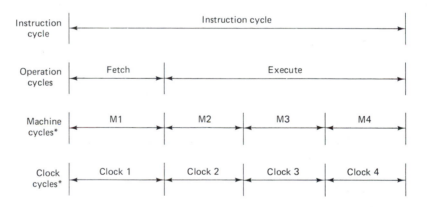

*These may vary for various instructions and between various microprocessors.

Figure 12.4   Complete instruction cycle breakdown.

cycle took 10 μs, the entire program would take 940 $\times$ 10 μs = 9400 μs to run. Being able to determine the length of time required for a program to run becomes important when discussing a special type of program, called a *timing loop*. A timing loop is used to generate a time delay. Timing loops are discussed in Chapter 13.

12.4 *DATA TRANSFER OPERATIONS*

The process of transferring data to and from the CPU is a continual microcomputer operation. Whenever the CPU fetches an instruction from memory, a data transfer is occurring. Whenever the CPU stores data in memory, a data transfer is occurring.

Probably 60% or more of the CPU's time is spent either reading information from, or writing information into memory. For this reason, it is important that you understand a few points about data transfer operations.

There are two registers involved in every data transfer operation. The register that contains the information to be transferred is called the *source*. The register that is to receive the information is called the *destination*. For example, when information is being transferred from the accumulator to a memory location, the accumulator is the source and the memory location is the destination. If information is transferred from a memory location to the accumulator, the memory location is the source and the accumulator is the destination. There is an important point that must be made regarding the source and destination registers involved in any data transfer operation: *In any data transfer, the contents of the destination register will change while the contents of the source register will not.* For example, if data is being transferred from the accumulator to a memory location, the data in the accumulator will not change. The contents of the memory location, however, will change and will now equal the data stored in the accumulator. If the contents of a memory location are transferred to the accumulator, the data in the accumulator will change to equal the contents of the memory location, while the contents of the original memory location will not change.

To help you understand this point better, consider the circuit shown in Figure 12.5. This circuit shows two parallel in/parallel out shift registers. The outputs of register A are connected to the inputs of register B. If the $\overline{\text{LOAD}}$ input to register B is activated, the values at the outputs of register A will be loaded into register B.

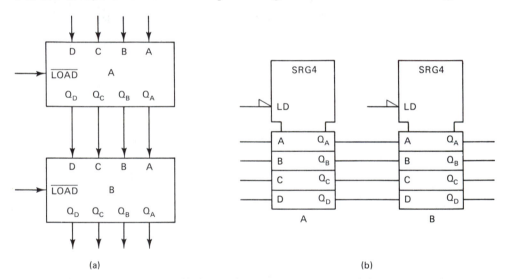

(a)   (b)

Figure 12.5 Two parallel in/parallel out shift registers: (a) conventional symbols; (b) DLN symbols.

While the contents of B (the destination) have been changed to equal the information at the B inputs, nothing has happened to change the value in register A (the source). Since we are dealing with similar registers in the CPU/memory relationship, the principles are the same. The destination contents will change, while the source contents will not.

The source/destination relationship just discussed accounts for the need to store the contents of the CPU when an interrupt service program must be run. If the contents of the CPU registers were not stored, they would be lost when the values needed for the interrupt program were loaded. Why? Because the CPU would be the destination for the interrupt program values, which means that the contents of the registers would change. *Note that anytime the CPU has important data in any of its internal registers, and that register is needed to store another value, the original value must be stored in another location before it can be used to hold the second value.* This same principle holds true for any register involved in the same situation.

Internal CPU Timing

The CPU performs certain operations internally at specific times in order to complete a data transfer operation successfully. Refer to the waveforms shown in Figure 12.6. The waveforms shown are those of the $\phi1$ and $\phi2$ clocks required by the MC6800.

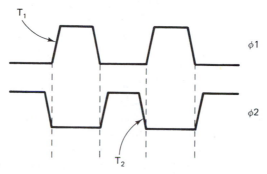

Figure 12.6 Clock cycles.

At time T1 the address code is transferred from the program counter to the address bus. The R/$\overline{\text{W}}$ line and VMA are also set to their proper levels. During the positive half-cycle of the $\phi1$ clock, these values settle on their respective lines. During the positive half-cycle of the $\phi2$ clock, the memory chips being addressed access the location and make the data from that location available on the data bus. At time T2 the CPU latches the information from the data bus and increments its program counter.

The write cycle is very similar to the process above. The only difference (in terms of timing) is that the CPU puts the data to be entered into the memory location during the positive half-cycle of $\phi2$. The R/$\overline{\text{W}}$ line then goes low and the memory chip latches the data.

12.5 A WORD ABOUT THE CPU INTERNAL CONTROL CIRCUITRY

One of the ideas that the average technician has the hardest time dealing with is the concept of how the CPU interprets instructions and carries them out. The control circuitry is extremely complex and is capable of carrying out operations that are much more involved than any other type of chip is capable of. But for all its complexity, this control circuitry works in the same basic fashion as every other type of circuit with which we have dealt. It receives a given input and responds to that input the way it was designed to respond.

There is absolutely no reason to get hung up on exactly how the control circuitry in the CPU decodes and executes instructions. Simply accept the fact that it does what it was designed to do, and leave it at that. Since no one will ever get into the CPU to fix a faulty control section, there is no point in worrying about how it works. If the CPU is faulty, you replace it, and that is that.

SUMMARY

The microprocessor consists mainly of the ALU, the instruction decoding circuitry, and a series of registers that each serve a specific purpose in the overall operation of the device. The program counter is used to store the address of the next instruction to be fetched from memory. This counter, together with the index register and the stack pointer, is connected directly to the address pins on the microprocessor. The stack pointer is used to store the starting address of the stack, a special area of memory that is used to save CPU data when an interrupt is being processed. The index register is a 16-bit general-purpose register that is used mainly for counting and a special type of addressing, called indexed addressing.

The main CPU register is the accumulator. The accumulator is used in a vast majority of CPU operations, including all arithmetic and logic operations. The MC6800 has two accumulators. The condition code register is an 8-bit register that contains the flags, individual flip-flops used to indicate that a given condition exists. In the MC6800, there are six flags. The two most significant bits in the CCR are not used and are always set. The final register is the instruction register, which is used to store the 8-bit instructions that are fetched by the CPU.

The time required for the CPU to fetch and execute a given instruction is referred to as an instruction cycle. During the fetch cycle, the CPU reads an instruction from memory and places it in its instruction register. It then increments its program counter. During the execution cycle, the CPU performs the operation called for by the instruction. The two cycles combine to form the instruction cycle. The instruction cycle is broken down further into machine cycles. A machine cycle is the time required for the CPU to perform one basic operation, such as a memory read. Machine cycles are defined in terms of real time in that a given CPU machine cycle will correspond to an exact number of clock cycles. For the MC6800, one machine cycle is equal, in time, to one complete cycle of the $\phi1$ and $\phi2$ clocks.

Data transfer operations will involve two registers, the source register and the destination register. The source register is the register that contains the data to be transferred, and the destination register is the register that is to receive the data. The source register contents are not changed by a data transfer operation, but the destination register contents are.

QUESTIONS

1. What determines the capabilities of the microprocessor?
2. List the 16-bit registers contained in the CPU.
3. What is the program counter used for?
4. What is the accumulator used for?
5. How are program instructions stored in memory?
6. What is the half-carry flag used to indicate? When is it used?
7. What is the interrupt flag used for?
8. When is the negative flag set?
9. If the contents of the accumulator equal 10000000 after a given operation, what is the state of the negative flag? The zero flag?
10. What is the overflow flag used for?
11. How many bits are stored in the instruction register? When are the contents of this register changed?
12. When is the program counter incremented?
13. What is the index register used for?

14. What purpose is served by the stack pointer?

15. Who determines the location of the stack in memory?

16. What is meant by the term *low byte*? What is meant by the term *high byte*?

17. Which register is the primary source of data used by the ALU?

18. What are the arithmetic operations performed by the ALU?

19. What are the logic operations performed by the ALU?

20. What is an instruction cycle?

21. What is a fetch cycle? What is the first step performed by the CPU during the fetch cycle? What is the last step performed by the CPU during a fetch cycle?

22. What is an execution cycle?

23. What is a machine cycle?

24. What always happens during the first machine cycle of any instruction cycle?

25. What is a source register?

26. What is a destination register?

27. Prior to a data transfer operation, the source register contains the value 10110110 and the destination register contains the value 11110001. What will be in each of the registers after the transfer has occurred?

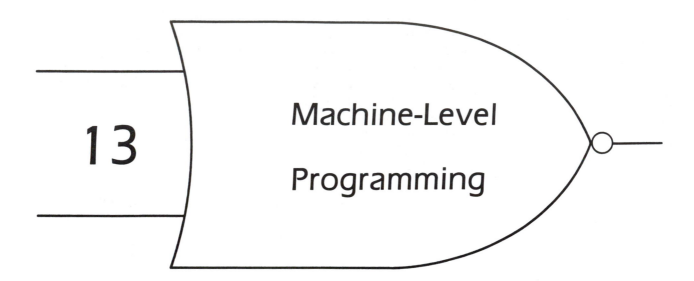

Machine-Level Programming

In Chapter 1, it was stated that microcomputer operation involves two distinct parts: *hardware*, the electronic circuits and mechanical parts that make up the machine, and *software*, the instructions that cause the hardware to perform a useful function. For the last 12 chapters we have focused on the hardware aspect of computer operation. In this chapter the emphasis is placed on software; specifically, machine-level (binary) programming. A machine-level program is *a series of binary instruction codes that control the basic operation of the CPU.*

There are as many different ways to program a computer as there are to build one. Microcomputer *languages* have been designed to fit almost every application. A language is defined as *a group of instructions that cause the microcomputer to perform a specific task or group of tasks*. Microcomputer languages are divided into two types: higher-level languages and lower-level languages. FORTRAN, COBOL, BASIC, and Pascal are examples of higher-level languages. A brief introduction to these languages is included at the end of this chapter.

Machine-level programming is a type of lower-level language. A lower-level language is one that is written in commands (instructions) that each cause one CPU operation to be performed. Machine-level programming is the writing of programs in the actual binary form to which the CPU responds. We will start our discussion of machine-level programming by going into the makeup of instructions inside the microcomputer. Again, the MC6800 will be the basis for the topics in this chapter.

13.1 INTRODUCTION TO MACHINE-LEVEL PROGRAMMING

The microprocessor is just like any other electronic circuit. It receives certain inputs and responds to those inputs in a very predictable manner. The inputs in this case are a series of binary codes called *operation codes*, or *op-codes*. When these codes are fed to the microprocessor in the correct sequence, the microprocessor will accomplish a useful task. If the op-codes are not fed to the microprocessor in the correct sequence, the results will not be those that were desired. *The key to getting the desired results from any microprocessor is to provide it with the correct sequence of op-codes.*

Every machine-level instruction has an op-code, and most of them contain other information as well. Instructions can contain from one to three bytes, as shown in Figure 13.1. One-byte instructions are instructions that require only an op-code. For

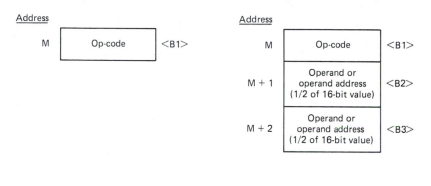

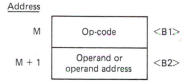

Figure 13.1 Instruction sizes and formats (typical).

example, an instruction to "clear the accumulator" would require only one byte, since there is no data or address required for the instruction to be executed. Two-byte instructions require an 8-bit data word or an 8-bit address in order for the CPU to be able to execute the instruction. The two bytes that make up the instruction are always stored in two successive locations in memory. Three-byte instructions require either a 16-bit data value or a 16-bit address in order for the instruction to be executed. Again, the bytes that make up the entire instruction would be stored in successive memory locations. *Regardless of the number of bytes contained in the instruction, the op-code always appears first.* As we cover the MC6800 instruction set, the reasons that these different instruction sizes are needed will become evident. For now, remember the following points:

1. Instructions range in size from one byte to three bytes depending on the information required by the CPU in order to execute the instruction.
2. The 8-bit op-code is always contained in the first byte of the instruction. The rest of the instruction contains either data or an address.

A machine-level program is made up of binary instructions such as those shown in Figure 13.1. These instructions are almost always stored in successive locations in memory. The microprocessor will fetch one instruction and perform the operation called for, will then fetch and execute the next, and so on, until the program is finished. If the program has been written correctly, the result of running that program will be of some benefit to the user. Writing a machine-level program correctly involves:

1. Determining how the problem to be solved can be broken down into a series of operations that the microprocessor can perform
2. Finding the op-codes required to perform that series of operations

This process may not seem to be too difficult at first, but there is a catch. Every microprocessor has a finite number of op-codes and thus a limitation on the number of operations that it is capable of performing. The MC6800 has approximately 72 op-codes, so *any task, no matter how sophisticated, must be performed using some combination of these 72 op-codes.* With this restriction, it should not be surprising that even relatively simple tasks can require the microprocessor to perform hundreds of steps.

The set of op-codes that a given microprocessor can respond to is referred to as its *instruction set.* The instruction set defines the absolute limits of what the microprocessor is capable of doing in a single step. What the system can do overall depends on what the machine-level programmer is capable of doing with the instruction set.

It should be noted that the instruction set varies from microprocessor to microprocessor. The binary codes that the MC6800 will respond to are not the same ones that another will respond to. Although we will be covering the MC6800 instruction set in this chapter, you should gain sufficient insight into machine-level programming to enable you to study the instruction types used by other microprocessors.

Flowcharts

A flowchart is a graphical representation of a program that shows two things:

1. The operations to be performed in the program
2. The order in which the operations are to be performed

A flowchart is used by the programmer as an aid in writing the program. It must show *every* operation that is to occur and the correct sequence of operations. If any step is left out, or the sequence of steps is incorrect, the program will not work.

A flowchart uses symbols to represent different types of operations. The most commonly used symbols are:

1. *Rectangle*: used to represent a process or action
2. *Diamond*: used to represent a decision that must be made
3. *Oval*: used to indicate the beginning and end of the program
4. *Circle*: used to show connections between different parts of the program
5. *Arrow*: used to show the path from one step to the next
6. *Parallelogram*: used to show an input or output function

The symbols listed can be seen in Figure 13.2.

The flowchart for a given program must not only meet the requirements listed at the start of this section, but must also provide for every possible set of circumstances that can arise during the time the program is being run. For example, consider the flowchart shown in Figure 13.3. This flowchart represents the problem of entering an apartment with two locks on the door. With two locks on the door, there are four possible combinations of conditions for the two locks:

Lock 1	Lock 2
Unlocked	Unlocked
Locked	Unlocked
Unlocked	Locked
Locked	Locked

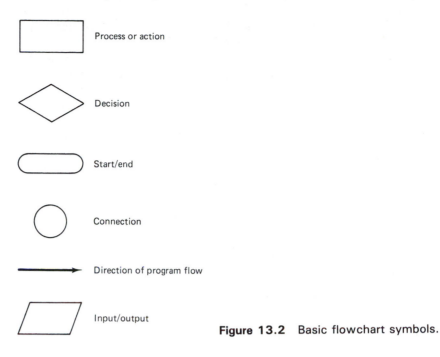

Figure 13.2 Basic flowchart symbols.

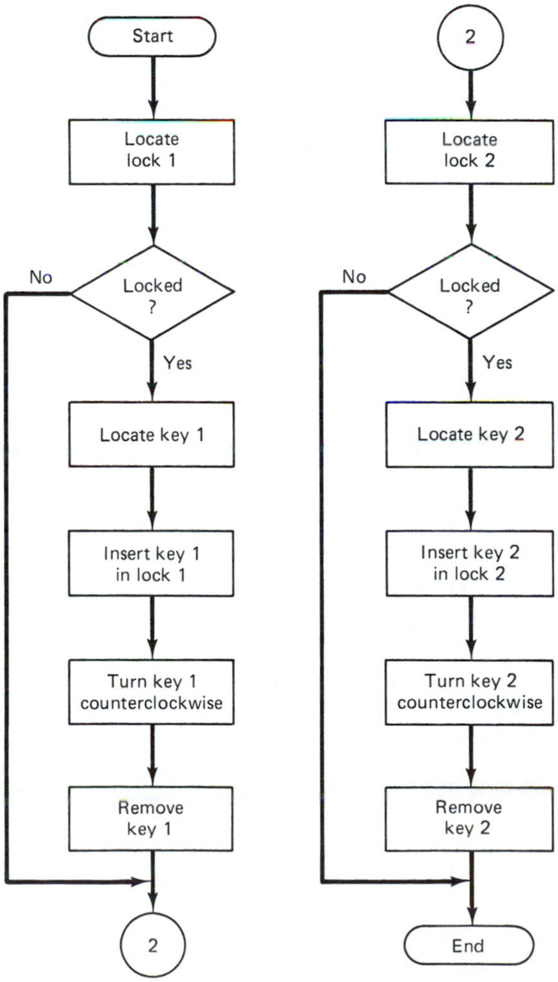

Figure 13.3 Flowchart for doorlock problem.

In any of the conditions shown, the flowchart must show the fastest possible series of steps to enter the apartment. The flowchart does this by initially asking if a given lock is locked—after locating the lock, of course. If the lock is locked, the flowchart directs you through a routine for unlocking the lock. If the lock is unlocked, it bypasses the routine and leads you to the next logical action. Note that the path taken from the decision blocks depends on the answer to the question contained in the block.

If you go through the four conditions listed for the locks, you will see that, in each case, the flowchart leads you to "end" in the minimum possible number of steps. In the cases where lock 1 is locked, you end up at the circle containing the number 2. When this circle is reached, you simply go to the circle numbered 2 on the right side and continue from there.

In the example, even a simple process such as opening an apartment door was broken down into a series of steps. The microprocessor works in a very similar manner. Having a limited number of operations that it is capable of performing, any and all problems must be solved using those operations. This is what makes machine-level programming a relatively difficult proposition. At the end of the chapter, there are problems in writing a flowchart. Go to these problems and see if you can solve them before going on. Just remember three things about a flowchart:

1. The flowchart must show *all* the steps required to solve the problem.
2. The flowchart must show the required steps in the correct sequence.
3. The flowchart must account for all possible conditions and give the fastest solution for each.

Mnemonics

A *mnemonic* is an abbreviation that is used to represent a given op-code. Op-codes are usually listed in their binary, octal, or hexadecimal form. In numeric form, it can be extremely difficult to remember which op-code is which. To make the process of reading a program easier, mnemonics are used. Another advantage of writing a program in mnemonic form is that the program can be written for any CPU, without regard to the actual op-code required. For example, the op-code for "load accumulator" varies for the three major 8-bit microprocessors as follows:

MC6800	8080A	Z80
96-H	7E-H	7E-H

The op-codes shown will cause their respective CPUs to load the accumulator from a specified source register. If a program were being written in machine code (binary), the process required to translate the program from one CPU to another would be long and tedious. However, using the mnemonic "LDA" to represent the "load accumulator" instruction allows the program to be written in general terms. Then, when you wish to use the program for one CPU or another, you would simply translate the mnemonic codes into the op-codes for that CPU.

Since mnemonics are easier to deal with than binary op-codes, most of the programs contained in this chapter are written in mnemonic form.

13.2 THE MC6800 INSTRUCTION SET

Recall that the instruction set for a given microprocessor is the sum total of the operations that the device is capable of performing in a single step. The instruction set for the MC6800 is shown in Figure 13.4. The instruction set for the MC6800 is broken down into four groups:

INDEX REGISTER AND STACK POINTER OPERATIONS	MNEMONIC	IMMED			DIRECT			INDEX			EXTND			INHER			BOOLEAN/ARITHMETIC OPERATION	5 H	4 I	3 N	2 Z	1 V	0 C
		OP	~	#	OP	~	#	OP	~	#	OP	~	#	OP	~	#							
Compare index reg.	CPX	8C	3	3	9C	4	2	AC	6	2	BC	5	3				$(X_H/X_L) - (M/M+1)$	•	•	⑦	‡	⑧	•
Decrement index reg.	DEX													09	4	1	$X - 1 \rightarrow X$	•	•	•	‡	•	•
Decrement stack pntr.	DES													34	4	1	$SP - 1 \rightarrow SP$	•	•	•	•	•	•
Increment index reg.	INX													08	4	1	$X + 1 \rightarrow X$	•	•	•	‡	•	•
Increment stack pntr.	INS													31	4	1	$SP + 1 \rightarrow SP$	•	•	•	•	•	•
Load index reg.	LDX	CE	3	3	DE	4	2	EE	6	2	FE	5	3				$M \rightarrow X_H, (M+1) \rightarrow X_L$	•	•	⑨	‡	R	•
Load stack pntr.	LDS	8E	3	3	9E	4	2	AE	6	2	BE	5	3				$M \rightarrow SP_H, (M+1) \rightarrow SP_L$	•	•	⑨	‡	R	•
Store index reg.	STX				DF	5	2	EF	7	2	FF	6	3				$X_H \rightarrow M, X_L \rightarrow (M+1)$	•	•	⑨	‡	R	•
Store stack pntr.	STS				9F	5	2	AF	7	2	BF	6	3				$SP_H \rightarrow M, SP_L \rightarrow (M+1)$	•	•	⑨	‡	R	•
Index reg. → stack pntr.	TXS													35	4	1	$X - 1 \rightarrow SP$	•	•	•	•	•	•
Stack pntr. → index reg.	TSX													30	4	1	$SP + 1 \rightarrow X$	•	•	•	•	•	•

JUMP AND BRANCH OPERATIONS	MNEMONIC	RELATIVE			INDEX			EXTND			INHER			BRANCH TEST	5 H	4 I	3 N	2 Z	1 V	0 C
		OP	~	#	OP	~	#	OP	~	#	OP	~	#							
Branch always	BRA	20	4	2										None	•	•	•	•	•	•
Branch if carry clear	BCC	24	4	2										C = 0	•	•	•	•	•	•
Branch if carry set	BCS	25	4	2										C = 1	•	•	•	•	•	•
Branch if = zero	BEQ	27	4	2										Z = 1	•	•	•	•	•	•
Branch if ≥ zero	BGE	2C	4	2										N ⊕ V = 0	•	•	•	•	•	•
Branch if > zero	BGT	2E	4	2										Z + (N ⊕ V) = 0	•	•	•	•	•	•
Branch if higher	BHI	22	4	2										C + Z = 0	•	•	•	•	•	•
Branch if ≤ zero	BLE	2F	4	2										Z + (N ⊕ V) = 1	•	•	•	•	•	•
Branch if lower or same	BLS	23	4	2										C + Z = 1	•	•	•	•	•	•
Branch if < zero	BLT	2D	4	2										N ⊕ V = 1	•	•	•	•	•	•
Branch if minus	BMI	2B	4	2										N = 1	•	•	•	•	•	•
Branch if not equal zero	BNE	26	4	2										Z = 0	•	•	•	•	•	•
Branch if overflow clear	BVC	28	4	2										V = 0	•	•	•	•	•	•
Branch if overflow set	BVS	29	4	2										V = 1	•	•	•	•	•	•
Branch if plus	BPL	2A	4	2										N = 0	•	•	•	•	•	•
Branch to subroutine	BSR	8D	8	2											•	•	•	•	•	•
Jump	JMP				6E	4	2	7E	3	3				} See special operations	•	•	•	•	•	•
Jump to subroutine	JSR				AD	8	2	8D	9	3					•	•	•	•	•	•
No operation	NOP										01	2	1	Advances prog. cntr. only	•	•	•	•	•	•
Return from interrupt	RTI										3B	10	1		———————⑩———————					
Return from subroutine	RTS										39	5	1	} See special operations	•	•	•	•	•	•
Software interrupt	SWI										3F	12	1		•	S	•	•	•	•
Wait for interrupt	WAI										3E	9	1		•	⑪	•	•	•	•

CONDITIONS CODE REGISTER OPERATIONS	MNEMONIC	INHER			BOOLEAN OPERATION	5 H	4 I	3 N	2 Z	1 V	0 C
		OP	~	#							
Clear carry	CLC	0C	2	1	$0 \rightarrow C$	•	•	•	•	•	R
Clear interrupt mask	CLI	0E	2	1	$0 \rightarrow I$	•	R	•	•	•	•
Clear overflow	CLV	0A	2	1	$0 \rightarrow V$	•	•	•	•	R	•
Set carry	SEC	0D	2	1	$1 \rightarrow C$	•	•	•	•	•	S
Set interrupt mask	SEI	0F	2	1	$1 \rightarrow I$	•	S	•	•	•	•
Set overflow	SEV	0B	2	1	$1 \rightarrow V$	•	•	•	•	S	•
Acmltr. A → CCR	TAP	06	2	1	$A \rightarrow CCR$	———————⑫———————					
CCR → Acmltr A	TPA	07	2	1	$CCR \rightarrow A$	•	•	•	•	•	•

CONDITION CODE REGISTER NOTES: (bit set if test is true and cleared otherwise)

① (Bit V) Test: result = 10000000?
② (Bit C) Test: result = 00000000?
③ (Bit C) Test: decimal value of most significant BCD character greater than nine (Not cleared if previously set.)
④ (Bit V) Test: operand = 10000000 prior to execution?
⑤ (Bit V) Test: operand = 01111111 prior to execution?
⑥ (Bit V) Test: set equal to result of N ⊕ C after shift has occurred
⑦ (Bit N) Test: sign bit of most significant (MS) byte of result = 1?
⑧ (Bit V) Test: 2's complement overflow from subtraction of LS bytes?
⑨ (Bit N) Test: result less than zero? (Bit 15 = 1)
⑩ (All)   Load condition code register from stack. (See special operations.)
⑪ (Bit I) Set when interrupt occurs. If previously set, a nonmaskable interrupt is required to exit the wait state
⑫ (All)   Set according to the contents of accumulator A

LEGEND:

OP	Operation code (hexadecimal)	00	Byte = zero	
~	Number of MPU cycles	H	Half carry from bit 3	
#	Number of program bytes	I	Interrupt mask	
+	Arithmetic plus	N	Negative (sign bit)	
−	Arithmetic minus	Z	Zero (byte)	
·	Boolean AND	V	Overflow, 2's complement	
M_{SP}	Contents of memory location pointed to be stack pointer	C	Carry from bit 7	
+	Boolean inclusive OR	R	Reset always	
⊕	Boolean exclusive OR	S	Set always	
$\overline{M}$	Complement of M	‡	Test and set if true, cleared otherwise	
→	Transfer into.	•	Not affected	
0	Bit = zero	CCR	Condition code register	
		LS	Least significant	
		MS	Most significant	

Figure 13.4 The MC6800 Instruction Set. *(Courtesy of Motorola, Inc.)*

1. *Accumulator and memory instructions*: used to perform all logic and arithmetic operations on the accumulator data, or the data contained in a specified memory location.

2. *Index register and stack manipulation instructions*: used to change the contents of the index register and/or the stack pointer.

INSTRUCTION SET*

ACCUMULATOR AND MEMORY OPERATIONS	MNEMONIC	IMMED OP	~	#	DIRECT OP	~	#	INDEX OP	~	#	EXTND OP	~	#	INHER OP	~	#	BOOLEAN/ARITHMETIC OPERATIONS (All register labels refer to contents)	H (5)	I (4)	N (3)	Z (2)	V (1)	C (0)
Add	ADDA	8B	2	2	9B	3	2	AB	5	2	BB	4	3				A + M → A	‡	•	‡	‡	‡	‡
	ADDB	CB	2	2	DB	3	2	EB	5	2	FB	4	3				B + M → B	‡	•	‡	‡	‡	‡
Add acmltrs	ABA													1B	2	1	A + B → A	‡	•	‡	‡	‡	‡
Add with carry	ADCA	89	2	2	99	3	2	A9	5	2	B9	4	3				A + M + C → A	‡	•	‡	‡	‡	‡
	ADCB	C9	2	2	D9	3	2	E9	5	2	F9	4	3				B + M + C → B	‡	•	‡	‡	‡	‡
And	ANDA	84	2	2	94	3	2	A4	5	2	B4	4	3				A · M → A	•	•	‡	‡	R	•
	ANDB	C4	2	2	D4	3	2	E4	5	2	F4	4	3				B · M → B	•	•	‡	‡	R	•
Bit test	BITA	85	2	2	95	3	2	A5	5	2	B5	4	3				A · M	•	•	‡	‡	R	•
	BITB	C5	2	2	D5	3	2	E5	5	2	F5	4	3				B · M	•	•	‡	‡	R	•
Clear	CLR							6F	7	2	7F	6					00 → M	•	•	R	S	R	R
	CLRA													4F	2	1	00 → A	•	•	R	S	R	R
	CLRB													5F	2	1	00 → B	•	•	R	S	R	R
Compare	CMPA	81	2	2	91	3	2	A1	5	2	B1	4	3				A − M	•	•	‡	‡	‡	‡
	CMPB	C1	2	2	D1	3	2	E1	5	2	F1	4	3				B − M	•	•	‡	‡	‡	‡
Compare acmltrs	CBA													11	2	1	A − B	•	•	‡	‡	‡	‡
Complement, 1's	COM							63	7	2	73	7	3				$\overline{M}$ → M	•	•	‡	‡	R	S
	COMA													43	2	1	$\overline{A}$ → A	•	•	‡	‡	R	S
	COMB													53	2	1	$\overline{B}$ → B	•	•	‡	‡	R	S
Complement, 2's (Negate)	NEG							60	7	2	70	6	3				00 − M → M	•	•	‡	‡	①	②
	NEGA													40	2	1	00 − A → A	•	•	‡	‡	①	②
	NEGB													50	2	1	00 − B → B	•	•	‡	‡	①	②
Decimal adjust, A	DAA													19	2	1	Converts binary add. of BCD characters into BCD format	•	•	‡	‡	‡	③
Decrement	DEC							6A	7	2	7A	6	3				M − 1 → M	•	•	‡	‡	④	•
	DECA													4A	2	1	A − 1 → A	•	•	‡	‡	④	•
	DECB													5A	2	1	B − 1 → B	•	•	‡	‡	④	•
Exclusive OR	EORA	88	2	2	98	3	2	A8	5	2	B8	4	3				A ⊕ M → A	•	•	‡	‡	R	•
	EORB	C8	2	2	D8	3	2	E8	5	2	F8	4	3				B ⊕ M → B	•	•	‡	‡	R	•
Increment	INC							6C	7	2	7C	6	3				M + 1 → M	•	•	‡	‡	⑤	•
	INCA													4C	2	1	A + 1 → A	•	•	‡	‡	⑤	•
	INCB													5C	2	1	B + 1 → B	•	•	‡	‡	⑤	•
Load acmltr	LDAA	86	2	2	96	3	2	A6	5	2	B6	4	3				M → A	•	•	‡	‡	R	•
	LDAB	C6	2	2	D6	3	2	E6	5	2	F6	4	3				M → B	•	•	‡	‡	R	•
Or, inclusive	ORAA	8A	2	2	9A	3	2	AA	5	2	BA	4	3				A + M → A	•	•	‡	‡	R	•
	ORAB	CA	2	2	DA	3	2	EA	5	2	FA	4	3				B + M → B	•	•	‡	‡	R	•
Push data	PSHA													36	4	1	A → M$_{SP}$, SP − 1 → SP	•	•	•	•	•	•
	PSHB													37	4	1	B → M$_{SP}$, SP − 1 → SP	•	•	•	•	•	•
Pull data	PULA													32	4	1	SP + 1 → SP, M$_{SP}$ → A	•	•	•	•	•	•
	PULB													33	4	1	SP + 1 → SP, M$_{SP}$ → B	•	•	•	•	•	•
Rotate left	RDL							69	7	2	79	6	3				M	•	•	‡	‡	⑥	‡
	ROLA													49	2	1	A	•	•	‡	‡	⑥	‡
	ROLB													59	2	1	B	•	•	‡	‡	⑥	‡
Rotate right	ROR							66	7	2	76	6	3				M	•	•	‡	‡	⑥	‡
	RORA													46	2	1	A	•	•	‡	‡	⑥	‡
	RORB													56	2	1	B	•	•	‡	‡	⑥	‡
Shift left, arithmetic	ASL							68	7	2	78	6	3				M	•	•	‡	‡	⑥	‡
	ASLA													48	2	1	A	•	•	‡	‡	⑥	‡
	ASLB													58	2	1	B	•	•	‡	‡	⑥	‡
Shift right, arithmetic	ASR							67	7	2	77	6	3				M	•	•	‡	‡	⑥	‡
	ASRA													47	2	1	A	•	•	‡	‡	⑥	‡
	ASRB													57	2	1	B	•	•	‡	‡	⑥	‡
Shift right, logic	LSR							64	7	2	74	6	3				M	•	•	R	‡	⑥	‡
	LSRA													44	2	1	A	•	•	R	‡	⑥	‡
	LSRB													54	2	1	B	•	•	R	‡	⑥	‡
Store acmltr.	STAA				97	4	2	A7	6	2	B7	5	3				A → M	•	•	‡	‡	R	•
	STAB				D7	4	2	E7	6	2	F7	5	3				B → M	•	•	‡	‡	R	•
Subtract	SUBA	80	2	2	90	3	2	A0	5	2	B0	4	3				A − M → A	•	•	‡	‡	‡	‡
	SUBB	C0	2	2	D0	3	2	E0	5	2	F0	4	3				B − M → B	•	•	‡	‡	‡	‡
Subtract acmltrs.	SBA													10	2	1	A − B → A	•	•	‡	‡	‡	‡
Subtract with carry	SBCA	82	2	2	92	3	2	A2	5	2	B2	4	3				A − M − C → A	•	•	‡	‡	‡	‡
	SBCB	C2	2	2	D2	3	2	E2	5	2	F2	4	3				B − M − C → B	•	•	‡	‡	‡	‡
Transfer acmltrs.	TAB													16	2	1	A → B	•	•	‡	‡	R	•
	TBA													17	2	1	B → A	•	•	‡	‡	R	•
Test, zero or minus	TST							6D	7	2	7D	6	3				M − 00	•	•	‡	‡	R	R
	TSTA													40	2	1	A − 00	•	•	‡	‡	R	R
	TSTB													50	2	1	B − 00	•	•	‡	‡	R	R

*Copied with permission of Motorola.

Figure 13.4 (Continued)

3. *Condition code register instructions*: used to change the contents of the condition code register. They are usually used prior to branch or jump instructions.

4. *Jump and branch instructions*: cause the microprocessor to go to a given memory location and start executing instructions from that point if a given condition exists. These instructions relate to the diamond shapes in the flowchart.

For each instruction in the set, there is quite a bit of information given, if you can read the chart. Beside each instruction name, the mnemonic for the operation is given, followed by the addressing modes. These addressing modes are discussed later in this section. However, in each addressing mode column, you will notice three columns. These columns contain the following information about the instruction:

OP: op-code for the instruction in that particular addressing mode

~: number of machine cycles required to complete the instruction

#: number of bytes contained in the instruction

In the *Boolean/arithmetic operation* column, there is a formula or expression that represents the operation being performed. These are also discussed later in this section. The *condition code register* column indicates the effect that a given instruction will have on the flags. A dot in the column indicates that the flag is not affected. The "↕" symbol indicates that the flag will SET or RESET, depending on the outcome of the instruction. The S or R indicates that the flag will definitely SET or RESET, regardless of the outcome of the operation. A number in the column refers you to the notes at the end of the instruction set chart. The Boolean/arithmetic and condition code register columns will appear throughout this chapter, and the contents of the columns discussed further.

Addressing Modes

The MC6800 has six addressing modes. This means that the data for a given operation can be obtained from one of several locations, depending on the addressing mode being used. The MC6800 distinguishes addressing modes by the op-code being used. For example, the "add to accumulator A," ADDA, instruction has four possible op-codes. Each op-code indicates the operation and the source of the value to be added to the contents of accumulator A. For each addressing mode, there is a slight variation in the op-code, as follows:

ADDA (immediate)	= 8B	=	1 0 0 0 1 0 1 1
ADDA (direct)	= 9B	=	1 0 0 1 1 0 1 1
ADDA (index)	= AB	=	1 0 1 0 1 0 1 1
ADDA (extnd)	= BB	=	1 0 1 1 1 0 1 1

If you look at the binary forms of the op-codes listed, you will see that they are identical, with the exception of the B5 and B4 values. These two bits are used to indicate the addressing mode being used. When the CPU decodes these two bits, it obtains the data to be added to accumulator A from the designated location. The method by which the data location is determined for each addressing mode is as follows:

1. *Immediate addressing*: In this addressing mode, the data to be used is the next value in the program. For example:

Address	Contents	
0020-H	8B	Instruction
0021-H	67	Data

The instruction, ADDA, is in the immediate addressing mode, as indicated by the op-code. Since the immediate mode of addressing is used, the microprocessor treats the next value in the program (67) as the data to be added to the contents of accumulator A. This type of addressing is useful when constant values are being used. *Note that the byte following an immediate mode instruction is always treated as data.*

2. *Direct addressing:* In this addressing mode, the second byte in the instruction is treated as an 8-bit address. The data is then obtained from this address. For example, if the op-code in the previous example had been 9B (direct addressing mode), the microprocessor would have gone to memory address 0067 to get the value to add to the accumulator. *Note that in this addressing mode, the high byte of the address is always set to 00-H.* Therefore, only addresses 0000 through 00FF can be used to store data if this addressing mode is used, since these are the only addresses that can be generated by direct addressing.

3. *Indexed addressing:* In this addressing mode, an 8-bit value, called an *off-set value,* is added to the contents of the index register to form a 16-bit address. The offset value is placed in the program as the second instruction byte. For example, if the index register contains the value 00A0, and the second byte of the instruction is 0B, the data address is determined as

$$00A0 \ + \ 0B \ = \ 00AB \quad (\text{the data address})$$

The applications of this addressing mode will be shown in a later example.

4. *Extended addressing:* In this addressing mode, every instruction is a three-byte instruction, with the instruction bytes being stored in successive memory locations. The first byte is the op-code, as always, and the second two bytes form a 16-bit data address. This has the advantage over direct addressing of allowing you to use the full range of memory addresses, but has the drawback of requiring three bytes per instruction. This drawback can become important when you are trying to use as little memory as possible to store a program.

5. *Implied addressing:* In this addressing mode, there are no address or data bytes contained in the instructions. The instructions themselves imply where the data to be operated on is located. For example, the INX (increment index register) instruction needs no data address since the instruction itself indicates where the data is located—in the index register. These instructions are *all* one-byte instructions.

6. *Relative addressing:* This is perhaps the most difficult of the addressing modes to understand. It is similar to indexed addressing, except for two points:
   a. The offset value is added to the *program counter.*
   b. The offset value is a two's-complement number that usually results in sending the CPU back to an instruction that was performed earlier in the program.

For example, consider the flowchart shown in Figure 13.5. The decision box requires that a NO answer return the CPU to an earlier instruction. Relative addressing would be used for this function. This is covered in greater detail in the section on jump and branch instructions later in this section.

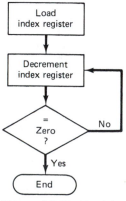

Figure 13.5 Decision signal flow.

Accumulator and Memory Instructions

These instructions involve the data stored in the accumulator or a given memory location. Many of these instructions can involve both the accumulator and a memory location, as will be shown. The instructions in this category are broken down into two basic types:

1. Arithmetic and logic operations
2. Data transfer operations

The arithmetic and logic operations cause some arithmetic or logic operation to be performed on the data, while the data transfer operations cause data to be moved from one location to another. In the case of each instruction, the expression listed in the Boolean/arithmetic column explains the operation to be performed. *It is important to remember that in this column, all register labels refer to the contents of that register.* For example, look at the ABA instruction (add accumulators) in Figure 13.4. The expression for this instruction is shown as

$$A + B \rightarrow A$$

This expression reads "the contents of accumulator A are added to the contents of accumulator B, and the result is stored in accumulator A." When the expression contains a numeric value, that numeric value is read as its exact value. For example, look at the "clear" (CLR) instruction. This instruction is used to clear (RESET) the contents of a given memory location. The expression for this instruction is

$$00 \rightarrow M$$

The expression in this case reads "store the value 00 in memory location M." This has the same effect as clearing the memory location. It should be noted that all the values listed in these expressions are in hexadecimal value, unless otherwise indicated.

Most of the instructions in the accumulator and memory group are fairly self-explanatory and can easily be analyzed using the Boolean/arithmetic expressions. There are, however, several instructions that need to be explained in greater detail than the expressions give. We will cover these instructions now.

1. *Add with carry:* The add with carry instruction takes into consideration the carry out from a previous addition operation. An "add" instruction does not. This point can be seen in their respective expressions. When would you use one instead of the other? Consider the problem of adding two 16-bit values:

$$0\ 1\ 1\ 0\ 1\ 0\ 0\ 1\ 0\ 0\ 1\ 0\ 1\ 0\ 0\ 1$$

and

$$0\ 1\ 1\ 1\ 0\ 1\ 1\ 0\ 1\ 1\ 1\ 1\ 0\ 0\ 0\ 1$$

Since the accumulator can hold only 8 bits, the addition of the two values will have to be done by breaking them into two bytes. The low bytes are added and the results are stored. Then the two high bytes are added, and together with the sum from the previous addition, yields the 16-bit sum of the two numbers. Now, if you add the two 16-bit numbers together yourself, you will notice that there is a carry-out of the B7 position. This carry would have to be involved in the addition of the two high bytes, or an incorrect answer would be obtained. The high bytes would therefore need to be added using the ADC (add with carry) instruction so that the carry-out from the low-byte addition would not be left out. The ADD instruction could be used for the low-byte addition, since there would be no carry into this addition operation.

2. *Logic instructions:* These are the AND, XOR, OR, and COMPLEMENT operations. In these instructions, the logic function is performed on each bit from one register, with the corresponding bit from the other register. For example, the ANDA (AND accumulator A) instruction calls for the contents of the A accumulator to be ANDed with the contents of a given memory location. Assume that this instruction is used on the following data values:

           accumulator A = 1 1 0 0 1 0 1 1

           memory data   = 0 1 1 0 1 0 0 1

           resulting data   = 0 1 0 0 1 0 0 1

Note that each result bit is determined by ANDing the two bits directly above it. The resulting data would be transferred to accumulator A, as indicated by the expression for the operation. Now you try it. The ORAA (OR accumulator A) instruction is being used on the following data. What will the result data equal?

           accumulator A = 1 0 0 1 1 0 1 0

           memory data   = 0 1 0 1 1 0 0 1

           resulting data   = _ _ _ _ _ _ _ _

Your result should equal 11011011, a value that would result by ORing each accumulator bit with the corresponding memory data bit. According to the expression for the ORAA instruction, where would the result of this operation be stored?

3. *Compare, Bit Test, and Test-Zero or Minus:* If you look at the expressions for these three instructions in Figure 13.4, you will notice that they do not show where the result of the operation is stored. This is due to the fact that the results of the operation are not stored anywhere. The operations are performed for the sole purpose of affecting the flags in the condition code register and thus giving some indication of the relationship between the two numbers. For example, the CMPA instruction is used to compare the contents of the accumulator with the contents of a given memory location. It does this by subtracting the contents of the memory location from the contents of the accumulator. *Note that the contents of the two registers are not changed.* The contents of the condition code register will be changed, however, in such a way as to indicate the relationship between the two numbers, as follows:

a. If the accumulator value is greater than the memory value, then A − M will yield a *positive* result and the N and Z flags will both be RESET.

b. If the accumulator value equals the memory value, A − M will result in an answer of 00000000, and the Z flag will SET.

c. If the accumulator value is less than the memory value, A − M will yield a negative result and the N flag will SET.

These three conditions are shown in the following chart:

Relationship	Result	N flag[a]	Z flag
A > M	Positive	0	0
A = M	Zero	0	1
A < M	Negative	1	0

[a]Note that the N flag will work according to this chart only when the compare instruction is being used on signed (two's-complement) binary numbers.

This allows the CPU to make decisions based on whether one value is greater than, less than, or equal to another value. In Section 13.3 the OIL PRESSURE program is based on this compare/decision operation.

The BIT TEST and TEST-ZERO OR MINUS instructions work in the same basic fashion, but the test method and value to be compared to have changed.

4. *Decimal adjust accumulator:* The DAA instruction is used in BCD arithmetic operations. When the MC6800 adds BCD values, it adds them according to the rules of binary arithmetic. This instruction is used to convert the binary formatted result into correct BCD form. Any time that BCD values are added in the MC6800, the DAA instruction must immediately follow the addition operation.

5. *Arithmetic and Logic Shift Operations:* In the case of each of these shift operations, the diagram in the Boolean/arithmetic column indicates where the shifted bits go. For example, in the "shift right, logic" operation, the bit in b0 goes to the carry flag and 0 is shifted into the b7 position. All bits in the accumulator are shifted right one position. The ROTATE instructions can be analyzed in the same fashion.

Index Register and Stack Instructions

There are six types of operations in this instruction group. They are the COMPARE, DECREMENT, INCREMENT, LOAD, STORE, and TRANSFER operations. The COMPARE instruction causes the microprocessor to compare the contents of the index register with the contents of two successive memory locations. The high byte of the index register is compared with the contents of the first memory location, then the low byte of the index register is compared with the contents of the next memory location. The contents of neither the index register nor the memory locations are affected, so again, this instruction is used for the sole purpose of affecting the flags. This instruction would be used for the same purpose as the CMP instruction and would have the same results. The big difference is that the CPX instruction allows you to compare two 16-bit values.

The DECREMENT instructions cause the contents of the addressed register to subtract (1) from its contents. This instruction is very useful in timing loops. The INCREMENT instruction causes the addressed register to add (1) to its contents.

The LOAD and STORE instructions perform READ and WRITE operations, respectively. When you load a register, you are reading a value from memory and putting the value into that register. When you store a register, you are writing the value contained in the register into the addressed memory location. The TRANSFER operations cause these registers to send data from one register to the other. Again, the source register contents do not change, and the contents of the destination register do.

The following program shows the index register being used in a *timing loop*. Recall that a timing loop is a program designed to provide a time delay. The time delay in this case is provided by tying up the microprocessor in a program. Since the BNE (Branch if not equal to zero) instruction has not been discussed yet, you must take it on faith that this instruction will send the microprocessor back to the DEX instruction as long as the index register contains any value other than zero. If the index register contains the value 0000-H, the BNE instruction will not be executed and the microprocessor will go on to the next instruction.

Address	Contents	Mnemonic
0000	CE	LDX
0001	C5	(C5)
0002	00	(00)
0003	09	DEX
0004	26	BNE
0005	FD	(FD)
0006	3E	WAI

The first instruction in the program is the LDX (load index register) instruction. If you look up the op-code CE, you will see that it is an immediate mode instruction. And according to the chart in Figure 13.4, the instruction takes three bytes. Since the immediate addressing mode is used, the next two bytes in the program make up the value to be loaded into the index register. The index register is therefore loaded with the value C500. The next instruction is located at address 0003. This is the DEX (decrement index register) instruction and causes the index register to be counted down by one.

The next instruction is the BNE instruction. This is a relative addressing mode instruction and is followed by the offset value, FD. If the index register equals anything other than 0000-H, this instruction will cause the program counter to be set back to 0003, where the DEX instruction will be fetched and executed again. This process repeats itself until the count of 0000-H is reached. At that time, the WAI instruction is fetched. This is the standard "program ending" command for the MC6800. When this instruction is fetched and executed, the CPU goes into the wait state and stays idle until an interrupt is received. Most MC6800 machine-level programs end with this instruction.

The program listed would follow the flowchart shown in Figure 13.6a. As you can see, this is almost exactly the same flowchart as the one shown in Figure 13.5. Only the labels and values have been changed. In Figure 13.6b, the program just

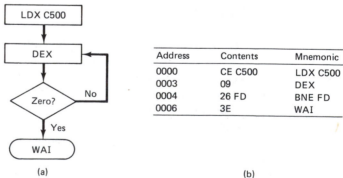

(a)   (b)

Figure 13.6 Timing loop flowchart and program listing.

discussed has been rewritten. The addresses shown are op-code addresses. The data or offset values that are part of the instruction are written on the same line. *The memory locations for these values are still accounted for, even though they are not listed in the program.* Writing a program in this fashion makes it easier to distinguish instructions from data.

The timing loop will "lock up" the microprocessor until the value C500 has been counted down all the way to zero. This would allow the external circuits to perform some operation without interference from the CPU.

Condition Code Register Instructions

These instructions are used to change the contents of the condition code register. Since the branch instructions all rely on the state of a given flag, it helps to make sure that the CCR is in the proper state before attempting to use it. *Each CCR instruction affects one flag, and all instructions are in the implied addressing mode.*

Jump and Branch Instructions

The BRANCH instructions cause the microprocessor to alter the course of the program, depending on the state of a given flag, or flags. All of the branch instructions are two-byte instructions that use relative addressing. Referring back to the instruction set in Figure 13.4, look at the column labeled *test conditions*. This column indicates the conditions under which a given branch will occur. If the test condition is not met, the branch instruction is not executed and the CPU goes on to the next program instruction.

It should be noted that no branch instruction will do anything to affect the flags. They only cause the contents of the program counter to be changed if one or more conditions exist.

Let's go back to the timing loop program. The program will be analyzed in detail here to show how the branch instructions work. The analysis of the program is as follows:

1. The CE at location 0000 causes the index register to load with the value C500, as was stated earlier. The next instruction, DEX, causes the value in the index register to be counted down by one, so the value now equals C4FF (C500 − 1 = C4FF). At this point, the register values are as shown below:

Program counter	Instruction register	Index register	Zero flag
0004*	09	C4FF	0

2. The CPU now addresses location 0004 and fetches the BNE instruction. As soon as the fetch is completed, the register contains the following values:

Program counter	Instruction register	Index register	Zero flag
0005	26	C4FF	0

The BNE instruction will cause the CPU to change the contents of the PC if the condition "Z = 0" exists. In this case, it does, so the CPU will execute the BNE instruction. To do so, it must now fetch the offset value. After fetching this value (FD), the register contents will be:

Program counter	Instruction register	Index register	Zero flag
0006*	26	C4FF	0

*This is due to the fact that the PC was incremented after fetching the DEX instruction.

3. Now the microprocessor will add the offset value to the *low byte* of the program counter. This addition is shown in both hexadecimal and binary form:*

Program counter	0006	00000000 00000110
Offset value	FD	00000000 11111101
New PC contents	0003	00000000 00000011*

*The carry-out from the low byte of the program counter does not carry over to the high byte.

As a result of the addition of the offset value to the low byte of the program counter, the value in the counter has been changed to 0003. As the next instruction cycle begins, this value is once again placed on the address bus and the DEX instruction is fetched and executed again. After the DEX instruction is complete, the BNE cycle repeats itself. This process will repeat itself until the contents of the index register equal 0000-H. At that time, the zero flag will be SET (Z = 1) and the BNE instruction will not be executed. *When the BNE instruction is not executed, the offset value that follows it in the program will be bypassed by the CPU. It will not be treated as an instruction.*

13.3 PROGRAM EXAMPLES

In this section two machine-level programs are analyzed. Although these programs are relatively simple, they will help you understand the way in which the CPU accomplishes the tasks set out for it in the program.

Program I: Oil Pressure Monitor

This program causes the microprocessor to monitor the pressure in an oil tank. If the pressure is too high, a release valve must be opened. If the pressure is as it should be, the system must do nothing but continue to check the pressure. The flowchart for the program is shown in Figure 13.7.

The program works by reading the oil pressure value and comparing the value with one that is held in the accumulator. The microprocessor then analyzes the results in the manner described on page 255. If the pressure is too high, the N flag will SET as a result of the comparison, and the CPU responds by turning the release valve on. If the pressure is as it should be, the Z flag will SET and the CPU will simply repeat the oil pressure reading process. If neither of the conditions above exists (i.e., if N = 0 and Z = 0), the CPU will turn on the pump in response to low pressure.

There are a few points that must be assumed to be true before actually analyzing the program. For the sake of discussion, we will assume:

1. The microprocessor obtains an 8-bit value that is equal to the oil pressure by reading the value at location A044. This address corresponds to the location of the input device.
2. The microprocessor controls the release valve and oil pump by sending specific data values to location A045. These control values are as follows:

no action = 1 1 1 1 1 1 1 1

pump on = 0 0 0 0 1 1 1 1

valve on = 1 1 1 1 0 0 0 0

*Since the offset value is data, and not an instruction, the contents of the instruction register have not been changed. The PC, however, has a new value.

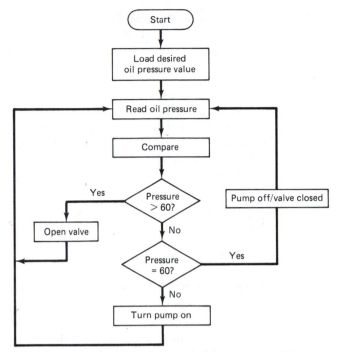

Figure 13.7 Flowchart for oil pressure problem.

3. The desired oil pressure is 60 psi.

The actual program is as follows:

Address	Contents			Mnemonic		Comment
0000	86	3C		LDAA	3C	Load accumulator A with 3C-H (60)
0002	CE	A0	44	LDX	A0 44	Load index register with A044-H
0005	A1	00		CMP	00	Compare accumulator with data from A044
0007	2B	OD		BMI	OD	Branch if minus to location 0016
0009	26	05		BNE		Branch if not zero to location 0010
000B	C6	FF		LDAB	FF	Load accumulator B with FF (11111111)
000D	E7	01		STAB	01	Store accumulator B at location A045
000E	20	F5		BRA	F5	Branch always to location 0005
0010	C6	OF		LDAB	OF	Load accumulator B with OF (00001111)
0012	E7	01		STAB	01	Store accumulator B at location A045
0014	20	EF		BRA	EF	Branch always to location 0005
0016	C6	FO		LDAB	FO	Load accumulator B will FO (11110000)
0018	E7	01		STAB	01	Store accumulator B in location A045
001A	20	E9		BRA	E9	Branch always to location 0005

The program can be divided into two parts. The first part consists of those instructions involved in checking the oil pressure, and deciding what action, if any, to take. This part of the program is contained in memory locations 0000 through 0009. The rest of the program is made up of the actions to be taken. If you look at the instructions in locations 000B through 001A, you will notice that there are three nearly identical cycles containing three instructions each. The three instruction cycle consists of loading accumulator B (ACCB), storing the contents of ACCB at A045 (the output to the pressure controls), and then branching back to location 0005, where the microprocessor restarts the cycle. Only two values vary from action cycle to action cycle. The value to be sent to A045 varies, since the actions themselves vary, and the offset value used to return to 0005 varies because of the difference in addresses where the BRA instructions occur.

The BRA (branch always) instruction is an *unconditional branch*. This means that there is no test condition under which the branch will occur. A BRA instruction will be executed every time that it is fetched, regardless of any conditions that may exist. In this program it is being used to return the microprocessor to the CMP instruction at location 0005 after every action cycle. This ensures that no matter what action is taken by the program, the next operation will be to check the pressure again. Each BRA instruction offset value is added to the program counter as follows:

0 0 0 1 0 0 0 0	0 0 0 1 0 1 1 0	0 0 0 1 1 1 0 0	PC values
1 1 1 1 0 1 0 1	1 1 1 0 1 1 1 1	1 1 1 0 1 0 0 1	respective
			offsets
0 0 0 0 0 1 0 1	0 0 0 0 0 1 0 1	0 0 0 0 0 1 0 1	new PC values

The original PC values shown are those that were in the low byte of the counter *after* the offset values were fetched. In every case, the resulting value in the PC was equal to 0005, the location of the CMP instruction.

The first part of the program starts out by loading the value 3C in accumulator A (ACCA). This is the hexadecimal equivalent of the decimal value 60, the desired psi. The program also loads the value A044 into the index register. This allows the use of indexed addressing mode instructions at locations 000D, 0012, and 0018, the store accumulator B (STAB) instructions. Why use indexed addressing for the STAB instructions? Each time the STAB instructions are used, a 16-bit address must be generated to address location A045. If extended addressing had been used for these instructions, it would have taken three instruction bytes for each of these instructions; a total of nine instruction bytes for the three STAB instructions. The CMP instruction also must be able to generate a 16-bit address. If extended addressing had been used for this instruction also, the total number of bytes for the four instructions would have been 12. Using the indexed addressing mode, the total number of instruction bytes for the four instructions and the LDX instruction totals up to 11. One less memory location was used by going with indexed addressing. This may seem like a lot of trouble to go through for one memory location, but if this program were being run by a system with limited memory capability, the effort would be worth it.

The CMP (compare) instruction reads the oil pressure, and compares it with the value in ACCA (60). If the pressure is too high, A − M will be negative and the negative flag will SET. If the pressure is correct, A − M will result in an answer of zero and the Z flag will SET. If neither of these two conditions exists, the program assumes that the pressure is too low and the appropriate action is taken. In summary:

Condition	Result of (A − M)	N flag	Z flag
Pressure high	Negative	1	0
Pressure correct	Zero	0	1
Pressure low	Positive	0	0

After the comparison, the program checks to see if N = 1 with the BMI instruction. If the condition (N = 1) exists, the program branches to location 0016. This is the starting point for the "open valve" process. If N = 0, the program simply bypasses the BMI instruction. The next instruction (BNE) will cause the program to branch to location 0010 if Z = 0. This location (0010) is the start of the "pump on" process.

If $Z = 1$ (pressure is correct), the program continues on to the first action cycle, which starts at location 000B. This cycle simply makes sure that neither the pump nor the valve are activated.

After the appropriate action has been taken, the program returns to the CMP instruction and starts the whole process over again. Let's take a look at how the program would run if the pressure in the tank was too low. The process would be as follows:

1. The CMP instruction would cause the conditions of $N = 0$ and $Z = 0$, as we stated earlier.
2. The BMI instruction would not be executed, because the condition of $N = 1$ does not exist.
3. The BNE instruction *would* be executed, because the condition of $Z = 0$ does exist. The PC is now set to 0010.
4. The CPU fetches the instruction at 0010 and loads the value 00001111 (0F) into ACCB.
5. The value in ACCB is now sent to location A045 by the STAB instruction.
6. The 00001111 at A045 causes the oil pump to turn on.
7. The program returns to location 0005 and starts the CMP instruction again.

The foregoing process will continue until the pressure is correct. At that time, the result of the CMP instruction will be $N = 0$ and $Z = 1$. When this happens, the process is changed as follows:

1. The BNE instruction at location 0009 is not executed because the condition of $Z = 0$ does not exist. The CPU continues on to the instruction at 000B.
2. The LDAB instruction at 000B causes the value 11111111 to be loaded into ACCB.
3. The STAB instruction causes the contents of ACCB to be stored at A045.
4. The 11111111 at A045 causes the pump to turn off.
5. The program now branches back to the instruction at 0005 and starts the whole process over again.

Program II: Binary Multiplication

If you look at the instruction set for the MC6800, you will see that there is no instruction for multiplication. Because of this, the microprocessor must run a program in order to multiply two numbers. There are two methods by which multiplication can be accomplished. One method is called a *shift-and-add algorithm*. An algorithm is a program that simulates a mathematical process. When the algorithm is used, the microprocessor does not actually multiply the numbers, but the results are the same as if it had. Another way of multiplying two numbers is to multiply by repeated addition. In this case, the multiplicand is added to itself over and over. The number of times that it is added to itself is determined by the multiplier. When the process is over, the microprocessor has the correct answer. In this program, we will multiply by repeated addition, simply because it is the easier of the two programs to follow. The flowchart for this program can be seen in Figure 13.8.

The multiplicand in this program will be stored in ACCA and the multiplier will be stored in ACCB. The product of the problem will be stored in two successive memory locations, 0020 and 0021. The program starts by clearing these two locations to ensure that the final product is correct. The two values are then loaded into

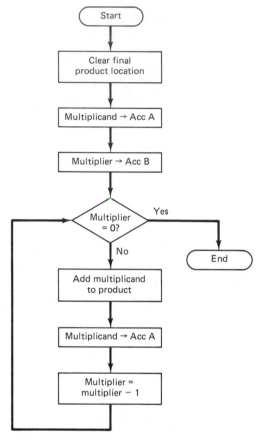

Figure 13.8 Multiplication by repeated addition.

their respective accumulators. The multiplier is then checked to ensure that it does not equal zero. If it does, the program ends and the two memory locations contain the correct answer 0000-H. If the multiplier is not equal to zero, the addition process begins. Each time the cycle is repeated, the multiplier is checked, the multiplicand is added to the product, and the multiplier is decremented. When the multiplier reaches zero, the program ends, and the correct answer is in the memory locations.

In this program, you will see the ADD and ADC instruction being used. Recall that the ADD instruction adds the contents of a memory location with the contents of the accumulator, while the ADC operation adds both of these values and the carry bit. Using the ADC instruction will allow the carry from the first addition (low byte) to be carried over into the second addition (high byte). The program itself is listed here:

Address	Contents	Mnemonic	Comment
0000	7F 00 20	CLR 00 20	Clears memory location (ML) 0020
0003	7F 00 21	CLR 00 21	Clears ML 0021
0006	96 23	LDAA	Load ACCA from direct address 0023
0008	D6 24	LDAB 24	Load ACCB from direct address 24 (0024)
000A	27 0F	BEQ	Branch if zero to location 001B
000C	9B 20	ADD 20	Add the contents of ML 0020 to ACCA
000E	97 20	STAA 20	Store ACCA in ML 0020
0010	96 21	LDAA 21	Load ACCA from ML 0021
0012	89 00	ADC 00	Add (with carry) 00-H to ACCA
0014	97 21	STAA 21	Store the result in ACCA in ML 0021
0016	96 23	LDAA 23	Reload multiplicand into ACCA
0018	5A	DECB	Decrement ACCB (multiplier)
0019	26 F1	BNE EB	Branch if not zero to ML 000C

Address	Contents	Mnemonic	Comment
001B	3E	WAI	Halt (wait for interrupt)
0020	DATA	DATA	Product low byte
0021	DATA	DATA	Product high byte
0023	DATA	DATA	Multiplicand
0024	DATA	DATA	Multiplier

The initial setup of all of the registers involved in the problem is handled by the instructions contained at locations 0000 through 0008. Once these instructions are executed, they are no longer used in the program. The next instruction, BEQ, causes the microprocessor to branch to the end of the program if the multiplier (which is in ACCB) is equal to zero. If the multiplier is not zero, the program continues by adding the contents of ML 0020 (the product low byte) to the multiplicand in ACCA. The result is then stored in ML 0020. The high byte of the product, which is contained in ML 0021, is then loaded into ACCA. This value is added with zero and the carry bit. The purpose of this is to cause any carry-out of the first addition to be added to the high-byte value of the product. The result of this addition is then returned to ML 0021. At this point, the multiplicand is returned to ACCA so that it is available for any further addition cycles of the program. The multiplier is now decremented and the microprocessor checks to see if it equals zero. If the multiplier is zero, the program branches to its ending instruction (WAI). If not, it branches back to repeat the entire addition cycle.

Let's go through the program using two values to see how it works. The values we will use are as follows:

$$\text{multiplicand} \quad = \quad 255 = 11111111 \text{ (stored in ML 0023)}$$

$$\text{multiplier} \qquad = \qquad 2 = 00000010 \text{ (stored in ML 0024)}$$

The program will start by loading the appropriate values in the given registers. After the instruction at ML 0008 has been executed, the register contents will be as follows:

ACCA	ACCB	ML 0020	ML 0021
11111111	00000010	00000000	00000000

The instructions at ML 000A is the BEQ instruction. This instruction would be executed only if Z = 1 after ACCB was loaded. Since the contents of ACCB ≠ 0, Z = 0, and the instruction is ignored. The program will go on to fetch the instruction at ML 000C. This instruction (ADD) causes the microprocessor to fetch the data in ML 0020 and add it to the contents of ACCA. Since ML 0020 contains the number 00000000, the result in ACCA will equal 11111111. This value is stored in ML 0020 by the STAA instruction. Also, the condition of the carry flag will be C = 0, since there was no carry-out of the ADD instruction. The register contents will now be:

ACCA	ACCB	ML 0020	ML 0021	C FLAG
11111111	00000010	11111111	00000000	0

The instructions at ML 0010 through 0014 cause the contents of ML 0021 to be transferred to ACCA, where the carry bit is added to the value. Immediate addressing is used for the ADC instruction to ensure that *only* the carry bit is added to the contents of ML 0021. As the chart in Figure 13.4 indicates, the expression for the ADC instruction is

$$A + M + C \rightarrow A$$

This indicates that the contents of the accumulator is added to the contents of a memory location and the contents of the carry flag. With immediate addressing, the M value comes from the second byte of the instruction. Since we are using the value 00000000 as our second instruction byte, the expression reduces to

$$A + C \rightarrow A$$

This is the operation we want. Using this process, the only time we add anything to the contents of ML 0021 is when there is a carry-out from the addition instruction at ML 000C. Since there was no carry-out on this round, the values listed for the registers after the STAA instruction at ML 000E are still valid. The next step (at ML 0016) reloads the multiplicand into ACCA so that it can be used on the next round of additions.

The instruction at ML 0018 decrements the contents of ACCB. After this operation is performed, the registers will contain the following data:

ACCA	ACCB	ML 0020	ML 0021	Z FLAG
11111111	00000001	11111111	00000000	0

The branch instruction at ML 0019 (BNE) will cause the microprocessor to go back to the instruction at ML 000C if Z = 0. Since the required condition for the branch does exist, the branch is executed. The CPU now adds the contents of ML 0020 to the contents of ACCA. The results of this operation are as follows:

ACCA	ACCB	ML 0020	ML 0021	C FLAG
11111110	00000001	11111111	00000000	1

The 1 in the carry flag is the carry out from the addition of 11111111 and 11111111, the contents of the two registers involved in the addition. The contents of ACCA are now stored in ML 0020, and the contents of ML 0021 are loaded into ACCA. As a result, the registers contain the following:

ACCA	ACCB	ML 0020	ML 0021	C FLAG
00000000	00000001	11111110	00000000	1

The ADC instruction at ML 0012 is now fetched and executed. As a result, the value is ACCA is 00000001, since zero was added to the 00000000 in ACCA, and then the carry bit (1) was added. This result (00000001) is now stored back in ML 0021, and the multiplicand is returned to ACCA by the LDAA instruction at ML 0016. The registers now contain the following:

ACCA	ACCB	ML 0020	ML 0021	C FLAG
11111111	00000001	11111110	00000001	0

At this point, ACCB is decremented by the instruction at ML 0018. The result of this operation is that the contents of ACCB will be 00000000, and the zero flag will be in the Z = 1 condition. Since Z = 1, the BNE instruction at ML 0019 will not be executed. The CPU now fetches and executes the WAI instruction, which is the program-ending instruction. Now let's take a look at the contents of ML 0021 and ML 0020. These two data values, when put together in the correct order, form the 16-bit value 0000000111111110. This binary number equals 510, the correct product for the original values given.

In both of the program examples, addressing modes have been mixed together. This is common to every machine-level program written for the MC6800. There are several problems at the end of the chapter that relate to analyzing machine-level programs. Go to those problems and see if you can solve them.

13.4 SUBROUTINES

A subroutine is *a program that performs a specific function which must be done more than once during the course of another program.* In a sense, a subroutine is a program that lies within another program. A subroutine is usually performed more than once during the course of the program that is using it. For example, refer back to the oil pressure program. What if the microprocessor had to perform this operation on four separate oil tanks? It would be much simpler to run the oil pressure program over and over than it would be to rewrite it for each of the tanks. If the oil pressure program were to be used as a subroutine, the flowchart for such a program would look as shown in Figure 13.9. The main program loop is on the left. The oil pressure program, which is the subroutine in this case, is shown on the right. The main program "calls up" (runs) the subroutine once for each of the oil tanks. When the oil pressure subroutine has ended, the microprocessor returns to the original program and continues with the instruction that immediately follows the one that called up the routine.

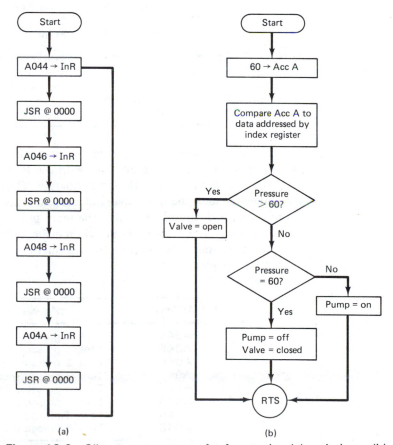

Figure 13.9 Oil pressure program for four tanks: (a) main loop; (b) subroutine.

There are several requirements for using subroutines. First, a special op-code must be used to call up the subroutine. For the MC6800, the two instructions that can be used are:

Branch to subroutine: op-code = 8D
Jump to subroutine: op-code = AD or BD

Either of these two instructions will cause the microprocessor to activate the stack, store all critical data from its internal registers there, and proceed to run the subroutine located at the address specified by the instruction. After the subroutine has ended, the CPU will get its data back from the stack and continue with the original program, provided that the subroutine ends with the *return from subroutine* instruction. This instruction *must* end all subroutines if the CPU is to return to the original program.

If the oil pressure program were to be used as a subroutine, it would have to be rewritten as follows:

Address	Contents		Mnemonic		Comment
0000	86	3C	LDAA	3C	Load ACCA with 3C-H (60)
0002	A1	00	CMP	00	Compare ACCA with oil pressure reading
0004	2B	0E	BMI	0E	Branch if minus to location 0014
0006	26	06	BNE	06	Branch if not zero to location 000E
0008	C6	FF	LDAB	FF	Load ACCB with data value 11111111
000A	E7	01	STAB	01	Store ACCB at pressure control location
000C	20	0A	BRA	0A	Branch always to location 0018
000E	C6	0F	LDAB	0F	Load ACCB with data value 00001111
0010	E7	01	STAB	01	Store ACCB at pressure control location
0012	20	04	BRA		Branch always to location 0018
0014	C6	F0	LDAB	F0	Load ACCB with data value 11110000
0016	E7	01	STAB	01	Store ACCB at pressure control location
0018	39		RTS		Return from subroutine

There are several changes in the program now that it is being used as a subroutine. First, the program ends with the RTS instruction. This will cause the microprocessor to return to the main program. The other change is that the program no longer contains the LDX (load index register) instruction that was in the first program. This is due to the fact that the main program will take care of loading the index register. The main program will put the addresses of the oil tank inputs and outputs in the index register prior to each run of the subroutine. These address values will be as follows:

Address	Addressed device
A044	Tank 1 pressure input device
A045	Tank 1 pressure control device
A046	Tank 2 pressure input device
A047	Tank 2 pressure control device
A048	Tank 3 pressure input device
A049	Tank 3 pressure control device
A04A	Tank 4 pressure input device
A04B	Tank 4 pressure control device

Each of the addresses listed will be used in the program to address the device that is being checked/adjusted. As the main program will show, we have come upon another advantage of indexed addressing. Using indexed addressing makes it simple for us to run a subroutine over and over, with a different device address being used during each subroutine run. The main program is as follows:

Address	Contents			Mnemonic			Comment
0020	CE	A0	44	LDX	A0	44	Load the index register with the value A044
0023	8D	DB		BSR	DB		Branch to subroutine at ML 0000
0025	CE	A0	46	LDX	A0	46	Load the index register with the value A046
0028	8D	D6		BSR	D6		Branch to subroutine at ML 0000
002A	CE	A0	48	LDX	A0	48	Load the index register with the value A048
002D	8D	D1		BSR	D1		Branch to subroutine at ML 0000
002F	CE	A0	4A	LDX	A0	4A	Load the index register with the value A04A
0032	8D	CC		BSR	CC		Branch to subroutine at ML 0000
0034	20	EA		BRA	EA		Branch always to ML 0020

This program does nothing more than continually run the oil pressure subroutine, providing a different index register value each time that the subroutine is run. On the first run, it provides the index register value needed for the subroutine to work on tank 1, on the second time it supplies the index register value needed to work on tank 2, and so on.

With the main program and the subroutine being written as they are, the microprocessor will take whatever action is called for on a given oil tank (i.e., opening the valve, turning on the pump, or no action at all), and then will proceed to the next tank, and so on. On some return check at a later time, the microprocessor will take whatever new action is necessary. For example, assume that the following conditions exist:

Tank 1: low oil pressure

Tank 2: correct oil pressure

Tank 3: high oil pressure

Tank 4: low oil pressure

The CPU would turn the oil pump on for tank 1 and go on to check tank 2. In the meantime, the pump for tank 1 stays on. Tank 2 is okay, so the CPU does nothing to change tank 2 and goes on to tank 3. With its oil pressure being high, the program causes the CPU to open the release valve for tank 3. The CPU now checks tank 4, detects that its oil pressure is low, and turns on the pump. Now the CPU returns to tank 1 and runs the subroutine again. If the pressure is okay, the CPU turns the pump off. If the pressure has gotten too high, the CPU will turn the pump off and open the release valve. If the pressure is still low, the CPU will leave the pump on. Now it goes on to tank 2, and so on. With this setup, the CPU is checking the other tanks while the action for a given tank is being taken. This makes the entire system much more efficient as a whole.

As you can see, the subroutine is a very handy type of program. Without subroutines, the entire oil pressure program would have to be rewritten for each oil tank. This would be a tremendous waste of memory space. If you continue to study machine-level programming beyond the scope of the book, you will come to see that a vast majority of CPU operations are contained in subroutines.

13.5 HIGHER-LEVEL LANGUAGES

As the previous discussions have shown, a machine-level program involves breaking a problem down into steps that the microprocessor can perform and entering the instructions that will perform those steps into memory in binary form. There are, however, computer languages that do not break down their problems into single microprocessor steps. These languages have basic commands that are oriented toward solving a specific type of problem, with the commands being broken down into machine-level commands by the computer. In these *higher-level languages,* the commands (instructions) are either in English or are very close. The English command is interpreted by a special type of program called a *compiler.* The compiler recognizes the command and calls up a subroutine that accomplishes the task called for by the command. For example, in Chapter 1, the example was given of a computer recognizing the ASCII codes for the command PRINT, and then taking the steps required to print the data. What would happen is that the CPU would call up the proper subroutine for the PRINT command and run that routine, using the data that the user wanted to have printed.

There are as many higher-level languages as there are applications. These languages each have a specific application, and all of them have made the microcomputer usable by almost anyone. Some of these languages use compilers, and some of them use a type of program that is very similar to a compiler, called an *interpreter.* The difference between the two types of programs is simple. While they both break the instructions down into machine-level subroutines, the interpreter will execute each higher-level instruction as soon as it has determined the subroutine to run. The compiler, on the other hand, will break the entire program down into a series of subroutines and then execute them all in sequence. But whether a language uses a compiler or interpreter, the end result is basically the same. The user has applied a problem-oriented language written in English, and the machine has broken that language down into a series of subroutines and accomplished the desired task.

BASIC

The *Beginner's All-Purpose Symbolic Instruction Code* (BASIC) is a higher-level language that provides the user with the capability to program the computer to accomplish "general-nature" operations using simple English. Using the correct sequence of BASIC commands, the user can program the system to accomplish just about any type of task. BASIC versions range from relatively simple types to extended versions that require a huge amount of memory to use. In general, the more sophisticated a higher-level language is, the more memory is required to store the compiler or interpreter. Many microcomputers being built today have their basic compilers stored in ROM, so it is not even necessary to enter BASIC into the system.

FORTRAN

FORTRAN stands for *FORmula TRANslation.* This language is used to solve mathematical and engineering problems. FORTRAN was one of the first of the higher-level languages. FORTRAN statements (instructions) are written specifically to solve complex mathematical and engineering problems. It is not a general-purpose language like BASIC.

COBOL

COBOL stands for *COmmon Business-Oriented Language.* This language, whose commands tend to be in straight English, is used for business applications, such as bookkeeping.

Pascal

Pascal is a system language that is much more structured than the other higher-level languages. It allows many of the same operations as BASIC, using different commands. It does not allow a great deal of subroutines within itself.

SUMMARY

A machine-level program is a series of binary-coded instructions that direct the activities of the microprocessor. These instructions are stored in successive memory locations, with the CPU fetching and executing the instructions in order.

Each instruction, regardless of the number of bytes it contains, starts with an operation code, or op-code. This op-code defines the action to be taken. The rest of the instruction either provides the data to be operated on or an address where the data can be obtained. In some cases, the second byte of the instruction may be an *offset* value that is added to the contents of a given register to form the address of the data.

Machine-level programming involves breaking a problem down into a series of operations that the microprocessor can perform and finding the op-codes required to perform those operations. These op-codes must be listed in the proper sequence if the program is to run as was intended by the programmer.

A *flowchart* is a programming aid that is used to give a visual representation of the program flow. The flowchart is designed from the problem to be solved, then the program is written from the flowchart. Another aid in machine-level programming is the *mnemonic*. A mnemonic is an abbreviation that indicates the operation to be performed. Writing machine-level programs in mnemonic form allows different programmers to relate the program to the microprocessor that they are using, without having to translate one machine code into another.

Some of the addressing modes used by the MC6800 are used by other microprocessors as well, and some are not. However, determining how a given addressing mode works is usually not a difficult task.

The decision-making process in a microcomputer program is accomplished by the use of *branch* instructions. There are two basic types of branch instructions: conditional and unconditional. A conditional branch is one that is executed only when a given set of conditions exist, such as BEQ (branch if equal to zero). An unconditional branch is executed anytime that it is fetched. There is no condition required for the execution of an unconditional branch.

A special type of program is the *subroutine*. A subroutine is a program that performs a specific task and is run as part of a larger program. The subroutine is called whenever the task it performs is needed by the main program. After the subroutine is completed, the RTS instruction returns the microprocessor to the main program. Every subroutine must end with the return instruction.

Subroutines are used extensively in higher-level languages. These languages are written so that users can command the computer using words or symbols that they are familiar with. Of the higher-level languages, BASIC is the most commonly used. This all-purpose language uses simple English words for commands.

Higher-level languages are broken down into machine codes by a type of program called a compiler. Another type of program used for this purpose is the interpreter. The difference between the two is the time at which they actually execute the instructions.

QUESTIONS

1. What is a machine-level program?
2. What is a language?
3. What is an op-code? Where does the op-code appear in a multibyte instruction?
4. In a multibyte instruction, what is contained in the second and third bytes of the instruction?
5. What is an instruction set? What is defined by the instruction set?
6. What is a flowchart? What are the symbols used in a flowchart, and what does each represent?
7. What is a mnemonic? What is the advantage of using mnemonics?
8. What are the MC6800 addressing modes? How is a given memory location addressed in each mode?
9. What is the restriction of direct addressing?
10. Which addressing mode actually changes the contents of the program counter?
11. What types of operations are performed by accumulator and memory instructions?
12. Explain how a given offset value is added to the contents of the program counter to provide a new address.
13. What is a conditional branch? What is an unconditional branch?
14. What are the two methods of performing binary multiplication?
15. What is an algorithm?
16. Explain the difference between the ADD and ADC instructions.
17. What is a subroutine? What is the advantage in using subroutines?
18. What instruction must every subroutine end with? Why?
19. What does the microprocessor do with the data from a main program when it calls up a subroutine?
20. What are the advantages of using indexed addressing?
21. What are higher-level languages?
22. What is a compiler? What is an interpreter?
23. What is the difference between a compiler and an interpreter?
24. What is BASIC? What is it used for?
25. What is FORTRAN? What is it used for?
26. What is COBOL? What is it used for?

PROBLEMS

1. Refer to Figure 13.4. For each of the instructions listed below, determine the expression and write the expression as an English statement.
   (a) CLRA
   (b) SUBB
   (c) DECA
   (d) INX
   (e) TBA
2. Using the flowchart symbols in Figure 13.2, draw a flowchart for the problem of determining which of three numbers is greatest. (Remember, the steps must be operations that the microprocessor can execute.) Assume that no two numbers are equal.
3. Complete the following chart, using the chart in Figure 13.4.
4. The LDAA instruction is being used. The op-code in this case is A6. If the index register value is A400 and the second instruction byte is B9, where will the microprocessor go to get the data?

Mnemonic	Op-code	Type of addressing	Second byte[a]	Third byte[a]
ADCA	89			
CBA		Implied		
LDAA	A6			
LDAB			Address	Address
STAA	97			

[a]Indicate whether these bytes would be data or an address, if used.

5. Listed below are the op-code addresses and offset values for a group of branch instructions. In each case, determine the PC value if the branch is executed.

Op-code address	Offset value
B397	F2
110B	FF
29D8	E6

Challenger Problems

6. In Figure 13.10 there is a flowchart for a *nested loop*. This is a timing loop contained in another timing loop. Write the MC6800 machine-level program that will perform the flowchart task.

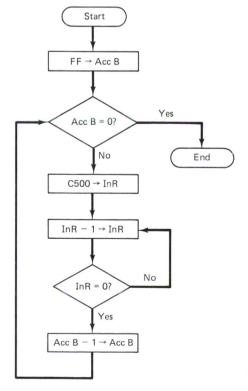

Figure 13.10 Nested loop (Problem 6).

7. In Figure 13.11, the flowchart for the shift-and-add multiplication algorithm is shown. Write the MC6800 machine-level program for this flowchart.

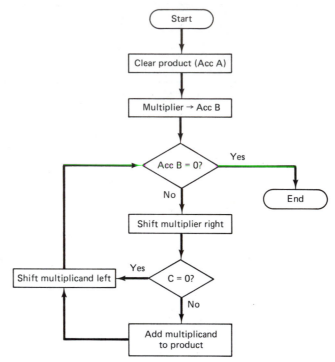

Figure 13.11 Shift-and-add algorithm.

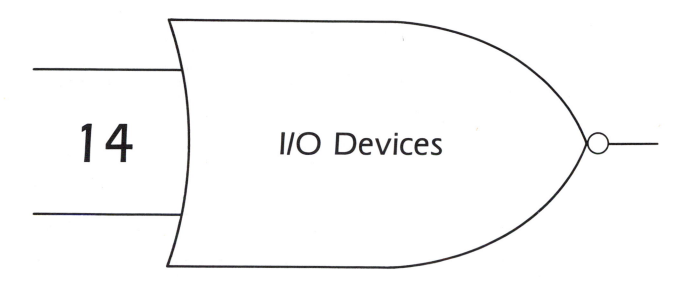

14   I/O Devices

The two units of the microcomputer that have not been covered up until now are the input unit and the output unit. Although these two parts of the system are separate entities, they are usually treated as one group of devices. The reason for this is the fact that they both provide a means by which the computer and user can communicate. The input unit allows the user to communicate with the computer, and the output unit allows the computer to communicate with the user. Since both sections are involved in this interaction, they are usually treated as the single *input/output,* or *I/O,* unit.

The input unit must be capable of not only accepting information from the user, but also of providing that information to the control unit in a form that can be understood by the control unit. By the same token, the output unit must be capable of not only accepting information from the control unit, but also of giving that information to the user in a form that is acceptable to the user. *In terms of these requirements, the input and output devices can be viewed as language translators.* The input unit translates the user's language into the system's language, and the output unit translates the system's language into the user's language. The exact method by which these translations are accomplished depends on which device is being used. The idea of "language translation" is discussed further in this chapter.

The number of I/O devices that are currently in use prohibits covering the operation and applications of every one of them, so we focus on the most common of the input and output devices. The most common input device is the keyboard, and the most common output device is the CRT. Both of these devices are covered in great detail, together with the circuitry that is used to control them. We will also briefly discuss modems and the methods used to connect them to microcomputers.

14.1 INTRODUCTION TO INPUT/OUTPUT INTERFACING

An *interface* is a physical connection between two or more circuits or systems. There are basically two ways in which input and output devices are interfaced with the control unit. One method, called *memory-mapped I/O,* has each input and output device wired so that it is treated by the control unit as a memory location. In this setup, the CPU does not distinguish between the I/O devices and any given memory location. It simply puts an address on the address bus, and either sends data to, or reads data from, the device. Obviously, the control unit would not try to read information from an output device. It would only write data to the output device. By the same token, it would only read information from an input device. It would never send information to an input device.

If you refer back to the ET-3400 system schematic, you will see a memory-mapped I/O system. The schematic is shown in Figure 11.5. A block diagram for this system is shown in Figure 14.1. According to the block diagram (and the system schematic), the input device (keyboard) and the output device (seven-segment displays) are connected to the memory decoding circuitry, just as ROM and RAM are. When the CPU is addressing either of the I/O devices, it goes through the same procedure as it does when it addresses a memory location. The advantage of using this type of I/O is simplicity. There is no special circuitry required to interface the control unit to the I/O devices. There is, however, a drawback. The input and output devices in a memory-mapped I/O system take up addresses that could be used for memory locations. In a system that needs a relatively large memory unit, this consideration can become critical. In a system with no need of a large memory, memory-mapped I/O is the best choice.

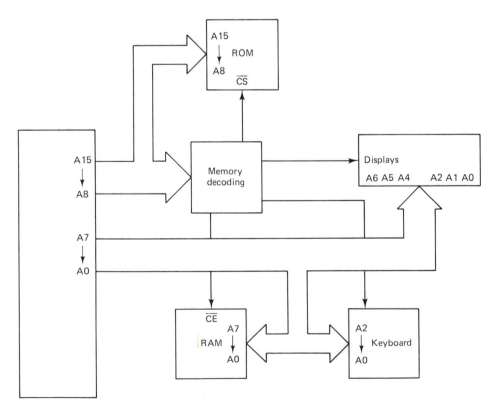

Figure 14.1 Block diagram of the Heath ET-3400 trainer. (© *1981 Heath Company. Reprinted by permission of Heath Company.)*

When memory-mapped I/O is not a feasible configuration, *isolated I/O* is used. In an isolated I/O system, the control unit communicates with a single controller. The controller then communicates with the I/O devices. Such a configuration is shown in Figure 14.2. In this setup, the control unit communicates only with the I/O device controller. The I/O device controller then communicates with all of the input devices and output devices. In many cases, this I/O device controller is simply another microprocessor. This microprocessor's only function would be to control the input and output devices. It would never be used to run any type of general-purpose programs. When an I/O device controller is used, the main system control unit needs only one address to communicate with all of the I/O devices. This eliminates the need to tie up several memory locations with I/O addresses. It also eliminates the need for the system CPU to tie up memory locations with the programs needed to interract with the input devices. These programs would be stored in memory that would be addressed and used only by the I/O device controller. The disadvantage of this type of system is the extra circuitry required to implement it.

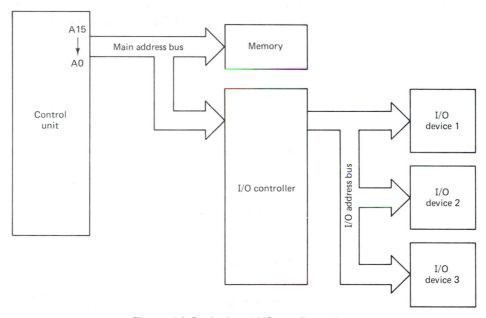

Figure 14.2   Isolated I/O configuration.

Input Interfacing

Input devices are interfaced with the CPU in one of two ways. The first method is the *scanned input*. In a system using a scanned input, the CPU sends out a signal to the various input devices, one at a time. When one of the input devices needs to communicate with the CPU, it acknowledges the scan signal and transfers the data to the CPU. The ET-3400, which constantly scans its keyboard, is a good example of this type of input interfacing. When the CPU is ready for an input from the keyboard, it constantly scans the keyboard and looks for an input value. This type of input has the advantage of not requiring a lot of circuitry. The disadvantage, however, is that the CPU spends a lot of its time being tied up in the scan routine when it could be doing other things. For this reason, the second input method, *interrupt I/O*, is usually used.

With interrupt I/O, the CPU goes about its business until an interrupt is received. At that time, it stops its current program and services the interrupt. This method, which has been discussed before, is by far the most common.

Another concept of input device interfacing is that of interrupt *priority*. Which of the input devices is to have the priority over the others? This is a question that is answered by the system designer. Some of the inputs are more critical to the operation of the system as a whole, and these inputs will always be recognized and dealt with before the others. For example, consider a computer in a hospital that is being used to monitor a patient's blood pressure and heart rate. If the blood pressure goes too high or the pulse rate becomes erratic, the microcomputer is to signal another system, which, in turn, informs the medical staff of the problem. You determine the priority. What is more important, high blood pressure or a stopped heart? Granted, this example is a bit extreme, but it helps show the idea of priorities.

The priority of the inputs is usually a hard-wired (circuit) function rather than a software function. A priority encoder can be used for establishing the priority of a group of inputs, as shown in the circuit in Figure 14.3. This is the interrupt logic for the Heath H-89A microcomputer. The interrupt circuit consists of U557, U558, U508B, and U553C. U557 is an 8-to-3-line priority encoder. When one of its input lines goes low, it provides two outputs: the GS output goes low, activating the $\overline{INT}$ (interrupt) input to the CPU, and the A0, A1, and A2 outputs provide a 3-bit code which is used to indicate which input line went low. The priority in this circuit is from 7 to 1 (i.e., the higher the input number, the higher the priority). If two inputs go low at the same time, the higher-numbered input will be the one to which the circuit (U557) responds. When the CPU detects the $\overline{INT}$ signal, it will finish its current instruction, store its internal data in the stack, and respond to the interrupt by driving its $\overline{M1}$ and $\overline{IORQ}$ outputs low. These two outputs are connected to the OR gate, U553C. With two low inputs, the output from the OR gate is low, which enables U558. This is a three-state inverter circuit which, when enabled, inverts the A0, A1, and A2 outputs and places the inverted signals on the data bus. At that point, the CPU latches the data and determines which input device needs to be serviced.

The use of the priority encoder has provided the system with several desirable characteristics. First, *all* the interrupting devices can be interfaced to the CPU on a single CPU input. Second, priority of the input devices has been established without having to use a program to do so.

Output Interfacing

The interfacing between the CPU and the output devices is usually a much simpler configuration than the interface between the CPU and the input devices. This is due to the fact that the output devices do not interrupt the CPU.

Output devices are usually controlled by circuits called *microcontrollers*. A microcontroller is essentially a dedicated microprocessor. While the microprocessor and the microcontroller are both capable of addressing memory and running programs, the microcontroller would be specially designed to run programs of a specific nature. For example, a CRT controller is a microcontroller that runs programs which are aimed specifically at controlling the microcomputer CRT. It has special inputs and outputs that direct it toward these activities. It provides vertical and horizontal sync signals for the CRT, and so on. The CRT controller could not be used for anything other than controlling CRT circuitry. This microcontroller is discussed in detail later in this chapter.

Also, we will be discussing the entire input/output logic for the Heath H-89A microcomputer later in this chapter. As you will see, each input and output device has a microcontroller that controls the device. These microcontrollers are, in turn, controlled by a microprocessor. This microprocessor is used specifically for controlling the I/O microcontrollers and is the only circuit that communicates directly with the main system microprocessor. Since we are building toward discussing this entire

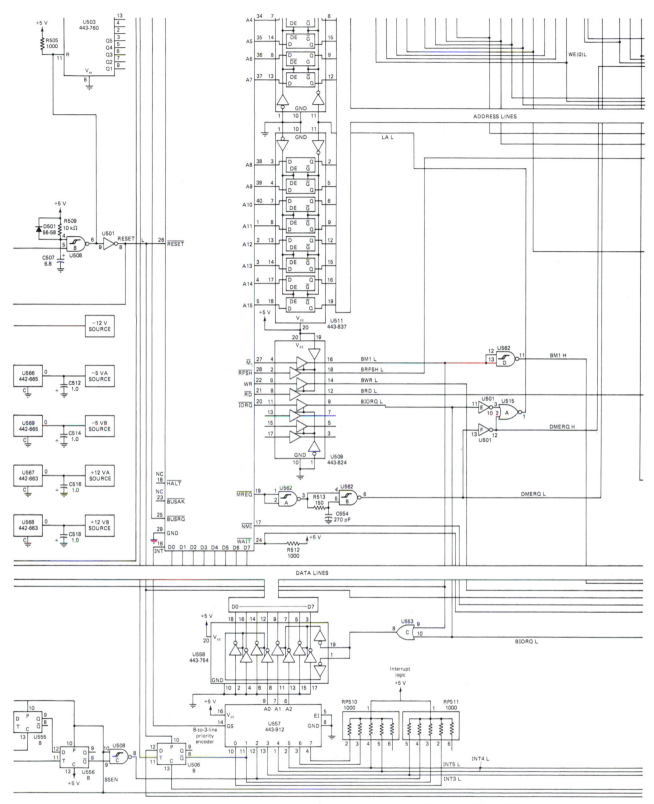

Figure 14.3 Interrupt circuitry for the Heath H-89A CPU Logic Board.

system, all the devices that we cover in this chapter will be related in one way or another to the H-89A configuration.

14.2 KEYBOARDS AND KEYBOARD ENCODING

Keyboards are the most common input devices used in microcomputers. They vary in size and in the functions that are available from pressing a given key, but all are set up in the same basic configuration as the keyboard discussed in the ET-3400 trainer. This keyboard is shown again in Figure 14.4 for convenience. As you can see see, the keyboard is set up as a switch matrix. Each column/row intersection contains a key that, when pressed, connects the column wire to the row wire. The CPU constantly scans the column wires, putting a low on the wires, one at a time. When a given key is pressed, the low passes through that switch and is applied to the data bus, indicating that a key has been pressed. The CPU uses the address/data combination to detect which key has been pressed. The program used to do this is actually a bit more involved than is indicated here, but the principle is the same.

There is more to encoding a key than simply determining which key has been pressed. The microcomputer must account for a problem that is inherent in *all* switches, including keypads. This problem is called *switch bounce*.

Switch Bounce

A switch is actually made up of two or more metal contacts that are connected when the switch is pressed. The action of the contacts is not as simple as one might think. When the switch is closed, the two contacts do not simply touch and stay together, but rather, act somewhat like a ball bouncing on the pavement. When one contact touches the other, it bounces, and the connection between the two is broken for a few milliseconds. They then touch again and the bounce occurs again. This touch/bounce action usually lasts for no more than about 10 ms, but that is long enough to cause some problems. Consider the $\overline{\text{RESET}}$ switch. When this switch closes, the CPU receives an active-low input and responds by starting to run its RESET program. However, if the signals from the switch bounce are allowed to make it to the CPU, the CPU will just be getting started in its RESET routine, when it will receive another low input. Each time the switch bounces, the output from the switch will go high as the connection is broken, and low as it is made again. The CPU will interpret these bounce signals as separate input signals, which can have an adverse effect on the system operation. The signal from a bouncing switch resembles the one shown in Figure 14.5. As you can see, the signal actually causes several low pulses to be generated. If the circuit to which the key is connected is a counter, for example, the count sequence will be thrown out of order. In one lab, a student was having trouble getting a counter to work. The problem was that the counter had an erratic count sequence. The student was using a switch to provide a clock input to the counter. As you have probably guessed by now, the problem was not the counter, but rather, the switch. It was providing quite a few clock signals every time that it was pressed. The solution was to use a circuit called a *switch debouncer*.

A switch debouncer is a circuit (or a program) designed to eliminate unwanted signals from the closing of a switch. A hardware switch debouncer is shown in Figure 14.6. The debouncer in this case is simply a 7474 D-type flip-flop. The switch is connected to the asynchronous inputs, PRESET and CLEAR. Recall that these inputs to the flip-flop work independently of the clock input and will have an effect on the output at the instant that they are activated. The PRESET input will cause the Q output to go high if the input goes low, and the CLEAR input will cause the Q output to go low if the input goes low.

When the switch connection is made, the low is applied to the CLEAR input of the flip-flop. This will immediately cause the Q output to go low. Any further low outputs from the switch will also be applied to the CLEAR input. Since the flip-flop is already in the low-output state, these pulses will not have any effect on the

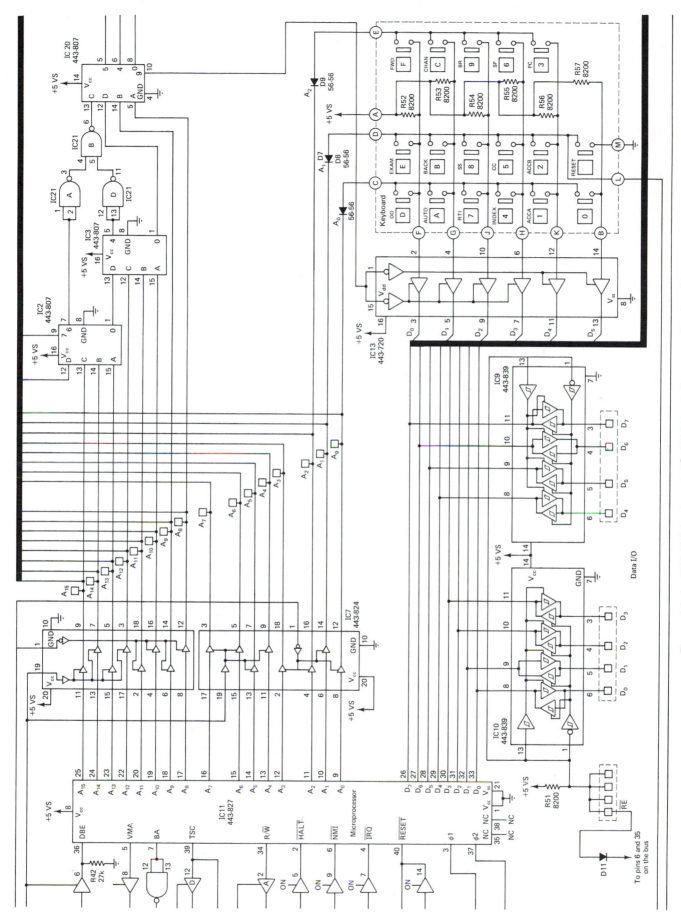

Figure 14.4 ET3400 keyboard. (© 1981 Heath Company. Reprinted by permission of Heath Company.)

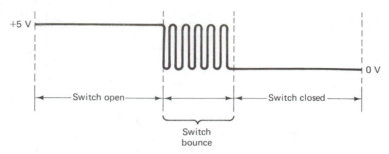

Figure 14.5 Switch bounce waveform.

flip-flop output. The end result is that the train of low pulses caused by the switch bounce has been changed by the flip-flop to a single low output. When the switch is released, it makes contact with the PRESET input to the flip-flop, which causes the output from the flip-flop to go high. Any further bounce activity at the PRESET input will also be ignored by the device, since it is already in the Q = 1 state.

While this technique works well for debouncing a single switch, consider the circuitry that would be required to debounce an entire keyboard. Each key would have to have its own debouncing circuit. Such a setup would hardly be worth the trouble. A much simpler way to debounce a switch is with *software debouncing*. When a switch is debounced by software (the program), there is no need for all the hardware that would otherwise be required to do the job. Software debouncing is based on the fact that switch bounce never lasts for more than 10 to 15 ms. The software debouncer waits until approximately 20 ms after a key closure has been detected to decode the key. By the time the program decodes the key, all the bounce activity has stopped. This takes some work by the CPU (running the program), but eliminates the need for hardware debouncing. In almost every system, keys and switches, in general, are now debounced by software routines. The only switches and keys that are still debounced by hardware are those that bypass the keyboard encoding circuitry and those that are used in specific-purpose digital circuits, such as beepers.

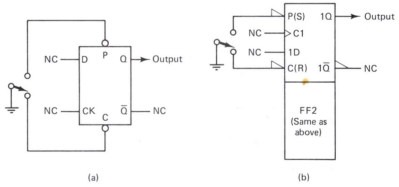

(a)   (b)

Figure 14.6 7474 switch debouncer: (a) conventional symbol; (b) DLN symbol.

Keyboard Encoders

When a key is pressed, the system must determine which key has been pressed and determine the code for that key. This is often done using a microcontroller, called a *keyboard encoder*. A keyboard encoder performs no function other than to handle the interfacing between the system and the keyboard. In doing this, the keyboard encoder must be able to:

1. Detect that a key has been pressed, and debounce the key.
2. Signal the control unit that there are data available from the keyboard.
3. Provide the correct system code for the key, that is, translate the key position code into ASCII, BCD, or whatever code the system uses.
4. Transfer the data to the CPU when the CPU signals that it is ready to accept the data.
5. Provide any control signals required by the system, such as CAPS LOCK, SHIFT, and so on.

An actual keyboard, together with its control circuitry, is shown in Figure 14.7. This is the keyboard circuitry from the H-89A microcomputer. The center of the entire circuit is the keyboard encoder, U444. This microcontroller has a 128-kHz clock input at pin 3. The circuitry that drives this clock input is not shown, but is part of the clock circuitry that drives all the circuits that are on the board which contains the keyboard circuitry. Lines X1 through X9 are outputs from the encoder, and lines Y1 through Y10 are inputs. The X lines and the Y lines are the encoder connections to the keyboard matrix. Lines X1 through X9 are constantly driven low, one at a time, and in order. When a key is pressed and the low appears at the correct output, the low will go through the key to the appropriate Y input. For example, assume that the L key is pressed (top row, third column from the left). When the X7 line (pin 6) goes low, that low will go through the L key to the Y9 input to the encoder. The keyboard encoder, detecting that a key has been pressed, waits approximately 20 ms, and scans the keyboard again. This allows enough time for any switch bounce to be eliminated. The encoder now uses the output/input combination X7/Y9 to determine which key has been pressed.

Once the encoder has determined which key has been pressed, it provides two output signals. An 8-bit code is provided at the B outputs, and a data strobe (DS) signal is provided at pin 13. The DS signal is used to signal the CPU that keyboard data is available. The DS signal is applied to the CPU via the D flip-flop, U448A, the NAND gate–U447B, and a NOR gate–U432C. The output from that NOR gate is applied to the $\overline{INT}$ (interrupt) input of the CPU. To understand how this circuitry works, let's take a look at the output states of the circuits *before* the DS signal occurs. Assuming that the U448A is RESET, its $\overline{Q}$ output is high. This high is applied to the input of the NAND gate, U447B. With the other input being at a constant high level, the NAND gate acts as if there were two high inputs, and has a low output. This low output is applied to the input of the NOR gate–U432C. This gate has two low inputs, and thus a high output, which is the inactive level for the $\overline{INT}$ input to the CPU. When the DS output makes its transition, it triggers the D flip-flop. The flip-flop SETs, due to the fact that the D input is tied high. When the flip-flop SETs, the $\overline{Q}$ output goes low. This low is applied to the NAND gate, causing its output to go high. The high output from the NAND gate is applied to the NOR gate input, causing its output to go low. This applies a low at the $\overline{INT}$ input to the CPU, interrupting the device.

While the DS signal has been signaling the CPU, the B outputs from the encoder have also been performing an important function. These outputs are applied to the address inputs of a 2k ROM chip, U445. This ROM chip stores the ASCII codes for the various keys. When the B output code is applied to the ROM, it addresses a memory location that contains the ASCII code for that particular key. So, as the DS is applied to the CPU, the encoder is also accessing the ASCII code for the key that was pressed.

When the CPU responds to the interrupt, it drives the $\overline{CS2}$ (chip select 2) input to the ROM low, taking it out of the three-state condition. This low is also applied to the input of the NAND gate, U447C, which is located directly below the ROM. With a low input, the output from this NAND gate goes high. This high is applied

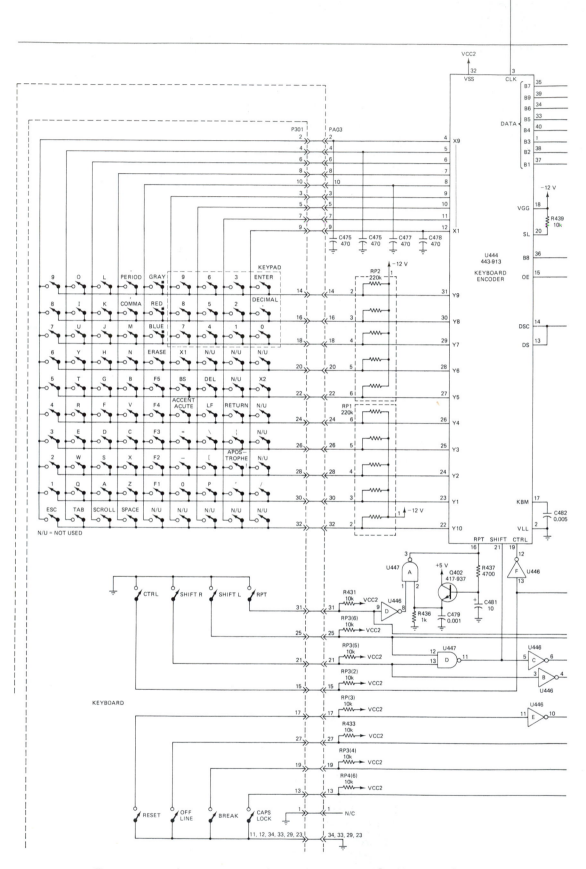

Figure 14.7 The Heath H-89A keyboard circuitry. (© *1981 Heath Company. Reprinted by permission of Heath Company.*)

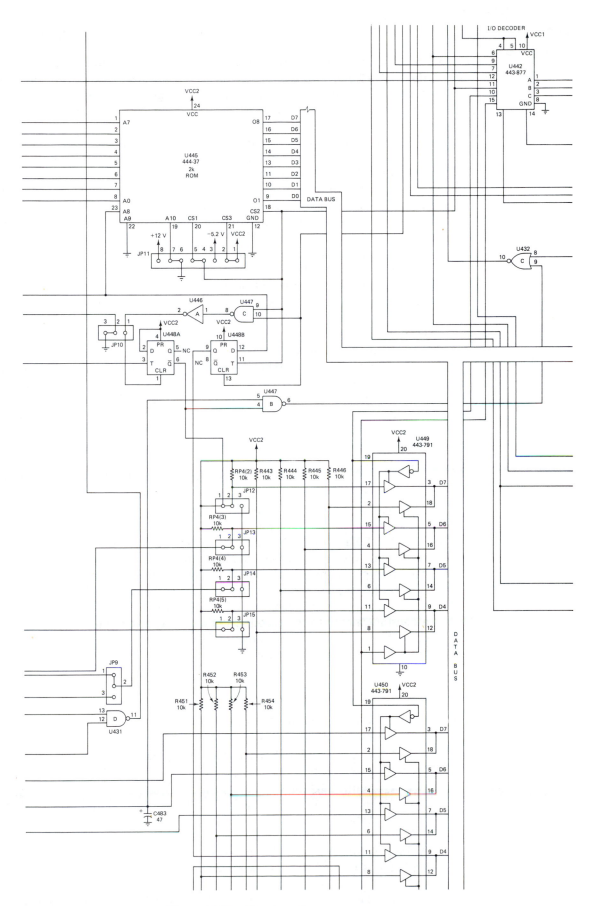

Figure 14.7 (Continued)

283

to the input of an inverter, U446A, driving its output low. This low is applied to the CLEAR input to U448A, clearing the flip-flop. This returns the interrupt circuitry to its initial state, (i.e., the interrupt signal is removed from the CPU). The CPU, having applied the $\overline{CS}$ signal to the ROM, latches the data from the chip, and the keyboard read sequence is complete.

Now, there are a few points that should be made about the circuitry shown. First, you may have noticed that the chips are all shown to be connected to a power supply labeled $V_{cc}2$. This is because there happens to be two separate power supply connections to the various chips on this board. Some of them are fed by the first supply, $V_{cc}1$, and some are fed by the second. Any time that you see numbered power supply connections, that simply means that there is more than one supply connection to the board, and the label identifies which power input feeds the chip.

Another point relates to the Y inputs to the keyboard encoder. You may have noticed that these inputs have "pull-up" resistors connected to them. The resistors are connected on the other side to a -12-V dc supply connection. While we are dealing with a TTL system, the keyboard encoder itself is a PMOS device and thus requires -12-V inputs. All of the other inputs and outputs from this circuit are at TTL levels.

Below the keyboard encoder, you will notice a lot of external circuitry which has not been covered at this point. There are three encoder inputs that are being driven by some of these circuits. These inputs are the $\overline{RPT}$ (repeat), shift, and CTRL (control) inputs. The shift input is activated when a capital letter is being entered into the system. The control input indicates that the key being pressed is a control character, not a letter input. You see, there are certain control functions within the computer which can be activated by pressing the CTRL key and the appropriate letter key on the keyboard. This is a programming function of the system. When the CTRL input to the encoder is activated, it changes the B code that is output for the letter key. This causes a control value, not an ASCII code to be addressed in the ROM. The CPU will use this control value to direct it to a given program rather than treating the keyboard input as a letter.

The $\overline{RPT}$ input to the keyboard encoder will cause a character to be repeatedly entered into the system. When this input is pulsed, whatever character has been pressed will be entered continuously into the system. The circuitry that is feeding this input is essentially a pulse generator. When the RPT key is pressed, the circuitry provides a pulse input to the keyboard encoder. When the RPT key is not pressed, it provides a constant high into the encoder. Let's take a look at how this circuit works. For convenience, the circuit is enlarged in Figure 14.8. When the RPT key is *not* pressed, the following conditions exist in the circuit:

1. The input to U446D is high and its output is low.
2. The low from U446D is applied to one of the inputs to the NAND gate, U447A, causing its output to be high. This high is applied to the $\overline{RPT}$ input of the keyboard encoder.
3. The high at U444-16 (encoder input) causes C481 to charge. As it charges, C481 turns Q402 on.
4. With Q402 on, C479 in its emitter circuit charges until it reaches approximately 4 V. This voltage is applied to the other input to the NAND gate, U447A-2

As long as the RPT key is not pressed, the conditions above will remain. When the RPT key *is* pressed, the following occurs:

1. The input to the inverter, U446D goes low, causing its output to go high.

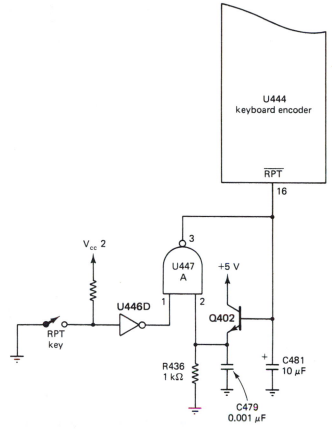

Figure 14.8 H-89A keyboard "repeat" circuitry. *(© 1981 Heath Company. Reprinted by permission of Heath Company.)*

2. The high out of U446D causes the output of the NAND gate, U447A to go low, since both of its inputs are high (see condition 4 above).

3. The low out of the NAND gate is applied to U444-16, and causes C481 to discharge simultaneously.

4. As C481 discharges, Q402 turns off. This causes C479 to discharge through R436 (on the NAND gate input).

5. When C479 discharges to approximately 0.8 V, the NAND gate output goes high. This applies a high into U444-16 and causes C481 to begin to charge again.

6. Q402 turns back on, which starts to charge C479 again. When the capacitor reaches sufficient charge, there will again be two high inputs to the NAND gate.

7. The NAND gate output goes low, and the cycle restarts back at step 3.

As long as the RPT key is pressed, the cycle above repeats continuously. The result is a steady stream of pulses at the $\overline{\text{RPT}}$ input of U444. This causes the character to be repeatedly entered into the system.

The majority of the control keys in this system bypass the keyboard encoder completely. These keys are read by the CPU when the CPU enables the three-state buffers, U449 and U450. Every time that the CPU reads data from the keyboard, it also reads these these buffer outputs to determine, which, if any, control characters have been activated.

Not every keyboard system operates in the exact same fashion as this one, but a majority of microcomputer keyboard interfaces use the same basic principles as this one. The keyboard encoder is a very common chip. Although they are not all exactly alike, most keyboard encoders are very similar to the one contained in the H-89A.

Troubleshooting Keyboard Circuits

Refer back to page 281 to the list of what the keyboard encoder circuitry must be able to do. The list applies to any keyboard circuit, not just the H-89A keyboard. When you come across a keyboard circuit that seems to be faulty, the first step is to analyze the circuitry and determine which lines carry which signals. Which line is used to interrupt the CPU? Which lines are used to scan the keyboard? Where is the data being provided for the CPU?

In this section you have been told all of the particulars on the keyboard circuitry. But what if you were faced with analyzing the circuit and had no one to tell you what the principles of operation for the circuit are? Remembering what a keyboard encoding circuit must do and analyzing the schematic would give you a good idea of where to look for the various signals. For example, let's go through the analysis that you would have to make on this circuit, using the list of requirements for a keyboard encoder circuit:

1. *Detect that a key has been pressed, and debounce the key.* Detecting a closed key means that it must be scanned. Looking at the schematic, it is obvious that the X and Y lines are used to scan the keys, since these are the only encoder connections to the keyboard. But which lines are the scan outputs and which are the scan inputs? The pull-up resistors at the Y connections indicate that they are the encoder inputs, since pull-up resistors are almost always placed on inputs, not outputs. Debouncing the keys is an internal function of the decoder, and thus you would not locate any debouncing circuitry. However, if, in another system, the key column or row lines go to a series of flip-flops, these are used either for hardware debouncing or as temporary latches.

2. *Signal the control unit that there is data available from the keyboard.* There must be an interrupt capability from the keyboard, unless the keyboard is continuously scanned by the CPU itself. This, however, is very rare. So the first step here is to search. Starting at the CPU, or the I/O controller, you must first identify the interrupt inputs to the device. When they have been identified, you must trace the lines from the CPU back to the keyboard circuitry. Now, here is the catch. As in the H-89A, the interrupt signal may have to go through several other circuits before it gets to the CPU. When tracing a signal, do not stop tracing if you get to an output other than one that is directly on the keyboard encoder. Keep tracing a given line until you reach its source. If the source is the encoder, you have found the interrupt line. If not, you have to keep looking. Also, you will save some time if you use a little common sense. If a line from the CPU leads in a direction other than toward the keyboard circuitry, it is probably not the interrupt line from the encoder. Check lines like these only if other line traces prove fruitless. Also, check the encoder first to see if there is any obvious interrupt labels or output lines. For example, in the circuit just discussed, the DS line would have to be the interrupt output, since it is the only single line out of the chip that goes anywhere.

3. *Provide the correct system code for the key.* If there is no ROM connection to the encoder, the encoder is providing the information required by

the system. If the encoder outputs are connected to the data bus, the control unit is decoding the key by means of a program. If, as in the H-89A, there is a ROM being addressed by the encoder, it is being used to provide a "code translation."

4. *Transfer data to the CPU when the CPU signals that it is ready to accept the data.* You need two connections for this operation. First, there must be a connection from the keyboard circuitry to the data bus. In this case, the connection was at the ROM outputs. In other systems, the connection may be at the encoder outputs. There must also be a connection from the CPU or controller to an enable input in the keyboard circuitry. This enable input will be located on the same chips that provide the path to the data bus. For example, in the H-89A, the ROM provides the connection to the data bus, and the $\overline{CS}$ on this chip is the enable that is needed. If the connection had been a series of three-state buffers, the enable inputs to the buffers would be the connection and so on.

5. *Provide control signals required by the system.* Here you would simply trace the paths from the control keys to the data bus, or the encoder, if applicable.

Once the connections have been determined, you must determine whether or not they are working. Using a dual-trace oscilloscope, a major check can be made with one test. Connect one oscilloscope input to the interrupt input to the CPU or controller. Connect the other oscilloscope input to the interrupt output from the keyboard circuitry. Now press a series of keys. Make sure that this series of keys includes one key in every column and one key in every row. Each time that you press a key, you should see a pulse out of the encoder circuitry and one at the CPU or I/O controller input. If, for every key closure, you see the two pulses, then the scan and interrupt sequences are good. If not, you may have to make some adjustments before assuming that there is a problem. The problem may be that the pulses are occurring too rapidly for the oscilloscope to react to them. To make sure that this is not the case, perform the following:

1. Turn up the oscilloscope intensity.
2. Turn the TIME/DIV setting on the oscilloscope to some value in the millisecond range—2 ms/div should be sufficient.
3. Repeatedly press the key in rapid succession to cause a series of pulses, or, holding the key down, press the repeat key, if there is one.

If this procedure does not change the results, there is a problem in the circuit. The following examples give some symptoms and their causes. Be sure to follow through the schematic in Figure 14.7 as you go through the examples.

EXAMPLE 14.1

Symptom: The microcomputer does not have any response to any keyboard letter input. The control characters, such as RESET, are functional.

Findings: Performing the test described above, the oscilloscope shows a series of pulses occurring at the DS output of the encoder when any key is pressed, but there is no pulse occurring at the CPU input. Testing of the interrupt circuitry is done by holding a letter key down and pressing the repeat key. While the encoder is pulsing the interrupt circuitry, these pulses are traced through the interrupt circuitry. The pulses are making it to the input of the NAND gate, U447B, but the output of this gate remains high.

Checking U447B-5 shows it to be a constant low, indicating that C483 is shorted. Replacing C483 corrects the problem.

EXAMPLE 14.2

Symptom: The microcomputer does not respond to any keyboard input, control or otherwise.

Findings: Performing the standard test shows no DS output from the encoder when any key is pressed. Checking the X outputs from the encoder shows them to be working properly (i.e., the encoder is scanning the keyboard). Checking the Y inputs show no low pulses when any key is pressed. The connector to the keyboard itself is checked and found to be loose. Reseating the connector solves the problem.

Before going on to the next example, an observation. The last example may have seemed a bit farfetched when the findings were stated. After all, connectors do not just jump off of sockets. However, consider the following situation. The computer you are working on was worked on by another person just hours before you were called in to look at it. The other technician had his or her mind on things other than the job at hand. After rushing through the repair, the other technician hurriedly put the microcomputer back together and did a poor job of seating the connector.

You should never assume that the only problems that occur in a microcomputer are those caused by circuit failure. Anytime that you work on a system, be sure to determine when it was last worked on by another technician. If the system had been worked on in the past 24 hours, start by checking the area where the previous technician had worked. Even if no one has worked on the system, always check all connectors.

EXAMPLE 14.3

Symptom: Keyboard inputs are erratic; that is, pressing a given key will result in an input one time, and not the next.

Findings: The interrupt inputs to the CPU occur at erratic intervals, as do the DS outputs from the encoder. Checking the X and Y lines indicate that these, too, are erratic. Checking the clock signal to the encoder shows the signal to be good; however, the V_{cc} line is unstable. Replacing a voltage regulator in the power supply connection to the circuit corrects the problem.

One final note on analyzing keyboard faults. Every microcomputer made displays the characters that are entered into the system on the CRT as soon as they are entered. When you enter information into the system and it fails to show up on the CRT, you need to determine whether the problem is in the keyboard or somewhere between the keyboard and the CRT. One simple way of determining where the problem lies is to act as if there is no problem (i.e., enter the commands that would make the disk drive or printer start up). If the system responds as it normally would, the problem is probably in the CRT circuitry. If not, it's time to check the keyboard and its related circuitry.

14.3 CRT OPERATION, CONTROL, AND TROUBLESHOOTING

The CRT circuitry of the microcomputer actually involves two parts: the CRT itself and video circuitry, and the logic that supplies information to the video circuitry. In this section we focus on the logic portion of the CRT circuitry.

Before discussing the logic circuitry that feeds the video circuitry, there are a few points that must be made regarding the operation of CRTs in general.

CRT Operation

A television CRT (cathode-ray tube) displays pictures by use of a single focused beam that scans from left to right and from top to bottom. The beam will be traced from left to right across the entire screen. At that time, it is moved down and traces from left to right again. This action is represented in Figure 14.9. When the beam has traced the entire screen, it returns to the top left of the CRT and starts the tracing process again. When the beam is returned from the right side of the CRT to the left, and from the bottom of the CRT to the top, it is *blanked*. This means that the beam is turned off while the deflection plates in the CRT reposition the beam.

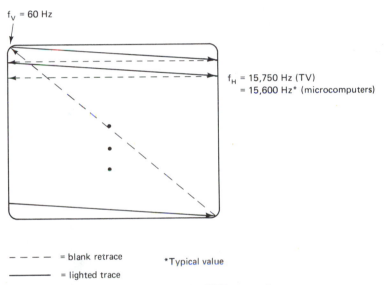

$f_V = 60$ Hz

$f_H = 15,750$ Hz (TV)
$= 15,600$ Hz* (microcomputers)

– – – – = blank retrace   *Typical value

———— = lighted trace

Figure 14.9 Basic CRT operation.

The computer CRT works in the same basic fashion as a television CRT, with a few exceptions. The television CRT has a horizontal scan frequency of 15,750 Hz, while the average computer CRT has a horizontal scan frequency of 15,600 Hz. This means that the beam traced from left to right across the CRT 15,600 times per second. The types of information they display also tends to be different, as you well know. The computer CRT is used to display characters and graphics almost exclusively. For now, it is important that you understand that there is a single beam being traced from left to right and top to bottom that produces the images you see.

If you have ever looked closely at the display on a microcomputer CRT, you may have noticed that the characters are actually made up of small "dots" of light. These dots combine to form the characters. This is represented in the diagram in Figure 14.10. The squares shown in Figure 14.10 represent positions on the CRT where a dot may appear if needed to display a given character. As you can see, the message "May I help you" has been formed by lighting certain positions and not lighting others. This means that at a given point, the beam will be either *on* or *off*—a conven-

Character positions

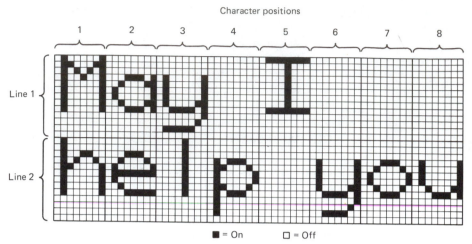

■ = On   □ = Off

Figure 14.10 CRT message.

ient situation when we are using binary values to display the needed characters. A logic 1, sent to the CRT circuitry, will cause the beam to light a point; and a 0 will cause the point to be blanked. Using this setup, binary numbers can be used to display characters on the CRT. To see how this is done, look at the character in Figure 14.11. The character shown is made up of a dot pattern that is seven dots wide and nine dots high. The entire space required to display the character is referred to as a *7 × 9*

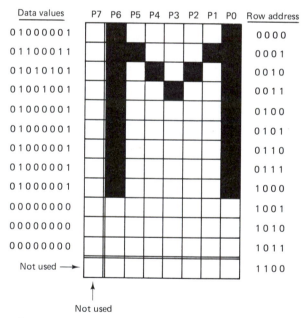

Figure 14.11 Typical CRT character format.

dot matrix. We are going to look at the entire space provided for the character as being a matrix that is made up of 13 rows by 8 columns. An address has been assigned to each row, as indicated to the right of the character itself. Now, assume for a minute that these address codes were the addresses of 13 separate memory locations. Each memory location would contain an 8-bit value—in this case, the values shown to the left of the character. Writing the 8-bit values into the memory locations shown would cause the appropriate points on the display to light. For example, look at the first row of the character. The first point is off, followed by one that is on, followed by five blank positions, and finally, another lit position. If a 1 is needed to light a given point, and a 0 is needed to blank one, the data value to the left of the character, 01000001, would light and blank the appropriate points on the display. The same can be seen for all the rows. In every case, the code needed to light the right points is shown to the left of the character.

Now, consider the beam tracing across the CRT from left to right. As the beam passes through a given row, picture the data word at the left being fed to the beam as it passes through the row. For example, as the beam starts to go across row 0001, the first point it hits is P7. At that time, the D7 bit bit would be fed to the beam. Since it is a zero, the beam would not light the P7 point. As the beam hits the P6 position in the same row, bit D6 would be fed to it. This one would cause the P6 position to be lit, and so on. After the beam passes the end of the row, it would move down one row, and begin the process all over again, this time being fed the data value for the dot pattern in the third row. This process would be continued over and over until the entire character had been displayed. This is the process used to light every character on the CRT. *The key here is to provide the proper dot pattern code at the right time,* that is, to provide the code for row 0001 exactly when it is needed, the code for row 0010 exactly when it is needed, and so on.

Now, let's go back to the message from Figure 14.10. This time we will look at it in terms of row addresses and data values. The process used to write an entire message (one line of characters) is almost exactly as described, with one catch. In writing the message in Figure 14.10, all the dot patterns in row 0000 would be written, than all the dot patterns in row 0001, and so on. This means that the following sequence must be followed:

1. The dot pattern code for row 0000 of the first character is sent to the beam.
2. When the beam reaches the P7 position of the second character, the dot pattern for its 0000 row is sent to the beam.
3. When the beam reaches the P7 position of the third character, its pattern for 0000 must be sent to the beam.
4. This process is repeated across the entire screen.

After row 0000 of all the characters have been displayed, the beam advances to row 0001 and the process starts again. This means that the beam makes 13 sweeps to complete a single row of characters. Each time that the beam passes through a given row, it must be fed a number of dot pattern codes equal to the number of characters in that row. Another point is that these dot pattern codes must be fed to the beam one bit at a time as the beam passes through the row. This process is repeated throughout the entire CRT scan. When the beam reaches the bottom of the CRT and returns to the top, the process starts all over again. To perform this operation successfully, the logic circuitry must perform the following operations:

1. It must determine the row that is being scanned by the beam.
2. It must determine the proper dot pattern codes for each row of each character.
3. It must supply the codes to the CRT circuitry, one at a time, in the proper sequence.

All these processes are controlled by a single chip, called a *CRT controller*. This chip is discussed in detail after a discussion of CRT formats.

CRT Formats

The characters displayed in the previous example were made up of a 7×9 dot matrix. However, as you may have noticed, an area of 8×13 dot positions was allowed for each character. The reasons for this are simple:

1. Space must be allowed for the space between letters and the space between rows of characters. Without leaving one column and one row blank, the results would be letters and rows of characters that ran together. Just as space between letters and lines have been provided in this book, they must also be provided on the CRT.
2. Even with one row and one column always being blank, that still leaves a marix that is 7 columns $\times$ 12 rows. The 7 columns are each used for one dot position of the character, but why 12 rows? Using 12 rows allows the use of both upper- and lowercase letters. A capital Y, for example, would extend from the baseline to the top available row, while a lowercase y would extend down toward the lowest rows.

Most microcomputer CRTs are capable of displaying either 12 lines of 32 characters or 24 lines of 80 characters. The CRT for the H-89A is a 24×80 display format.

Character Generators and CRT Controllers

Character generators and CRT controllers are two of the most critical logic circuits in CRT operation. The CRT controller is a microcontroller that is responsible for supplying the horizontal and vertical sync signals, row addresses, and character addresses. It essentially runs the whole show. The *character generator* is a ROM that stores all of the dot pattern codes for the microcomputer. We will look at this chip first. The character generator for the H-89A is shown in Figure 14.12a. The character generator has 11 address inputs (A0 through A10), and thus is a 2K ROM. This ROM stores all of the dot patterns that the CRT is capable of displaying. The address inputs to this chip are actually divided into two groups. A4 through A10 accept a 7-bit address that corresponds to the character to be displayed. The ASCII code for the character is applied to these address inputs, identifying the character to be displayed. The other four address inputs (A0 through A3) are used to apply the row address. So if the fifth row of the letter "A" was to be displayed, the input address to the character generator would be:

$A10$	$A9$	$A8$	$A7$	$A6$	$A5$	$A4$	$A3$	$A2$	$A1$	$A0$
1	0	0	0	0	0	1	0	1	0	1

where 1000001 is the ASCII code for the letter A, and 0101 is the row address. At address 1000010101 in the character generator ROM would be the dot pattern code for the fifth row of the letter A. All of the characters/rows are addressed in the same manner. This includes the space that is entered between letters when the space bar on the keyboard is used. The space between words has an ASCII code, just like any other character. In this case, however, the dot pattern codes would consist of all zeros.

When a dot pattern code is addressed, the character generator provides the dot patterns at its Q_1 through Q_8 outputs. From here, other circuitry is used to provide the dot pattern code to the beam one bit at a time. This is covered later in this section. At this time, let's take a look at the CRT controller.

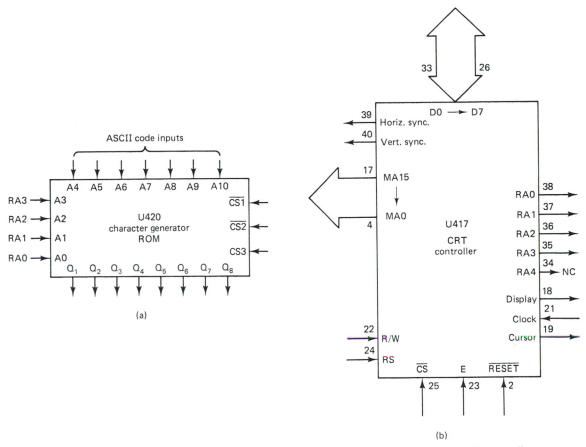

Figure 14.12 H-89A character generator (U420) and CRT controller (U417). *(© 1981 Heath Company. Reprinted by permission of Heath Company.)*

The CRT controller is a microcontroller that is used specifically to direct the activities of the entire CRT logic circuitry. It is a 40-pin chip that has address and data lines and an internal memory that is programmed by the main CPU when power is first applied to the system. This internal program controls the operation of the device. The logic symbol for the CRT controller is shown in Figure 14.12b.

The MA (memory address) outputs from the chip are used to address external RAM. This RAM would be used to hold the ASCII codes for the characters to be displayed. The R/$\overline{\text{W}}$ line allows the CPU to program the device at power-up. The RA (row address) outputs are used to drive the four row address inputs of the character generator. The horizontal sync and vertical sync outputs from the chip supply 15,600 Hz and 60 Hz, respectively, to the CRT circuitry. The DISPLAY output (pin 18) enables the circuitry that transfers the dot pattern codes to the CRT. Essentially, this output acts as a display enable. The CLK pin (pin 21) is the clock input to the device. The CURSOR output (pin 19) is used when the address on the MA outputs corresponds to the position of the cursor on the screen. The *cursor* is the flashing line or square that indicates where the next entered character will be displayed. When the beam reaches the cursor position on the CRT, this output from the CRT controller goes high, causing the cursor to appear.

The $\overline{\text{CS}}$ and E inputs to the CRT controller are activated when the main CPU is attempting to communicate with it. These essentially enable the data inputs to the CRT controller.

The Complete CRT Logic Circuitry

To show how all the elements of the CRT logic circuitry combine to cause the characters to be displayed on the screen, we will now discuss the operation of the entire group of circuits. Again, we will be using the circuit from the H-89A as the basis of our discussion. The circuit is shown in Figure 14.13.

The center of the CRT control circuitry consists of the CRT controller, U417, and the character generator, U420. The video shift register, U421 (located directly below the character generator), is used to convert the parallel data from the character generator into serial data. Recall that the CRT must be fed the dot pattern codes one bit at a time. U421 will fulfill this requirement by taking the 8-bit dot pattern code and shifting it out to the video circuitry one bit at a time. This is a parallel in/serial out shift register that is clocked at a 12.288-MHz rate. Why such a high frequency? Consider the fact that the CRT in this microcomputer is capable of displaying 80 characters across the screen. Each one of these characters is 8 dot positions wide, and thus there are 640 dot positions in any given row. This means that in the time that it takes for one horizontal trace, the video shift register must be capable of sending 640 individual bits to the video circuitry. The trace time for one horizontal sweep is $1/15,600 \, Hz = 64.1 \, \mu s$. The dot pattern bits must therefore be shifted to the video circuitry at a rate of approximately 10 bits per microsecond. The minimum clock rate to the video shift register that will accomplish this transfer rate is 9.98 MHz. The clock rate into the video shift register is well above the minimum required.

The clock signal to the video shift register is often referred to as the *dot clock* and is usually the highest frequency within the system. The fact that it is usually the highest frequency within the system makes sense when you consider the fact that none of the other circuits in the system require as high an operating frequency as the video shift register.

The $\overline{LD}$ (load) input to the video shift register is clocked at 1.538 MHz. This makes the circuit load in a new dot pattern code once for every eight cycles of the dot clock. With this setup, the video shift register will load in a new dot pattern code as soon as the last bit of its current code is shifted out. Since the output is taken from the Q_H output, and this output will reflect the MSB of the new code as soon as it is entered, there is no delay between the LSB of one dot pattern code and the MSB of the next. This is important because there is no space between character positions on the CRT (i.e., the last dot position for one character is followed immediately by the first dot position for the next character). As a result, there must be no delay between dot pattern codes.

The series of basic gates and flip-flops below and to the lower right of the video shift register is discussed later in this section. For now, we will shift our attention to the circuitry located to the left of the CRT contoller. On the far left of the logic diagram, there are four lk RAM chips. These RAM chips are used to store the ASCII codes of the characters to be displayed. Each chip is a lk × 4 RAM, and thus the ASCII code for a given character will be contained in two of these chips. For example, look at the two top chips, U408 and U409. For a given ASCII code, U408 would be used to store the four least significant bits, while U409 would be used to store the three most significant bits. The MSB would be a 1* for every code stored, in order to provide a dark space between the letters on the CRT, as was discussed earlier. U408 and U409 make up a lk × 8 RAM, and U410 and U411 make up another lk × 8 RAM, for a total of 2k × 8. The display RAM is therefore capable of storing 2048 8-bit words. This would be the smallest possible display RAM, because of the fact that there must be an ASCII code stored for every character displayed on the CRT. Since this system is capable of displaying 1920 characters, a 2k RAM is required.

---

*This 1 is inverted by circuitry that will be discussed later in this section.

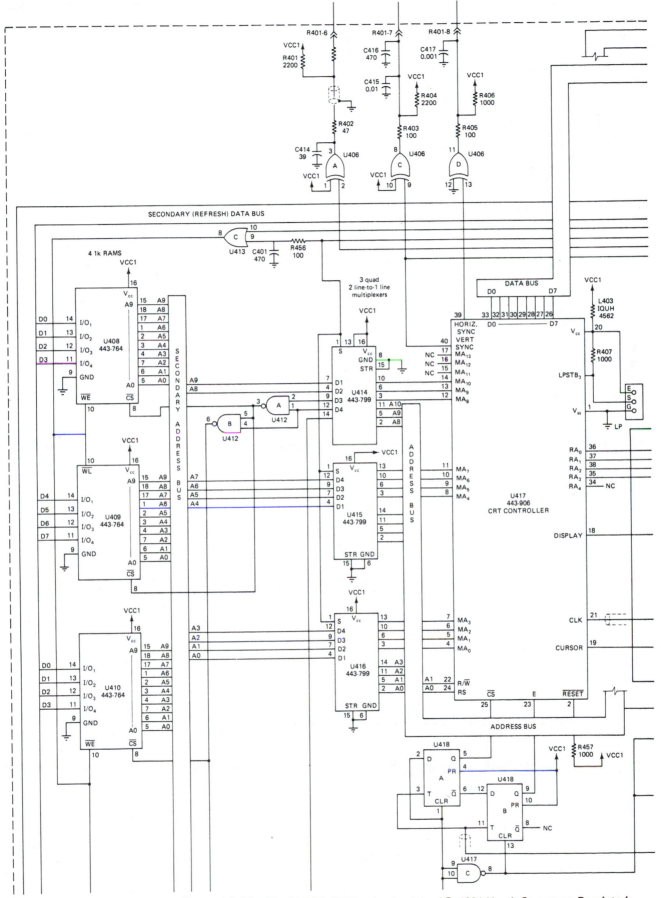

Figure 14.13 The H-89A CRT logic circuitry. (© *1981 Heath Company. Reprinted by permission of Heath Company.)*

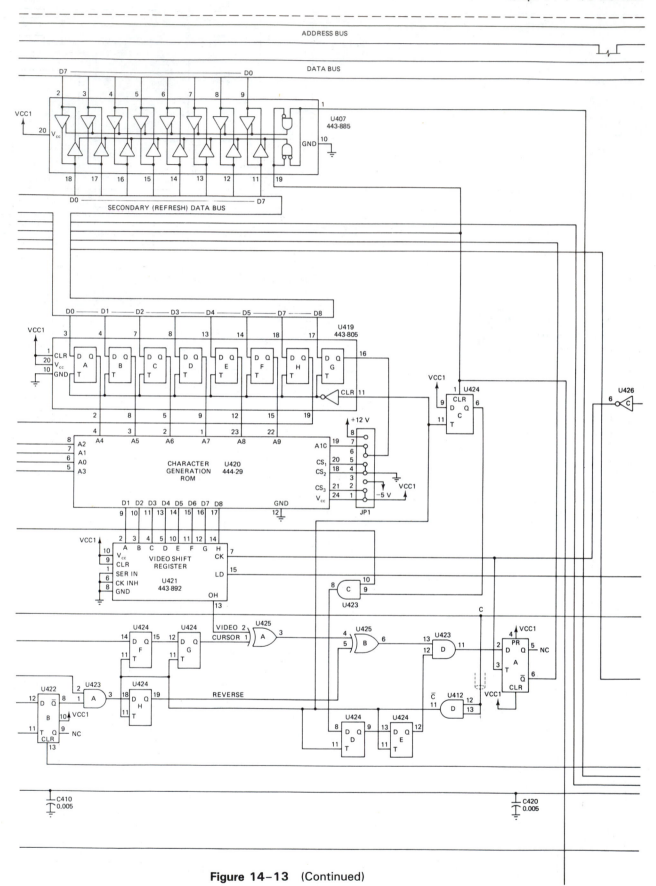

Figure 14–13 (Continued)

The display RAM can be addressed by both the CPU and the CRT controller. The CPU must be able to address the RAM in order to store the ASCII codes for the characters to be displayed, and the CRT controller must be able to address the RAM in order to send the codes to the character generator. The multiplexers, U414, U415, and U416, are used to allow the two different devices to address the display RAM. Each of the multiplexers has eight inputs, four outputs, and a select (S) input. When the S input is low, the multiplexers will connect the CPU address bits to the outputs. When the S input is high, the CRT controller address bits will be connected to the outputs. The three multiplexers are used to provide a 10-bit address code and a $\overline{CS}$ to the RAM chips. The $\overline{CS}$ is provided by the D_3 and D_4 pins of U414. These pins will both be high whenever the MSB of the address is high. When the MSB of the address is low, D_3 will be low. These multiplexer outputs are connected to two NAND gates that work according to the following truth table:

D_3	D_4	U412A-1	U412A-2	U412A-3	U412B-6[a]
0	1	1	0	1	0
1	1	1	1	0	1

[a]The inputs for this chip are equal to the values in the U412A-3 and D_4 columns.

The last two columns of the table indicate that the output from one of the NAND gates will be low and the other will be high, depending on the output D_3. When D_3 is high, U408 and U409 will receive a low $\overline{CS}$ signal and will react to the address and control signals. When D_3 is low, U410 and U411 will receive a low $\overline{CS}$ signal and will also react accordingly. D_3 is therefore used to select between the two RAM chip pairs. As the truth table indicates, the D_4 output from the multiplexer, U414, is always high. This is due to the fact that the input pins that are connected to this output have been left open.

The S inputs to the multiplexers are controlled by the CPU. When the CPU addresses the display RAM, it drives this line low, causing the CPU address codes to be applied to the display RAM chips through the multiplexers. The CPU will address these chips only during the time when the CRT is in a vertical retrace. This address timing is a function of the program that the CPU is running when it is sending data to the display circuitry.

The $\overline{WE}$ (write enable) inputs to the display RAM chips are the same thing as a R/$\overline{W}$ input. These inputs are driven by the OR gate, U413C. One of the inputs to this OR gate is being driven by the same CPU line that drives the S inputs to the multiplexers. The other input is driven by the R/$\overline{W}$ output of the CPU. These chips will therefore be write enabled only when being addressed by the CPU and when the CPU is in the write mode of operation. At that time, data can be entered into the display RAM. *The CRT controller would never enter information into the RAM. It would only cause the RAM to output data.* When the CRT controller addresses a given display RAM location, the ASCII code that is stored in that location is output onto the *secondary data bus.* This bus is used to allow data transfers between the CPU and the CRT circuitry and between the RAM and the character generator. A separate data bus is needed for the RAM/character generator data transfers so that these data transfers will not interfere with the data transfers between the other units in the system. If only one data bus was used, it would be tied up most of the time by the display circuitry sending data to the character generator. This would be unacceptable, and thus the need for another data bus. Data is transferred between the two data buses by way of U407 (above the character generator), an octal three-state buffer. When the CPU selects the address multiplexers by driving the S line low, the same line also selects U407, connecting the two buses.

Assuming that the ASCII codes for the display data are already in the display RAM, let's take a look at how the display circuitry goes about sending that data to the video circuitry. The sequence is as follows:

1. The CRT controller (CRTC) addresses the display RAM, causing the ASCII code for the character to be displayed to be sent to U419, an octal D flip-flop.

2. On the next transition of the CRTC clock (1.536 MHz), the ASCII code is entered into U419. The clock input to U419 is connected to the CRTC clock by way of the NAND gate, U412D.

3. The ASCII code and row address (supplied by the CRTC) are both applied to the character generator, addressing the appropriate dot pattern code.

4. On the next LD signal to the video shift register, the dot pattern code is loaded into the video shift register and starts being shifted out to the video circuitry.

5. During the time required for steps 3 and 4 above, the CRTC has addressed the next location in the display RAM.

One important point: The first 80 locations in the display RAM correspond to the character positions on the top line of the CRT display. These 80 locations must be addressed over and over, until the CPU has sent the 13 dot pattern codes for each character out to the CRT. In other words, the CRTC supplies row address 0000. While this row address is out, the CRTC must address the display RAM to obtain the ASCII codes for all 80 characters that are to be displayed on the CRT. After the row is traced, the CRTC advances the row address value to 0001 and addresses the 80 ASCII codes again. This process is repeated until all 13 rows of all 80 characters have been supplied to the video circuitry. The process is then repeated for the ASCII codes in the next 80 RAM locations, as these codes correspond to the second display line on the CRT, and so on.

Now, let's take a look at the collection of basic gates and flip-flops that are located in the lower section of the circuitry. These circuits are used mainly to provide time delays and enable signals. For our discussion, we will divide these circuits into groups. After discussing the groups one at a time, we will combine them to show how they interact. The five groups of circuits, and their basic functions, are as follows:

Circuits	Function
U418A, U418B, U412C	Enables the CRT circuitry
U422B, U423A, U424H	Reverse video circuitry
U424F, U424G, U425A	Cursor circuitry
U425B	Combines cursor/video and reverse video signals
U424D, U424E, U423D, U422A	Final time delay and enable

There are two inputs to the circuitry used to enable the CRTC. These are a select signal from the CPU and a clock signal that is at 2.048 MHz. The purpose of the circuitry, which consists of U418A, U418B, and U412C, is to provide the $\overline{CS}$ and E signals that are shown in Figure 14.14. The two signals shown are needed to allow the CPU to enter information into the CRTC when it is programmed at power-up. When the system is first turned on, the CRTC is programmed for its operation by the CPU, as we explained earlier. Any time that the CPU needs to enter any information into the CRTC, it must supply the signal shown in Figure 14.14. Notice how the E (enable) signal occurs within the half cycle of the $\overline{CS}$ signal. This timing relationship is supplied by the circuits listed above. The select signal from the CPU (active low) is applied to U418A-1 and the inputs to the NAND gate, U412C. The 2.048-MHz clock is applied to the T inputs of the two flip-flops. As an exercise, try to determine for yourself how the circuitry develops the waveforms shown in Figure 14.14. Assume that the low signal from the CPU occurs before the clock signal. The operation is covered at the end of this section, but try it for yourself first.

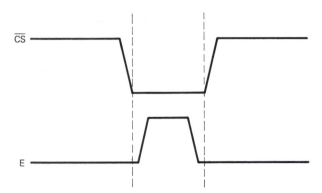

Figure 14.14 CPU control inputs to the CRT controller.

The H-89A has *reverse video* capability. This means that instead of the standard light letters on a dark background, it can display dark letters on a light background. Whether or not the screen is in reverse video is determined by a switch that the user sets in the system. If this switch is set, the CPU will program the system for reverse video. Here is how the circuitry works. If the reverse video switch is set, the CPU will address the CRTC and program the circuitry for reverse video. It does this during the normal power-up routine. As it addresses the CRTC, the CPU outputs the address bit A3 = 0. This 0 is applied to the D input of U422B, and when the select signal from the CPU is applied to the input of U412C, the 0 is clocked into U422B. With U422B being RESET, the $\overline{Q}$ output from the device is high. This high output is applied to the lower input of the AND gate, U423A. The other AND input is being fed by the MSB of each data word in RAM. Recall (from page 292) that this MSB of each data word is always a 1. The two 1's into the AND gate will cause a high output, which is applied to the D input of U424D. When clocked, the output of U424D will go high, and this high will be applied to the lower input of U425B. The effect it has at this point will be discussed when we cover the combining of signals throughout this circuitry. For now, the bottom line is that a high at U425B-5 will cause the reverse video effect, and a zero at this input will cause normal CRT operation.

The third group of circuits listed were those associated with the cursor. When the CRTC is addressing a RAM location that corresponds to the cursor position on the screen, it will drive its cursor output high. This high output goes through U424F and U424G, which together form a two-clock pulse time delay. The purpose for the time delay is to ensure that the cursor is positioned in the correct row of the 13-row scan sequence. When the cursor position is addressed, there is no data in the RAM location associated with it, so if the cursor were not present, the entire space would be blank. However, when the proper row is addressed, the Q output of U424G will have just gone high. This puts a 1 into U425A. The result of this is that the rest of the video circuitry will react as if the dot pattern code had been 11111111. When the cursor has been displayed, the CRTC removes the high cursor output. This will prevent a misdisplay at another point in time.

U425B is used to combine the outputs of the reverse video circuitry and the cursor/video circuitry. If the reverse video bit is a 1, the XOR gate will invert the data at the other input. This will cause the points that should have been dark to be light, and vice versa. If the reverse video bit is a 0, the XOR gate will not invert the values on the other input, and the display will work normally.

The AND gate, U423C, is used to combine the display signal from the CRTC, and the enable signal from the flip-flop, U424C, to enable the final data output from the CRT circuitry. The flip-flop will be continually set, except when the CPU is entering information into the CRT circuitry. This means that during normal operation, the only bit needed to enable the final output is the DISPLAY output from the CRTC. When this bit is high, the output from the AND gate, U423C, will be high. This high is delayed for two clock signals by U424D and U424E in the same way that the cursor signal was delayed. After two clock cycles, the Q output from U424E will go high. This high goes to U423D, the AND gate, enabling the output from the gate. With a high in on the lower input of the AND gate, and video data being applied to the other input, the output from the AND gate will equal the video data. The video data now go through the D flip-flop, U422A, where it is inverted and sent to the video board through the XOR gate, U406A.

Now, here is the explanation of the CRTC enable circuitry. When the CPU goes to enable the CRTC, the following process occurs:

1. The low input from the CPU clears U418A, driving its Q output low. This provides transition A in Figure 14.14.
2. When U184A is cleared, its $\overline{Q}$ output goes high. This high is clocked into U418A on the next positive-going transition of the clock, causing the Q output of U418B to go high. This causes transition B.
3. After the CPU finishes its routine with the CRTC, it returns its select line to the high state. This high is inverted by U412C, and the low clears U418B. This causes transition C.
4. The high line from the CPU has also been applied to the D input of U418A. On the next clock transition. U418A SETs again, causing its Q output to return to the high state. This causes transition D, which completes the cycle.

The final circuits contained in the CRT circuitry are the XOR gates, U406A, C, and D. These circuits are used for buffering and current amplification. U406A is the path taken by the bits of the dot pattern codes, U406C is used as a path for the vertical sync signal, and U406D is used as a path for the horizontal sync signal.

The discussion of the CRT control circuitry has probably been somewhat difficult for you to follow. This is understandable, considering the amount of activity that goes on in this circuit. Given the number of possible problems that could arise in this circuit, it would seem to be a troubleshooting nightmare. However, although more tests may be required to find a given fault in this circuit than in circuits discussed previously, it can still be effectively diagnosed when it malfunctions.

Troubleshooting the CRT Logic Circuitry

As in troubleshooting any group of logic circuits, the first step in troubleshooting the CRT logic circuitry is to determine the functions that the circuitry was intended to perform and to find the points where the performance of those functions can be verified. The three main functions of the CRT logic circuitry are:

1. To provide horizontal and vertical sync signals to the video circuitry
2. To fetch the ASCII codes for the characters to be displayed and provide the dot pattern codes for those characters
3. To ensure that the proper dot pattern codes are sent to the display at the proper time

Problems with the horizontal and vertical sync signals are the easiest to diagnose. First, any trouble in the horizontal or vertical sync signals would be immediately evident on the CRT. If the vertical sync signal is out, the display will roll vertically. For the H-89A, loss of the horizontal sync signal will prevent the CRT filament from lighting. This is a part of the operation of the video circuitry itself. For other systems, it may simply cause a loss of horizontal control, or stability. In either case, the first step would be to verify that the appropriate sync signal is getting to the video circuitry. If it is, the problem is in the video circuitry. If not, the appropriate pin on the CRTC should be checked. If the sync signals are being generated by the CRTC as they should, the problem lies between the CRTC and the video circuitry. All you would need to do is trace the signal toward the video board until it is lost. When you lose the signal, you are at the cause of the problem.

In order for the ASCII codes to be transformed into dot pattern codes, several operations occur, involving several circuits. A summary of the operations required is as follows:

1. The CPU must store the display character ASCII codes in RAM.
2. The CRTC must fetch the ASCII codes from RAM and transfer them to the character generator.
3. The CRTC must supply the proper row address to the character generator.
4. The character generator must take the ASCII code and the row address and, based on that information, provide the proper dot pattern code.

One of the problems in troubleshooting this sequence of events is the fact that a failure in any one of the steps will produce the same results as a failure in any other. If any of the steps listed above fail to occur, the display will be filled with a series of random characters. The photo shown in Figure 14.15 shows the display of the H-89A

Figure 14.15 A faulty CRT display.

when the CPU has failed to load the ASCII codes into the display RAM. Although this picture was taken under the condition stated, failure of *any* of the four steps listed above would have had the same results. It would follow, then, that the display problem shown would require quite a bit of testing. Let's take a look at the circuits that would be involved in each of the steps listed above. For this discussion, refer back to the circuit shown in Figure 14.13.

1. *The CPU must store the display character ASCII codes in RAM.* Assuming that all other units of the microcomputer are working, this step involves the display RAM, the address multiplexers, the NAND gate (U412), the OR gate (U413C), and the three-state buffer (U407).

2. *The CRTC must fetch the ASCII codes from RAM and transfer them to the character generator.* This operation involves the CRTC (U417), the address multiplexers, the NAND gate (U412), the display RAM, the D-type flip-flop (U419), and the CRTC clock circuitry. Since the CRTC must be enabled and programmed at power-up to perform its basic operations, the D-type flip-flop (U418) is also considered to be part of the circuitry involved in the stated operation.

3. *The CRTC must supply the proper row addresses to the character generator.* Assuming that all of its inputs are good, this operation involves only the CRTC.

4. *The character generator must take the ASCII code and the row address and based on that information, provide the dot pattern code.* Assuming that all of its inputs are good, this is a function of only the character generator.

Since the end result of these operations should be a dot pattern code being present at the outputs of the character generator, this would be the best place to start the troubleshooting procedure. Remember that the data rate coming out of this circuit is approximately 1.536 MHz, so the outputs from this chip will apear to be "garbage signals" that vary between the high and low limits for the system. If any output from the character generator appears to be faulty, you should check *all* of the address inputs to the chip.

When checking the inputs to the character generator, the address inputs can be used to direct you toward the cause of the problem. The row addresses should form a divide-by-13 count. This can be checked using the technique discussed in Chapter 8 on troubleshooting counters. If the row addresses are not good, the CRTC must be checked. If they are good, and the $\overline{CS}$ inputs and power supply inputs to the character generator are good, you have two possible situations: Either the character generator ROM is faulty, or the information coming from RAM is faulty. Obviously, if the address inputs to the character generator that come from RAM are dead, the problem lies somewhere other than in the character generator itself. But what if all of the inputs to the character generator appear to be good? Do you replace the character generator ROM, or do you continue troubleshooting back toward the RAM circuitry? Statistically, you would be better off checking out the RAM circuitry. The reason for this is the fact that ROM chips tend to be extremely reliable.

If we assume that the address bits reaching the character generator are not the ASCII codes that were intended to be there, we assume that we are troubleshooting a data problem; that is, since ASCII codes are data values that are supplied to this circuitry by the CPU, the assumption that they are not reaching their final destination (the character generator) indicates a problem in a data transfer sequence. As you may recall, this can be one of the most difficult types of problems to troubleshoot. The first step after making this assumption would be to check all of the control inputs to the chips that are involved in the ASCII codes getting from the CPU to the character generator.

If you check back to the list of the circuits involved in transferring the ASCII codes from the CPU to the CRT logic circuitry and then to the character generator, you will see that quite a few control lines need to be checked. Excluding clock inputs, a list of the control signals that would need to be checked is as follows:

U417-25	U407-1	U415-1	U408-10	U410-8	U411-10
U417-23	U424C-1	U416-1	U409-8	U410-10	
U407-19	U414-1	U408-8	U409-10	U411-8	

The control inputs listed include all those involved in the ASCII code transfers. If any of these inputs prove to be faulty, that signal should be traced to the source of the fault. If they all prove to be good, the next step would be to check the address inputs being supplied to the RAM chips. Every address input to each RAM chip would be checked and should appear to be a series of signals that the oscilloscope cannot lock in on. If any address input appears to be bad, trace the signal back to its source, using the technique discussed in Chapter 10 on address line troubleshooting. *One note:* In this circuit, you are dealing with multiplexed addresses. You would need to check out the multiplexers if any RAM address inputs appeared to be bad.

Assume now that you have checked all the address and control lines and that they all appear to be good. By doing this, you have narrowed down the problem to one of three causes:

1. One or more of the RAM chips are bad.
2. The character generator ROM is bad.
3. The ASCII codes being supplied to the CRT circuitry are bad.

Once again, you are at the point of swapping chips. The best place to start would be to replace the RAM chips one at a time. Each time that you replace one, power-up the system and see if the problem has been corrected. If replacing all of them does not correct the problem, you would replace the character generator ROM. If this does not correct the problem, the trouble lies in the ASCII codes being sent to the CRT logic circuitry, and another section of the system is faulty.

Although the checking of the power and clock connections within the group of circuits has not been mentioned up to this point, that does not mean that they need not be checked. As several previous discussions have stated, these connections should be checked at the start of any troubleshooting procedure. As was done in this discussion, all future troubleshooting procedures in this text will assume that these checks have been made and that no difficulty in these lines was found.

As you may have noticed, nothing was said in the procedure about the flip-flop and basic gates that are located between the character generator and the video circuitry. This was due to the fact that we are discussing the problems that would make themselves evident by causing the display shown in Figure 14.15. If the video shift register, or any of the circuitry that follows it were to go bad, the symptoms would be different from the display shown.

If the video shift register or any of the basic logic located in the lower right section of the schematic goes bad, there will be symptoms in one of three areas:

1. The cursor will not be displayed as it should.
2. The screen will be stuck in reverse video.
3. There will be no output to the video circuitry (i.e., a totally blank or totally bright CRT display).

Any problems with the cursor or reverse video are not difficult to troubleshoot, since these problems could only be caused by a handful of dedicated circuits; (that is, those circuits involved in the cursor and reverse video functions are used only for those functions, and thus are easily identified and tested). The third system listed above would be caused by there being no output to the video circuitry. In this case, the output to the video circuitry would be at either a constant 1 or a constant 0. This would cause the screen to be either completely on (all dot positions lighted) or off (all dot positions blank). When this happens, the first step would be to check for a changing output from the video shift register. If there is no output, and the inputs to the register are as they should be, the register itself must be replaced. If there is an output from the video shift register and no output to the video circuitry, the problem lies between the register and the final output. In this case, you would simply trace the signal from the register toward the output until the bad circuit was located.

The Bottom Line

All of the CRT logic circuitry troubleshooting has been directed toward the H-89A. However, the basic principles of this system are the same as those for any microcomputer. There are specific functions which are performed by the CRT logic circuitry. These functions, which are listed on page 301, are performed by one group of circuits or another in the CRT section of every microcomputer.

When faced with troubleshooting a system for the first time, start by determining which groups of circuits perform the functions listed on page 301. Then determine the connections between the various groups of circuits. Once this has been done, you have the means to trace the various signals through the CRT logic circuitry. When trying to determine the group of circuits that is most likely the cause of the problem, remember the following:

1. Loss of the horizontal or vertical stability can be caused by the CRT controller. If the CRTC is not the cause of the problem, the source of the problem is in the video circuitry.
2. Displays that consist of random characters are caused by a break in the normal sequence of converting ASCII codes to dot pattern codes. This break can occur at any point between the CPU transfer of the ASCII codes to the display RAM and the character generator's operation.
3. Total loss of display characters is probably caused by the circuitry that is involved in transmitting the serial dot pattern codes to the video circuitry.

Using these three statements as a guideline, you should have a fair idea of where a problem lies before even getting out your oscilloscope. However, you must be sure to remember that these statements are meant as guidelines, and nothing more. Simply because the symptoms listed are *usually* caused by the circuits mentioned does not mean that these are the only possible causes. Reading the technical data on a given system before attempting to troubleshoot it will show you the ways in which that system differs from the one just discussed.

14.4 SERIAL I/O FOR PRINTERS AND MODEMS

As shown in the preceding section, the video circuitry that drives the microcomputer CRT requires serial data transmission from the CRT logic circuitry. The process of changing the dot pattern codes from parallel to serial form was performed by the video shift register.

There are other I/O devices that require serial data transmission in order to function properly. Two of these devices are *modems* and *line printers*. A line printer is a device that produces a hard copy (paper copy) of the results of a given microcomputer operation, and a modem (modulator/demodulator) is a device that allows a given microcomputer to communicate with another system over the telephone. In order for data to be transmitted to either a line printer or a modem, several requirements must be met:

1. The parallel data in the microcomputer must be converted to serial data. In the same category, the serial data being sent to a terminal must be converted to parallel data within the receiving terminal (microcomputer).

2. The data must be transmitted from one device to the other in the same manner and at the same rate.

3. The connectors between the two devices must be set up in some standard way so that the proper connections are made.

The first requirement is met by a type of chip called a UART (universal asynchronous receiver/transmitter). A UART converts the parallel micrcocomputer data into serial form so that it may be transmitted, and converts received serial data into parallel form for suitable microcomputer use. The second requirement may also be met by the UART, as it is used to determine the rate at which data is transmitted and is usually used to determine the manner in which it is transmitted. The third requirement is met by use of a connection and data transmission standard called the *RS-232-C interface*. This interface standard is discussed later in this section.

The UART

A UART is a device that is used as the main controlling element in serial data communications. It receives parallel data from the internal microcomputer circuitry and converts it to serial form. Similarly, it receives serial data from outside sources and converts it to parallel form for internal microcomputer use. The device is shown in Figure 14.16 as it is connected in the H-89A to help in our discussion of its basic operation. As you can see, it has an 8-bit parallel data input/output set of pins (pins 1 through 8). These pins are connected to the main CPU of the system and are the means by which data is transmitted to and from the UART. Pin 14, $\overline{CS2}$, is used to select the device. When the CPU needs to communicate with the UART, it drives this input low. There are also three address inputs to the UART, A0, A1, and A2, which allow the CPU to address one of eight internal UART registers. This is needed because the CPU must program some values into the UART when the system is first turned on.

One such value is called the *baud rate* of the system. The baud rate for a given system is the rate at which it transmits data, in bits per second. The UART controls the baud rate, which is programmed into the device by the CPU. *The baud rates of the two communicating devices are critical, because they must be equal if successful data transmission is to occur.* This will be discussed in more detail later.

Two of the control inputs to the UART are DISTR (pin 21) and DOSTR (pin 18). These are strobe inputs that cause the UART to input data from the CPU and output data to the CPU, respectively. For example, when the CPU drive the DISTR pin low, the UART will accept the value that the CPU is providing on the data bus. Similarly, when DOSTR goes low, the UART will output a given 8-bit data value to the CPU. These inputs control the UART-to-CPU communication.

The MR input to the UART (pin 35) is used to reset the internal data registers of the UART. This pin would be activated immediately prior to programming the device. The INTRPT (interrupt) output of the UART is used to signal the CPU that data from an external device has been received. The CPU would respond to this signal by activating the DOSTR input to the UART and reading the data output from the device.

The UART sends serial data to the external devices by way of the S OUT (serial output) pin and accepts data from the devices by way of the S IN (serial input) pin.

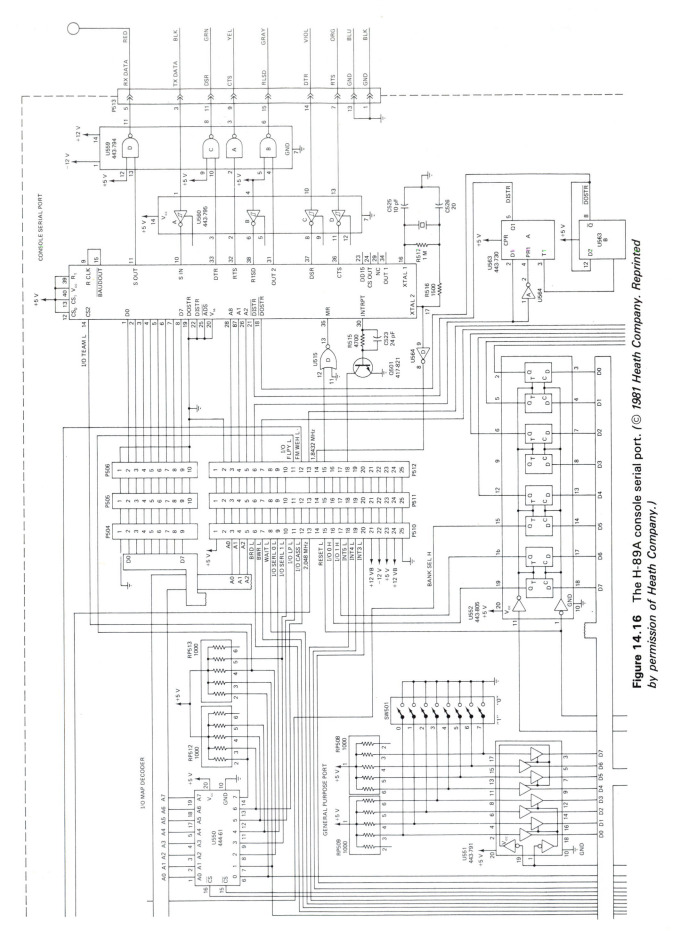

Figure 14.16 The H-89A console serial port. (© 1981 Heath Company. Reprinted by permission of Heath Company.)

The rest of the pins on the right-hand side of the UART are control signals that are sent to and received from the external device that is communicating with the microcomputer.

The DTR (data terminal ready) pin, when low, informs the external device that the UART is ready to receive data. The RTS (request to send) output of the UART is used to inform the external device that the UART is ready to send serial data to the device. This output is also an active-low output. RLSD (received line signal detect) is a UART input that is used to inform the UART that a modem has detected an input carrier from the telephone line. Essentially, it informs the system that another system is attempting to communicate with it.

The $\overline{DSR}$ (data set ready) pin, when low, informs the UART that the modem has data that it is ready to transmit to the UART. The UART would respond to this active-low input by driving its $\overline{DTR}$ output low. The $\overline{CTS}$ input to the UART informs the device that the modem (or other external device) is ready to receive data from the UART. When this input goes low, the UART will respond by sending the serial data to the external device.

Data is transmitted at a given rate from the UART and is received at the same rate. By the same token, the external device would be programmed to send and receive data at a specific rate. These baud rates must be equal in order to ensure that each device will be looking to receive a given data bit at the same time that the other is transmitting it. This is why it is critical that the baud rates of the two devices be equal.

The same UART as shown in Figure 14.16 is used on the terminal logic board of the H-89A. In this case, however, it is labeled as the ACE (asychronous communications element). Even though it is labeled differently, it is still being used for the purposes described previously.

The H-89A Serial Interface Board

To give you an idea of how the UART is used in serial I/O data communications, let's take a look at the serial interface board for the H-89A. This board is used as the communication link between the system and either a modem, line printer, or another system. The schematic of this board is shown in Figure 14.17. There are three separate UARTs on this board, U602, U603, and U604. Each of these devices is used to provide the communication link between the system and the output or input/output device to which it is connected. U602 is used to transmit data from the system to a line printer, while U603 and U604 would be used for two-way data transmissions with a modem and another system, respectively. Each of these UARTs operates in the same manner as the one discussed previously.

U606, U608, and U611 are used to convert TTL voltage levels to those required for RS-232-C interface standards. In this case, the voltages for a logic 0 and a logic 1 are +10 V and -10V, respectively. This point is discussed further in the next section. U605, U607, and U609 are used to convert the RS-232-C voltage level inputs from the external devices to TTL levels which are compatible with the system. P603, P604, and P605, the external connectors, are located on the back of the system. These connectors are designed in such a way as to conform to RS-232-C interface standards. This allows the system to be connected to any external device that also conforms to these standards, since their pin configurations would be completely compatible. This is discussed further later in this section.

U610A and U610B are D-type flip-flops which are used to latch the DISTR and DOSTR signals. These two signals, as well as all of the other control signals for the board, are provided to the serial interface board via the connector P602. Data is transferred to and from the devices by way of P601.

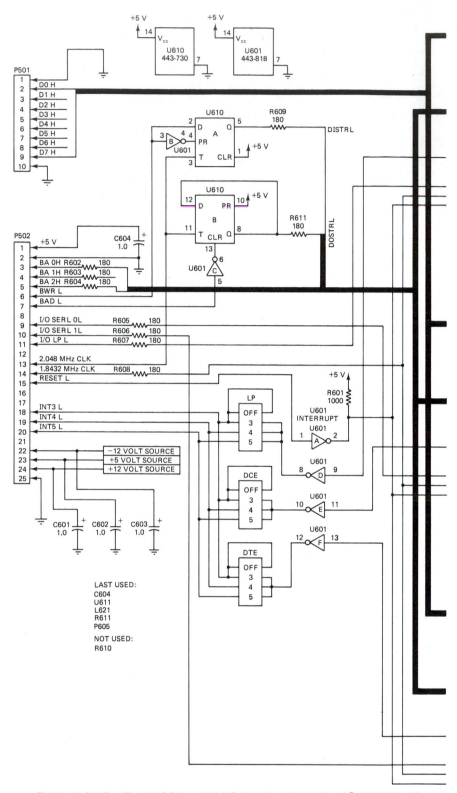

Figure 14.17 The H-89A serial I/O board schematic. (© 1981 Heath Company. Reprinted by permission of Heath Company.)

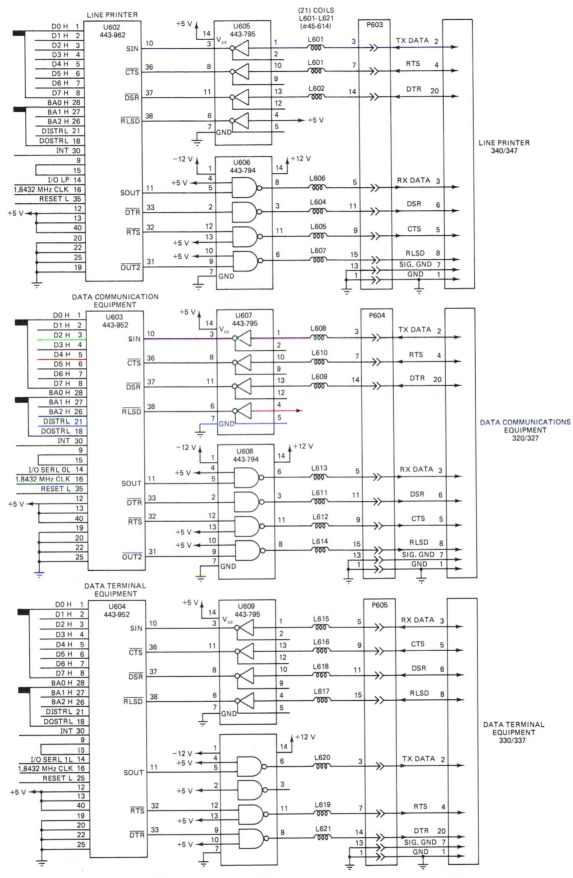

Figure 14.17 (Continued)

The RS-232-C Interface

Continuous reference has been made to the RS-232-C interface standard. This standard, which was set up by the Electronics Industries Association (EIA), defines several interfacing requirements. These requirements are as follows:

Voltage levels: The RS-232-C standard sets voltage limits for data transmission. With the RS-232-C interface, a logic 0 is represented by any voltage between +3 and +25 V. A logic 1 is represented by any voltage between −3 and −25 V. The typical microcomputer will use +10 V and −10 V to represent logic 0 and logic 1, respectively.

Handshake signals: Handshake signals are simply a series of signals that are transmitted between the two communicating devices to establish communications. They are all the basic input and output signals discussed previously: DTR, DSR, and so on. These signals are transmitted in specific sequences to establish the communication link between the two communicating devices.

Connectors: The RS-232-C interface uses standard pin connectors to ensure that the proper output signals from one device are received on the proper input lines of the other, and vice versa. The pin configuration for an RS-232-C connection is shown in Figure 14.18.

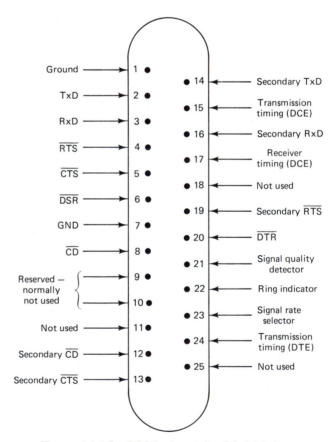

Figure 14.18   DB25 pinout for RS-232-C.

Each of the pin connections are labeled as to its functions. These functions are listed and identified as follows:

Transmitted data (T × D): This is the pin at which the device outputs the data it is transmitting.

Received Data (R × D): This is the pin at which the device receives serial data from the other device.

Request to Send (RTS): This is the connection for the UART RTS output.

Clear to Send (CTS): This is the connection for the UART CTS input.

Data Terminal Ready (DTR): This is the connection to the UART DTR output.

Received Line Signal Detector (CD): This connector provides a path for the UART RLSD input signal.

Signal Ground (GND): This connection provides a common ground reference between the two systems.

The main advantage of using the RS-232-C interface is that it provides a standard by which computers and other digital devices can communicate without having to use any type of code or connector modifications. Nearly every digital device produced has RS-232-C capabilities.

Modems

As we stated at the beginning of this section, serial I/O circuits are used primarily to help a system to communicate with modems and line printers. Line printers are discussed in Chapter 15 and are not discussed further at this point. However, we will look at some of the basic operating principles of modems.

Modems are devices that convert digital data into audio tones and audio tones into digital data. The modem is the link between the microcomputer and the telephone, as shown in Figure 14.19. When system A in the diagram wishes to transmit data

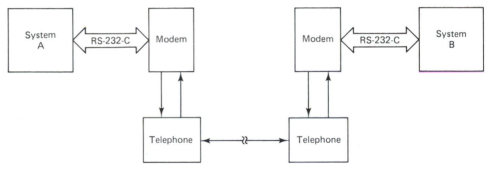

Figure 14.19 Modem I/O connections.

to system B, it sends the proper data and control signals to the modem. The modem then takes the data, converts it to a series of audio tones, and transmits those tones over the telephone line. Conversely, when audio tones are received by the modem, it converts those tones to digital data and provides that data to the system.

When two systems communicate via modems, one of the modems is designated as the *originate modem* and the other is designated as the *answer modem*. The choice of which modem is the originate and which is the answer is determined either by a switch on both modems or by a software routine that the two systems go through as soon as communication between the two is established. The designation of the two modems is important because it determines the audio frequencies that the two will use to transmit and receive data. The frequencies which are used are standard frequencies, meaning that specific frequencies have been established for modem data transmission. These standard frequencies are as follows:

Direction of transmission	Logic 1 f	Logic 0 f
Originate modem to answer modem	1270 Hz	1070 Hz
Answer modem to originate modem	2225 Hz	2025 Hz

Each modem is set up to transmit the frequency designated for that modem and to receive the transmitted frequency of the other modem. Thus the answer modem would transmit frequencies of 2225 Hz and 2025 Hz for logic 1 and logic 0, respectively, and would receive frequencies of 1270 Hz and 1070 Hz for logic 1 and logic 0, respectively. The situation is reversed for the originate modem. Since both systems are transmitting and receiving different frequency ranges, both systems can receive and transmit data simultaneously. This is due to the fact that the nonharmonically related frequencies used will not mix on the telephone lines. The simultaneous transmission of data between the two systems greatly reduces the time required for the data transmission process. The process of transmitting data simultaneously using nonharmonically related frequencies is referred to as *frequency shift keying*. Frequency shift keying is always used with modems, using the standard frequencies listed on page 000.

QUESTIONS

1. What is the difference between memory-mapped I/O and isolated I/O?
2. What are the advantages and disadvantages of using the types of I/O interfacing in Question 1?
3. What is the difference between a scanned input and an interrupt-generating input?
4. What are the advantages of using a hardware priority-interrupt system such as the one shown in Figure 14.3?
5. What is a microcontroller?
6. What is switch bounce? How is it corrected?
7. Refer to Figure 14.7. How does the keyboard encoder detect that a key has been pressed? How does it respond to a keyboard input?
8. What purpose is served by the ROM shown in Figure 14.7? How does it accomplish its purpose?
9. Describe the basic operation of a CRT.
10. Describe the process of lighting a character on the CRT.
11. What is a character generator?
12. What is a CRT controller?
13. Describe the method by which the character generator in Figure 14.13 is addressed.
14. Describe the function of the inputs and output of the CRT controller shown in Figure 14.13.
15. Discuss the troubleshooting procedure for the CRT circuitry in Figure 14.13.
16. What are the data transmission frequencies for modems?
17. What is frequency shift keying?
18. What are the requirements for effective serial data communications between two digital systems?
19. What is a UART? Which data transmission function does it perform?
20. What is meant by the term *baud rate?*
21. Describe the function performed by the various pins shown on the UART in Figure 14.17.
22. What is the RS-232-C interface?
23. What voltage levels are used with the RS-232-C interface?

15 Printers and Disk Drives

Up to this point, our discussion of I/O devices has been limited to some of the simpler circuits used to enter data into and obtain results from a microcomputer. In this chapter we take a look at two of the more complicated I/O devices: *line printers* and *floppy disk drive units*. A line printer is a device that is used to provide the operator with a *hard copy* (paper printout) of the results of a system operation. A floppy disk drive unit is used to transfer data to and from a floppy disk. The floppy disk is a long-term data storage device. Data is recorded and stored on a floppy disk in a manner that is somewhat similar to the method by which music is recorded and saved on magnetic tape.

Disk drives and printers are similar to a modem in that they are actually separate units from the microcomputer itself. In the case of the printer, the fact that it is a separate unit is obvious. The disk drive unit may or may not be cased in the microcomputer terminal itself; but in either case, it is still a separate unit. This can be seen in Figure 15.1, which shows a disk drive unit both in and out of the microcomputer terminal.

Printers and disk drive units differ from other I/O devices in that they are *electromechanical* devices. This means that a given printer or disk drive may experience malfunctions that are either electronic or mechanical in nature. The procedures used to diagnose and repair faults in the mechanical parts of a given printer or disk drive unit vary from one type to another and thus cannot be discussed in any realistic sense in this chapter. It is best to have any major mechanical breakdowns repaired by the manufacturer of the device. However, with the proper background information and troubleshooting techniques, it is possible for the field technician to diagnose and repair a vast majority of the electronic problems that may arise.

15.1 INTRODUCTION TO LINE PRINTERS

As we stated earlier, a line printer is a device that accepts data from a digital system and provides a printout of that data. Most printers are designed to accept ASCII codes which are transmitted to the printer in serial form (one bit at a time) via an

Figure 15.1   Photo of disk drive (in and out of computer). (© *1981 Heath Company. Reprinted by permission of Heath Co.)*

RS-232-C interface. When an ASCII code is transmitted to a printer, the printer converts the serial data back into parallel, and then stores the data in its own internal memory until the device is actually ready to print the character. At that time, the printer sends the appropriate signals to the actual printing circuitry and the character is printed on the paper.

There are basically two types of printers, which are classified according to the method by which they print characters on the paper. *Impact printers* use a mechanical printing device that actually comes into contact with the paper. The other type, *nonimpact printers*, use a mechanical printing device that does not come into contact with the paper.

Impact Printers

There are basically two types of impact printers: *face character* and *dot character*. A face character printer uses a printing mechanism which contains a solid hammer for each character that can be printed. Just as a typewriter has a separate hammer for each character, the face character printer has a hammer for each of its characters. One type of face character printing mechanism, the daisy wheel, is shown in Figure 15.2. The daisy wheel is made up of "spokes" which have the various characters

Figure 15.2   Photo of daisy wheel.

formed around the outer edges. When a given character is to be printed, the wheel is revolved so that the correct character is in position. The spoke containing the character then strikes a ribbon, which causes the character to be printed on the paper.

Another type of face character is the *rotating-type head*. If you have ever used an IBM Selectric typewriter, you have seen the "ball" that contains all of the characters that are used. This "ball" is the rotating-type head. A code is fed to the circuitry that controls the type head. The circuitry then turns the ball until the proper character is in position, and causes it to strike the ribbon. The maximum print rate for this type of printing device is approximately 16 cps (characters per second), compared to approximately 60 cps for the daisy wheel.

There are several other types of face character printers. The other face character printers are used mainly with larger computer systems and thus will not be discussed here. Rather, we will concentrate on the dot character printer, which is the most commonly used type of impact printer.

The dot character printer works in a manner that is very similar to the way in which characters are printed on a CRT. Each character is formed by a series of dot positions, as shown in Figure 15.3. Recall from the discussion on CRTs in Chapter

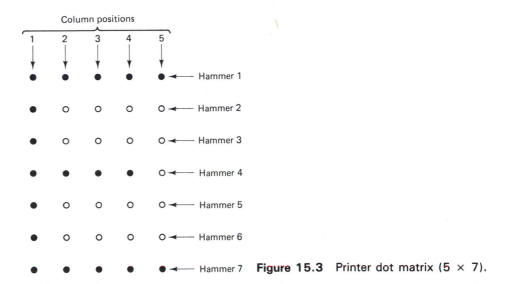

Figure 15.3   Printer dot matrix (5 × 7).

14 that a given character is formed by lighting dot positions that form the character to be displayed. A dot character printer works in much the same fashion. Each character position is made up of a dot matrix. The printing mechanism is made up of a series of hammers that each correspond to a given dot position in the matrix. When a given character is to be written, the appropriate hammers are activated and strike the ribbon. The pattern formed by the dots make up the character. For example, take a look at the character shown in Figure 15.3. The letter "E" has been formed by the darkened dot positions in the 5 × 7 matrix. When the character was printed, the hammers corresponding to the darkened dot positions were all caused to strike the ribbon. The result was the letter "E" being printed on the paper.

One of the advantages of using the dot character format is that the printer can be made to print virtually any type of character. Since the printing head is controlled by the logic and programming of the device, changes in the programming can be used to allow a given printer to print characters that a face character printer could not. Virtually any character that can be printed in the space provided by the matrix can be printed using a dot character printer. Another advantage of dot character printers is that they are faster than face character printers. Since the same hammers are used in printing each character, the machine does not have to perform the rotation that is required by daisy wheel and rotating-type printers. Since the rotation time is eliminated, the dot character printer can operate at much higher speeds. Some dot character printers can print at a rate as high as 250 cps.

Nonimpact printers

As we stated earlier, nonimpact printers have printing mechanisms that do not actually come in contact with the paper itself. One of the most common nonimpact printing techniques is the *face character nonimpact* printing technique. This printing technique is used mainly by office copiers. The basic process involves transferring a dry ink compound to the paper and then fusing the ink into the paper with heat. The document being copied is essentially photographed on an electrostatic type of film. The charges on the film then attract the ink compound (called "toner"), which forms complete characters on the film in the same positions that the characters appeared on the original document. Paper is then placed near the film and a large potential is generated behind the paper, causing the toner to "jump" to the paper, again retaining the character shapes from the original document. Heat is then applied to the paper, causing the toner to fuse into the paper.

Another type of nonimpact printer is the *ink-jet printer*. This type of printer forms characters on the paper in a dot character configuration using short jets of ink. For all practical purposes, the ink is sprayed onto the paper in a dot matrix. The result is a printed character.

Of all the printing techniques introduced here, the most common is the dot character impact printer, with the 5 × 7 dot character size being the most common. The Heath WH14 printer utilizes this printing format, as will be seen in Section 15.3.

15.2 MICROCOMPUTER/PRINTER INTERFACING

It was stated earlier that line printers are usually interfaced to a microcomputer using the RS-232-C interface. Before we discuss the actual connections between the microcomputer and the printer, let's take a look at some of the general principles involved in transferring data to a printer.

Data Transfers

In Chapter 14 you were introduced to the term *baud rate*. The baud rate of a given microcomputer was defined as the rate at which information is transferred, in bits per second (bps). Some of the common baud rates for microcomputers are 110, 150, 300, 600, 1200, 2400, 4800, and 9600 bps. To show you the main consideration in transferring data to a printer, let's consider the case of a microcomputer with a 4800-baud rate being connected to a printer that is capable of printing characters at a 165-cps rate. This setup is represented by the drawing in Figure 15.4. As shown, the data transmission rate from the microcomputer is 4800 bps. If a single character

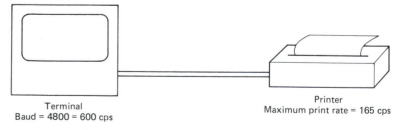

Terminal
Baud = 4800 = 600 cps

Printer
Maximum print rate = 165 cps

Figure 15.4 Terminal/printer interface. (© *1981 Heath Company. Reprinted by permission of Heath Co.*)

is represented by an 8-bit value, the microcomputer shown is capable of transmitting characters to the printer at a rate of 600 cps. However, the printer is capable of printing only 165 cps. This would cause characters to be lost if it were not for two things:

1. The printer has internal memory which is capable of storing character codes until the print head is ready to print them.
2. The printer sends a signal to the microcomputer when its memory is full, indicating that the condition exists. The microcomputer then waits for the removal of this signal to send any more character codes to the printer.

There is another condition that you must keep in mind regarding data transfers to a printer. Recall that the baud rates for all the devices involved in a data transfer must be equal for the transfer to occur without any errors. If the baud rate for the printer is set to a different value than that of the microcomputer, the printer will be looking for data bits at different times than the microcomputer will be sending them. For example, assume that the microcomputer in Figure 15.4 is transmitting data at a rate of 4800 bps, and the baud rate for the printer is set to 2400 bps. The result would be that the microcomputer would be transmitting one bit every 208 μs (approximately), and the printer would be looking for a data bit every 506 μs. Thus two data bits would be transmitted by the microcomputer during each time period that the printer was looking for one. As a result, the printer would receive only every other data bit that the microcomputer was transmitting, and the printout would be bad.

Baud-rate problems usually occur only when a printer is being installed for the first time. However, since baud rates are determined by the UARTs of the two communicating devices, baud-rate problems could also be caused by a bad UART or a faulty UART crystal. It is therefore a good idea to check the baud rates using an oscilloscope, whether the printer is a new installation or not.

The RS-232-C Microcomputer/Printer Interface

The communication link between the microcomputer and the printer is just as important to understand as the printer itself if you are going to deal effectively with printer malfunctions. Since most microcomputer/printer interfaces are RS-232-C interfaces, we are going to concentrate on this method of connecting the two devices together. As a starting point, let's take a look at the UART circuitry of the Heath WH14 printer. This circuitry is shown in Figure 15.5. The chips that we will be concerned with in Figure 15.5 are U103, U104, and U105. U103 is a three-state Schmitt trigger inverter, U104 is a quad two-input NAND gate, and U105 is the UART itself. To help you trace the signals through U103 and U104, their pin diagrams are shown in Figure 15.6.

The connector, S102, may seem to be a bit confusing at first since all of the arrows are pointing outward. Although this may lead you to believe that all of the lines are printer outputs, this is not the case. The arrows are indicating that these lines go to a connector. The connector pins for the lines are designated as follows:

Pin number	Input/output[a]	UART signal
11	Input	$\overline{\text{DSR}}$
5	Input	S_{IN}
4	Input	$\overline{\text{CTS}}$
7	Output	$\overline{\text{RTS}}$
14	Output	DTR
3	Output	S_{OUT}

[a]I/O is determined with respect to U105 (i.e., these lines are either U105 inputs or outputs).

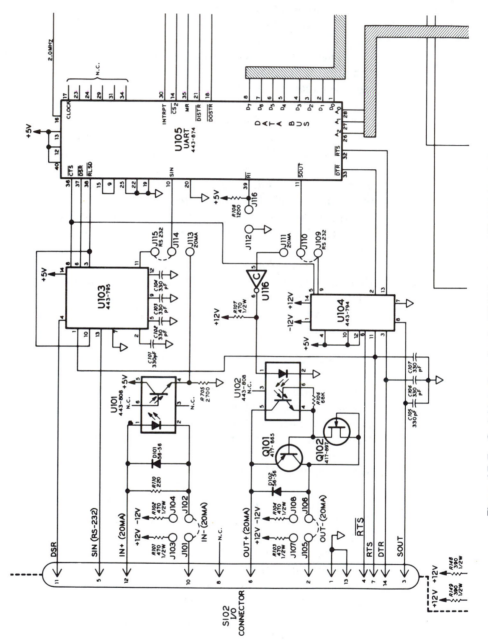

Figure 15.5 Serial interface for the WH14 printer. (© *1981 Heath Company. Reprinted by permission of Heath Co.*)

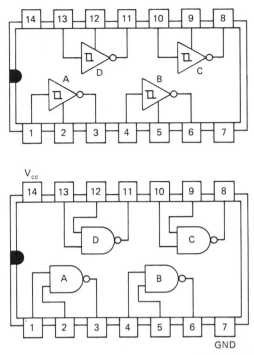

Figure 15.6 U103 and U104 pin diagrams. (© *1981 Heath Company. Reprinted by permission of Heath Co.*)

In our discussion of this circuitry, we will be dealing only with the results of a given set of control signal applications. If you have trouble following the discussion on the UART responses to a given set of signals, refer to the discussion on UARTs in Chapter 14. U105 is the same type of chip as the UART discussed in Chapter 14. There is one point in the operation of the UART which was not discussed in Chapter 14 that is important for the discussion of the microcomputer/printer interface. The $\overline{RLSD}$ input to the UART must be low before the UART can transmit or receive data. As you will see, this input will be used to affect the starting operation of the UART.

Let's start our discussion of the circuit shown in Figure 15.5 by assuming that the printer is not printing any data, and the internal memory of the printer is empty. The UART will signal the microcomputer that it is ready to receive data by driving its $\overline{RTS}$ output (pin 32) low. This low output is inverted by U104D and sent to the microcomputer via the RS-232-C interface cable. This cable is connected from the printer to the RS-232-C connector on the microcomputer. The RTS input to the microcomputer signals the system that the printer is ready to receive data. The high output from U104D is also applied to the input of U103A. U103A inverts the signal and applies the low output (pin 3) to the RLSD input of the UART. This indicates to the UART that the microcomputer is attempting to send data, so the UART constantly awaits data at its S_{IN} input (pin 10). When the UART starts receiving data, it converts the serial data to parallel, and then sends the data to the printers memory via its data I/O pins (pins 1 through 8). If the data is being transmitted to the printer at a slow enough rate, the printer will be able to print the characters as they are received, and the data transmission will proceed uninterrupted until all characters have been transmitted and printed. At that time, the microcomputer will quit transmitting data and the UART will continue to look for more data.

But what happens when the microcomputer is transmitting data faster than the printer can print it? The WH14 printer can continually print transmitted data as long as the baud rate is not greater than 110 bps. What happens when the baud rate is at some value greater than 110 bps? When the data is being transmitted at a higher rate than the printer can handle, the UART will respond by driving its $\overline{\text{RTS}}$ line high when the printer memory is nearly full. This high output is inverted and sent to the microcomputer as a low, causing the microcomputer to stop transmitting data. The low is also applied to the input of U103A, which then puts a high on the $\overline{\text{RLSD}}$ input of the CPU. This high indicates to the UART that valid data is no longer being transmitted. The high output of U103A is also applied to the input of U103C, and the low output from that gate is applied to the $\overline{\text{CTS}}$ input of the UART. The UART sees this signal as an indication that the microcomputer is attempting to communicate with it. The result is that the UART will once again drive its $\overline{\text{RTS}}$ output low when the printer has printed the received characters and is once again ready to receive data. At this time, $\overline{\text{RLSD}}$ and $\overline{\text{CTS}}$ are returned to their original states, and the microcomputer, having received the RTS signal, returns to transmitting data. This cycle will continue to repeat itself until all the data has been transmitted and printed.

There are several ways in which the control signals that are transmitted between the printer and microcomputer can be used. Although the example here has been only one method by which the two devices can be interfaced, it demonstrated several points about microcomputer/printer interfacing:

1. *The microcomputer must be able to signal the printer that it is ready to transmit data, unless this signal is not required by the printer.* In the circuit just discussed, the microcomputer did not need to send a $\overline{\text{RTS}}$ signal to the printer, since the printer is normally in the input mode anyway. However, that does not mean that this signal would not be sent. Consider the diagram shown in Figure 15.7. This figure shows the wiring between the microcomputer UART and the printer UART. In the case of the circuitry discussed, the $\overline{\text{RTS}}$ output of the printer is normally at its active level, so the microcomputer is receiving a $\overline{\text{CTS}}$ signal. As discussed in Chapter 14, the UART normally puts an active low $\overline{\text{RTS}}$ signal out when it is ready

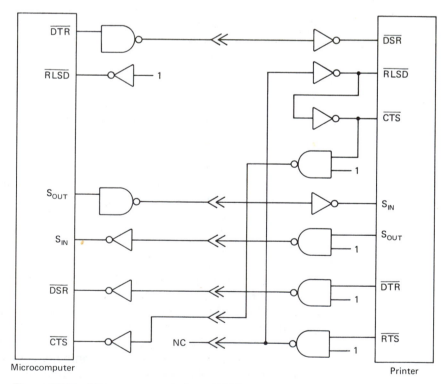

Figure 15.7 Microcomputer/printer UART connections. (© *1981 Heath Company. Reprinted by permission of Heath Co.*)

to transmit data, and actually starts the transmission after receiving an active low $\overline{CTS}$ input. When the microcomputer represented in Figure 15.7 drives its $\overline{RTS}$ line low, it immediately senses an active low $\overline{CTS}$ input and responds by sending data. The $\overline{RTS}$ signal from the microcomputer was generated, but was not needed by the printer, since the printer's $\overline{RTS}$ signal was already low. This low, being applied to the $\overline{CTS}$ input of the microcomputer, enabled the data transmission process as soon as the microcomputer was ready.

2. *The printer must be able to indicate to the microcomputer that the printer cannot accept any more data.* This signal is required whenever the data transmission rate of the microcomputer exceeds the maximum rate at which the printer can instantly print the characters as they are received. In the case of the serial interface just discussed, the printer removed the active-low $\overline{CTS}$ signal from the microcomputer when its internal memory was nearly full. This prevented the microcomputer from transmitting data until the $\overline{CTS}$ input to the microcomputer went low again.

The control signals that are sent back and forth between the microcomputer and the printer are referred to as *handshake signals*. Handshake signals may be single control lines, as was the case with the circuitry shown, or they may consist of data codes which are sent back and forth via the S_{IN} and S_{OUT} lines of the two devices.

15.3 THE HEATH WH14 PRINTER

To start our discussion of the circuit operation of a working printer, let's take a look at the block diagram of the Heath WH14 printer, shown in Figure 15.8. As you can see, there are quite a few circuit groups which are used to complete the printer circuitry. However, just as with any other digital system, each circuit group serves a specific purpose. The purpose served by each circuit group is as follows:

Functional block	Purpose
Print head drive circuitry	Drives the strike hammers in the printing head; the print head contains seven striking hammers, each with its own drive circuit
Stepper drive circuitry	Drives the stepper motors which are used to advance the printer paper
Print head position circuitry	Used to move the print head back and forth across the paper; the forward line moves the print head from left to right; the reverse line, from right to left
Ribbon motor circuitry	Advances the ribbon used for printing
Detectors	
Print head home	Detects that the print head has returned to the leftmost position; this position is the starting point for a given line of characters
Paper out	Detects when there is no paper in the printer
Paper jam	Detects when the paper has jammed in the printer (i.e., when the paper cannot be advanced as it should be)
High temperature	Detects when the temperature of the print head has exceeded a given limit
Logic circuitry	
Power-up switches	Used to program the CPU for baud rates when the printer is first turned on
Control switches	These switches (on line, wide character, etc.) are used to determine certain operating characteristics of the printer; the various switches will be covered as needed to discuss

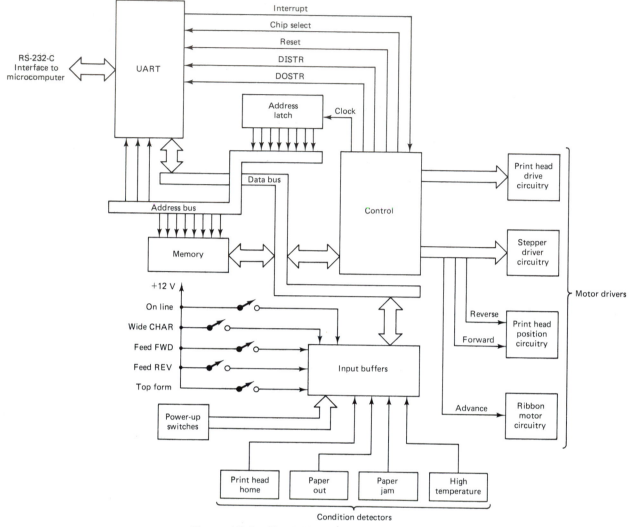

Figure 15.8 Heath WH14 printer block diagram. (© *1981 Heath Company. Reprinted by permission of Heath Co.*)

Functional block	Purpose
	the various circuits.
Input buffers	These three-state buffers are enabled when the CPU needs to check the status of the various switches
Memory	Used to store the data sent from the microcomputer until the printer CPU is ready to print the data
Address latch	Used to provide the memory addresses
UART	Used to provied the communication link between the printer and the microcomputer
Control	This is a specially designed CPU (a microcontroller) which is used to control the overall operation of the printer; it continually runs programs which are contained in internal ROM.

Due to the size of the printer schematic, it is not practical to reproduce the entire circuit in a single figure. Because of this, we will be discussing the printer in terms of its circuit groups. Whenever a circuit group is covered, take a look at Figure 15.8 to relate the circuit group to the overall system diagram. Since we have already discussed the UART and its connections to the microcomputer, we will start with taking a look at how the UART, the CPU, and the memory work together. This circuitry is shown in Figure 15.9.

The CPU, U106, is a specially designed microcontroller that controls all of the printer operations. It contains an internal ROM which provides all of the printer programs. These programs are used for all of the basic printer functions, such as receiving data from the microcomputer, transferring this data to the printer RAM, and controlling the print head. The CPU also detects certain operating conditions, such as high temperature, paper out, and so on.

One of the characteristics of the CPU which can be seen on the schematic is the fact that it has no address bus per se. This leads to a bit of a problem, since the CPU must be able to address the memory locations in the RAM. RAM addressing is accomplished in a rather round-about way in the printer, with RAM addresses actually being supplied by the CPU data bus. To clarify this, take a look at the pin diagram of U111, the address latch, which is shown in Figure 15.10. The address latch is a series of eight D-type flip-flops. The D inputs to the flip-flops are connected to the data outputs of the CPU, and the clock inputs to the flip-flops are driven by U106-24. When the CPU needs to address a given RAM location, it supplies the 8-bit RAM address on its data pins, then provides a clock pulse to the address latch. The data at the D inputs of the flip-flops then appear at the Q outputs of the chip. These Q outputs are connected to the address bus. The CPU data value then becomes a RAM address. For example, assume that the CPU needs to address RAM location 10110001. The value 10110001 would be put out on the CPU data pins and U111 would receive a clock pulse. At that time, the internal flip-flops of U11 would latch the value, causing its Q outputs to equal 10110001. These Q outputs, being connected to the address bus, would apply the address value to the RAM chips. Data could then be entered into the RAM chips, or read from them, depending on whether the CPU was performing a read or a write operation.

The RAM chips are each 256×4 chips, giving the printer a total of 256×8 memory locations. When these chips are nearly full during a data transfer from the microcomputer to the printer, the CPU will cause the data transfer to stop until the characters being stored in the RAM are printed. The RAM read cycle is performed when the CPU must fetch a RAM character in order to provide the print head with the appropriate signals to cause the character to be printed. This cycle is basically as described on the preceeding page. The CPU addresses the RAM location as described and then provides the $R/\overline{W} = 1$ and $\overline{CE} = O$ signals. After the RAM data appears on the data bus, the CPU latches the data and the read cycle is complete.

The write cycle is a bit more complicated. This is due to the fact that the CPU itself is not the source of RAM data. Rather, the UART is the source, since all data being stored in the RAM come from the microcomputer terminal via the UART. Therefore, a complete RAM write cycle consists of a UART read cycle, followed by the actual RAM write cycle. For example, assume that the UART has data which must be stored in RAM. When the UART has the complete character, it provides an interrupt signal to the CPU by driving U106-38 low. After the CPU finishes its current operation, it provices a $\overline{CS}$ signal to the UART, together with the address value A2 = 0, A1 = 0, A0 = 0. Just as with any RAM address, this address must be supplied via the address latch. The address value 000 addresses the internal data latch of the UART. At that time, the CPU drives the $\overline{DISTR}$ (data in strobe) pin of the UART low and reads the character data from the UART. Once the character data is latched, the CPU addresses the next available RAM location (i.e., the first

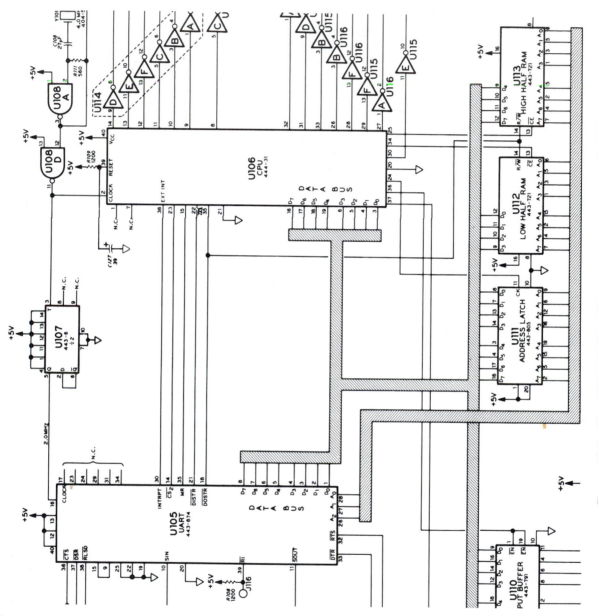

Figure 15.9 The WH14 UART, CPU, and memory circuitry. (© 1981 Heath Company. Reprinted by permission of Heath Co.)

324

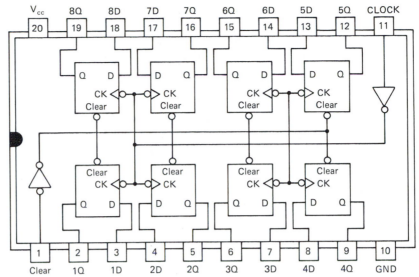

Figure 15.10 U111 pinout. (© *1981 Heath Company. Reprinted by permission of Heath Co.*)

RAM location that does not already contain valuable data). When the address value is provided by the address latch, the CPU provides the RAM with the proper R/$\overline{W}$ = 0 and $\overline{CE}$ = 0 signals. After the RAM location latches the character data, the write cycle is complete.

As the operations described on the write cycle would indicate, the CPU basically treats the UART like a memory location. When interrupted by the UART, the CPU performs a read operation on the device. It then follows with either a write operation to the RAM, or it sends the data directly to the print head. Which of these two courses of action is taken depends on the baud rate of the microcomputer. If data is being transferred to the CPU at a slow enough rate, the CPU will simply read the data from the UART and send the appropriate signals to the print head. If not, the CPU will store the character data in RAM until it is ready to use it.

As you may have figured out by now, UART read cycles, RAM read cycles, and RAM write cycles are performed at various times during the overall operation of the printer. When these operations are actually performed depends on when data is being transferred to the printer, the baud rates of the two systems, and so on. But when is a write operation performed on the UART, if ever? The only time that the CPU writes to the UART is when the printer is first turned on. At that time, the CPU programs the UART for baud rates, parity, and other internal operating characteristics. When writing data to the UART, the CPU drives the $\overline{DOSTR}$ pin (data out strobe) of the UART low. This is the equivalent of a $\overline{WRITE}$ signal. The CPU then addresses the proper internal latches of the UART (via the address latch), provides a $\overline{CS}$ signal, and sends the appropriate data to the UART. Again, this operation is performed only at power-up.

Now that we have discussed the way in which data is received by the printer, transferred to and from the CPU, and stored in RAM, we will take a look at the actual printing circuitry. This circuitry consists of the blocks in Figure 15.8 labeled *print head drive circuitry* and *stepper drive circuitry*.

Print Head Drive Circuitry

Before we discuss the circuitry used to drive the print head of the printer, it is necessary to take a look at the printing process itself. The WH14 is an *impact printer*, which, as you may recall, means that there is actual contact with the paper. As is the case with all impact printers, "hammers" are used to strike a ribbon, driving the ribbon against the paper. This contact leaves a mark on the paper that is shaped just like the hammer that struck the ribbon. For example, a typewriter uses hammers which have heads that are shaped like the letters of the alphabet. When a given hammer is caused to strike the ribbon, the ribbon causes the letter struck to be printed on the paper.

In the case of the WH14, printing is accomplished using a *dot matrix* similar to that used in CRT operations. A given letter is printed on paper by a series of dots which are positioned in the shape of the character to be printed. This can be seen in Figure 15.11a. The "M" character shown is formed using a 5×7 dot matrix.

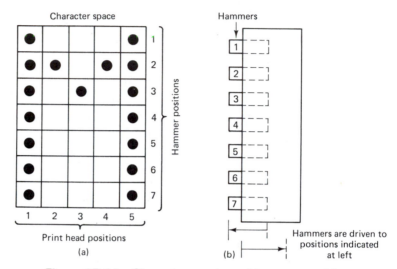

Figure 15.11 Character matrix and hammer positions.

The print head used to form the character has seven hammers that are in a vertical line, as shown in Figure 15.11b. Assuming that the hammers are being used to print the character shown, the actual print process would be as follows:

1. The first vertical line of print (labeled A in Figure 15.11a) is printed by causing all seven hammers to strike the ribbon. The print head now moves one position to the right.
2. In the B position, only hammer 2 is activated. After striking the paper, the print head again moves one position to the right.
3. In position C, only hammer 3 is used.
4. In position D, hammer 2 is used.
5. In position E, all hammers are again used.

The result is that the letter M is printed on the paper. Although the process may seem very simple, there are a few points about the operation of the printer which can now be understood:

1. The printing process is simply a matter of striking a given hammer at a point or not striking the hammer. In other words, at a given point on the paper, a given hammer is either enabled or disabled.
2. The seven hammers used must be able to be activated independently of each other. Thus, the CPU must have a separate control line for each hammer.

We can now take a look at the circuitry that is actually used to control the striking hammers on the print head. This circuitry is shown in Figure 15.12. The CPU drives

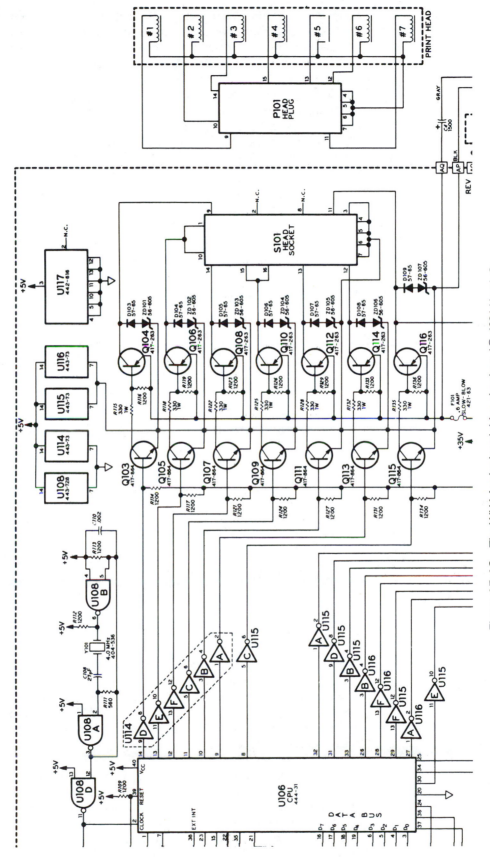

Figure 15.12 The WH14 print head drive circuitry. (© *1981 Heath Company. Reprinted by permission of Heath Co.*)

the print head using output pins 8 through 14. Each of these lines is inverted and applied to a pair of driver transistors. All seven of the circuits are identical, so we will discuss only one of them. For ease of discussion, the circuitry that is driven by U106-14 is redrawn in Figure 15.13. When the CPU is actively attempting to drive hammer 1, it drives pin 14 low. This low is inverted by U114D and the resulting high output is applied to the base of Q103. When Q103 gets a high input, it saturates, dropping its collector potential to approximately +0.3 V. This low is applied to the base of Q104, a PNP transistor that has its emitter connected to a +35-V supply. The low on the base of Q104 saturates the transistor, causing its collector to rise to approximately +35 V. This potential, applied to the hammer relay, causes the hammer to strike ribbon.

The diodes in the Q104 collector circuit are there to short the *counter EMF* produced by the inductor, L1, when it turns off. This protects Q104 from having

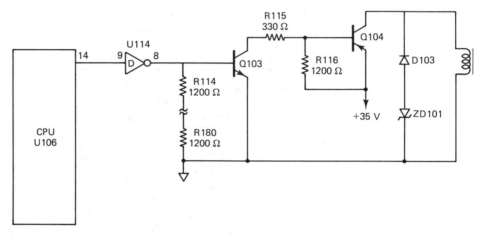

Figure 15.13   WH14 print head driving circuit. (© *1981 Heath Company. Reprinted by permission of Heath Co.*)

a large reverse bias applied to its collector, a situation that could destroy the transistor. This principle was discussed in Chapter 4.

All of the hammer driver circuits are the same, and each is driven by a different CPU output, as can be seen in Figure 15.12. This situation allows the CPU to activate as few or as many hammers as are needed to produce a given vertical line of print.

Stepper Drive Circuitry

The stepper driver circuitry is used to advance the paper through the printer. After each line of print is completed, the CPU will activate the appropriate circuit to advance the paper a fixed distance. The printer can then continue printing on the next line. CPU output pins 27, 29, 28, 26, 33, 31, and 32 are used to supply control signals to the *stepper driver circuit board*, the logic board that contains the actual drive circuitry for the stepper motor.

Before we can actually begin discussing the driver circuitry for the stepper motor, we need to take a look at the motor itself. A *stepper motor* is a motor that rotates in fixed increments rather than in a continuous rotation. The "steps" can range anywhere from approximately 1 to 30°, depending on the motor being used. Stepper motors are rated in degrees of rotation in the same way that standard motors are rated in terms of rotational speed. In other words, a given stepper motor will be rated at x° of rotation. This rotational value is not variable.

Stepper motors are very useful in such applications as printer paper positioning, where a spool must be rotated by a fixed amount in order to have equal spacing between lines of print. There are many other applications for stepper motors. Stepper motors can be found in any robotic system, and in disk drive units, as will be seen later in this chapter.

A basic understanding of the operation of stepper motors can be gained by discussing the motor represented in Figure 15.14. The diagram shown is not a standard schematic symbol, but rather, a representative circuit that has been drawn in this manner to help you understand how a stepper motor works. The motor, represented by the circle in the middle of the diagram, can be made to move so that the internal inductor faces A, B, C, or D, by turning on the appropriate outer inductor. For example, turning on inductor C would cause the point of the motor labeled X to face inductor C. Turning on inductor D in addition to C would cause point X to rest halfway between inductors C and D, and so on. The various positions of X, together with the conditions of the outer inductors, are also represented in Figure 15.14. As you can see, moving the stepper motor in fixed increments is merely a matter of turning the motors on and off in the correct sequence. In the WH14, as well as other printers, the stepper motor driver circuitry is used to provide the proper signals to the inductors represented in Figure 15.14.

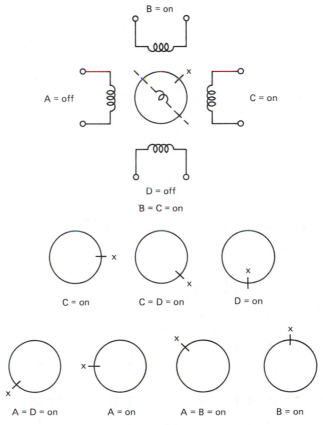

Figure 15.14 Stepper motor operation.

Now, let's take a look at the stepper driver circuitry. The circuit board containing this circuitry is represented by the schematic diagram shown in Figure 15.15. There

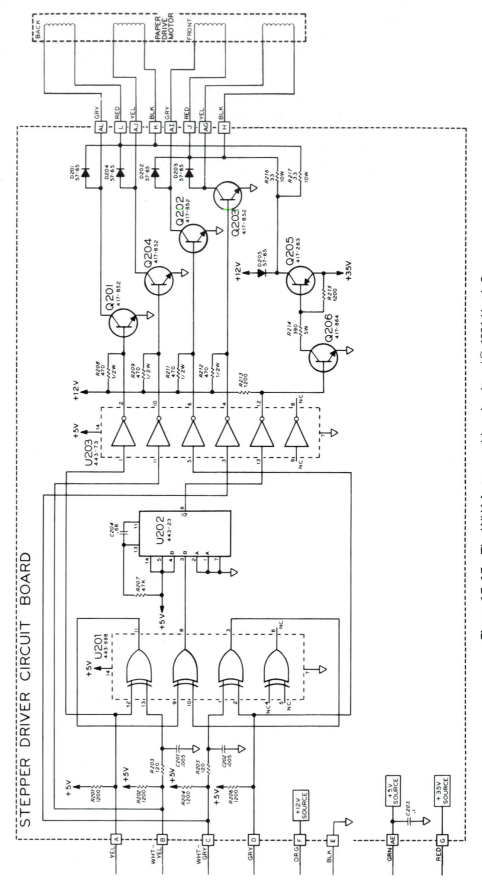

Figure 15.15 The WH14 stepper drive circuitry. (© *1981 Heath Company. Reprinted by permission of Heath Co.*)

are four control inputs to the logic board, indicated by the blocks labeled A, B, C, and D. These inputs are driven by the CPU outputs as listed below:

Board input	CPU output
A	U106-28
B	U106-26
C	U106-29
D	U106-27

The CPU outputs listed, together with the inverters that are on each of the given lines, can be seen in Figure 15.12.

There are several operating characteristics of this circuit which should be established right away. These are:

1. The input points to the board (A, B, C, and D) are all active low.
2. The two inputs to U201A (pins 1 and 2) are always at opposite logic levels. When pin 1 is low, pin 2 is high, and vice versa. The same condition exists for U201D, pins 12 and 13.

These two facts, although not evident in the schematic, are stated in the operators manual on the printer, and thus would be available to any technician working on the printer.

The motor inductors are being driven by Q201, Q202, Q203, and Q204. When the output from any one of the transistors is low, the indicator to which it is connected will conduct. To understand the process completely, you must analyze what is happening on *both* sides of the inductor. For example, let's take a look at the top inductor in Figure 15.15. The points labeled *AL* and *L* are the points at which the inductor is connected to the stepper drive circuit board. In order for the inductor to conduct, *AL* and *L* must be at different potentials. In this case, the inductor will conduct when AL = 0 V (approximately) and L = +35 V. With these two potentials present, the inductor will conduct, causing the stepper motor to move. Now, we'll look at the way these two potentials are developed.

AL = 0 volts: When input block A to the circuit board goes low, this low is applied to U203-1. This inverter produces a high output at pin 2, driving the base of transistor Q201 high. When Q201 gets this high input, it saturates, causing its collector to drop to approximately 0 V. This provides the needed low voltage to point AL.

L = +35 volts: The low in at point A was also applied to U201-12. Assuming that the other input to this XOR gate is high, the output of the circuit will also go high. This high output is applied to another XOR gate at U201-9. Assuming that the other input to the gate (U201-10) is low, the output at pin 8 will go high. This high output is applied to U202, a one-shot. This one-shot is wired to drive its $\overline{Q}$ output low for approximately 10 ms whenever the output from the XOR gate goes high. When the $\overline{Q}$ output of U202 goes low, the low is applied to the input of inverter U203D (pin 13), causing its output to go high. This high is applied to the base of Q206, saturating that transistor. When Q206 saturates, a low is applied to the base of Q205, causing it to saturate; Q205 is a PNP transistor, thus the low-input saturation condition. When Q205 saturates, its collector goes to approximately +35 V, the voltage that is applied to its emitter. This +35 V potential is applied to the *L* connection via the 33-Ω resistor.

As we stated earlier, these two potentials being applied to the opposite sides of the top inductor in the diagram cause the inductor to conduct. This causes the stepper motor to turn. If you look closely at the diagram, you will see that the other inductor drive inductors are wired in the same way, and thus can be turned on in the manner just described. The key is to apply the correct input to drive one of the driver transistors (Q201 through Q204) into saturation and to cause the one-shot to fire. When the one-shot fires, the +35 V is applied to connectors *L, K, J,* and *H.* Thus the lower side of *all* the inductors will be at +35 V. Q201 through Q204 are then used to drive the other side of the selected inductors low, causing current to flow through the selected inductors. The diodes are placed in the transistor collector circuits to protect the transistors from the EMF produced when the inductors turn off.

Head Motor and Ribbon Motor Drivers

There are two more driver circuits that should be discussed: the *head motor driver* and the *ribbon motor driver.* The head motor driver is used to move the print head back and forth across the paper, and the ribbon driver circuit is used to advance the ribbon. Both of these circuits are shown in Figure 15.16. The *head motor driver* is capable of moving the printing head in either direction. Since both of these circuits are the same, we will discuss the operation of the FWD (forward) motor driver circuit. The REV (reverse) motor works in the same manner.

There are a few facts that must be established in order for you to see how the circuitry for the FWD driver motor works:

1. The common connection for the two inductors in the block labeled "head motor" is connected to approximately +12 V at a point not shown in the diagram.

2. The FWD motor inductor will conduct, moving the print head forward, when Q118 is on.

3. Q117, Q118, and Q119 are all *triacs.* As a review, their operation is as follows:

   a. A high at the *gate* (G) input causes the triac to conduct.

   b. When the gate to the triac goes low, the triac will continue to conduct until the current from pin 1 and pin 2 drops to zero. This is controlled by circuits external to the triac itself.

   c. Once the triac turns off, the G input must go high before the triac will again conduct.

4. The triac, Q118, is normally on. An active output from the CPU is used to turn it off.

5. C517, which is connected across the two inductors, normally has a plate to plate charge of +12 V. Depending on the circumstances, either the upper plate of the capacitor will be at +12 V and the lower plate at 0 V, or vice versa.

For our discussion, we will assume that the upper plate of the capacitor is at +12 V and that Q118 is already on. With Q118 on, current flows through the device and through the lower, or forward, inductor, causing the print head to move from left to right across the paper. When the CPU detects that the print head is nearing the end of the paper, it drives its output pin 35 low. This low is applied to the diode (D111), causing it to turn off. When the diode turns off, the gate potential of Q118 drops to zero, turning Q118 off. The lower inductor will continue to conduct until C517 charges. At that time, the current flow through Q118 stops and the triac turns off. When the CPU wishes to start the FWD motor again, it simply drives output pin 35 high. This turns diode D111 on again, turning the triac on. Once again, current flows in the circuit, the capacitor charges, and we are back to the starting point.

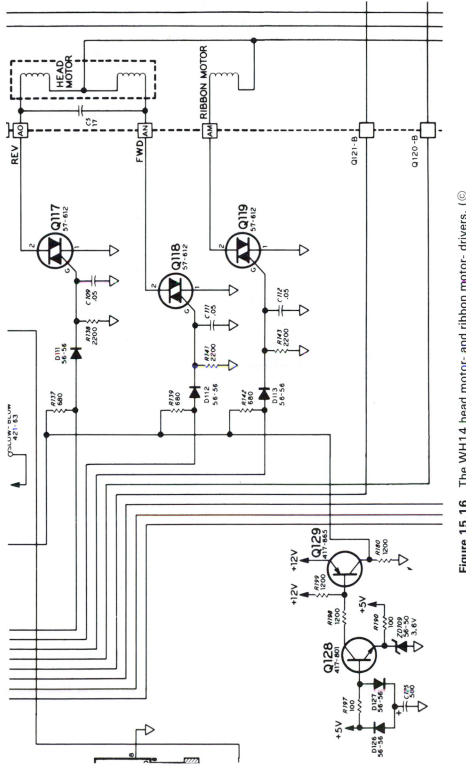

Figure 15.16 The WH14 head motor- and ribbon motor- drivers. (© 1981 Heath Company. Reprinted by permission of Heath Co.)

333

Whenever the print head gets to the right end of the paper, the CPU is informed of this fact by a detector. At that time, it turns Q118 off and turns Q117 on. With the same type of circuit action as just discussed, the REV motor turns on and the print head is returned to the left side of the paper. The paper is then advanced by the stepper driver circuit board and the FWD motor is reactivated. The ribbon motor is activated to advance the ribbon as the ink on it is used.

At this point, we can summarize the action of the driver circuits that have been discussed in this section. The action summary is as follows, starting at the point when the printer is first starting a new line of print:

1. The FWD motor is activated, causing the print head to advance from left to right across the paper.

2. As the print head moves, the print head hammer drivers cause the hammers to strike the ribbon, printing the desired characters on the paper. The ribbon is also advanced to provide consistency in the print.

3. When the print head reaches the right side of the paper, the FWD motor is turned off and the REV motor is turned on, returning the print head to the left side of the paper.

4. The stepper driver circuit board is activated to advance the paper by one line, and the process listed here repeats itself for the next line of print.

The process just listed is a fairly common sequence of events (i.e., quite a few of the printers used follow this sequence). One very common variation from this sequence would be found in *dual-direction* printers. These printers print both from left to right and from right to left. While the circuitry required for this type of printer is more complicated, the result is that the printing process is completed in a shorter period of time. Instead of just printing in one direction and then returning the print head to start another line of print, the printer will advance the paper when the print head returns to the starting, or *home*, position. As you may have guessed, the logic circuitry needed to print a line backwards, as the printer is doing on the REV line, is more complicated than that discussed here. However, the overall process really is not that much different than the operation for the printer we have covered.

Detector Circuits

The only circuits that still need to be covered from the original block diagram are the *detector circuits*. These circuits are used to inform the CPU when a given set of circumstances exist so that the CPU can take the appropriate action. The detector circuits for the WH14 printer are shown in Figure 15.17. The *head home detector* and the *paper out detector* are both located on the left side of the diagram. Both of these detectors use optical switches formed by an LED and a phototransistor. The head home detector will provide a high input to U109-6 when the print head is in the home, or leftmost, position. When the print head is in this position, the light path between the LED and Q3 is blocked and Q3 turns off. This causes the line to Y109-6 to go high. When the CPU detects this condition, it turns the REV motor for the print head off.

The *paper out detector* is actually used to detect one of two conditions. This circuitry will cause the printer to stop printing if it is out of paper or if the paper is jammed in the printer. The optical switch for this circuit is placed on both sides of the paper so that the sprocket holes on the edge of the paper cause the transistor to turn on and off as the paper is advanced. When the sprocket hole is between the LED and the transistor, the transistor is saturated, sending a low to U109-13. When a sprocket hole is not lined up between the two components, the transistor will be off and U109-13 will be high. In the case of this detector, the CPU looks for *changes*

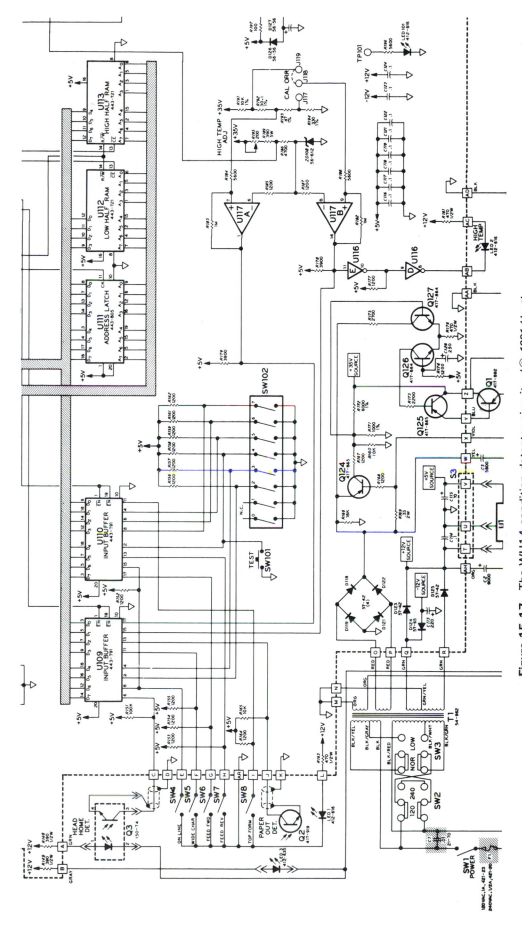

Figure 15.17 The WH14 condition detector circuits. (© 1981 Heath Company. Reprinted by permission of Heath Co.)

in the input to U109-13. If a constant high is felt at U109-13, then the paper is jammed and the CPU will stop printing. If a constant low is felt at U109-13, then either the paper is jammed or the printer is out of paper. In either case, the printer stops printing.

The third detector circuit is the *high-temperature* detection circuit. This circuit is much more sophisticated than the other two. The high-temp circuit detects a high-temperature condition by constantly comparing the resistance of the copper winding in one of the print head circuits to a specified value. As you may recall, the resistance of copper increases with any increases in temperature. Therefore, by checking the resistance of the copper winding and comparing that value to a known resistance, the system can detect when the temperature of the winding is getting too high. When the temperature is determined to be too high, the printer will shut down and light an LED, indicating the problem.

The actual circuitry used (shown in Figure 15.17), consists of U117 and its input components, and U109-15 and U109-17. Under normal circumstances, the output from U117A is high and output from U117B is high. These high outputs are felt at U109-15 and U109-17, indicating to the CPU that the temperature of the print head is within specified limits. When the temperature of the winding increases to an unacceptable limit, the condition is detected at the (−) inputs to the comparators. The point between R186 and R189 in the comparator circuit is tied to the copper winding in the print head. When the resistance of this winding increases, the voltage at the tie-in point increases, causing the two (−) comparator inputs to go more positive. When they reach a potential equal to the potential at the (+) inputs, the comparator outputs go low. This indicates a "high temp" condition to the CPU, causing it to stop the printing process. The high output from U117B is also inverted twice, by U116D and U116E, causing the "high temp" LED to light.

15.4 PRINTER TROUBLESHOOTING

One of the nice things about troubleshooting a printer is the fact that so many of the problems that can develop in a printer are easy to diagnose to the section (circuit group) level. Since so many of the circuits are dedicated to performing a specific function, the absence of that function leads right to the faulty circuit group. For example, look at the print line represented in Figure 15.18. The sentence should read

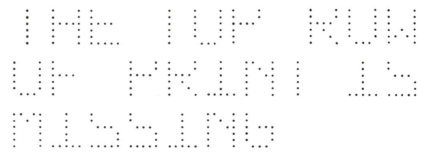

Figure 15.18   Printing caused by defect in hammer 1 or its drive circuitry.

"The top line of print is missing." By looking closely at the matrix of each letter, it becomes obvious that the characters are 5 × 6 instead of 5 × 7. Since the line is exactly as it should be with the exception that the top line of the matrix is missing, the problem must be in the circuitry that drives the hammer for the top line of print. Or the problem could be in the print head itself. Either way, the problem has already been narrowed down a great deal just by looking at the printout.

Not all of the problems that can develop in a printer are as easy to diagnose as the ones just described, but a vast majority of them are. In most cases, you can narrow the problem down to a circuit group just by looking at the result of the printer operation and using a little deductive reasoning. Those problems that cannot be rapidly identified in this manner are usually caused by one of three things:

1. A fault in the control unit
2. A fault in the power supply
3. A fault in the microcomputer/printer interface

Even these problems tend to have some strong identifying symptoms, as will be seen in some of the examples in this section.

The basic process for troubleshooting the circuitry in a printer is just as described for other circuits and circuit groups. First, you have to narrow the problem down to a group of circuits. In many cases, this can be done with a printer by simply looking at a sample printout. If the problem does not make itself evident in the printout, the problem is located in one of the three sections listed above. Once you narrow the problem down to a circuit group, then determine which output line, or lines, from that section went bad. If only one line is bad, trace that line back until the faulty component is found. If more than one output line is bad, try to locate the point at which the lines meet and start tracing back from there.

Let's go through some example problems to help you get a grasp of printer troubleshooting. In many of these examples, we will be referring back to the block diagram of the WH14 printer shown in Figure 15.7.

PROBLEM 1

Symptom: The printer paper does not advance. The printer prints over one line several times and then stops, indicating a paper jam.

Analysis: The printer can be tested for its overall operation by pressing the "TEST" button shown in Figure 15.17. This button (SW101), located on the inside of the printer, causes lines of characters to be pressed continuously when held down. While testing with this switch, it became evident that the printer was printing as it should, but the paper was not being advanced. The assumption at this point is that the problem is located somewhere on the stepper driver circuit board.

Tests: Inputs A, B, C, and D to the circuit board (shown in Figure 15.15) proved the previous assumption to be correct, since all of these points showed signal activity. Recall that, in most cases, simply determining that there is activity on the line is a good indication that the line is functioning as it should.

Further tests indicate the inputs to the driver transistors (Q201 through Q204) are active. When checking the high side of the motor inductors, all lines were shown to be at less than +12 V, when they should be at +35 V, indicating that Q205 is not turning on. Tracing the signal back showed the following conditions to exist:

Q205 off.

Q205 (base) low.   At this point, Q205 is assumed to be good.

Q206 off.

Q206 (base) low.   At this point, Q206 is assumed to be good.

U203-12 low.

U203-13 high.   At this point, U203 is assumed to be good.

U202-6 high.

Q202-3 active.   At this point, there is reason to suspect Q202.

To verify that Q202 is the problem, the rest of the inputs to the chip were checked. All the supply, ground, and control connections to the chip were at the proper levels, but there was not output from the one-shot.

Conclusion: U202 is faulty and must be replaced.

In problem 1, all of the paper drive motor inductors had the same + 12-V condition, so the troubleshooting process actually started at the point where they all meet: Q205. From that point, it was simply a process of determining which chip had all of the proper inputs and no output. Let's try another one.

PROBLEM 2

Symptom: The printer prints several lines and then stops. When "reset," the symptom repeats itself.

Analysis: This problem is not as evident at first as the last one, but could be diagnosed through knowledge of the system. The system is set up to stop after approximately 1 inch of lines of print if the paper is out or if a paper jam exists.

Tests: The first step was to verify that approximately 1 inch of print had been completed before the shutdown occurred. By using the test switch, the symptom was verified. In three test runs, the printer accomplished approximately 1 inch of lines of print when it shut down. This lead to the checking of the "paper out" detector. Checking the input to the input buffer from the detector at U109-13, the line was seen to be at a constant high. Since the line should have been changing whenever the sprocket holes passed the LED/phototransistor detection circuit, the circuit was checked, with the following results:

Q2 (collector) high.

Q2 (emitter) low.

LED 3   not lit.

Conclusion: LED 3 is bad.

With LED 3 being out, no light was being produced to activate Q2. Since Q2 could not be saturated, the system responded as if there were a paper jam in the printer. *A word of caution:* The symptoms just described could have also been caused by the LED having shifted its position. Photo-detection circuits such as the one used here depend on the LED and phototransistor being properly aligned to work correctly. If the mounting for the transistor or the mounting for the LED comes loose, the results will be the same as if the electronic circuitry had failed.

PROBLEM 3

Symptom: The printer is printing "garbage" characters with no apparent reason. The printing occurs at odd intervals.

Analysis: There are several things that could cause this problem. This is one of those problems that would be caused by either the printer power supply, the printer control circuitry, or the microcomputer/ printer interface. This conclusion is drawn because none of the dedicated circuits discussed would be capable of causing the problem (i.e., none of the detectors, drives, or motor control circuits would cause the random printing of characters). The printing of characters, which characters are printed and when, is controlled by the interface between system and the printer control circuitry itself.

Tests: When the printer was tested with the "test" button, the system operated correctly. All of the symptoms disappeared. This lead to the conclusion that the problem was in the microcomiputer/ printer interface. Checking both systems showed that the printer was set to a different baud rate than the system which was feeding it data.

Although this may seem like a short problem analysis, the fault indicated is a common one. When the baud rates of the printer and the microcomputer are set to different values, the printer will randomly print garbage. If the baud rate had not been the problem, the UART circuitry, together with the rest of the circuitry associated with the microcomputer/printer interface, would have to have been tested. *Note that a problem of this sort may originate in the microcomputer rather than in the printer itself.* If there seems to be an interface problem, you may have to go to the microcomputer before finding the cause of the fault.

Not all the printers have a "test" switch, but all of them do have another means by which interface problems may be isolated. There is a switch on this printer, and almost all printers for that fact, called the *off-line* switch. This switch is used to electrically isolate the printer from the microcomputer. If a printer is behaving eratically, press the off-line switch. If the problem disappears, the problem is in the interface. If the problem persists, it is in either the control and memory circuitry of the printer or in the printer power supply.

Although the operation and troubleshooting discussions on printers have been restricted mainly to the WH14 printer, most of the principles covered here pertain to a vast majority of impact printers. You will, of course, encounter some variations, such as printer with parallel data inputs, dual-direction printers, and so on. But with a grasp on the basic of printer operation, you should not have too much trouble analyzing and troubleshooting almost any printer designed for use with a microcomputer.

15.5 INTRODUCTION TO FLOPPY DISKS

A *floppy disk* is a magnetic memory device which is used to store data on a long-term basis. Most microcomputers being marketed have one or more floppy disk drive units, devices that are used to handle the floppy disks themselves. A disk drive unit causes the disk to rotate (much like a record), writes data onto the disk, and reads data from the disk. The reading and writing of data is handled by a read/write head, a device that strongly resembles the play/record head on a tape player.

The floppy disk itself is extremely thin (several thousandths of an inch thick) and pliable, thus the name *floppy*. The disk is housed in a lightweight jacket which has several openings in it to provide access to the disk itself. A diagram of the floppy disk and the disk jacket can both be seen in Figure 15.19. The disk shown in Figure 15.19 is a $5\frac{1}{4}$-inch floppy disk. The jacket it would be housed in (shown in Figure 15.19b) measures $5\frac{1}{2}$ inches square. Another standard-size floppy disk is the 8-inch floppy, but since the $5\frac{1}{4}$-inch floppy is more commonly used, we will discuss flop-

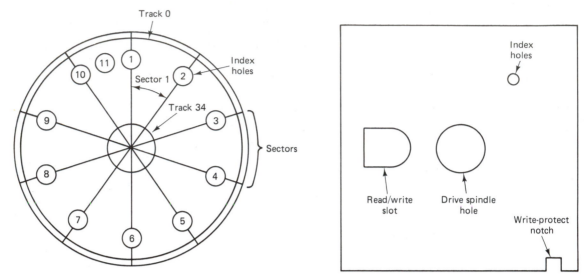

Figure 15.19 Floppy disk (hard-sectored).

py disk operation in terms of this size disk. As you will discover when actually work-ing with floppy disks, there is little difference between the two standard types of floppy, other than their sizes.

The disk shown in Figure 15.19a is made of 40 grooves, called *tracks*. Unlike a record, which has one continuous groove per side, the 35 to 40 tracks found on a standard $5\frac{1}{4}$-inch floppy are independent of each other (i.e., each track is a separate physical groove with a length equal to one revolution of the disk). The outermost track would be labeled track 00, while the innermost track would be either track 34 or track 39, depending on the disk being used.

Each track on the disk is divided into groups of memory locations, called *sectors*. Thus a given group of data bytes would be identified and located using both the track number and sector number. In the disk shown, sectors are identified by the holes that circle the inside of the disk, called *index holes*. These holes pass the single index hole shown in the jacket in Figure 15.19b. When the disk is placed in the disk drive unit, the positioning of the disk is such that there is an LED on one side of the jacket index hole and a phototransistor on the other side. As the holes in the disk pass the hole in the jacket, light from the LED passes through the disk, saturating the phototransistor. The output from this transistor is then used to signal the system that the disk has rotated to a given sector. This point is discussed further later in this section.

Since there are a number of tracks, each containing data, there must be some way for the read/write head of the disk drive unit to be positioned above the proper track. This is accomplished by the use of a stepper motor. The read/write head is moved in and out over the top of the disk by the stepper motor. The motor is con-trolled by the microcomputer. When a given disk drive is first turned on the read/write head is moved to track 00. The system can then locate a given track by pulsing the stepper motor a number of times equal to the track number. For example, assume that a system wants to access data which is stored on track 5. The stepper motor would be pulsed continuously until the read/write head is positioned over track 00. Then the stepper motor would be pulsed five times. Since each pulse to the stepper motor causes the read/write head to move in by a single track, the read/write head would be over track 05 when the fifth pulse was applied. When the read/write head is positioned over a desired track, the rotation of the disk, as indicated by the index holes, will place the read/write head over the desired sector. Data can then be written onto or read from the disk.

The disk is rotated by a *drive spindle* which comes into contact with the disk through the *drive spindle hole*. The drive spindle is rotated at a constant 300 rpm.* As the disk is turning, the read/write head comes into contact with the disk through the *read/write slot* in the disk jacket. The *write protect notch* in the disk jacket is used to prevent the system from entering data onto a disk which already has critical data on it. When the disk is placed in the disk drive, the positioning of the disk places the write protect notch between another LED/phototransistor pair. When the write protect notch is covered with *opaque* tape, the light from the LED cannot get to the phototransistor. As long as the light is blocked, the drive unit will not allow data to be written on the disk. If the notch is not covered, light goes through the slot and the system will allow data to be entered.

Sectoring

As we stated earlier, tracks are identified by the number of times that the read/write head stepper motor is pulsed in or out from a given track. However, the means by which the sector is identified is a bit more complicated. Referring back to Figure 15.19, it was stated that when a given disk index hole passes the jacket index hole, the system knows that a given sector is now under the read/write head. Although this principle may seem relatively easy to grasp, there still remains one problem. How does the system know *which* sector is the one that is in position? When index hole 5 (Figure 15.19a) passes through the jacket index hole, how does the system know that sector 5 is now in position under the read/write head? The problem of sector identification for the disk shown is accomplished by the positioning of the eleventh hole in the disk. If you take a close look at the disk, you will see that the spacing between holes 1 through 10 is uniform around the disk. If the disk is rotated at a constant 300 rpm, one of these holes will pass the jacket index hole every 20 ms. For example, 20 ms after hole 1 passes through the jacket index hole, hole 2 in the disk will pass the jacket index hole. This relation exists for all of the holes in the disk. However, hole 11 is placed halfway between 10 and 1. Thus 10 ms after hole 10 passes, hole 11 will pass. This change in timing is detected by the system and indicates that the next pulse of light through the jacket index hole represents the start of sector 1. It is then simply a matter of counting pulses through the index hole until the desired sector is reached. The following example will help you see how the track/sector circuitry is used to find a given data set.

EXAMPLE 15.1

A given disk drive is set with the read/write head positioned over sector 5 of track 00. The system needs to read data from sector 3 of track 03. Since the read/write head is over track 00, the stepper motor is pulsed three times, moving the read/write head over track 03. As the disk is rotating, the system waits for the 10-ms light pulse detection through the index hole. After this pulse occurs, the system counts out three more pulses through the index hole. The first pulse indicates the start of sector 1, the second indicates the start of sector two, and the third indicates the start of sector three. The system will now start to read the needed data.

---

*Some drive units are set to operate at 360 rpm. The rotational speed for a given unit will be specified in the operator's manual for the drive.

The type of disk shown in Figure 15.19, and used in the previous discussions, is referred to as a *hard-sectored* disk. The name comes from the fact that hardware (electronic circuitry) is used to inform the system of the start of each sector. Another type of disk, the *soft-sectored* disk, uses only one index hole in the disk to establish the start of the first sector. The rest of the sectors are established by *identification bytes* on the disk. In other words, certain codes are placed on the soft-sectored disk which inform the system that the read/write head is over the start of another sector. The only sector which is identified by the index hole is sector 1. *It should be noted that whereas some disk drives are designed to handle both hard-sectored disks and soft-sectored disks, most disk drives are designed to handle only one type or another. You cannot always substitute one type for another.* There have been many instances in which a disk drive as believed to be bad, when the only problem was the type of disk being used. Disks are usually labeled as to the type of sectoring used, so be sure to check the sectoring of the system versus that of the disk when you think that there is a problem with the disk drive.

Data Recording on Floppy Disks

It was stated earlier that a floppy disk is a *magnetic* memory type. Data is recorded on a floppy disk in much the same way as music is recorded on tape. Magnetic flux is imposed on the disk by the read/write head just as it is on a tape. In the case of data being recorded on a disk, data bits (ones and zeros) are represented by flux *direction* in most cases. For example, consider the diagram representation of a read/write head shown in Figure 15.20. In the circuit shown, a coil is placed around an iron

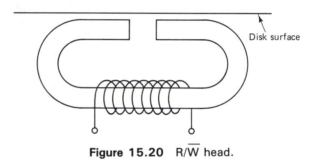

Disk surface

Figure 15.20 R/W head.

core. When current is caused to flow in the direction indicated in the diagram, the resulting direction of flux is induced in the core. Causing current to flow in the opposite direction would cause a flux to be induced which is 180° out of phase with the flux direction shown. If the read/write head shown is placed against a disk, the flux directions will be imposed on the disk. All we need to do to change the flux directions on the disk is to change the direction of current through the winding that surrounds the iron core.

By the same token, when a disk is being read, the direction of flux on the disk at a given point will cause a current to be induced in the wire in one direction or another. The changes in current direction can be detected, and the disk drive can generate the appropriate logic level. For example, assume that data are recorded so that a magnetic flux with a polarity such as that shown in Figure 15.21a is a logic 1 and the flux polarity shown in Figure 15.21b represents a logic 0. When the current flow through the coil in Figure 15.21a is applied, the logic 1 flux direction is imposed on the disk. The same principle applies to the flux direction/current flow relationship shown in Figure 15.21b. Later, when the disk is read, the indicated flux directions will cause the resulting currents to flow through the wires. These current flow

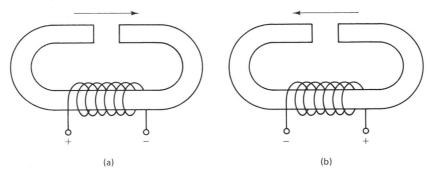

Figure 15.21 Flux/current relationships.

directions are then converted to the logic levels indicated and the data is sent to the microcomputer.

One common disk recording mode is called *non-return to zero* (NRZ). In NRZ data is stored as described above. The name refers to the fact that current is always being applied to the read/write head. The only thing that changes is the direction of the current flow.

15.6 DISK DRIVE UNITS AND DISK DRIVE INTERFACING

It should be noted from the start that disk drive units are very complex devices which are prone to many types of electronic and mechanical failures. There are a great many significant differences in the ways in which disk drives are designed and built, so knowledge of one type of disk drive will not necessarily help you in any way when trying to repair another. Also, there are quite a few mechanical devices which are set to specific tolerances within a disk drive. The LED/phototransistor pair used with the index hole must be set at specific points or the system will not be able to distinguish sectors. If the drive spindle revolves at the wrong speed, data may be read from the disk incorrectly, and so on. *For these reasons, it is recommended that you do not attempt to repair a disk drive yourself. Rather, whenever possible, simply replace the bad drive unit and send the original back to the manufacturer for repair.* In this section we treat the drive unit itself as a "black box" that must receive signals from and transmit signals to the microcomputer. We concentrate on these signals and how they are interfaced to the microcomputer. With a working knowledge of these signals, you should be able to isolate a disk drive problem down to the unit itself or to the microcomputer interface. If the interface is the problem, fix it. If the drive is the problem, replace the drive and return the faulty drive to the manufacturer for repair. Remember, you stand to lose a lot more by trying to repair a disk drive than you do by simply replacing it and having the manufacturer fix it.

Disk Drive Signals

There are several signals that must be provided between the disk drive unit and the microcomputer in order for the devices to interact. These signals are represented in the diagram shown in Figure 15.22. The signal lines shown are defined and used as follows:

Write data: Used to transmit data to the disk drive.
Read data: Used to transmit data from the disk drive.
Index: This line is pulsed low each time that light passes through the index hole.

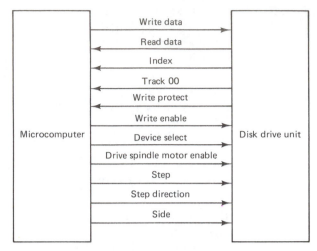

Figure 15.22   Disk drive/microcomputer interfacing.

It informs the microcomputer that a new sector is now passing under the read/write head. It is activated only once per revolution in a system using soft-sectored disks.

Track 00: This line is pulsed low when the stepper motor has positioned the read/write head over the outermost track, track 00.

Write protect: This line is held low when the disk being used is write protected. For a given disk, it will be either constantly high or constantly low.

Write enable: This line is driven low by the microcomputer whenever it is sending data to the disk, indicating that a write operation is in progress. This line is disabled when a write protected disk is in the drive.

Device select: When low, this line indicates that the microcomputer is attempting to communicate with the drive. Acts like a standard $\overline{CS}$ line.

Device spindle motor enable: When low, this line causes the drive spindle motor to start revolving. The motor will stop when this line returns to the one state. This ensures that the spindle motor is using power only when it is needed.

Step: This line pulses low to cause the stepper motor to take one step in the indicated direction.

Step direction: This line will cause the stepper motor to step toward the outside of the disk when at one logic level, and toward the center when at the other.

Side: This line is used when the floppy being used is a double-sided disk. The logic level on this line would indicate which side of the disk the read/write head was reading data from or writing data to.

These lines are not very complicated in nature. When working with a disk drive, however, you need to pay attention to which lines should be showing activity and which lines should be at stable logic levels. For example, the *side* line should not be showing any activity if the disk drive unit is set for single-sided disks. The write protection line should be constantly high unless a write-protected disk is being used. In that case, it should be constantly low.

Also, the *index* line should be changing at a rate of one pulse per revolution in a soft-sectored sytem, and at a much higher rate if hard-sectored disks are being used. The *write data* line should be active only when a write operation is being performed by the microcomputer. Otherwise, it should be at a constant high. The *track 00* line will go low only when the read/write head is over the outermost track, so there is no telling how often this line will be pulsed. It will *always* be pulsed, however, when the disk drive is first activated, since the read/write head must be stepped out in order for the system to get a bearing on exactly where the read/write head is located.

Troubleshooting the Disk Drive Interface

When a disk drive fails to operate as it should, there are three possible sources of trouble:

1. The microcomputer may not be able to communicate with the disk drive because of an internal fault (i.e., the fault may be located in the microcomputer itself).
2. The interface between the microcomputer and the disk drive may be faulty.
3. The disk drive unit itself may be faulty.

When there seems to be a malfunction in the disk drive circuitry, the first thing you should check is the floppy disk itself. If the floppy disk is bad, it will seem that the drive unit is failing. To check the disk, replace it with another. If the system works, the disk was the problem. If not, you need to check further.

There are several types of drive malfunctions that will make themselves evident with relative ease. If you cannot enter data onto a disk which is not write protected, check the write protect signal line. If it shows the disk to be write protected, the problem lies in the disk drive. If not, the problem lies in either the microcomputer or in the microcomputer/disk drive interface. If the read/write head cannot locate a given track, the track 00 line should be checked. If it shows activity, the problem is not in the disk drive unit. If not, the problem is in the drive unit. Other lines that would cause obvious symptoms are the index line and the step direction line. If the stepper motor keeps driving the motor in one direction, even though the motor has reached its limit in that direction, the step direction line should be checked. If the system keeps indicating that a given sector cannot be located, the index line or its associated circuitry may be faulty. In any case, the microcomputer and the interface should be verified as being good. If they are both in working condition, the disk drive is the source of the fault and should be replaced. If not, trace the signal down until you reach the source of the fault, and repair it.

In the following table, some common disk drive failures are listed. By each one, you will see some of the microcomputer/disk drive interface signals that could cause the given fault.

Symptom	Possible fault line
Data cannot be written onto the disk	Write data, write protect, write enable, device select
Stepper motor does not work	Device select, step, step direction
Drive spindle does not rotate	Drive spindle motor enable
Read/write head moves in and out at a constant rate	Track 00, step
System cannot locate sector	Index
System cannot read data from the disk	Read data, device select

A FINAL WORD

It may seem that the operation of the disk drive was sidestepped in this section, but the topic has been avoided due to the fact that there would be little gained from a long and drawn discussion of the internal operation of the drive unit. Since disk drive units vary considerably, any discussion included here would be of little benefit, unless you happened to be working with the one discussed. So, rather than involve you in a lengthy discussion of this type, you have been introduced to the basics of floppy disks and disk drive operation, together with the basic interfacing principles. *It is sincerely recommended that you do not attempt to repair a disk drive unit unless you have been trained to work on that specific unit.* If you have not been trained on a specific unit, you should refer any repair of that unit to the manufacturer.

QUESTIONS

1. What overall function is served by a printer? A disk drive?
2. How do printers and disk drive units differ from other microcomputer I/O devices?
3. What type of breakdowns are printers and disk drives subject to that the rest of the system is not?
4. What are the two main classifications of printers?
5. What are the two types of impact printers? How is information printed in each of these types?
6. What is a daisey wheel? What is a rotating-type head?
7. In what type of machines are the two types of printing heads named in Question 6 used?
8. What is the main advantage of using a dot character printer?
9. What is the most commonly used character format for dot character printers?
10. When is face character nonimpact printing used?
11. How is information printed on paper using the face character nonimpact printing technique?
12. Discuss the main considerations involved in transferring data from a microcomputer to a printer.
13. Why does a printer need internal RAM?
14. What are handshake signals?
15. Describe the microcomputer/printer handshake signals discussed in this chapter.
16. Refer to Figure 15.8. Describe the operation of the print head drive circuits.
17. With regard to the same diagram, discuss the operation of the stepper drive circuitry.
18. Discuss the operation of stepper motors.
19. What is a triac? What purpose is served by the triacs shown in Figure 15.16?
20. Discuss the operation of the high-temperature circuitry shown in Figure 15.17.
21. Why are most printer malfunctions relatively easy to diagnose?
22. What is a floppy disk?
23. What are the standard sizes of floppy disks?
24. What is a track? What is a sector?
25. Refer to Figure 15.19. If the disk shown can store 256 bytes per sector and the disk is single sided, how many data bytes can be stored on the entire disk?
26. Discuss the purpose for the index holes in a floppy disk.
27. What is hard-sectoring? Soft-sectoring?
28. When are hard-sectored and soft-sectored disks interchangeable?
29. What are the standard rotational speeds for $5\frac{1}{4}$-in. floppy disk drive systems?
30. How does a system using hard-sectoring know when sector 1 is positioned under the read/write head?
31. How is the read/write head positioned above a given track?
32. How are sectors established on a soft-sectored disk?
33. Discuss the method by which data is recorded on a floppy disk.
34. Discuss the microcomputer/disk drive interface signals covered in this chapter.

16

Analyzing and Troubleshooting the System

Now that we have covered all of the units contained in a typical microcomputer, it is time to begin discussing the steps you should take when confronted with troubleshooting a down system. There are two types of systems that you will encounter as your experience in troubleshooting microcomputers grows: those systems with which you are familiar, and those with which you have no experience. As you will learn, the methods you use to troubleshoot will vary significantly between the two types.

Troubleshooting a system with which you are familiar can be a relatively simple task. Having worked with the system before, you will undoubtedly have gained a great deal of insight as to which circuits cause specific types of problems. This reduces troubleshooting time, as the symptoms will lead you directly to a given group of circuits. If you have diagnosed that group of circuits before, determining the proper test points will be no trouble at all.

But how do you go about analyzing and troubleshooting a system that you have never dealt with before? What is the starting point? Troubleshooting a system that you have never dealt with involves a great deal of analysis. You must gather as much information as you can and put that information to use as you work on determining the cause of the problem. Before you can do this, however, you must know what type of information is relevant to fixing the system and where to go about obtaining that information.

In this chapter we discuss the methods by which you can effectively analyze and troubleshoot a system with which you are unfamiliar. We will go from the point at which you are first presented with the system to the point of finding and replacing the faulty component.

16.1 THE STEP-BY-STEP PROCEDURE

Although there is a fair amount of analysis and tesing involved in troubleshooting microcomputers, the basic procedure can be summed up as follows:

1. Gather all the information that you can using the available sources.
2. Break down the logic diagram into groups of circuits that perform specific functions.
3. Perform a visual check of the system.
4. Using information that you have gathered from the three steps above and your test equipment, isolate the problem to a single printed-circuit (PC) board.
5. Test the circuit groups on the PC board to determine which is the source of the trouble.
6. Once a group of circuits has been isolated, perform the tests required to determine which component is faulty.
7. Replace the faulty component and check out the system to ensure that it is working properly.

In the following sections of this chapter we take an in-depth look at the steps listed above and the operations that are involved in each one of them. Before we do this, however, let's take a look at the philosophy behind troubleshooting in general.

Troubleshooting any device is the process of determining which of possibly hundreds of components is causing the device to malfunction. Rarely does a technician take one look at a malfunctioning system and immediately determine the exact cause of the problem. A great deal of testing is usually required to isolate the cause of the problem. But which tests are required, and when? How do you go about isolating one out of so many components? The best way to effectively isolate a problem down to one component is to use what is called the *divide-and-conquer* approach. With this approach, you troubleshoot the system at three levels: the board level, the section level, and the component level. At each level, you constantly divide the possibilities by checking the input/output relationships, and thus locate the cause of the fault. For example, take a look at the process represented by the blocks in Figure 16.1. The first level of troubleshooting is the board level. At this level, the signals

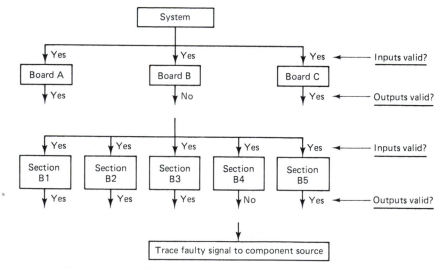

Figure 16.1 Divide-and-conquer troubleshooting procedure.

are checked between the three printed circuit boards to determine which has a faulty input/output relationship. A faulty input/output relationship exists when all of the inputs to the PC board are good and the board has one or more faulty outputs. Once the faulty PC board is located, the circutiry on the board is broken down into groups of components that together perform a specific function. The input/output relationships of these sections are then checked to determine which group of circuits on the board contains the fault. As with isolating the faulty PC board, you are looking for the section that has all of the proper inputs and one or more faulty outputs. Once the faulty section has been located, the section is checked to determine which component is faulty.

The divide-and-conquer approach is a logical method of troubleshooting because it constantly divides the problem into groups of circuits that can easily be isolated. It also provides the fastest path to the fault, since time is not wasted by troubleshooting on a board or in a section where it is not needed. When you use this approach, you are guaranteed of finding the greatest number of faults in the least amount of time. For these reasons, we stress the divide-and-conquer approach throughout this chapter.

Where to Begin

If you are going to be effective in troubleshooting a microcomputer, you must start by gathering all of the information that you can about the system. You must determine what the microcomputer does when it is working and how it has varied from that operation. You must determine which circuits are involved in performing the various system operations and where those circuits are located within the microcomputer. When gathering this information, you have three indespensable sources: the *system schematics,* the *technical manual,* and the *operator.*

The operator of the system is the best initial source of information, especially if you ask the right questions. This person may have some bit of information that will save you hours of troubleshooting or fighting with the manual on the system. Some of the questions that you should ask the operator are:

> What does the computer normally do when you are using it?
> How do you normally go about getting the system to perform the functions for you?
> What has the computer failed to do?
> Is the computer functioning normally otherwise?
> Did the problem happen suddenly? If it did, did you hear, see, or smell anything?
> Has this problem happened before? If so, who repaired the system for you?

Each of the questions listed can provide you with information that is vital to the troubleshooting process. Let's take a look at the information that can be gained from each of the questions.

1. *What does the computer normally do when you are using it?* To determine what is wrong with a given microcomputer, you must first have a good idea of what it does when everything is all right. The answer to this question will not only give you a start on understanding the overall operation of the system, but will give you a means of checking the operation of the system after completing the repair. Be sure to find out what type of display is present when the system is first turned on, what audio tones occur, and so on.

2. *How do you normally go about getting the system to perform the functions for you?* Although this question will not really save you any time in most instances, there is always that occasion when the problem is not the system, but the operator of the system. If the operator has recently purchased the system, it is possible that he or she has not been operating it properly. When the answer to this question is obtained, check the opera-

tor's manual to see if there are any steps that should performed which were not mentioned by the operator. There may also be an instruction in the manual which states "If the system fails to respond to this command, try. . . ," which the operator may not have tried.

3. *What has the computer failed to do?* What you are looking for with this question is an indication of which section of the system is not working (i.e., is the CRT blank, is the disk drive not turning off, etc.). The operator's answer can indicate where the problem is located. For example, the operator complains that nothing happens when the power is turned on. With all functions being completely out, there is good reason to suspect that the computer has a power supply problem.

4. *Is the computer functioning normally otherwise?* What you are trying to determine here is if more than one part of the system is faulty. Knowing that only one part of the computer is malfunctioning can save you a good deal of time in troubleshooting. For example, say that a given computer has a blank CRT. The operator then assumes that the system is completely down, and calls you. When you ask the operator to try to operate the system as if nothing was wrong, the operator discovers that all of the other system operations are good (i.e., the disk drive is operating, the printer is printing, etc.). By knowing that all of the other system operations are good, you have already narrowed the problem down to the CRT section of the system.

5. *Did the problem happen suddenly? If so, did you hear, see, or smell anything?* When a problem develops gradually, there is probably no visible sign of where the problem is. When it happens suddenly, there may be distinct evidence as to where the problem is, such as a burned resistor, a cracked IC, and so on. Also, if the operator smelled smoke, there is probably going to be evidence of something having burned. It is much easier to look for such evidence than to try to locate it with test equipment. A visual symptom that can save you some trouble is a CRT that flashed brightly before going blank. Such a symptom is characteristic of a problem on either the video board or the power supply. If all other system operations are normal, the problem is probably on the video board. If not, the problem is probably in the power supply.

6. *Has this problem happened before? If so, who repaired the system for you?* If the problem has happened before, the operator may have some idea of what caused it. If the technician who repaired the system can be contacted, that person may have some information that will help you. Perhaps the most important point is this: If the problem occurred several times in the past, this may indicate that the technician who repaired the system has been fixing the problem but not the cause of the problem. For example, say that a given chip is drawing too much current from a voltage regulator, which eventually causes the regulator to go out. The technician replaces the regulator, the system starts to work, and the computer is returned to the operator. After a few hours, the new regulator goes out because of the same current draw. The regulator is again replaced, and again the system works. The technician in this example has been fixing the problem (the regulator) but not the cause of the problem (the chip that is drawing the current). *It is important that you not only fix a problem, but also determine its cause.* If the problem was caused by another circuit, that circuit must also be repaired.

As you can see, you can gain quite a bit of information from the operator. Whenever you get an answer to any of the questions listed, you have probably saved yourself a good bit of research. The word here is *dig*. Get every bit of information that the operator has which can help you. The next step is to obtain the technical manual and schematic diagrams of the system. These can be found in a public library or can be purchased from the manufacturer.

16.2 BREAKING DOWN THE LOGIC DIAGRAM

After obtaining the documentation on the microcomputer, the logic diagram must be broken down into groups of circuits and types of connections. The manual on the system will help you determine which chips are contained in the control/ALU, memory, input, and output sections. You need to determine exactly which chips are contained in each section. You may even consider marking the chips in a given section using a colored high-lighter. Marking the IC number in each chip using a different color for the various sections of the system gives you a map in the logic diagram. This will save you the time required to recheck the manual constantly to determine which section a given chip is considered to be a part of.

One problem that you will run into is the way in which ICs are labeled on most system schematics. Most manufacturers label the ICs with their company part numbers, not the actual numbers of the ICs themselves. You saw this in the schematics used from the H-89A. Whereas such ICs and NAND and NOR gates (together with the other basic gates) are easily identified, some of the more complex circuits are not so easily identified. You will usually find, however, that there is a cross-reference chart somewhere in the documentation. Use this cross-reference to label the ICs that cannot be identified simply by looking at them in the schematic. This again will save you time in rechecking and will also save you time in the event that you work on the same system again in the future.

Even though you have identified the chips in each section, there is another step that will help you a great deal. Using the same high-lighter color that you used to mark the chips, draw a dotted border around the sections. This time, however, break down the system further. Draw a border around the groups of circuits that are dedicated to a specific purpose. For example, rather than grouping all the output circuits together, group them into sections such as CRT circuitry, keyboard circuitry, modem circuitry, and so on. You will now have a detailed outline showing the specific functions associated with every IC in the system. Once you have determined which chips are associated with each computer function, it is time to analyze the way in which the various sections are interconnected.

Determining the Control Line Interfacing

When you have grouped the circuits into sections, you will see that there are quite a few interconnections between those sections. As you know, those connections can be grouped as address, data, and control lines. The next step in the troubleshooting process is to determine which lines are the control lines.

The control section of the system will be connected to every other section of the system. Generally, the control signals will be $\overline{CS}$ and R/$\overline{W}$ signals. These signals, however, do not always originate at an output that is labeled $\overline{CS}$ or R/$\overline{W}$. The signals may come from a multiplexer or some other type of circuit. They may not even seem to originate at the microprocessor itself (i.e., the source of the signal may not appear to be associated with the CPU). In any event, you must trace all control signals to their source.

Now, which signals do you trace at this point? Trace only those signals that are entering the section from another section. Do not mark the control lines that are used within a section, only those that connect one section of the system to another.

If you are color coding the system, use the color of the section that the line is being used to control, not the color of the section where the line originates. It is also advised that if you are color coding the control lines, you trace the line all the way to its source before marking the line. This will ensure that your schematic does not end up being a collection of "wrong turn" markings.

Once the control lines have been marked, trace out the clock signals from the master clock of the system. Remember that this clock is usually a crystal-controlled oscillator and will have an output that goes in various directions to feed several circuits. If the clock goes to a counter, you must trace *every* output from the counter to its final destination. This is due to the fact that the counter may be used to provide different "divide-by-N" counts, as discussed in Chapter 8. After tracing out these clock lines, go through the schematic again and make sure that each clock input in the system has been accounted for. Again, we are concerned only with those clock lines that enter a given section of the system. At each of these inputs, write the frequency that should appear there. If you cannot determine the frequency from the schematic, check the manual. If the manual does not contain the information, it may be necessary to contact the manufacturer to obtain the information.

You do not need to determine the address and data interfacing at this point. These connections can be located later if necessary. Besides, address and data connections are usually fairly obvious, due to the fact that they are represented by the thick bus symbols that you have seen in previous diagrams. It is the control and clock line interfacing that will tend to be the most confusing and thus must be mapped out carefully. Once the system has been broken down carefully in the manner discussed, you are ready to start checking the system.

16.3 INITIAL CHECKOUT PROCEDURES

After you have gathered as much information from the operator as possible and have broken down the system schematic, you are ready to start the initial check of the system. In this step, you are looking for obvious signs of trouble and isolating the trouble location to a single PC board. There are two basic test procedures which are used in the initial checkout. First, a *visual inspection* is performed to locate any obvious signs of trouble. Then, *signal tracing* is performed on the connections between the boards contained in the system to determine which board has the proper inputs and one or more faulty outputs. This board then becomes the next level for analyzing in the divide-and-conquer scheme.

Visual Inspection: What to Look For

In most cases, the visual inspection of a system will yield little or no results (i.e., you will find no evidence as to what the problem is). However, when there *is* evidence of trouble, you will quite possibly save yourself hours of work by inspecting the system. For this reason, a visual inspection should be performed on every system that you troubleshoot. The inspection does not take a great deal of time, and the results may be well worth the effort.

When you perform a visual check of the system, what you are looking for are signs of excessive current flow and physically damaged components. The common signs of excessive current flow are:

Burned resistors
Copper runs that have lifted up off the board
Wires whose color has grayed near the connections
Brown areas on the printed circuit board

A resistor that has turned solid black is obviously a sign of excessive current. However, the damage to a resistor may not be as obvious as this. Sometimes, excessive current flow through a resistor will not turn it black, but rather, will cause the color code bands on the resistor to lose a lot of their color. If you have ever looked inside any piece of electronic equipment that is beginning to age, you may have noticed that some of the resistors have lost the brightness that was originally in the color code bands. This has occurred due to years of operation and the heat that the resistor has been exposed to during that time. When a resistor is exposed to a large current for a relatively short period of time, the same fading of color can occur. When a given resistor seems to be very faded compared to other resistors in the immediate area, there is reason to suspect that the current flow through the resistor has been excessive. However, before you decide that there is a problem, check the system schematic to make sure that the resistor in question was not intended to handle more current than the others in the area. For example, a resistor that is connected to the output of a voltage regulator will be exposed to much more current than will a typical pull-up resistor. The first resistor would therefore be expected to be more faded than the latter. However, if a given pull-up resistor was to show signs of excessive fading, there is probably a problem, since these resistors should, under normal circumstances, be exposed to little current flow.

When a copper run on a printed circuit board is exposed to a high amount of current, it may lift up off the board or burn itself open altogether. The circuit shown in Figure 16.2 shows the effect of this excessive current flow. The copper run that

Figure 16.2   Damage caused by excessive current flow.

is pointed out was destroyed by excessive current flow. When this type of damage is evident, you must closely check out *every* IC that is connected to the copper run. There is a high probability that one or more of these ICs were destroyed by the same current surge that lifted the copper run. The advantage of finding a copper run like the one shown in Figure 16.2 is the fact that it gives you an immediate indication of exactly where the problem lies. This can save you a great deal of time analyzing the overall system.

Wires can be faded in the same manner that resistor color bands are faded. When excessive current flow does not burn out a wire completely, it may fade the color of the wires near the point at which they were soldered to the board. Again, there is a judgment that you must make. Was the wire faded by excessive current flow, or was it faded by the technician who soldered it onto the board? As a rule, compare the wire to those that were soldered to the same board. If the wire in question is obviously more faded that any of the others, there may be reason to check it out.

The last sign of excessive current flow is the appearance of brown areas on the printed circuit board. This is usually caused by a current surge that is not large enough to lift a copper run off the board but is large enough to singe the board around the run. Just as any other sign of excessive current flow, the components in the area of the singed spot on the board must be checked completely.

Another sign of trouble that you should look for is physical damage to the components on each printed-circuit board. An IC that has been exposed to high current may crack. Or, when the IC has not cracked, its numbering may be burned away or extremely faded. Again, faded numbering is not conclusive evidence of trouble, but what you are attempting to do at this point is collect some evidence of where the problem *may* be. There are more tests that must be performed before any conclusions can be drawn, except in the case where the physical damage to an IC or a burned wire of copper run is so severe that there is no room for doubt as to where the problem lies.

Isolating the Problem to a Board

There are usually several printed circuit boards in a given microcomputer, which means that a given problem must be isolated to a specific board before the problem itself can be diagnosed. In isolating the problem to a board, you are actually determining which boards are working rather than one that is not. For example, consider the block diagram of the H-89A, shown in Figure 16.3. This block diagram is set up by printed-

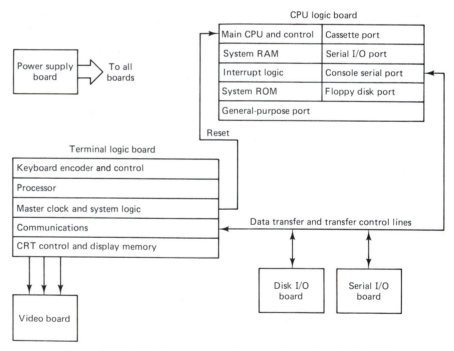

Figure 16.3   Basic board breakdown of the Heath H–89A.

circuit boards rather than by circuit functions. Inside each block, the groups of circuits contained on that board are listed. To isolate a problem in this system to one of the boards, you would use two tools: your oscilloscope and the information that was supplied to you by the operator. The information from the operator would be used as a basis for determining a starting point in the troubleshooting procedure. For example, if the operator stated that the system was completely operational except for the disk drive unit, you would not start checking out the system at the CPU logic board. The place to start would be the point where the disk drive I/O board is connected to the power supply and the CPU logic board. If all of the inputs to the disk drive I/O board were good, the board with the trouble would be the disk drive I/O board itself or the disk drive unit. If an input to the disk drive I/O board was determined to be bad, the inputs to the source board would be checked. For example, if an input that was being supplied by the CPU logic board was determined to be bad, you would then check the inputs to the CPU logic board. These inputs come from the CPU logic board and the power supply board, as indicated in the block diagram. If these inputs were all good, the problem would be located on the CPU logic board. If not, you would have to continue in the direction of the bad input.

How do you determine when an input to a board is good or bad? Some inputs to a board are used only at specific times or under specific circumstances. These inputs may appear to be bad when checked but may actually be good. For example, the RESET input to the CPU logic board originates on the terminal logic board. When checking this line, it should appear to be a constant high, since the only time it would go low is during a manual or power-up reset operation. But how do you know which lines are used in this way and which ones are not? Most control lines are used at fairly regular intervals. Although they may not be constantly changing, they should be changing at a rate that can be observed on an oscilloscope. For example, a given line may be used by the system only once every couple of milliseconds, a slow rate for the average microcomputer. Viewing that line with the oscilloscope set on a microsecond TIME/DIV setting may lead you to believe that there is a problem, since you may not see any activity on the line. However, by changing the TIME/DIV setting on the oscilloscope into the high-millisecond range, you would see considerable activity on the line. This would indicate that the line is all right. *Whenever a given control line appears to be faulty, check it on higher TIME/DIV settings on the oscilloscope.* If the line shows activity, it is probably good. If not, check the source of the signal and then look that chip up in the system manual. If the line is the type that is used only at specific times, this fact will be stated in the manual on the system. If there is no indication that the line is used only under specific circumstances, it is probably bad.

There is another important point that should be made regarding the checking of signals between printed-circuit boards. The boards in a given system are interconnected using either cables and cable connectors or edge connectors and sockets. Regardless of which method is used to interconnect the boards, the connections themselves can sometimes be the source of the trouble. An edge connector may not be seated properly in the socket, a cable connector may have been pulled loose, or a wire may have been pulled loose in a cable connector. Because these possibilities exist, you should check the inputs to a board on the board itself. If a given input does not seem to be there, check the output from the other board that is feeding the input. If the signal is present on the other board, the problem is the connection between the boards. Edge connectors between boards can cause a type of problem that is readily repaired. Sometimes the edge connectors on the board develop a residue that can cause intermittent breaks in the signal flow through the connector. Whenever dealing with edge connectors, check to see if they appear slightly tarnished. If they do, remove the tarnish with a pencil eraser and then reseat the edge connector into the socket. Cleaning the edge connectors in this fashion has been known to completely repair a number of microcomputers.

The Bottom Line

The step-by-step procedure for initially checking out the system involves finding any obvious troubles and isolating the problem down to a board. In many cases, the problem can be isolated to a board from the operator's description of the trouble. However, even when the problem board seems obvious, you should verify the information you received from the operator with your own testing. The procedure is as follows:

1. Inspect the boards for signs of excessive heat, such as lifted copper runs, burned components, discolored wires, and brown areas on the boards themselves.

2. If any signs of excessive heat are present, check all components in the area that is suspect.

3. Starting with the board that you suspect is the source of the problem, check all outputs from the board. If they are all good, check to make sure that they are getting to the boards to which they are sent.

4. When a bad output is located, check all inputs to that board on the board itself. If an input appears to be bad, check the input again at the output of the board that is the source of the signal.

5. If the output from the source board is bad, repeat the output/input check procedure on the source board. Keep repeating this procedure until you locate a board that has all of the correct inputs and one or more incorrect outputs. This board is the source of the problem.

6. Any time that an input to a board appears to be bad and the output of the board that is the source of that signal appears to be good, carefully check the interconnections between the two boards, as this is probably the source of the problem.

7. If the interconnection between the boards appears to be the source of the problem, check all the wires for continuity when wires are being used, and clean edge connectors when they are being used.

Make sure that your signal checking on the board inputs includes the V_{cc} and ground connections to the power supply. A bad power supply is as common as any problem you may encounter in microcomputer troubleshooting.

16.4 ISOLATING THE PROBLEM TO A SECTION

Once you have determined which board is the source of the problem, the next step is to determine which group of circuits on the board contains the faulty component. The starting point for determining the section that contains the problem is to think about the symptoms and the circuits that relate to those symptoms. For example, look at the block diagram in Figure 16.4. In the block diagram, the control section is used to control all the other sections, as is usually the case. Because of this, *the control unit must be considered a possible cause of the problem, regardless of which area of the board seems to be faulty.* For example, a problem in the display could originate in one of three areas: the video circuitry, the CRT logic circuitry, or control. The following chart shows the possible sources of a variety of symptoms:

Symptom	*Possible fault locations*
Display faulty	Video circuitry, CRT logic circuitry, control
System does not respond to keyboard input	Keyboard circuitry, control

No output to printer	Serial I/O circuitry, control
Faulty disk drive operations	Disk drive I/O circuitry, control
Two or more of the above	Control

In every case, the control unit is suspect, so the logical place to start is to ensure that the control unit is providing the signals needed by the other circuitry to perform its function. For example, if the keyboard does not seem to be working, the first step would be to ensure that the signals needed from control are making it to the keyboard section. If they are all there, the problem is in the keyboard section; if not, the problem is in the control section.

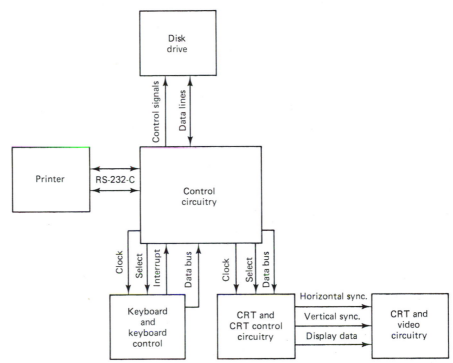

Figure 16.4 Example control circuitry connections.

Of any of the possibilities listed above, the control unit is probably the hardest to diagnose, perhaps because it is responsible for so many operations. As a review, let's take a look at what the control unit would have to do to control the units to which it is connected. The control unit must do three basic things: address the various sections, transfer data to/from the sections, and provide the clock and enable signals to the various chips in each section. These three operations involve a large number of ICs and lines, all of which must be suspect when the control unit seems to be the source of the trouble. All of this is complicated further by the fact that the control unit probably contains some amount of memory that is used in conjunction with any and all operations that it performs, so this memory must also be suspect.

The circuit represented by the block diagram in Figure 16.4 would be relatively easy to diagnose in terms of section failures, simply because each section of the circuit is dedicated to performing a very visible function. A problem in the display would lead directly to a certain group of circuits, a problem in the keyboard would lead directly to another group of circuits, and so on. But what about the case where the functions of the circuit groups are not so easily identified? Such a circuit is represented in the block diagram shown in Figure 16.5. This block diagram represents the circuitry on the H-89A CPU logic board. This logic board contains the logic that makes up all but the main I/O logic of the system (i.e., the main control unit, the main memory, and the main processing circuitry are all located on this board). Since this board is responsible for the overall operation of the system, it is much more difficult to isolate a problem on the board down to a specific group of circuits. Most of the groups of circuits on this board are involved in *all* computer operations, not just one or two. However, if you look closely at the block diagram, it is possible to come up with a grouping of circuits by basic functions. The best place to start is at the CPU, located on the left side of the block diagram. If you look at the circuits surrounding the CPU, you will notice that some of the circuits are being fed by the CPU and some of them are feeding signals *to* the CPU. The first group of circuits that will be considered a section will be those that are feeding signals to the CPU. This section would consist of the following:

    System clock
    Power Up and Reset
    Interrupt Logic
    Single Step and 2-ms Clock

With the exception of the single step and 2-ms clock circuitry, all of the circuits listed have outputs that go to the CPU control and clock inputs. The single step and 2-ms clock circuitry is still considered to be a part of this section, because it has outputs that go to two of the other circuits listed and therefore must be a part of the section. The next section will be those circuits that are fed *directly* by CPU control and address outputs. These circuits are as follows:

    Address Latches
    Control Logic

The memory section of the board would consists of the memory chips themselves and the memory decoding circuitry. From the block diagram, the section consists of the following:

    Memory-Map Decoder
    Dynamic RAM Address MUX (multiplexer)
    System ROM, Floppy Disk ROM
    System RAM, Floppy Disk RAM

A circuit that must be grouped by itself is the general-purpose port. This circuitry is used by the CPU to provide enable signals for several of the other sections on the board. The reason that this circuitry was not included in the group of circuits fed directly by the CPU outputs is the fact that it gets its information via the data bus. The address latches and control logic are independent of the data bus and thus were grouped separately.

The remainder of the board consists of circuits used to provide I/O for the CPU logic board. This group of circuits consists of the following:

    I/O Map Decoder
    Cassette Port
    Three-Port Serial
    Console Serial Port
    Floppy Disk Port

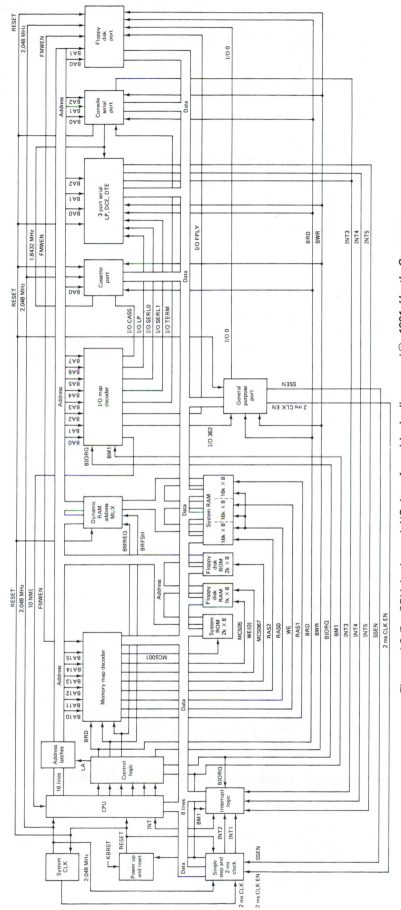

Figure 16.5 CPU logic and I/O interface block diagram. (© 1981 Heath Company. Reprinted by permission of Heath Co.)

Now that the circuitry has been grouped into sections, the next step would be to isolate the bad section by checking the input and output lines to each section. Since the majority of the sections on this board interact in every operation performed, it is difficult to determine the correct place to start trying to isolate the faulty section. However, there are general symptoms that will *usually* lead you to the section. These symptoms and their causes are as follows:

Symptom	Possible cause
Nothing works	Power supply, CPU, control inputs and outputs to/from CPU
I/O circuitry out	Control, I/O circuitry
Board does not perform its functions, but no major problems are apparent	Memory

The last of the symptoms listed deserves further attention. There is a saying that "when everything works, but nothing works, the problem is memory." This is the best indication of a memory problem. When memory fails, the sections of the system will appear to be working individually (i.e., control signals, clock signal, addresses, and changes on the data bus will all be apparent). However, the system as a whole will not work. The overall functions normally performed by the system will not occur. Therefore, the best indication of a memory problem is the fact that everything else seems to be working.

When checking a given section, you determine that the outputs from that section are bad. The next step is to check the inputs to that section. The best procedure to follow, is to check the following types of inputs, in order:

V_{cc} and ground connections
Control inputs to the section
Address inputs to the section
Data inputs to the section

It can be argued that the order in which you check the types of inputs is not important, but consider the following: The power supply connections are the easiest to check and take the shortest time. Control inputs are checked next because they are unique to each section and thus are likely to be the inputs that would cause a section to malfunction, assuming that any input is the cause of the problem. The address and data inputs to a section are not likely candidates as the cause of *one* section going bad, because they are common to all sections. If a given address or data bus line fails, the problem will most likely show up in *all* sections, not just one. All things considered, checking the lines in the order listed above will probably lead you to a bad line faster than any other order of input testing.

The block diagram is useful not only as a tool for grouping the sections on the board, but is also very useful in determining the control line interfacing. By using this block diagram while analyzing the board schematic, you will save yourself a great deal of time and trouble in determining the control line connections throughout the board. When trying to isolate the problem down to a section, you would use the block diagram as your guide and use the system schematic to help you locate the various check points (section inputs and outputs) on the board.

16.5 ISOLATING THE PROBLEM TO A COMPONENT

Once you have narrowed a given problem down to a specific section of a board, there is only one thing left to do: Find and replace the faulty component. Techniques have been shown throughout this book for troubleshooting the various types of circuits which are used in a microcomputer, and from time to time you may have to refer back to these techniques in order to troubleshoot on the component level.

The best place to start troubleshooting a group of circuits is to start at the point where the problem first became evident. In the preceding section we discussed the fact that a section is isolated as the cause of the problem by the lack of one or more output signals while all of the section input signals are present. It would make sense to start troubleshooting the circuits in the section at the output or outputs which are not as they should be.

In most cases, troubleshooting down to the component level is simply a matter of tracing a signal back to the component that has a bad output while having a valid input. For example, consider the CRT logic circuitry which was discussed in Chapter 14. For convenience, this circuit is shown again in Figure 16.6. The following example is designed to take you through the entire troubleshooting procedure. Pay close attention to the conclusions that are drawn at each step in the procedure.

EXAMPLE 16.1

Symptoms: The CRT is blank. No data can be displayed.

Operator Input: All other system functions are normal (i.e., the disk drive works, etc.).

Visual check: Results are negative. There are no signs of excessive heat.

Since the problem seems to be isolated to the CRT and its associate circuitry, the logical place to start is at the connections between the CRT logic circuitry and the video circuitry, which is located on a separate board. Checking the system schematics shows the only connections between the two sections (the video circuitry and the CRT logic circuitry) to the outputs of the exclusive-OR gates, U406A, U406C, and U406D. These gates are shown at the top of the schematic in Figure 16.6. Checking the outputs of these gates shows that the output from U406A is being held at a constant low, indicating a problem. The outputs from the other two exclusive-OR gates are as they should be.

Observation: Note that the U406C and U406D outputs were also checked, even though the output of U406A has already been determined to be bad. This was done for the purpose of determining if the problem was on one single line, or on several. *Never assume simply because you have located one faulty output line that it is the only one. Verify the condition of all output lines from a given board or section.*

Since all system functions seem to be normal other than the CRT operations, the problem is assumed to be in either the control inputs to the CRT logic circuitry or in the CRT logic circuitry itself. The control inputs to the CRT logic circuitry are now checked, and all of them are functioning normally.

Observation: Why didn't the technician go straight from the bad output and troubleshoot the CRT control circuitry? The output of U406A was obviously bad, so why not just start checking from there? The reason is simple. Imagine that the technician *had* started from U406A, and had gone through an entire troubleshooting process only to discover that the reason the original output was

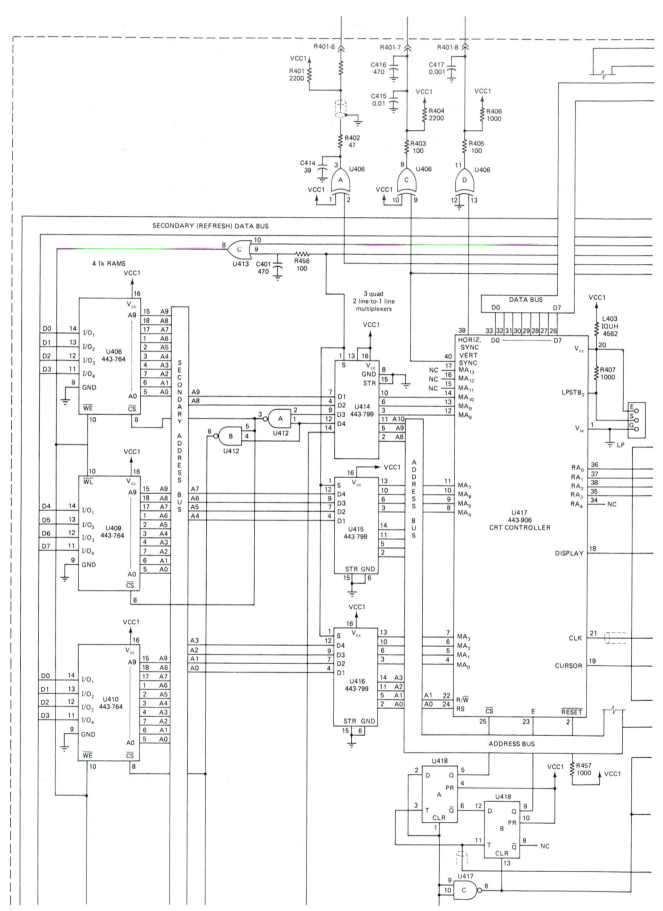

Figure 16.6 The Heath H–89A CRT logic circuitry. (© *1981 Heath Company. Reprinted by permission of Heath Co.*)

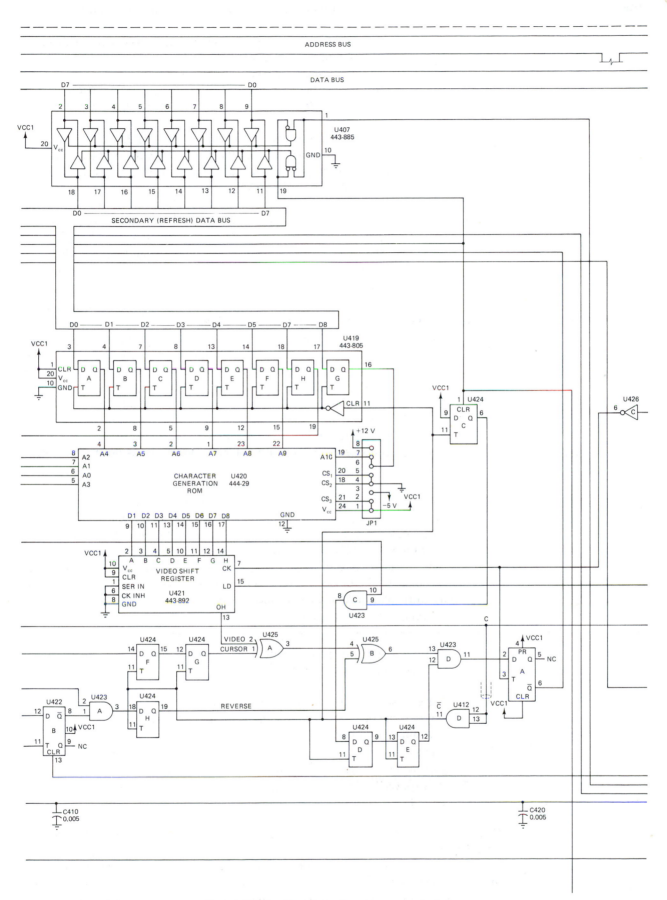

Figure 16.6 (Continued)

bad was because the CRT logic circuitry has been disabled by some input from control. A great deal of time would have been wasted because the technician would not have to repeat the entire process on the control circuitry. *Always verify that the problem lies in a specific condition before going on to find the faulty component.*

Now that the problem has been isolated to the CRT logic circuitry, the logical place to start troubleshooting is at the point where the problem was first discovered. The next check performed is at U406A-2 (U406A, pin 2). This input is at a constant high, as is U406A-1.

Conclusion:　U406A is not faulty, since it is operating as it should. An exclusive-OR gate with two high inputs should have a low output. The fault must lie somewhere in the circuitry that provides the signal to U406A-2, since this line should be changing at a varying rate as the dot pattern bits are shifted to the video circuitry.

U406A-2 is connected to the output of the D-type flip-flop, U422A-6. This point is now checked and is also at a constant high.

Observation:　Why check the output from the flip-flop when the other end of the copper run is at a constant high? It would seem that the next place to check would be the input to the flip-flop, since the output would *have* to be bad for U406A-2 to be held at a constant high. However, the possibility always exists that the copper run between the two circuits was the cause of the problem. For this reason, the two ends of the run must *both* be checked to make sure that the copper run is not the problem. *Always verify that the source of a bad input is a bad output from another circuit, not the connection between the two.*

The D input to the flip-flop, U422A-2 is checked, and is at a constant low. This accounts for the $\overline{Q}$ output of the device being at a constant high. The low is found to also be present at the output of the AND gate, U423D-11. Checking the inputs to U423D shows that U423D-12 is being held low. This low is also present at the output to the D-type flip-flop, U424E-12. Checking the D and T inputs to the device shows them both to be good. The V_{cc} and ground inputs to the chip are at their proper levels.

Conclusion:　U424E is faulty and should be replaced.

There were three major points made in the example that pertain to component level troubleshooting. As a summary:

1. Never assume simply because you have located one faulty output line that it is the only one. Verify the condition of *all* output lines from a given board, section, or component.
2. Always verify that the problem lies in a specific section before going on to find the faulty component.
3. Always verify that the source of a bad input is a bad output from another circuit, not the connection between the two.

Failure to apply any one of these principles can result in a great deal of unnecessary troubleshooting.

In most cases, isolating the problem down to a component is a relatively simple task if you keep the principles listed above in mind, and starting at the bad section output (or outputs), trace back until you find the chip with valid inputs and one or more bad outputs. In some cases, however, a given IC may fail in such a way as to make it appear to be good when it is really faulty. Sometimes the output of a given chip may become erratic after a lot of use. Such an output may appear on the oscilloscope to be acting properly when it actually is not. Some ways in which you can deal with such a problem are discussed in the next section.

16.6 WHEN ALL ELSE FAILS

One point must be made from the start: The techniques discussed in this section are *not* considered by most computer professionals to be valid troubleshooting procedures. They should be used only when all of your valid troubleshooting efforts have failed to produce any tangible results.

Every digital technician has seen it: a circuit that, despite all efforts, refuses to be repaired. Tests all indicate that everything is working, all input and output relationships seem good, and the circuit still refuses to work. So, what do you do now? You obviously cannot return a down system to the user while apologizing for your failure to fix it. The alternative is to try some "desperate measures" that may repair the fault. These measures (procedures) are discussed in this section.

Chip Swapping

Although chip swapping is considered to be a rather shoddy method of repairing a down system, you may be surprised to learn that a great majority of digital technicians must resort to this procedure a lot more often than they would care to admit. Chip swapping simply means to replace the chips on the faulty section, one at a time, until the problem disappears. The problem with using this method of troubleshooting is the fact that it can be very expensive. If you have to replace quite a few chips in a section before it works, you have spent a great deal of money on replacement chips. You also have to deal with the fact that you must buy *all* of the chips that are in the section, whether you need them or not. Why? Because, sure enough, the one you do not buy when you go to the parts store will be the one you need. So if you are going to use chip swapping as a troubleshooting technique, you have to be prepared to lay out a good deal of money for chips that you may or may not need. And if you work for anyone other than yourself, you may find it embarrassing having to explain to your supervisor why you use so many chips whenever you repair a given system. It would seem then, that, all things considered, chip swapping is not a good practice to get into.

There is one circumstance when chip swapping can be your best troubleshooting tool. When you have a great deal of experience working on one specific microcomputer, you usually gain a great deal of insight as to which chips cause specific types of problems. Say, for example, that you have worked on a specific brand and model of microcomputer and you have learned that a given problem is always caused by one of three chips. It is much faster and easier to go ahead and replace those three chips than to go ahead and perform a troubleshooting procedure to isolate the problem to one specific chip. In terms of cost-effectiveness, it is better to replace three chips quickly than it is to troubleshoot the system for a given period of time and then replace only one chip. The time saved by chip swapping in this case can be used to repair another system. This results in greater profits to you or your company.

Piggybacking

In any microcomputer systems, quite a few of the chips are soldered onto the printed-circuit boards. For these chips, chip swapping is hardly a practical alternative, since it would involve desoldering all the old chips and soldering in the potential replacements. There is, however, a method by which you can effectively swap chips without actually having to do so. This method is called *piggybacking*.

To piggyback a given chip, you take the replacement chip and press it down on the suspect chip in such a way as to have each pin of the replacement chip seated firmly on the corresponding pin of the suspect chip. A photo of two chips that have been put together in this manner can be seen in Figure 16.7. With the replacement

Figure 16.7 Piggybacking. (© *Heath Company. Reprinted by permission of Heath Co.*)

chip placed firmly on the suspect chip, turn the power on and see if the problem has been corrected. If it has, you have located the faulty chip. If not, you must perform the same operation with another chip. A couple of important points:

1. Make sure that the power is off before putting the replacement chip on the suspect chip. Otherwise, the replacement chip may be instantly destroyed and you may receive a nasty shock.
2. As soon as the operation of the system is verified, turn it off. In most cases, the replacement chip will be taken out by the faulty chip if left to operate for more than a few seconds.

Again, this is not a technique that is approved by most computer professionals. As with chip swapping, it should only be used *when all else fails*.

16.7 REMOVING AND REPLACING THE FAULTY IC

All of the ICs in any microcomptuer are either soldered into the printed circuit board or are placed in sockets that are soldered to the board. In a great number of microcomputers, there is some combination of the two. In either case, you need to know the proper technique for removing and replacing a faulty IC from the circuit.

The easiest situation to deal with is replacing the IC that is placed in a socket. IC sockets are soldered to the board and act as holders for the chips themselves. Removing a chip from one of these holders is easier than desoldering the chip from the board. However, there are still correct and incorrect ways to remove ICs from sockets. The main rule regarding the removal of ICs from their sockets is as follows: *Never remove an IC from its socket without using the proper tool for the job.* It is a great temptation to simply flip the end of an IC up with your thumb, and then pull the IC from its socket. However, removing an IC in this manner can give you a thumb full of IC pins. IC pins are sharp and will puncture the skin with very little pressure.

There are two tools that make the removal of ICs safe, and the use of either removal technique takes very little time. The first tool is an IC pulling tool, shown in Figure 16.8a. The IC pulling tool is inserted under the two sides of the IC, as shown in Figure 16.8b. Then, holding the IC firmly with the tool, the IC is lifted *straight* up out of the socket. Lifting it straight up is important so that the pins are not bent in the removal process. You want to be sure not to bend the pins so that the IC can be used again if you discover that it was not really faulty to begin with.

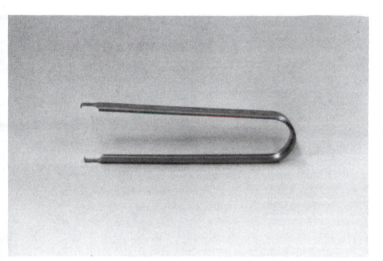

Figure 16.8 (a) IC pulling tool; (b) proper use. (© *1981 Heath Company. Reprinted by permission of Heath Co.*)

Another method for removing an IC from a socket involves the use of a small flathead screwdriver. The screwdriver is wedged under one end of the IC and rotated to practically lift the end of the IC from the socket. The procedure is then repeated on the other end of the IC. Once the IC is up and loose in the socket, it can safely be removed by hand.

Placing the new IC in the pocket is a relatively easy task. All you need to do is position the pins so that they will not be bent in the process. ICs are constructed in such a way that their pins tend to point slightly outward. When left in this way, the pins can easily be bent when trying to insert the IC into the socket. The best thing to do, then, is to bend the pins in until they point straight down, as shown in Figure 16.9. Bending the pins in as shown is best done by laying the IC on the table so that the pins are facing you and are flat on the table. Then roll the top of the IC slightly toward you. This will cause the pins to bend in a uniform manner. Once the pins on both sides of the IC have been bent inward, the IC can be placed in the socket with very little trouble. Simply line up the pins with the socket holes and press the IC down into the socket using light, even pressure. Do not force the IC if it does not seem willing to go into the socket. There is probably a pin that is catching. When

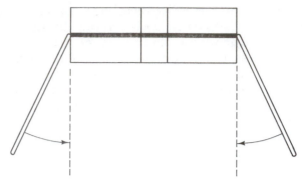

Figure 16.9 End view of an IC.

the IC does not easily go into the socket, check the pins, realign them if necessary, and try again.

Soldering and Desoldering ICs

Replacing ICs that are soldered onto the PC board is much like replacing any other type of component that has been soldered into a circuit, with one possible exception: *ICs have a very low tolerance for heat.* Because of this, they must be soldered into a circuit quickly and efficiently. You cannot spend a great deal of time soldering one specific pin, nor can you be sloppy in applying the solder to the component.

Rather than going through a complete course on soldering, let's just take a look at some of the pitfalls that you can run into when soldering ICs onto a PC board and how using the proper soldering techniques can help you avoid some of these pitfalls. First, the type of soldering iron that you use is important. You want to use a soldering iron that has a low wattage rating. Since ICs and copper runs need little heat to get hot enough to accept the solder, there is no reason to use a high-wattage soldering iron. Also, make sure that the soldering iron is properly tinned so that the maximum transfer of heat will occur in the shortest period of time.

When soldering a new IC onto a PC board, touch the tip of the iron to *both* the pin and the copper run. After a few seconds, touch the solder to the point where the soldering iron, the pin, and the PC board all meet. This will cause the solder to flow onto the point where the heat is the greatest.

It takes very little solder to connect an IC permanently to the PC board. One of the greatest mistakes that is usually made when soldering ICs to a PC board is using too much solder. The copper runs that are connected to the IC pins are very close together. Because of this, it is very easy to connect two adjacent pins by using too much solder on the pins. After soldering a given pin, be sure that no solder has run from one pin to another.

Figure 16.10 illustrates two circuits that have been soldered. The one shown in Figure 16.10a has been soldered correctly; the one shown in Figure 16.10b has not. In the circuit shown in Figure 16.10a, the solder connections were done in such a way to prevent any cold solder joints (caused by uneven heating of the pin and copper run), and with the proper amount of solder. There are no connections between the IC pins and the solder lays almost flat on the PC board. The circuit shown in Figure 16.10b has several cold solder joints, which are characterized by the balls of solder on the pins, and has several solder connections between pins. This type of soldering job guarantees that the "repaired" circuit will not work.

There is a tendency for technicians to think that desoldering an IC does not require any special technique, since you are removing a faulty IC that will be thrown away. However, nothing could be further from the truth. When desoldering an IC, you run the risk of ruining the copper run connections to the IC if you are not care-

Figure 16.10 (a) Proper solder connections; (b) poor solder connections.

ful. Whenever desoldering an IC, use a desoldering tool, commonly called a solder sucker. Place the iron tip on the solder joint and hold it there just long enough for the solder to become fluid. Then use the solder sucker to quickly remove all of the solder. It is not recommended that you use a soldering braid, since the heat must be applied to the solder joint for a longer period of time when using this tool. The extra time with heat applied to the circuit could cause damage to the copper run connections on the PC board. After carefully removing all of the solder from the IC, lift the IC out of the circuit *carefully*. If it resists being removed, make sure that you got all of the solder out of the connections. If all of the solder has been removed and you still have trouble removing the IC, try applying a little more pressure to the IC.

SUMMARY

Troubleshooting a system that you have never dealt with before involves a great deal of analysis that usually is not required to troubleshoot a system with which you are familiar. But regardless of whether you are familiar with the system or not, there is one important source of information: the operator. The operator of the system can give you information that may lead you directly or indirectly to the source of the malfunction. However, you must take the time to ask the operator for specific bits of information, since the operator may overlook some information that would be useful to you. The questions listed at the beginning of this chapter should give you an idea of the types of questions to ask.

After obtaining the information available from the operator, you have two other key sources of information: the system schematics and the system manual. Both of these sources are crucial if you are to troubleshoot the system systematically and effectively. When the schematic is obtained, it is a good idea to break it down into sections using a high-lighter. This will give you a reference that can be used in the future, as well as simplifying the task at hand. Breaking down the schematic into sections is best accomplished using the block diagrams of the system. After determining the sections, mark the control and clock inputs to the various sections for a quick reference. This can also be done using the system block diagram.

After determining the system control and clock signal interfacing, the next step is to perform a visual inspection of the system. At this point, you are looking for signs of excessive heat. It is also a good idea to check to see that all the connectors are properly seated. After the visual insepction, you want to determine which board contains the problem. This is done by checking the outputs and inputs of the boards. *Remember to check the interconnections between the boards at both the source and destination of the signal lines.* The interconnections between the boards can sometimes be the problem, and checking the lines at both ends can eliminate the possibility that the connection itself is bad.

Some board inputs and outputs will be used only under specific circumstances. These lines may appear to be bad when checked but may actually not be in use at the time you checked them. For this reason, if you are unsure what a given control line does, and it appears to be bad, check the manual to see if the line is used only at specific times. If the manual does not indicate this fact about a given line, odds are that you have a bad line and that further checking is required. This same situation may exist within sections on a given board, so whenever you feel that a line may be bad, check the manual if you do not know the purpose served by the line.

Once you have narrowed the problem down to a given board, the next step is to locate the faulty section. This task is simple when the sections all serve dedicated purposes, and not so simple when the sections are general purpose. In either case, check the lines into the section with a bad output to see if all the inputs are good. If they are and the outputs are bad, you have found the faulty section. If the inputs to the suspect section are bad, you have to go to the section that is providing the faulty inputs.

The order of testing for section inputs is as follows: Check the V_{cc} and ground connections, followed by the control inputs, the address inputs, and finally, the data inputs. Once the problem has been narrowed down to a given section, you are ready to test for the faulty component.

The best place to start testing for the faulty component is at the output or outputs that are bad. Starting at this point, trace the faulty signal to the circuit that has the correct inputs but not the correct outputs. Once the faulty component has been located, it is removed and replaced. If replacing a faulty component fails to correct the overall system malfunction, or if the system develops new problem symptoms, one of two situations exists: Either the component you replaced was not the source of the malfunction, or there was more than one problem in the system to begin with. In either case, you should start the troubleshooting procedure again at the circuit you replaced. For example, say that you are troubleshooting a circuit and replace a NAND gate because it has the correct inputs but not the correct output. After replacing the NAND gate, the system develops some symptoms other than those you saw when you first checked the system. Checking the NAND gate, you see that the output is now correct for the input signals. Since the NAND gate is working but the overall system is not, there must be another problem. The best move at this point would be to check the circuits connected to the NAND gate, since the original NAND gate may have taken out another chip when it went bad.

The key point to remember when troubleshooting is this: *You are not finished until the computer is totally operational.* When you feel that you have corrected the problem, you should go through the entire system operation to make sure that the system actually works.

It is acknowledged that the troubleshooting techniques discussed in this chapter are not the only valid techniques for microcomputer troubleshooting. When you are extremely familiar with a given microcomputer, *shotgunning* may be a more valid technique than those discussed here. Shotgunning is a repair method where the technician simply opens a computer and, based on previous experience with the system, simply replaces three or four chips. This is done because the technician knows that these chips usually cause the type of problem that is present. When it works, shotgunning saves a great deal of troubleshooting time and therefore gives you time to work on another project. *Diagnostic programs,* programs that are written specifically to help you locate the source of a system malfunction, can also help shorten the troubleshooting process. However, it is unwise to become too dependent on these programs because the microcomputer can malfunction so severely that running the diagnostic program is impossible. If you do choose to use them, diagnostic programs can often be purchased from the microcomputer manufacturer.

A FINAL NOTE

There is a way to save yourself a great deal of time in troubleshooting a given system. It has been suggested that a log be kept of all your repair experiences, including a list of symptom/fault relationships. This log could then be used to help you reduce troubleshooting time when you encounter a reoccuring problem. Remember, the more documentation you have (including your own records), the more effectively your time can be spent.

QUESTIONS

1. Which three sources of information are required to troubleshoot a system malfunction effectively?
2. What types of information can be obtained directly or indirectly from the operator?
3. What is the first step in breaking down a logic diagram?
4. After breaking down the logic diagram into sections, which lines do you trace?
5. When you initially check out the system, what check do you make?
6. When performing a visual check, what do you look for?
7. While performing a visual check, you find a copper run that has been lifted up from the board. After repairing the run, what must you check?
8. When isolating a problem to a board, how do you determine whether the problem is on the board or in the interconnections between boards?
9. When a given control or address line appears to be inactive, what oscilloscope adjustment should be made before deciding the line is bad?
10. If the adjustment in Question 9 shows the line still to be inactive, can you assume that the line is bad? If not, what else must be done before drawing any conclusions?
11. What special maintenance is required by edge connectors?
12. What is the step-by-step procedure for isolating a problem down to a given printed-circuit board?
13. When isolating a problem down to a given section, what is the first thing you should check?
14. Why are problems in the control unit the hardest to diagnose?
15. After you have determined a given section of a board to be bad, where should you begin to look for the faulty component?
16. How should ICs be removed from their sockets?
17. What problem is encountered when soldering and desoldering ICs?
18. When is shotgunning considered to be a valid troubleshooting technique?

17 Introduction to 16-Bit Microprocessors

Until now, our discussions have all centered around systems that are controlled by 8-bit microprocessors. These microprocessors all transfer data in 8-bit word lengths and have a maximum addressing capability of 64k (due to a 16-bit address bus). Although these microprocessors are fine for most applications, developments have been made in the past several years that may render them obsolete. The 16-bit microprocessor is the first of these developments and the 32-bit microprocessor is the second. In this chapter we take a brief look at the 16-bit microprocessor, specifically, the Motorola MC68000.

In 1979, Motorola introduced the first microprocessor capable of dealing with 16-bit and 32-bit word lengths. This microproceessor, the MC68000, is as radically different from its predecessor, the MC6800, as an Indy 500 racer is from a soapbox derby coaster. The internal structure of the MC68000 is far more sophisticated than that of the MC6800, as are its address bus, data bus, and control lines. The instruction set of the MC68000 allows it to perform operations that were previously accomplished using subroutines, such as multiplication and division.

The complete discussion of the MC68000 would take far more time and space than will be alloted for it in this text. In this chapter we take only an introductory look at the MC68000. Further information on the device can be found using the references listed at the end of the chapter. For now, we will deal only with the way in which the MC68000 differs from 8-bit microprocessors in terms of control functions, basic operations, internal construction, and data word length.

17.1 INTRODUCTORY CONCEPTS

There are five versions of the MC68000 available, and the four differ only in their maximum clock frequency. The MC68000 microprocessors and their maximum clock rates are as follows:

MC68000L4	4 MHz
MC68000L6	6 MHz
MC68000L8	8 MHz
MC68000L10	10 MHz
MC68000L12	12.5 MHz

The pin configuration and basic block diagram for all of the chips above can be seen in Figure 17.1. For the remainder of this chapter, we will simply refer to the MC68000, without distinguishing between the versions of the chip listed above.

The block diagram shows the input and output signals for the MC68000. The various inputs and outputs have been grouped according to the purpose served by the lines. The address lines and data lines have been grouped, as have the various control inputs and outputs. The 23 address lines (A1 through A23) allow the MC68000 to directly access 2^{23} = 8,388,610 memory locations. The 16-bit data bus can be used to read or write data values of either 8-bit or 16-bit length, depending on the instruction being executed. The address bus pins and the data bus pins are all three-state pins. As usual, the address bus is unidirectional and the data bus is bidirectional.

MC68000 Control Lines

The first group of control lines that we will look at is the group labeled *asynchronous bus control*. The term "asynchronous" in this case means something a little different than has been defined earlier. In this case, the term is used to indicate that the length of the read/write cycle may vary, according to the response time of the memory or I/O device that the CPU is communicating with. For example, consider the two circuits shown in Figure 17.2. The circuit in Figure 17.2a is a block diagram showing the MC6800, one memory location, and one I/O device. The time required to access information from each of the devices is shown in the respective blocks. The access time for information from the memory location is 100 ns, and the access time for information from the input unit is 20 μs. Since the MC6800 uses a set number of machine cycles for a memory read operation, it must be set up for the slowest device so that all devices can be read from or written into accurately. In this case, the minimum read/write cycle time is 20 μs. Figure 17.2b shows the MC68000 in the same basic block diagram, with one very important feature added. The memory location and the input device have an output that goes to the DTACK input of the MC68000. This input to the CPU indicates that a read/write cycle is complete. When it goes low, the CPU can go on to its next operation. Using this input, the CPU would spend 100 ns in the read/write cycle for memory, and 20 μs in the read cycle for the input device. Thus, no time is wasted as it is with the MC6800. Instead of the MC68000 being stuck with a set read/write cycle time, it can adjust the total cycle time to fit the device with which it is communicating. It will end any given read/write cycle as soon as DTACK goes low. Garnted, this means additional external circuitry (required to provide the DTACK signal), but it also results in a much faster overall system operation. A summary of the control lines in this group and their functions, is as follows:

Line	Name	Function
$\overline{AS}$	Address strobe	Indicates that there is a valid address on the address bus
R/$\overline{W}$	Read/write	Controls the direction of data flow, as usual

Line	Name	Function
UDS	Upper data strobe	A CPU output that works as described below
LDS	Lower data strobe	A CPU output that works in conjunction with UDS, as described below
DTACK	Data transfer acknowledge	This CPU input is used by an external device to indicate that valid data have been transferred; a read/write cycle is terminated when this input goes low

The $\overline{\text{UDS}}$ and $\overline{\text{LDS}}$ outputs from the CPU are used to indicate the type of data transfer that is being performed. These lines are combined with the $R/\overline{W}$ signal to indicate the following conditions:

UDS	LDS	D8 through D15	D0 through D7
1	1	No valid data	No valid data
0	0	Valid data	Valid data
1	0	a	Valid data
0	1	Valid data	a

aDuring a read cycle there will be no valid data on these lines. During a write cycle, the values on these lines will be the same as the values on the other 8-bit group of data pins.

The state of these two lines is determined by the instruction being executed. If the instruction calls for an operation to be performed by an 8-bit value, only the LDS line will be low. If the instruction calls for an operation to be performed on a 16-bit value, both lines will be low, assuming that the system has 16-bit memory locations. If the system memory has 8-bit memory locations, one byte of the 16-bit word will be fetched (or written) first and then the other. This is discussed further in a later section.

The next group of control lines is the group labeled *bus arbitration control*. These lines are used in systems where more than one device needs to be able to control the address and data buses. A summary of these lines is as follows:

Line	Name	Function
BR	Bus request	This input requests control of the buses when active low
BG	Bus grant	This CPU output acknowledges that it has turned control of the buses over to the device requesting bus control
BGACK	Bus grant acknowledge	This CPU input informs the CPU that the external device that requested control of the buses has done so

When an external device needs to gain control of the system buses, it sends a $\overline{\text{BR}}$ signal to the CPU. At the end of the current instruction cycle, the CPU will send a $\overline{\text{BG}}$ signal back to the device. It then responds by sending a $\overline{\text{BGACK}}$ signal back to the CPU. The device requesting control of the buses then retains control of them until the $\overline{\text{BGACK}}$ is driven back to its inactive level. At that time, the CPU returns to normal operation. *Note that the CPU three-state lines are all disabled while $\overline{\text{BGACK}}$ is low.* This prevents them from being damaged due to a wire-AND situation on these lines.

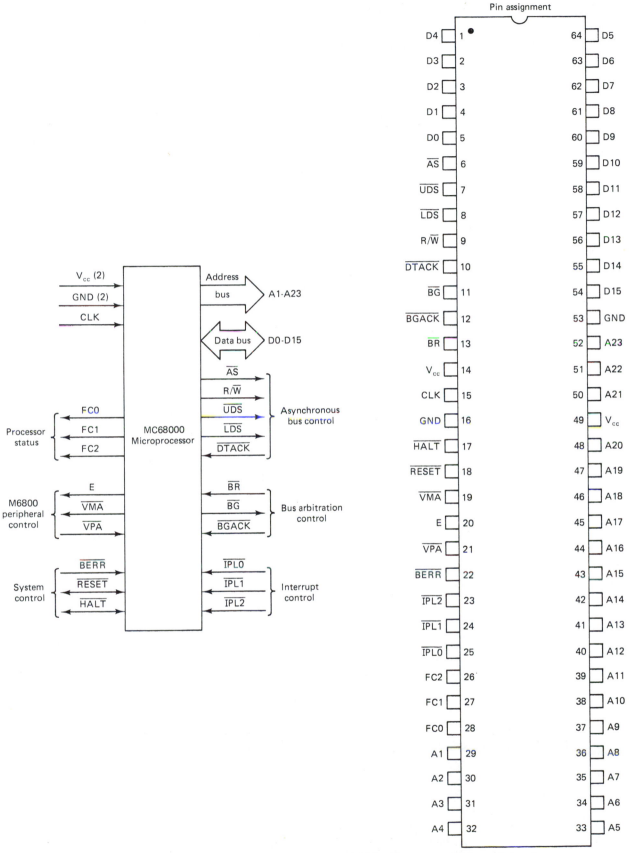

Figure 17.1 MC68000. *(Courtesy of Motorola Inc.)*

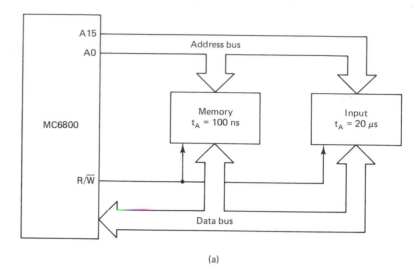

(a)

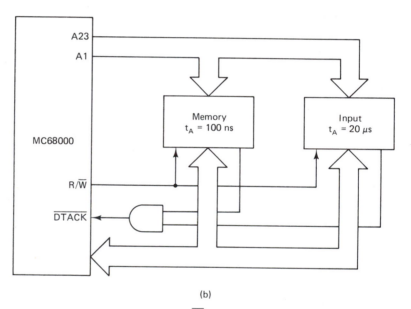

(b)

Figure 17.2 R/$\overline{W}$ timing examples.

The next group of control lines is the group labeled *interrupt control*. These interrupt inputs are used to determine the priority of the interrupting device, according to the following table:

IPL2	IPL1	IPL0	Interrupt level	Priority
1	1	1	7	Highest
1	1	0	6	Second
1	0	1	5	Third
1	0	0	4	Fourth
0	1	1	3	Fifth
0	1	0	2	Sixth
0	0	1	1	Lowest
0	0	0	0	No interrupt

This method by which interrupts are generated and handled is discussed further in a later section.

The next group of control lines is the group labeled *system control*. These lines are used to RESET or HALT the CPU (or system) and to inform the CPU that a bus error has occurred. A summary of these lines and their operations is as follows:

$\overline{\text{RESET}}$. For the MC68000, the $\overline{\text{RESET}}$ line can be either a CPU input or a CPU output. When it is used as a CPU input, it causes the same type of action as the $\overline{\text{RESET}}$ input on the MC6800. The CPU clears its internal registers and fetches and executes a specific RESET program. When used as an output, this line will go low, causing all of the devices to which it is connected to RESET. In this case, the internal registers of the CPU are not affected. Note that this line will be used as a CPU output only when the CPU fetches and executes the RESET instruction.

$\overline{\text{HALT}}$. When this pin is used as a CPU input, it acts just as the $\overline{\text{HALT}}$ input to the MC6800. When it is used as a CPU output, this line is used to indicate to all external devices that the CPU has stopped operating.

$\overline{\text{BERR}}$ (bus error). This input to the CPU indicates that an error has occurred during the course of a read or write cycle. If it goes active low, the CPU will try to perform the operation again, as long as the $\overline{\text{HALT}}$ input to the CPU has not been activated. If both inputs have been activated, the CPU will respond by halting its operation.

The group of control lines labeled *peripheral control* is used to allow peripherals to be interfaced with the CPU. Most peripherals are synchronous and thus must be wired in a special way to the asynchronous CPU. The lines in this group are summarized as follows:

E (enable). This active-high output is used to enable any peripherals that are connected to it. It will stay high for 10 clock cycles after it is initially driven high.

$\overline{\text{VMA}}$ (valid memory address). This CPU output is used to indicate that there is a valid address on the address bus and that the CPU data transfer operation has been synchronized to the enable output.

$\overline{\text{VPA}}$ (valid peripheral address). This CPU input is used to indicate to the CPU that the device (peripheral) that is involved in the data transfer is a synchronous device and that the CPU must therefere synchronize any data transfer operation with the occurrence of the enable signal.

The final group of control signals are the *processor status* signals. These CPU outputs are used to indicate the type of cycle that is currently being performed. The following table indicates what the various output codes on these three lines indicate.

FC2	FC1	FC0	Cycle type
0	0	0	X
0	0	1	User data
0	1	0	User program
0	1	1	X
1	0	0	X
1	0	1	Supervisor data
1	1	0	Supervisor program
1	1	1	Interrupt acknowledge

For you to understand the chart, a distinction must be made between *user* and *supervisor*. A user program is one that the user has entered into the system. A supervisor program is one that is stored in ROM, which the CPU runs only under specific circumstances. For example, the RESET program would be a supervisor program. Other supervisor programs may or may not be stored in ROM. These programs, however, would still be used in the supervisor mode of operation, to prevent the user from gaining access to them. For example, consider the system that is used to allow access to the accounts of a given bank. The programs used to allow this access would be stored as supervisor programs, to prevent any user from altering the program. Data associated with such a program would also be inaccessible to the user. This data would be called *supervisor data.*

The codes in the table that contains an "×" under cycle type are undefined and are not used. The other codes are used to indicate whether the CPU is fetching or writing user data, fetching a user program instruction, or performing one of the two operations on supervisor data or program instructions. The only remaining control lines on the CPU are V_{cc} and ground, which are not actually control lines, and clock. Note that the MC68000 needs only a single clock input, which is another improvement over the MC6800.

As you have probably been able to see for yourself, the MC68000 is capable of performing a much wider variety of control functions than the MC6800. These control functions are used in almost every phase of CPU operation, from read/write cycles to interrupt handling. These topics are discussed in Section 16.3. At this point, we will take a look at the internal construction of the MC68000, as well as the way in which data is stored in memory.

17.2 INTERNAL CONSTRUCTION AND DATA STORAGE

The basic internal register configuration of the MC68000 is shown in Figure 17.3.

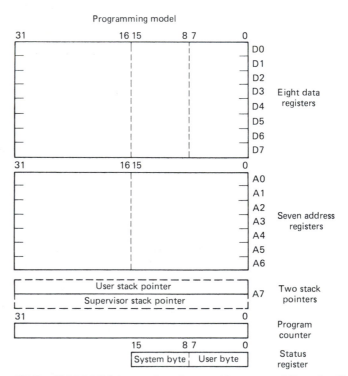

Figure 17.3 MC68000 internal registers. *(Courtesy of Prentice-Hall)*

As you can see, the CPU consists of eighteen 32-bit registers and a 16-bit status register. The 32-bit registers are broken down into the following groups:

Eight 32-bit data registers
Seven 32-bit address registers
Two 32-bit stack pointers
One 32-bit program counter

When discussing the operation of these registers, we will use the following terms to describe data values of varying lengths:

Byte: an 8-bit value
Word: a 16-bit value
Long word: a 32-bit value

Each of the data registers in the MC68000 can be used to store a byte, word, or long word. When a single byte is stored in any data register, that byte is automatically placed in the lowest 8 bit positions. When a single word is stored in a data register, it is placed automatically in the lowest 16 bit positions. A 32-bit long word would obviously fill the entire data register. When a value that is byte or word length is stored in any data register, only those bit positions that contain the byte or word are affected. For example, assume that the following value is stored in data register DO:

1111000010101111   1111111100000000   (F0AF FF00-H)

If the CPU were now to load the 16-bit value 1101001111110001 (B3F1-H) in the register, the new contents of Do would be

1111000010101111   1101001111110001   (F0AF B3F1-H)

Note that only the lowest 16 bit positions were affected by the operation. The highest 16 bit positions contain the same data before and after the operation. The same operating principle applies to all eight of the internal data registers.

The internal address registers differ from the data registers in that they are capable of handling only word or long-word values. A single byte cannot be loaded into any of the address registers. When a word is loaded into any address register, the higher 16 bits are set to equal the sign of the number. When a positive number is loaded, the higher 16 bits are set to zero, and are all set to ones otherwise. These operating principles also hold true for the stack pointers. All of the registers described to this point can be used as index registers.

The 32-bit program counter operates in the same manner as any program counter. It is used to store the address of the next instruction to be fetched from memory, and is incremented at the end of every fetch cycle. The program counter of the MC68000 is affected by branch instructions in the same way as the program counter for the MC6800, for all practical purposes.

The status register is divided into two bytes. The high byte makes up the *system byte* and is used in conjunction with supervisor programs. The low byte is designed as the *user byte* and is used in conjunction with user programs. The detailed breakdown of the status register can be seen in Figure 17.4. The Negative, Zero, Overflow, and Carry flags work exactly as described in Chapter 12. The Extend bit is an operand

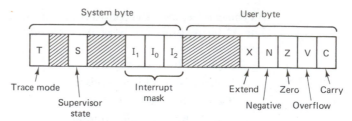

Figure 17.4 MC68000 status register. *(Courtesy of Prentice-Hall)*

for multiprecision arithmetic operations. The Interrupt bits are used for two purposes: First, they indicate the level of priority of any received interrupt. Second, they disable any lower-priority interrupts. For example, assume that interrupt level 3 is activated (at the IPL2 through IPL0 inputs). The bits in the status register should be set to the value at the IPL0 through IPL2 inputs and would disable any lower- or equal-priority-level interrupts (i.e., any interrupt-priority level less than or equal to level 3 would be disabled). Any higher-priority interrupts would still work.

The Status bit indicates whether the CPU is operating in the user or supervisor mode. When this bit is equal to a 1, the CPU is in the supervisor state; when 0, it is in the user state. The tracer bit is used for a special operation called *tracing*. This operation will be discussed in Section 17.3.

You will note that there is no accumulator in the MC68000. This is due to the fact that all operations can be performed using a value contained in any of the data or address registers in the CPU. Which register is used as the source of a given operand is determined by the lowest 6 bits in a given instruction. For example, take a look at the instruction format shown in Figure 17.5. In the instruction shown, the bits

Figure 17.5 MC68000 instruction format.

labeled "×" are the operation code and are used to identify the operation being performed. The lowest 6 bits are used to specify the location of the value that the operation is to be performed on. These bits are broken into two groups; the *mode* and *register*. When the mode value is 000, the register value is used to select one of the eight data registers. When the mode value is 001, the register bits select one of the seven address registers as the operand source. The addressing modes become much more involved when addressing external memory locations.

Memory Data Organization

As has been indicated, the internal registers of the MC68000 are capable of storing data values of byte, word, and long-word length. But how would these values be stored in a memory system capable of storing only 8-bit values? The method by which the various word lengths are stored in memory is shown in Figure 17.6. As shown, words are stored in successive memory locations, with the high byte appearing first. When the CPU is fetching a word, it fetches the high byte and places it in the high-byte position of the appropriate register. It then fetches the low byte and places it in the low-byte position of the same register. The high-word position of the register (bits 16 through 31) is not affected by the data transfer.

When long words are stored in memory, they are stored as shown in Figure 17.6b. Note that the long word, which is made up of four bytes, is stored in four consecutive memory locations. The first two bytes make up the high word and the

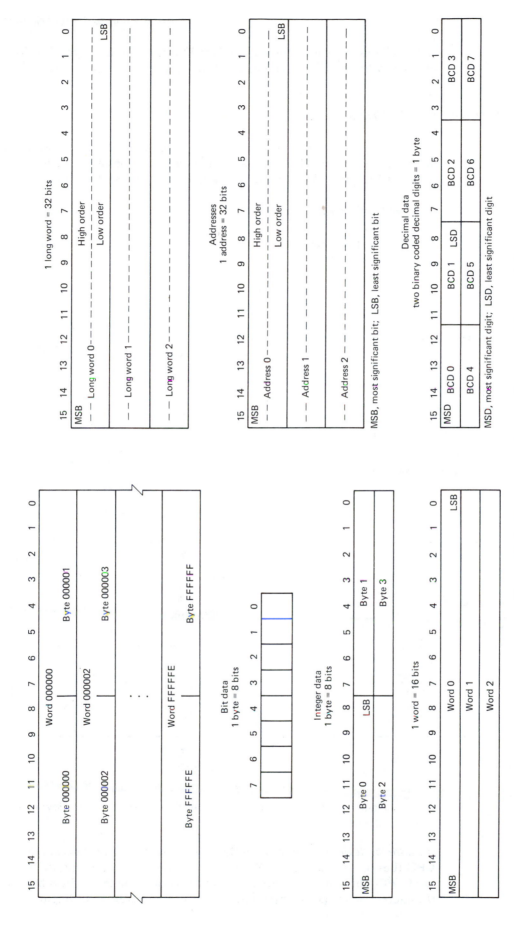

Figure 17.6 Memory organization. *(Courtesy of Prentice-Hall)*

381

last two bytes make up the low word. In a 32-bit data transfer, the four bytes would
be fetched by the CPU and would fill the appropriate 32-bit register.

17.3 COMMON CPU OPERATIONS

In this section we take a brief look at some of the common CPU operations as they
are performed by the MC68000. Among these operations are read/write cycles and
interrupt handling. We will also take a look at a special operation, called *tracing*.

Read/Write Cycles

The flowcharts for the read-byte and read-word cycles are shown in Figure 17.7. In

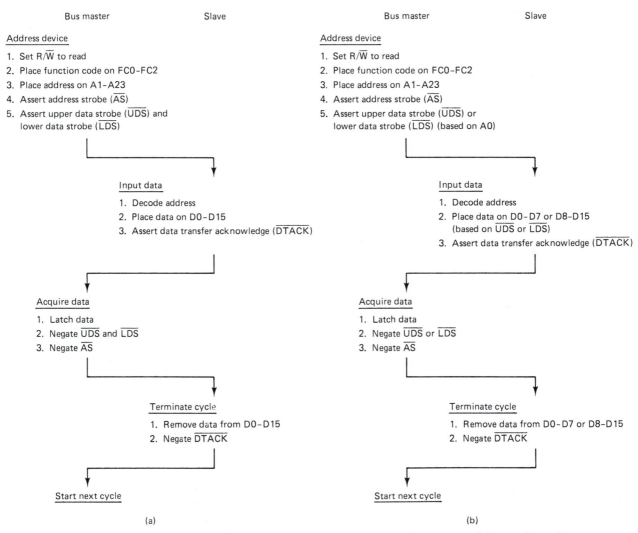

Figure 17.7 Read cycles: (a) word flow chart; (b) byte flow chart.
(Courtesy of Prentice-Hall)

the *address device* section of both flowcharts, the first four steps are the same. The
CPU (bus master) sets the R/W line to read, places the appropriate function code
on the FC0 through FC2 outputs, places the address on the address bus, and drives
the address strobe (AS) output low. The fifth step varies according to the length of

the value being fetched. If a word is being fetched, both UDS and LDS are driven low. If a single byte is being fetched, either UDS *or* LDS will be driven low, and the other will remain high. If UDS is driven low, the byte that is fetched will be placed in the high-byte position of the word destination. If LDS is low, the byte that is fetched will be placed in the low-byte position of the word destination. The output (UDS or LDS) that will be low depends on the state of an internal address bit, A0. When A0 is low, UDS will be low. When A0 is high, LDS will go low. This ensures that the correct byte appears in the correct location.

The slave (memory unit or peripheral) responds by performing the actions listed under *input data*. The address is decoded, then the data are placed on the appropriate data lines, and the DTACK input to the CPU is driven low. The CPU uses the DTACK signal as the indicator that it is time to latch the data on the data bus.

The *acquire data* operations are started when DTACK goes low. After the data is latched from the appropriate data lines, the UDS and/or LDS signals are driven back to their inactive levels and the AS output returns to the high (inactive) level. The slave device responds by entering the *terminate cycle*. During this time, it removes the data from its data outputs and removes the DTACK signal from the CPU. The CPU, upon detecting that the DTACK signal is no longer active, starts the next instruction cycle.

The write-cycle flowcharts, which are shown in Figure 17.8, are fairly similar to the read-cycle flowcharts. Note that in the *address device* sequence, the function code, address, and address strobe (AS) are all active before the R/W line is driven low. The value to be written into memory (or to a peripheral device) is then placed on the appropriate data lines, and UDS and LDS are placed at their proper values. As with the read cycle, the UDS/LDS states are determined by the length of the value being written, and in the case of a write-byte cycle, upon the value of the internal A0 bit.

The slave device responds with the *input data* cycle. After decoding the address, the slave device places the value being written into the appropriate location(s) and then drives the DTACK input to the CPU low. Again, the CPU responds to this input by initializing the *terminate output transfer* sequence. In this case, it removes the active UDS/LDS signals and the AS signal. It then removes the data from the appropriate data lines and places a 1 on the R/W line. The slave device then responds by driving the DTACK input to the CPU high, which informs the CPU that the next instruction cycle is to begin.

Interrupts

The flowchart for the sequence of events that occur when an interrupt is received can be seen in Figure 17.9. Note that this sequence does not include the possibility of a second interrupt being received while the first one is being serviced. This case will be discussed after the flowchart. When an interrupt is received, the CPU goes into the *grant interrupt* sequence immediately after completing its current instruction. At that time it compares the priority of the interrupting device with the value contained in the interrupt bits of the status register. It then places the interrupt level on the address bus (to be used to address the device) and places the same value in the interrupt bit positions of the status register. The R/W line goes high and then the function code outputs all go high, indicating that the CPU is acknowledging the interrupt. The address strobe output is then driven low, followed by the LDS output.

When the LDS output goes low, the interrupting device responds by going into the *provide vector number* cycle. The interrupt vector is placed on the data bus, indicating which device is interrupting the CPU, and DTACK is driven low. The address vector is needed to inform the CPU as to the exact source of the interrupt signal, since several devices can have the same priority.

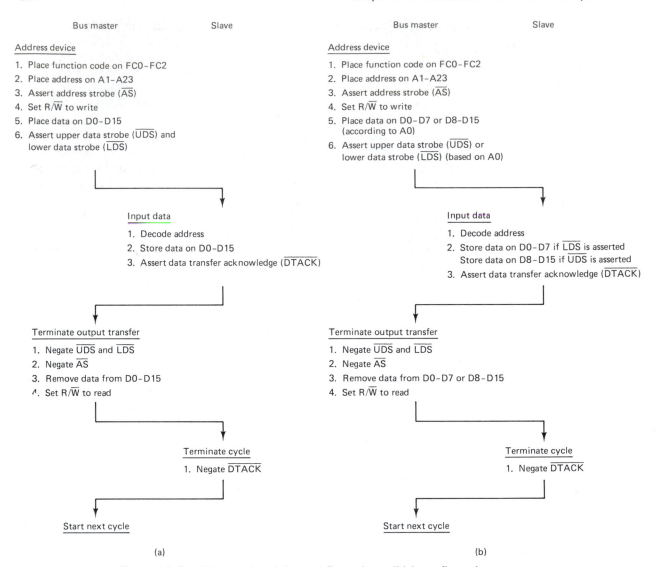

Figure 17.8   Write cycles: (a) word flow chart: (b) byte flow chart.
(Courtesy of Prentice-Hall)

When the CPU receives the DTACK signal, it enters *acquire vector number* cycle. It latches the interrupt vector and returns LDS and AS to their inactive (high) levels. The interrupting device then returns the DTACK line to its inactive (high) level. Using the vector number, the CPU identifies the interrupting device and runs the appropriate supervisor program that was written to service the device.

If another interrupt is received while the first is being serviced, the process shown in the flowchart is started again. However, if the priority number for the new interrupt is equal to or less than the one for the interrupting device being serviced, the CPU will ignore the interrupt input until the current interrupt cycle is complete.

Tracing

The trace function is a feature of the MC68000 that helps the system programmer to develop programs. When the tract bit in the status register is set to a 1, the CPU is in the trace mode. In this mode, the CPU will run a separate program (in the supervisor state) after each instruction execution in the user program. The program that is run between instruction cycles would be a program debugging (troubleshooting)

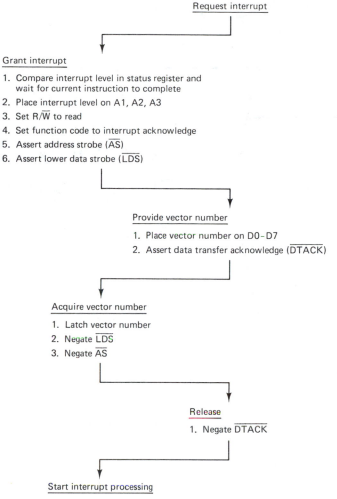

Figure 17.9 Interrupt cycle. *(Courtesy of Prentice-Hall)*

program. This program would be used to check the results of each step, making sure that no errors occurred during the execution of the program under test. If an error occurred, the trace program would indicate which step caused the error. If none occurred, there would be no indication from the trace program. The trace program is disabled when the trace bit is low.

SUMMARY

As has been shown, the MC68000, as well as all 16-bit microprocessors, is capable of performing many more operations than the typical 8-bit machine. The 32-bit internal registers, the 23-bit address bus, the 16-bit data bus, and the increased control line functions combine to allow many operations that were not possible previously.

Not all 16-bit microprocessors work in the exact same fashion as the MC68000, but you should be capable of reading the technical manuals available for any 16-bit microprocessor and gain a fair degree of understanding of the operation of the device.

REFERENCES

16-Bit Microprocessor User's Manual; Prentice-Hall, Inc. Copyright 1982. Third edition.

IC Master; Hearst Business Communications, Inc./UTP Division. Copyright 1983.

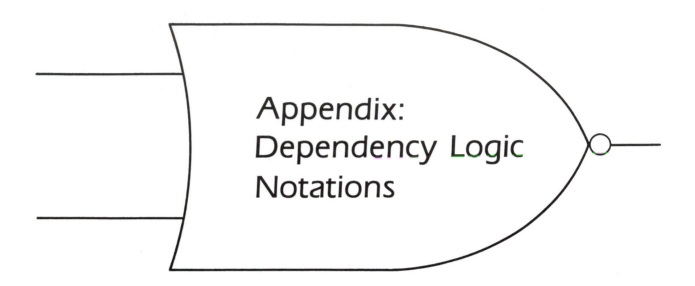

Appendix: Dependency Logic Notations

The information contained herein was reproduced in its entirety from the Texas Instruments, Incorporated 1984 TTL Data Book, Volume 1. This information appears as a courtesy of Texas Instruments Incorporated.

If you have questions on this Explanation of Logic Symbols, please contact:

F.A. Mann, MS 49
Texas Instruments Incorporated
P.O. Box 225012
Dallas, Texas 75265

Telephone (214) 995-2867

IEEE Standards may be purchased from:

Institute of Electrical and Electronics Engineers, Inc.
IEEE Standards Office
345 East 47th Street
New York, N.Y. 10017

International Electrotechnical Commission (IEC) publications may be purchased from:

American National Standards Institute, Inc.
1430 Broadway
New York, N.Y. 10018

1.0 INTRODUCTION

The International Electrotechnical Commission (IEC) has been developing a very powerful symbolic language that can show the relationship of each input of a digital logic circuit to each output without showing explicitly the internal logic. At the heart of the system is dependency notation, which will be explained in Section 4.

The system was introduced in the USA in a rudimentary form in IEEE/ANSI Standard Y32.14-1973. Lacking at that time a complete development of dependency notation, it offered little more than a substitution of rectangular shapes for the familiar distinctive shapes for representing the basic functions of AND, OR, negation, etc. This is no longer the case.

Internationally, Working Group 2 of IEC Technical Committee TC-3 has prepared a new document (Publication 617-12) that consolidates the original work started in the mid 1960's and published in 1972 (Publication 117-15) and the amendments and supplements that have followed. Similarly for the USA, IEEE Committee SCC 11.9 has revised the publication IEEE Std 91/ANSI Y32.14. Now numbered simply IEEE Std 91-1984, the IEEE standard contains all of the IEC work that has been approved, and also a small amount of material still under international consideration. Texas Instruments is participating in the work of both organizations and this document introduces new logic symbols in accordance with the new standards. When changes are made as the standards develop, future editions will take those changes into account.

The following explanation of the new symbolic language is necessarily brief and greatly condensed from what the standards publications will contain. This is not intended to be sufficient for those people who will be developing symbols for new devices. It is primarily intended to make possible the understanding of the symbols used in this data book and is somewhat briefer than the explanation that appears in several of TI's data books on digital logic. However, it includes a new section (6.0) that explains several symbols for actual devices in detail. This has proven to be a powerful learning aid.

2.0 SYMBOL COMPOSITION

A symbol comprises an outline or a combination of outlines together with one or more qualifying symbols. The shape of the symbols is not significant. As shown in Figure 1, general qualifying symbols are used to tell exactly what logical operation is performed by the elements. Table 1

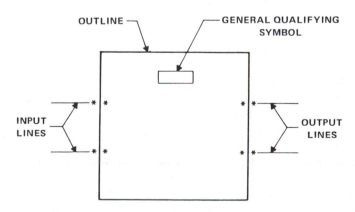

*Possible positions for qualifying symbols relating to inputs and outputs

Figure 1. Symbol Composition

shows general qualifying symbols defined in the new standards. Input lines are placed on the left and output lines are placed on the right. When an exception is made to that convention, the direction of signal flow is indicated by an arrow as shown in Figure 9.

3.0   QUALIFYING SYMBOLS

3.1   General Qualifying Symbols

Table 1 shows general qualifying symbols defined by IEEE Standard 91. These characters are placed near the top center or the geometric center of a symbol or symbol element to define the basic function of the device represented by the symbol or of the element.

X/Y is the general qualifying symbol for identifying coders, code converters, and level converters. X and Y may be used in their own right to stand for some code or either or both may be replaced by some other indication of the code or level such as BCD or TTL. As might be expected, interface circuits make frequent use of this set of qualifying symbols.

Table 1.   General Qualifying Symbols

SYMBOL	DESCRIPTION
&	AND gate or function.
≥ 1	OR gate or function. The symbol was chosen to indicate that at least one active input is needed to activate the output.
= 1	Exclusive OR. One and only one input must be active to activate the output.
1	The one input must be active.
▷ or ◁	A buffer or element with more than usual output capability (symbol is oriented in the direction of signal flow).
⎍	Schmitt trigger; element with hysteresis.
X/Y	Coder, code converter, level converter.

The following are examples of subsets of this general class of qualifying symbol used in this book:

BCD/7-SEG	BCD to 7-segment display driver.
TTL/MOS	TTL to MOS level converter.
CMOS/PLASMA DISP	Plasma-display driver with CMOS-compatible inputs.
MOS/LED	Light-emitting-diode driver with MOS-compatible inputs.
CMOS/VAC FLUOR DISP	Vacuum-fluorescent display driver with CMOS-compatible inputs.
CMOS/EL DISP	Electroluminescent display driver with CMOS-compatible inputs.
TTL/GAS DISCH DISPLAY	Gas-discharge display driver with TTL-compatible inputs.

SRGm	Shift register. m is the number of bits.

3.2   Qualifying Symbols for Inputs and Outputs

Qualifying symbols for inputs and outputs are shown in Table 2 and will be familiar to most users with the possible exception of the logic polarity and analog signal indicators. The older logic negation indicator means that the external 0 state produces the internal 1 state. The internal 1 state means the active state. Logic negation may be used in pure logic diagrams; in order to tie the external 1 and 0 logic states to the levels H (high) and L (low), a statement of whether positive logic (1 = H, 0 = L) or negative logic (1 = L, 0 = H) is being used is required or must be assumed. Logic polarity indicators eliminate the need for calling out the logic convention and are used in this data book in the symbology for actual devices. The presence of the triangle polarity indicator indicates that the L logic level will produce the internal 1 state (the active state) or that, in the case of an output, the internal 1 state will produce the external L level. Note how the active direction of transition for a dynamic input is indicated in positive logic, negative logic, and with polarity indication.

Table 2. Qualifying Symbols for Inputs and Outputs

Logic negation at input. External 0 produces internal 1.

Logic negation at output. Internal 1 produces external 0.

Active-low input. Equivalent to ―◁ in positive logic.

Active-low output. Equivalent to ▷― in positive logic.

Active-low input in the case of right-to-left signal flow.

Active-low output in the case of right-to-left signal flow.

Signal flow from right to left. If not otherwise indicated, signal flow is from left to right.

Bidirectional signal flow.

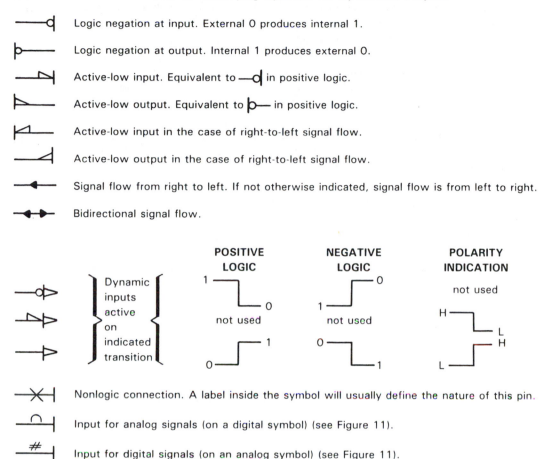

Nonlogic connection. A label inside the symbol will usually define the nature of this pin.

Input for analog signals (on a digital symbol) (see Figure 11).

Input for digital signals (on an analog symbol) (see Figure 11).

When nonstandardized information is shown inside an otline, it is usually enclosed in square brackets [lilke these]. The square brackets are omitted when associated with a nonlogic input, which is indicated by an X superimposed on the connection line outside the symbol.

3.3   Symbols Inside the Outline

Table 3 shows some symbols used inside the outline. Note particularly that open-collector (open-drain), open-emitter (open-source), and three-state outputs have distinctive symbols. ALso note that an EN input affects all of the outputs of the element and has no effect on inputs. An EN input affects all the external outputs of the element in which it is placed, plus the external outputs of any elements shown to be influenced by that element. It has no effect on inputs. When an enable input affects only certain outputs, affects outputs located outside the indicated influence of the element in which the enable input is placed, and/or affects one or more inputs, a form of dependency notation will indicate this (see 4.9). The effects of the EN input on the various types of outputs are shown.

It is particularly important to note that a D input is always the data input of a storage element. At its internal 1 state, the D input sets the storage element to its 1 state, and at its internal 0 state it resets the storage element to its 0 state.

The binary grouping symbol will be explained more fully in Section 6.11. Binary-weighted inputs are arranged in order and the binary weights of the least-significant and the most-significant lines are indicated by numbers. In this document weights of input and output lines will be represented by powers of two usually only when the binary grouping symbol is used, otherwise decimal numbers will be used. The grouped inputs generate an internal number on which a mathematical function can be performed or that can be an identifying number for dependency notation . This number is the sum of the weights $(1, 2, 4 \ldots 2^n)$ of those input standing at their 1 states. A frequent use is in addresses for memories.

Reversed in direction, the binary grouping symbol can be used with outputs. The concept is analogous to that for the inputs and the weighted outputs will indicate the internal number assumed to be developed within the circuit.

Table 3. Symbols Inside the Outline

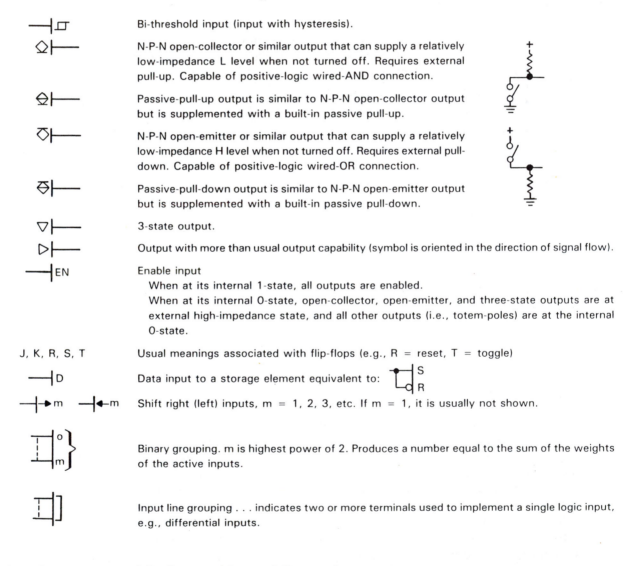

	Bi-threshold input (input with hysteresis).
	N-P-N open-collector or similar output that can supply a relatively low-impedance L level when not turned off. Requires external pull-up. Capable of positive-logic wired-AND connection.
	Passive-pull-up output is similar to N-P-N open-collector output but is supplemented with a built-in passive pull-up.
	N-P-N open-emitter or similar output that can supply a relatively low-impedance H level when not turned off. Requires external pull-down. Capable of positive-logic wired-OR connection.
	Passive-pull-down output is similar to N-P-N open-emitter output but is supplemented with a built-in passive pull-down.
	3-state output.
	Output with more than usual output capability (symbol is oriented in the direction of signal flow).

EN	Enable input
	    When at its internal 1-state, all outputs are enabled.
	    When at its internal 0-state, open-collector, open-emitter, and three-state outputs are at external high-impedance state, and all other outputs (i.e., totem-poles) are at the internal 0-state.

J, K, R, S, T	Usual meanings associated with flip-flops (e.g., R = reset, T = toggle)
D	Data input to a storage element equivalent to:
m m	Shift right (left) inputs, m = 1, 2, 3, etc. If m = 1, it is usually not shown.
	Binary grouping. m is highest power of 2. Produces a number equal to the sum of the weights of the active inputs.
	Input line grouping . . . indicates two or more terminals used to implement a single logic input, e.g., differential inputs.

3.4   Combinations of Outlines and Internal Connections

When a circuit has one or more inputs that are common to more than one element of the circuit, the common-control block may be used. This is the only distinctively shaped outline used in the IEC system. Figure 2 shows that unless otherwise qualified by dependency notation, an input to the common-control block is an input to each of the elements below the common-control block.

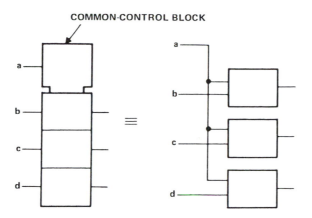

Figure 2. Common-Control Block

The outlines of elements may be embedded within one another or abutted to form complex elements, in which case the following rules apply. There is no logic connection between elements when the line common to their outlines is in the direction of signal flow. There is at least one logic connection when the line common to two outlines is perpendicular to the direction of signal flow. If no indications are shown on either side of the common line, it is assumed that there is only one logic connection. If more than one internal connection exists between adjacent elements, the number of connections will be clarified by the use of one or more of the internal connection symbols from Table 4 and/or appropriate qualifying symbols or dependency notation.

Table 4. Symbols for Internal Connections

Internal connection. 1 state on left produces 1 state on right.

Negated internal connection. 1 state on left produces 0 state on right.

Dynamic internal connection. Transition from 0 to 1 on left produces transitory 1 state on right.

Dynamic internal connection. Transition from 1 to 0 on left produces transitory 1 state on right.

Table 4 shows symbols that are used to represent internal connection with specific characteristics. The first is a simple noninverting connection, the second is inverting, the third is dynamic. As with this symbol and an external input line, the transition from 0 to 1 on the left produces a momentary 1-state on the right. The fourth symbol is similar except that the active transition on the left is from 1 to 0.

Only logic states, not levels, exist inside symbols. The negation symbol (o) is used internally even when direct polarity indication (◿) is used externally.

In an array of elements, if the same general qualifying symbol and the same qualifying symbols associated with inputs and outputs would appear inside each of the elements of the array, these qualifying symbols are usually shown only in the first element. This is done to reduce clutter and to save time in recognition. Similarly, large identical elements that are subdivided into smaller elements may each be represented by an unsubdivided outline. The MC3446 symbol illustrates this principle.

4.0 DEPENDENCY NOTATION

Some readers will find it more to their liking to skip this section and proceeed to the explanation of the symbols for a few actual devices in 6.0. Reference will be made there to various parts of this section as it is needed. If this procedure is followed, it is recommended that 5.0 be read after 6.0 and then all of 4.0 be reread.

4.1 General Explanation

Dependency notation is the powerful tool that sets the IEC symbols apart from previous systems and makes compact, meaningful, symbols possible. It provides the means of denoting the relationship between inputs, outputs, or inputs and outputs without actually showing all the elements and interconnections involved. The information provided by dependency notation supplements that provided by the qualifying symbols for an element's function.

In the convention for the dependency notation, use will be made of the terms ''affecting'' and ''affected.'' In cases where it is not evident which inputs must be considered as being the affecting or the affected ones (e.g., if they stand in an AND relationship), the choice may be made in any convenient way.

So far, eleven types of dependency have been defined but only the eight used in this book are explained. They are listed below in the order in which they are presented and are summarized in Table 5 following 4.10.2.

Section	Dependency Type or Other Subject
4.2	G, AND
4.3	General Rules for Dependency Notation
4.4	V, OR
4.5	N, Negate (Exclusive-OR)
4.6	Z, Interconnection
4.7	X, Transmission
4.8	C, Control
4.9	EN, Enable
4.10	M, Mode

4.2 G (AND) Dependency

A common relationship between two signals is to have them ANDed together. This has traditionally been shown by explicitly drawing an AND gate with the signals connected to the inputs of the gate. The 1972 IEC publication and the 1973 IEEE/ANSI standard showed several ways to show this AND relationship using dependency notation. While ten other forms of dependency have since been defined, the ways to invoke AND dependency are now reduced to one.

In Figure 3 input **b** is ANDed with input **a** and the complement of **b** is ANDed with **c**. The letter G has been chosen to indicate AND relationships and is placed at input **b**, inside the symbol. A number considered appropriate by the symbol designer (1 has been used here) is placed after the letter G and also at each affected input. Note the bar over the 1 at input **c**.

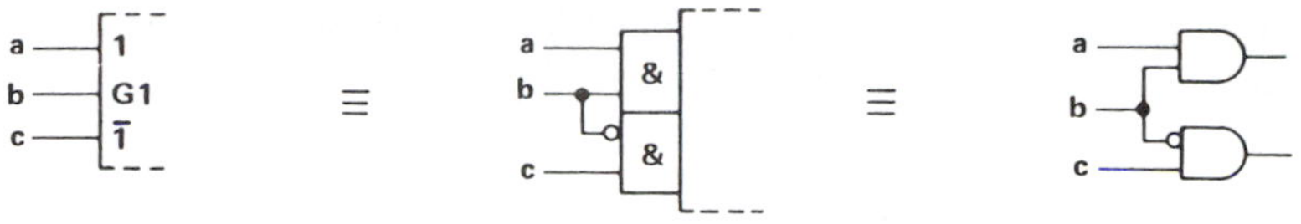

Figure 3. G Dependency Between Inputs

In Figure 4, output **b** affects input **a** with an AND relationship. The lower example shows that it is the internal logic state of **b**, unaffected by the negation sign, that is ANDed. Figure 5 shows input **a** to be ANDed with a dynamic input **b**.

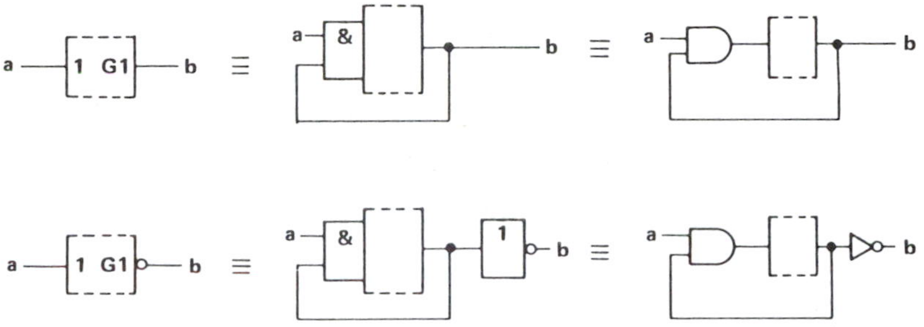

Figure 4. G Dependency Between Outputs and Inputs

Figure 5. G Dependency with a Dynamic Input

The rules for G dependency can be summarized thus:

When a Gm input or output (m is a number) stands at its internal 1 state, all inputs and outputs affected by Gm stand at their normally defined internal logic states. When the Gm input or output stands at its 0 state, all inputs and outputs affected by Gm stand at their internal 0 states.

4.3 Conventions for the Application of Dependency Notation in General

The rules for applying dependency relationships in general follow the same pattern as was illustrated for G dependency.

Application of dependency notation is accomplished by:

1) labeling the input (or output) *affecting* other inputs or outputs with the letter symbol indicating the relationship involved (e.g., G for AND) followed by an identifying number, appropriately chosen, and

2) labeling each input or output *affected* by that affecting input (or output) with that same number.

If it is the complement of the internal logic state of the affecting input or output that does the affecting, then a bar is placed over the identifying numbers at the affected inputs or outputs (Figure 3).

If two affecting inputs or outputs have the same letter and same identifying number, they stand in an OR relationship to each other (Figure 6).

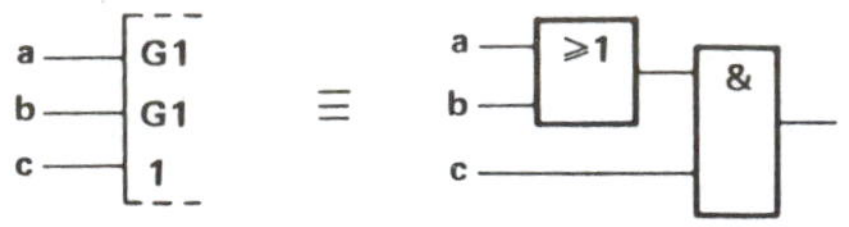

Figure 6. ORed Affecting Inputs

If the affected input or output requires a label to denote its function (e.g., "D"), this label will be *prefixed* by the identifying number of the affecting input (Figure 12).

If an input or output is affected by more than one affecting input, the identifying numbers of each of the affecting inputs will appear in the label of the affected one, separated by commas. The normal reading order of these numbers is the same as the sequence of the affecting relationships (Figure 12).

4.4   V (OR) Dependency

The symbol denoting OR dependency is the letter V (Figure 7).

When a Vm input or output stands at its internal 1 state, all inputs and outputs affected by Vm stand at their internal 1 states. When the Vm input or output stands at its internal 0 state, all inputs and outputs affected by Vm stand at their normally defined internal logic states.

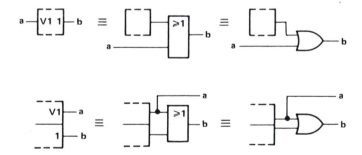

Figure 7. V (OR) Dependency

4.5   N (Negate) (Exclusive-OR) Dependency

The symbol denoting negate dependency is the letter N (Figure 8). Each input or output affected by an Nm input or output stands in an Exclusive-OR relationship with the Nm input or output.

When an Nm input or output stands at its internal 1 state, the internal logic state of each input and each output affected by Nm is the complement of what it would otherwise be. When an Nm input or output stands at its internal 0 state, all inputs and outputs affected by Nm stand at their normally defined internal logic states.

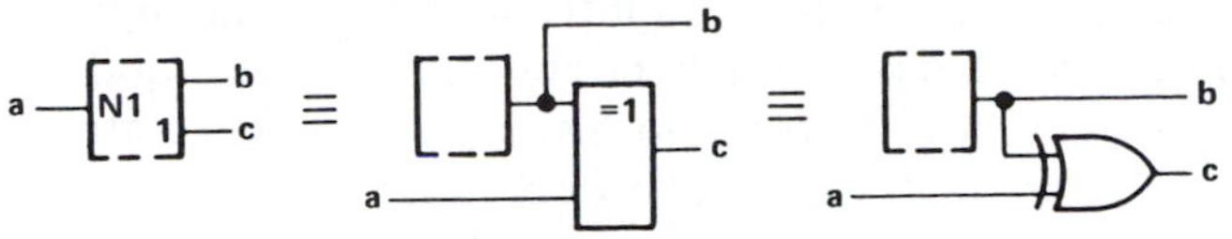

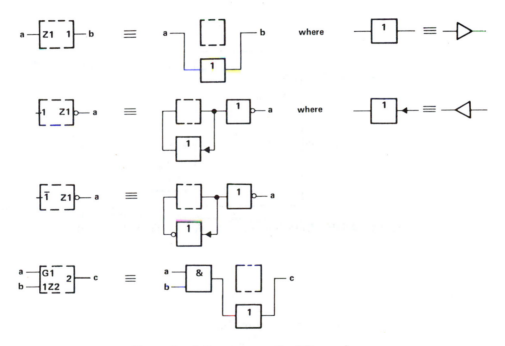

If a = 0, then c = b
If a = 1, then c = $\overline{b}$

Figure 8. N (Negate) (Exclusive-OR) Dependency

4.6 Z (Interconnection) Dependency

The symbol denoting interconnection dependency is the letter Z.

Interconnection dependency is used to indicate the existence of internal logic connections between inputs, outputs, internal inputs, and/or internal outputs.

The internal logic state of an input or output affected by a Zm input or output will be the same as the internal logic state of the Zm input or output, unless modified by additional dependency notation (Figure 9).

Figure 9. Z (Interconnection) Dependency

4.7 X (Transmission) Dependency

The symbol denoting transmission dependency is the letter X.

Transmission dependency is used to indicate controlled bidirectional connections between affected input/output ports (Figure 10).

When an *Xm* input or output stands at its internal 1 state, all input-output ports affected by this *Xm* input or output are bidirectionally connected together and stand at the same internal logic state or analog signal level. When an *Xm* input or output stands at its internal 0 state, the connection associated with this set of dependency notation does not exist.

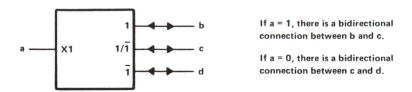

Figure 10. X (Transmission) Dependency

Although the transmission paths represented by X dependency are inherently bidirectional, use is not always made of this property. This is analogous to a piece of wire, which may be constrained to carry current in only one direction. If this is the case in a particular application, then the directional arrows shown in Figures 10 and 11 would be omitted.

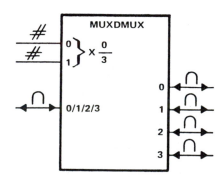

Figure 11. Analog Data Selector (Multiplexer/Demultiplexer)

4.8   C (Control) Dependency

The symbol denoting control dependency is the letter C.

Control inputs are usually used to enable or disable the data (D, J, K, R, or S) inputs of storage elements. They may take on their internal 1 states (be active) either statically or dynamically. In the latter case the dynamic input symbol is used as shown in the second example of Figure 12.

When a *Cm* input or output stands at its internal 1 state, the inputs affected by *Cm* have their normally defined effect on the function of the element, i.e., these inputs are enabled. When a *Cm* input or output stands at its internal 0 state, the inputs affected by *Cm* are disabled and have no effect on the function of the element.

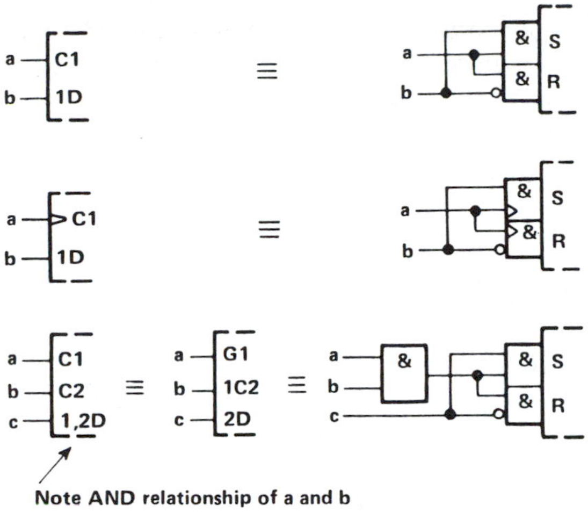

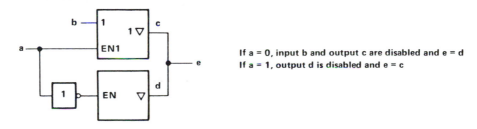

Figure 12. C (Control) Dependency

4.9 EN (Enable) Dependency

The symbol denoting enable dependency is the combination of letters EN.

An ENm input has the same effect on outputs as an EN input, see 3.3, but it affects only those outputs labeled with the identifying number m. It also affects those inputs labeled with the identifying number m. By contrast, an EN input affects all outputs and no inputs. The effect of an ENm input on an affected input is identical to that of a Cm input (Figure 13).

If a = 0, input b and output c are disabled and e = d
If a = 1, output d is disabled and e = c

Figure 13. EN (Enable) Dependency

When an ENm input stands at its internal 1 state, the inputs affected by ENm have their normally defined effect on the function of the element and the outputs affected by this input stand at their normally defined internal logic states, i.e., these inputs and outputs are enabled.

When an ENm input stands at its internal 0 state, the inputs affected by ENm are disabled and have no effect on the function of the element, and the outputs affected by ENm are also disabled. Open-collector outputs are turned off, three-state outputs stand at their high-impedance state, and all other outputs (e.g., totem-pole outputs) stand at their internal 0 states.

4.10 M (MODE) Dependency

The symbol denoting mode dependency is the letter M.

Mode dependency is used to indicate that the effects of particular inputs and outputs of an element depend on the mode in which the element is operating.

If an input or output has the same effect in different modes of operation, the identifying numbers of the relevant affecting Mm inputs will appear in the label of that affected input or output between parentheses and separated by solidi, e.g., (1/2)CT = 0 ≡ 1CT = 0/2CT = 0 where 1 and 2 refer to M1 and M2.

4.10.1 M Dependency Affecting Inputs

M dependency affects inputs the same as C dependency. When an Mm input or Mm output stands at its internal 1 state, the inputs affected by this Mm input or Mm output have their normally defined effect on the function of the element, i.e., the inputs are enabled. When an Mm input or Mm output stands at its internal 0 state, the inputs affected by this Mm input or Mm output have no effect on the function of the element. When an affected input has several sets of labels separated by solidi (e.g., C4/2 → /3 +), any set in which the identifying number of the Mm input or Mm output appears has no effect and is to be ignored. This represents disabling of some of the functions of a multifunction input.

The circuit in Figure 14 has two inputs, **b** and **c**, that control which one of four modes (0, 1, 2, or 3) will exist at any time. Inputs **d, e,** and **f** are D inputs subject to dynamic control (clocking) by the **a** input. The numbers 1 and 2 are in the series chosen to indicate the modes so inputs **e** and **f** are only enabled in mode 1 (for parallel loading) and input **d** is only enabled in mode 2 (for serial loading). Note that input **a** has three functions. It is the clock for entering data. In mode 2, it causes right shifting of data, which means a shift away from the control block. In mode 3, it causes the contents of the register to be incremented by one count.

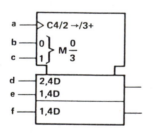

Note that all operations are synchronous.

In MODE 0 (b = 0, c = 0), the outputs remain at their existing states as none of the inputs has an effect.

In MODE 1 (b = 1, c = 0), parallel loading takes place thru inputs e and f.

In MODE 2 (b = 0, c = 1), shifting down and serial loading thru input d take place.

In MODE 3 (b = c = 1), counting up by increment of 1 per clock pulse takes place.

Figure 14. M (Mode) Dependency Affecting Inputs

4.10.2 M Dependency Affecting Outputs

When an Mm input or Mm output stands at its internal 1 state, the affected outputs stand at their normally defined internal logic states, i.e., the outputs are enabled.

When an Mm input or Mm output stands at its internal 0 state, at each affected output any set of labels containing the identifying number of that Mm input or Mm output has no effect and is to be ignored. When an output has several different sets of labels separated by solidi (e.g., 2,4/3,5), only those sets in which the identifying number of this Mm input or Mm output appears are to be ignored.

Figure 15 shows a symbol for a device whose output can behave like either a 3-state output or an open-collector output depending on the signal applied to input **a**. Mode 1 exists when input **a** stands at its internal 1 state and, in that case, the three-state symbol applies and the open-element symbol has no effect. When **a** = 0, mode 1 does not exist so the three-state symbol has no effect and the open-element symbol applies.

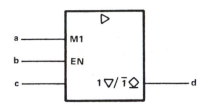

Figure 15. Type of Output Determined by Mode

Table 5. Summary of Dependency Notation

TYPE OF DEPENDENCY	LETTER SYMBOL*	AFFECTING INPUT AT ITS 1-STATE	AFFECTING INPUT AT ITS 0-STATE
Control	C	Permits action	Prevents action
Enable	EN	Permits action	Prevents action of inputs ◇ outputs turned off ▽ outputs at external high impedance Other outputs at internal 0 state
AND	G	Permits action	Imposes 0 state
Mode	M	Permits action (mode selected)	Prevents action (mode not selected)
Negate (Ex-NOR)	N	Complements state	No effect
OR	V	Imposes 1 state	Permits action
Transmission	X	Bidirectional connection exists	Bidirectional connection does not exist
Interconnection	Z	Imposes 1 state	Imposes 0 state

*These letter symbols appear at the AFFECTING input (or output) and are followed by a number. Each input (or output) AFFECTED by that input is labeled with that same number.

5.0 BISTABLE ELEMENTS

The dynamic input symbol and dependency notation provide the tools to identify different types of bistable elements and make synchronous and asynchronous inputs easily recognizable (Figure 16).

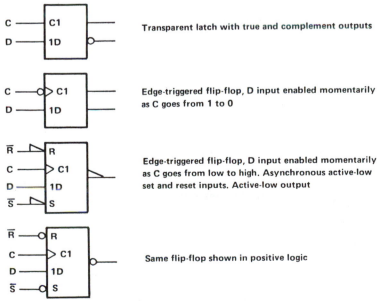

Transparent latch with true and complement outputs

Edge-triggered flip-flop, D input enabled momentarily as C goes from 1 to 0

Edge-triggered flip-flop, D input enabled momentarily as C goes from low to high. Asynchronous active-low set and reset inputs. Active-low output

Same flip-flop shown in positive logic

Figure 16. Latches and Flip-Flops

Transparent latches have a level-operated control input. The D input is active as long as the C input is at its internal 1 state. The outputs respond immediately. Edge-triggered elements accept data from D, J, K, R, or S inputs on the active transition of C.

Notice that synchronous inputs can be readily recognized by their dependency labels (a number preceding the functional label, 1D in these examples) compared to the asynchronous inputs (S and R), which are not dependent on the C inputs. Of course if the set and reset inputs were dependent on the C inputs, their labels would be similarly modified (e.g., 1S, 1R).

6.0 EXAMPLES OF ACTUAL DEVICE SYMBOLS

The symbols explained in this section include some of the most complex in this book. These were chosen, not to discourage the reader, but to illustrate the amount of information that can be conveyed. It is likely that if one reads these explanations and follows them reasonably well, most of the other symbols will seem simple indeed. The explanations are intended to be independent of each other so they may seem somewhat repetitious. However each illustrates new principles. They are arranged more or less in the order of complexity.

6.1 SN75430 Dual Peripheral Positive-AND Driver

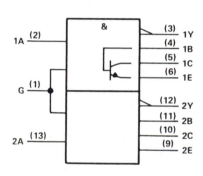

There are two identical sections. The symbology is complete for the first element; the absence of any symbology for the second element indicates it is identical. The two elements share pin 1 as an input. Had there been more than two elements this would have been indicated more conveniently with a common input block.

Each of the two elements is indicated by the & to be an AND gate. The output, pin 3, is active low so to this point the device is what would commonly be called a NAND gate. An extension of symbology used for analog devices has been used to show a floating transistor. Its emitter, base, and collector are shown lined up with the terminals to which they are connected; they are not connected internally to anything else. The device is usually used with pin 3 connected to pin 4 providing an inverting driver output and converting the NAND to AND.

6.2 SN75437 Quadruple Peripheral Driver

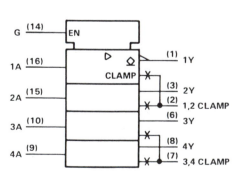

There are four identical sections. The symbology is complete for the first element; the absence of any symbology for the other elements indicates they are identical. The top two elements share a common output clamp, pin 2. This is shown to be a nonlogic connection by the superimposed X on the line. The function for this type of connection is indicated briefly and not necessarily exactly by a small amount of text within the symbol. The bottom two elements likewise share a common clamp.

Each element is shown to be an inverter with amplification (indicated by ▷). Taking TTL as a reference, this means that either the input is sensitive to lower level signals, or the output has greater drive capability than usual. The latter applies in this case. The output is shown by ⎐ to be open collector.

All the outputs share a common EN input, pin 14. See Figure 2 for an explanation of the common control block. When EN = 0 (pin 14 is low), the outputs, being open-collector types, are turned off and go high.

6.3   SN75128 8-Channel Line Receiver

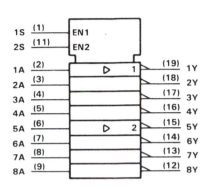

There are eight identical sections. The symbology is complete for the first element; the absence of any symbology for the next three elements indicates they are identical. Likewise the symbology is complete for the fifth element; the absence of any symbology for the next three elements indicates they are identical to the fifth.

Each element is shown to be an inverter with amplification (indicated by ▷). Taking TTL as a reference, this means that either the input is sensitive to lower level signals, or the ouput has greater drive capability than usual. The former applies in this case. Since neither the symbol for open-collector (◇) or 3-state (▽) outputs is shown, the outputs are of the totem-pole type.

The top four outputs are shown to be affected by affecting input number 1, which is EN1, meaning they will be enabled if EN1 = 1 (pin 1 is high). See 4.9 for an explanation of EN dependency. If pin 1 is low, EN1 = 0 and the affected outputs will go to their inactive (high) levels. Similarly, the lower four outputs are controlled by pin 11.

6.4   SN75122 Triple Line Drivers

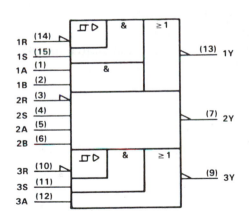

There are two identical sections. The symbology is complete for the first section; the absence of any symbology for the next section indicates it is identical. Likewise the symbology is complete for the third section, which is similar, but not identical, to the first and second.

The top section may be considered to be an OR element (≥ 1) with two embedded ANDs (&), one of which has an active-low amplified input (▷) with hysteresis (⊓), pin 14. This is ANDed with pin 15 and the result is ORed with the AND of pins 1 and 2. The output of the OR, pin 13, is active-low.

The third section is identical to the first except that pin 12 has no input ANDed with it. Since neither the symbol for open-collector (◇) or 3-state (▽) outputs is shown, the outputs are of the totem-pole type.

6.5   SN75142 Dual Line Receivers

There are two identical sections. The symbology is complete for the first section; the absence of any symbology for the second section indicates it is identical.

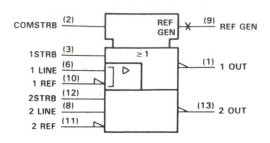

Each section may be considered to be a 3-input OR element (≥ 1). The first input, pin 2, is common to both OR elements. See Figure 2 for an explanation of the common-control block. The second input in the case of the first section is pin 3. The third input is a differential pair shown coming into an embedded element with amplification ($\triangleright$). Since neither the symbol for open-collector ($\diamondsuit$) or 3-state ($\triangledown$) outputs is shown, the outputs are of the totem-pole type. The outputs are active low.

The common control block is sometimes used as a point of placement for an output that originates with either more than one or, as in this case, none of the elements in the array. Pin 9 is shown to be a nonlogic connection by the superimposed X on the line. The function for this type of connection is indicated briefly and not necessarily exactly by a small amount of text within the symbol.

6.6   DS8831 Quad Single-Ended or Dual Differential Line Drivers

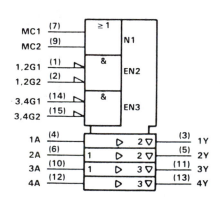

There are four similar elements in the array. Each element is shown to be noninverting with amplification (indicated by $\triangleright$). Taking TTL as a reference, this means that either the input is sensitive to lower level signals or the output has greater drive capability than usual. The latter applies in this case. The outputs are shown by $\triangledown$ to be of the 3-state type.

The top two outputs are shown to be affected by affecting input number 2, which is EN2, meaning they will be enabled if EN2 = 1. See 4.9 for an explanation of EN dependency. If EN2 = 0, the affected outputs will go to their high-impedance (off) states. EN2 is the output of an AND gate (indicated by &) whose active-low inputs are pins 1 and 2. Both pins 1 and 2 must be low to enable pins 3 and 5. Likewise both pins 14 and 15 must be low to enable pins 11 and 13 through EN3.

Input pins 6 and 10 are shown to be affected by affecting input number 1, which is N1, meaning they will be negated if N1 = 1. See 4.5 for an explanation of N (negate or exclusive-OR) dependency. If N1 = 0, the input signals are not negated. N1 is the output of an OR gate (indicated by ≥ 1) whose acive-high inputs are pins 7 and 9. Thus if either of these pins are high, then the second and third elements become inverters.

6.7   SN75113 Differential Line Drivers with Split 3-State Outputs

There are two similar elements in the array. The first is a 2-input AND element (indicated by &); the second has only a single input. Both elements are shown to have special amplification (indicated by $\triangleright$). Taking TTL as a reference, this means that

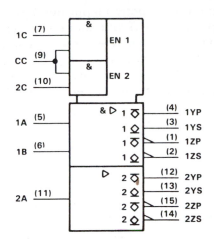

either the input is sensitive to lower level signals, or the output has greater drive capability than usual. The latter applies in this case.

Each element has four outputs. Pins 4 and 3 are a pair consisting of one open-emitter output ($\diamondsuit$) and one open-collector output (φ). Relative to the AND function, both are active high. Pins 1 and 2 are a similar pair but relative to the AND function, both are active low. All outputs of a single, unsubdivided element always have identical internal logic states determined by the function of the element except when otherwise indicated by an associated symbol or label inside the element. Here there is no such contrary indication. All four outputs are shown to be affected by affecting input number 1, which is EN1, meaning they will all be enabled if EN1 = 1. See 4.9 for an explanation of EN dependency. If EN1 = 0, all the affected outputs will be turned off. EN1 is the output of an AND gate (indicated by &) whose active-high inputs are pins 7 and 9. Both pins 7 and 9 must be high to enable the outputs of the top element. Assuming they are enabled and that pins 5 and 6 are both high, the internal state of all four outputs will be a 1. Pins 4 and 3 will both be high, pins 1 and 2 will both be low. The part is designed so that pins 3 and 4 may be connected together creating an active-high 3-state output. Likewise pins 1 and 2 may be connected together to create an active-low 3-state output.

All that has been said about the first element regarding its outputs and their enable inputs also applies to the second element. Pins 9 and 10 are the enable inputs in this case.

6.8   SN75163A Octal General-Purpose Interface Bus Transceiver

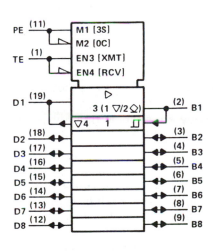

There are eight I/O ports on each side, pins 2 through 9 and 12 through 19. There are eight identical channels. The symbology is complete for the first channel; the absence of any symbology for the other channels indicates they are identical. The eight bidirectional channels each have amplification from left to right, that is, the outputs on the right have increased drive capability (indicated by $\triangleright$), and the inputs on the right all have hysteresis (indicated by $\mathcal{\Pi}$).

The outputs on the left are shown to be 3-state outputs by the ∇ . They are also shown to be affected by affecting input number 4, which is EN4, meaning they will be enabled if EN4 = 1 (pin 1 is low). See 4.9 for an explanation of EN dependency. If EN4 = 0 (pin 1 is high), the affected outputs will go to their high-impedance (off) states.

The labeling at pin 2, which applies to all the outputs on the right, is unusual because the outputs themselves have an unusual feature. The label includes both the symbol for a 3-state output (∇) and for an open-collector output (φ), separated by a slash indicating that these are alternatives.

The symbol for the 3-state output is shown to be affected by affecting input number 1, which is M1, meaning the ∇ label is valid when M1 = 1 (pin 11 is high), but is to be ignored when M1 = 0 (pin 11 is low). See 4.10 for an explanation of M (mode) dependency. Likewise the symbol for the open-collector output is shown to be affected by affecting input number 2, which is M2, meaning the $\ominus$ label is valid when M2 = 1 (pin 11 is low), but is to be ignored when M2 = 0 (pin 11 is high). These labels are enclosed in parentheses (used as in algebra); the numeral 3 indicates that in either case the output is affected by EN3. Thus the right-hand outputs will be off if pin 1 is low. It can now be seen that pin 1 is the direction control and pin 11 is used to determine whether the outputs are of the 3-state or open-collector variety.

6.9   SN75161 Octal General-Purpose Interface Bus Transceiver

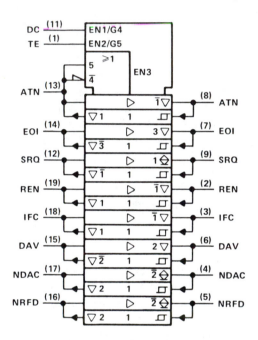

There are eight I/O ports on each side, pins 2 through 9 and 12 through 19. Pin 13 is not only an I/O port; the lines running into the common-control block (see Figure 2) indicate that it also has control functions. Pins 1 and 11 are also controls. The eight bidirectional channels each have amplification from left to right, that is, the outputs on the right have increased drive capability (indicated by $\triangleright$), and the inputs on the right all have hysteresis (indicated by $\sqcap$). All of the outputs are shown to be of the 3-state type by the $\triangledown$ symbol except for the outputs at pins 9, 4, and 5, which are shown to have passive pullups by the $\ominus$ symbol.

Starting with a typical I/O port, pin 18, the output portion is identified by an arrow indicating right-to-left signal flow and the three-state output symbol ($\triangledown$). This output is shown to be affected by affecting input number 1, which is EN1, meaning it will be enabled as an output if EN1 = 1 (pin 11 is high). See 4.9 for an explanation of EN dependency. If pin 11 is low, EN1 = 0 and the output at pin 18 will be in its high-impedance (off) state. This also applies to the 3-state outputs at pins 13 and 19 and to the passive-pullup output at pin 9. On the other hand, the outputs at pins 8, 2, 3, and 12 all are affected by the complement of EN1. This is indicated by the bar over the 1 at each of those outputs. They are enabled only when pin 11 is low. Thus one function of pin 11 is to serve as direction control for the first, third, fourth, and fifth channels.

Similarly it can be seen that pin 1 serves as direction control for the sixth, seventh, and eighth channels. If pin 1 is high, transmission will be from left to right in the sixth channel, right to left in the seventh and eighth. These transmissions are reversed if pin 1 is low.

The direction control for the second channel, EN3, is more complex. EN3 is the output of an OR (≥ 1) function. One of the inputs to this OR is the active-high signal on pin 13. This signal is shown to be affected at the input to the OR gate by affecting input number 5, which is G5, meaning that pin 13 is ANDed with pin 1 before entering the OR gate. See 4.2 for an explanation of G (AND) dependency. The other input to the OR is the active-low signal on pin 13. This signal is ANDed with the complement of pin 11 before entering the OR gate. This is indicated by the G4 at pin 1 and the 4 with a bar over it at pin 13. Thus for EN3 to stand at the 1 state, which would enable transmission from pin 14 to pin 7, both pins 13 and 1 must be high or both pins 13 and 11 must be low.

6.10   SN75584 7-Segment Cathode Driver with Latched Inputs

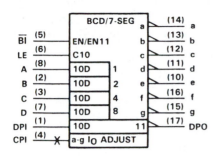

The heart of this device and its symbol is a BCD to 7-segment decoder. Supplying the inputs to the decoder are four elements with D inputs. A D input indicates a storage element. All four D inputs are shown to be affected by affecting input number 10, which is C10, meaning they will all be enabled if C10 = 1. See 4.8 for an explanation of C dependency and 5.0 for a discussion of bistable elements. Since the C input is not dynamic, the storage element is a transparent latch. While C = 1, meaning in this case while pin 6 is high, the outputs of the latches (and hence the inputs of the decoder) will follow the input pins 8, 2, 3, and 7. When C = 0 (pin 6 goes low), those inputs are latched.

The BCD inputs to the decoder are labeled **1**, **2**, **4**, and **8** corresponding to the weights of the inputs. The outputs are labeled **a** through **g** corresponding to the accepted segment designations for 7-segment displays. When the decoder is in operation, an internal number is produced that is equal to the sum of the weights of the BCD inputs that stand at their 1 states. This causes those outputs corresponding to the segments needed to display that number to take on their 1 states. For example, if pins 8 (weight 1) and 7 (weight 8) were high and pins 2 and 3 were low while pin 6 was high, the internal number would be the sum of 8 and 1. All the segment outputs except **e** would be active (low).

The remaining input to the decoder, pin 5, is an EN input. An EN input affects all the outputs of the element in which it is placed. When EN = 0, all the segment outputs take on their 0 states. Being active low, that means they are forced high.

Located below the decoder is another transparent latch. In this case its active-low output is brought out to a terminal. This latch is also under the control of C10 (pin 6). The output, pin 17, is shown to be affected by affecting input number 11, which is EN11, meaning it will be enabled if EN11 = 1 (pin 5 is high). See 4.9 for an explanation of EN dependency. Notice that while the effect of pin 5 is the same for the latch output as for the decoder outputs, it is necessary to use EN dependency for the latter since an EN input affects all outputs of the element in which it is placed and any other elements shown to be affected by that element. The latch is shown to have no logic connection to the decoder making it necessary to use dependency notation to show that its output is also controlled by pin 5.

Located below that latch is another element whose function is defined by its single input, pin 4. This is shown to be a nonlogic connection by the superimposed X on the line. The function for this type of connection is indicated briefly and not necessarily exactly by a small amount of text within the symbol. In this case the function of the element is to adjust the output current of the decoder, but not that of the latch.

6.11   SN75500A AC Plasma Display Driver with CMOS-Compatible Inputs

The heart of this device and its symbol is an 8-bit shift register. It has a single D input, pin 2, which is shown to be affected

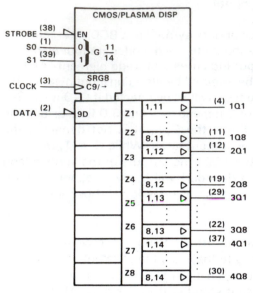

by affecting input number 9, which is C9, meaning it will be enabled if C9 = 1. See 4.8 for an explanation of C dependency and 5.0 for a discussion of bistable elements. Since the C input is dynamic, the storage elements are edge-triggered flip-flops. While C = 1, which in this case will occur on the transition of pin 3 from low to high, the state of the D input will be stored. Pin 2 is shown to be active low so to store a 1, pin 2 must be low.

In addition to controlling the D input, pin 3 is shown by $/\rightarrow$ to have an additional function. As pin 3 goes from low to high, data stored in the shift register is shifted one position. The right-pointing arrow means that the data is shifted away from the control block (down).

On the right side of the symbol an abbreviation technique has been used that is practical only when the internal labels and the pin numbers are both consecutive. Thus it should be clear that the input of the element whose output is pin 5 is affected by affecting input number 2, just as the input of the element whose output is pin 4 is affected by affecting input number 1. Affecting inputs 1 through 8 are Z inputs (Z1 through Z8), which means their signals are tranferred directly to the output elements. See 4.6 for an explanation of Z dependency.

The inputs of the 32 implicitly shown output elements are also shown to be affected by affecting inputs numbers 11, 12, 13, and 14 in four blocks of eight each. These inputs will be found in the common control block preceeded by a letter G and a brace. The brace is called the binary grouping symbol. It is equivalent to a decoder with outputs in this case driving four G inputs (G11, G12, G13, and G14). The weights of the inputs to the coder are shown to be 2^0 and 2^1 for pins 1 and 39, respectively. The decoder has four outputs corresponding to the four possible sums of the weights of the activated decoder inputs. If pins 1 and 39 are both low, the sum of the weights = 0 and G11 = 1. If pin 1 is low while pin 39 is high, the sum = 2 and G13 = 1 and so forth. G indicates AND dependency, see 4.2. Only one of the four affecting G inputs at a time can take on the 1 state. The block of eight output elements affected by that G input are enabled; the 0 state is imposed on the other 24 output elements and externally those output pins are low.

Because of their high-current, high-voltage characteristics, the outputs are labeled with the amplification symbol $\triangleright$. All the outputs share a common EN input, pin 38. See Figure 2 for an explanation of the common control block. When EN = 0 (pin 38 is high), the outputs take on their internal 0 states. Being active high, that means they are forced low.

6.12 SN75551 Electroluminescent Row Driver with CMOS-Compatible Inputs

The heart of this device and its symbol is a 32-bit shift register. It has a single D input, pin 24, which is shown to be affected by affecting input number 40, which is C40, meaning it will be

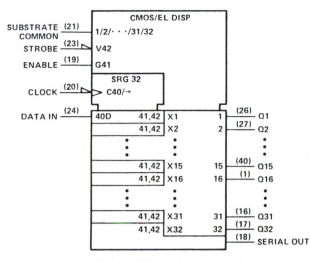

enabled if C40 = 1. See 4.8 for an explanation of C dependency and 5.0 for a discussion of bistable elements. Since the C input is dynamic, the storage elements are edge-triggered flip-flops. While C = 1, which in this case will occur on the transition of pin 20 from high to low, the state of the D input will be stored. Pin 24 is shown to be active high so to store a 1, pin 24 must be high.

In addition to controlling the D input, pin 20 is shown by /→ to have an additional function. As pin 20 goes from high to low, data stored in the shift register is shifted one position. The right-pointing arrow means that the data is shifted away from the control block (down). The internal outputs of the shift register are all shown to be affected by affecting inputs 41 and 42. Affecting input 41 is G41, meaning that pin 19 is ANDed with each of the internal register outputs. If pin 19 is high, the affected outputs are enabled. If pin 19 is low, the 0 state is imposed on the affected outputs. See 4.2 for an explanation of G (AND) dependency. Affecting input 42 is V42, meaning that pin 23 (active low) is ORed with ech of the internal register outputs. If pin 23 is high, V42 = 0 and the affected outputs are enabled. If pin 23 is low, V42 = 1 and the 1 state is imposed on the affected outputs. See 4.4 for an explanation of V (OR) dependency. The affect of V42 is taken into account after that of V41 because of the order in which the labels appear. This means tha the imposition of the 1 state by pin 23 would take precedance over the imposition of the 0 state by pin 19 in case both inputs were active. Pin 18 is shown to be an output directly from the thirty-second stage of the shift register. The dependency label 41,42 does not apply to this output, so pins 19 and 23 do not affect it.

An abbreviation technique has been used for the shift register elements, the output lines, and the associated dependency notation. This technique is practical only when the internal labels and the pin numbers are both consecutive. Thus it should be clear that the output at pin 28 is affected by affecting input number 3, just as the output at pin 27 is affected by affecting input number 2. Affecting inputs 1 through 32 are X inputs (X1 through X32). If one of these X inputs stands at the 1 state, there is a connection established between the ports labeled with the number of the X input. In the case of X2, there would be a connection between pin 27 and pin 21. Pin 21 (labeled 1/2. . ./31/32) is the common point for all the connections indicated by X dependency in this symbol. See 4.7 for an explanation of X dependency.

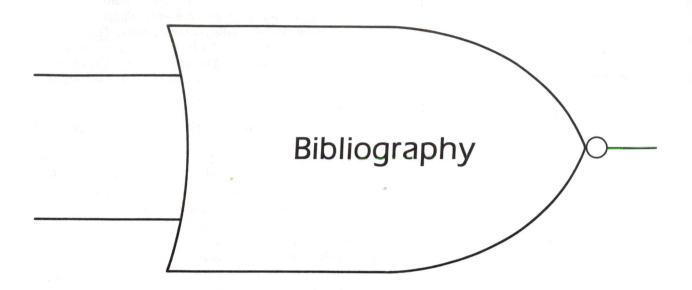

Bibliography

Digital Logic Circuits: Tests and Analysis, by Robert G. Middleton. Howard W. Sams & Co., Inc. Copyright 1982.

16-Bit Microprocessor User's Manual; Third Edition. Prentice-Hall, Inc. Copyright 1982.

Basic Microprocessors and the 6800, by Ron Bishop. Hayden Book Company, Inc. Copyright 1979.

Microcomputer Dictionary, Second edition, by Charles J. Sippl. Howard W. Sams & Co., Inc. Copyright 1981.

Microcomputer Design and Troubleshooting, by Eugene M. Zumchak. Howard W. Sams & Co., Inc. Copyright 1982.

Understanding and Troubleshooting the Microprocessor, by J.W. Coffron. Prentice-Hall, Inc. Copyright 1980.

Digital and Microprocessor Technology, by Patrick O'Conner. Prentice-Hall, Inc. Copyright 1983.

The Complete Motorola Microcomputer Data Library. Motorola Semiconductor Products, Inc.

McGraw-Hill Encyclopedia of Electronics & Computers, Sybil P. Parker, Editor-in-Chief. McGraw-Hill Book Company. Copyright 1982.

Computers for Technicians, by Marcus & Lenk. Prentice-Hall, Inc. Copyright 1973.

Microprocessors and Digital Systems, by Douglas Hall. McGraw-Hill Book Company. Copyright 1983 (Second Edition).

Heathkit Manual for the Microprocessor Trainer Model ET-3400. Heath Company. Copyright 1977.

Heathkit Manual for the Digital Computer Model H-89A. Heath Company. Copyright 1981.

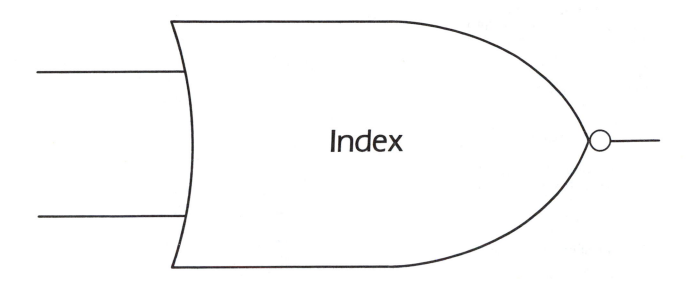

Index

A

Access time, 179
Accumulator
  general, 234
  MC6800, 234–35
Addition (*see also* Binary arithmetic)
  binary, 16–17
Address bus, 179
  MC6800, 214–15
  MC68000, 373
Address decoding
  general, 181, 193–98
  internal
    RAM, 188–90
    ROM, 182
Addressing modes
  direct, 252
  extended, 252
  immediate, 251–52
  implied, 252
  indexed, 252
  relative, 252
Address multiplexing, 197–98
ALU (Arithmetic/Logic Unit), 4
AND gate, 32–33 (*see also* Logic circuits)

B

BASIC, 268
Baud rate, 305
BCD (Binary Coded Decimal), 20–21 (*see also* Binary codes)
Binary arithmetic, 16–20
  addition, 16–17
  division, 19–20
  multiplication, 19–20
  subtraction, 17
  two's complement arithmetic, 17–19
Binary codes, 20–24
  ASCII, 5, 21–23
  BCD, 20–21
  Gray code, 22
  Hollerith, 21–22
Binary number system, 11, 13–16, 136 (*see also* Number systems)
Buffers, 31–32 (*see also* Logic circuits)

C

Capacitors, 50–53
  discharge curve, 52
Carry flag, 235

CCO (Crystal Controlled Oscillator)
  advantages of, 116
  outputs, 117
  troubleshooting, 117–18
Central processing unit (*see* CPU)
Character generator, 292
Chip swapping, 365
Clock signal
  applications, 111
  defined, 111
  fanout, 111
  minimum frequency, 112
Counter
  output sequence (binary), 135–36
  presettable, 144, 146, 150–51
    74176, 146
  troubleshooting, 150–51
  up/down, 141–42
CPU (Central Processing Unit)
  internal registers, 233–38
  MC6800, 212–17
  MC68000, 372–85

D

Darlington pair, 64
Data, 2
Data bus, 4, 179
Data transfer operations, 240–41
Decoder/drivers, 170–73
  7447, 170–73
  troubleshooting, 173
  types, 171
Decoders (*see* Demultiplexers)
Delay time, 8–9, 63
Demultiplexers, 167–70
  applications, 167
  74138, 167–68
  troubleshooting, 167–70
Dependency logic notation, 71–76
Differentiator (*see* RC circuits)
Duty cycle, 8

E

ECL (Emitter-Coupled Logic) (*see* Logic families)
Encoders, 173–76
  applications, 175
  priority, 173
  74148, 173–75
  troubleshooting, 176

Exclusive-NOR (XNOR) gate (*see* Logic circuits)
Exclusive-OR (XOR) gate (*see* Logic circuits)

F

Fall time, 8–9, 63
Fanout, 81–82
555 timer
  astable operations, 115–16
  block diagram, 113
  internal circuitry, 112–13
  internal operation, 112–13
  monostable operation, 113–15
Flip-flops
  applications, 111, 129–33
    frequency divider, 130–32
    one-bit memory, 129–30
    operation sequencer, 132
  D-type, 125–27
    asynchronous inputs, 126–27
    logic symbol, 125
    7474, 126
  description (general), 111
  J-K, 127–28
    input states, 127
    logic symbol, 127–28
    master-slave, 127
    waveforms (typical), 128
  NAND gate S-R, 124–25
  NOR gate S-R, 123–24
  output states, 123
Floppy disks, 339–45
  drive units, 343–45
  sectoring, 341
Flowcharts, 246–48
FORTRAN, 268

I

ICs (Integrated Circuits), 68–98
  levels of integration, 69
  manufacturing, 68–69
  open collector (*see* Open collector logic)
  three state (*see* Three state logic)
  TTL, 76–87
  types, 70–71 (*see also* Logic families)
Information
  binary, 1, 5
  types, 2
Input unit, 3, 273–76
  interfacing, 275–76

Instruction cycles, 238–40
Instructions, 2, 5
Integrated injection logic (I²L) (*see* Logic families)
Integration, 69
Integrator (*see* RC circuits)
Interrupt I/O, 275
Inverter (*see* Logic circuits)
Inverter (programmable), 39–40
Isolated I/O, 275

K

Keyboard
    encoders, 280–86
    troubleshooting, 286–88

L

Logic analyzers, 110
Logic circuits, 1–2, 30–47
    alternate logic symbols, 41, 43–45
    AND gate, 32–33
    buffers, 31–32
    combinations, 37–39
    faults in, 45–47
    inverters, 30–31
    NAND gate, 34–36
    NOR gate, 36–37
    OR gate, 33–34
    output states, 41–45
    waveform analysis, 37–39
    XNOR gate, 40
    XOR gate, 39–40
Logic families, 67–98
    CMOS logic, 93–96
        characteristics, 94–96
    ECL, 96
    I²L, 97
    MOS logic, 90–93 (*see also* CMOS logic)
        MOS transistors, 91–92
    NMOS, 92–93
    PMOS, 93
    TTL, 76–87
        numbering, 79–80
        parameters, 80–84
        subfamilies, 84–87
Logic gates (*see* Logic circuits)
Logic levels, 1, 2, 5–6
    high impedance (*see* Outputs, three-state)
Logic probes
    B & K model DT-57, 109

operation, 109
Logic symbols
    alternate, 41, 43–45
    DLN (*see* Dependency Logic Notation)

M

MC6800, 212–17, 232–38, 248–58
    instruction set, 248–58
MC68000, 372–85
Memory, 4, 178–208, 209–10
    addressing, 179, 193–204
    cell, 178
    dynamic RAM, 192–93
    maps, 204
    non-volatile, 180
    organization, 180–82
    read-only, 180, 182–88
    sequential access, 180
    static RAM, 180, 188–92
    troubleshooting, 178, 204–7
    volatile, 180
Memory mapped I/O, 274
Microcomputers, 209–12
    ET-3400, 217–30
    troubleshooting, 4, 230–31, 347–71
    units, 209–12
Mnemonics, 248
Modems, 311–12
MOS logic (*see* Logic families)
Multiplexers, 161–67
    applications, 163
    74151, 161
    74153, 162
    troubleshooting, 165–67
Multivibrators
    astable, 111
    bistable (*see* Flip-flops)
    defined, 111
    monostable (*see* One-shots)

N

NAND gates (*see* Logic circuits)
NMOS logic (*see* Logic families)
NOR gates (*see* Logic circuits)
Number systems
    binary, 11, 13–16, 136
    binary-to-decimal conversion, 13–14
    decimal, 11–13
    decimal-to-binary conversion, 15–16

Number systems (*cont.*)
  hexadecimal, 25–26
  octal, 24–25
  octal-to-binary conversion, 25

O

One-shot
  applications
    clock enable, 121
    pulse narrowing, 122
  description (general), 111, 118
  logic symbols, 119
  retriggerable, 121
  74121, 118–21
  triggering, 118, 120
  troubleshooting, 122–23
Open collector logic, 89–90
  troubleshooting, 90
OR gate (*see* Logic circuits)
Oscilloscopes
  ac/dc coupled displays, 103–4
  ac/dc/gnd control, 103
  dc voltage checks, 105
  digital testing, 104–5
  display
    open input, 107
    short duration signals, 109
    typical digital, 102
  external triggering, 106–7
  high voltage checks, 105
  inverter testing, 106
  Tektronix model T922
    description, 100–103
  triggering modes, 101–2
  triggering source, 101
  volts/div control, 102–3
Outputs
  active versus inactive, 41–45
  interfacing, 276–78
  three state, 6, 87–89
Output unit, 3

P

Parity, 24
Parity generator, 40
Piggybacking, 366
PMOS logic (*see* Logic families)
Power dissipation, 83–84
Printers, 314–39

data transfers, 316–17
  impact, 314–16
  non-impact, 316
  print head drive circuitry, 326–28
  RS-232-C interface, 317–21
  stepper drive circuitry, 328–30
  troubleshooting, 336–39
  WH14, 321–36
Programs, 2
  machine level, 244–68
Propagation delay, 83–84
Pulse delay circuit, 57–58
Pulse repetition rate, 7
Pulse shaping circuit, 58
Pulse width, 6–7

R

RAM (Random Access Memory) (*see* Memory, static RAM)
RC (Resistive-Capacitive) circuits, 50–59
  applications, 50, 57–59
  circuit operation, 50–52
  differentiator, 56–57
  integrator, 54–55, 57
  pulse inputs, 54–57
  time constants, 53–54
Read-only memory (*see* Memory, read-only)
Read operation, 179
Register
  applications, 135
  MSI, 153–57
    7495, 153–56
  parallel in/parallel out, 153–54
  parallel in/serial out, 156
  serial in/parallel out, 155
  serial in/serial out, 156
  shift left, 153
  shift left/right, 153
  shift operations, 151–53
  shift right (8-bit), 152
  troubleshooting, 157–59
RESET circuit, 58
Rist time, 8–9, 63
ROM (*see* Memory, read-only)
RS-232-C, 310–11

S

Serial I/O, 304–12
Seven-segment displays, 171

Shift registers (*see* Registers)
Signals (*see* Waveforms)
16-bit microprocessors (*see* MC68000)
Software, 2–3 (*see also* Programs)
Stepper motors, 328–30
Storage time, 8–9, 63
Subroutines, 265–69
Switch bounce, 278–80

T

Three state logic, 87–89
   applications, 88
   troubleshooting, 89
Time constants (*see* RC circuits)
Transistors (bipolar), 59–66
   applications, 63–64
   darlington pair, 64
   output states, 59–60

   pulse waveforms, 62–63
   switching, 61–62
   troubleshooting, 65–66
TTL (*see* Logic families)

U

UART, 305–7

W

Waveforms
   basic types, 1, 2
   pulse, 2, 6–9
      RC circuit response, 55–57
      types, 7–8
Wire-AND, 90
Word (memory), 180
Write operation, 179